THE PAPERS OF

WOODROW WILSON

VOLUME 67

DECEMBER 24, 1920 - APRIL 7, 1922

SPONSORED BY THE WOODROW WILSON
FOUNDATION
AND PRINCETON UNIVERSITY

THE PAPERS OF

WOODROW WILSON

ARTHUR S. LINK, *EDITOR*

JOHN E. LITTLE, *ASSOCIATE EDITOR*

L. KATHLEEN AMON, *ASSISTANT EDITOR*

PHYLLIS MARCHAND, *INDEXER*

Volume 67
December 24, 1920 - April 7, 1922

PRINCETON, NEW JERSEY
PRINCETON UNIVERSITY PRESS
1992

Printed in the United States of America
by Princeton University Press
Princeton, New Jersey

INTRODUCTION

THIS volume opens on Christmas Eve 1920, in the waning days of the Wilson administration. Wilson and his advisers have no program other than to bring the administration to a decent end. In foreign affairs, the only still controverted issue is the award of the Island of Yap to Japan by the Supreme Council at the peace conference. As if bowing to the wishes of the voters in the Republican landslide of the month before, Wilson ends even informal liaison with post-war Allied commissions and refuses to engage in any direct dialogue with the Council of the League of Nations. Using the Executive prerogative for the last time, Wilson vetoes a number of bills. One provides for reviving the War Finance Corporation in order to stimulate agricultural exports; Congress overrides this veto. Another imposes high duties on the import of agricultural products; this veto is sustained. Another measure provides for severe restriction of immigration; Wilson is able to give it a pocket veto. The Cabinet meets for the last time on March 1, 1921. Emotions run high as various members recall the battles they have fought with their chief, and Wilson, tears rolling down his cheeks, dismisses them with the benediction: "Gentlemen, it is one of the handicaps of my physical condition that I cannot control myself as I've been accustomed to do. God bless you all."

The end of the Wilson presidency evokes an outpouring of letters to Wilson and editorials in leading newspapers. From the immediate vantage point of seeming wreckage, these friends and spokesmen look back over Wilson's public career, from the presidency of Princeton to the end of his presidency of the United States, and describe what remains of the Wilsonian legacy: high standards of educational and public service, courageous leadership in domestic reform, constancy of principle, and a new vision of the world united for progress, democracy, human rights, and peace.

Wilson is able to participate in the final formalities preceding Harding's inauguration. He is then driven to his new home on S Street in his beloved Pierce-Arrow limousine, which old friends on the board of trustees of Princeton have bought for him. In addition, a group of ten friends, headed by Cleveland Dodge, have contributed a purse of $100,000 to help the Wilsons pay for their new home.

The transition from the White House to S Street goes smoothly, and Wilson is soon settled into a congenial regime. He is still depressed and partially bedridden because he is still severely handicapped and does not get proper exercise. But Mrs. Wilson, Dr.

Grayson, and others manage remarkably well in helping Wilson to adjust to a life of retirement. His new private secretary, also his brother-in-law, John Randolph Bolling, takes care of his schedule and personal affairs. Each passing day sees Wilson dictating more and more letters as he seeks to reach out and create a world beyond his walls of old and new friendships. He finds it difficult to read because his left hand is useless, but Mrs. Wilson, Stockton Axson, and others read to him daily. Every afternoon, at a strictly appointed time, and in all kinds of weather, he and Mrs. Wilson are driven around Washington and through the surrounding countryside on routes that Wilson has chosen. As strength returns, Wilson is able to receive an increasing number of visitors and to attend the theater occasionally and Keith's every Saturday night.

The event that most energizes and excites Wilson is the formation in the spring of 1921 of a law partnership with his former Secretary of State, Bainbridge Colby. Wilson is admitted to the bar of the District of Columbia by regular procedure and to the New York bar by special action of the legislature of that state. He watches with great interest as Bolling oversees the outfitting of elaborate offices in Washington. By the end of this volume, the business of Wilson & Colby is not flourishing. However, overtures are beginning to come in from foreign governments, but Wilson establishes the policy of taking no cases involving any issue in which his administration had been concerned diplomatically. This will spell the doom of the firm.

Wilson views events at home and abroad with increasing interest and concern. He sends occasional brief messages to Democratic dinners and rallies; he begins to work with Brandeis, Colby, Houston, and Baruch in drafting "The Document," a statement which he thinks might be the Democratic platform of 1924, on which he would run for a third term. He tries to arrange the ouster of George White, the present chairman of the Democratic National Committee. He also tries to work through friendly senators to achieve defeat of the Treaty of Berlin, which the Harding administration has negotiated for a separate peace with Germany. He keeps a careful eye on the Conference on the Limitation of Armament of 1921-1922, known as the Washington Naval Conference. He then tries quietly to defeat one of that conference's principal achievements, the Four Power Treaty, designed to maintain the status quo in the Pacific. But the Democrats in the Senate are leaderless, and, for the most part, oblivious to his overtures, and the Senate consents to the ratification of what Wilson thinks is a disgraceful separate peace and a balance-of-power treaty for the Far East. And in spite of the urgings of friends like Frank Cobb of the New York *World*, Wilson maintains an absolute public silence on affairs of state. As he says over and over, he will speak only when the time is right, and when his voice will be heard.

Meanwhile, friends across the country have already begun to do Wilson honor. There is a movement out of Harvard to organize a national Woodrow Wilson College Club network. It fails, but the groundswell of admiration for Wilson on college campuses is palpable. A group consisting mainly of Wilsonians organize the Council on Foreign Relations in New York to perpetuate concern for world affairs and work for an end to American isolation from them. A group of women in New York start a movement for a permanent organization to perpetuate Wilsonian ideals. It burgeons into a nationwide and successful effort, which is near its culmination as this volume ends, to organize and raise an endowment for the Woodrow Wilson Foundation. Franklin D. Roosevelt and Hamilton Holt lead this effort, but it would have failed without the support of women across the country.

Wilson also becomes a prophet with honor in his own city. When he arrives at his home on S Street on Harding's inaugural day, he is greeted by a throng of several thousand persons. After participating in the ceremonies attending the burial of the unknown soldier on Armistice Day 1921, he returns home to find some 20,000 persons gathered there to acclaim him as "the greatest soldier in the world" and as "a wounded soldier of the war." He is so overcome with emotion that he can only thank the crowd for its tribute and call down God's blessing on it. Two months later, on January 15, 1922, several thousand men and women, led by Samuel Gompers, who have just attended a fund-raising meeting for the Woodrow Wilson Foundation, walk two miles, four abreast, to S Street to tell Wilson that the League of Nations is not dead and that they live by his spirit and vision. In his first public remarks on the League of Nations since his retirement, Wilson thanks his well-wishers for their greetings and assures them that the League of Nations is very much alive.

Life is not always serene in the handsome house on S Street. Still suffering from the effects of his stroke, Wilson has good days and bad ones of discontent and irritability. He harbors old grudges, against the present French government and Marshal Foch, for example. However, Wilson's depression grows less and less enervating as this volume progresses, and its ending finds him not only more at peace with himself but eager to become more involved in affairs than he has been since leaving the White House.

Manfred F. Boemeke, Associate Editor, resigned effective March 1, 1991, to accept the position of Director of Publications of the

German Historical Institute in Washington, D. C. Dr. Boemeke
came to the Wilson Papers in 1977 as a part-time Research Assistant and served in that capacity until 1982, when he received the
Ph.D. degree from Princeton University and was appointed Research Assistant and Assistant Editor. He served as Associate Editor from 1985 to 1991. Dr. Boemeke made a contribution to the
success of the Wilson Papers during these years, the importance
of which it is impossible to exaggerate. We wish him all success in
his new career.

We here note with gratitude the kindness of Dr. Steven Lomazow in giving us copies of a portion of the papers of Dr. Francis X.
Dercum, which he has recently acquired. We are able to include
several of these documents in the Addenda to this volume and also
to print from several original Wilson letters to Dercum instead of
from carbon copies. In addition, Dr. Lomazow's collection includes
Dr. Dercum's handwritten and revised typed version of his memorandum concerning his examinations of Wilson in October 1919,
the final version of which we print in Volume 64, pages 500-505.
Readers will be interested to know that Dr. Dercum deleted the
following paragraph from his penultimate draft:

"THE DIAGNOSIS made October 2nd and confirmed at the subsequent examinations was that of a vascular lesion involving the internal capsule of the right cerebral hemisphere."

Dr. Dercum also deleted the following final sentence from his
memorandum: "Mrs. Wilson, the President's wife was absolutely
opposed to detailed statement being given to the public."

We extend our sincere thanks to persons who have given invaluable assistance in the preparation of this volume: James Gordon
Grayson and Cary T. Grayson, Jr., for giving us documents from
their father's papers; Timothy Connelly, Archivist of the National
Historical Publication Records Commission, for indefatigable research in numerous archives and collections and for supplying us
with most of the photographs reproduced in this volume; Michael
T. Sheehan, Director of the Woodrow Wilson House in Washington, for supplying us with the photographs of the Wilson house;
John Milton Cooper, Jr., William H. Harbaugh, August Heckscher,
Richard W. Leopold, Bert E. Park, and Betty Miller Unterberger of
our Editorial Advisory Committee, for carefully reviewing the manuscript of this volume; Margaret D. Link, for her careful reading of
the galley proofs of this volume; and Alice Calaprice, our editor at
Princeton University Press, for keeping things on track.

                                                    THE EDITORS

Princeton, New Jersey
February 6, 1992

CONTENTS

Diplomatic, Military, and Naval Affairs

Personal Affairs

To Wilson from

CONTENTS

ILLUSTRATIONS

Following page 292

A much touched-up photograph taken during the last days in the White House

Another much touched-up photograph

Wilson and his Cabinet, February 15, 1921

On his way to the Capitol, March 4, 1921, with Harding, Cannon, and Penrose

The house on S Street

The library in the S Street house

In the Armistice Day parade, 1921

Leaving his home on the arm of Isaac Scott

Out for a drive in his Pierce-Arrow

ABBREVIATIONS

AL	autograph letter
ALI	autograph letter initialed
ALS	autograph letter signed
AMP	Alexander Mitchell Palmer
ASB	Albert Sidney Burleson
BC	Bainbridge Colby
CC	carbon copy
CCL	carbon copy of letter
CCLS	carbon copy of letter signed
CLSsh	Charles Lee Swem shorthand
DFH	David Franklin Houston
EBW	Edith Bolling Galt Wilson
EBWhw	Edith Bolling Galt Wilson handwriting, handwritten
FDR	Franklin Delano Roosevelt
FR	*Papers Relating to the Foreign Relations of the United States*
Hw, hw	handwriting, handwritten
JPT	Joseph Patrick Tumulty
JRB	John Randolph Bolling
JRT	Jack Romagna typed
MS, MSS	manuscript, manuscripts
NDB	Newton Diehl Baker
NHD	Norman Hezekiah Davis
PPC	*Papers Relating to the Foreign Relations of the United States, The Paris Peace Conference, 1919*
RG	record group
T	typed
TCL	typed copy of letter
TI	typed initialed
TL	typed letter
TLS	typed letter signed
TS	typed signed
TWL	Thomas William Lamont
WBW	William Bauchop Wilson
WGM	William Gibbs McAdoo
WW	Woodrow Wilson
WWhw	Woodrow Wilson handwriting, handwritten
WWsh	Woodrow Wilson shorthand
WWshL	Woodrow Wilson shorthand letter
WWT	Woodrow Wilson typed
WWTLS	Woodrow Wilson typed letter signed

ABBREVIATIONS FOR COLLECTIONS AND REPOSITORIES

Following the National Union Catalog of the
Library of Congress

CtY	Yale University
CtY-D	Yale University Divinity School
DLC	Library of Congress

ABBREVIATIONS

DNA	National Archives
ICU	University of Chicago
IEN	Northwestern University
KyBB	Berea College
KyLoU	University of Louisville
LDR	Labor Department Records
MH	Harvard University
MH-Ar	Harvard University Archives
MH-BA	Harvard University Graduate School of Business Administration
NjP	Princeton University
NHpR	Franklin D. Roosevelt Library
PHC	Haverford College
PMA	Allegheny College
RSB Coll., DLC	Ray Stannard Baker Collection of Wilsoniana, Library of Congress
SDR	State Department Records
ViU	University of Virginia
VtU	University of Vermont
WC, NjP	Woodrow Wilson Collection, Princeton University
WHi	State Historical Society of Wisconsin
WP, DLC	Woodrow Wilson Papers, Library of Congress

SYMBOLS

[Jan. 4, 1921]	publication date of published writing; also date of document when date is not part of text
[*March 4, 1921*]	composition date when publication date differs
[[Nov. 10, 1921]]	delivery date of speech when publication date differs
**** ***	text deleted by author of document

THE PAPERS OF

WOODROW WILSON

VOLUME 67

DECEMBER 24, 1920-APRIL 7, 1922

To Norman Hezekiah Davis

My dear Davis: The White House 24 December, 1920

Pardon me for not having replied to your letter about the Key West-to-Habana cable.[1] I meant to indicate that I would be perfectly satisfied with your judgment as to whether the action was consistent with our treatment of the Western Union or not, and I certainly am satisfied to abide by that judgment.

Faithfully yours,   Woodrow Wilson

TLS (SDR, RG 59, 811.73/484, DNA).
[1] NHD to WW, Dec. 23, 1920 (third letter of that date), Vol. 66.

To Samuel Gompers

My dear Mr. Gompers: The White House 24 December, 1920

It is very kind of you to offer to be of service in the Santo Domingo matter,[1] but our relations with Santo Domingo have been adjusted recently by the State Department in a way which promises to be entirely satisfactory.

Sincerely yours,   Woodrow Wilson

TLS (RSB Coll., DLC).
[1] See S. Gompers to WW, Dec. 21, 1920, Vol. 66.

From Newton Diehl Baker

My dear Mr President: Washington December 24, 1920

Mrs Baker[1] and I beg you and Mrs Wilson to accept our hearty Christmas greeting and New Year wishes for your health and happiness

Almost every day now seems to close some chapter in the wonderful drama of world affairs in which you have been the leader and in which I am gratefully happy to have been permitted to play a part. The years to come will be rich in recognitions of the genius, the wisdom and the justice with which you have led and I pray that you may be long spared both to realize these recognitions and to impress further the lessons you have taught us us [sic] all.

For my part I have gathered imperishable recollections of a great man dealing highly with great affairs which will enrich all the rest of my life so that my affectionate wishes for your welfare are also an expression of deep and abiding gratitude

Respectfully yours,   Newton D. Baker

ALS (WP, DLC).
¹ Elizabeth Leopold Baker.

From Evangeline Cory Booth

Dear Mr. President: New York. December 24, 1920

We have shared to the uttermost what we know to be a nation-wide regret that you should have been, during the past year, so much held a prisoner, when every ambition of your heart must have been for action, and, if you will permit me to say so, I cannot help but feel you must have suffered from terrible depression as a result.

This makes me venture to intrude upon your crowded and burdened days at this season with Christmas greetings from the Salvation Army, and to assure you that individually, as well as as [sic] a people, we are praying for you.

How difficult it is to understand God's purposes from the beginning to the end, and what a struggle we often have to trust where we cannot trace; yet our knowledge of God, in the midst of darkness and mystery, does enable us to say He is Wisdom and Love, and I am sure you would tell me that His ways are not only right but that they will prevail, no matter to what extent erring human judgment may lead men to attempt to thwart Him and delay the glad arrival of good-will between all peoples, and universal peace.

How often lately I have thought upon those words of Lowell's, "Truth is ever on the scaffold."¹ So it is. Those who lead in ideals, in the discovery and taking possession of new lands of human progress, and in the development of age-old principles for the good of man and the glory of God, in advance of their own day—those who have the greater vision—are more often martyred than approved in their own time, though the future sees them canonized.

I believe, Mr. President, that the things you have seen of international justice and unity for the promotion of good and the prevention of evil, are in God's plan for the world; and though we may not be spared to witness the complete triumph of those glorious ideals for which you have so earnestly striven, and for which you have so heroically sacrificed, there are no forces that can prevent their ultimate crowning.

Let me assure you of the affectionate and respectful regard of the tens of thousands of Salvationists who, with myself, through your term of office have learned to know, to honor, and to love you.

We pray that upon this day of the birth of all Grace the blessing of God, which maketh rich and addeth no sorrow, may be the strength and joy of your heart.

I have the honor to be,

Yours sincerely   Evangeline Booth

TLS (WP, DLC).
[1] From James Russell Lowell, *The Present Crisis*.

From the Diary of Josephus Daniels

December Saturday 25 1920

Addie[1] told of story of the President that when he returned from Paris she said "I regret the capitol is not illuminated[."] "The more important thing is that there are some people under the capitol who are more in need of illumination[."]

HW bound diary (J. Daniels Papers, DLC).
[1] Addie Worth Bagley (Mrs. Josephus) Daniels.

From Edith Bolling Galt Wilson

[The White House] Dec. 25, 1920

Just a thought for my precious one—to reflect only love and happiness.   E.

ALI (WP, DLC).

From Eleanor Randolph Wilson McAdoo

My darling Father,   [New York, c. Dec. 25, 1920]

You are so very, very dear and generous to send me all that money again for Christmas. I can't tell you how much it means to me to have your dear message and to know that you are thinking of me, as I am thinking of you, on Christmas Day. When I think of all the happy, happy Christmases we have had together I don't think there ever was such a happy family as ours. I get desperately homesick. In spite of my dear husband and children[1] and our lovely times here, I long to be with you again, darling Father. You don't know how much I love you and what you and all your wonderfulness mean to me. This letter is full to the brim with love and thanks to you and some especially extra love because it will reach you on your birthday. Many many happy returns, darling—we are all thinking of you with deepest love and gratitude for all you mean to us.

We have had a most exciting Christmas. Santa Claus brought Ellen a doll's house and it has caused a thousand thrills. She ignored everything else—tree and other presents and all—and fell on her knees in front of it where she remained rooted for hours. She said "Heavens—Mother" and was oblivious to all the world from then on. The baby had a terrible time deciding which was the most alluring—the tiny doll-carriage that Santa Claus had brought *her* or some dancing dolls from Uncle Stock[2] and ended by a mad attempt to push one and pull the other at the same time—with disastrous results and loud screams. Now she runs across the room as fast as she can go pushing the doll carriage—brings [it] up with a bang against a piece of furniture and is indignant because it got in her way. We are completely exhausted trying to keep her pacified. Nona's little girl[3] is with us, too, and was also greatly excited—so we have had the most strenuous Christmas possible!

I have written to Edith asking if I might take the children down after New Years—I hope I can because I am so eager to see you all and to have them see and be seen. I was terribly disappointed over not being able to go down before Christmas.

With all my love, darling darling Father, and all the dearest wishes in my heart for you from

Your adoring daughter   Nell.

Mac and the babies send their love, too and their loving wishes for a happy, happy birthday.

ALS (WC, NjP).
  [1] Ellen Wilson McAdoo, born May 21, 1915, and Mary Faith McAdoo, born April 6, 1920.
  [2] That is, Stockton Axson.
  [3] Daughter of Nona Hazelhurst McAdoo (Mrs. Ferdinand) de Mohrenschildt.

From Bainbridge Colby

Rio de Janeiro [Dec. 25, 1920]

Please accept, my dear Mr. President, my sincere and affectionate Christmas greetings. My visit at Rio is finished to-day and I am sailing for Montevideo where we are due to arrive on the 29th. Our visit here has been marked by the most elaborate, dignified and cordial hospitality. Every speech that has been made has contained a reference to you of the most appreciative character and with a striking touch of genuine and intimate regard.

Bainbridge Colby.[1]

T telegram (WP, DLC).
[1] "Please ask Davis, as soon as he gets in touch with Colby by telegram again, to thank him for his message to me and tell him how happy it has made me to note the success of his visit to the various capitals he has so far reached. The President." WW to JPT, c. Dec. 27, 1920, TL (WP, DLC). This message was conveyed in JPT to NHD, Dec. 27, 1920, TLS (SDR, RG 59, 033.1132/59, DNA).

To John Spargo

My dear Mr. Spargo: The White House 27 December, 1920

I have your letter of December twenty-second[1] and am heartily in sympathy with the protest against the anti-Semitic movement. I beg that you will add my name to the signatures.

With best wishes,   Sincerely yours,   Woodrow Wilson

TLS (J. Spargo Papers, VtU).
[1] Printed at that date in Vol. 66.

To Ray Stannard Baker

My dear Baker: [The White House] 27 December, 1920

Thank you for your letter of December twenty-third,[1] which gave me a great deal of pleasure. I have a trunk full of papers, and the next time you are down here I would like to have you go through them and see what they are and what the best use is that can be made of them. I plunked them into the trunk in Paris and have not had time or physical energy even to sort or arrange them. I am looking forward with great satisfaction to the work you are purposing to do, and have no doubt that it will be of the highest value.

With the best wishes of the season,
    Cordially and faithfully yours,   [Woodrow Wilson]

CCL (WP, DLC).
[1] Printed at that date in Vol. 66.

To Charles Zeller Klauder

My dear Mr. Klauder: [The White House] 27 December, 1920

We are very much pleased with the rearrangements you are effecting of our rooms at the western end of the second story, and the private stair is just what I desired.[1] But you have assigned to the valet the room which I had intended for a billiard room. The staircase will be none the less useful and in the right place, but I don't like to give up to the valet a room which would be so suitable for the use I have mentioned.

Your plan for an entrance to the sitting room above the porte cochere through a wide arch centering on the upper portion of the great hall strikes us as admirable. We hope that you will carry it out.

I think it would be best to have the garage open on the north side into the road, rather than on the west into the fore court, because of the unsightly stains which seem inevitably to gather about the doorsill of a garage.

I am sorry to say that in sending back the books you mentioned we overlooked the one on the Cotswold District. It will now follow, however, and I hope that you have not been inconvenienced by the lack of it in your library.

Mrs. Wilson joins me in the warmest good wishes of the season and the hope that you are well, as well as in an expression of appreciation of the pains you are taking to perfect the plans.

With warm regard,
Very sincerely yours,   [Woodrow Wilson]

CCL (WP, DLC).
¹ Wilson was replying to C. Z. Klauder, Dec. 23, 1920, Vol. 66.

To Norman Hezekiah Davis

My dear Mr. Secretary: [The White House] 27 December, 1920

I think it highly desirable that the contemplated visit of the Duke D'Aosta should be postponed.¹ I am sure the new administration will desire an opportunity for a splurge, and such a visit would afford it. I am sure you will be able to suggest to Johnson² the best way of conveying the intimation.

Cordially and faithfully yours,   [Woodrow Wilson]

CCL (WP, DLC).
¹ Wilson was replying to NHD to WW, Dec. 23, 1920 (second letter of that date), Vol. 66.
² That is, Ambassador Robert Underwood Johnson.

From Norman Hezekiah Davis

My dear Mr. President: Washington December 27, 1920.

Mr. Young,¹ the American commissioner to the Baltic Provinces, has been telegraphing that the situation in that district is very threatening and that there is grave fear of a Soviet occupation of Esthonia and Latvia, and he has requested that some American naval vessels be sent to Riga or Reval to assist Americans in case of an emergency.²

I have been reluctant to ask the Navy Department to send a ship into the Baltic Sea, but I am informed that the destroyer KANE is at present in dry dock in a Swedish port and about to put to sea with orders to leave the Baltic. I have therefore taken the liberty to request the Secretary of the Navy not to hasten the departure of the KANE from the Baltic Sea.

If this meets with your approval, we will hold this destroyer in a friendly neutral port until the situation clears up.

Faithfully yours,   Norman H. Davis

TLS (WP, DLC).
  [1] Evan Erastus Young.
  [2] E. E. Young to NHD, Dec. 24, 1920, T telegram (SDR, RG 59, 760N.61/3, DNA); printed in *FR 1920*, III, 666-67.

From William Bauchop Wilson

My dear Mr. President: Washington December 27, 1920.

I am enclosing you herewith cablegram from Albert Thomas, relative to the appointment of a representative of the United States on the International Emigration Commission.[1]

Faithfully yours,   W B Wilson

TLS (WP, DLC).
  [1] A. Thomas to WBW, Dec. 24, 1920, T telegram (WP, DLC). Thomas urged that an American representative be appointed to the commission as soon as possible in order to prevent further delay in the beginning of its work.

From the Diary of Josephus Daniels

1920 Tuesday 28 December

Cabinet. Bristol[1] had telegraphed from Constantinople that Greek King was going to Athens & should he salute him? Is he King? asked the President. If King, salute. France and England will not salute. Bristol telegraphed to avoid Greek fleet & let recognition be extended in some other way.

Presidents birthday. In answer to congratulations he said rather sadly that he did not know whether he deserved to be congratulated.

Wilson brt up immigration bill[2] WW said he wished to send back those who were not Americans—he wished he had an X ray to determine where ones heart was—in this country or some other.

  [1] Rear Adm. Mark Lambert Bristol.
  [2] Albert Johnson, Republican of Washington, had introduced H.R. 14461 in the House of Representatives on December 6. This bill prohibited the immigration of all aliens to the United States for a period of two years. In the course of debate in the House, the measure was amended to cut the period of prohibition to one year. The bill

was intended as a stopgap until Congress could evolve more studied immigration leg-islation. The House passed the measure on December 13. At this time, it was under consideration by the Senate Committee on Immigration. *Cong. Record*, 66th Cong., 3d sess., pp. 10, 135-38, 188-92, 285-86, 308.

From Norman Hezekiah Davis

My dear Mr. President: Washington December 28, 1920.

The issue has arisen as to what attitude this Government should take toward King Constantine, recently returned to Greece. The American Minister has asked for new letters of credence.

King Constantine returned to Greece as a result of a Parliamentary election and a subsequent plebiscite which our Minister at Athens reports as showing that 55% of all the Greeks and 75% of the population of old Greece desire his return.[1] You will remember that the Government of the United States, unlike that of Great Britain and France, took no active participation in the disputes which occurred prior to the expulsion of King Constantine. The records of the Department show that Mr. Droppers, the American Minister at Athens was duly accredited on October 9, 1914 to King Constantine and that subsequently, after the expulsion of the King, was given a new letter of credence to King Alexander on November 23, 1917. I am informed by my legal advisors that though new letters of credence are technically necessary on the installation of the new monarch, the Government of Greece as existing under Venizelos may legally be considered as continuing.

I have been informed that the Ministers of Great Britain and France had been ordered to leave Athens immediately but that the orders of recall were subsequently revoked, apparently owing to the influence of Italy.

The French Embassy, stating that a decision had been reached by Great Britain and France to give no further credits to the Government of King Constantine, suggested the desirability of the United States also suspending further credits. You will recall that a credit of $38,000,000 was granted the Venizelos Government which amount was to be paid after peace was made. Though a ratification of the Treaties of Peace by the United States was considered a condition precedent to this obligation, a temporary arrangement was made to advance certain sums against this credit for the purchase of goods in the United States for consumption in Greece. Payments amounting to $15,000,000 have already been made under this arrangement and a further advance of $5,000,000 has now been requested. The Treasury has asked me whether the Department of State has any objection to the Treasury's proceeding to make the requested advance and whether the Treasury may deal with the new Government in Greece through the Charge d'Affaires of the Legation for the purpose of negotiating this credit.

I am inclined to believe that letters of credence should be issued to Mr. Capps, our Minister at Athens; that the credit obligation negotiated with the Venizelos Government should be considered as still binding, and that the Greek Charge d'Affaires, on proper application, should be recognized as representing the Government of King Constantine.   Faithfully yours,   Norman H. Davis

I concur <u>W.W.</u>[2]

TLS (SDR, RG 59, 868.001C76/49, DNA).
[1] Edward Capps to NHD, Dec. 6, 1920, printed in *FR 1920*, II, 708.
[2] Davis, on December 30, instructed Capps to extend recognition to Constantine once he assumed office and formally announced his accession to the throne to the United States Government.

To Evangeline Cory Booth

My dear Miss Booth: [The White House] 28 December, 1920

Your letter of December twenty-fourth is very generous and has given me cheer and strength, both because of my warm esteem for you and because of my great admiration for and confidence in the Salvation Army, which has rendered services of the finest kind in so many fields. Thank you with all my heart.

With the warmest good wishes of the season,
            Cordially and sincerely yours,   [Woodrow Wilson]

CCL (WP, DLC).

From Felixiana Shepherd Baker Woodrow[1]

My dear Tommy: Columbia, S. C., Dec. 28, 1920.

Just a line to let you know that I am thinking of you, and sympathising with you and to tell you how glad I am that you are so much better.

With love to your devoted Wife,
                  Yours affectionately,   "Aunt Felie."

Excuse pencil. Rheumatism is one of the things that does not improve with age!

ALS (WP, DLC).
[1] Wilson's aunt, the widow of James Woodrow.

To Alexander Mitchell Palmer

The White House
My dear Mr. Attorney General: 29 December, 1920

Thank you for the list of the names of those who have endorsed William Ryan for appointment as United States Judge for the Western District of Wisconsin.[1] I would very much like to know whether he is being urged by either Senator LaFollette or Senator Lenroot. Do you know whether these gentlemen desire his appointment?

Cordially and sincerely yours,   Woodrow Wilson

TLS (A. M. Palmer Papers, DLC).
[1] Wilson was replying to AMP to JPT, Dec. 24, 1920, TLS (WP, DLC). Palmer enclosed a list of eleven men, all of them from Wisconsin and mostly judges, who had endorsed Ryan.

A Veto Message

To the Senate: The White House 30 December, 1920.

I return herewith without my signature Senate Bill No. 4526,[1] amending section 501 of the Transportation Act, by extending the effective date of section 10 of the Clayton Act.

The Clayton Anti-Trust Act was responsive to recommendations which I made to the Congress on December 2, 1913, and January 20, 1914,[2] on the subject of legislation regarding the very difficult and intricate matter of trusts and monopolies. In speaking of the changes which opinion deliberately sanctions and for which business waits, I observed:

It waits with acquiescence, in the first place, for laws which will effectually prohibit and prevent such interlockings of the *personnel* of the directorates of great corporations—banks and railroads, industrial, commercial, and public service bodies—as in effect result in making those who borrow and those who lend practically one and the same, those who sell and those who buy but the same persons trading with one another under different names and in different combinations, and those who affect to compete in fact partners and masters of some whole field of business. Sufficient time should be allowed, of course, in which to affect these changes of organization without inconvenience or confusion.

This particular recommendation is reflected in section 10 of the Clayton Anti-Trust Act. That Act became law on October 15, 1914, and it was provided that section 10 should not become effective until two years after that date, in order that the carriers and others affected might be able to adjust their affairs so that no inconvenience or confusion might result from the enforcement of its provisions. Further extensions of time, amounting in all to more than four years and two months have since been made. These were in part due to the intervention of federal control, but ten months have now elapsed since the resumption of private operation. In all, over six years have elapsed since this enactment was put upon the statue book, so that all interests concerned have had long and ample notice of the obligations it imposes.

The Interstate Commerce Commission has adopted rules responsive to the requirements of section 10. In deferring the effective date of section 10, the Congress has excepted corporations organized after January 12, 1918, and as to such corporations the Commission's rules are now in effect. Therefore, it appears that the necessary preliminary steps have long since been taken to put section 10 into effect, and the practical question now to be decided is whether the partial application of those rules shall be continued until January 1, 1922 or whether their application shall now become general, thus bringing under them all common carriers engaged in commerce, and at last giving full effect to this important feature of the Act of October 15, 1914.

The grounds upon which further extension of time is asked, in addition to the six years and more that have already elapsed, have been stated as follows:

That the carrying into effect of the existing provisions of section 10 will result in needless expenditures on the part of carriers in many instances; that some of its provisions are unworkable, and that the changed status of the carriers and the enactment of the transportation act require a revision of section 10 in order to make it consistent with provisions of the transportation act.

When it is considered that the Congress is now in session and can readily adopt suitable amendments if they shall be found to be necessary, such reasons for further delay appear to me to be inadequate. The soundness of the principle embodied in section 10 appears to be generally admitted. The wholesome effects which its application was intended to produce should no longer be withheld from the public and from the common carriers immediately concerned, for whose protection it was particularly designed.

Woodrow Wilson.

CC MS (WP, DLC).
¹ Section 10 of the Clayton Act of 1914 had provided that no common carrier should, after two years from the approval of the measure, have any dealings or contracts of more than $50,000 in any one year with another corporation having a director or other officer who was also a director or officer of the common carrier. By various acts, the effective date of Section 10 had been extended to January 1, 1921. Senate Bill No. 4526 extended

the nonoperation of Section 10 for another year. Palmer, in transmitting the above facts to Wilson, said that he knew of no objection to approval of Senate Bill No. 4526. AMP to WW, Dec. 22, 1920, TLS (WP, DLC).

Wilson asked Tumulty to refer Palmer's letter to "somebody" who would advise him (Wilson) "as to whether this is a perfectly perfunctory report, containing a thing that I already knew." WW to JPT, c. Dec. 22, 1920, TL (WP, DLC).

Wilson's concern about the matter was probably aroused by Tumulty, who had just received a letter from Robert W. Woolley, warning that the Republicans and some reactionary Democrats were "trying to do some pretty bold things," and that this measure was one of them. R. W. Woolley to JPT, Dec. 20, 1920, TLS (WP, DLC). Woolley saw Tumulty on December 21 and then wrote him a letter saying that Wilson should veto the bill and that certain members of the Interstate Commerce Commission opposed the measure. R. W. Woolley to JPT, Dec. 22, 1920, TLS (WP, DLC).

We do not know who wrote Wilson's veto message, but Tumulty and Woolley probably had a large hand in it.

The veto message is printed in *Cong. Record*, 66th Cong., 3d sess., p. 811. There was apparently no attempt to override the veto.

² Wilson's Annual Message and his address on antitrust legislation are printed at these dates in Vol. 29.

To William Gibbs McAdoo

My dear Mac: The White House 30 December, 1920

Your telegram on my birthday¹ was very delightful to read and I thank you for it most affectionately.

It was very delightful to have a day or two with Nell, and she is certainly looking fine and strong, to our great delight.

With the season's affectionate greetings to you all,

Faithfully yours,   Woodrow Wilson

TLS (W. G. McAdoo Papers, DLC).
¹ WGM to WW, Dec. 28, 1920, T telegram (WP, DLC).

From Alexander Mitchell Palmer

My dear Mr. President: Washington December 30, 1920.

Referring to the inquiry contained in your letter of December twenty-ninth, so far as our records show, neither Senator LaFollette nor Senator Lenroot has endorsed William Ryan for appointment as United States Judge in the Western District of Wisconsin.

I have learned nothing about the attitude of Senator LaFollette but it has been represented to me that another candidate, who is a fellow-townsman of Senator Lenroot, says that he can be confirmed "because Senator Lenroot would be for him."

Faithfully yours,   A Mitchell Palmer

TLS (WP, DLC).

From Ray Stannard Baker

Amherst Massachusetts
December 30, 1920.

My dear Mr. Wilson:

I assume from your letter of the 27th, in which you speak of the "next time" I am down, that you are willing to have me come any time—even before March 4th. This, indeed, I should like to do, for the sooner I get at the work, the sooner we can have something to show for it. I think I can do it, or the preliminary part of it, without much interference with your manifold duties. If I am not right in this supposition, please correct me.

I have got a piece of writing on hand that will take me ten days or possibly two weeks to finish, and then I am free and quite prepared for the fine adventure you suggest.

The mention of the trunk quite takes hold of one's imagination. I shall search that trunk with far more interest than I should if it were treasure trove of the Spanish Main and contained pieces-of-eight!

The more I think of it, the more certain I am that here is a great and useful work to do: to try to present, with the sturdy thrust of the actual documents, facts, reasons, the first really great clash of America and American ideals with world affairs, and this from the American point of view. I have had the conviction all along that it was only necessary to set down the truth of the matter to convince reasonable human beings of the essential wisdom of your course at Paris.

The primary trouble at Paris, so far as America was concerned (as I see it) was a blinding ignorance on the part of our people of foreign problems. It was an outgrowth, of course, of our traditional isolation. I saw this vividly symbolized by our newspaper correspondents, many of them exceptionally good men and the best of them as able, or abler, than either British or French writers, but vastly inferior to either in knowledge of the history, politics and psychology, of Europe. I think a vigorous outline of what Europe was, as I saw it intimately during the year preceding the Peace Conference, would form a proper background for the picture of the Peace Conference. Only thus can we make clear the stupendous problems you had to face there: the forces you met: and the logic of your course.

My own general view of the Conference and of your course in it, I expressed in an address I delivered at Boston last summer.[1] I venture to enclose a copy with the essential paragraphs on pages 6 and 7 scored in blue so that you will not need to read the entire address, unless you care to do so.

In this address and in my little book,[2] I have set forth the general point of view with which I should wish to approach the development of the larger book. I think it might sometime be interesting to discuss the question as to how far these general views coincide with your own.

With cordial best wishes for a Happy New Year, I am

Sincerely yours,   Ray Stannard Baker

TLS (WP, DLC).

[1] *Should the United States Remain Outside the League of Nations? Address Delivered at the Annual Meeting of the League for Permanent Peace . . . Boston June 8th, 1920,* printed pamphlet (WP, DLC). In the paragraphs marked by Baker, he said that, in essence, the problem of the peace conference was the effort "to apply clear-cut moral principles . . . to the turgid and intractable realities of life." Although all the participants at the conference had agreed to make peace on the basis of Wilson's Fourteen Points, the nature and the multitude of problems made it impossible to arrive at easy and clear-cut solutions. Wilson and his colleagues had tried sincerely to achieve the best results they could and had faced problems "in the spirit of the highest and wisest statesmanship." After all, Baker continued, the American delegation was not in Paris for the purpose of correcting all ancient grievances or satisfying all national ambitions, but to establish machinery for the settlement of future problems. Thus, the League of Nations was "the inexorable minimum" of Wilson's demands, because, through the League, future changes and corrections in the various settlements could always be made. The treaty as adopted embodied all the unimaginative greeds, fears, vanities, and petty interests of the victorious nations. However, it also included "the finest aspirations and hopes of the world." "And the aspirations, the hopes, the forward-looking, the moral aspects," Baker concluded, "would not have been there if it had not been for America and American influence."

[2] *What Wilson Did at Paris* (Garden City, N. Y., 1919).

To Felixiana Shepherd Baker Woodrow

My dear Aunt Felie: The White House 31 December, 1920

Thank you for your birthday letter. I wish you could have said in your letter that you were getting stronger. I hope you are and that the New Year will bring you complete restoration of health and strength.   Affectionately yours,   Woodrow Wilson

TLS (received from James Woodrow).

From Thomas William Lamont

Dear Mr. President: [New York] December 31st, 1920.

WAR FINANCE CORPORATION

I note that both Houses of Congress have passed the Bill to revive the powers of the War Finance Corporation. In view of this fact, it is barely possible that it may be of some interest to you to have before you an advance copy of a report on this very subject that the New York Chamber of Commerce, Committee on Finance and Currency, is planning to present next week.[1] It so happens that, somewhat to my discomfort, I am Acting Chairman of this Committee. I am always reluctant to take a view contrary to that of Congress, but my view is, in effect, that already expressed by Secretary Houston, and we are, therefore, obliged in our report to adopt this position. We take occasion to say that any real revival of foreign trade must necessarily be dependent upon the settlement of certain factors in Europe, particularly that of German reparations. The opinion expressed in the report, of course, is not simply my own, but that of all the members of the Committee.

With great respect, I am, dear Mr. President,
Very truly yours,   Thomas W. Lamont

Happy New Year!

TLS (WP, DLC).
[1] *Report of the Committee on Finance and Currency, to be acted upon at the Meeting of the Chamber of Commerce of the State of New York, Jan. 6, 1921* (New York, 1920).

From Edmund Munroe Smith[1]

My dear Dr. Wilson: New York December 31 1920

I am writing, as you see, not to the President, but to a colleague. After the campaign of misrepresentation to which you have been exposed for two years, I feel moved to say that I, for one, share the ideals embodied in the League Covenant; believe that they will persist and prevail; and am confident that history will do you justice and give you full credit for the first great step towards a better world order.

May the New Year bring you health and strength,
Yours sincerely   Munroe Smith

ALS (WP, DLC).
[1] Wilson's old friend and critic, Professor of Roman Law and Comparative Jurisprudence at Columbia University since 1891.

From Håkon Löken and Others

Kristiania the 31st of December 1920

Highly appreciating the decision made by the Nobel Committee of the Norwegian Storting in awarding to you, Mr. President, the Alfred Nobel Peace Prize, for the year 1919, we the undersigned members of the Central Committee of Norges Fredsforening[1] venture to express our hearty congratulations and our unreserved admiration of the great work you have done since 1916 in bringing to accomplishment in the world's political life the great idea of the

international organization of nations, in order to secure the oblig-
atory settlement of all conflicts through peaceful means instead of
through war.

The statement made in your telegram read before the Storting[2]
by the honored Minister of your country, that the world as yet is
only at the beginning of this new evolution, is undisputable but,
like you, we place trust in this evolution as the one way to procure
happiness for humanity.

Hoping that the League of Nations will soon extend to all civilized nations and that its spirit of democracy will be intensified
from year to year, we present to Your Excellency our most hearty
good wishes for yourself and your family, for your great nation,
which contains so many of our kinsmen, and for the whole of mankind to which you have contributed so mighty a work.

Yours most respectfully

Håkon Löken	N. B. Thvedt	Hans B. Klaeborg
President	Vice president	Bernhard Nanssen
Hanna Isaachsen	Johanne Biörn Bording	Memb. of the Norw. parl.
Editor of "Folkefred"		F. F. Lövland

ALS (received from Robert R. Cullinane).
   [1] The Norwegian Peace Society.
   [2] See the Enclosure printed with NHD to WW, Dec. 8, 1920, Vol. 66. For a graphic
account of the ceremony in the Norwegian Parliament on December 10, at which Wilson's letter of acceptance was read, see A. G. Schmedeman to SecState, Dec. 13, 1920,
enclosed in NHD to WW, Jan. 13, 1921, TLS (WP, DLC).

From Eleanor Axson Sayre

Dear Grandfather   [Cambridge, Mass., c. Jan. 1, 1921]
   I love you so much
   Thank you for the nice Xmas present
                         Love and X X   Eleanor Sayre

ALS (WP, DLC).

A Veto Message[1]

                                        THE WHITE HOUSE,
To the Senate of the United States: 3 *January, 1921.*
   I am returning, without my signature, Senate joint resolution
212, "Joint resolution directing the War Finance Corporation to
take certain action for the relief of the present depression in the
agricultural sections of the country, and for other purposes."
   The joint resolution directs the revival of the activities of the War

Finance Corporation. This corporation is a governmental agency. Its capital stock is owned entirely by the United States. It was created during hostilities for war purposes. The temporary powers which it is now proposed to revive were conferred in March, 1919, to assist if necessary in the financing of exports. The general powers of the corporation expire six months after the termination of the war and the special powers with respect to the financing of exports expire one year after the termination of the war. While we are technically still in a state of war, it unquestionably was presumed, when this added power was granted, that peace would have been formally proclaimed before this time and that the limitation of one year would have expired.

In May, 1920, in view of the fact that export trade had not been interrupted, but had greatly expanded, and that exports were being privately financed in large volumes, the War Finance Corporation, at the request of the Secretary of the Treasury, and with my approval, suspended the making of advances.

This resolution was passed by the Congress apparently in view of the recent sudden and considerable fall in prices, especially of agricultural commodities, with the thought that some European countries to which certain products were customarily shipped before the war might again be enabled to resume their importation, and that larger masses of domestic exports to European countries generally might be stimulated, with the resulting enhancement of domestic prices. I am in full sympathy with every sound proposal to promote foreign trade along sound business lines. I am not convinced that the method proposed is wise, that the benefits, if any, would offset the evils which would result, or that the same or larger advantages can not be secured without resort to Government intervention. On the contrary, I apprehend that the resumption of the corporation's activities at this time would exert no beneficial influence on the situation in which improvement is sought, would raise false hopes among the very people who would expect most, and would be hurtful to the natural and orderly processes of business and finance.

Large Government credits were extended during the war to certain European governments associated with us in the struggle. These ceased several months after the armistice, except for commitments already made. They should not now be resumed, either directly or indirectly. The recent Brussels conference,[2] composed of experts from many European countries and from other nations, itself expressed the opinion that further credits should not be accorded directly by governments. I do not believe that they should be accorded indirectly.

Exports of domestic products have not declined since the armistice. On the contrary, they have greatly increased. From an aggregate value before the war of less than two and one-half billions of dollars, and of about six billions the last year of hostilities, they rose in the calendar year 1919 to more than $7,900,000,000, and this figure will probably be exceeded for the last calendar year. For the first eleven months of the last calendar year we exported more than seven and one-half billion dollars' worth of domestic merchandise. These have been largely privately financed. The difficulty in the way of still larger exports does not seem to lie so much in the lack of financial ability here as in Europe's lack of means to make payment. Her productive energies and the services which she renders have not yet reached a point where they balance the value of commodities taken from this Nation, and her ability to furnish for additional exports securities which business men would feel justified in taking is restricted. The experts of the Brussels conference reported that "one of the chief obstacles to the granting of credits is the absence in borrowing countries of sufficient securities for ultimate repayment." Until this obstacle is removed, it is difficult to see how materially larger exports to Europe are to be made even if exporters, aided or unaided by Government finance, stand ready to do their part. It is remarkable that Europe is able to make an effective demand for as large a volume of our goods as she is making. It is gratifying evidence of her recovery and progress toward full production and sounder financial conditions.

Under the law, if the activities of the corporation were resumed, no direct advances could be made to producers and, if they could be, they would not accomplish the objects in view. They would not create demand for our products. They could be made only to exporters or to banks engaged in financing exports and if they did in some measure stimulate exports they would probably not have the effect apparently most desired of substantially increasing those of agricultural commodities. Already, with the larger volume of exports which Europe is taking from us, she is exercising her option of taking a smaller volume of some of our principal agricultural products, such as meats, presumably because she herself has become more largely self-sufficient, or is again providing herself with supplies from distant countries which, with the opening up of shipping since the armistice, have once more found their place in the markets of the world.

It is highly probable that the most immediate and conspicuous effect of the resumption of the corporation's activities would be an effort on the part of exporters to shift the financing of their operations from ordinary commercial channels to the Government. This would be unfortunate. It would continue the Government as an active factor in ordinary business operations. If activities of any considerable magnitude resulted, they would necessitate the imposition of additional taxes or further borrowing, either through the War Finance Corporation or by the Treasury. In either case new burdens would be laid upon all the people. Further borrowing would in all likelihood tap the very sources which might otherwise be available for private operations or which the Treasury is now compelled to reach to meet current obligations of the Government. There is no question that the borrowing of the Government should be limited to the minimum requirements, and that the Government should not be called upon further to finance private business at public expense. To the extent that Europe is able to furnish additional securities, private financial institutions here will doubtless find means of giving the necessary accommodation. The way has been opened for added legitimate efforts to promote foreign trade. Financial agencies in aid of exports, privately financed, have already been planned to operate under the act approved December 24, 1919, authorizing the organization of banking corporations to do foreign banking business. One corporation has been organized in the South and a second of large scope is in course of development. These agencies may be expected to act as promptly and as liberally and helpfully as sound business conditions will permit. Through reliance on such enterprises, rather than through Government intervention, may we expect to secure a return to stable business relations. For many months there has been a demand that war agencies should be abolished and that there should be less Government interference with business. I have sympathized with this view, and believe that it is applicable to foreign trade as well as to domestic business. I am of the opinion that now, more than two years after the armistice, the Nation should resume its usual business methods and return to its reliance on the initiative, intelligence, and ability of its business leaders and financial institutions.

We shall not witness an immediate satisfactory adjustment of domestic and international trade relations. The burdens of war are not lifted when the fighting ceases. One sad thing about war is that it leaves behind a legacy of economic ills and of suffering from which there is no escape. Conditions, however, are improving both here and abroad. The difficulties with which we are now confronted are of small consequence in comparison with those which we have met and overcome. Fuller restoration awaits the adoption of constructive measures of large consequence; the secure establishment of a just peace in the world; the cessation of fighting everywhere; the more complete resumption in Europe of the normal courses of industry, the return of her people to sounder fiscal and banking policies, and the breaking down within her border of harmful restrictions.   Woodrow Wilson.[3]

Printed in *Cong. Record*, 66th Cong., 3d sess., p. 876.
    [1] We have found no evidence relating to the drafting of the following document. Presumably, Houston drafted it.
    [2] About which, see D. F. Houston to WW, Sept. 7, 1920, n. 1, Vol. 66.
    [3] The Senate and House overrode Wilson's veto on January 3 and 4, 1921, respectively.

To Alexander Mitchell Palmer

                                                    The White House
My dear Mr. Attorney General: 3 January, 1921
    I suppose, in view of the facts you lay before me, it would be wise for me to assent to the appointment of William Ryan for the Western District of Wisconsin, and I will be obliged if you would have the proper form of nomination made out.
                            Sincerely yours,   Woodrow Wilson

TLS (A. M. Palmer Papers, DLC).

To William Gibbs McAdoo

My dear Mac: The White House 3 January, 1921
    I need not tell you that your message of the first[1] gave us a great deal of pleasure. You and Nell and the babies have been very much in our hearts, and we hope that the New Year will bring everything that is delightful and comfortable.
    I suspect you of the intention of settling down in California. Don't do it.   Affectionately yours,   Woodrow Wilson

TLS (W. G. McAdoo Papers, DLC).
    [1] WGM to WW, Jan. 1, 1921, T telegram (WP, DLC).

To Eleanor Axson Sayre

My dear little Granddaughter: The White House 3 January, 1921
    I was so much pleased by your letter. It was very nicely written and it was a pleasure to know that you are all right and getting on finely. I love you very much and hope that the New Year will be very happy for you.

Give my love to Francis and Woodrow. I wish that I might see you sometime soon.   Your loving   Grand-Father

TLS (received from Francis B. Sayre).

From Norman Hezekiah Davis, with Enclosure

My dear Mr. President: Washington January 3, 1921.

I am enclosing a cable received from Secretary Colby, which I think may be of interest to you.

Faithfully yours,   Norman H. Davis

TLS (WP, DLC).

E N C L O S U R E

For Norman Davis.   Montevideo, Received January 1, 1921.

Your message of greetings and news greatly appreciated. Dominican delegation not the least troublesome.[1] I can take care of them. You can have no conception of the intelligent appreciation in South America of President Wilson and unfeigned affections which he is held. He would never believe it himself. My stay here has been touching in its cordiality. Bringing beautiful present from Uruguay to Mrs. Wilson. Please advise her. Reach Buenos Aires tomorrow morning, leaving there Monday night for home. Find three days adequate for all functions and not prolonging stay at any point in order not to burden hosts. Happy to be coming home but President's judgement of importance of this trip fully vindicated and entirely beyond my previous conception. Thank Grayson his message which made me happy. Please convey my New Year's Greetings to President.[2] With warmest regards for yourself.

Colby.

T telegram (WP, DLC).

[1] A news report, datelined Santiago, Chile, December 27, 1920, described this situation as follows: "Secretary Colby has been preceded through South America by [Francisco] Henríquez [y] Carvajal, former President of Santo Domingo, who is heading a propaganda commission charging that the United States has committed atrocities in Haiti and Santo Domingo and attempting to persuade the South American republics to champion the islanders against the United States. Carvajal has just reached Buenos Aires, following trips to Rio [de] Janeiro and Montevideo, leaving his declarations fresh in the minds of each capital before Secretary Colby's arrival." *New York Times*, Dec. 28, 1920.

[2] Wilson responded to Colby's greeting in an undated T MS attached to the above document, which reads as follows: "Please ask Secretary Davis, the next time he communicates with Colby, to give him my warmest good wishes for the New Year, my thanks for the fine work he is doing, and an expression of my impression that that work

has been doing a great deal of good. The President. C.L.S." This was conveyed to Davis in JPT to NHD, Jan. 5, 1921, TLS (SDR, RG 59, 811.458/656, DNA).

From Charles Homer Haskins

Cambridge, Massachusetts
Dear President Wilson: 3 January 1921

Some time when you have leisure for matters historical you may be interested in the enclosed report of a lecture[1] which I gave last week in Philadelphia and which is to be printed with others of the series in book form next spring.[2] I have tried to make clear how you maintained your fundamental position on the Left Bank and the Sarre, thus correcting the perspective of Tardieu's articles in *l'Illustration*, which were brought to my attention by the Secretary of State in the summer.[3] If anything in my own statement needs correction or supplementing, I am particularly anxious to gets its final form accurate.

With all best wishes for the New Year, believe me
Sincerely yours,   Charles H. Haskins

TLS (WP, DLC).
[1] Tear sheets from the Philadelphia *Public Ledger*, Dec. 31, 1920, WP, DLC.
[2] Haskins gave the fourth lecture at the Academy of Music in Philadelphia in a series organized by Colonel House, sponsored by Edward W. Bok, and known as the Public Ledger Forum on the Peace Conference. The lectures were published as Edward M. House and Charles Seymour, eds., *What Really Happened at Paris: The Story of the Peace Conference, 1918-1919, by American Delegates* (New York, 1921).
[3] About Tardieu's articles, see BC to WW, July 23, 1920, n. 1, Vol. 65; for Colby's letter to Haskins, see WW to BC, July 24, 1920, n. 2, *ibid.*

Norman Hezekiah Davis to Joseph Patrick Tumulty, with Enclosure

Dear Mr. Tumulty: Washington January 3, 1921.

In accordance with a suggestion from the President, I am enclosing herewith a statement to be given out from the White House regarding General Crowder's mission to Cuba.[1] As the newspaper men have already heard something and are making inquiries, I suggest that this be given out for the afternoon papers.
Sincerely yours,   Norman H. Davis

TLS (WP, DLC).
[1] The Cuban presidential election had been held on November 1, 1920, with Alfredo Zayas y Alfonso and José Miguel Gómez as the contestants. The results were inconclusive, and there were widespread allegations of fraud, voter intimidation, and violence. Complaints about the conduct of the election in a great many voting districts were sub-

mitted to provincial election boards, to the national election board, and finally to the courts. This process proceeded so slowly that by this time it was widely believed that the imbroglio could not be resolved before the time set for the presidential inauguration in May 1921. At the same time, an economic crisis brought on by a steep decline in the price of sugar threatened to force Cuba's banks to close and plunge the country into financial chaos. In this situation, Norman Davis decided to send Maj. Gen. Enoch H. Crowder, who in 1919 had been primarily responsible for formulating the existing Cuban election law, to Havana to inform President Mario Garcia Menocal of the concern of the American government over the political and financial situation in Cuba, and to discuss remedial measures. Crowder sailed for Cuba on January 1. See Dana G. Munro, *Intervention and Dollar Diplomacy in the Caribbean, 1900-1921* (Princeton, N. J., 1964), pp. 517-22, and David A. Lockmiller, *Enoch H. Crowder: Soldier, Lawyer and Statesman* (Columbia, Mo., 1955), pp. 228-30. Davis' instructions to Crowder are printed in *FR 1920*, II, 41-43.

E N C L O S U R E

Upon instructions of the President, Major General Enoch H. Crowder has sailed for Havana, Cuba, on the u.s.s. MINNESOTA. General Crowder goes to Cuba to confer with President Menocal regarding conditions in Cuba. The moratorium and financial crisis in Cuba continue, the solution of which appears more difficult on account of the unsettled Presidential election. A continuation of the present situation would prove most detrimental to the prosperity of Cuba and harmful to the relations between the United States and Cuba. As this cannot but be a matter of the closest concern to this Government because of the special relations existing between the two countries, the President has instructed General Crowder to confer with President Menocal as to the best means of remedying the situation.

T MS (WP, DLC).

From the Diary of Josephus Daniels

[Jan. 4, 1921]

Jan 4. W.W. said he did not wish to make position of Sec or Asst Sec a stepping stone to a place on a commission (Woodbury exit)[1]

Shall Eugene Meyers be appointed?[2] Burleson & others seemed to think "yes" & Houston said he would not like to work with a liar.[3] Burleson said "offer place to Senators who were active in putting it over the veto." WW no. He said Dems. had better traditions than Republicans but did not live up to them. H——— evidently not keen to make loans & doubtful if Corporation functions with spirit to make it meet the needs.

Davis talked about Cuba. Is Gomez[4] part negro? WGH[5] Sent

Gen. Crowder down on ship to confer with Menocal to secure set-tle[men]t of presidential election. Moritorium ordered, ships in harbor unloaded, & conditions bad. I said Marines had 4 yrs ago helped keep Menocal in when he was not elected.

Should Morgan's offer of house in London for Am. Embassy be accepted?[6] He said he would hold it open only till March. WW said yes

Coontz went before Com.[7] & said Japan & England were working together & Japan was finding ships in GB. Japs here troubled when they learned we knew it—said they were not *war* ships

[1] Gordon Woodbury, who had succeeded Franklin D. Roosevelt as Assistant Secretary of the Navy, was eager for appointment to the Interstate Commerce Commission, to succeed Robert W. Woolley. Wilson did not view such ambition favorably. In reply to a letter from Carter Glass recommending Woodbury for the I. C. C., Wilson replied somewhat testily: "I have no doubt that what you say of Mr. Woodbury is true. I should believe it whether I knew anything of him or not, but, as you know, I have already appointed him Assistant Secretary of the Navy and I had supposed that that was sufficient indication of my high esteem for him. I do not think it would be wise at present to take him away from the Navy Department and put him in the Interstate Commerce Commission, and hope that you will not too strongly disagree with this judgment." C. Glass to WW, Dec. 23, 1920, TLS (WP, DLC), and WW to C. Glass, Dec. 24, 1920, CCL (WP, DLC).

[2] Eugene Meyer, Jr., who had been managing director of the War Finance Corporation, had been very active in the movement to reestablish that agency in order to promote the export of American farm products.

[3] Houston undoubtedly referred to something Meyer had said to congressional committees and public groups in his campaign to reestablish the W.F.C.

[4] To repeat, Gen. José Miguel Gómez, President of Cuba, 1901-1913, who was contesting the election of Alfredo Zayas y Alfonso.

[5] Probably a reference to the rumor that Harding had some Negro ancestry.

[6] J. Pierpont Morgan, Jr., in a letter to Lansing of April 17, 1919, had offered to donate his London home at 13-14 Lancaster Gate, Hyde Park, to be used as the American Ambassador's residence in the British capital. Wilson had directed that the letter be turned over to Vice President Marshall and Speaker Clark. See WW to RL, June 3, 1919 (first letter of that date), and the notes thereto, Vol. 60; also the *New York Times*, Jan. 21, 1921.

Having received no reply to his letter, Morgan announced in early January 1921 that he would withdraw his offer unless it was acted upon by March 4. The House of Representatives, on January 29, accepted an amendment to the Diplomatic and Consular Appropriations bill to permit the government to accept Morgan's offer. *New York Times*, Jan. 30, 1921. This provision was in the final version of the bill that Wilson signed on March 2. 41 *Statutes at Large* 1214.

[7] Rear Adm. Robert Edward Coontz, Chief of Naval Operations, testified on January 3 before an executive session of the Senate Foreign Relations Committee on a resolution introduced by William E. Borah calling for a conference of the British, Japanese, and American governments for the purpose of agreeing on a program of reduction of naval armaments. Coontz asserted that any reduction should preserve the present proportionated standing of the United States, Great Britain, and Japan.

From Jan Christiaan Smuts

Dear Mr President   Pretoria. 4 Jan. 1921

I take the liberty to send you a memo which has also gone to the New York Evening Post to be published on your retirement from the Presidency.[1] I have asked the Editor to give it publicity also in other papers. It expresses my confidence in the permanance of the great work you have rendered for humanity in our age. America does not seem to appreciate yet that the foundations of a new world order has been laid by one of her own sons on the ruins of the war. But she will do so yet.

We have all watched your illness with deep and grave anxiety. My wish for you is that you may have peace and happiness at the last, and a return of strength to continue the great human work to which your life has been dedicated.

Ever yours sincerely   J. C. Smuts

ALS (WP, DLC).
¹ This article, entitled "Woodrow Wilson's Place in History," was an attempt to assess that subject in the context of the passions and greed which Smuts said carried the day in Paris and resulted in the imposition of a "Punic" treaty on Germany. It was not Wilson who had failed in Paris, Smuts argued, but the human spirit and humanity itself. Although overwhelmed by atavistic forces, Wilson, by sheer will power, had succeeded in defending and protecting the Covenant, "one of the great creative documents of human history," Smuts was sure that all nations would eventually fall in behind the Covenant's banner in a "march forward to triumphs of peaceful organisation and achievement undreamt of by us children of an unhappier era." Smuts concluded with a mighty tribute to Wilson: "And the leader who, in spite of apparent failure, succeeded in inscribing his name on that Banner, has achieved the most enviable and enduring immortality. Americans of the future will yet proudly and gratefully rank him with Washington and Lincoln, and his fame will have a more universal significance than theirs." CC MS (WP, DLC). Smuts' article was printed widely in American newspapers on March 3 and 4, 1921.

To Ray Stannard Baker

My dear Baker: [The White House] 5 January, 1921

I have yours of December thirtieth, and you have correctly interpreted my meaning. My idea is that you should come down at your own convenience, and then we should immediately get together to make the arrangements which I indicated in my last letter.

Thank you for the copy of the address which you were thoughtful enough to send me.

I hope that the New Year will bring you everything that is helpful and delightful.

Cordially and sincerely yours,   [Woodrow Wilson]

CCL (WP, DLC).

To Thomas William Lamont

My dear Friend: [The White House] 5 January, 1921

Thank you for your letter of December thirty-first with its enclosure. I think the very weighty objections which the Committee on

Finance and Currency of the New York Chamber of Commerce urge against the recent financial action of the Congress are substantially embedded in the veto which has just been overridden. I sincerely hope so. Certainly, the objections should have prevailed, but unhappily they did not.

With the warmest regards and best wishes for the New Year to both Mrs. Lamont[1] and yourself from both of us,

Cordially and sincerely yours,   [Woodrow Wilson]

CCL (WP, DLC).
    [1] Florence Haskell Corliss Lamont.

To Samuel M. Johnson[1]

My dear Doctor Johnson: [The White House] 5 January, 1921

It gives me real pleasure to express my interest in the association of which you are the General Director. It is certainly most appropriate that there should be a national memorial to General Lee. It is one of the happy circumstances of our national life that the bitterness of the Civil War has disappeared and that General Lee is now recognized as a man worthy of the admiration of the whole nation. Certainly his heart was true to the nation, and he did all in his power to heal the wounds which were made by the bitter civil strife in which he was obliged to take part.

It is a happy old saying that sectional lines are obliterated only by the feet that cross them, and this great highway should contribute to that much-to-be-desired result.

Cordially and sincerely yours,   [Woodrow Wilson]

CCL (WP, DLC).
    [1] A civil engineer of Roanoke, Va., and general director of the Lee Highway Association of the same city. The objective of the association was the promotion of a southern transcontinental highway to be named in honor of Robert Edward Lee and similar in concept to the previously projected Lincoln Highway. The Lee Highway was to extend from New York to San Francisco, via Washington, Memphis, and San Diego. For a detailed description of the project, see S. M. Johnson, "GREAT LEE HIGHWAY," *New York Times*, Jan. 15, 1922, Sect. VI, p. 7. As it turned out, the Lee Highway as thus envisioned never materialized.

To Edmund Munroe Smith

[The White House]
My dear Professor Smith: 5 January, 1920 [1921]
Your kind letter of December thirty-first gratified me very much indeed and I want to thank you for its expression of friendship and confidence, which cheers and strengthens me.
With the best wishes for the New Year.
Sincerely yours,   [Woodrow Wilson]

CCL (WP, DLC).

From Gordon Woodbury

My dear Mr. President: Washington. January 5, 1921.
My Chief, Mr. Daniels, has told me of his conversation with you regarding my desire to serve on the Interstate Commerce Commission, and of your feeling that my appointment should not be made. I have long been accustomed to accept your views upon all matters with unvarying concurrence in your wisdom. And I do so now, much as I am disappointed. The greatest honor I have ever had is the opportunity you gave me to serve here and as a part, though for but a short time, of your administration, the most notable in high purpose and accomplishment in our history.
Allow me, Sir, to say to you in this way, as I may not see you face to face, that your exalted character and brilliant achievements are and long have been, an inspiration to me, as they have been to many others. And I beg to say that I still venerate you, admire and respect you, and I cherish the hope that still greater benefits are yet to come to this country and to all the World through your great leadership and devotion to mankind.
Very respectfully yours,   Gordon Woodbury

TLS (WP, DLC).

From Charles Stedman Macfarland

My dear Mr. President: New York January 5, 1921
Your message to the Federal Council of the Churches of Christ in America,[1] recently assembled in session at Boston, was received with the deepest appreciation, the entire Council rising and manifesting its deeply sympathetic and prayerful spirit.
I think I may say that the meeting in Boston did and will fulfill the hope which you so confidently expressed and that the Federal

Council, representing so large a body of the churches, has been strengthened and will be strengthened so that it may become an increasing power in the nation and in the world.

If you should have opportunity to read the official records when they appear later I am sure you would be gratified at the manner in which the Council met questions affecting both national and international affairs.

The Council not only deeply regretted your absence but with prayerful sympathy still more regretted that it should be caused by the physical burdens which you have so long and so patiently borne.

It was very clear that entirely aside from points of view on political questions, the members of the Council desired to express their personal appreciation of yourself and your service.

Faithfully yours,   Charles S. Macfarland

TLS (WP, DLC).
[1] Macfarland was replying to WW to C. S. Macfarland, Nov. 18, 1920, Vol. 66.

From the Shorthand Diary of Charles Lee Swem

5 January, 1921

This morning the President expressed irritation at a note the Secretary[1] sent him asking him to send a message of condolence to somebody who was dying. The President said that the people the Secretary said were dying never turned out to die. One case he cited was Roosevelt, another was Cardinal Gibbons, both of whom revived and lived for some time after. The Secretary was always going off half-cocked.

JRT transcript (WC, NjP) of CLSsh (C. L. Swem Coll., NjP).
[1] That is, Tumulty.

From Charles Zeller Klauder

My dear Mr. President: Philadelphia January 6th, 1921.

Your appreciative letters of December 23rd and 27th[1] have been received. I am glad to know that you liked the little portfolio of drawings and also the basement plan. The book on the Cotswold District has also come safely to hand. It is indeed gratifying to learn of your satisfaction with the house you have purchased and I look forward with pleasure to seeing it.

I am entirely in accord with your suggestion to use for the entrance from the road to the western cloister, the type of door with the wrought iron hinges and big nails as found at Sulgrave Manor. Your suggestion to open the garage on the main road is excellent. To do so will not only be the means of avoiding the unsightly stains from cars but will give a sense of privacy to the fore court.

The problem of locating the valet's room is a difficult one, but I think we can solve it very interestingly. The space is now too small for a billiard room, the minimum size of which should be 14′ x 19′ for a small table, and 15′ x 20′ for a table of standard size, in order to leave a playing space 5′ wide all around the table. The study above is not to [so] large as this. Nevertheless, we could make the billiard room most attractive by supporting the west wall of the study on a great wide arch, the crown of which would make its appearance above the terrace floor. A small sketch is enclosed to show you our idea in details.

Another suggestion which offers itself is to place the billiard room under the south end of the great hall, in which case the main stair of the house and the elevator would lead directly into this room. It would be a most interesting room and it could have a window of the semi-bay type like the one in the great hall. It could also readily have a large fireplace even though this involves shifting the fireplace in the dining room to the front wall near the porte cochere. This may cause some difficulty in Mrs. Wilson's suite but I think we can suggest an acceptable solution of this also.

We should like to know whether the location indicated for the vault opening into the sitting room commends itself to you. We shall develop the sitting room above the porte cochere with its wide arch-way leading to the gallery in the upper portion of the great hall.   Sincerely yours,   Chas Z Klauder

P.S. Prints sent are Set No. 6, basement plan, revisions A and B,
       ”   ”   ” section through billard room
          looking east.
       All dated January 3rd, 1921.[2]

TLS (WP, DLC).
    [1] Wilson's letter of December 27, 1920, is printed in this volume; his letter to Klauder of December 23, 1920, is printed in Vol. 66.
    [2] They are missing.

To Gordon Woodbury

My dear Mr. Woodbury: [The White House] 7 January, 1921

Your letter of January fifth has gratified me very much. You may be sure that I am happy to have had you associated with my administration.[1]

Cordially and sincerely yours,   [Woodrow Wilson]

CCL (WP, DLC).

[1] Actually, Woodbury stayed on as Assistant Secretary of the Navy until March 4, 1921.

To Charles Stedman Macfarland

My dear Mr. Macfarland: [The White House] 7 January, 1921

I read with pleasure your letter of January fifth and am very glad indeed that the session in Boston should have been so successful in every way. You may be sure it was a pleasure to send my greetings to the assembly.

In haste   Sincerely yours,   [Woodrow Wilson]

CCL (WP, DLC).

From Norman Hezekiah Davis

My dear Mr. President: Washington January 7, 1920 [1921].

For your information, the Cuban Minister[1] has informed us of the receipt of a cable today stating that President Menocal would receive General Crowder with much pleasure.

Yours faithfully,   Norman H. Davis

TLS (WP, DLC).

[1] That is, Carlos Manuel de Céspedes.

To Norman Hezekiah Davis

My dear Davis: The White House 7 January, 1921

I was cheered to read that Menocal had concluded to act like a gentleman in receiving Crowder, and I hope that this closes what might have been an unpleasant incident.

Cordially and faithfully yours,   Woodrow Wilson

TLS (SDR, RG 59, 837.00/2118, DNA).

From Norman Hezekiah Davis, with Enclosure

My dear Mr. President: Washington January 7, 1921.

I am enclosing for your information and consideration a letter from Ambassador Wallace relative to our withdrawal from participation in various commissions in Europe.

As suggested by you, I told Ambassador Jusserand several days ago of our concern and attitude regarding the latest manipulations in France looking to occupation of the Ruhr coal basin.[1] I think it had a good effect. He told me he would communicate with his Government immediately. Yesterday he called and told me that while his Government wished to have a thorough discussion with the Allied Powers regarding Germany's failure to comply with her obligations, and while he hoped that this Government would give most friendly and sympathetic consideration to the French contention, his Government would take no action without the consent of such Powers. I told him under those circumstances we would consider all the facts in relation to the subject, but that as long as there is agitation regarding French permanent occupation of the Rhine provinces or of an occupation of the Ruhr coal basin, confidence and stability cannot be restored which is so essential for the economic rehabilitation of Europe and France. I also explained that in case of wilful failure by Germany to comply it would be necessary to consider the expediency of taking any action.

The French Ambassador has sent me a copy of a note from the French Government sent to Germany on December thirty-first, defining the various failures on the part of Germany to comply with her obligations under the Treaty and under the Spa Protocol. He also informs us that the Supreme Council will meet on the seventeenth to consider this question and his Government hopes the United States will be represented at this meeting. I presume that you do not wish to have a representative at this meeting.

If, however, for the reasons advanced by Ambassador Wallace, and the fact that the above questions raised by France are to receive consideration in the very near future, you should determine to postpone withdrawal from the Council of Ambassadors, I presume you would want me to instruct Ambassador Wallace as to your views regarding this question.[2]

Faithfully and cordially yours,   Norman H. Davis

[1] Talk about an imminent French occupation of the Ruhr Valley had been in the air since late December 1920, when a report by Gen. Charles-Marie-Edouard Nollet, head of the Interallied Commission of Control in Germany, to the Conference of Ambassadors had charged the German government with a violation of the disarmament agreement concluded at Spa in July 1920. According to this agreement, Germany was to reduce its regular army to 100,000 men and its so-called citizen police to 150,000 men by January

1, 1921. In the event Germany failed to carry out these provisions, France would have the right to occupy additional German territory. According to Nollet's report, not only was the citizen police force still larger than stipulated, but militia units in East Prussia and Bavaria also had not been disbanded. Although the German government had denied Nollet's allegations and insisted that the militia units were needed to protect East Prussia from Bolshevism and prevent civil war in Bavaria, the Conference of Ambassadors, in a move that clearly worried the Germans, had instructed Foch to look into the whole question of German disarmament. In addition, the French government, on December 31, 1920, sent a note to the German government, charging that Germany had failed to live up to the disarmament requirements of the Versailles Treaty and had not fulfilled the promises made at the Spa conference.

As a result of Nollet's report, the State Department conducted its own investigation and made it known that the United States would oppose any proposition further to punish Germany for the violation of provisions that the German government could not possibly execute. According to news reports, the American government regarded French intentions to occupy the Ruhr Valley "with genuine concern" and would "take positive action" if France should proceed unjustly against Germany.

In an apparent effort to head off American, British, and Italian criticism of its independent action, the French government, on January 5, asked for a meeting of the Allied Prime Ministers in Paris on January 19 to discuss the question of German disarmament and, two days later, asked the United States to be represented at the conference. A report in the *New York Times*, January 8, 1921, stated that Wilson was considering the French request, but that it was generally understood that he would not authorize American participation in the Paris meeting. See also *ibid.*, Dec. 30 and 31, 1920, and Jan. 6, 1921.

2 The following is typed at the top of the carbon copy of this letter in the State Department files (SDR, RG 59, 763.72119/11136A, DNA):

"The President called by telephone and informed me that the reasons given by Wallace were not controlling, and that they should be instructed to carry out his former instructions to get off the Council of Ambassadors. NHD."

E N C L O S U R E

Hugh Campbell Wallace to Norman Hezekiah Davis

Personal and Confidential.

My dear Mr. Secretary: Paris, December 17, 1920.

In my cable reply to your secret telegram No. 1073 of December 15th, 5 P.M.,¹ I am asking that you defer final decision as regards the withdrawal of our representation on the Council of Ambassadors until you receive this letter.

While I can only conjecture as to the reasons actuating your decision not only to withdraw from the Ambassadors Conference, but also from the Reparations Commission and all other commissions in Europe, I presume the proposal is based on the result of the elections. I realise that in that sense the decision is logical, but I venture to point out the reasons why such action would in my opinion be a mistake.

The question is briefly this: either we maintain our representation or we effect immediate withdrawal.

In the first case, the new administration upon their advent to power can do one of two things: it can either maintain our representation on commissions in Europe and thereby endorse the wisdom of the present administration, or it can withdraw our representation, which will be regarded here as a signal that America was deserting Europe. This will also bring down upon it the condemnation of our former associates as well as the criticism of American commercial and financial interests which, aside from the humanitarian aspects of the question, are deeply interested in the rehabilitation of Europe for commercial purposes.

The alternative now under consideration is the immediate withdrawal of all American representation on the commissions in Europe.

Aside from the manifest benefit which accrues to our interests both political, commercial and financial by being represented on these commissions particularly on the Reparations Commission, there is another aspect of the matter which I deem it my duty to lay before you.

To go back a little, last summer when my predecessor, Mr. Myron T. Herrick, was here, he obtained considerable publicity. On more than one occasion he intimated that the many difficulties with which the French Government and people were faced would be rectified by the Republican administration. For instance, in one of his addresses he begged France to have patience and wait a little longer. This was said while the campaign was in progress. Generally speaking, such statements as this led the majority of French political opinion to expect that the advent of the new administration would right all ills for France. It would not be an exaggeration to say that the French, if not every European statesman, are anxiously waiting to see what the United States will do. France is expecting a great deal.

It was in this atmosphere that Medill McCormick[2] landed recently. He had been heralded as the special representative of the new administration. He met many members of the Government. He had conversations with Marshal Foch and prominent members of the general staff; he saw senators and representatives. He expressed his contempt for the League of Nations. It is true he approved in general terms some idea of an Association of Nations to prevent war. On the other hand, he gave them no hope of the ratification of the defensive treaty of alliance.[3] He forecasted the withdrawal of our troops on the Rhine after March 4th. His general attitude towards European affairs and his opposition to American participation therein has already caused people to ponder. I think they are already beginning to see the contrast between this administration and what is likely to follow.

Under the circumstances, if we now withdraw, this administration will voluntarily incur an obloquy which may well be passed to other shoulders. If the new administration should replace our representatives, it would be argued here and in America that we had not only been remiss in safeguarding American interests but also that we had deserted Europe and that the new administration had come to the rescue of a situation brought about by us.

I have been somewhat pressed for time in making this reply to your telegram which I only received yesterday, and no doubt could enlarge upon what I have said in this letter, but I feel so strongly my duty to the President and the administration in this matter, not to mention what appears to me to be the best interests of our country, that I cannot help fervently to express the hope that you will reconsider your decision.

If you see fit I should be very glad for you to show this letter to the President.

I beg that you will not place this letter on the files of the Department.

Believe me, my dear Mr. Secretary,

Yours very sincerely,   Hugh C. Wallace

TLS (WP, DLC).
[1] "SECRET, for Ambassador. It has practically been decided to discontinue participation in the meetings of the Council of Ambassadors. I should be glad to have your views as to best procedure if and when decision is put into effect." NHD to H. C. Wallace, No. 1703, Dec. 15, 1920, T telegram (SDR, RG 59, 763.72119/10799a, DNA).
Wallace replied to this message saying that he was sending a personal letter by pouch, which he thought Davis should have before making a final decision on the question of withdrawal from the Conference of Ambassadors and the Reparation Commission. H. C. Wallace to NHD, No. 2021, Dec. 17, 1920, T telegram (SDR, RG 59, 763.72119/10801, DNA).
[2] Republican senator from Illinois.
[3] That is, the so-called French Security Treaty, about which see index references to it in preceding volumes under the heading "France," or "France and the United States."

Three Letters from Norman Hezekiah Davis

My dear Mr. President: Washington January 7, 1921.

I believe Secretary Colby informed you that Ambassador Davis agreed to return to London, and to remain as long as his services are required by this Administration, but that in case of unforeseen developments he would be released before the fourth of March, so as not to have to remain until his successor takes office.

I am in receipt of a confidential letter from him,[1] saying that he would like very much to arrange to sail from London about the middle of February, and that if it meets with our approval he would like to place his resignation in your hands at once, to take effect upon his departure. As he has requested a reply by cable I should be glad to have your views.

Faithfully yours,   Norman H. Davis

[1] J. W. Davis to NHD, Dec. 16, 1920, TLS (N. H. Davis Papers, DLC).

My dear Mr. President: Washington January 7, 1921.

I am in receipt of a note from Judge Elkus, announcing his return and his willingness to come here and give an unofficial and confidential account of the work of the Aland Commission. He says that he would be glad to tell you personally or write you about it. I shall be glad to communicate your wishes in the matter.

Faithfully yours,   Norman H. Davis

My dear Mr. President: Washington January 7, 1921.

A rather embarras[s]ing and perplexing situation has developed relative to Donal O'Callaghan, claiming to be Lord Mayor of Cork,[1] who arrived at Newport News, Virginia, on January fourth, as a stowaway from Cork on board an American steamship, but without a passport.

The Department of State received today a communication from the Immigration Inspector at Norfolk giving the facts in the case, and requesting a decision as to whether or not the passport regulations would be waived. Before this reached me for consideration it was learned that the Secretary of Labor had allowed O'Callaghan to enter the United States on parole, without awaiting the decision of the Department of State. I called the Secretary of Labor by telephone to ascertain his reasons for taking such action. He informed me, in substance, that on account of the political and other embarrassing aspects of the question he thought the best way to dispose of it was to grant a parole, theoretically keeping the Lord Mayor within the custody of the Department of Labor, pending a decision as to his entry into the United States. As you are no doubt aware, he comes to testify before the Committee of One Hundred which is investigating Irish conditions. A parole would enable him to testify pending Secretary Wilson's decision.

I reminded Secretary Wilson of the fact that under existing law and regulations the power of the Immigration Bureau is limited to determining whether or not an alien is admissible to the United States under the immigration laws, and that the power to determine whether or not an alien may enter without a passport or visa is reserved to the Secretary of State. Secretary Wilson then stated that he understood that the Secretary of State would not be called upon to pass on the matter at all until after the Secretary of Labor has made his decision. This is not to the point, because the Secretary of State may very well refuse entry to an alien without a passport or a visa whom the Secretary of Labor may consider admissible under the immigration law, in which case the Immigration Bureau has nothing to decide. In this particular case, however, the Immigration Bureau has already referred the question to the Secretary of State. I therefore inquired of Secretary Wilson if I should now determine that O'Callaghan cannot be admitted to the United States without a passport and order his deportation, he would feel that he had a right to give the matter any further consideration, and if he would therefore issue the orders for deportation. To this he replied that he would be inclined to defer action until he had all the facts in the case.

I am informed that under existing legislation and decrees issued by you thereunder, any person who attempts to enter the country without a passport or a visa, or without permission of the Secretary of State, is liable to arrest, fine and imprisonment. It would seem, therefore, that unless the policy of the Department is reversed and an exception made of this case, it is my duty to refuse entry to O'Callaghan and to order his deportation. This case has already received considerable publicity, and any action is going to cause more publicity.

Unfortunately, Secretary Wilson informed me he will be absent until Monday, but I feel that in so far as the Department of State is concerned, a decision should be made without further delay, and I should therefore be pleased to have your guidance and instructions.   Faithfully and cordially yours,   Norman H. Davis

TLS (WP, DLC).
    [1] O'Callaghan, who was indeed the new Lord Mayor of Cork, had come to the United States to testify before the American Commission on Conditions in Ireland, commonly known as the Committee of One Hundred, on events in Cork in December 1920 (about which, see NHD to WW, Dec. 15, 1920 [first letter of that date], n. 3, Vol. 66). The Committee of One Hundred (later called the Committee of One Hundred and Fifty), established on September 25, 1920, was sponsored by Oswald Garrison Villard and the New York *Nation* and included a distinguished and broad-based membership, among which were Cardinal Gibbons, Senator David I. Walsh of Massachusetts, Senator Robert M. La Follette of Wisconsin, Senator James D. Phelan of California, Jane Addams, etc. The committee's hearings were conducted by eight non-Irish members headed by Levi Hollingsworth Wood, New York lawyer, active in the American Friends Service Committee and social-reform and peace groups.

The White House Staff to Joseph Patrick Tumulty

Memo. for Mr. Tumulty: The White House, January 7, 1921

Will you kindly indicate what is to be done with the Trenton file? The letters were all gone over in 1913 and such as could be so disposed of were sent to the Departments; the rest—6 drawers-full is in the attic.

We have 150 drawers full of the general office files. This includes routine letters, file cards showing stuff sent to the Departments, etc. It has been the practice in the past to destroy this file by burning. Shall this course be followed with the present file? Of course the more important letters are kept in the "Numbered" file—this file is treated as a permanent office record.

If the general file is to be destroyed, permission is requested to burn the four years' accumulation—1913 to 1917—at this time, as it is a slow process and will take considerable time.

It is assumed that the President will take with him his personal file of which we have four drawers, card indexed and arranged numerically, and that you will take your personal file which has been kept in the File Room which is likewise arranged numerically.[1]

T MS (WP, DLC).
  [1] Swem's note at the top of this letter reads: "Jan 12/20 President says send his file & the Trenton file to his new home. OKeh to burn old general office files. C.L.S."

William Edward Dodd to Virginia Le Roy[1]

My dear Mrs. Le Roy: [Chicago, c. Jan. 7, 1921]

Your letter of last fall has remained unanswered on my desk all this time, not for want of interest but because of too many pressing things and the realization that we were in accord and no immediate reply would be of particular importance. Besides Mrs. Dodd[2] was twice in the hospital during the autumn threatened with some trouble that seemed ominous. She is better now and we are sure it is not what we at one time feared.

Has it not been a marvellous year, this last one? Our generation will surely be weighed in the balances one of these days and found wanting, found to have abandoned its best faith and even its moral obligations to a world broken and prostrate. If ever a nation returned to its flesh-pots ours has done so since November, 1918. My only consolation consists in the full confidence that we shall all come back to our former ideals, even if it is too late to reap the fruits of ideals put into practice.

At present I am engaged in adding two chapters to my *Wilson and His Work*, which is to appear in a fifth edition revised and enlarged as soon after March 4th as I can get the proof and the composing done. Perhaps the newspapers will not have so strong a motive to suppress the book this time, and I am hoping the publishers may have the courage to advertise this time—which they did not have before. Anyway I shall do my part and some people will buy the book. The record will be kept straight.

Last week[3] I lunched with the President and then spent two hours talking with him in his bedroom, where he lay in bed reviewing some of the ordeals he went through at Paris and later in Washington. It almost overcame me and more than once the tears welled up in his eyes, as he told of the near-ness to success and then of the ways men had to prevent success. He says all mankind deserted him at Paris.[4] The fact is that mankind deserted its ideals in the flush of victory that came sooner than men had expected. It was awful to me those days of heartless talk and receding ideals of October and November 1919. Since that time, one long wilderness of despair and betrayal, even by good men.

But I was talking of Wilson. I do not quite know how I shall handle those two years, 1919–1920. But Wilson and his illness, his errors and his ignorance of what was doing while he was ill, the Senate and its practical conspiracy and the two conventions, with a brief survey of the resulting election will be my subjects. He could not give me much that I did not know. He did however let me see the depth of his disappointment and his child-like faith in the plain people who, he says, have been fooled and befuddled. I saw and talked with the President in September 1918, when he was the embodiment of will and faith and power—sure that all the world was coming to a better way of dealing with its affairs. I saw and talked with Wilson, the man, broken, yet keen of mind, too ill to walk, save for a few moments at a time, absolutely alone in his chamber, the famous room where so many of his predecessors, great and small, lived and worried and even prayed. I could not help thinking of the famous Wolsey passage in Shakespeare, of the scene in Second Faust where the old statesman witnesses the foolish conduct of people whom he had endeavored to save. If the periodicals would publish it, I would draw that picture for the public. But the editor of *The Atlantic*,[5] our liberal periodical, says only harm would follow, so bitter are the people! I do not believe the people are bitter. Only everybody thinks everybody else bitter and so everyone fears to confess his own heart. How human?

This is a rather long letter to a busy editor. It is a late one too; but you will pardon me all, when I say that it is the best I have been able to do.   Yours sincerely   William E. Dodd

CCLS (W. E. Dodd Papers, DLC).
   [1] Of Streator, Ill., a speaker on the Chautauqua circuit, supporter of Wilson and the League of Nations.
   [2] Mattie Johns Dodd.
   [3] On December 30, 1920.
   [4] Wilson also said to Dodd on this occasion: "What more could I have done? I had to negotiate at Paris with my back to the wall. Men thought I had all power. Would to God I had had such power. The 'great' people at home wrote and wired every day that they were against me. But we shall come back, return to those high levels we have abandoned. No good cause is ever lost. Is there anything I can do? I am still ready to serve." W. E. Dodd, *Woodrow Wilson and His Work* (New York, 1932), p. 434.
   [5] Ellery Sedgwick.

To Norman Hezekiah Davis

My dear Mr. Secretary: The White House 8 January, 1921

I think it would be very well indeed for Judge Elkus to come down and give you a confidential account of the work of the Aland Commission. I do not think that it would be necessary for me to see him personally.

Cordially and sincerely yours,   Woodrow Wilson

TLS (SDR, RG 59, 758.6114A1/144, DNA).

Norman Hezekiah Davis to Hugh Campbell Wallace[1]

Washington, January 8, 1921.

For the Ambassador. Your 2021, December 17, 9 p.m. and your letter of December 17, relative to withdrawal from Council of Ambassadors, which was referred to the President. After due consideration of all the circumstances it has been definitely decided ⟨that we shall⟩ *to* discontinue our representation on the Council of Ambassadors. In announcing this action to your colleagues and to the President of the Council of Ambassadors, you may state that the United States had participated in the conferences primarily for the purpose of dealing with questions relating to the armistice, and also to keep conversant with questions relating to the treaty, pending the action of the United States on the treaty. As the most important questions relating to the armistice have been disposed of and as the United States has not ratified the Treaty of Versailles, there appears to be no further occasion for a continued representation by the United States on the Council of Ambassadors. You may also express the sincere appreciation of your Government ⟨of⟩ *for* all the courtesies extended to you under the circumstances. For your information and that of Boyden,[2] he will until further instructions, continue ⟨to represent us⟩ unofficially on the Reparation Commission.   Davis Acting.

T telegram (SDR, RG 59, 763.72119/10801, DNA).
  [1] Words in angle brackets in this telegram deleted by Wilson; words in italics added by him.
  [2] Roland William Boyden, American liaison to the Reparation Commission.

From Norman Hezekiah Davis

Dear Mr. President: Washington January 8, 1921.

I am enclosing a communication to be transmitted to Congress,[1] if you approve, recommending Congressional authorization for the

United States to be represented in the Permanent Association of International Road Congresses. This communication has the favorable endorsement of the Secretary of Agriculture and would entail the small annual membership fee of 15,000 francs.

Faithfully yours,   Norman H. Davis

TLS (WP, DLC).
  [1] A T MS (WP, DLC).

From Emily Greene Balch

Dear Mr. President,   Geneva, January ninth 1921.

I hope that it may not be too much out of the way if I venture to write a brief letter to you not as holder of your high office but purely personally.

During the sessions of the first Assembly of the League of Nations, which I have had the great privilege of attending,[1] I cannot but think that it would have given you deep satisfaction to have heard and felt the evidence of men's feeling about you and about what the League owed and owes to you.

Bitter as must be the suffering and disappointment that you have been called upon to undergo yet it may be that these will at last appear to you, if they do not now, small indeed compared to the privilege of having, under God, called into being a new organ of human life, capable of incalculable service.

While the fact that our country and certain other great peoples are not yet in the League, and other peculiarities of the present political situation prevent the League from being all that it might be and all that one trusts that it will become, surely it marks an historic advance. For the first time the Governments of a great part of the world have gathered to consider—not merely, as at the Hague, how to avoid fighting and how to fight if war should come—but how to further their common interests by common action. The difference is crucial.

For my self my hopes for the League were much greater, my fears much less, after the experience of the Assembly meetings. There is much in the atmosphere of such a gathering which is clearly perceptible yet hard to define or prove. There was little oratory and much honest effort to get work done. The idealists were conspicuous by their ability and energy and by the respect that they inspired. There was a visibly growing sense of corporate internationalism. There was patience and a willingness to build slowly if necessary.

Quite apart from the Assembly, the world has in the Secretariat of the League a constant quiet force at work creating a new type of public servant, a new plane of statesmanship, a new temper in international affairs.

In these days of illness and of political reverses may you find sustenance and courage and compensation in the hope of the world in this great undertaking so largely due to your vision and to your persistence.   Yours very faithfully   [Emily G. Balch]

I write purely in my own person not on behalf of the Womens International League for Peace and Freedom of which I have the honor to be the international secretary but which has given me no mandate to address you.

TCL (J. Addams Papers, PSC-P).
  [1] She attended in her capacity as international secretary-treasurer of the Women's International League for Peace and Freedom, which had its headquarters in Geneva.

William Edward Dodd to Alexander Frederick Whyte[1]

My dear Whyte: University of Chicago January 9, 1921.

If you will pardon the use of a type-writer, I will burden you with a letter from one of your American friends and admirers. Many, many times since I saw you I have been upon the point of writing you but "one thing or another" intervened to prevent my doing so.

You are now under orders for India I judge from the statement made in The New Europe quite a while since. It is a good thing, if a risky one, for a liberal like yourself. You will be out of England at the critical moment of the merging of all the liberal forces, a merging that must come, and you must succeed in a task as difficult as was that of Wilson at Paris, if not quite so spectacular. But you did right in accepting the post. You have all my good wishes. Make your mission a success. Let it appear that Great Britain really seeks the good of India and is willing to let the Indians decide things against both their own and the empire's good and you will have done a great thing. Nor does this remark imply that Britain is not equal to that. She has more than once done that very thing.

May I tell you that in speaking with President Wilson last week with whom I lunched and spent some three hours I related to him your own story to me about your first and continued admiration of him, your speeches in this country and your present mission to India. He was greatly pleased and asked me to give you his blessing and best wishes. He liked to think of such a man setting the new Indian parliament on the ways.

And while I am on this theme, let me say that the President is sure a broken man. He thinks and speaks clearly and without that thickness of voice which generally marks those who have suffered strokes. He showed me how his ailments distress and hamper his movements and he seemed to think that it was not a permanent thing. Yet in his conversation, a little later, he indicated that he was disposing of his papers in a certain way and that he was about to give up the idea of writing his own narrative of recent history. That spoke louder than words. I was almost overcome at times as he rehearsed the story of Paris, of the difficulties there, of the blind imperialism of the French and the "unscrupulousness" of Lloyd George who, he thinks, thwarted him in the great programme—he more than Clemenceau, more even than the recent election in his own country. The President still feels and thinks in terms of persons rather more than I do in studying such situations as that at Paris. He told me March 1, 1919 that the British delegation was at one with him. From this I at that time drew much comfort. Last week he said Lloyd George was the real cause of the defeat—for defeat he indirectly allowed it to be. Yet in another connection he spoke as if the whole outcome were a liberal victory. But whether a defeat or a victory, Wilson can not talk ten minutes without reverting to Paris. That word means the summation of a life struggle to him. There he had the world for his parish; there he says the world abandoned him. As he retold the story two or three times the tears filled his eyes. He was lying in bed with an electric button in his right hand, looking straight at me and apparently anxious that I, as a historian, might understand.

This is going to be a long letter if I rehearse what was said that day. But I must mention one or two things. And the biggest thing was the insistance that the Irish had wrecked his whole programme for adoption of the work at Paris. "Oh, the foolish Irish," he would say. "Would to God they might all have gone back home," was another sentence. And I was more disposed to see in this the cause of the difficulty both at Paris and in the Senate than to see it in Lloyd George, for I am not sure that the prime minister could have held office ten days if he had agreed with Wilson and the two made a peace in full harmony with the terms of the armistice. Nor do I believe that Wilson himself could have retained office, if we had had a responsible system that would have allowed public opinion to recall him, when he succeeded at Paris. The Irish! What have they not done; the American Irish, for now it appear[s] from your last White papers that it was they, cooperating with von Bernstorff, who set the Irish at home upon the wrong road in 1914! And Wilson knew of all this too—how much more difficult does it now appear was his rôle of bringing his party and his country to aid the hard-pressed allies!

I have said in my book that the Irish que[e]red things at Paris. They defeated the treaty and the League in America, for I learned recently that Lodge was more than once on the point of adopting the treaty, when Irish, Italian and German influences, speaking always through the Irish of Massachusetts took him in hand. To a man they voted against all that Wilson had done. It was the drift their open abandonment of their party allegiance set going that started the landslide.[2] So three or four million Irish in this country govern both Great Britain and America. Is not that logic? Too much of it true logic. Self determination permits a few people strategically placed to defeat the purposes of all the liberals of the world.

An interesting thing: Wilson reverted to Gladstone, whom he has always considered a sort of political saint to himself. Gladstone he said was right in most he tried to do. You know how perfectly the Irish trouble defeated Gladstone in his life-work. It is like that closing scene in Second Faust. Wilson is another Gladstone and he feels it.

But you allowed the *New Europe* to go down. Could you not carry it around the world with you? I was just getting ready to send one of my pessimistic articles to it and was going to replenish my exchequer from the returns! You know how much I feel the need of our two countries getting on well together. If we are to do so men of your type, and what I consider to be mine, must cultivate the most friendly understandings. If the Irish problem is to be solved, and I believe it will be now that Wilson has been broken and the American election past, we shall have easier sailing. Only our imperialists and your Bourbons will find other causes of trouble. And I do not see in your periodicals any increasing tendency to make allowances for our follies. Most of your "best people" seem to make a good deal of our wickedness. Nearly all them seem to be yielding to the campaign of Hearst and his kind. Therefore I am the more sorry the *New Europe* is no more. Yet? How can mere print turn the currents set going by the Paris defeat and the worse defeat of November? Man won't see and learn except through disaster, nor even much from that. Our old South had to go to Appomattox. Nothing could dissuade them. But Appomattox did not cure the disease.

Sometimes I think I would like to visit England again and see your fine old country better than I did when I was a student hard pressed to find enough means to procure my tea and steak at the nearest restaurants, at the British Museum. If your people and our people could only make headway together in the great world! But what could a mere student do in a world of business, the very centre of that commerce that covers the earth!

On our side, we surely need more of your type. Not so many of certain types who had preceded you. You certainly did more to make the better British understood here than a score of others who have visited us. But then one must not expect only the cream of a country to travel in "foreign parts." Ramsey Muir[3] is to come next summer. I hope he is of the right sort. Surely he is.

If I could tell you the gossip in Washington, when I was there, it would interest you. Harding is in all kinds of trouble. He wants Fall for State and that means Mexico and a way round European troubles by war or semi-war nearer at home! In this he has been baulked for the moment by the counter move for Hughes as Secretary of State. That would mean our entering the league of nations. That would be to me a great thing. Only it would stir our politics to the depths. Think of the Irish and the Germans! They boast in the press every day that they put Harding "across" and the boast is a just one. If Hughes goes in, he will later go back to the bench as Chief Justice and then Fall for Secretary of State, and then Mexico. And this will be popular in Europe, unless Americans take too much of the good things to the south of Texas.

Is it not a strange fact: Wilson held the Germans and Irish away, in the main, from the Republican ticket in 1916 by preaching, "he kept us out of war," and that as soon as he entered the war these same Irish and Germans combined to punish him and the whole world for our entering the war. And now Harding, who won by appealing to these elements, in much the same way Wilson did, must defeat the purposes of the better element of his party by pleasing them or defeat himself, and make his administration one continued row, by displeasing them. Our coalition is even more coalition than yours; but we have no such magician to conjure it.

Now, is not this an unconscionable letter to a man who writes three lines to his best friends, when he writes at all? You see I have imagined you the British Liberal party, or part of a party, and belabored you after the manner of McDuff. And you quite defenseless. But you have not suffered from me before, and being far away in India, if anything is far away in the modern world, I am immune. Really, won't you take a bit of time, while some Indian grandee is making a speech which you can not understand, and write me a letter, directed, if you please, at my wing of the Democratic party? That would be a treat.

All of us here think and speak of you and Mrs. Whyte,[4] do not forget this, constantly. All send love and regards and especially best wishes for success in your new task.

Yours sincerely   William E. Dodd

CCLS (W. E. Dodd Papers, DLC).

¹ President of the Legislative Assembly of India; one of the founders and joint editor of *The New Europe* in 1916, a liberal journal devoted to Central European affairs.
² About the massive defection of Irish-American and German-American voters from the Democratic party in 1916 to the Republican and Socialist parties in 1920, see David Burner, *The Politics of Provincialism: The Democratic Party in Transition, 1918-1932* (New York, 1968), pp. 234-35, *passim*.
³ Professor of Modern History at the University of Manchester, member of the Calcutta University Commission, 1917-1919.
⁴ Margaret Emily Fairweather Whyte.

To Norman Hezekiah Davis

My dear Mr. Secretary: The White House 10 January, 1921

I have taken the liberty of not approving the recommendation to Congress to grant authority for the United States to be represented in the Permanent Association of International Road Congresses, because I think it is inadvisable at this time to seek any permanent association with the European nations in view of the uncertainty of the basis upon which all such relations will rest in the future, an uncertainty which does not seem to me to be very rapidly clearing even in the minds of those who would invent something new.
          Cordially and faithfully yours,   Woodrow Wilson

TLS (SDR, RG 59, 515.4Ala/18, DNA).

To Charles Zeller Klauder

My dear Mr. Klauder: [The White House] 10 January, 1921

Thank you for your letter of January sixth. I have been studying the changes indicated in the set of drawings No. 6.

The problem of the billiard room is, I see, a very difficult one. My great objection to the plan you suggest is that it leaves no access free to the elevator for a servant carrying wood up from the cellar. I have always felt that it was only fair to let the servants use the elevator for heavy loads, and the cellar plan first drawn was admirably adapted for service in that respect. Then, too, I would very much regret to see the fireplace moved from one end of the great hall to the other. I think it is ideally placed in the original drawing.

Would it be possible, without excessive cost, to enlarge the little square addition which contains the study and Mrs. Wilson's dressing room above, and thus make the room below the study big enough for a billiard room? By the way, as I explained to you, I shall not really need a study. I could use the library perfectly well, and I am ready to give up the study for use as a billiard room if it can without too great cost be made large enough.

I suppose there is no way of enlarging the bedrooms upstairs without increasing the width or length of the whole house in that portion of it. Mrs. Wilson's room is rather too small, I fear, and I suggest that the space taken out of it for her bathroom might be taken out of my room instead of out of hers. Could that be worked out conveniently?

Returning to the basement again, we shall, I fear, need three maids' rooms, and therefore in that respect drawing No. 6 is most convenient. I notice you have sent no drawing for the third story, and you have provided in the second story no staircase leading to the third. Would not such a staircase be wise in any case, even if we did not develop the third story into rooms? It ought to be accessible, if only for storage. And, you remember, we agreed that it was to be made quite light by the free use of glass "slates." I hesitate to suggest a maid's room on the third floor because that would, I suppose, involve putting a toilet up there and running the plumbing arrangements to that floor, which I assume would be rather costly.

I am sorry to submit so many minor problems to you, but I know how resourceful you are in working them out, and hope I am not burdening you. I feel that we are approaching and are about to get exactly what we want in these plans, and I feel greatly indebted to you for the interest you have taken in developing them. We hope soon to have the pleasure of showing you the house we have purchased.

Please present my compliments to Mr. Day[1] and accept for yourself and for him also our warm best wishes for the New Year, which I hope will bring us into frequent association as the plans are converted into brick and mortar.

Cordially and sincerely yours,   [Woodrow Wilson]

CCL (WP, DLC).
  [1] Harry Kent Day, retired member of the firm of Day and Klauder, the architectural firm of Philadelphia. Wilson and Day had corresponded in 1920.

From William Bauchop Wilson

My dear Mr. President: Washington January 11, 1921.

I regret that a misunderstanding has arisen between the Department of State and the Department of Labor relative to the case of Donal O'Callaghan, who arrived at the Port of Newport News, or Norfolk, some time last week, and who was denied admission to the United States by a Board of Special Inquiry at Norfolk on the ground that he was a stowaway and without passports.

He appealed to the Department of Labor against the decision of the Board of Special Inquiry. Under the immigration law a stowaway has the right of appeal. The case has not yet been determined by me, and I am not familiar with all of the facts. I directed that he should be paroled upon his own recognizance pending a decision of his appeal. Such action does not constitute admission to the United States within the meaning of the law.

We have no suitable immigration detention station at Norfolk. He was, therefore, from the time of his arrival until I directed that he should be paroled, detained in the custody of immigration officers in a hotel in that city. He was just as much within the United States in a hotel in Norfolk as he would be in a hotel in New York or Washington. He was in the custody of the Department of Labor, and it seemed to me that there could be no question of my legal right to parole him. The wisdom of it is another matter. I have no doubt in my own mind about either.

Holding this viewpoint, I can see no basis for the belief entertained in the Department of State that I have violated the law and may be subject to its penalties.[1] I have tried to impress upon the Acting Secretary, Mr. Davis, that I have not admitted Mr. O'Callaghan, have not even passed upon his appeal, have not expressed an opinion of the law as applied to the facts in his case, and have simply paroled him pending a decision concerning the law and the facts.

While the absence of passports is prima facie evidence that the alien is not entitled to admission, it is not conclusive evidence. There is a large number of individuals and groups of persons not required to have passports. For instance, Section 7 of Title I of your Executive Order of August 8, 1918, says:

"The term 'seamen' as used herein includes, in addition to persons ordinarily described thereby, seagoing fishermen and all owners, masters, officers, and members of crews and other persons employed on vessels which, for purposes of business or pleasure, cruise on tidal waters beyond the shore line or on the Great Lakes."

Paragraph (c) of Section 10 of Title II says:

"(c) Aliens who are seamen on vessels arriving at ports of the United States and who desire to land in the country shall apply to an immigrant inspector. They shall submit to such immigrant inspector satisfactory evidence of their nationality and furnish such photographs and execute such forms and applications as the immigrant inspector shall require. The immigrant inspector may thereupon issue identity cards authorizing such seamen to land in the United States, unless the Secretary of State directs that they be kept on their vessels."

The only way in which I could determine whether or not Mr.

O'Callaghan came within this or any other exception to the passport requirements was to examine into the facts and apply the law to them as I found them. He was a subject of the British Empire. We were at peace with Great Britain. The person in question was alleged to be the Mayor of a great city. He was not likely to abscond or be lost sight of, and I could conceive of no advantage to the United States by holding him in physical custody at Norfolk.

This case, together with a number of others that have come to my attention, has led me to the conclusion that there should be some changes made in the passport regulations to conform to the changed conditions that have arisen since your Proclamation and Order were issued. At that time Great Britain, France, Italy, Japan, and a number of other nations were associated with us in the war with Germany and Austria. Since then these other countries have made peace. We alone are at war, though the Administration has striven with all its energy to secure the ratification of the same peace terms adopted by the other countries. While we had a common enemy, we might very properly say to the other nations, because of our community of interest, that we would not admit into the United States any person to whom they thought it unsafe to give passports. The same community of interest does not now exist, and by continuing the passport regulations we are permitting other countries, who now have no such community of interest, to determine for us whom we shall not admit into the United States. They have but to refuse passports to accomplish that purpose.

Under the ordinary immigration laws stowaways may be admitted to the United States in the discretion of the Secretary of Labor. The unusual economic conditions existing in Europe have resulted in a large number of stowaways seeking entrance to the United States. They are frequently persons of more than ordinary vigor who are willing to endure temporary hardships in order to get away from the hardships at home. They, of course, have no passports, and under the rulings of the State Department are not admissible. There are cases of Ukrainians and other Russians escaping from bolshevik rule without passports, children born in transit who could not possibly secure passports, and numberless other complications that seem to me should be dealt with in accordance with the usual discretion exercised in immigration cases.

As I have already stated, there is a number of circumstances under which passports are not required, and that naturally raises the question: If a passport is not required by the law or the regulations, does the determination of the question of admission rest with the Immigration Service of the Department of Labor, or the Passport Service of the Department of State? The whole question of immigration policy is involved in the determination as to which of these services shall pass upon the admission of aliens under the exceptions provided in the passport regulations. The policy of the Department of Labor has been to exercise a humanitarian discretion in the application of the immigration laws where it was clear that no menace to the United States Government could possibly result from the admission of the alien. On the other hand there has been a disposition to utilize the passport and visa regulations as a means of securing the total exclusion of immigrants. It has been pointed out by representatives of the State Department in conference with us that a refusal on the part of the State Department to visa any passports would accomplish the same purpose that is sought to be accomplished by the Johnson Bill[2] now pending in Congress. Whatever the value of total exclusion may be, I do not believe it is wise policy to achieve that end by such administrative action.

Personally, I can see no reason for a continuance of the passport regulations, except insofar as they apply to alien enemies.

Faithfully yours,   W B Wilson

TLS (WP, DLC).
    [1] "I feel that in the discharge of the functions entrusted to this Department by the above mentioned Executive regulations, which have the effect of law, it is my duty to take appropriate action looking to the enforcement of the law, which was violated by Mr. O'Callaghan's improper entry into the United States." Last paragraph of NHD to WBW, Jan. 11, 1921, TCL (WP, DLC).
    [2] About which, see n. 2 to the extract from the Daniels Diary printed at Dec. 28, 1920.

From the Shorthand Diary of Charles Lee Swem

12 January, 1920 [1921]

In connection with the awarding of the Nobel Peace Prize: previously the Nobel Committee had sent the President a form of order for the amount of the prize—in Swedish crowns. The President had put the order in the bank. But this morning a representative of one of the banks in Sweden came to the office with a draft which the Nobel Committee had drawn on his bank in favor of the President. Before the order which the President had placed in his bank could be honored he would have to sign the draft on the other bank.

The President had evidently had some correspondence with the American representatives of this bank[1] on which the draft had been drawn, and when this morning I took the draft to him to be signed he summarily waved the whole thing aside saying, or rather intimating, that the firm handling the matter didn't know what they were talking about. I tried to tell him that, whether they did or not, he couldn't receive his money until he had signed the draft which I placed before him. But he would hear no more and directed me to send the whole thing to Randolph Bolling, who had handled the matter for him in the first place.

After discussing the matter with Mrs. Wilson and after she had herself failed to change him, I sent the representative with his papers over to John Randolph Bolling.

While I was sitting in the President's study taking his dictation Randolph came over with the draft and made the same argument that I did.

"I don't believe a word of it," said the President, taking his pen and signing his name!

After Bolling had gone he turned to me and said "They pay me in Swedish crowns instead of American money—which aren't worth anything at all, the exchange has gone down so with them."

Then he allowed it to remain in a Swedish bank getting a check book and pass book for it—evidently in the hope that by allowing it to remain there later on he might gain a better rate of exchange.

And in notifying the Swedish bank that he would place it in their bank, he said, "My bankers here tell me that I may expect a very liberal rate of interest—probably 5 percent."

JRT transcript (WC, NjP) of CLSsh (C. L. Swem Coll., NjP).
    [1] Brown Brothers & Co. of New York. See Brown Brothers & Co. to WW, Jan. 11, 1921, TLS (WP, DLC).

To William Bauchop Wilson

My dear Mr. Secretary: The White House 12 January, 1921

I am sorry that any difference of opinion should have arisen between the Department of State and your own department with regard to the admission of the stowaway, O'Callaghan, but I must say that I do not concur in the conclusions of your argument about making more liberal exceptions to the rules regarding passports. I believe that they ought to be applied with great care and with practically no exceptions. Exceptions inevitably lead to vagueness in administration and to complaints of favoritism.

I, of course, do not wish to interfere with the legal jurisdiction of the Department of Labor, and I think it would be very unwise to make an exception in the case of O'Callaghan. In the present state of Ireland, we should have a whooping lot of stowaways descending upon us if we admit them without passports. I think passports are particularly necessary in the present disturbed state of the world.   Cordially and faithfully yours,   Woodrow Wilson[1]

TLS (LDR, RG 174, DNA).

¹ W. B. Wilson yielded to Woodrow Wilson and the State Department only technically in what had by now become a *cause célèbre.* A memorandum by the Assistant Secretary of Labor, Louis Freeland Post, for the Acting Commissioner General of Immigration, dated January 15, 1921 (CC MS, WP, DLC), reviewed the facts in the O'Callaghan case, declared that O'Callaghan was a stowaway, but also a seaman within the meaning of the law. Under the President's Proclamation of August 8, 1918, and Executive Orders issued pursuant to it, the Secretary of State had the right to direct that alien seamen be kept on their vessels. In accordance with the decision of the State Department, the memorandum continued, O'Callaghan would be allowed to land for the purpose of reshipping on board any vessel bound for a foreign port or place. The federal judge who had heard O'Callaghan's case was directed to surrender him to the immigration officer in Norfolk. Upon the surrender of O'Callaghan, his parole would be canceled, and the officer in charge would carry out these instructions.

W. B. Wilson did have the last word, if only rhetorically. In a letter to Davis on January 17, Wilson asserted that, for reasons explained in this letter, he did have the right to admit O'Callaghan permanently. Wilson went on to say that he had, however, decided that such a course would not be wise "in the present circumstances" and had, therefore, permitted him to land for the purposes of reshipping. "Taking all of the law and the facts into consideration," Wilson said in a parting shot, "I can not concur in the judgment of the State Department that Mr. O'Callaghan has improperly entered into the United States, or that the law has been violated in his case." WBW to NHD, Jan. 17, 1921, CCL (WP, DLC).

This was not the end of the matter. Woodrow Wilson, W. B. Wilson, and Norman Davis conferred about the case at the White House on January 18, following a Cabinet meeting, and President Wilson supported Davis in the decision that O'Callaghan had to leave the United States. W. B. Wilson ordered O'Callaghan to report to Norfolk and to ship out from there. O'Callaghan refused to do so, and there were mass meetings of Irish-American societies to protest against his deportation. Reelected Lord Mayor of Cork on January 31, he embarked upon a speaking tour and on one occasion went into hiding. On February 15 he appealed to Bainbridge Colby and W. B. Wilson to change his status from seaman to political refugee, and Secretary Wilson extended his stay in the United States to permit him to appeal the order for his deportation. O'Callaghan then went on an extended speaking tour and was barred from speaking in some cities. After the State Department refused to grant him political asylum, he finally left the United States on an unknown date and arrived in Ireland on June 18, 1921.

The above is based upon news reports in the *New York Times,* Jan. 5-June 19, 1921, *passim;* Alan J. Ward, *Ireland and Anglo-American Relations, 1899-1921* (London, 1969), pp. 238-40; and Charles C. Tansill, *America and the Fight for Irish Freedom, 1866-1922* (New York, 1957), pp. 409-14.

From Norman Hezekiah Davis, with Enclosure

My dear Mr. President: Washington January 12, 1921.

I desire to call your attention to the enclosed cable from the Embassy at London embodying a note from the British Foreign Office regarding the Island of Yap, apparently in reply to our cable despatch of December fourth for transmission by the Ambassador to the Foreign Office.¹ In case you should desire to refresh your memory, I am also enclosing a copy of the latter cable.

This flippant and unresponsive rejoinder from the British Government, which indicates not only a most unsatisfactory and improper attitude but also a complete disregard of our rights and contentions, merits most serious consideration. Apart from the Treaty, as the principal participant in the war, the United States has maintained its right to a voice in the disposition of the ex-German colonies. The League has ruled, with regard to mandates, that the

principal Allied and Associated Powers may designate the mandatory and that the powers interested may decide on the terms of the
mandate subject to the approval of the League. The British Government took the same position in the oil note recently answered
by Mr. Colby's communication to Lord Curzon,[2] which was communicated to the other principal powers for their information. In
his reply Mr. Colby specifically stated that the United States, as
one of the powers interested, had a right to be consulted regarding
the mandate terms before their submission to the League. Ignoring the claims of the United States, and without even answering
our contention or indicating their intentions, the British and apparently certain of the other powers have presented to the League
the mandate terms for the Pacific Islands, agreed upon by themselves, which have been approved by the Council. This action involves also a ratification of the alleged allocation to Japan, under
mandate, of the Island of Yap to which we cannot consent. The
behavior of the Allies in this connection seems to me not only unjustifiable but impertinent.

After we hear from the other Allies and get all of the facts you
may possibly consider it advisable to lay the situation before Congress. It seems to me, however, that you should at least furnish the
facts regarding the Island of Yap as defined in the enclosed cable
of December fourth. In my conference with the Foreign Relations
Committee regarding the disposition of the ex-German cables,
someone inquired regarding the status of the Island of Yap, and I
indicated very briefly that there existed a difference of opinion regarding the decisions taken, but which we hoped to clear up satisfactorily by communications already sent on the subject. I judge
from this experience that the Foreign Relations Committee, some
of whom apparently had read the Minutes, concurred in the position taken by us. If you concur in the advisability of making a full
report regarding Yap, would you prefer to send a formal message
on the subject, or to have me, under your direction, give the facts
to the Foreign Relations Committee of the Senate? It is probable
that the latter course would avoid extended discussion in the Senate and obtain more satisfactory results.

In the meantime, I think a reply should be sent to the British to
the effect that we are astonished at the action which has been
taken, and that, as you may consider it necessary to bring the facts
to the attention of Congress, this Government would like to be informed whether in submitting this question, the Council of the
League was advised that the claim of the United States to a voice
in the matter had been ignored and also whether it was apprised
of the attitude of this Government with respect to the Island of

Yap; and that the United States does not consider the mandate over Yap and its terms a matter purely between the United States Government and Japan, but on the contrary primarily one of good faith on the part of the Allies.

I propose to call in the Allied Ambassadors and inform them orally of our attitude with regard to this matter, and indicate that if it becomes necessary for you to bring the subject before Congress it may probably destroy the last hope of this country entering into any further plans of cooperation with them.

Good
W. W.

I am, my dear Mr. President,

Faithfully yours,   Norman H. Davis

TLS (WP, DLC).
[1] It is printed as Enclosure III with NHD to WW, Dec. 3, 1920, Vol. 66.
[2] Printed as an Enclosure with BC to WW, Nov. 19, 1920 (first letter of that date), *ibid.*

E N C L O S U R E

London. January 7, 1921.

18. Your 1199, December 4, 12 noon.

Following note from Foreign Office received this morning dated January 5th:

"As your Excellency is doubtless aware, all the 'C' mandates granted under the treaty of Versailles have now been formally approved by the Council of the League of Nations, and the mandate for the ex-German islands in the Pacific north of the equator has been conferred upon Japan in accordance with the recorded and published decision of the Supreme Council of May 7th, 1919.

"In these circumstances I can only assume that the question of the grant of cable rights on the Island of Yap will be brought by the United States Government, if they so desire, before the Cable Conference when it resumes its sittings, or that the matter will form the subject of direct negotiation between the United States and Japanese Governments."   Davis.

T telegram (WP, DLC).

From Peter James Hamilton

San Juan, P. R.

My dear Wilson: January twelfth, Nineteen twenty-one.

First of all let me wish you a Happy and Prosperous New Year. I was not within reach of the mails for your birthday and was not able to write you on that occasion.

My only sister, Mrs. Mary H. Goodman, of Mobile, died a few days before Christmas and I went over to Santo Domingo in order to get away from the noise and festivity of Christmas here. I spent a quiet two weeks with friends and came back much refreshed. It has occurred to me that you might care to hear an outside impression of conditions over there. I was at San Pedro de Macoris the day that Governor Snowden issued his proclamation announcing that the government would be shortly returned to the Dominicans and that a committee would be appointed to devise the necessary means, such as a proper election law and some amendments to the constitution.[1] One would have supposed that this would have been received with rejoicing, and I am quite sure that this was your idea in promulgating it, but over there there is no public opinion; there is only class opinion, and the talkative class being editors and politicians, who are much in accord. I came in contact with these leaders in Macoris, and afterwards with some at the capital, and from newspaper accounts see that the same feeling prevails among them all over the Island. This was that the United States had taken away their government in 1916 and should get out of the Island as quickly as it could, leaving them to reestablish their own government under Henríquez,[2] who has been dispossessed. The idea that the United States had acted not only for the good of Santo Domingo but in order under the Monroe Doctrine to protect all America did not occur to them and when I mentioned it did not appeal to them in any way. Their idea was what they call the patriotic one of having their own country without reference to anybody else upon the face of the earth.

I enclose translation of a characteristic paper,—resolutions adopted by the only public body they have, practically refusing to cooperate with the Admiral's proclamation as to getting public affairs in shape for withdrawal of the Americans.[3] This is Latin-America all over.

I called on Admiral Snowden at the time and found him a most attractive man, alive to the situation and anxious only to do what was best for Santo Domingo. I saw him at nine o'clock in the morning on which the committee he was convoking was to meet at eleven, and did not see him afterwards. From newspaper reports this committee had the same idea that the politicians had, or rather was made up of the politicians, and wanted to make impossible conditions before they would help save their own country! I do not know how it worked out; I know what I would have done in his place. I would have told them to help on my terms or go home and let me work it out myself.

The Latin-American temperament is doctrinaire and not practical. We see it on every hand here in Porto Rico, although they have got somewhat used to American methods here. Here they talk a great deal and do very foolish things, but they realize that there is a limit which they cannot pass. I think that limit has been reached even here and it is possible a firmer stand should be taken. However, I did not mean to discuss Porto Rico.

As to my own future I know nothing. The papers I sent you seem to reflect the real feeling and I hope I shall be retained. Even if I am not, your kind words, almost amounting to "Well done, good and faithful servant!",[4] gratify me very much and will always be cherished by me and my family.

Very sincerely,   Peter J. Hamilton.

TLS (WP, DLC).
[1] Following the discussions in high administration circles during the preceding months about the restoration of some measure of home rule to the Dominican Republic (about which see the index references to "Dominican Republic" in Vol. 66), Rear Adm. Thomas Snowden, Military Governor of the Dominican Republic, on December 23, 1920, issued a proclamation (printed as an Enclosure with BC to WW, Nov. 27, 1920 [second letter of that date], Vol. 66) announcing that the United States Government believed the time had come to inaugurate the rapid withdrawal from responsibilities assumed in connection with Dominican affairs. Snowden further said that a commission of representative Dominicans would be appointed to set under way the reconstitution of a constitutional state in the island republic.
[2] That is Francisco Henríquez y Carvajal.
[3] A CC MS, WP, DLC, this is a translation of a statement by the National Dominican Union, dated Dec. 24, 1920.
[4] "It would gratify me very much indeed to see you continued indefinitely in your present usefulness." WW to P. J. Hamilton, Dec. 4, 1920, CCL (WP, DLC).

From Douglas Wilson Johnson

Dear Mr. President,   New York January 12, 1921

I take the liberty of sending you a complete copy of the address which I delivered in the Academy of Music at Philadelphia January 7th, in the series conducted by Colonel House.[1] In this address, which is published quite widely in America and in Europe, I endeavored to place before the public the solid grounds which justified your strong position on the Adriatic question, and to correct some widespread misapprehensions as to the supposed rigidity of the American attitude toward the Italians, as contrasted with a supposed leniency toward other claimants to alien territories. I am not responsible for the newspaper version of my answers to questions, where this over emphasizes the *extent* to which the President called upon me and my colleagues; but I did seek to correct the widespread assertion that "the President took many experts to Paris, but did not use them."

It is my hope that the address will contribute at least a little toward a better appreciation of the splendid fight you made, against overwhelming odds, in favor of a new and higher conception of morality in international dealings; and I only hope that you will find in what I said nothing to cause you embarrassment.

With sincere wishes for your early restoration to perfect health, I am, my dear Mr. President,

Your obedient servant,   Douglas Johnson.

ALS (WP, DLC).
    [1] Tear sheets from the Philadelphia *Public Ledger*, Jan. 8, 1921, WP, DLC. Johnson's lecture was reprinted in House and Seymour, eds., *What Really Happened at Paris*, pp. 112-39.

To Norman Hezekiah Davis

My dear Mr. Secretary: The White House 13 January, 1921

I have read your letter of January twelfth about the British action in regard to Yap, and agree to all that you say in your letter. I am glad that you are calling in the Allied Ambassadors and I hope that you will speak very plainly to them.

I would also be very much obliged if you would act upon your suggestion that you give the facts to the Foreign Relations Committee of the Senate very fully. I think they will be interested and stirred up.

Cordially and faithfully yours,   Woodrow Wilson

TLS (SDR, RG 59, 862i.01/82, DNA).

From James Hamilton Lewis, with Enclosure

Dear Mr. President: Chicago Jan. 13, 1921.

I enclose you a card containing a poem that is written by William Church Osborne [Osborn], former chairman of the Democratic State Committee, New York. He has always felt you treated him badly, neglected him or placed him at a great disadvantage by some form of ignoring his service and position,—yet nevertheless shows the attitude of mind he bears to you and to your service, status and standing, to say nothing of his expression as to those who pursue you.

His poem, I am informed, has lately appeared in many magazines. I saw Osborne and asked him if it really was his poem and that I wanted to send you one, that you might know who was the author. Thus it is I enclose you this card now,—when I hestitated to do so before when you were ill,—lest the suggestion of your illness would be discouraging, but am glad to send it now that you are recovered and where no expression could serve discouraging as to your health.

Your obedient servant,   Jas Hamilton Lewis

TLS (WP, DLC).

ENCLOSURE

AFFLICTION.

When I do think upon his high emprise,
    And call to mind the grandeur of his thought,
Then view the wreckage that around him lies,
    How that his mighty task has come to naught,
While he, pale, broken shadow sits,
    Impotent to rebuff injurious scorn
And oft his darkened message flits
    Batlike among the shades, of illness born;
Lo! all the losses borne by men of old
    Crowd the sad fancies of my dreaming mind,
How some lacked courage, some were overbold
    But most fell, broken, under fortune blind,
Blind fate that waits on greatness; wild, insane,
    Wearer of tragic mask, bearer of bitter pain.

November, 1920

Printed copy (WP, DLC).

To Charles Homer Haskins

My dear Haskins: The White House 14 January, 1921

Thank you for your thoughtfulness in sending me a copy of your Philadelphia address.[1] I had heard of it before your letter arrived through friends in Philadelphia who had heard it and admired it very much. I want you to know that I am truly proud to have the support of a judgment like your own in the critical matters of which you were speaking. I believe that in the course of time the air will clear and all the misrepresentation which is now being thrown around the Paris Conference will clear away like a mist.

With the most cordial good wishes from both Mrs. Wilson and myself for you and yours for the New Year,

Cordially and sincerely yours,   Woodrow Wilson

TLS (C. H. Haskins Papers, NjP).
    [1] Wilson was replying to C. H. Haskins to WW, Jan. 3, 1921.

From the Shorthand Diary of Charles Lee Swem

14 January 1921

This morning I spoke to the President about the book which Lansing will bring out the day after the President retires from office—concerning the peace commission.[1] The book reviews say it will be unmerciful criticism of the President and his course at Paris.

I called the President's attention to this and asked if Ray Stannard Baker's book might not be ready for publication at that time.

The President smiled about Lansing's book, saying it could amount to nothing as far as he was concerned. Lansing was a "dismissed Secretary of State" and would be written down as a Grouch. Also he said that some day "Everybody would know what a liar he was anyway."

JRT transcript (WC, NjP) of CLSsh (C. L. Swem Coll., NjP).
    [1] Robert Lansing, *The Peace Negotiations: A Personal Narrative* (Boston and New York, 1921).

From Norman Hezekiah Davis, with Enclosures

My dear Mr. President: Washington January 14, 1921.

In compliance with your verbal instructions, I cabled Ambassador Davis that you thought it would be most ill advised and detrimental to the public service for him to leave such an important post before he can be replaced in the customary manner.[1] Knowing that his principal reason for desiring to take this action was a financial one, I spoke to Frank Polk, who is one of the partners in the law firm[2] which Ambassador Davis intends to enter when he is out of the service, and added to the cable that Polk, after consulting his partners, concurred in your view of what he should do. The personal letter to me from the Ambassador was dated December sixteenth,[3] but in some way was considerably delayed in reaching me, and on the day following the despatch of my cable to him I received a formal letter of resignation, under date of December twenty-third, to be delivered to you.[4] I then cabled him[5] that his letter to you had just been received, but that unless and until I hear from him further I would consider my former despatch as a reply from you to his letter of December twenty-third. I am enclosing for your information the reply received from him,[6] and also his letter of resignation.

When he was here he informed me confidentially that it was costing him about $4,000. a month and that he had exhausted nearly all of his capital. I am sure that this is what is worrying him, and the controlling reason for his desire to be released. I may say, however, that I concur entirely in your view.

I think he should communicate to Mr. Harding, explaining his situation and requesting that steps be taken to release him; but as he cannot properly leave his post even on March fourth without permission from the Secretary of State, I am by no means sure that it would be wise for us to grant him a leave of absence, say, from March first. May I ask if you have any further suggestions to make?   Faithfully yours,   Norman H. Davis

[1] See Enclosure II.
[2] Stetson, Jennings & Russell, of New York.
[3] Cited in NHD to WW, Jan. 7, 1921 (third letter of that date), n. 1.
[4] It is printed as Enclosure I.
[5] NHD to J. W. Davis, Jan. 12, 1921, T telegram (SDR, RG 59, 123D296/68, DNA).
[6] J. W. Davis to NHD, Jan. 13, 1921, T telegram (WP, DLC). Davis said that he was still unconvinced of the necessity of his remaining at his post until March 4 but would remain at it until that date, although not a day longer, if Wilson so insisted.

E N C L O S U R E   I

From John William Davis

My dear Mr. President: London, December 23, 1920.

I beg to tender for your acceptance, as early as may be compatible with the public interest, my resignation of the position of Ambassador to the Court of St. James. I am the more disposed to urge its acceptance because of the fact that in any interim which may occur before the arrival of my successor, the affairs of the Embassy will be in the hands of Mr. J. Butler Wright as Chargé who is entirely familiar with all the current business of the Embassy and in whose judgment and discretion I have complete confidence.

When I returned to my post in November, I did so with the understanding that I would remain until the fourth of March if the state of public business demanded it. I indicated, however, my desire to return without delay to private life and since it does not appear to me that the public interest would suffer by my earlier departure, I submit my resignation for such action as you may deem appropriate.

I am,   Faithfully yours,   John W. Davis

TLS (WP, DLC).

E N C L O S U R E   I I
Washington, January 10, 1921.
15 CONFIDENTIAL, FOR AMBASSADOR ONLY.

Upon receipt of your letter December sixteenth, I consulted the President, who thinks it would be most ill-advised and detrimental to the public service for such an able representative to leave such an important post before the vacancy can be filled. I explained to him the conditions under which you returned to London and asked if he would not be willing for you to tender your resignation now, to take effect on March fourth, to which he replied that he thought this would be also ill-advised because it would lay us open to charge of abandoning the ship and leaving an embarrassing situation for the incoming Administration. The President strongly urges that you therefore remain and tender your resignation to Harding. I have discussed this with Frank Polk, who, after consulting his partners, concurs in my view that under the circumstances it would be advisable for you not to resign until March fourth.

Davis Acting.

TS telegram (SDR, RG 59, 123D296/68, DNA).

To Alexander Mitchell Palmer

The White House
My dear Mr. Attorney General: 15 January, 1921

Before signing the nomination of C. W. Miller to be United States Attorney for the Eastern District of Oklahoma, I should like very much to know whether he has the support of Senators Owen and Gore, either or both of them. The support of either would make it impossible for me to make the nomination.

Cordially and sincerely yours,   Woodrow Wilson

TLS (A. M. Palmer Papers, DLC).

To Douglas Wilson Johnson

My dear Major: [The White House] 15 January, 1921

I appreciate your thoughtful courtesy in sending me a copy of the address which you delivered in the Academy of Music in Philadelphia on the seventh. I had heard of it through friends who spoke most highly of it and of the impression that it had made. I am sincerely glad that men like yourself are seeking to give the

public the right information with regard to the matters which have
been so vilely misrepresented.

With the best wishes,

Cordially and sincerely yours,   [Woodrow Wilson]

CCL (WP, DLC).

From Norman Hezekiah Davis, with Enclosures

My dear Mr. President: Washington January 15, 1921.

As I stated to you this morning, I have been obtaining all the
information possible which would have a bearing on your mediation between Armenia and the Kemalists,[1] and have come to the
conclusion that it would be futile to direct yourself to those two
contending factions who have little, if any, control over their destiny or activities. Nothing can be accomplished without eliminating the principal causes of the trouble, and this cannot be done
without the actual moral and diplomatic support of the principal
powers, and possibly the elimination of the Bolshevist influence. A
definite acceptance of all the conditions under which you proposed
to mediate has not yet been given. My judgment, therefore, is that
you should either drop the matter, indicating your reasons for
doing so, or that you should endeavor to present the problem to the
world in the hope that some good may come of it. Probably not
knowing what else to do, the Allies and the Council of the League
of Nations simply endeavored to shift the burden from their own
shoulders and to give the impression that they were not in any way
responsible for the existing situation.

I feel therefore that in the adoption of either plan the responsibility and blame should be thrown back on them. I am therefore
transmitting, with many apologies, the two proposed despatches
embodying the two indicated plans. If either one of these plans
meets with your approval I can probably improve the wording, and
shall be glad to transmit the one corresponding to the procedure
you may determine upon.

Faithfully yours,   Norman H. Davis

TLS (N. H. Davis Papers, DLC).
[1] That is, the Turkish nationalists led by Mustapha Kemal Pasha (later Kemal Ata-
türk), who had conquered Armenia and, on December 3, 1920, had imposed a peace
treaty on Armenia by which it was reduced to the province of Erivan.

E N C L O S U R E   I

Paul Hymans,   (I)
   President of the Council of the League of Nations,
   Geneva, Switzerland.

Your telegram of December 26, 1920,[1] transmitting a message received by the Council from the British Government, concerning Armenia, stating that Armenia is reported to be under the control of Soviet Russia, and suggesting that the President instruct the American High Commissioner at Constantinople to take the matter up with the Allied High Commissioners, has been received and read with interest by the President, who instructs me to reply as follows:

The President does not deem it practicable to instruct the American High Commissioner at Constantinople to act for him in this matter. As was stated in my telegram of December 16, 1920,[2] he has chosen the Honorable Henry Morgenthau, who has been prepared to act for him in such steps as may be taken. Before instructing him to proceed, however, the President has been awaiting the definite assurances and information from all the principal Powers interested as requested in his cable of November 30, 1920,[3] defining the conditions under which he would endeavor to mediate.

The message from the British Prime Minister transmitted by you on December 26th would seem to indicate the impracticability or futility of the President's directing himself, at least in the first instance, to the Armenians and Kemalists. The President is inclined to share this view and to feel that no solution can be had without first getting at the source of the trouble.

The President has been most desirous of rendering any possible assistance in this unfortunate situation, but he believes that any effort on his part would now be impracticable in view of the fact that he has not yet received all the necessary information and assurances asked for and that there is not sufficient time remaining before he retires from public office, to deal with this question effectively and comprehensively.

[1] It is printed in FR 1920, III, 809.
[2] Actually, NHD to P. Hymans, Dec. 15, 1920, printed in ibid., p. 807.
[3] Printed as Enclosure II with BC to WW, Nov. 29, 1920 (first letter of that date), Vol. 66.

ENCLOSURE II

Paul Hymans,   (2)
    President of the Council of the League of Nations,
        Geneva, Switzerland.

Your telegram of December 26, 1920, transmitting a message received by the Council from the British Government, concerning Armenia, stating that Armenia is reported to be under the control of Soviet Russia, and suggesting that the President instruct the American High Commissioner at Constantinople to take the matter up with the Allied High Commissioners, has been received and read with interest by the President, who instructs me to reply as follows:

The President does not deem it practicable to instruct the American High Commissioner at Constantinople to act for him in this matter. As was stated in my telegram of December 16, 1920, he has chosen the Honorable Henry Morgenthau, who has been prepared to act for him in such steps as may be taken. Before instructing him to proceed, however, the President has been awaiting the definite assurances and information from all the principal Powers interested as requested in his cable of November 30, 1920, defining the conditions under which he would endeavor to mediate.

The message from the British Prime Minister transmitted by you on December 26th would seem to indicate the impracticability or futility of the President's directing himself, at least in the first instance, to the Armenians and Kemalists. The President is inclined to share this view and to feel that no solution can be had without first getting at the source of the trouble.

Pending receipt of information and assurances requested by the President in his despatch of November 30, 1920, it is deemed wise to state the problem as the President views it, its causes and possible remedies. It would appear that the immediate cause of trouble in Armenia and Turkey has been the Treaty of Sevres. Admittedly, this was a difficult question with which to contend, but the Treaty was drafted by the Allied Powers and the trouble has arisen over the failure of certain factions to accept this Treaty, and of the Allies to enforce it. This is a question over which the President has no control, and any measures which he might take or recommend in this direction would be dependent upon the hearty cooperation and support of the Allied Powers. It would now appear that another complication has developed through the dependence of Armenia on Soviet Russia.

The British Prime Minister calls attention to the report that Armenia is under the control of Moscow. In regard to the relations

between Armenia and Soviet Russia, the President sees no action
he could take without the moral and diplomatic support of the principal powers which holds promise of bringing peace and accord to
the contending parties.

There is bitter distrust and fear of war along all the Russian borders. It seems futile to attempt to bring peace to the Caucasus, if
the result is merely to free the forces there engaged for new campaigns on other sectors of this long front. The distressful situation
of Armenia is but one detail of this vast Russian problem, and the
President most earnestly urges his conviction that it is only by a
general and comprehensive treatment of the whole problem, only
by full and generous cooperation of the principal powers, that a
hopeful approach to the pacification and independence of Armenia
can be found.

The attitude of the President towards those now in power in
Russia has been frequently and clearly expressed. He regards the
Bolsheviki as a violent and tyrannical minority, by no means representing the real desires and purposes of the Russian people. But
he has never believed that the problems raised by this *coup d'etat*
could be solved by military action from outside. He now hopes that
the recent tragical events on the Polish front and in the Crimea
have convinced all the world that armed invasion is not the way to
bring peace to the people of Russia.

The rapidly shifting events of recent months have only strengthened his conviction that the Russian Revolution, beneficent in its
main purposes, must be developed to a satisfactory conclusion by
the Russians themselves. Help may from time to time be given
from outside and voluntarily received, but attempts at military
coercion can but end in disaster.

There are elements in the present situation which give added
hope to projects of pacification. All the world is weary of war, and
the conviction grows among the peoples of all countries that the
military method offers very little promise of solving the grave problems of reconstruction which face us. There is at present no overt
civil war in Russia. It is now a problem of the relations between
Central Russia and the surrounding smaller national groups.

The unrest and instability along the border are caused by bitter
and mutual distrust. The struggling new nationalities, which were
formerly part of the Russian Empire, are afraid to disarm and return to the works of peace because they distrust the Bolsheviki and
fear new aggressions. The Soviets contend that they are afraid to
demobilize because they fear new attacks.

The great impediment to peaceful reconstruction in these troubled border territories, the imminent danger of new hostilities, is

caused by the utter confusion between offense and defense. Unless this distinction can be clearly defined, there is not only small hope of peace, but no hope of a clear perception of who is responsible for new wars.

It is therefore the thought of the President that the present moment offers a peculiarly pressing challenge to an attempt at general pacification on the Russian borders along these lines. Such an attempt seems to the President the logical outgrowth—in fact, the only logical development—of the request to mediate in the Armenian conflict, and he feels bound in conscience once more to call this matter to the attention of the Associated Nations.

It is obvious to all that these small struggling border states will not attack Great Russia unless encouraged by promise of support from the stronger powers. The President therefore believes that the *sine qua non* of an attempt at pacification must be a public and solemn engagement among the Great Powers not to take advantage of Russia's stricken condition and not to violate the territorial integrity of Russia nor to undertake themselves any further invasions of Russia, nor to tolerate such invasions by others.

Such a public agreement would in effect say to those now in power in Russia: "You are not menaced from outside. The Great Powers have voluntarily guaranteed you from attack. You can have peace if you want it."

The responsibility for any new war which might break out on the Russian border would then be clearly placed.

If the principal powers represented on the Council of the League find themselves in accord with the President in this matter and will assure him of their moral and diplomatic support, he will instruct his personal representative, Mr. Morgenthau, to proceed at once on his mission.[1]

T MSS (N. H. Davis Papers, DLC).
[1] "This is the one to send. Excellent! Thank you W.W." WWhw note attached to this draft. It was sent Jan. 18, 1921.

From the Shorthand Diary of Charles Lee Swem

15 January, 1921

The President these days is much given to gratifying whatever petty prejudices he has. He won't sign a nomination but what he asks the Attorney General if so and so or this, that, or the other senator is behind the man recommended. If such a senator is found to be a sponsor or even to have sent a routine letter in support of him—that man is not appointed. He doesn't merely ask who is supporting the man but singles out the person who might support him and asks if he is the guilty party. And this is but an example of his whole course nowadays.

JRT transcript (WC, NjP) of CLSsh (C. L. Swem Coll., NjP).

William Edward Dodd to Dice Robins Anderson[1]

Dear Anderson: University of Chicago January 16, 1921.

. . . The meeting of the [American] Historical Association was rather more pleasant than I had expected. The committee on nominations has before it the proposition to make President Wilson second vice president next time. While this is confidential in a sense, I do not wish you to keep it still if you know people, especially in the North who would like to have Wilson read the annual address three years from now. There was a certain silly opposition made to the proposition in the committee. This gave way, but it would help a great deal if people who really understand President Wilson would write F. H. Hodder, University of Kansas,[2] later in the year requesting the nomination, if it seems feasible. Hodder, the chairman, is enthusiastic about the idea. And I saw President Wilson and secured his consent to serve if nominated. There may or may not be a referendum this year. If there should not be one, suggestions from various elements would be very helpful. You know a good many people in the North who would welcome the nomination. You also know that nearly all Southerners would be glad of the nomination. I am hoping Hamilton[3] will let the situation be known to as many as come within his range.

The President may not live to see the day when we wish him to address us. He walks with great difficulty, but he was most interesting, keen in his conversation and he apparently expects to be able to meet the occasion. I spent nearly the whole afternoon of the 30th with him in his sick room, after being with the family, including himself, at luncheon. It was a most affecting scene, the man whom I had talked with when all mankind did him obeisance was now broken, plainly broken by the stubborn wills of imperialistic and selfish men, and no man anywhere speaking a word of good will. I have sat and listened to him talk about his hopes and purposes when exgovernors, archbishops and business magnates were literally shouting about the White House, trying to get in. They were trying to wreck him and his cause. He would not see them. Now they have wrecked his cause, they endeavor to make out that it was he who betrayed the world. More than once as he talked this time, his eyes filled with tears; and mine were not dry.

I could not help thinking of that famous saying: "how oft would I have gathered you, like a hen doth her brood, under my wings but ye would not."

These words came into my mind especially when he rehearsed the ordeal of Paris and told how all of our own delegation, except Henry White, abandoned him at critical moments and especially when he reported how leaders and simple folk of this country cabled him to do this or the other in contravention of the American promises. And again when he said: "Men of all nations and all causes pressed upon me daily to save them from the powers of imperialism as if I had all power. Would to God I had had the power." But people would not do what they knew was right and noble. They agreed to Christian principles to be applied to others but not to themselves. Wilson made the remark, if men only knew the principles of Christian conduct. "Why, they are so simple, so attractive that they are catching, Christianity is catching, if it only be understood."

It is a long letter I am writing. I did not intend so to write. Only, Wilson stands out as such a tragic figure, such a near approach to that other great figure of mankind who was put to death because he would do good and not evil, that I can not abbreviate my words when I write of him. And it will not be many years before you find all parties in this country citing his words and his plans as the great models for the country. He said to me more than once: "you university men must keep up the fight. These ideas must win. If you stand together and continue to preach them and write them, men will listen to you; they can not help doing so. If I only knew how best to help, it would be the one work of my remaining years to aid in this cause."

While I am aware of the weakness of Wilson's leadership, I am not in the least inclined to blame him, even for his mistakes. They were made in the hope of winning men to the right cause. If he hates any eminent men, and he does hate some, they are the very men you and I have opposed and even despised these many years. I am vain enough to think they are the men whom history will utterly condemn.

With all good wishes,   [William E. Dodd]

CCL (W. E. Dodd Papers, DLC).
   [1] President of Randolph-Macon Woman's College, 1920-1931.
   [2] Frank Heywood Hodder, Professor of American History at the University of Kansas.
   [3] Joseph Gregoire de Roulhac Hamilton, Kenan Professor of History and Government at the University of North Carolina.

To James Hamilton Lewis

My dear Senator: [The White House] 17 January, 1921

Your letter was most welcome, as indeed any letter from you would be. I am warmly obliged to you for sending me the copy of the poem which was enclosed. I hope that you will express my appreciation also to the author if you have an opportunity.

With the most heartfelt good wishes for the New Year for yourself and for all you represent.

               Cordially and sincerely yours,   [Woodrow Wilson]

CCL (WP, DLC).

From Alexander Mitchell Palmer

Dear Mr. President: Washington January 17, 1921.

I have your letter of the 15th instant in reference to the proposed nomination of C. W. Miller to be United States Attorney for the Eastern District of Oklahoma, and asking whether he has the support of Senators Owen and Gore.

I have not heard from Senator Gore in reference to this vacancy. Senator Owen, however, has written me a letter indorsing Mr. Miller, who is now Acting United States Attorney under appointment by the court.   Cordially yours,   A Mitchell Palmer

TLS (WP, DLC).

From the Diary of Josephus Daniels

                              January Tuesday 18, 1921

Cabinet—W of M[1] suggests——— for War Finance Corporation. Said Houston, "Nothing doing. Never anything else to do with him.["]

Will you ride with Harding asked Baker. ["]I hope you will not go if it is a cold & sleety day." "O that will not matter. I will wear a gas mask anyhow.["]

Davis talked of how Lloyd George asked him to talk to Brit rep. & ask him to agree with Am on G. reparation   Davis said he had done so & if L.G. could not influence him D could not. LG said he had a letter from the former Presidt of Bk of England saying G ought to pay 25 billion. "Give him that letter & you may influence him.["] But LG would not give up letter

WW did not want army reduced—said France would yet involve

Europe in another war—that Foch and his party were determined to take the Rhine territory.

WW gave two limericks. Houston said his daughter had found new book of limericks. W.W. said let me know the name of the publisher.

[1] Probably Walsh of Montana, that is, Senator Thomas J. Walsh.

From the Diary of Ray Stannard Baker

[Washington] Wednesday Jany 19th [1921].

I found the President & Mrs. Wilson enjoying a moving-picture show in the great ball-room of the White House—just the two, sitting in the middle of the great dark room. I joined them there. It was a blood-curdling "crook" melodrama laid in San Francisco, showing how certain criminals, a man and a girl, were made to "go straight" by the teaching of a Chinese Confucian. The President is far better than when I saw him in November. His speech is almost normal & he looks better & walks better. At luncheon he was really lively and talked with evident pleasure of leaving the White House & getting settled in the new home in S. street. We talked of the difficulty Mr. Harding is having in selecting a cabinet. "I can look on," he said, "with a good deal of dispassionate interest." I told him that I had heard from a friend who had known Mr. H. for years that he was indolent minded & that it wore heavily upon him to have to meet such irritating problems. "Has he any mind?" asked the President caustically. He spoke of Hughes,[1] as prospective Secretary of State, as a poor selection because he was "legally-minded: had no knowledge of foreign affairs; and none of the larger constructive imagination." But he was bitterest about Penrose[2]: said he was "the most sinister influence to-day in our public life."

We discussed the work I am planning to do. Mrs. Wilson said he had been quite stirred by my enthusiasm to have a proper record made of his service in Paris. I again urged him to do it himself.

"Well," he said, "if I do anything at all, it will be a long time in the future." We went up to his study, one of the men bringing along a shining steel cabinet-box which the President said he had got in Paris. He had to shut up all his private papers there, he told me, because "all the servants in that house were spies." I said I had presumed as much. "They were," he said, "I know they were: and I left no important papers around anywhere." I found that there was not only the "trunk-ful" of Paris documents to which the President had referred but *three* trunkfuls, besides the steel cabi-

net, and a precious box which Mrs. Wilson has in a bank vault. I
began at once sorting out the papers in one of the trunks, working
in the President's study. I can see a tremendous job ahead of me,
& no very good warrant that I shall have a free hand in doing it.
The President ought to do it himself!

The President spoke again as I have often heard him do before
of the "power of the word" to influence men. "It was the statement
of our principles in 1917-18," he said, "not anything that I did, that
was effective in Europe, that undermined the morale of Germany."

His faith in the thing said is profound.

Hw MS (R. S. Baker Papers, DLC).
   [1] That is, Charles Evans Hughes.
   [2] That is, Senator Boies Penrose, Republican of Pennsylvania.

From Edward William Bok

                                        Philadelphia Pennsylvania
My dear Mr. President: January nineteenth 1921

You have doubtless seen the enclosed.[1] Naturally you will not
care to make any answer, but may I, in connection with this and
my own personal inclinations, recur to my suggestion made to you
last summer, i.e. that upon your retirement from office you will
come to Philadelphia and speak on The League of Nations?[2] This
would come most à propos in connection with the remarkable series on "What Really Happened at Paris," which we are now holding here and which is attracting such attention.

The last talk in this series is on the evening of March 18th, when
Mr. David Hunter Miller will speak on The Making of the League
of Nations. It would therefore be appropriate in every way if, on the
following evening, Friday, March 25th, we could put on an "extra"
to the series and have you speak. In this way your talk could be
made as an addition to the series, and need in no respect take any
cognizance of Mr. Lansing's material, which will then be in process of being published, and will yet give you an opportunity of
presenting your side of the question.

I need not add that Colonel House is just as keen to have you do
this as I am, and that I can assure you one of the most distinguished audiences in Philadelphia.

May I not know how the idea strikes you? You may of course
depend upon me to handle it in a way that will be in every respect
favorable to your interests, and as I said in my previous letter I
would expect to send you an honorarium of One Thousand Dollars.

With every assurance of personal regard, believe me
                              Very sincerely yours,   Edward W. Bok

TLS (WP, DLC).
¹ Frederick William Wile, "LANSING TO REVEAL PARIS PEACE STORY AS WILSON RE-
TIRES," tear sheet from the Philadelphia *Public Ledger*. Wile briefly summarized the
contents of Lansing's forthcoming *The Peace Negotiations* and characterized the book
as being highly critical of Wilson's conduct of the Paris negotiations. Bok also enclosed
three printed announcements of the *Public Ledger* Forum on the Paris Peace Conference.
² E. W. Bok to WW, Aug. 13, 1920, Vol. 66.

To Norman Hezekiah Davis, with Enclosure

My dear Davis: The White House 20 January, 1921

I wish you would read this extraordinary message from Samuel
Gompers and give me your opinion with regard to it and any sug-
gestions that you may see fit to make. Of course, the word "domin-
ion" in the message should read "Dominican." Apparently the
American Federation of Labor is as willing to rule the world as the
Soviets are.

Cordially and faithfully yours,   Woodrow Wilson

TLS (SDR, RG 59, 839.00/2386, DNA).

ENCLOSURE

From Samuel Gompers

Mexico DF Jan 17, 1921.

The third Pan-American Congress in convention assembled has
instructed the undersigned to transmit to you the following declaration with reference to the subject mentioned therein:

"Whereas the Pan-American Federation of Labor believes it to be
indispensable that the administration of the dominion affairs in
all of their manifestations must be in the executive hands of the
dominion people with the especial cooperation of the organized
labor movement which must exercise this inalienable right, and

"Whereas the dominion people have declined to accept President Wilson's proclamation because they consider it detrimental
to their right of self-determination. Therefore, the third Pan-
American Labor Congress, assembled in Mexico City, being in
complete sympathy with the sentiment of the dominion people
protests against the continued occupation by armed force of the
United States of the Dominion Republic and urgently requests
that her sovereignty and complete independence be immediately
restored to her."

Samuel Gompers,   President,
Pan-American Federation of Labor.

T telegram (SDR, RG 59, 839.00/2386, DNA).

To Raymond Blaine Fosdick, with Enclosure

My dear Fosdick: The White House 20 January, 1921

Will you not read the enclosed and give me your frank opinion of the suggestion? It is a serious matter to divert funds from the purpose for which they were originally intended, but I would like to know your judgment, nevertheless, with regard to Mr. Lamont's friendly suggestion.

With the most cordial good wishes for the New Year,
                    Faithfully yours,   Woodrow Wilson

E N C L O S U R E

From Thomas William Lamont

Dear Mr. President: [New York] January 17th, 1921.

In your kind note to me of December 18th[1] you say, "I have looked about in vain for any fund that I am at liberty to divert for that purpose.[2] I wish there were such a fund." In this connection, it occurs to me that there is at present undistributed and idle a considerable fund that belongs, not to the Government, but that is controlled by a Board upon which Secretaries Baker and Daniels both have seats.

I understand that there is in the old United War Work Campaign Fund an undistributed amount of $4,500,000, and that there are further sums originally purposed for this same Fund still in the hands of the various local committees. There have, I believe, been some technical difficulties in getting one or two of the constituent bodies to agree as to the disposition of the total Fund, but there seems to be little doubt that if the right representation were made from sufficiently high quarters, the difficulty might be solved. It does seem a shame, if the facts given to me are correct, that this Fund should lie idle when it might be so nobly utilized.

In order to bring the matter up, I am wondering whether you would feel warranted in addressing a personal and private line to Raymond Fosdick, Chairman of the trustees of this United War Work Campaign Fund, and indicating your own views in the matter—that is to say, assuming that you have views. I have sketched out in a suggested letter to Mr. Fosidck [Fosdick][3] the main points as they were given to me, and I venture to submit them to you. I can well imagine that in your own mind there may arise some reason against making this recommendation, but the need continues to be so urgent and the present business difficulty is so heavy that the Hoover Fund[4] and the China Famine Fund are both suffering. It would, of course, be my idea that if the War Work Fund could be converted to these pressing needs it should be divided up properly between the China Famine Relief, European Relief, with something also for the Near East.

Sincerely yours,   Thomas W. Lamont   Chairman

TLS (WP, DLC).
    [1] WW to T. W. Lamont, Dec. 18, 1920, Vol. 66.
    [2] Lamont was writing as chairman of the American Committee for China Famine Fund.
    [3] T MS (WP, DLC). Lamont outlined the same proposal discussed in his letter to Wilson.
    [4] The European Children's Relief Fund.

To Peter James Hamilton

My dear Hamilton: [The White House] 20 January, 1921

I have your letter of January twelfth and am very much distressed to hear of the death of your only sister.

Thank you for what you tell me of the condition of affairs in Santo Domingo and Porto Rico. We are in constant touch with those two little republics and are following the development of affairs very closely.

With the best wishes for the New Year, in haste
                              Sincerely yours,   [Woodrow Wilson]

CCL (WP, DLC).

William Edward Dodd to Margaret Woodrow Wilson

My dear Miss Wilson: [Chicago] January 20, 1921.

Since talking with you and learning how you and your sister felt about part of my first chapter of my book on your father and his work, I have reviewed all my sources for that chapter and looked at the comment of Professor Axson on the margins of the manuscript. I recall also very well the statement of the President about that part of the book in which he said that his father was not so orthodox as I had made him out.

In view of all this I am revising the part that refers to Doctor Joseph Ruggles Wilson but leaving what is said in general about the strenuous character of the group out of which your father grew. This seems to be necessary. The sermons, the songs and the conversation, see Mrs. Andrews in her book, *A War Time Journal of a Georgia Girl*,[1] pages 381-382, all make it clear beyond a peradventure that my general narrative is correct. But I would not have you think I am s[a]ying this as particularly applying to the Presbyterians. In my history of the United States,[2] the volume entitled, *Expansion and Conflict*, pages 216 and on, I have made it plain that all the important denominations, except the Catholics and Northern Episcopalians and Unitarians, taught the same sort of religious orthodoxy, the same ideas of a personal devil, going about seeking whom he might devour.

It was just this firm faith, that thought men might remove mountains by prayer, which made this country great. It was, in my judgment, this sort of religious training that gave Woodrow Wilson that strength of character, as well as those abiding principles, which gave him such a place in the cynical atmosphere of Paris and which will award him, or cause historians to award him, the foremost place in American history after Washington, the first place in world history among all those who have labored and fought for the good of all men since Luther. I am not an orthodox churchman of any creed, but it is one of the special contributions that I have made, if I I [*sic*] have made any at all, to American historical writing that religious convictions, even when wrong, are among the greatest things in the world. And in this view I was heartily sustained by the President on September 13, 1918 in a long and to me memorable conversation. He then said, "it was religious training and the fact of the general poverty around me that made me what I am." I have a record of the conversation somewhere,[3] but it hardly seems necessary to quote it *verbatim* at length here.

Of course I know Doctor Joseph Ruggles Wilson was not an extremist in religious orthodoxy; and I knew that Doctor James Woodrow was highly unorthodox, but I did not know till you told me that the former defended the latter in his views. So it seems right for me to make the change. Only, I would not have you or the President or Professor Axson, to whom I am indebted for so much assistance, think that I wrote as I did in any sense of light-hearted or semi-fun making. The volume of mine already referred to, and which has run the gauntlet of very close criticism, in the chapter entitled *American Culture* shows how much importance I attach to the subject.

If this seems satisfactory, may I add a word more? The President told me he was about decided what disposition he would make of his papers. As a student of history and one who thinks his papers must become the most important sources for determining many very important matters, I am a little disturbed at what he said. Not disturbed at the risks due to the character of the gentleman[4] to whom the papers are to be consigned, but at the absence of historical knowledge of any particular range in the mind of the man who must have final authority. President Wilson's work is going to be the object of the fiercest attack during the next twenty years. Already a score of volumes upon one or two other contemporaries and thousands of articles have been published with the purpose of filling the public mind with disparaging statements and with rubbish in the hope of obliterating the great record your father has made. There are diaries and journals of which I have knowledge, more than a hundred and fifty thousand letters from one of his predecessors in office already in the Library of Congress[5] and a great mass of pictures and collections of anecdotes being gathered. Say what you will about the justice of history, this material is going to have effect. More than one historian of national and international reputation has lamented this effort. Some have protested to publishers who are aiding and abetting.

I do not believe there are any intimate diaries or other material to make clear to the people who come after us, just what President Wilson was endeavoring to do. More than once, in the early years of his presidency I urged upon Colonel House the wisdom of bringing this to the attention of people in a position to keep records. I have no inkling from any source that such was done.

Now, if it was not done, the President's papers are going to be the one source, for I believe there are going to be books and reminiscences from his own circle that will attempt to blur the record against him, from which historians will draw the facts. If this be true, it seems proper for me to say (although I know I risk the charge of intermeddling) that his papers ought to go to the Library of Congress as soon as may be possible and that some historian ought to have some say, along with Mr. Baker, as to what shall see the light early. I have no doubt that Wilson's name will ere long be ranked among the very greatest of modern times; but I think the high rank which is his due ought not to be postponed in the interest of semi-charlatans, now deceased, in whose name so much capital is being made. If I have made myself clear, and you feel like risking it, won't you bring this to your father's attention?

[William E. Dodd]

CCL (W. E. Dodd Papers, DLC).

[1] Eliza Frances Andrews, *The War-Time Journal of a Georgia Girl, 1864-1865* (New York, 1908).

[2] Dodd was the editor of "The Riverside History of the United States," published in four volumes by Houghton Mifflin Co. He himself wrote *Expansion and Conflict* (Boston, etc., 1915).

[3] If Dodd kept a memorandum of this conversation, we have not found it in his papers. In a "thank-you" letter to Mrs. Wilson after this visit, he wrote: "The remarkable manner in which the President revealed his mind and ideals the other day and the

realization that his time is the country's and the world's prevented me from explaining the character of the work I have it in mind to do and, therefore, the reason for my being there at all." W. E. Dodd to EBW, Sept. 15, 1918, CCL (W. E. Dodd papers, DLC). In another letter, he wrote: "But on September 13, I had luncheon with Mr. and Mrs. Wilson and remained two hours afterwards. Of course a letter would not be the proper medium to repeat what he said about important matters. One thing I will say: he is a man of immense passion and deep democratic purpose. His public utterances do not indicate the volcanic nature beneath. He has some rather simple traits. For example, although he is a historian much abler than his history of the United States shows him to be, he does not realize the complexity of our historical evolution; he was absolutely on the right course when he was made president of Princeton, about to become a great historian, but that event cut short his research. He was ahead of Turner in his great method, the most fruitful of any in all our historical writing." W. E. Dodd to L. F. Post, Dec. 5, 1918, CCL, *ibid.*

4 That is, Ray Stannard Baker.

5 Theodore Roosevelt, and later his biographer, James Bucklin Bishop, had deposited large portions of his papers in the Library of Congress between 1917 and 1920. William Howard Taft also had donated a large portion of his papers accumulated to date in 1919 and 1920.

To Thomas Lincoln Chadbourne, Jr.

My dear Chadbourne: [The White House] 21 January, 1921

We have been delighted to hear of your new happiness,[1] and I write to send you for Mrs. Wilson and myself our heartiest congratulations. Knowing you as I do, I should like to congratulate Mrs. Chadbourne also. Please say to her that I regard you as one of the finest men I ever knew and one of the most loyal friends.

We join in wishing for you both the greatest happiness and all sorts of good fortune for the New Year.

With the warmest regard,

Cordially and sincerely yours,   [Woodrow Wilson]

CCL (WP, DLC).

1 Chadbourne had married Marjorie Allen Curtis in New York on January 15, 1921.

Three Letters from Norman Hezekiah Davis

My dear Mr. President: Washington January 21, 1921.

I have received your letter of January 20, transmitting a telegram from the Pan American Federation of Labor, signed by Samuel Gompers as President.

I have seen in the newspapers that Mr. Gompers refused to consent to transmit this message to you,[1] and I assume that it must have been sent by certain of the delegates to the Pan American Congress without his knowledge. I am particularly inclined towards this view since Mr. Gompers, before his departure for Mexico City, at his request, was informed by the Department of the policy which you had determined should be adopted in regard to the gradual withdrawal of the United States from continued intervention in Santo Domingo, and expressed himself as being in entire accord with the policy determined upon by this Government.

I presume that very few of the delegates who agreed to this declaration have been in Santo Domingo and that they are not conversant with the conditions which brought about the intervention of the United States in Santo Domingo and that they are likewise totally unaware of the steps which have already been taken towards preparing the way for the Dominican people to establish on a firm basis an independent government. It does not seem to me that in the circumstances this message merits any reply.

Faithfully yours,   Norman H. Davis

TLS (WP, DLC).
  [1] See, e.g., the *New York Times*, Jan. 18, 1921.

My dear Mr. President: [Washington] January 21, 1921.

In accordance with your instructions,[1] I am going before the Senate Committee on Foreign Relations next Tuesday morning to explain the situation relative to the Island of Yap.[2] Some time before that I should like to discuss the matter briefly with you, and hope you will let me know if and when it is agreeable for you to see me.   Cordially yours,   [Norman H. Davis]

CCL (N. H. Davis Papers, DLC).
  [1] See WW to NHD, Jan. 13, 1921.
  [2] There is no record of their discussion. However, Davis met with the Foreign Relations Committee on January 25 and reviewed the controversy and negotiations over Yap in great detail. *New York Times*, Jan. 26, 1921.

My dear Mr. President: Washington January 21, 1921.

I doubt if Mr. Hymans will give out for publication the reply I sent to him several days ago on your behalf, relative to Armenian mediation. In my judgment, nothing can be accomplished without full publicity, and unless you instruct me to the contrary I shall give this to the press on Saturday for release next Sunday morning.

Faithfully and cordially yours,   Norman H. Davis

Approved   W.W.

TLS (SDR, RG 59, 760j67/85, DNA).

From Thomas William Lamont

Dear Mr. President: [New York] January 21st, 1921.

I should like to ask your counsel as to whether you think there is any chance of approaching Congress to put through a resolution appropriating simply sufficient funds to transport to China the several millions of bushels of corn that the farmers have now offered to give us. I venture to attach herewith a clipping, which gives the gist of this proposition.[1] Mr. Howard, the President of the American Farm Bureau Association,[2] came in to see me recently and he stated that the surplusage of corn in the hands of the farmers is so great that he probably could arrange for a donation of from ten to twenty-five millions of bushels for China.

Gifts for the China Fund have, under present business conditions, been coming in so slowly, that there are no funds available to use for the transportation of food. The very limited amount that has been collected up to date has been transmitted at once to China to enable the Relief Committee there to purchase food which is available on the spot and which will alleviate immediate distress. This we considered much better than to exhaust these limited funds in transporting a very small amount of food from this country.

This is a fine offer on the part of the farmers, and should, if possible, be availed of. Howard, the head of their Association, expresses himself as quite willing to co-operate in behalf of the farmers, making such representations to Congress as might be necessary to pass any Resolution necessary to provide this transportation. I quite realize that this may be another case where it is impossible for you to move, and you may not feel even like giving your good counsel in the matter, but, with the necessity so appalling and with this bountiful supply of food at hand, I am not at all sure that Congress might not feel the appeal to the extent of providing transportation.

Were you ever able to look into the matter of the fund in the Sugar Equalization Board?[3]

With great respect,

Sincerely yours,   Thomas W. Lamont

TLS (WP, DLC).
[1] Unidentified newspaper clipping (WP, DLC). It reported that James Raley Howard had announced on January 14 that he was authorized by the "American Farm Bureau Association" to offer enough corn grown in the United States to feed the starving millions of Europe and China. The organization would provide the corn gratis, but American urban dwellers should pay for its transport.
[2] Actually, the American Farm Bureau Federation.
[3] See TWL to WW, Dec. 14, 1920, Vol. 66. Wilson did reply to this letter in WW to TWL, Dec. 18, 1920, *ibid.*

From Thomas Gilbert Pearson[1]

Dear President Wilson: New York City January 21, 1921.

I inclose copy of a telegram I have just sent you.[2]

On January 17 the House passed a bill (S.793) authorizing and directing the Secretary of the Interior to issue a patent to the Milk River Valley Gun Club, which is supposed to be a corporation organized under the laws of Montana, the members of which are located in and around Helena. The land involved consists of 76.69 acres and will cover lots 5 and 6 and the southeast quarter of the southwest quarter of section 32, township 31 north, range 31 east, Montana Meridian. The patent is to be issued upon the payment of $1.25 an acre. The bill has passed both Houses and has gone to you for approval.

The debate in the House shows that the objects and purposes of the bill are to create a game preserve where birds are to be protected at all times; but several Congressmen pointed out, and Mr. Riddick,[3] who introduced the bill, conceded, that it would give the members of the club the exclusive right to hunt on the land. This is a very dangerous precedent to establish. If the true purpose is to establish a game preserve, it can be carried out through a proclamation by the President without any action by Congress, in the same manner as other Federal Bird Reservations are created.

The bill having passed both branches of Congress before we learned of it, only one course remains open and that is to appeal to you. We most respectfully and earnestly urge that you veto this bill which is nothing short of an amazing attempt to secure private shooting grounds under the guise of making them a bird reservation.

Evidently the members of this Club are quite willing to pay $1.25 an acre to secure the right to shut out all other hunters from Montana and elsewhere and have the exclusive shooting privileges for themselves.   Yours very sincerely,   T. Gilbert Pearson

TLS (WP, DLC).
  [1] President of the National Association of Audubon Societies.
  [2] T. G. Pearson to WW, Jan. 21, 1921, T telegram (WP, DLC).
  [3] Carl Wood Riddick, Republican congressman from Montana.

From the Diary of Josephus Daniels

January Saturday 22, 1921

George Creel here—talked about his visit to Mexico at request of Wilson & how the plans written out came to naught because Davis insisted on treaty,[1] thus leaving matter in hand of Republican Senate when Wilson might have settled it now. Of course now Obregon thinks it is better to come to terms with Harding. He says Doheny[2] wishes intervention & speaks of adding 28 stars to our flag by adding Mexico. McAdoo represents Doheny, who is in with or has close relations with S. O. Co.[3]

[1] About this matter, see the index references to "Mexico and the United States" in Vol. 66.
[2] That is, Edward Laurence Doheny.
[3] The Standard Oil Company of New Jersey.

From the Diary of Ray Stannard Baker

Saturday the 22nd [January 1921]

Working at White House: still wading neck deep in disordered papers. I begin to see some light. I am making both a chronological arrangement (of the dated letters & less bulky documents) and a subject arrangement for the more important matters, like Shantung, Italy, Russia, Reparations &c

Mrs. W. came up toward noon and asked me come down for the moving-pictures, said the President had suggested it. Afterwards I staid on to luncheon. The President was quite the most cheerful I have seen him. Repeated Riley's[1] "The Man in the Moon" for us with great spirit. Told of his experience at Princeton. Asked me about Meiklejohn[2] of Amherst. I told him I thought he was doing a fine work but trying to do it too fast.

"That was my trouble at Princeton," said the President. "Trying to change old institutions too fast."

I thought he said the latter with a sense of a wider application than universities!

When he speaks of public men, and indeed, of the Paris experience, he at once turns acid, bitter. Referring to the new arrangement in Fiume,[3] he said:

"Well, they are sowing the seeds of new wars."

I had an opportunity to refer to the "Freedom of the Seas" as expressed in the fourteen points.

"With the League of Nations accepted the problem of free seas disappears," he said.

This is no explanation: & not satisfying as history!

Mrs. Wilson is splendid. Good sense, a fine spirit, devotion! What has she not gone through these last months. The President could not have lived without her—literally. The relationships between them are beautiful. To-day while the moving pictures were going on, I saw him raise her hand to his lips and kiss it.

¹ James Whitcomb Riley.
² That is, Alexander Meiklejohn, the controversial President of Amherst College since 1912.
³ About which, see BC to WW, Nov. 13, 1920 (fourth letter of that date), and its Enclosure, Vol. 66.

To Warren Gamaliel Harding

[The White House]
My dear Mr. President-elect: 22 January, 1921

It has been customary, I understand, for a luncheon to be arranged by the outgoing President for the incoming President and his guests on the fourth of March, the day of inauguration. Mrs. Wilson and I would be very glad, indeed, to arrange such a luncheon if it would be agreeable to you and Mrs. Harding.¹ Of course, the invitations would go from you and Mrs. Harding, and we would only have to know approximately the number of guests you invite so that proper arrangements may be made. Hitherto the guests have adjourned after luncheon to a stand erected on the Avenue immediately in front of the White House to review the inaugural parade.

I know through the newspapers of the interest you have taken in the whole programme of the day, and wish therefore to submit this part of the programme to your consideration at as early a date as possible.

If it meets with your approval, I should be glad to direct one of the gentlemen in the office, familiar with the customary arrangements at the White House, to call upon you in Florida at your convenience and go over with you any of the details of this or any other matter connected with the White House which you and Mrs. Harding may care to know about.

Mrs. Wilson joins me in hoping that Mrs. Harding and you are well and that you will in every way enjoy your residence in the White House.   Sincerely yours,   Woodrow Wilson

TLS (Letterpress Books, WP, DLC).
¹ Florence Mabel Kling DeWolfe Harding.

To Edward William Bok

My dear Friend: [The White House] 22 January, 1921

Thank you for your letter of the nineteenth and your renewal of the suggestion that I speak in Philadelphia on the League of Nations after my retirement from office. I think it depends very much upon the development of affairs whether it would be profitable for me to speak upon the League of Nations or not, but you may be sure that I shall avail myself of every proper opportunity to press a cause which I am sure must win in the long run. The Republicans are going to make this Government cut a very poor figure outside the League, that is certain.

With warmest regards and most cordial good wishes for the New Year,   Sincerely yours,   [Woodrow Wilson]

CCL (WP, DLC).

From Charles Zeller Klauder

My dear Mr. President: Philadelphia January 22nd, 1921.

Thank you for your letter of January 10th. I have been giving consideration to the possibilities opened up by your suggestion to release the study for use as a billiard room, and have found a solution which commends itself to me as resulting in a distinct improvement in this plan as well as causing an improvement in the other stories.

Under separate cover are being sent plans in blue print form,[1] together with a slight sketch of the billiard room interior, all dated today, which incorporate the following salient features:

Basement Plan. As originally drawn with such minor changes as are necessitated by the lengthening of the end wings on the floors above.

First Floor. The increased space in the wings is well used at one end in the kitchen services which were slightly crowded before. At the other extremity, the study can now be turned into an ample sized billiard room, the north end of which, with its fireplace, forms a beamed or vaulted alcove from which one may in comfort watch the game without interfering with the players.

The garage has been changed in accordance with your previous suggestion, with both openings to the north.

Second Floor. By enlarging the plan for the billiard room, Mrs. Wilson's room above has now become a liberal size for a bed room, thus utilizing the space of the former bed room for a splendid dressing room for Mrs. Wilson. However, should she prefer the original arrangement with the bed room to the north, but larger in size, it will now be possible to remove her bath to a location above the main portion of the billiard room as shown on the alternate flap. Should this be done, it would still leave a dressing room nearly as large as the one shown on the old plans.

Third Floor. It has always been my intention to run the main stair to the third floor. This space is susceptible of various arrangements. We have indicated two bed rooms with baths, all lighted as shown without the use of dormers.

Respecting the one to the west, we thought you might regard it as a suitable room for a valet should more general servants' rooms be desired in the basement, and in order that you may see the full possibilities of the suggestion, the small stair has also been carried to the third floor.

Under the main part of the roof, the space could be arranged to provide ample storage lighted, in large part, as you suggest by glass slates. You will note a small portion of this glass slate already shown on the front elevation in the sketches you now have.

I am sending these drawings with the thought that after you have had a full opportunity to study them, I can make a trip to Washington to rehearse with you the aspects of all the plans, to the end that by conferring we may then evolve a set of plans which would represent completely your cherished ideas.

Looking forward with pleasure to talking over these details at your convenience with you, and to seeing your new house, I am, with kindest regards,   Sincerely yours,   Chas Z Klauder

TLS (WP, DLC).
    [1] They are missing.

From Francis Bowes Sayre

Dear Father,   Cambridge, Mass. Jan. 23, 1921

I had a long talk with some of the Y. M. C. A. people yesterday; and they are a bit worried lest, as a result of certain propaganda, pressure be brought against you to get you to issue a statement recommending that the money now in the treasury of the United War Work campaign[1] be turned over to Mr. Hoover for European Relief work. This of course would put the Y. M. C. A. in a very unfortunate situation, since the money was given for Army work, and they have already committed themselves and budgeted the money for work among the armies of occupation, the Polish army, the Greek army, etc., and their legal advisers tell them they would have no right to devote the money to ordinary relief work.

I told the Y. M. C. A. people that I felt very sure you would issue no such statement without going into the facts of the case; but to satisfy them I promised to drop you a line about the matter. I enclose a memorandum,[2] which please do not bother to read unless you *are* pressed for such a statement. And please forgive my breaking my rule not to write you as to public matters.

Jessie and the children are all well, and, with me, send you our deepest love and devotion.

Ever affectionately yours,   Frank

We are planning tentatively to go down to Princeton to pack your things on the vans on February 14th. F.B.S.

ALS (WP, DLC).
  [1] About this fund, see the Enclosure printed with WW to R. B. Fosdick, Jan. 20, 1921.
  [2] A. S. Taylor, "Report of YMCA Work in Poland. Month of October, 1920," T MS (WP, DLC).

To Samuel Gompers

My dear Mr. Gompers: The White House 24 January, 1921

I am in receipt of your message dated Mexico, January seventeenth, and find myself a good deal puzzled about it. I had understood that the delegates of the labor convention you have been attending had declined to send such a message to me when it was proposed that they should. Perhaps I have been misinformed.

The Under Secretary of State informs me[1] that before you departed for Mexico City you were at your own request informed by the Department of State of the policy which I had determined should be adopted with regard to the gradual withdrawal of the United States from continued intervention in Santo Domingo, and that you expressed yourself as being in entire accord with the policy determined upon by this Government there.

Very truly yours,   Woodrow Wilson

TLS (photostat in RSB Coll., DLC).
  [1] NHD to WW, Jan. 21, 1921 (first letter of that date).

To Charles Zeller Klauder

My dear Mr. Klauder;   [The White House] 24 January, 1921

There are two points about which perhaps I had better drop you just a line or two. I think perhaps the position you have chosen for the safe or vault is a little too conspicuous, being so near the door of the sitting room into and out of which strangers will constantly be passing. What would you think of adopting some such screen as is very much in vogue in the movies, namely, a sliding bookshelf or a glass door with imitation books behind it? My thought would be that the basement was the best place for it.

Could we not, without very great cost, put quarters for two men servants over the garage? It occurs to me that a picturesque access to such quarters should be provided leading by an exterior staircase from the fore court and sustained by a wooden structure of some interesting design. What do you think of that suggestion? I have, of course, in mind a chauffeur and perhaps a butler.

With warm regard,

Sincerely yours,   [Woodrow Wilson]

CCL (WP, DLC).

From Raymond Blaine Fosdick

My dear Mr. President: New York City January 24th, 1921.

I have your letter of January 20th enclosing the letter from Mr. Lamont in regard to the question whether the undistributed balance of $4,500,000 now in the treasury of the United War Work Campaign committee can be used for such purposes as the China Famine Relief, the European Relief, etc. This is a question to which we have already given considerable attention, and I have had the matter up with the seven organizations which participated in the United War Work Campaign in the fall of 1918. With one exception, these societies are all opposed to releasing their claim to this fund. They say—some of them with apparent good reason—that the purposes for which the fund was contributed have not been entirely fulfilled, and that in justice to their own constituents and to their own plans, they cannot consent to its alienation to other ends.

You will appreciate that this has been a very delicate situation to handle, and it is complicated by the friction which unfortunately developed between some of the societies during the war. I felt, therefore, that inasmuch as legal questions would probably be involved we ought to consult counsel, and we have been advised by Mr. George Welwood Murray, who has been acting as our counsel since 1918, that the United War Work Campaign Committee could not, without the unanimous consent of the seven organizations, turn over this surplus to any other agency. Our only course, therefore, I believe, is to give this surplus to the societies in the percentages agreed upon in 1918, and leave to them individually the responsibility of acting upon any appeals which Mr. Hoover or Mr. Lamont may make.

Fortunately the matter does not end here. In addition to the $4,500,000 now in our campaign treasury, there are large sums running into the millions still in the possession of local war chests. These sums were collected for the United War Work Campaign but were not turned over to us because it was felt that we had all the money we could properly use. They have therefore remained in the possession of local treasuries. Buffalo, for example, has approximately $700,000, Philadelphia has $900,000 and other cities have similar amounts, so that the aggregate total is quite large. These cities will not make any further payments to the United War Work Campaign, and unless some project can be discovered, connected, of course, with the purposes for which the money was raised, the funds will probably be returned to the donors. Mr. Hoover has already made some approach to these local treasuries and has been advised in one or two cases that if he could secure a release from our committee and from the seven organizations, the war chests would be glad to turn part of their surplus over to him. Our committee has already taken favorable action on this matter and we are now in the course of securing the assent of our seven participating societies. If to these papers can be added a letter of consent from yourself, I believe that it will open the door to the use of these funds by the European Relief.

Whether the China Famine Fund would have access here I very much doubt. This money was raised on the distinct understanding that it would be used for war purposes, or for purposes growing out of the war, and this condition was written into the pledges. The European situation grows distinctly out of the war; apparently the China situation does not. As a member of Mr. Lamont's committee, to which you generously appointed me, and as a member, too, of his smaller executive committee, I am most anxious to help him in any way I can. At the same time I am afraid that we are confronted with a legal situation which may make it impossible for these particular funds to be used in China. The matter of course is not definitely settled, but what I have expressed seems to be the opinion of the various attorneys who are guiding the war chest representatives and the United War Work Campaign Committee.

I have talked this matter over at length with Mr. Hoover and I understand that he hopes to secure from you a letter of approval as far as his participation in these war chest funds is concerned. I am also taking the matter up with Mr. Lamont so that he will understand thoroughly the peculiar position in which my committee finds itself.

I hope I have made this entirely clear. If anything occurs to you in the way of a further step that we might take, or if I can be of any service to you in this situation, I trust you will not hesitate to let me know.

I return Mr. Lamont's letter herewith.

With warm personal regards,

Ever faithfully yours,   Raymond B. Fosdick

TLS (WP, DLC).

From Ray Stannard Baker

My dear Mr. President: Washington, D. C. 24 January, 1921

In making an exploration of the material brought back from the Paris Peace Conference, I have made a crude arrangement in two groups, the first consisting of letters, memoranda and many of the shorter documents arranged according to their dates. There are 9 packages of these, beginning with October 1918 and running through to and including June, 1919. There are also two or three packages of minutes and reports of the later sessions of the Peace Conference held in August and September, 1919.

The second grouping is made up of documents and reports concerning certain specific subjects dealt with by the Peace Conference. These packages are as follows:

1. Papers relating to the Shantung settlement and the relationships between China and Japan.

2. Papers relating to the League of Nations and the meetings of the Commission of the League of Nations.

3. Papers relating to the Saar Valley decision.

4. Reports of the various plenary sessions.

5. Papers relating to the financial, economic, and reparations clauses in the Treaty.

6. Papers relating to the military, naval and air terms of the Treaty.

7. Papers relating to ports, waterways and railways.

8. Papers relating to submarine cables.

9. Papers relating to labor clauses in the Treaty.

10. Papers relating to colonies and the mandatory system.

11. Papers dealing with the negotiations with the German Peace Delegates at Versailles.

12. Turkey.

13. Russia.

14. Italy.

15. Greece.

16. Denmark.

17. Belgium.

18. Papers relating to the Austrian Treaty.

19. Papers relating to the clauses in the Treaty dealing with the responsibility of the authors of the war.

Besides these packages, there is a small number of the weekly intelligence summary of the War Department and a package of the bulletins of the American Commission to Negotiate Peace.

One complete set of the bound volumes of the minutes of the
Council of Four is in Safety Box No. 1. The volumes are as follows:

No. 1. April 19-26.

No. 2. April 28-May 7.

No. 3. May 8-17.

No. 4. May 19-22.

No. 5. May 23-31.

No. 6. June 2-11.

No. 7. June 12-16.

No. 8. June 17-24.

The minutes of the meetings from June 25 to June 28 are unbound and unindexed, but are filed with this set. They include
Nos. 91, 92, 93, 95, 96, 96a, and 97: I find no record of any No.
94.

There are two volumes of indexes with this set, the first an index
of the minutes from April 19 to May 7. This index is only for volume No. 1 and No. 2 of the minutes, and reference is made to the
key numbers of the daily report (with paging) from 171d to 181f.

Volume No. 2 of the index covers minutes from May 8 to June
24. This index is for Volumes No. 3 to No. 8 of the minutes, inclusive. References are to side-tabbed numbers, beginning with No. 1
in Volume 3 to No. 90 in Volume 8.

Minutes from June 25 to June 28 are unbound and unindexed.

I found one duplicate set and part of another of the minutes of
the Council of Four. These I have grouped in packages by months,
from April to June. I have placed the extra duplicates in the packages according to their dates.

This arrangement has been hastily done, with the aim merely to
explore the material. When I go further into it, I can make a more
accurate and careful arrangement.

The documents according to both groupings are in Safety Box
No. 2 and in the George Washington trunk.

Sincerely yours,   Ray Stannard Baker

TLS (WP, DLC).

From the Diary of Josephus Daniels

1921 Tuesday 25, January

Cabinet. Palmer told of German Doctor in Wash. whose property
was taken over by the Alien property custodian. His wife was
American & under recent act of Congress she is entitled to her
property if not obtained through German sources. It was all returned, but when he examined [it] he complained it lacked a price-

less possession—the appendix of Alice Roosevelt Longworth in alcohol.

Houston said British evidently intended not to deal with this administration on debt due this country. Twice they had made date for Lord Chalmers[1] & twice postponed. He wished to give Congress Lloyd George's letter & the Presidents.[2] Davis objected because it contained something bearing on French affairs and WW said that part should be omitted. Decided to give facts & show this administration had left no stone unturned. . . .

WWs new house. Among other things I can look down on Phelan.[3]

[1] Robert Chalmers, 1st Baron Chalmers of Northiam; Joint Permanent Secretary of the Treasury, 1916-1919.
[2] D. Lloyd George to WW, Aug. 5, 1920, printed as an Enclosure with BC to WW, Aug. 18, 1920, Vol. 66; and WW to D. Lloyd George, Nov. 3, 1920, *ibid.*
[3] Senator Phelan's Washington residence was at 2249 R Street, N.W.

To Charlotte D. Wilbur

My dear Miss Wilbur: [The White House] 25 January, 1921

I have your letter of January twenty-second[1] and am very glad to send a contribution to the fund of which you speak. I hope that the plans for a testimonial to Mr. Beach will be in every way successfully carried out, and that, if you have an opportunity, you will express to Mr. Beach my congratulations and best wishes.

Sincerely yours,   [Woodrow Wilson]

CCL (WP, DLC).
[1] Charlotte D. Wilbur to WW, Jan. 22, 1921, ALS (WP, DLC). Miss Wilbur, who lived at 27 University Place, Princeton, N. J., was soliciting donations toward the purchase of an automobile for the Rev. Dr. Sylvester Woodbridge Beach, in honor of his fifteen years of service as pastor of the First Presbyterian Church of Princeton. The automobile, she explained, would greatly assist Beach in making some seven hundred annual pastoral visits in and around Princeton, which at present he performed with only the aid of a bicycle and flashlight.

To George Foster Peabody

My dear Friend: [The White House] 25 January, 1921

Your letter[1] has given me the greatest pleasure, for I see happiness for yourself written in every line of it and that rejoices me. I have every reason to believe that the most delightful things are in store for you, and I hope I may convey my warm congratulations not only but my affectionate good wishes.

I hope that you will convey to Mrs. Trask my affectionate greetings. I have valued her friendship more than I can say and am very proud indeed that she should believe in me as she does, for I know the truth and sincerity of her nature.

With the warmest good wishes,

Cordially and sincerely yours,   [Woodrow Wilson]

CCL (WP, DLC).
¹ It is missing in both the Wilson and Peabody Papers, but as EBW to Kate N. Trask (printed as an Enclosure with Kate N. Trask to WW, Jan. 30, 1921) reveals, it told of his coming marriage to Mrs. Trask on February 5, 1921.

From Norman Hezekiah Davis

My dear Mr. President: Washington January 26, 1921.

In my letter of December 6,¹ I advised you that the Department was informed that the Bolivian Congress elected in November was to meet in convention on December 20, to revise the Constitution and to elect a provisional President. I submitted for your consideration the advisability of recognizing the Bolivian Government, after the election of the provisional President, as the *de facto* Government of Bolivia, postponing entering into formal relations with that Government until it was permanently established. You will recall that you expressed your approval of this procedure.

The Department has today been advised that the Congress amended the Constitution of the Republic so as to permit the election of the Constitutional President by the Congress, thus avoiding the necessity of electing a provisional President to hold office pending the election of a Constitutional President next May in accordance with the former provisions of the Constitution. Dr. Bautista Saavedra was yesterday elected President by the Congress and will be inaugurated on January 28th.

Under these circumstances, I submit to you the desirability of extending formal recognition to the Government of Dr. Saavedra as the Constitutional Government of Bolivia. I beg to request your instructions as to the course you desire followed.

Faithfully yours,   Norman H. Davis

What do you advise?   W.W.

TLS (SDR, RG 59, 824.00/181a, DNA).
¹ NHD to WW, Dec. 6, 1920 (second letter of that date), Vol. 66.

From Walker Downer Hines

Dear Mr. President: Paris January 26th, 1921.

I have just made my first decision as Arbitrator of the questions pertaining to river shipping under the Peace Treaties,—the position to which you did me the honor to appoint me. I, therefore, take pleasure in submitting to you the enclosed copy of this decision,[1] which relates to the Rhine, and which probably involves more tonnage than any other decision I shall make.

While the French and German Delegations showed a spirit of courteous co-operation in establishing the statistical facts, they were very far apart on the principles involved. The result was that France asked for a Rhine fleet of about 776,000 tons, while Germany conceded a fleet of only 111,000 tons, and my decision resulted in allotting a fleet of about 254,000 tons. I had anticipated that my action would prove extremely disappointing and distasteful to both sides, but, as far as I have been able to learn, I have been gratified to find no marked evidence of serious discontent on either side.

The decisions as to the Elbe, the Oder, and the Danube, are yet to be made.

My stay in Europe has been most stimulating and enlightening, and I have been increasingly confirmed in the view that the United States, both on moral and material grounds, must establish a basis for continuous counsel and co-operation with the rest of the world.
                    Cordially yours,   Walker D. Hines.

TLS (WP, DLC).
    [1] *In the Matter of the Cessions by Germany to France under Article 357 of the Treaty of Versailles . . . Walker D. Hines, Arbitrator, Paris, January 8th 1921*, printed pamphlet (WP, DLC).

From the Diary of Ray Stannard Baker

Jany 27th [1921]

I had a talk this morning at 11 with the President. I have seen him several mornings sitting at his desk signing papers, Mrs. Wilson standing at his side & turning them over as he signed. We discussed the documents and he said he would help me in cases where the intent was not clear. I also referred to the notes in his hieroglyphics (short-hand) of which I had found quite a number and he said he would "translate" them for me. I could have access to the documents at any time, both here at the White House & after they had moved to the new home in "S" Street. I wanted to have it perfectly clear as to where I stood with regard to the book, and just what I could & could not assume. Either I should write with his supervision & authority: or I should write my own book in my own way. It could not be both. The President saw this clearly. "If I authorize the book or even read it to criticize it," he said, "it would be the same as though I wrote it myself." "Then it is to be my book, with my own interpretations & conclusions."

"Yes," he said.

I am glad of this: I can now go ahead & set down exactly what I find, what I know, what I believe. The great thing is not to defend or excuse every act of the President: which I have never done: but to present this strong, able, fallible man struggling with vast events, in a torn world. I want to exhibit America in contact with Europe for the first time on a really vital scale: the clashing character, ideals, methods. It can be no better dramatized than at this Conference. Here is a real thing to do.

I can also add the chapter or chapters on Publicity & Communications which I have always wanted to write. This is most important.

—The President was in cheerful mood: told about his visit with Mr. Cox yesterday:[1] said he liked him. Tumulty came in & the talk shifted to politics. The President is pretty acid when he discusses the various leaders. He thinks the Republicans are due to split as soon as the pressure of administration rests upon them. "That will be the chance," said Tumulty, "for the democrats."

"If the democrats had any leaders," said the President.

"Why not Cox?" I asked

"Not Cox," said Tumulty.

Various democratic senators were referred to: & the President spoke of most of them slightingly or bitterly. He called McKellar a "scoundrel." Hoover was mentioned as a possible member of Harding's cabinet. "Hoover," he said, "is a fakir. He is not real." Of course Hoover is not a fakir.

The question of the treaty came up, and the President expressed absolute confidence that it would have to be ratified by the new administration & that we should have to go into the League. He made light of Harding's "sinuosities" on this matter.

[1] James M. Cox visited Wilson at the White House on January 26. After the meeting, he told reporters that Wilson was "heavier and more robust in every way" than he was the last time Cox saw him, when Cox and Franklin D. Roosevelt paid a ceremonial call on Wilson on July 18, 1920 (about which, see the extracts from the Grayson and Swem diaries and the news reports printed at July 18, 1920, Vol. 65). Cox described his visit as merely a "friendly" call and refused to go into the details of his conversation with Wilson. He did say that he and Wilson had talked about Cox's trip to Europe in June and that he would not take any messages to Europe for Wilson. He also told Wilson that he had come to the White House to tell him that he had decided "not to move in." *New York Times*, Jan. 27, 1921.

To Kate Nichols Trask

My dear Mrs. Trask: The White House 27 January, 1921

Mrs. Wilson was gracious enough to let me read her last letter to you[1] and [it] so perfectly expressed what I could have wished to say that I greatly desired a copy of the letter, but I spoke of it, unfortunately, after the letter had got into Uncle Sam's hands and was on its way to you. If it is not too much trouble, I would be very much obliged if you would let your secretary send me at your convenience a copy of the letter. I should like to keep it for its own sake and for the sake of what it expresses to two dear friends.

With the most cordial good wishes and with great gratitude for your generous friendship,

Cordially and sincerely yours,   Woodrow Wilson

TLS (Yaddo).
[1] That is, the Enclosure printed with Kate N. Trask to WW, Jan. 30, 1921.

From Norman Hezekiah Davis

My dear Mr. President: Washington January 27, 1921.

I apologize for not having conveyed more clearly my recommendation regarding the extension of recognition to the Constitutional Government of Bolivia upon the inauguration of Dr. Saavedra as President. I do recommend that recognition be extended. I may also say that I have just discussed the matter with Secretary Colby, who concurs in my view, and that the governments of Argentina and Brazil, with whom we have been acting in concert, have advised us that they favor taking such action concurrently with this Government.   Faithfully yours,   Norman H. Davis

I concur   W.W.

TLS (SDR, RG 59, 824.00/181b, DNA).

From Bainbridge Colby

My dear Mr. President: [Washington] January 27, 1921.

The first thing that I wish to do on reaching my desk this morning is to advise you of my safe return. Our trip was concluded yesterday afternoon without mishap, and the members of my little party are all well.

I have much to relate to you. I am also the bearer of many messages, some of importance, all of the most cordial feeling for you. I shall be so happy to see you, which I hope I may do at your early convenience. My first inquiry on landing was as to your health, and I am gratified to receive good reports.

Your messages to me, which were faithfully transmitted by the State Department, gave me a great deal of pleasure.

Very respectfully yours,   Bainbridge Colby

CCL (B. Colby Papers, DLC).

To Thomas William Lamont

My dear Lamont: The White House 28 January, 1921

I took up the matter you wrote me about with Raymond Fosdick and am now sending you a copy of his reply.[1] In the letter he says that he has already been in communication with you and it may be that this is a work of supererogation.

Cordially and faithfully yours,   Woodrow Wilson

TLS (T. W. Lamont Papers, MH-BA).
[1] R. B. Fosdick to WW, Jan. 24, 1921.

From Raymond Blaine Fosdick, with Enclosure

My dear Mr. President: New York City January 28, 1921

With reference to my letter to you of January 24th in regard to the use by the European Relief Council of the funds now in the hands of community War Chests, I have been requested by my committee to ask whether you would be willing to write me some such letter as I enclose herewith. The more we go into this matter, the more it seems probable that these funds cannot be used for the China Famine Committee, but that they will probably be available for Mr. Hoover's purposes. As I told you the other day, there are in these War Chests amounts of money running up into the millions, and inasmuch as they are no longer available for the purposes of the seven organizations affiliated with the Committee of Eleven, it would seem as if they ought to be used in this positive work of relief. With the resolution that is being passed by the Committee of Eleven and the seven societies, together with a letter from you, I think we would have ammunition enough to induce these War Chests to turn their surpluses, or large portions of them, over to Mr. Hoover.

You will understand, of course, that this has nothing to do with funds already in the treasuries of the seven participating organizations or in the treasury of the United War Work Campaign Committee. It relates only to funds that have not been paid over to us and that we cannot collect for ourselves.

With warm personal regards,

Ever cordially yours, Raymond B. Fosdick[1]

TLS (WP, DLC).

[1] Fosdick wrote the following at the bottom of the carbon copy of this letter in his papers in NjP: "President Wilson did not write to Mr. Hoover, as I suggested. I was told that it was due to his personal feeling against Hoover. R.B.F." Moreover, Wilson did not answer Fosdick's letter in any way.

ENCLOSURE

My dear Mr. Fosdick:

I am encouraged to learn from you that the purposes for which the United War Campaign Fund was raised have been so nearly accomplished, and that the unity of spirit and of action requested in my letter to you of September 3, 1918[1] have been so finely maintained throughout the whole business.

You tell me that certain local organizations, such as War Chests, have not yet paid in full the amount of their subscriptions to the United Fund, and that in view of these circumstances and of the overwhelming suffering and danger of famine in southeastern Europe caused by the War some of these organizations desire to turn over part of their subscriptions to the European Relief Council, which is now making an appeal to the generosity of our people for the relief of these suffering populations, especially children, and I understand that the Committee of Eleven, the central body of the United War Work Campaign, and the seven societies cooperating in that Campaign assent to this course.

May I add that, under the circumstances and in view of the undoubted need of southeastern Europe, such payments would meet with my approval as in a broad and general sense reasonably related to the purposes for which the United War Campaign Fund was raised. Sincerely yours,

T MS (WP, DLC).

[1] WW to R. B. Fosdick, Sept. 3, 1918, Vol. 49.

From Newton Diehl Baker

My dear Mr President   Washington January 29, 1921

This resolution[1] is not as good as the one which passed the Senate[2] but under all the circumstances I am sure it should receive your approval. The disposition of the House is such that a much greater reduction would be ordered if the resolution were vetoed and another opportunity given to consider the subject. Indeed the appropriation bill, reported in the House this morning provides for only one hundred and fifty thousand men.

By approving this you have an impregnable position if you find it wise to veto the appropriation bill later.

Respectfully yours, Newton D. Baker

ALS (WP, DLC).

¹ H.J. Res. 440, which directed the Secretary of War to cease enlisting new recruits in the Regular Army until the number of enlisted men had gone down to 175,000. Only men previously enlisted were to be allowed to reinlist. Introduced on January 5 by Julius Kahn, Republican of California, the resolution was approved by the House on January 17 and by the Senate on January 22. It was sent to the White House on January 28. See *Cong. Record*, 66th Cong., 3d sess., pp. 1019, 1533-38, 1544, 1855-56, and 2179.

The question of the number of enlisted men in the Regular Army had developed into a controversy between Congress and the War Department due to a discrepancy between the provisions of the Army Reorganization Act of June 4, 1920, and the Army Appropriations Act approved on June 5, 1920. While the former stipulated that, "in time of war or similar emergency," the size of the Regular Army was to consist of up to 280,000 enlisted men, the latter had appropriated funds for the enlistment of only 175,000 men. On the assumption that the absence of a peace treaty with Germany constituted an emergency situation, the War Department had engaged in an active recruiting campaign with the result that, by early January 1921, the Regular Army had reached a strength of over 230,000 men. For a detailed discussion of the situation, see NDB to WW, Dec. 17, 1920, Vol. 66.

² S.J. Res. 236, introduced by Senator Harry S. New, Republican of Indiana, on January 4, 1921, and adopted, with amendments, on January 17, 1921. Although this resolution was very similar to the House resolution and also limited the number of enlisted men to 175,000, it provided that this restriction was to be in effect only "until a further and specific appropriation for the pay of enlisted men shall be made by Congress." See *Cong. Record*, 66th Cong., 3d sess., pp. 919, 1186-95, 1347-59, 1416-17, and 1494-1513.

From Alexander Mitchell Palmer

IN THE MATTER OF THE APPLICATION FOR PARDON
In behalf of EUGENE V. DEBS.

Sir: Washington, D. C. 29 January, 1921.

Petitioner, hereinafter called the defendant, was convicted in the United States District Court for the Northern District of Ohio, at Cleveland, of violating Section 3, Title 1, of the Espionage Act of June 15, 1917, as amended by the Act of May 16, 1918, and on September 14, 1918, was sentenced to imprisonment for ten years in the State Penitentiary at Moundsville, West Virginia. On appeal the Supreme Court of the United States affirmed the judgment of the District Court March 10, 1919, and he began to serve his sentence April 12, 1919, in the West Virginia State Penitentiary, but was later transferred to the United States Penitentiary at Atlanta, Georgia, where he is now confined. He will be eligible for parole August 11, 1922. His term, with the allowances for good conduct, will expire December 28, 1925.

In view of the prominence of the defendant and the publicity that has been given to his case, I do not feel it is necessary to more than briefly refer to the facts upon which his conviction was secured. The facts fully appear in the transcript of record filed in the Supreme Court (vol. 35, Records and Briefs in United States Cases, U. S. Supreme Court, October term 1918, No. 714), and the case is reported in 249 U. S., 211.

Mr. Justice Holmes,[1] who delivered the opinion of the Court, after reciting that the indictment had been cut down to two counts, originally the 3rd and 4th, states the case as follows:

"The former of these alleges that on or about June 16, 1918, at Canton, Ohio, the defendant caused and incited and attempted to cause and incite insubordination, disloyalty, mutiny and refusal of duty in the military and naval forces of the United States and with intent so to do delivered, to an assembly of people, a public speech, set forth. The fourth count alleges that he obstructed and attempted to obstruct the recruiting and enlistment service of the United States and to that end and with that intent delivered the same speech, again set forth."

Mr. Justice Holmes states that the main theme of the speech was socialism and that the defendant began by saying that he had just returned from a visit to the workhouse in the neighborhood where three of their most loyal comrades were paying the penalty for their devotion to the working-class—these being Wagenknecht, Baker and Ruthenberg,[2] who had been convicted of aiding and abetting another in failing to register for the draft; that these men were paying the penalty for standing erect and for seeking to pave the way to better conditions for all mankind and that he was proud of them; that he expressed opposition to Prussian militarism in a way that naturally might have been thought to be intended to include the mode of proceeding in the United States.

Mr. Justice Holmes states that the defendant then took up the case of Kate Richards O'Hare,[3] convicted of obstructing the enlistment service, praised her for her loyalty to socialism and otherwise, and said that she was convicted on false testimony, under a ruling that would seem incredible to him if he had not had some experience with a Federal Court, and in referring to war the defendant said that "You have your lives to lose; you certainly ought to have the right to declare war if you consider a war necessary."

Mr. Justice Holmes states that the defendant next mentioned Rose Pastor Stokes,[4] convicted of attempting to cause insubordi-

[1] That is, Oliver Wendell Holmes, Jr.
[2] Alfred Wagenknecht, Charles Baker, and Charles Emil Ruthenberg.
[3] About her case, see Enclosure II with WW to AMP, Aug. 29, 1919, Vol. 62.
[4] About her case, see n. 1 to W. Kent to WW, June 3, 1918, Vol. 48.

nation and refusal of duty in the military forces of the United
States and obstructing the recruiting service, saying that she went
out to render her service to the cause in this day of crises, and they
sent her to the penitentiary for ten years; that she had said no more
than the speaker; that if she was guilty so was he and that he
would not be cowardly enough to plead his innocence, but he says
that her message that opened the eyes of the people must be suppressed, and so, after a mock trial before a packed jury and a corporation tool on the bench, she was sent to the penitentiary for ten
years.

Mr. Justice Holmes states that the defendant then gave personal
experiences and illustrations of the growth of socialism, a glorifi-
cation of minorities, and a prophesy [prophecy] of the success of
the international socialist crusade, with the interjection that "you
need to know that you are fit for something better than slavery and
cannon fodder." He says that the rest of the discourse consisted of
sneers at the advice to cultivate war gardens, attribution to pluto-
crats of the high price of coal, etc., with the implication running
through it all that the working men are not concerned in the war,
and a final exhortation "Don't worry about the charge of treason to
your masters; but be concerned about the treason that involves
yourselves."

Mr. Justice Holmes refers to the fact that the defendant addressed the jury himself, and while contending that his speech did
not warrant the charges said, "I have been accused of obstructing
the war. I admit it. Gentlemen, I abhor war. I would oppose the
war if I stood alone."

The foregoing is, in brief, the substance of what the defendant
said, and I therefore deem it unnecessary to review the facts as
reported by the United States Attorney further than to state his
reasons for recommending adversely to any executive clemency
being shown him.

United States Attorney Wertz[5] states in a letter dated October 4,
1920, that he feels the offense committed by the defendant was a
very serious one; that he was well known and enjoyed a large following among a certain class of the population of this country; that
his prominence and eloquence caused many of the people of this
nation to be persuaded from their path of duty during the world
war, and that he committed the crime with full deliberation and
premeditation. He says his traitorous remarks did incalculable
damage to the country to which he owed allegiance and service

[5] Edwin Slusser Wertz, United States Attorney for the Northern District of Ohio.

and gave an immense amount of comfort and aid to the nations with which we were then at war.

Mr. Wertz states that knowing the harm which the defendant's gospel caused in the Northern District of Ohio and throughout the nation he cannot bring himself to believe that executive clemency should be extended and that he therefore recommends against it, in which recommendation he says Assistant United States Attorney J. C. Breitenstein and former Assistant United States Attorney Francis B. Kavanagh[6] concur.

Hon. D. C. Westenhaver,[7] the trial judge, states in a letter dated October 6, 1920, that since the conviction was justified by the evidence the question of whether executive clemency should be extended becomes one peculiarly for the Executive branch of the Government to determine. He says that it seems to him the real question to be determined is whether or not, in the light of subsequent developments a sentence of ten years may not be regarded as heavier than the interests of a just and efficient law enforcement policy might require. He says in the light of the situation when the sentence was imposed, particularly the widespread and secret, as well as open, organization having for its objects the commission of the acts made a crime by the Espionage Law, a heavy sentence seemed to be called for, and that the deterring influence of the sentence upon others seemed to him to be of unusual weight and importance.

Judge Westenhaver states that a similar violation of the Espionage Law at this time, under changed conditions, when the deterring influence of the sentence upon others is not so important, would not seem to call for a sentence of more than two to five years. He says this aspect of the situation is the only one, it seems to him, that should now be given much consideration and in that light he says that it does not seem to him that it would be improper to commute the sentence proportionately.

Any contention that the defendant was improperly convicted cannot be maintained. Nor can it be said that the sentence was excessive, for at that time the country was at war and the words uttered by the defendant, a man of influence and with not an inconsiderable following, only a few months preceding the sentence, were well calculated to create a spirit of disloyalty, if not actual resistance to the war aims of the United States.

The defendant has now been incarcerated since April 12, 1919,

[6] Joseph C. Breitenstein and Francis Bernard Kavanagh.
[7] David Courtney Westenhaver.

a little over one year and nine months. He was sixty-three years of age at the time of beginning his sentence. The only question to be considered is whether or not the punishment he has undergone adequately satisfies the demands of justice and he can, in the public interests, be safely released.

I have examined a number of cases involving violations of the Espionage Act on which you have acted. I find that in the cases of thirteen defendants who were sentenced for ten years each with the exception of one who was sentenced for eleven years, you have, by commutation of sentence or pardon, reduced their respective terms on an average to two years and one month. Of five defendants sentenced to fifteen years each you have commuted their sentences on an average to one year and ten months, and of eight defendants sentenced to twenty years each you have commuted their sentences on an average to four years. The average for the 10, 15, and 20 year sentences considered as a whole would be approximately two years and seven months.

While the defendant here has served less than the average time to which you have commuted the terms of those defendants sentenced for ten and twenty years, and less than the average sentences as commuted, he will, on February 12, 1921, have served one year and ten months, which is the average term to which you have commuted the sentences of those defendants sentenced for fifteen years.

I have examined the cases to which I have referred in relation to this case and in my judgment to require this defendant, in the light of the action taken on them, to serve out any further considerable portion of his sentence would be to invite criticism of a discriminating character. The only argument that could be advanced by way of avoidance would be that Debs was a leader, with a following, and should, because of that fact, be held to a stricter accountability than others convicted of like offenses.

Debs is now approaching 65 years of age. If not adequately, he has surely been severely punished. In view of these and the foregoing considerations, and in the light of the statement of the trial judge himself that it would not be improper to commute the sentence proportionately, having reference to, and drawing a distinction between, the conditions at the time sentence was imposed and those existing at the present time, I advise that the sentence be commuted to expire February 12, 1921.

Respectfully,   A Mitchell Palmer[8]

TLS (Records of the Office of the Pardon Attorney, RG 204, DNA).

[8] Wilson filled in the date of the application for executive clemency in behalf of Debs and wrote: "Denied. W.W."

From the Shorthand Diary of Charles Lee Swem

30 January, 1921

It would seem that the President's illness has but hastened the period of senility that comes with old age. He is intensely proud of his past glories, which perhaps is as it should be—for no man has greater justification—but he does not display his pride with the discreetness that one would expect from such an intellect. I have seen him developing since he came into office much as Caesar or Napoleon would, but always he has shown his conceit with good grace, but now he will sit and dream about his greatness much as a child looks to what the future will hold for him—or rather as an old war veteran seeking favor in the eyes of children by the tales of his prowess—much exaggerated of course.

A case in point: the Signal Corps has given to the President a copy of the army films taken of his trip abroad. It consists of five reels dealing with the actions of the President in Paris, Italy, England, and Belgium. So great is the President's delight to see himself portrayed in these weekly news that he has sat and seen them at least seven times—on the pretext of exhibiting them to visitors of the house. He has shown them to Nellie, Jessie, Eleanor, Dr. Grayson, Dr. Dercum, the nerve specialist, and Mr. Klauder, the architect, on separate occasions—besides to others who he thinks ought to witness them.

And the other day a double set taken by the Pathe News came in and when I tried to make off with them myself for my own memoirs and when Brooks[1] told him of their arrival he asked me for them and directed that they should be put with the others.

It may be that the inordinate delight he takes in seeing these pictures arises from the feeling said to be innate in cripples—a pride for the time when he had two good legs and two good arms, but I am inclined to think that that is only incidental.

Mrs. Wilson encourages him in all these weaknesses, for of course she is intensely proud of his achievements and surrounds him with all the symbols of his greatness—illuminated presentations from English cities, plaster of paris casts of him and his deeds, glorifying cartoons of him with sword uplifted in a crusader's garb and looking into the sun.

Another result of the President's illness is his loss of initiative: nowadays—when I know he is perfectly able to perform such tasks—he will excuse himself by reason of his illness to write short messages to associates that he would have written before. He whined to me the other day that "he was too ill to do that sort of thing." That seems to be his entire attitude toward all kinds of work. Even tonight's. I am not trying to overlook the serious nature of the disease he has suffered from and from which he has not yet altogether recovered—but still I can't help but see him as a child, humored, petted, and coddled and justifying all his weaknesses by the plea that he is sick.

About two weeks ago a joint resolution came down from Congress for the President's signature to which he took an aversion immediately. My recollection is that it was a bill granting to companies incorporated outside of a particular state the same rights of timber cutting as enjoyed by companies organized within the state itself.[2] The President sent the bill to Secretary Payne of the Interior Department for advice, and Payne wrote that there was no objection at all to the bill. The President was not satisfied with this and asked for some advice as to the policy behind the bill, to which Payne replied that it was nothing more than a routine bill, doing nothing more than it stated on the face of it—that there was no reason why companies incorporated outside of one state should not be accorded the same privileges as companies incorporated within the state itself.

As it was the last day on which the President had to sign the bill, I took up the matter with Payne personally and got his letter specifically recommending the signing of the bill and took it to the President. The President read the letter and said he would not sign the bill, he didn't think it ought to be a law. I then asked if he didn't want it vetoed. He replied by stating that he did not have the material with which to veto it and therefore he would let it become a law without his signature. In other words, he had no reason for opposing the bill himself other than it was a prejudice he had formed. And because nobody else could furnish him with the material with which to veto it, he would let it become law without his signature. An ingenious way out of it!

JRT transcript (WC, NjP) of CLSsh (C. L. Swem Coll., NjP).
    [1] That is, Arthur Brooks, Wilson's valet.
    [2] There had been such a bill, S.1, which Wilson received on December 30, 1920, and became law without his signature on January 11, 1921, 42 *Statutes at Large* 1088. But it is clear that Swem confused this bill with S.793, about which see T. G. Pearson to WW, Jan. 21, 1921. Wilson, through Tumulty, did indeed send this bill for the Milk River Valley Gun Club to Payne on January 22, and Payne replied that he saw no objection to its approval. J. B. Payne to WW, Jan. 24, 1921, TLS (WP, DLC). Wilson or Tumulty then sent the bill to the Secretary of Agriculture, who in his reply explained the policy behind the bill and recommended that Wilson veto it, mainly on the ground that it conferred a special privilege on a small group and did not promote the benefit of all the people. E. T. Meredith to WW, Jan. 29, 1921, TLS (WP, DLC). What Wilson told Swem on January 30 about letting the bill become law without his signature reflected momentary fatigue and irresolution. As will be seen, Wilson asked Payne to draft a veto message for him. It is printed at February 3, 1921.

To Thomas William Lamont

My dear Friend: The White House 30 January, 1921

I have yours of the twenty-first of January. In reply, I can only say that I hesitate to make any suggestions to the present Congress because they have shown themselves so ready to treat everything I suggest with something less than consideration. I think that an appropriation in aid of the relief of famine in China would be justified from every point of view, but do not feel that my influence is sufficient to obtain it.

Cordially and faithfully yours,   Woodrow Wilson

TLS (T. W. Lamont Papers, MH-BA).

To Newton Diehl Baker

My dear Mr. Secretary: [The White House] 30 January, 1921

Notwithstanding your indulgent opinion of it,[1] I do not think I would be justified in signing the Joint Resolution directing you to cease enlisting men in the Regular Army of the United States. I believe this to be a most inopportune time for such action, to say nothing more of it, and the conversation I recently had with the Secretary of State about the matter confirms me in that feeling and leads me to request that you and he will be generous enough to collaborate in formulating for me a veto message.

Cordially and faithfully yours,   [Woodrow Wilson]

CCL (WP, DLC).
[1] Wilson was replying to NDB to WW, Jan. 29, 1921 (first letter of that date).

To Duane Reed Stuart[1]

My dear Professor Stuart: The White House 30 January, 1921

I am writing to ask if you will help me out a little on my Greek. Is the following the correct form of Greek for the number thirteen, and have I succeeded in forming the letters correctly?

τριόηαίδεχα[2]

Let me explain. The number thirteen has been associated with some of the most important turning points in my life and I want the Greek form of it to serve as a name for a home we are hoping to build a little way outside of Washington.[3] I am, therefore, very anxious to get the letters in exactly the correct form.

I began my thirteenth year of service at Princeton as the thirteenth President of the University, and became President of the United States in 1913.

Hoping that all goes well and will continue to go well with you in the New Year,

Cordially and sincerely yours,   Woodrow Wilson

TLS (received from D. R. Stuart, Jr.).
  [1] Wilson's old friend, now Professor of Classics at Princeton University.
  [2] WWhw.
  [3] Perhaps about this time Wilson typed a list of names of persons to invite to a house-warming when his mansion on Conduit Road was completed. The list, which included many of the authors he was then reading, follows: Robert Bridges, A. G. Gardiner, Archibald Marshall, Christopher Morley, Don Marquis, Samuel McChord Crothers, George Bernard Shaw, John Drinkwater, John Galsworthy, Sir Gilbert Murray, Nancy S. Toy, the Rev. and Mrs. A. W. Hazen, Bernard Baruch, Mr. Bird Grubb, Norman Davis, Henry B. Fine, Charles W. McAlpin, Thomas W. Lamont, George Foster Peabody, Sir James Barrie, Rudyard Kipling, Henry Morgenthau, William Watson, G. K. Chesterton, Wilson Harris, Sir Robert Borden, Sir Maurice Hankey, Capt. Sir Charles Cust, Stanley Weyman, James Lane Allen, Anthony Hope, Stephen Leacock, Joseph Conrad, Lord Robert Cecil, Gen. Jan C. Smuts, and E. K. Vénisélos. WWT MS (WP, DLC). Another list of "guests" included the names of Frank I. Cobb, Rabbi Stephen S. Wise, Augustine Birrell, W. B. Maxwell, Elbert Hubbard, Ray Stannard Baker, and Philip Kerr. WWT and WWhw MS (WP, DLC).

From Kate Nichols Trask, with Enclosure

My dear Mr. President—   Yaddo Saratoga January 30 [1921].

I send you in great haste a copy of this beautiful letter for which you ask. Is it not a beautiful, a dear letter? It went to my heart and brightened these days already full of sunshine and made music in these hours of song.

Thank you for asking me to share it with you. It gives me great pleasure to do so.   With my homage,   Katrina Trask.

TLS (WP, DLC).

E N C L O S U R E

Edith Bolling Galt Wilson to Kate Nichols Trask

Copy—
Dearest "Ladye"

After reading your beautiful letter yesterday with its wonderful secret, I folded the pages reverently feeling that I had for a moment been permitted to enter a shrine on whose Altar a flame had been kindled whose white light blinds for the moment even the eyes of the Spirit who dwells there—but to whom it brings inward light which glorifies the darkness, and the glory of which you share with only those who have seen and understand!

We are so happy and content in your happiness—and my husband and I have talked of little else since we were honoured with your confidence.

We went for a long drive yesterday and all the time spoke of you two dear friends who have found the same priceless thing that has been granted to us.

You ask for your "Hero's" blessing. You have it in all its rich abundance and he asks me to say to you and Mr. Peabody that his letter to him in no sense represents what he felt—but what that is lies too deep for speech.

I shall always keep your letter to me for it is like a great poem— and I love to read it over and over.

The only sad note is the one you touch so lightly when you say you can never leave "Yaddo"—God grant this is a mistake—but if not, then surely we will come to you—for I feel there are brighter days ahead—and "Love" is a wonderful healer!

Of course we will guard your secret but we keep it close in our hearts where it warms and cheers our own lives.

May the same happiness that is ours come to you, and a greater wish I could not make—as always

Yours faithfully   Edith Bolling Wilson.[1]

TCL (WP, DLC).
     [1] The ALS of this letter is at Yaddo, Saratoga, N. Y.

From Bainbridge Colby

My Dear Mr President.   Washington Jan'y 31, 1921

Your remark the other day about a possible plan for the future[1] has gripped my thought and interest very powerfully. You spoke a little casually—I know—and I hope I am not pursuing the subject too energetically.

It presents thrilling possibilities, and I want to talk to you further about it, as soon as I may.

Faithfully always   Bainbridge Colby

ALS (WP, DLC).
     [1] That Wilson and Colby go into the practice of law as partners.

From Jessie Woodrow Wilson Sayre, with Enclosure

Dearest Father,   Cambridge Jan 31 [1921].

Our first snow storm of the year greets our eyes this morning! January felt that on the last day at least she must give us a little winter, and of course the children are very happy. I can visualize you all out on the portico in almost summer weather if your days have been correspondingly warm.

We have all been very well. The children love their school and are learning apace. Eleanor is the cutest thing reading aloud. She is perfectly thrilled by being able to do it. When I suggest reading aloud to her she says "No *I*'ll read to you" and even the Little Red Hen on its hundredth reading has some charm from her enthusiasm! I am enclosing a poem which she dictated to me and which I was able to get down almost exactly as she gave it. It opens with a "poem" from her reader which took her fancy greatly.

Frank and I are looking forward to our trip to Princeton on the 13th. We expect to load everything up on the 14th. We shall stay at the Scott's.[1]

On the 22nd we are going up for snowshoeing into the mountains with our friends the Hazens.[2] We do that every Washington's birthday, though I suppose when little Woodrow is old enough to know that that is his birthday too we shall not be able to go, or at least not so happily and conscience-free!

So many people up here have told me that they have dined or lunched or called in your new house and how entirely charming it is that it makes me very happy.

Just one month more now! Isn't it fine—and we shall have you all to ourselves again as in the old days! Dr. Davis[3] was here for supper yesterday. He comes up once a month to visit a patient in Milton and we always have a glimpse of him. He brought good news of you and the little circle down there and it was good to hear first hand.

Dearest, dearest love from us all to you both,

Adoringly   Jessie

ALS (WC, NjP).
  [1] With the William Berryman Scotts, old family friends of the Wilsons. Jessie was particularly close to the two Scott daughters, Mary and Sarah.
  [2] Maynard Thompson Hazen and Marjorie Frances Howe Hazen. Hazen, a lawyer of Hartford, was the son of Wilson's old friend and former pastor, the Rev. Dr. Azel Washburn Hazen of Middletown, Conn.
  [3] That is, Edward Parker ("E. P.") Davis of Philadelphia.

E   N   C   L   O   S   U   R   E

"Good night, sleep tight,
Wake up bright, in the morning light,
And do what's right with all your might"
The stars shine in the heavens bright
The little children play in morning light,
    The little children do what's right,
        With all their might.
The little birdies play in the trees because
    it is day.

Where do you come from little birdies?
Let me put my hand on your heads.
The little birdies flew away into the
    heavens because it is night.
God put his hand on their heads.
    It is night now
      "Good night, sleep tight etc"

                          Amen

"It begins and ends just alike. Some poems *do*, you know, mother."

Hw MS (WC, NjP).

From the Diary of Josephus Daniels

February Tuesday 1, 1921

Cabinet. Burleson urged President to protest against allies compelling Germany in addition to 54 bil dollars to pay 12% on all exports.[1] This makes impossible our trading with Germany & injuriously affects all countries not receiving indemnity. Houston said WW had offered the way and Senate had rejected it. WW said nations would laugh at our protest & it would have no effect. W.B.W. said we should protest. Otherwise when Harding comes in & plan injurious to us has been settled we will be charged with not having done our duty. W.W. told State & Treasury to study proposed settlement & let him have the facts.

Colby said S. A.[2] feels we are not helping & not cordial.

Should Cabinet officers resign? WW said he would not accept any of our resignations if we did.

There was a young man of St Louis
Who married a beautiful Jewess
Her talk was so bold
And her stories so old
He called her Chauncey Depewess.

There was a monk in Siberia
His lot was dreary and drearier,
So he broke from his cell
With a hell [of a yell]
And eloped with the mother superior

France will ask us to accept or float German bonds—If England & F cannot pay us.

[1] At the behest of Lloyd George, the Allied Premiers meeting in Paris had agreed on January 29 that Germany should pay reparations of 226,000,000,000 marks in gold or

its equivalent, in graduated installments over the next forty-two years. In addition, they decided that Germany was to pay to the Allies an annual tax of 12 per cent on the total value of its exports, also for a period of forty-two years. The plan was to be presented to the Germans for their approval at a meeting in London to begin on March 1. See the *New York Times*, Jan. 29 and 30, 1921; Rohan Butler, J. P. T. Bury, and M. E. Lambert, eds., *Documents on British Foreign Policy, 1919-1939*, First Series, XV (London, 1967), 73-104; and Marc Trachtenberg, *Reparation in World Politics: France and European Economic Diplomacy, 1916-1923* (New York, 1980), pp. 188-89.
    [2] That is, South America.

To John Barton Payne

My dear Mr. Secretary: [The White House] 1 February, 1921

I would be very much obliged if you would do me the kind service of formulating a veto message on the enclosed bill.[1] It seems to me vicious legislation in its character, because it seeks to direct an executive officer how he shall exercise a discretionary power vested in him by law; but besides that, I fear, from a communication I have received from the Audubon Society,[2] that this if it became law would very seriously affect the birds of the country whom other laws seek to protect. No doubt other aspects of the proposed legislation will occur to you.
                Cordially and sincerely yours,   Woodrow Wilson

TLS (Letterpress Books, WP, DLC).
    [1] About which, see T. G. Pearson to WW, Jan. 21, 1921.
    [2] See the letter just cited.

From Thomas William Lamont

Dear Mr. President: New York City February 1, 1921.

Thank you very much for your letter of January 28th enclosing me a copy of Raymond Fosdick's reply in the matter of unexpended charitable war fund. I am still in touch with Mr. Fosdick and he is doing everything he can to counsel with me in this matter.

I am going over to Washington Friday with my wife to spend the week-end with Norman Davis, and, as I told Tumulty over the telephone yesterday, I should very much like to pay my respects to you some time Saturday,[1] if you feel like seeing me and can spare five minutes.

My wife joins me in affectionate good wishes to you and to Mrs. Wilson.

With hearty thanks again for your recent letter, I am,
                Sincerely yours,   Thomas W. Lamont

TLS (WP, DLC).
    [1] The Lamonts lunched with the Wilsons either on Saturday, February 5, or very soon afterward; see T. W. Lamont to WW, Feb. 21, 1921.

A News Report

[*Feb. 1, 1921*]

WILSON RECEIVES OVATION AT THEATRE
Audience Rises and Cheers

Washington, Feb. 1.—President Wilson attended the theatre to-night for the first time since he became ill more than sixteen months ago. John Drinkwater's play, "Abraham Lincoln," with Frank McGlynn in the title part, was the attraction that caused the President to come out of the forced retirement due to his break-down.

A few minutes before the curtain rose on the first act a White House limousine, bearing the great red, white and blue crest of the United States on its side panels, passed from Pennsylvania Avenue into E Street and entered the narrow alleyway leading to the stage entrance of the National Theatre. In it were the President, Mrs. Wilson and John Randolph Bolling, Mrs. Wilson's brother.

The President, leaning on a cane, walked from behind the scenes to the second box from the stage in the right-hand lower tier of boxes. He seemed able to get along without assistance other than from his cane. Almost instantly he was recognized, and the audience rose and began a round of hand-clapping that was soon drowned by cheering. The audience was extremely enthusiastic and kept up its applause for several minutes.

The President, who had seated himself, rose in response to the demonstration and remained standing while the cheering went on. He bowed and smiled and waved his hand. It was evident that he was greatly pleased with the heartiness of his welcome. The audience wanted to keep up its demonstration, but followed the President's example when, with a wave of the hand, he sat down again. The curtain rose on the first act a few seconds later.

The President remained throughout the performance and gave close attention to it. He showed deep interest in everything that took place on the stage. When the performance was over there was a parting demonstration.

The members of the audience on rising turned generally to face the President and cheered and applauded. There were some who thought the sentiments, evoked by the stage portrayal of the assassination of Lincoln, influenced the audience as they gazed upon the countenance of the present Chief Executive.

Tonight was raw and cold, with a suggestion of snow. The fact that the President ventured out of doors in such weather showed that his physician considered that he had overcome the tendency to take cold that was one of the causes of concern during the early stages of his long illness. He looked much better than had been generally understood, and was apparently in condition to carry out his determination to take part in the inaugural of his successor on March 4.

Printed in the *New York Times*, Feb. 2, 1921.

From Newton Diehl Baker

My dear Mr. President: Washington February 2, 1921.

I wrote the attached suggested veto message and then considered it with the Secretary of State, as you suggested in your note yesterday.[1] Mr. Colby approves of it in this form.

You will observe that I have ventured to set forth in the veto message[2] both the particular objections to the form of the resolution and also the general objection to its substance. The first of these, that is as to the form of the resolution, was pointed out to the Congress and the Senate amended its resolution to overcome the difficulty but later abandoned its position and passed the House resolution, apparently fearing that delay would lead the House to take a more extreme position.

Respectfully yours,   Newton D. Baker

TLS (WP, DLC).
    [1] Actually, WW to NDB, Jan. 30, 1921.
    [2] It is printed at Feb. 5, 1921.

A Veto Message

To the Senate: THE WHITE HOUSE, *3 February, 1921.*

I return herewith without my approval S.793, an act authorizing the issuance of patent to the Milk River Valley Gun Club, which proposes to direct the Secretary of the Interior to issue patent to the Milk River Valley Gun Club for 76.69 acres of land in Montana for a game preserve.

In my opinion the legislation proposed is not in the public interest and is objectionable, because it would, by a special act of Congress, pass title to a tract of public land to a private interest for a private purpose. Moreover, I am informed that the lands in question are used by ducks and other game birds as a resting place and breeding ground, and the turning over of the land to a private gun club would be likely to destroy its use for this purpose and seriously affect the birds and water fowl, which existing laws seek to protect.

I think, therefore, that the bill should not become a law and that the tract should be made a Federal bird reservation for the protection of the birds which now frequent the lands.

Woodrow Wilson.[1]

Printed in *Cong. Record*, 66th Cong., 3d sess., p. 2480.
[1] The Senate failed to override this veto by a vote of nine to forty-seven on February 7, 1921.

From the Shorthand Diary of Charles Lee Swem

3 February, 1921

Apropos of the difficulty of getting an Executive Order through the President: he asked me to read him a letter[1] requesting an Executive Order for a woman. After listening to the first paragraph, which cited the needs of the woman and her unfortunate circumstances, the President would hear no more. He said, "The people of the departments would break down the Civil Service. They conceive the government as an institution of charity." It reminded him of the action of a judge in Georgia who in rendering a dissenting opinion said he despaired of ever seeing justice done in that court where a woman was involved.

JRT transcript (WC, NjP) of CLSsh (C. L. Swem Coll., NjP).
[1] Probably J. B. Payne to WW, Feb. 1, 1921, TLS (WP, DLC). Payne requested that Wilson sign an Executive Order to allow Myrtle N. (Mrs. Francis J.) Parke to be appointed to a civil service job "without regard to civil-service rules." Mrs. Parke was the widow of a long-time employee in the General Land Office and had two small children to support. The Civil Service Commission soon supported Wilson in his adverse opinion of the case. Martin Andrew Morrison *et al.* to WW, Feb. 5, 1921, TLS (WP, DLC). Wilson then refused to sign the Executive Order.

From Bainbridge Colby

My dear Mr. President: Washington February 4, 1921

Referring to the suggestion, discussed at Tuesday's Cabinet, of addressing to the Entente Governments something in the nature of a protest or caveat upon the recently formulated terms of German reparation, I have given the subject careful reflection since you asked my opinion and can reach no other conclusion than that your disinclination at the present time to make such a protest is correct and sound.

Mr. Davis and I together have sought to gauge the proposal from every angle and he is of this opinion also.

The measure of reparation and the terms of payment have not yet been finally determined. The meeting to be held in London[1] with representatives of Germany will not necessarily register final judgment in favor of the terms agreed upon by the Allied Premiers. As I understand it, Germany has been notified of the action of the Entente Prime Ministers and is to have an opportunity to express her objections at the London meeting. Thus the case is still open and in view of the strong criticisms which have been voiced not alone in England but in France as well, it does not by any means appear that the matter is in final form.

Of course it is the duty of the Executive to take timely action to protect American interests at any point where they are menaced and no one would for a moment think of omitting such protest merely because a partisan Congress had, as the result of prejudice or error, refused or lost the opportunity to participate effectively in the earlier stages of the discussion. We must, no doubt, take the country's position as we find it from day to day and make the best case we can. Thus, despite the fact that if we had ratified the Treaty, we could have exercised a veto upon any disposition of the question of reparations, which did not seem just or scientific, we might nevertheless be under the duty of filing a protest, now or at some time hereafter, if by so doing we could safeguard the country's position in the future and avert injurious results to our trade. Were we, however, at this stage to make such a protest, we would of course encounter a reminder of the very influential relation to the discussion which was ours without asking and which we have so flatly renounced.

Furthermore, we were invited to send a representative to the recent Paris Conference,[2] and a protest at this time might simply result in a renewal of the invitation, already declined, to participate in the discussions. Anything therefore that we might now urge by way of objection or proposal would logically involve some disclosure of our own theory as to our relation to the European settlement. But this, we are not in a position to make in view of the state of mid-air suspension in which Congress has left the whole question of peace.

The further thought occurs to me that inasmuch as our protest would proceed upon the impracticability of such a settlement as the Allied Ministers propose, this impracticability must be revealed, and promptly, by the course of events. A protest from us at this moment is therefore not necessary as a practical measure of protection against future contingencies.

I think that public opinion throughout the world still hopes for unity among the Allies in their treatment of Germany. The fact that the Allied Premiers were able to reach any kind of agreement after so much divergence of opinion is a source of satisfaction and favorable remark in many quarters. If we have nothing practical to suggest, and if in interposing in the discussion today we are not able to indicate the lines or the extent of our future cooperation with the Allies, all that we would accomplish would be to puncture this solidarity, so much desired and so difficult of achievement, encourage Germany to a program of resistance and thus distinctly hurt rather than improve the situation.

The subject is receiving the closest study by all the interested Governments, and something may arise between now and the date of the London meeting to put a different light upon it. Meanwhile we have cabled Mr. Boyden,[3] our representative on the Reparations Commission, to send us all the information he can gather on every phase of the subject.

Very respectfully yours,   Bainbridge Colby

TLS (WP, DLC).
  [1] March 1-7, 1921.
  [2] See NHD to WW, Jan. 7, 1921, with Enclosure (first letter of that date), and NHD to H. C. Wallace, Jan. 8, 1921.
  [3] That is, Roland William Boyden.

From Duane Reed Stuart

Princeton, New Jersey

My dear President Wilson: February 4, 1921.

It gave me deep pleasure to hear from you and to realize that you had thought of turning to me for assistance. As a matter of fact, however, you do not stand in need of help; as to the Greek equivalent for thirteen, I have but to confirm the accuracy of your recollection. The form may be written either as you give it,

τρισηαίδεχα

or

τρεισηαίδεχα

The latter is, perhaps, more common, but either is impeccable Greek. While my Greek shuttle is working, I might transcribe the form in capitals, thus:

ΤΡΙΣΚΑΙΔΕΚΑ or ΤΡΕΙΣΚΑΙΔΕΚΑ

You and Mrs. Wilson may decide which characters better suit your purpose artistically. In case you prefer the capitals, you will note that no accent is used. The accent may well be omitted with the minuscules, since you are to use the word as a name.

I am greatly tempted to indulge myself in a malicious thought. It seems that, although Princeton University has recently seen fit to adopt a skeptical attitude toward the serviceableness of a knowledge of Greek to the educated man,[1] the President of the United States finds something that he can express in that discredited tongue with satisfaction. I trust that you will not think of me as transgressing the proper bounds of an answer to your question if I venture to assure you of my joy at the reports of your return to health and strength, and to confess to my great interest in your plans. I hope that you realize the devotion and the homage that you command from us, youngsters when you knew us, but now each year approaching more closely the head of the roster of Princeton Faculty, who were so fortunate as to work with you here. Those stimulating years, I realize, mark the great epoch in my own life. I am proud to recall that everything good that has happened to me in my professional career is derivable from your tenure in Princeton.

I beg to reciprocate your cordial wishes for the New Year, and to cherish the hope that, as you lay down the fasces, you may enjoy the life earned by one who can say, in the words of a great Roman ex-consul: "praeclara conscientia sustentor cum cogito me de re publica meruisse optime."[2]

Yours ever faithfully,   Duane Reed Stuart.

TLS (WP, DLC).
  [1] President John Grier Hibben had announced on March 18, 1919, that the faculty of Princeton University had decided that the study of Greek would no longer be required either for entrance to the Bachelor of Arts program or for graduation with the A.B. degree. *New York Times*, March 19, 1919.
  [2] "My conscience then is clear and helps to support me, when I think that I have always rendered my country good service." Cicero, *Letters to Atticus* 10.4.5. Courtesy of Alison Frantz.

Cleveland Hoadley Dodge to Cary Travers Grayson

My dear Admiral Grayson: New York February 4, 1921.

I owe you an apology for not having written you before regarding that delightful proposition you suggested for buying the Pierce-Arrow car[1] for the President. I had expected to see Mr. McCormick[2] when he came to New York in January, but his wife[3] was taken seriously ill and died two weeks ago, and I have not been able to see him. But, nevertheless, I hope you consider that the President's friends want to give him the car, and that you have arranged with the Pierce-Arrow people so there will be no chance of losing it. I am writing to Mr. Jones[4] today and ask[ing] him to take the matter up with his brother,[5] and Mr. McCormick, and will let you know later just which ones of the President's friends participate in the gift. I understand that the price is $3500, and I hope you will let me know whenever you need the money to make the payment, as I can send you a check at any time, and arrange with the others later.

It was most gratifying to read in the papers about the President's going to see the play "Abraham Lincoln" and I sincerely hope that he is really making good progress. With warm regards

Very sincerely yours,   Cleveland H Dodge

TLS (received from James Gordon Grayson and Cary T. Grayson, Jr.).
¹ A Pierce-Arrow touring car, which the White House had leased from the Pierce-Arrow Company in June 1919. It was the one hundred twentieth of the Series 51 of the vestibule suburban limousine. The sale price of the car when new was $9,250. There were two bodies for the car—a vestibule suburban body and an open touring body. The bodies had to be changed at the factory in Buffalo. The car had a right-hand steering wheel and was powered by a 48 h.p. six-cylinder engine.
About the time Wilson left the White House, the seal of the United States of America on one of the rear passenger doors was painted over, and orange stripes were painted on the body and the wheel spokes, and a Princeton tiger hood ornament adorned the front. The automobile, restored as the presidential limousine, is now in the museum facilities of the Woodrow Wilson Birthplace in Staunton, Virginia. *Woodrow Wilson's Pierce-Arrow: The Story of the President's Car Exhibited at His Birthplace* (Staunton, Va., 1990).
² Cyrus Hall McCormick, Jr.
³ Harriet Bradley Hammond McCormick.
⁴ That is, Thomas Davies Jones.
⁵ David Benton Jones.

From the Shorthand Diary of Charles Lee Swem

5 February, 1921

The President this morning said to me: "Swem, I wish you would explain to Tumulty that the other day, when he asked me if George Foster Peabody was not going to marry Mrs. Trask, that I knew the marriage was going to take place. But it had been told to me as a profound secret, and therefore I felt it necessary to lie to him about it." I asked: "Do you think it necessary to tell him that, Mr. President?" The President thought a moment and said, "Yes, I want him to know that I wouldn't lie to him about it without a reason."

JRT transcript (WC, NjP) of CLSsh (C. L. Swem Coll., NjP).

A Veto Message

THE WHITE HOUSE,
To the House of Representatives: 5 *February, 1921.*

I return herewith, without my approval, House joint resolution No. 440, directing the Secretary of War to cease enlisting men in the Regular Army of the United States, except in the cases of those men who have already served one or more enlistments therein.

The text of the joint resolution discloses that its purpose is to cause a discontinuance of enlistment in the Regular Army until the number of enlisted men shall not exceed one hundred and seventy-five thousand. No provision is made in the resolution for the preservation of any proportionate strength in the combatant corps of the Army and a mere discontinuance of enlistment would, for a long time, preserve the Staff corps disproportionately enlisted and the combatant corps insufficiently manned to maintain the instruction and training which ought to be assured if an Army of one hundred and seventy-five thousand men is to be efficient in proportion to its aggregate number.

On the fourth day of June, 1920, I signed a bill passed by the present Congress, providing for the reorganization of the Army.[1] Because of the profoundly disturbed condition of the world and in order that full benefit might accrue to the people of the United States from the lessons of the world war as to what, under modern conditions, is required to be the nucleus of an efficient army, the War Department had recommended an Army of approximately five hundred thousand men. The Congress, after prolonged consideration, determined to authorize, and did authorize, the reorganization of the Army on the basis of an enlisted strength of approximately two hundred and eighty thousand men, including in the organization new arms like the Air Service and the Chemical Warfare Service, the use of which were developments of the war and provision for which is a necessary addition to the prewar strength of the Army. The act authorized for the first time in our history a tactical organization of the Army, resting upon divisions as tactical units, and required the training of the National Guard and the organized reserve in territorial areas of the United States in association with the divisions of the Regular Army. At that time the Congress plainly regarded the provision then made as the minimum which would provide for the added arms and new duties imposed on the Army, and for that efficiency which the peace-time Army of the United States should have as the nucleus of mobilization in the event of a national emergency. I regret that I am not able to see in the condition of the world at large or in the needs of the United States any such change as would justify the restriction upon that minimum which is proposed by the House joint resolution.

Woodrow Wilson.[2]

Printed in *Cong. Record*, 66th Cong., 3d sess., p. 2684.

[1] About this bill, see NDB to WW, June 3, 1920 (first letter of that date), n. 1, Vol. 65.

[2] The House overrode Wilson's veto on February 5 and the Senate did the same on February 7.

Joseph Patrick Tumulty to Edith Bolling Galt Wilson, with Enclosures

Dear Mrs. Wilson: [The White House] 5 February 1921.

Judge Payne agrees that the attached is the right kind of a telegram to send to the railroad men. I think it would be well to get it out today.   The Secretary

TL (WP, DLC).

ENCLOSURE I

John Barton Payne to Joseph Patrick Tumulty

My dear Mr. Tumulty: Washington February 4, 1921

I have given careful consideration to the labor matters you sent over, and my suggestion is that a telegram such as the enclosed be sent.

No other action seems feasible.
                              Cordially yours,   John Barton Payne

TLS (WP, DLC).

ENCLOSURE II

4 February 1921.

Mr. E. F. Grable,
Grand President of the United Brotherhood
of Maintenance Employees and Railway Shop
Laborers, Chicago, Illinois.

I have carefully considered the several telegrams addressed to me dealing with the labor questions and railroad management now under consideration by the Railroad Labor Board in Chicago.[1]

The Transportation Act approved February 28, 1920, to a greater extent than any previous legislation, places all questions dealing with finances and railroad management and necessary rates under the jurisdiction of the Interstate Commerce Commission; hence all questions involving the expense of operation, the necessities of the railroads, and the amount of money necessary to secure the successful operation thereof, are now under the jurisdiction of the Commission. At the same time, the Act placed all questions of dispute between carriers and their employees and subordinate officials under the jurisdiction of the Railroad Labor Board, now sitting in Chicago. This Board is composed of three members constituting the Labor Group, representing the employees and subordinate officials of the carriers; three members constituting the Management Group, representing the carriers; and three members constituting the Public Group, representing the public. So far as I am advised the board may be relied on to give careful and intelligent consideration to all questions within its jurisdiction. To seek to influence either of these bodies upon anything which has been placed within their jurisdiction by Congress, would be unwise and open to grave objection.

It would be manifestly unwise for me, therefore, to take any action which would interfere with the orderly procedure of the Interstate Commerce Commission or of the Railroad Labor Board; and all the matters mentioned in your telegrams are within the jurisdiction of one or the other of these bodies; and in their action I think we may repose entire confidence.

In view of the foregoing, it does not seem wise to comply with your suggestion that the matter be submitted to the Congress, and the only action deemed necessary is to submit copies of the telegrams received from you and from the representatives of the railroad executive to the Interstate Commerce Commission, and to the Railroad Labor Board, for such action as these bodies may deem wise in the premises. This will be done.   Woodrow Wilson.

Send same telegram to

Mr. Thomas DeWitt Cuyler, Chairman,
   Association of Railway Executives,
   Hotel Blackstone, Chicago, Illinois.
Mr. J. F. Anderson, Vice President,
   International Association of Machinists,
   Chicago, Illinois.

T MS (WP, DLC).
   [1] J. F. Anderson *et al.* to WW, Jan. 31, 1921; Edward Frank Grable to WW, Feb. 1, 1921; Thomas DeWitt Cuyler to WW, Feb. 1, 1921; and J. F. Anderson *et al.* to WW, Feb. 2, 1921; all T telegrams (WP, DLC). Anderson, the vice-president of the International Association of Machinists, and six other union officials initiated the correspondence with a lengthy telegram in which they informed Wilson that William Wallace Atterbury, a vice-president of the Pennsylvania Railroad, had suddenly appeared before a meeting of the United States Railroad Labor Board on January 31 to present on behalf of the Association of Railway Executives a demand that the wages of railway workers be lowered and the existing rules on working conditions be abrogated immediately in order to save the railroads from financial collapse. The labor leaders suggested that, if the situation of the railroads was as dire as Atterbury had suggested, the Association of Railway Executives should present their case with supporting documents to the Interstate Commerce Commission and to President Wilson. If Wilson then considered the situation to be acute, he should present the matter to Congress for appropriate legislative action. However, the union leaders continued, they believed the railroad executives were using the current economic recession as an excuse to drive down wages and destroy the railroad unions. They accused the executives of having deliberately operated their systems in a financially extravagant manner and then seeking to place the blame for high costs on the unions. Grable, the president of the United Brotherhood of Maintenance Employees and Railway Shop Laborers, made similar accusations in his telegram.
   Cuyler, the chairman of the Association of Railway Executives, sent his telegram in

response to press reports of the labor leaders' telegrams. He denied that the railroads had been operated in an inefficient and extravagant manner and asserted that the reduction of railroad labor costs was indeed a matter of dire necessity. Thus, he said, Atterbury's presentation to the Railroad Labor Board had been entirely justified. Moreover, Cuyler declared, each railroad company should negotiate necessary changes in work rules with its own employees; uniform rules covering the entire country, whether determined by the Railroad Labor Board or anyone else, were unworkable. The second telegram from Anderson and the other labor leaders, based upon press reports of Cuyler's telegram, was a point-by-point refutation of Atterbury and Cuyler's arguments.

To Oscar Wilder Underwood

My dear Senator: [The White House] 5 February, 1921

I have your letter of February third and will, of course, take into consideration Mr. McConville's suggestion.[1]

I hope you will not think me inconsiderate or presuming if I ask that you will do me the great kindness to get ready for me a veto of the pending tariff bill.[2] You can give the right reasons for vetoing it better than any man I know of, certainly very much better than myself, and I would be under great obligation if you would do me this great service.

With warm regard,
Cordially and sincerely yours,   [Woodrow Wilson]

CCL (WP, DLC).
[1] O. W. Underwood to WW, Feb. 3, 1921, enclosing H. A. McConville to O. W. Underwood, Jan. 29, 1921, both TLS (WP, DLC). McConville, of Montgomery, Ala., chairman of the Louisville & Nashville Railroad Council of the International Association of Railroad Supervisors of Mechanics, recommended one W. F. Milligan (or Miligan), an official of the council, for a vacancy on the Railroad Labor Board.
[2] The House Ways and Means Committee had agreed on December 18, 1920, to the introduction of an emergency tariff bill which would impose prohibitive duties upon imports of wool and a limited number of other agricultural products. Joseph Warren Fordney, Republican of Michigan, chairman of the Ways and Means Committee, introduced H.R. 15275 in the House on December 20. As introduced, the bill set the new rates for a period of ten months. Its objective, according to its supporters, was to provide temporary assistance to American farmers during the current economic recession, pending the passage of permanent tariff legislation in the coming Harding administration. The House passed the bill by a large margin on December 22. In the Senate, where there was more serious opposition to the bill, it was not referred to the Finance Committee until December 27. The Finance Committee held hearings on the bill January 6-11, 1921. The committee voted on January 15 to report the bill to the Senate with amendments which extended high tariff rates to virtually all farm products. The bill was tied up on the Senate floor in late January and early February by a filibuster of its opponents. Following the defeat of a vote for closure of debate on the bill on February 2, senators of both parties reached a tentative agreement on February 3 that it would be brought to a vote on or about February 15. *New York Times*, Dec. 19, 21, 23, 28, 1920; Jan. 16, 27-30, Feb. 1-5, 1921.

From Thomas DeWitt Cuyler

Chicago, Ills., Feb. 6, 1921.

I acknowledge with thanks the courtesy of your telegram of today. Your conclusion that the United States Railroad Labor Board is the appropriate body to settle the questions now properly before it and that the Interstate Commerce Commission is the appropriate body to settle any other questions regarding the responsibility of the railroad companies for the character of their operation is in our judgment the sound and proper conclusion. We appreciate your promoting the cause of orderly procedure by the position which you have taken.

I assume that your statement, "It does not seem wise to comply with your suggestion that the matter be submitted to the Congress." was intended as a reply only to the representatives of the railway employes as we have never at any time made such suggestion.

Aside from the adjustment of wages of unskilled labor in accordance with now existing conditions our effort is to secure a prompt decision on one fundamental point, namely, that the managements responsible for efficient and economical railway operation shall have the opportunity to adjust rules and working conditions to meet the differing needs of the railroads and of the territories which they respectively serve.

The evidence which we have already presented to the United States Railroad Labor Board demonstrates beyond question that it is economically unsound and can only be fraught with disaster to attempt to compel all of the railroads of the country regardless of their differing conditions to operate under rigid and uniform working arrangements. It has also demonstrated that the existing wartime working arrangements not only deny this necessary right of variation but that they scandalously inflate the labor cost of railway operation and result in enormous waste and inefficiency.

Upon their termination the railroads stand ready to readjust their rules and working conditions in accordance with the differing normal needs of the country, each carrier in orderly conference and negotiation with its own employes and in obedience to the letter and spirit of the Transportation Act.

The railroads are also prepared to fully meet before the Interstate Commerce Commission any responsible charges or inquiries regarding their operation. They do, however, strongly object to the obvious attempt of certain leaders of the railway employes to evade the real questions at issue and to delay and becloud their settlement by irrelevant and unfounded charges.

Thomas DeWitt Cuyler

T telegram (WP, DLC).

From Oscar Wilder Underwood

My dear Mr. President: [Washington] February 7, 1921.

I received your note of the 5th inst., and thank you for the compliment you pay me in asking me to make suggestions in reference to the veto of the present tariff bill. I shall be more than glad to comply with your request, and, in ample time before the bill reaches the White House, I will send you my views in reference to the matter.

In my judgment, under the guise of helping a distressing situation in the country, no more vicious bill has ever been proposed than the so-called Emergency Tariff Bill. Its construction is bad from every angle, and it violates every principle of tariff legislation, whether viewed from a Republican or a Democratic standpoint. Its enactment in my judgment would not be beneficial to the real producers of farm products, and on the other hand, it would undoubtedly, without warrant, greatly increase the cost of many of the necessities of life to the people of the country, without the increased cost being reflected into the Treasury of the United States.

With kindest regards, I am

Sincerely yours,   O W Underwood

TLS (WP, DLC).

From Sylvester Woodbridge Beach

My very dear Friend: Princeton New Jersey Feb. 7. 1921

It was not until Friday evening that I knew of your generous & beautiful letter[1] and the enclosure in behalf of a fund that was being raised in recognition of my fifteenth Anniversary.

The outpouring of the people, and the warm expressions of appreciation & affection were almost more than I could endure—as they surely were more than I deserved.[2]

A purse of $1800 was handed to me, not a small kindness at a time when all our resources are being so heavily taxed by appeals that none can resist.

I do so much thank you for what you did.

May God's richest blessing follow you into the well-earned rest from public cares that now awaits you. The American people & the world will never fail to keep green the memory of the greatest administration in our history, and of the noblest type of the true American that God has ever given to America.

Hoping some time to see you all again, and with loving appreciation of your goodness to me, I am

Cordially & faithfully yours   Sylvester W. Beach

ALS (WP, DLC).
   [1] WW to Charlotte D. Wilbur, Jan. 25, 1921.
   [2] The celebration of Beach's fifteenth anniversary as pastor of the First Presbyterian Church was held on February 4. See the *Princeton Packet*, Feb. 12, 1921.

From the Diary of Josephus Daniels

1921 Tuesday 8, February

Each cabinet officer should send his resignation to the President on March 4th.

W.W. said a newspaperman said he had been much with Harding—he had good intentions & good character—all he lacked was "mentality" WW said he hated the word "mentality."

Dawes[1] & his profanity. When Judge [Samuel Chase] was under impeachment, the charge against him [was] that he said "Damn" & his attorney contended that "damn" was in no sense profane— only a word of emphasis.

Payne & Baker said Dawes had talked that way all along & Burleson thought Dawes talked as he did because it was sour grapes because he did not get assurance [of] office WW said he had heard Dawes had written to Harding he did not want his G——d office.

[1] Charles Gates Dawes, president of the Central Trust Co. of Chicago, former chairman of the General Purchasing Board of the A.E.F. and member of the United States Liquidation Commission, soon to become Director of the new Bureau of the Budget in the Harding administration.

From Franklin Randolph Mayer[1]

My dear Mr. President: New York February 8th, 1921.

It is with great pleasure that I find myself able to tell you after diligent search, we recovered possession within the last few days of the desk used by you on the "S.S. GEORGE WASHINGTON."[2] Knowing the personal and historic interest that this desk must have, instructions have been given to have it forwarded by express to you at the White House.

It is believed that the desk is the one that was in your cabin, and I trust that when the desk arrives in Washington this belief will be found correct.

The opportunity of being able to be of some slight service in this matter is most gratifying to our Company.

I have the honor to remain,

Very truly yours,   F. R. Mayer

TLS (WP, DLC).
    [1] President of the United States Mail Steamship Co., Inc.
    [2] For earlier correspondence on this matter, see G. C. Cook to WW, Nov. 13, 1920, and WW to G. C. Cook, Nov. 15, 1920, both in Vol. 66.

To Duane Reed Stuart

My dear Stuart: The White House 9 February, 1921

I am immensely relieved to find that my Greek had not altogether decayed, and thank you sincerely for your careful reply to my inquiries about the Greek thirteen. Having got accustomed in my mind to the form ΤΡΙΣΚΑΙΔΕΚΑ, I think I shall adopt it rather than ΤΡΕΙΣΚΑΙΔΕΚΑ. It gives me great satisfaction, you may be sure, to be one of the last to turn away from the use of Greek, in which I have always firmly believed as a medium of education.

With the best wishes for you and yours,

Cordially and sincerely yours,   Woodrow Wilson

TLS (received from D. R. Stuart, Jr.).

To Jessie Woodrow Wilson Sayre

My dear little Girl: [The White House] 9 February, 1921

The poem by Eleanor[1] is really delicious and I hope and believe gives promise of very delightful productions in the future. Please give her, and keep for yourselves, my warmest love.

Affectionately your devoted   [Father]

TCL (WC, NjP).
    [1] Printed as an Enclosure with Jessie W. W. Sayre to WW, Jan. 31, 1921.

To Jan Christiaan Smuts

My dear Friend: The White House 9 February, 1921

It was a great pleasure to hear from you through your letter of the fourth of January, and the paper you enclosed gave me, you may be sure, the deepest gratification. I know of no one I have met whose good opinion I value more than I value yours. I wish there might be someone to write discerningly and with knowledge of your own actions and influence at the Peace Conference, which were wholly admirable.

With the most cordial and affectionate good wishes,

Sincerely yours,   Woodrow Wilson

TLS (J. C. Smuts Papers, National Archives, Praetoria).

From Joseph Patrick Tumulty

Dear Governor: The White House, 9 February 1921.

Members of the Cabinet, after returning from the White House on yesterday, said that you had informed them that you would be willing to come over to the White House on next Tuesday to sit for a new picture.

I sincerely hope that you can see your way clear to do this. It will have a wonderful effect on the country. I think it would be unwise, however, to have the Cabinet meeting at four in the afternoon, and think it would be better if the picture can be taken in the morning.

Will you let me know your wishes in the matter.

Sincerely,   J. P. Tumulty

TLS (WP, DLC).

To Joseph Patrick Tumulty

Dear Tumulty: The White House [c. Feb. 9, 1921]

I don't think it would be dignified to change the meeting hour of the Cabinet just to suit the photographers. They can take the picture when it is four o'clock and use the kind of lights that the movies use.[1]   The President.

TL (WP, DLC).

[1] The Cabinet portrait was taken on February 15 and is printed in the illustration section of this volume.

To Sylvester Woodbridge Beach

My dear Friend: [The White House] 9 February, 1921

Thank you for your letter of the seventh. You may be sure it was a pleasure to do anything that I could to show my friendship and appreciation.

Cordially and sincerely yours,   [Woodrow Wilson]

CCL (WP, DLC).

From the Shorthand Diary of Charles Lee Swem

9 February, 1921

In acknowledging a book, "Allen's Synonyms and Antonyms,"[1] this morning the President said: "I haven't the least idea what an antonym is." And then: "I suppose it is the opposite of a synonym."

[1] Frederic Sturges Allen, *Allen's Synonyms and Antonyms* (New York and London, 1921). A copy of the book had been sent to Wilson by William Harlow Briggs, an executive of Harper & Brothers. W. H. Briggs to WW, Feb. 5, 1921, TLS (WP, DLC). Wilson acknowledged the gift in WW to W. H. Briggs, Feb. 9, 1921, CCL (WP, DLC).

10 February, 1921

Upon asking the President the immediate purpose he had in mind when taking up shorthand, he said, "I had none. I thought it would be a useful thing to do. I was a youngster about fifteen at the time and I got a textbook—Standard Phonography[1]—and learned it myself. I copied books for practice—a particular one that I remember was a complete treatise on geology."

JRT transcript (WC, NjP) of CLSsh (C. L. Swem Coll., NjP).
[1] Andrew Jackson Graham, *Hand-Book of Standard or American Phonography* (New York, 1858). See the Editorial Note, "Wilson's Study and Use of Shorthand, 1872-1892," Vol. I.

Two News Reports

[*Feb. 11, 1921*]

WILSON VISITS NEW HOME

Washington, Feb. 11.—President Wilson spent several hours today at the house where he will make his home after his retirement from office on March 4.

It was the President's second visit to the house since he purchased it, and, with Mrs. Wilson, he spent considerable time in going over his belongings which have recently been brought here from Princeton, N. J., and indicating where he desired them to be placed. The President paid particular attention to the books of his library and to their arrangement in the racks.

All of Mr. Wilson's furniture which was in storage in Princeton has been received, and there remains only the moving of the few personal effects of the President and Mrs. Wilson from the White House.

[*Feb. 11, 1921*]
Shallow-Minded Visitor
Reminds Wilson of Bungalow

Washington, Feb. 11.—The best "inside story" in Washington today is one of President's Wilson's witticisms.

Recently the President listened patiently to a man who impressed him as having little intellectual depth.

"That man," said the President, "is a simple bungalow. He has no upper story whatever."

Printed in the *New York Times*, Feb. 12, 1921.

To Franklin Randolph Mayer

My dear Mr. Mayer: [The White House] 11 February, 1921

I appreciate very much your kind letter of February eighth and the intention expressed in it. As a matter of fact, I think I ought to say that the desk you speak of has all along been my personal property, inasmuch as it was made for a committee headed by Mr. Rodman Wanamaker on the model of a desk of General Washington's and put on the Steamship George Washington as a present to me when I took passage to Europe.

These circumstances, however, render me no less appreciative of your thoughtful and generous kindness. I shall value the desk all the more highly because of the combined kindnesses which it will represent.   Sincerely yours,   [Woodrow Wilson]

CCL (WP, DLC).

Laurence E. Rubel[1] to Joseph Patrick Tumulty

Dear Sir: Washington, D. C. February 11, 1921.

In arranging for photographs on March 4th, we understand that it is necessary for us to get permission for making photographs within the White House Grounds.

We should like, for instance, to make photographs of Mr. Wilson as he will stand in the doorway before entering the automobile which will take him to the President's Room in the Capitol where we are told he will sign the last minute measures.

We should like also to make other photographs which might suggest themselves at the time within the White House Grounds.

May we ask for your early consideration of this so that our plans for the disposition of our men can be laid well in advance?

Very respectfully yours,

Underwood & Underwood, by L Rubel[2]

TLS (WP, DLC).
[1] Manager of the Washington office of Underwood & Underwood, Inc., photographers.
[2] An undated note attached to this letter reads as follows: "No more pictures. C.L.S."

Edward Parker Davis to Cary Travers Grayson

My dear Grayson.   [Philadelphia] Feby. 11 1921.

Cyrus H. McCormick has just dined with me and gone on to New York. He asked me to tell you that the house project is going on well, and he is hopeful of accomplishing what is desired. We do not know whether the President knows of this, but if he is anxious and worried about the future, his anxiety should be relieved. If you can, give him my love.

Will you send me, when you can conveniently, the street and number of the new house, and can you tell me where Professor Axson can be reached by letter? I hope you and yours are well.

Sincerely yours,   Edward P. Davis.

ALS (received from James Gordon Grayson and Cary T. Grayson, Jr.).

From the Diary of Ray Stannard Baker

[Washington] Feby 12, [1921].

I arrived in Washington this morning. I have been away a week, very busy, mostly at home, where I have been at work on my own large collection of documents relative to the Peace Conference.

Yesterday I was busy in New York with the publishers,[1] talking over the methods of using the materials I have.

At the Century[2] I ran across Sir Horace Plunkett and had an interesting talk with him on the Irish question. He is rather despondent about it. Also talked with Thomas Mott Osborne, the prison reformer: an interesting man.

Called on Colonel House & had a long talk. He is as busy as ever seeing people of all kinds. It is his genius. He still talks much about his break with the President: & now seems to blame the President more & more for what has happened since Paris. I like him very much: yet I always wonder a little how much of a real part he played at Paris. He saw innumerable people, arranged innumerable meetings: but his only real effect came through his influence with the President which in the latter part of the Conference was slight. His great service was in keeping the President informed & especially in contributing some of the human relationships which the President never had.

The Colonel is now worried over the reports that he was against the inclusion of the Covenant with the treaty, or that in the month while the President was away from Paris, he accepted the idea of a treaty separate from the Covenant. I think he did.

He is now at the stage of trying to correct or defend his record: or to explain what a large part he really had in it all. He told me how he had argued Clemenceau over to the League: and how much better it would have been if, at this crisis or that, Wilson had followed his advice. He is a diarist! How different all this from that grim, powerful, bitter man in the White House! He never defends or excuses: (has he not acted?) he has no need of proving the importance of the place he occupied: nor to shine by the reflected glory of association with personages. He kept no records of what he did: and will write no account of it. He will abide by the event.

Wilson said once: "I have a great affection for Colonel House." And he had. Colonel House helped him greatly with information about men & things: never with principles. Where the Colonel gave advice (as distinguished from information) at Paris—and I knew of most of the instances—it never made the least difference in the President's course. Sometimes he acted as the Colonel thought he should: Sometimes he acted quite contrary to the Colonel's ideas. And whatever he did the Colonel defended him! How different from Walter Page—who was clear.

Yet, while I see these things, I never meet the Colonel without a new sense of personal liking such as I have never at any time felt for the President. He is a human soul: he is generous: he is kindly: he wants good in the world: and he has a kind of common-sense (not wisdom) which grows out of his knowledge of what human beings are. His intellectual equipment is small: he has no real mind of his own: his instincts & feelings keep him generally upon the liberal & democratic side, but when confronted with real events & hard-set personalities—as often at Paris—he compromises everything away in order to preserve "harmony" & keep people liking one another. He has no *inner structure*: no bony framework: and yet a lovable man. Such men, with the best intent in the world, often do as much harm as good.

[1] Doubleday, Page & Co.
[2] That is, the Century Association (Club).

From Newton Diehl Baker

My dear Mr. President: Washington. February 12, 1921.

Ambassador Wallace cabled me this morning that he is planning
to lay a wreath on the grave of the unknown French soldier whose
remains are buried under the Arc de Triomphe on the 22nd day of
February, Washington's birthday. He suggests that it would be "a
most graceful act if the President would grant authority to confer
upon the nameless soldier the Distinguished Service Cross." I have
examined the statutory authority in such cases and find it ample
to authorize you to confer the Distinguished Service Cross upon
any member of the forces allied with us in the war, under any rules
and regulations to be prescribed by you. The fact that this soldier
is nameless and that his deeds of personal valor cannot be recited
need not, in my judgment, deter you from authorizing the decoration. I therefore concur in the suggestion of Ambassador Wallace
and ask your authority to cable him that he may make the award
in your name. I will also cable, as a citation for the award, the following, if it meets with your approval:

"By the authority of the President of the United States, I confer upon this nameless soldier the Distinguished Service Cross.
He was a member of the great Armies of France. He has been
selected to typify to this and all succeeding generations the imperishable glory won by the valor of the soldiers of his country.
In his sacrifice is revealed the resolute spirit with which France
faced the enemy. His death illustrates the price which it is necessary to pay for liberty. The triumph of the cause for which he
fought is the final assurance that liberty, resting on right, is to
be the enduring portion of the children of men."

Respectfully yours,   Newton D. Baker

TLS (WP, DLC).

John Randolph Bolling to the Skandinaviska
Kreditaktiebolaget

Gentlemen: [The White House] 12th February, 1921.

My brother-in-law, President Woodrow Wilson, asks me to acknowledge your kind letter of January 24th,[1] and the cheque-book
which accompanied same.

He appreciates your courtesy in allowing him your highest deposit rate of 6% per annum, and notes that a statement of the account will be rendered half-yearly showing the accrued interest
credited.

Please note on your records that after March 4th, 1921, the permanent address of The President will be:

Honorable Woodrow Wilson,

2340 S Street, N.W.,

Washington, D. C.

and send all statements, and communications, there.

Cordially yours,   [John Randolph Bolling]

CCL (WP, DLC).
   [1] Skandinaviska Kreditaktiebolaget to WW, Jan. 24, 1921, TLS (WP, DLC).

From Bainbridge Colby

My dear Mr. President: Washington 13 February 1921

There is a new development to record in the Mexican situation. Although I have little confidence that it will bring us to the point of recognition, it points that way and I wish to lay it promptly before you.

I received a visit today from Senor Manuel Vargas, who presented a very friendly and polite letter of introduction from President Obregon, describing Mr. Vargas as his confidential agent and private secretary. Mr. Vargas exhibited a copy of a declaration which President Obregon purposes issuing broadcast and which apparently he thinks contains sufficient assurance to warrant recognition of Mexico by all foreign nations. I beg to enclose the copy of the proposed declaration which was handed me.[1] It is a little untidy and pocket-worn, but to save delay I will send it just as I received it.

You will observe that the declarations are a little grandiose in style and very general and amount to little more than the similar declarations which were contained in the letter of Mr. Pesqueira.[2]

It was apparently the idea of Mr. Vargas that if a personal meeting could be arranged at the Mexican border between President Obregon and a representative whom you might designate, that President Obregon could give convincing assurance by word of mouth of his sincerity in making this declaration.

I made the statement in reply that we entertain no doubt of President Obregon's sincerity and that these declarations unquestionably represented his purposes. I added, however, that there was only one thing to be done, and that was to carry out the program outlined in the final letter given Mr. Pesqueira on the eve of his departure in November.[3] In other words, the only justification for such a meeting as was suggested would be for the purpose of signing a treaty expressing in that form the assurances which Mr. Pesqueira had proffered us and which we had indicated our cordial willingness to accept.

There is some telegraphing going on tonight with President Obregon, and something may come of it, but I am not very hopeful. There is a faction in Mexico which insists upon regarding anything in the nature of a treaty stipulation as compromising Mexican dignity, and I seriously doubt whether President Obregon is ready to expose himself to such a criticism or able to perceive how he would grow beyond its reach by the statesmanlike course which has been outlined to him, obediently to your suggestions and instructions.

I will, of course, keep you instantly advised as to any further developments in the matter.

Very respectfully yours,   Bainbridge Colby[4]

TLS (WP, DLC).
[1] CC MS (WP, DLC). This undated document declared that the Obregón administration was acting "in strict adherence to the laws of morality and right" and listed ten of its "achievements" to date which, its author believed, should encourage all other nations to accept Mexico as a part of the international community.
[2] R. V. Pesqueira Morales to BC, Oct. 26, 1920, the text of which is printed in n. 1 to Enclosure I printed with BC to WW, Oct. 28, 1920 (first letter of that date), Vol. 66.
[3] See the Enclosure printed with WW to BC, Nov. 25, 1920, *ibid.*
[4] Wilson wrote at the top of this letter: "Ackn & file W.W."

To Newton Diehl Baker

My dear Mr. Secretary: [The White House] 14 February, 1921

The message you suggest sending to Ambassador Wallace about the unknown French soldier is excellently conceived in every way, but I feel so strongly disinclined just now to show any additional courtesies to France, in view of her unreasonable and threatening attitude, that I do not think it would be wise for me to do what is suggested in your letter. Wallace will represent us at the ceremonies, and I think that will be sufficient.

Cordially and faithfully yours,   [Woodrow Wilson]

CCL (WP, DLC).

To Edith Bolling Galt Wilson

The White House, 14 Feb'y, 1921

My lovly Valentine, I cannot let Sweetheart's Day pass without again pledging you my deep love forever—so long as my spirit is conscious at all—and begging you to be my sweetheart as long

Your own Woodrow

ALS (EBW Papers, DLC).

From Warren Gamaliel Harding

My dear Mr. President: St. Augustine, Fla. February 14, 1921

I beg to gratefully acknowledge your esteemed letter of January twenty-second, which should have had my acknowledgment long ago and would have been given attention but for the fact that I was on a house-boat cruise and only a few days ago returned to headquarters here at St. Augustine to find a considerable quantity of mail awaiting my notice.

It was very thoughtful of you to write as you did respecting the customary luncheon arrangements for inauguration day and very gracious of you to express the readiness of yourself and Mrs. Wilson to aid in any manner possible. I know of no reply to make other than to thank you in all sincerity.

In view of the cancellation of any inaugural celebration, we have thought that there should be no luncheon party at the White House, as has been a part of the previous custom, and there will be no occasion to trouble you and Mrs. Wilson to make any arrangements. It is our expectation to go to the White House immediately after the inaugural at the Capitol, and we expect to be joined at luncheon and at dinner that evening by the immediate members of our own family. If you will simply say to the housekeeper that we will be grateful if arrangements are made for family luncheon and dinner, no other preparation is required. I will thank you to have conveyed this information because I should feel reluctant to communicate in any way with any of the attaches of the White House until coming into responsibility. It is exceedingly good of you to suggest sending one of the force to confer with me here in Florida, but I think the plans which we have in mind will make such a trip quite unnecessary.

I read with very great interest the newspaper statement that you had so far recovered as to be able to attend the theatre, and I share with your countrymen the rejoicing at this manifestation of your progress toward recovery.

Again expressing my appreciation of your thoughtful courtesy and reciprocating your good wishes, I am
                    Very truly yours   Warren G Harding

TLS (WP, DLC).

A Tribute, with Enclosure

[c. Feb. 14, 1921]

TO THE PRESIDENT
OF
THE UNITED STATES

We the undersigned, a few women of New York, send the enclosed quotation from the article by Lowes Dickinson in the February Atlantic,[1] as a means of expressing our convictions.

We beg the honor of enrolling our names among those who feel that in the judgement of posterity, the name of Woodrow Wilson will be added to those of Washington and Lincoln as the men of vision in American history.[2]

Hw MS (WP, DLC).

[1] Goldsworthy Lowes Dickinson, "SOS—EUROPE TO AMERICA," *Atlantic Monthly*, CXXVII (Feb. 1921), 244-49. The quotations in the Enclosure are all from p. 246.

[2] Attached to the scroll on which the tribute appeared were five sheets containing 105 signatures. Among the signers were Jeanie North (Mrs. Charles R.) Henderson, Sara Delano (Mrs. James) Roosevelt, Eleanor (Mrs. Franklin Delano) Roosevelt, Katrina Brandes Ely (Mrs. Charles Lewis) Tiffany, Edith Minturn (Mrs. Isaac Newton Phelps) Stokes, Carlotta Russell Lowell, Emily Sinkler (Mrs. Nicholas Guy) Roosevelt, Helen MacGregor Byrne (Mrs. Hamilton Fish) Armstrong, Edith Parsons Morgan, Amey Aldrich, Elizabeth Sturgis Potter (Mrs. Frank Lyon) Polk, Anne Hyde Clarke (Mrs. Arthur Osgood) Choate, Maud Bonner (Mrs. Francis Higginson) Cabot, and Martha Bagby (Mrs. George Gordon) Battle. Virtually all of the signers were listed in the *New York Social Register*.

ENCLOSURE

"Mr. Wilson may have committed this or that minor error of tactics. But all that is dust in the balance compared to the main fact, that he had vision where the others had passion; that he looked to the future, while they looked to the past; that he drew his inspiration from reason and truth, while they drew their expertness from hatred, greed, and fear. * * *

And what of the people of America? Did they know what a man had been vouchsafed to them as a leader? Were they really behind that great voice? Was it, after all, their soul that spoke in him? It does not look like it. It looks as if, once more, a prophet had appeared, and been without honor among his own people. * * * Would that my voice were strong and authoritative enough to bear to him, while he yet lives, that verdict of posterity which will acclaim him as the first statesman who ever came to an international conference of victors, to put humanity above country, the interest of the peoples above that of their rulers, reason above passion, justice above revenge, and reconciliation and peace above all. The powers of this world defeated him, and men will pay, and are paying, dearly for it. But if there is to be any continuing civilization for mankind, if there is to be any movement toward a better and juster society, his name will live when those of his adversaries are lost in ignominy; his star will shine from the heaven of our fixed lights when their marsh-fires are vanished, together with the swamp on which they fed."

T MS (WP, DLC).

From Charles Zeller Klauder

My dear Mr. President: Philadelphia February 14th, 1921.

I have delayed answering your letter of January 24th because I felt that you would understand that the suggestions you made in respect to the location of the vault, and the two rooms for the chauffeur and butler could be taken care of in the manner suggested. An outside staircase leading to the two rooms would be very interesting and would give us much pleasure to design.

Concerning the vault, it would be quite possible to place it in the basement but I am wondering whether you may not think the second story a much safer place for it inasmuch as members of your family would always be in that part of the house and since in the last scheme the billiard room was transferred from the basement to the first floor, it seems unlikely that any of the family would be in the basement. It is quite possible to cover or shield the door of the vault by a sliding book case or panel as you suggest and furthermore, it would be possible to have an opening into the safe from the closet next to Mrs. Wilson's room, should that be deemed more desirable.

In my last letter, I suggested that you might wish carefully to look over the plans last sent you and that you might then care to confer with me. I shall hold myself in readiness to come at any time.   Sincerely yours,   Chas Z Klauder

TLS (WP, DLC).

Cleveland Hoadley Dodge to Cary Travers Grayson

My dear Admiral Grayson: New York February 14, 1921.

About ten days ago I wrote you a letter[1] regarding the matter we spoke of in December, namely, the purchase of the Pierce-Arrow car. I addressed the letter to what I thought was your residence in

Washington, but as I have had no answer from you, I fear possibly you did not get the letter. I told you in that letter I hoped you would at once close the matter with the Pierce-Arrow people and that I would let you know later exactly who would participate in the gift. Since then I have seen Mr. McCormick and heard from Mr. Tom Jones & his brother David B. and Mr. Sheldon,[2] and all I want to know now is whether the matter is all right, and whether I shall send the check to you, and when, and for how much.

Mr. McCormick also spoke to me about the larger scheme which you had suggested to him and Mr. Baruch,[3] and I think that is working out satisfactorily. I of course want to do my share in it, and others have responded to the idea so generously that I hope it is going to be all right.

I was thinking today, however, that if all the money for the purchase of the house could not be secured, and there is to be a mortgage on the house, whether we could not perhaps buy the mortgage and present the mortgage, or something of that kind which would not involve quite such a large sum, and put the President under so much obligation. As I have not assumed any particular responsibility, and the matter is in the hands of Mr. McCormick and Mr. Baruch, I am just throwing this out as a suggestion in case the whole sum could not be readily secured.

Hoping to hear from you soon, with warm regards to everybody
Yours sincerely,   Cleveland H. Dodge

TLS (received from James Gordon Grayson and Cary T. Grayson, Jr.).
[1] C. H. Dodge to C. T. Grayson, Feb. 4, 1921.
[2] That is, Edward Wright Sheldon.
[3] The "larger scheme" was Grayson's idea of rallying Wilson's intimate friends to help pay for the house on S Street. From various sources, it is clear that Grayson, or perhaps Grayson and his collaborators, hoped to raise two thirds of the purchase price, or $100,000, from ten individuals, who would each buy a "share" of $10,000 in the house fund. Grayson asked Cyrus H. McCormick, Jr., to canvass Wilson's Princeton friends and Baruch to approach certain other people. For his part, McCormick donated one share and raised shares from his mother, Nettie Maria Fowler McCormick; Thomas Davies Jones; and probably from his sister, Anita McCormick (Mrs. Emmons) Blaine. See B. M. Baruch to C. H. McCormick, Jr., April 9, 1921, CCL (B. M. Baruch Papers, NjP). In this same letter, Baruch says that Thomas Lincoln Chadbourne, Jr., had declined, but that "another man" had come in. We have not been able to identify this individual, but he was almost certainly Charles R. Crane. Dodge himself needed no urging from McCormick to contribute. He sent McCormick $20,000, all of which McCormick kept. C. H. McCormick, Jr., to B. M. Baruch, April 21, 1921, TLS ibid.; Phyllis B. Dodge, Tales of the Phelps-Dodge Family: A Chronicle of Five Generations (New York, 1987), p. 333. As for Baruch, he gave one share and collected another from Jesse H. Jones. J. H. Jones to B. M. Baruch, March 19, 1921, TLS (B. M. Baruch Papers, NjP). We do not know who gave the final share, but it might well have been Hugh Campbell Wallace, Vance C. McCormick, or George Foster Peabody, all of whom are mentioned as potential donors in C. H. McCormick, Jr., to B. M. Baruch, April 21, 1921, cited above.
We do not know when and to whom this money was sent. C. T. Grayson to E. P. Davis, Feb. 10, 1921, makes it clear that Wilson was ignorant of Grayson's little campaign up to the time that Grayson wrote this letter. And we can be certain that Wilson never knew about the benevolence of his friends. He thanked each person who had

helped to buy the Pierce-Arrow for him, and he certainly would have thanked the donors to the house fund if he had known that such a fund was collected and who the
donors were. It might be added that Gene Smith, *When the Cheering Stopped: The Last
Years of Woodrow Wilson* (New York, 1964), p. 174, says that Baruch bought the lot
adjacent to the S Street house in order to assure privacy for the Wilsons. This may or
may not have been true; Smith gives no evidence for this statement.

A News Item

[*Feb. 15, 1921*]

Wilson Goes to Cabinet Office;
Is Photographed With Advisers

Washington, Feb. 15.—President Wilson today for the first time
since his illness went to the Cabinet room in the White House Executive offices for the weekly Cabinet meeting. Since he has been
able to attend the weekly sessions, the President has met the Cabinet members at the Executive Mansion.

The meeting was held at the Executive offices today for the purpose of permitting a last photograph to be made of the President
with his Cabinet. Shortly before the time fixed for the meeting, the
President, accompanied by Secret Service men, left the Executive
Mansion and with the aid of his cane walked across the short path-
way separating the Executive offices from the Executive Mansion.
He took his seat at the head of the table in the Cabinet room before
any of the other Cabinet officers had arrived. After the photogra-
pher had retired, the regular Cabinet meeting was called to order
by the President.

Printed in the *New York Times*, Feb. 16, 1921.

To Armistead Mason Dobie[1]

My dear Mr. Dobie: [The White House] 15 February, 1921

Allow me to express my very deep interest in the effort to collect
a centennial endowment fund for the University of Virginia.[2] I
should suppose that there will be a very general interest in this
effort, for the service of the University of Virginia not only to the
state, but to the nation, is so well known. There are very few institutions of which it can be said, as it can be said of the University
of Virginia, that two-thirds of its graduates enter some form of public service, and there are very few so admirably adapted to mediate
between North and South by reason of their position and traditions. The University of Virginia is particularly adapted to play
such a part, and is in a very real sense a national institution.

Hoping that the efforts to secure this fund will be abundantly successful,

Cordially and sincerely yours,   [Woodrow Wilson]

CCL (WP, DLC).
¹ Professor of Law at the University of Virginia.
² Wilson was replying to A. M. Dobie to WW, Feb. 14, 1921, TLS (WP, DLC).

To Joseph Patrick Tumulty

Dear Tumulty: The White House [c. Feb. 15, 1921].

I do not think they will respond to anything I suggest or request,¹ but if you will consult with some trustworthy friends of ours in each house and get their advice, I will be very much obliged. Please get not only their advice as to whether I should do it, but also as to how I shall do it, in a letter to whom, for example.

The President.

TL (WP, DLC).
¹ Carl Vrooman, whose letter is printed as the next document, had talked to Tumulty about the American Farm Bureau Federation's offer to donate corn for relief purposes, and Tumulty had written or spoken to Wilson about it. After receipt of Wilson's letter, Tumulty talked to Vrooman and asked him to write to Wilson, as C. V. Vrooman to JPT, c. Feb. 15, 1921, ALS (WP, DLC), reveals.

From Carl Schurz Vrooman[1]

Dear Mr. President: Washington, D. C. 15 February 1921.

The farmers of the country, through the American Farm Bureau Federation, have offered to give the starving peoples of the world all the corn that the city folk or other agencies, will ship abroad.

The American Relief Council is being given a million bushels; the Polish Relief Committee is being given a million bushels; the Near East Committee is to be given a half million bushels; the China Relief Committee was offered any amount of corn from a million bushels up. But as it has been able to raise very little money, the only hope of sending corn to the famine districts of China is through Congressional action.

The Railway Brotherhoods have offered their services in transporting the gift corn, free; the railroads have also offered the use of cars, locomotives and other facilities, free; the elevators are offering part of their services free and the rest at cost. Under these circumstances, it would seen a shame not to be able in some way to solve the problem of ocean transportation.

Therefore, in behalf of the American Farm Bureau Federation, I suggested to several Senators that a Joint Resolution of Congress be passed, appropriating either a half million, or a million dollars, to be expended by the U. S. Grain Corporation, the American Farm Bureau Federation, and the China Relief Committee,—shipping as much corn as possible to the starving millions of the famine districts of China.

Senators Kenyon and Jones,[2] after conferring with members of both Houses of Congress, said that if such a suggestion were embodied in a communication from you, it would be passed at once without any opposition.

I asked Senator Kenyon if he felt sure that such a letter from you would help matters. He replied that every Senator and Congressman to whom he had spoken on the subject, felt that the response to such a word from you would be instantaneous and overwhelmingly in favor of the project.[3]

Respectfully yours, Carl Vrooman

TLS (WP, DLC).
[1] Former Assistant Secretary of Agriculture, at this time a "publicist" and director of the American Farm Bureau Federation Corn Gift Project.
[2] That is, William Squire Kenyon of Iowa and Andrieus Aristieus Jones of New Mexico, both members of the Senate Agriculture Committee.
[3] "Mr. Vrooman is going out of the city today; he asks that Senator Kenyon be notified of the action taken by the President in the matter of the attached." W. F. Johnson to JPT, Feb. 16, 1921, TL (WP, DLC). "The attached" was either Vrooman's letter to Tumulty of c. February 15 or his letter to Wilson of the same date.
We have not discovered what Wilson's "action" was. Perhaps he wrote at once to Kenyon; if so, his letter is missing. Perhaps he had Tumulty talk to Kenyon to urge him to take some action. In any event, Kenyon, on February 17, introduced a joint resolution appropriating $500,000 to pay for the transportation of cereals for the relief of China. *Cong. Record*, 66th Cong., 3d sess., p. 3293. The Senate approved the resolution on February 25, 1921, but it died in the House Appropriations Committee at the end of the lame-duck session. However, John D. Rockefeller, Jr., and the Laura Spelman Rockefeller Memorial Fund had meanwhile donated $500,000 to China Famine Relief, and other contributions followed. *New York Times*, Feb. 28, 1921. President and Mrs. Harding, the American Red Cross, churches, etc., took up the cause in March and throughout the spring. See *ibid.*, passim.

Tom Scott to Charles Lee Swem

My Dear Sir, Grasmere, Westmorland. Feby 15-21.

Further to your letter of November 1st 1920[1] I shall be glad to know if the President would like anything extra doing for his visit; i.e. Has he any choice of foods or any special wishes; If so it will give me great pleasure to fulfill. Is his party the same as per his first visit?.

I may mention that I have up-to-date Motors and a very nice Garage should he come with his own car.

Will you please assure him of a very hearty welcome and I am looking forward with great pleasure to seeing him again.

Assuring you of my best attention, I am,

Yours sincerely, Tom Scott

TLS (WP, DLC).
[1] It is missing, but see T. Scott to WW, Oct. 18, 1920, Vol. 66.

George Creel to Edith Bolling Galt Wilson

[New York]

Dear Mrs. Wilson: February Fifteenth, Nineteen Twenty-one.

I have been giving a good deal of thought to our matter, and more and more the conviction comes home that the President will *have* to write. Not only does he owe it to himself and those who have followed him, but he owes it to the world. It is not necessary to set any hard and fast time for this writing, but it *is* necessary to make the decision.

The books that the President ought to write are very clear in my mind: (1) his story of the Peace Conference: (2) his story of the war from the White House, taking in the period between August 1914 and the Armistice: (3) the bringing up to date of his History of the American People.

A first thing to consider in this connection is that even were the President in perfect physical condition, his time and strength are too precious to waste on the drudgeries of routine research. Strangely enough, when he comes to writing, the President still thinks of himself as a professor at Princeton, just starting in literature and unable to employ secretarial assistance. This point of view should and must be changed.

Under no circumstances should the President be permitted to lose the services of Swen [Swem]. It is not only that he needs him, but he is *used* to him, and the irritation of accustoming himself to a new personality is something that he should be guarded against.

In the second place there is the very huge task of preparing his papers. This is not a job for volunteer effort, but a daily routine that calls for highly specialized ability. A couple of trained historians should be employed and put to work as soon as possible. I have in mind such men as Guy Stanton Ford, Dean of the University of Minnesota, and Samuel G. Harding[1] of the University of Indiana, the two men who ran my pamphlet division throughout the war.

These men will not only put the President's papers in order and in sequence, but they can make the proper notations, researches and digests, not only with reference to the President's papers, but at the Congressional Library and elsewhere.

In all of the suggested books, the aid of two trained assistants would cut down the work to a minimum and particularly would this be the case in connection with the history.

With all my heart I feel that the President must write these three books. And just as deeply I feel that these three books *cannot* be written unless his strength is guarded by relieving him of drudgeries to which he has been used in the past. And if the books are written, *someone* is going to make money out of it. There is no way in which he can give them as a gift to the people. Therefore, I want the President to make this money himself.

I am leaving my mind open as to the best method of sale. There can be magazine publications of salient chapters, then book publication, and after that serial publication in the newspapers. The process adopted in this country would, of course, apply to the rest of the nations of the world. These, however, are details to be worked out later.

What I want to get now is the President's decision to *write*, and the President's decision to accept the *aid* that he ought to have. I am willing to assume this expense and the matter of a contract between us presents few difficulties. I want the President to make the money. On the strength of his decision to write, I can raise any amount of money, not only for the expense, but for such delivery to the President as he may think fair.

I am going to Chicago on Friday to deliver a series of three speeches and will be back in New York on February twenty-second. May I come down the latter part of that week and see you and the President with respect to these matters?

Believe me,   Always sincerely,   [George Creel]

CCL (G. Creel Papers, DLC).
    [1] Actually, Samuel Bannister Harding, Professor of History, Indiana University, 1895-1918.

Edith Bolling Galt Wilson to George Creel

My dear Mr. Creel: The White House [c. Feb. 16, 1921]

I have your letter, and have talked to my husband of your suggestions and he is very happy for you to come and talk to him as his ideas in regard to the kind of writing he will do are not on the same line as yours and he thinks a talk will clear things up. However he suggests that instead of the end of next week, as you suggest you make it the first of the following week. My own idea would be for Monday 11 a.m. the 27th[1] but if that is not convenient to you Wednesday is better than Tuesday, as that is Cabinet day

Forgive a brief note. With warm assurances,

Hastily,   EBW

ALI (G. Creel Papers, DLC).
    [1] She meant Monday, the twenty-eighth.

From the Shorthand Diary of Charles Lee Swem

17 February, 1921

Somebody sent to the President a very bad portrait of him, and this morning Mrs. Wilson received a letter asking if it had been received. The President told me to say in reply that "unfortunately it had been received in good shape." Mrs. Wilson suggested that we send some word of appreciation of it. He said, "No, I will not lie to these people. They ought to do something honest like digging ditches."

JRT transcript (WC, NjP) of CLSsh (C. L. Swem Coll., NjP).

To Warren Gamaliel Harding

[The White House]
My dear Mr. President-elect: 17 February, 1921

Allow me to thank you for your courteous letter of February fourteenth and to say that, of course, I will in every way conform to your wishes with regard to the luncheon at the White House. We shall take pleasure in instructing the housekeeper to make the arrangements you suggest for a family luncheon and dinner.

Hoping that the fourth of March will be a bright day in every way,   Sincerely yours,   [Woodrow Wilson]

CCL (WP, DLC).

To Jeanie North Henderson

My dear Mrs. Henderson: [The White House] 17 February, 1921

The paper sent me by you and the ladies of New York[1] has given me the deepest gratification. I am very much moved that these women should entertain so generous a judgment of what I have attempted to do. It will help to strengthen me in spirit for the days to come. I hope that there will be some occasion when you can convey to the ladies associated with you an expression of my very profound and grateful appreciation.

Cordially and sincerely yours,   [Woodrow Wilson]

CCL (WP, DLC).
[1] See the tribute printed at Feb. 14, 1921.

From Norman Hezekiah Davis, with Enclosure

My dear Mr. President: Washington February 17, 1921.

In compliance with your suggestion made at a Cabinet meeting some weeks ago, Secretary Houston and I have examined your undertaking to recommend to Congress that German bonds be accepted in exchange for Belgian obligations for sums borrowed from the United States during the war and up to November 11, 1918. I am, therefore, transmitting a suggested draft of a message to be sent by you to Congress on the subject.

Final arrangements have not as yet been made for the delivery by Germany to the Reparation Commission of the necessary bonds. The Department is informed that no action with regard to the agreement has yet been taken by the French and British Governments, though responsible officials of both governments have informally stated their belief that appropriate action to fulfill the commitments entered into will be taken at the proper time. Considering the uncertainty as to what arrangements will finally be made by the Allied Governments with regard to reparations and the impossibility, therefore, of estimating the future value of obligations issued by the German Government, we are not prepared to take any position at present with regard to the advisability of the arrangement contemplated. I believe, however, that in view of your commitment, it would be wise to present the matter, in somewhat the form suggested, to the Senate before the termination of your Administration.   Faithfully yours,   Norman H. Davis

TLS (WP, DLC).

ENCLOSURE[1]

TO THE SENATE:

I herewith call your attention to an agreement with Belgium made by the British and French Premiers and myself, which is embodied in the following letter:

"June 16, 1919.

M. Hymans,
   Ministre des Affaires Etrangers,
      Hotel Lotti, Paris.

Sir:

The Reparation Clauses of the draft Treaty of Peace with Germany obligate Germany to make reimbursement of all sums which Belgium has borrowed from the Allied and Associated Governments up to November 11, 1918, on account of the violation by

Germany of the Treaty of 1839. As evidence of such an obligation Germany is to make a special issue of bonds to be delivered to the Reparation Commission.

Each of the undersigned will recommend to the appropriate governmental agency of his Government that, upon the delivery to the Reparation Commission of such bonds, his Government accept an amount thereof corresponding to the sums which Belgium has borrowed from his Government since the war and up to November 11, 1918, together with interest at 5% unless already included in such sums, in satisfaction of Belgium's obligation on account of such loans, which obligation of Belgium's shall thereupon be cancelled.

We are, dear Mr. Minister,

Very truly yours,

(signed) G. Clemenceau
                Woodrow Wilson
                D. Lloyd George."

In recommending to you that Congress take appropriate action with regard to this agreement, certain facts should be brought to your attention.

The neutrality of Belgium was guaranteed by the Treaty of London in 1839. In considering the reparation to be made by Germany it was agreed that the action of Germany in grossly violating this Treaty by an attack on Belgium, obligated the German Government under international law to repay to Belgium the costs of war. On this principle the Treaty of Versailles (Art. 232) provided that in accordance with Germany's pledges already given as to the complete restoration for Belgium, Germany should undertake, in addition to the compensation for material damage, to make reimbursement of all sums which Belgium had borrowed from the Allied and Associated Governments up to November 11, 1918, together with interest at 5% per annum on such sums. This obligation was to be discharged by a special issue of bearer bonds to an equivalent amount payable in gold marks on May 1, 1926, or at the option of the German Government on the 1st of May in any year up to 1926.

For various reasons the undertaking defined in the above letter was embodied in the Treaty. Belgium's obligations to the United States for advances made up to the date of the Armistice amounted to approximately $171,000,000, and to England and France they amounted, I am informed, to about §164,700,000. In view of the special circumstances in which Belgium became involved in the war and the attitude of this country toward Belgium, it was felt that the United States might well agree to make the same agreement respecting pre-Armistice loans to Belgium as England and France offered to do.

Advances made by the Treasury to the Belgian Government from the beginning of the war to the Armistice amounted to $171,780,000. This principal sum, however, includes advances of $499,400 made to enable the Belgians to pay the interest due November 15, 1917, and $1,571,468.42 to enable the payment of the interest due May 15, 1918. The interest on the advances has been paid up to April 15, 1919, the interest due from May 15, 1918, to that date having been paid out of Treasury loans for which the United States holds Belgian obligations, which, however, were made after November 11, 1918, the date of the Armistice. This latter advance would not come within the terms of the Agreement above mentioned. If, therefore, the United States accepts payment of Belgian obligations given before the Armistice by receiving a corresponding amount of German obligations, it would seem that it should receive German obligations amounting to $171,780,000 with interest from April 15, 1919.

Although it is understood that England and France will take their share of the German bonds when received by Belgium, I am informed that the Reparation Commission has not as yet finally determined the details of the issuance of the necessary bonds by the German Government. A recommendation at this time that suitable legislative action should be taken may appear somewhat premature, but in view of the approaching termination of my Administration I have brought this matter to your attention, hoping that suitable action may be taken at the appropriate time.

Respectfully submitted,

T MS (WP, DLC).
    [1] The following message was sent to the Senate and House of Representatives on February 22, 1921, and is printed, verbatim (except that the "Respectfully submitted" was omitted), in *Cong. Record*, 66th Cong., 3d sess., p. 3598.

From Franklin Randolph Mayer

My dear Mr. President: New York February 18th, 1921.

It is with a feeling of disappointment that I am compelled to admit that the good news regarding the believed recovery of the desk you used on the "s.s. GEORGE WASHINGTON" which I gave you in my letter of the 8th instant is not confirmed by the latest reports I have just received on the matter.

We have been able to secure a photograph of your desk and the comparison of it with the desk believed to be the one you used on the "s.s. GEORGE WASHINGTON" convinvingly [convincingly] demonstrated that unfortunately our original thought was erroneous.

Being now in possession of a photograph of your desk we will be in a position to continue our efforts to locate the original with better chances of success.

Hoping that our continued endeavors may at last bring about the recovery of this historic desk, I have the honor to remain,

Very truly yours,   Franklin Randolph Mayer

TLS (WP, DLC).

From Norman Hezekiah Davis

My dear Mr. President: [Washington] February 19, 1921.

I desire to call your attention to the enclosed telegram from Ambassador Wallace,[1] and to submit for your consideration the attached cable to be sent to Ambassador Wallace for transmission to the Council of the League of Nations.[2] I had hesitated about sending a direct communication to the League of Nations, at least without your approval, but in view of the fact that the Allies apparently submitted the terms and allocation of the mandates for the Pacific Islands and certain African territories to the Council of the League, which officially approved them, I have come to the conclusion that it is necessary, in order to complete our record, to make this direct communication to the Council of the League of Nations. Such action seems necessary since in the approved form of the mandate covering the Island of Yap the WHEREAS clauses preceding the mandate terms contain the unwarranted statement that "the Principal Allied and Associated Powers" have conferred the mandate for all the islands in the Pacific north of the Equator on Japan and have proposed the terms to the Council of the League. As the Council is to meet on Monday, the twenty-first, I should appreciate a word from you at your earliest convenience.

Faithfully yours,   [Norman H. Davis]

CCL (SDR, RG 59, 862i.01/106A, DNA).
[1] H. C. Wallace to SecState, No. 116, Feb. 17, 1921, T telegram (SDR, RG 59, 862i.01/34, DNA). Wallace warned that the League Council would next meet on February 21 and would soon afterward be giving final approval of both "A" and "B" mandates, and it was reasonable to assume that the Council would consider American views on the whole mandate question. He also thought that it would be advisable to file a formal protest against the Council's action on December 17, 1920, in designating Japan as the mandatory for all former German islands north of the equator, including Yap, in spite of the State Department's earlier protest against the award of Yap to Japan. Wallace's telegram is printed in FR 1921, I, 87-88.
[2] A CC MS (N. H. Davis Papers, DLC; CC MS, SDR, RG 59, 862i.01/106A, DNA). This proposed telegram to the President of the Council of the League restated the American position on the question of Yap. It was never sent. Wilson, Colby, and Davis probably discussed the proposed telegram and decided that Colby should rewrite it in order to restate the American position more strongly and at greater length, and also to use it as a means of officially conveying the Secretary of State's message to Lord Curzon of

Nov. 20, 1920, to the League Council. For whatever reason, this is what Colby did in the telegram that was sent. It is printed as BC to H. C. Wallace, Feb. 21, 1921, n.2 to which cites the message to Curzon.

Cary Travers Grayson to Cleveland Hoadley Dodge

Dear Mr. Dodge: The White House February 19, 1921.

I received both of your letters—February 4th and 14th. My delay in acknowledging them has been due to the fact that I have been confined to bed for over three weeks with pleurisy and have been very sick. I have been unable to do anything during this time, and this is the first letter I have written since my illness.

Concerning the Pierce-Arrow car, I had communicated with the Company and they offered to let the President have it, with all of the equipment, for $3500, which is a great bargain. Since you and Mr. McCormick and other friends of the President are considering the matter to which you refer in your letter, I am wondering if this automobile proposition might not be imposing too much upon the good nature of yourself and the others mentioned by you. You have certainly shown a fine and generous spirit in interesting yourself in these matters, which, I know, will add so much to the pleasure and comfort of the President and Mrs. Wilson after they leave the White House.

When I regain my strength I am going to try to visit New York for a few days. If I do, I shall take the liberty of calling you up, as I am anxious to have a talk with you similar to the one we had when you were here in Washington last.

The President is making steady improvement every week, and I am sure you would notice a decided improvement in his appearance and in his movements.

With warm personal regards, believe me,

Sincerely yours,   Cary T. Grayson

TLS (received from Phyllis Boushall Dodge).

Cary Travers Grayson to Edward Parker Davis

Dear Doctor Davis: [The White House] February 19, 1921.

I have received your letter of February 11th and have read it with a great deal of interest. I have been confined to bed for three weeks with an attack of grippe and pleurisy but am up and about again. I have had a pretty hard time of it and am now improving daily.

What you say about your talk with Mr. McCormick is most interesting. The President does not know anything about the proposition. I am happy to be able to report that he is steadily improving. He has made more improvement in the last month than in any previous month.

The President's house is located at 2340 S Street, N.W. Dr. Axson can be reached at the Rice Institute, Houston, Texas.

With warm personal regards both to Mrs. Davis and yourself,
                              Sincerely yours,   [Cary T. Grayson]

CCL (received from James Gordon Grayson and Cary T. Grayson, Jr.).

From Warren Gamaliel Harding

                                        St. Augustine, Florida.
My dear Mr. President: February 20, 1921.

I gratefully acknowledge your note of February seventeenth, and thank you very sincerely for expressing our wishes to the house-keeper at the White House concerning arrangements for the first day of our coming there. You have been very considerate and ex-ceedingly kind, and I should like you to know of my grateful appre-ciation.

If it is becoming to take note of some of the expressions carried in the press, I note that you are hesitant about your participation in such inaugural ceremonies as are to be observed on March 4th. I want to take this opportunity of saying that whatever program for yourself best suits your convenience will be wholly agreeable to me in every way. I realize quite well that in your convalescence it is quite impossible for you to stand throuhgout [throughout] an in-augural address, and I can well believe your presence, except un-der the most genial weather conditions, would be attended by dan-ger to you. I would not wish you to take such a risk merely to be courteous to me. Perhaps all this is unnecessary, but I have wished you to know that I am not unmindful of the situation, and to assure you that any program which best suits your personal convenience will be accepted by me in the same spirit in which I take your cour-teous note to be written.
                    Very truly yours,   Warren G Harding

TLS (WP, DLC).

From the Shorthand Diary of Charles Lee Swem

21 February, 1921

Ike Hoover says about the President that he more nearly resembles McKinley than any other of the Presidents in the White House in that, like McKinley, he is more human and more natural. Ike says: "With Roosevelt there was a lot of slapping on the back and 'good fellow' business, but that was the end of it. You could not approach Roosevelt on the common ground of humanity, whereas on the contrary I can go up to the President and talk to him just as I would with you—but there is always the feeling present that you have got to do right."

JRT transcript (WC, NjP) of CLSsh (C. L. Swem Coll., NjP).

From the Diary of Josephus Daniels

February Monday 21, 1921

Talked over some tribute to the President. Baker thought a letter signed by all—Wilson agreed. Meredith a separate letter but to be bound.

Colby thought something in silver. Why not his chair?

I suggested that all members of cabinet meet & talk it over for Colby to ask them.

"One Secy of State was bounced for calling a cabinet meeting— Did I wish to get rid of him?"

To Paul Brunett[1]

My dear Mr. Burnett: [The White House] 21 February, 1921

We have now seen on the screen the pictures of my two official trips to France which you were generous enough to send to us, and I want to express my grateful appreciation of the generous attitude towards myself which is evidenced by the titles to the pictures. It gave me very great gratification.

                    Cordially and sincerely yours,   [Woodrow Wilson]

CCL (WP, DLC).
   [1] Of the Pathe Exchange, New York. About these films, see the Swem shorthand diary, Jan. 30, 1921.

To Walker Downer Hines

My dear Hines: [The White House] 21 February, 1921

Thank you for your letter of the twenty-sixth of January.

You may be sure that it was a pleasure to show my confidence in you by assigning you to the important duty to which you are now giving such earnest and successful attention. I shall look forward, when I have the necessary leisure of mind, to make myself acquainted with the results of your arbitration.

With the most cordial good wishes for the New Year,

Faithfully and sincerely yours,   [Woodrow Wilson]

CCL (WP, DLC).

From Thomas William Lamont

Dear Mr. President   Thomasville, Ga. 21 February '21

You may or may not have seen the enclosed statement[1] which I gave out at St. Augustine last Tuesday, following a brief conference that I had with Senator Harding. He telegraphed me to see him, and when I got there he said he wanted to ask me about these rumors that were going about as to some possible commitment at Paris, in the matter of the Allied indebtedness to the United States.

Of course I explained to him in detail that there was not the shadow of a commitment; that in fact you and all your staff had consistently taken a strong position against any suggestion of cancellation or debt-consolidation.

Mr. Harding said that he had already inferred that such had been our attitude. Then he added: "I think it only fair to Pres't Wilson and to his advisers that the fact be made clear at once." He asked me whether I would not issue a statement on the subject, and gave it as his opinion that such a statement, coming from a layman, so to speak, would have fully as much weight as if issued by a member of the administration itself.

He suggested further that if issued at once, following my interview with him, it would probably gain wide publicity. So I at once wrote out this statement which he read over, and then I handed it to the newspaper men.

I hope, my dear Mr. President, that you have not thought me going beyond proper bounds in making this published denial of persistent & false reports as to our attitude at Paris? Senator Harding said that "international bankers" so-called, were popularly supposed to be the ones—if any—who favored debt cancellation and therefore he thought it wise for one of *them* to make this declaration as to our Paris attitude.

I recall with great pleasure our luncheon with you and Mrs. Wilson a fortnight ago. It did my heart good—and my wife's too—to talk & visit with you once again in the old way. I have been getting a rest here[2] for a few days; but shall be back at my office in New York on Feby 24.

With great respect & deep regard I am, as always, dear Mr. President,   Very Sincerely Yours   Thomas W. Lamont

ALS (WP, DLC).
    [1] In this statement, Lamont said that he had assured Harding that there was absolutely no truth in the oft-repeated rumor that there had been some secret understanding in Paris between Wilson and his advisers, on the one hand, and French and British representatives, on the other hand, to the effect that the Allied indebtedness to the United States should be canceled in whole or in part. "To repeat," the statement added, "there was no commitment, expressed or implied, near or remote, moral or otherwise, as to the handling of the allied indebtedness to the United States." CC MS (WP, DLC). See also the *New York Times*, Feb. 16, 1921.
    [2] At Springwood Plantation.

From Jesse Holman Jones

My Dear Mr President   Washington, Monday Feby 21st 1921

You and Mrs Wilson gave my wife[1] and me a pleasure today that we greatly appreciate—and will never forget.

The sight of you or the sound of your voice especially if speaking to me, has always been the greatest inspiration to me. You came at a time when you and the qualities you possess were especially needed, you gave more to mankind & the world than is now realized or appreciated except by the unbiased thinking people. You fell in the great battle—wounded—but not until you had carried the flag to Victory.

The principles that you have paid so dearly for—and with such poor assistance and understanding in many instances, will—must ultimately survive.

I salute you The Commander in Chief of a great cause as well as of our great country
          Sincerely & Affectionately Yrs   Jesse H Jones

ALS (WP, DLC).
    [1] Mary Gibbs Jones of Houston, Texas, whom Jones had married on December 15, 1920. The Wilsons had just had them to lunch. About this occasion, see also S. Axson to EBW, Feb. 26, 1921.

Bainbridge Colby to Hugh Campbell Wallace

Washington, February 21, 1921.

No. 107 Referring again to your 116, February 17, and our Number 103, February 20, 1921, 11 p.m.,[1] you will please deliver the following note immediately to the President of the Council of the League of Nations, setting it forth exactly as herewith transmitted, including ascription and signature.

The reason for this careful instruction is that as Ambassador you have no official contact with the League and no recognized capacity even as a conduit for the transmission of communications. It is desired that the communication should be presented and delivered as coming directly from this Government. We have recourse to the method of sending it through you in order to expedite and assure its delivery to the President of the League, to whom it is addressed.

You will observe that the communication contemplates the delivery at the same time of a copy of the note of this Government dated November 20, 1920, addressed to Curzon, British Secretary of State for Foreign Affairs,[2] on the subject of the nature of a mandate. It is desired that you will deliver with the communication set forth below a clear copy of said note of November 20, of which you have a copy.

QUOTE. To the President and Members of the Council of the League of Nations:

1. The Government of the United States has received information that the Council of the League of Nations at its meeting which is to be held in Paris on this date, proposes to consider at length the subject of mandates, including their terms, provisions and allocation, and accordingly takes this opportunity to deliver to the Council of the League of Nations a copy of its note addressed under date of November 20, 1920, to His Excellency Lord Curzon of Kedleston, the British Secretary of State for Foreign Affairs, in which the views of the United States are quite fully set forth regarding the nature of the responsibilities of mandatory powers.

The attention of the Council of the League of Nations is particularly invited to the request therein made on behalf of this Government that the draft mandate forms intended to be submitted to the League of Nations be communicated to this Government for its

[1] BC to H. C. Wallace, No. 103, Feb. 20, 1921, T telegram (SDR, RG 59, 862i.01/34, DNA), instructing Wallace to ask the President and Council of the League of Nations to defer any action on mandates until they had received the communication from the United States Government which would be transmitted on February 21.

[2] Colby's note to Curzon is printed as an Enclosure with BC to WW, Nov. 19, 1920 (first letter of that date), Vol. 66.

consideration before submission to the Council of the League, in order that the Council might thus have before it an expression of the opinion of the Government of the United States on the form of such mandates, and a clear indication of the basis upon which the approval of this Government, which is essential to the validity of any determinations which may be reached, might be anticipated and received. It was furthermore stated in said note that the establishment of the mandate principle, a new principle in international relations and one in which the public opinion of the world is taking especial interest, would seem to require the frankest discussion from all pertinent points of view, and the opinion was expressed that suitable publicity should be given to the drafts of mandates which it is the intention to submit to the Council in order that the fullest opportunity might be afforded to consider their terms in relation to the obligations assumed by the mandatory powers and the respective interests of all governments who deem themselves concerned or affected.

A copy of this note was transmitted to the Governments of France and Italy requesting an interpretation by each government of the provisions of the agreement between Great Britain, Italy and France signed at Sevres on August 10, 1920, relating to the creation of spheres of special interests in Anatolia, in the light of this government's note to the British Government, of November 20, 1920. A reply has thus far been received only from the French Government,[3] in which attention is directed to Article X of the so-called Sevres Treaty, which provides, in favor of nationals of third Powers, for all economic purposes, free access to the so-called zones of special interest.

2. This Government is also in receipt of information that the Council of the League of Nations, at its meeting at Geneva on December 17, last, approved among other mandates a mandate to Japan embracing "all the former German islands situated in the Pacific Ocean and lying north of the Equator." The text of this mandate to Japan which was received by this Government and which, according to available information, was approved by the Council, contains the following statement:

Quote.

Whereas the principal Allied and Associated Powers agreed that in accordance with Article XXII, Part One, (Covenant of the League of Nations) of the said Treaty, a mandate should be conferred upon His Majesty the Emperor of Japan to administer the

[3] H. C. Wallace to NHD, Jan. 14, 1921, with Enclosure, printed in FR 1920, II, 674-75.

said islands, and have proposed that the mandate should be for-mulated in the following terms: Et cetera.[4]

Unquote.

The Government of the United States takes this opportunity re-spectfully and in the most friendly spirit to submit to the President and Members of the Council of the League that the statement above quoted is incorrect and is not an accurate recital of the facts. On the contrary, the United States which is distinctly included in the very definite and constantly used descriptive phrase "the Prin-cipal Allied and Associated Powers," has not agreed to the terms or provisions of the mandate which is embodied in this text, nor has it agreed that a mandate should be conferred upon Japan covering all the former German islands situated in the Pacific Ocean and lying north of the Equator.

The United States has never given its consent to the inclusion of the Island of Yap in any proposed mandate to Japan, but, on the other hand, at the time of a discussion of a mandate covering the former German Islands in the Pacific north of the Equator, and in the course of said discussion, President Wilson, acting on behalf of this Government, was particular to stipulate that the question of the disposition of the Island of Yap should be reserved for future consideration. Subsequently, this Government was informed that certain of "The Principal Allied and Associated Powers" were un-der the impression that the reported decision of the Supreme Council, sometimes described as the Council of Four, taken at its meeting on May 7, 1919, included or inserted the Island of Yap in the proposed mandate to Japan. This Government in notes ad-dressed to the Governments of Great Britain, France, Italy and Ja-pan, has set forth at length its contention that Yap had in fact been excepted from this proposed mandate and was not to be included therein. Furthermore, by direction of President Wilson, the respec-tive governments, above mentioned, were informed that the Gov-ernment of the United States could not concur in the reported de-cision of May 7, 1919, of the Supreme Council. The information was further conveyed that the reservations which had previously been made by this government regarding the Island of Yap were based on the view that the Island of Yap necessarily constitutes an indispensable part of any scheme or practicable arrangement of ca-ble communication in the Pacific, and that its free and unham-pered use should not be limited or controlled by any one Power.

While this Government has never assented to the inclusion of the Island of Yap in the proposed mandate to Japan, it may be

[4] E. Drummond to W. G. Harding, Feb. 17, 1921, printed in *FR 1921*, I, 118-20.

pointed out that even if one or more of the other Principal Allied and Associated Powers were under a misapprehension as to the inclusion of this island in the reported decision of May 7, 1919, nevertheless the notes, above mentioned, of the Government of the United States make clear the position of this Government in the matter. At the time when the several notes were addressed to the respective governments above mentioned, a final agreement had not been reached as to the terms and allocation of mandates covering the former German islands in the Pacific. Therefore, the position taken in the matter by the President on behalf of this Government and clearly set forth in the notes referred to, necessarily had the result of effectively withdrawing any suggestion or implication of assent, mistakenly imputed to this Government, long before December 17, 1920, the date of the Council's meeting at Geneva.

As one of the Principal Allied and Associated Powers, the United States has an equal concern and an inseparable interest with the other Principal Allied and Associated Powers in the overseas possessions of Germany, and concededly an equal voice in their disposition, which it is respectfully submitted cannot be undertaken or effectuated without its assent. The Government of the United States therefore respectfully states that it cannot regard itself as bound by the terms and provisions of said mandate and desires to record its protest against the reported decision of December 17 last, of the Council of the League of Nations in relation thereto, and at the same time to request that the Council, having obviously acted under a misapprehension of the facts, should reopen the question for the further consideration, which the proper settlement of it clearly requires.   Bainbridge Colby
Secretary of State
of the
United States.
End Quote.
Colby

T telegram (SDR, RG 59, 862i.01/34, DNA); printed in *FR 1921*, I, 89-92.

Cleveland Hoadley Dodge to Cary Travers Grayson

My dear Admiral Grayson: New York February 21, 1921.

I thank you very much for your good letter of February 19th, and am only sorry to hear that you have been knocked out yourself. It is a wonder that you have stood the strain as long as you have, and

I only hope you are going to be all right again soon, and that I may have the pleasure of seeing you here in New York.

The matter of the automobile is such a small one compared with the other big thing,[1] that we all certainly want to carry that out, and I sincerely hope, therefore, that you will close the matter with the Pierce-Arrow people at once, and if you will just drop me a line and tell me when you want the money, I can send you a check at short notice.

The news you give regarding the President is perfectly splendid and I earnestly hope that he is not going to knock himself out by trying to do too much in the last days of his administration and in all the functions at the time of the new inauguration.

With warm regards and best wishes

Yours sincerely,   Cleveland H Dodge

TLS (received from James Gordon Grayson and Cary T. Grayson, Jr.).
[1] That is, raising the money to help to pay for the Wilsons' new house.

From the Shorthand Diary of Charles Lee Swem

22 February, 1921

The Secretary[1] was responsible for the action of Palmer in recommending to the President a pardon for Debs.[2] He coaxed the Attorney General into doing it—either believing that the President would act favorably or hoping that the action of the Attorney General would have the effect of causing him to do so. The Secretary was "mum" about the whole matter after the President turned it down so emphatically and blamed Palmer for a foolish action.

JRT transcript (WC, NjP) of CLSsh (C. L. Swem Coll., NjP).
[1] That is, Tumulty.
[2] See AMP to WW, Jan. 29, 1921.

To William Faulkner McCombs

[The White House, Feb. 22, 1921]

I have heard with great distress of the death of your distinguished son,[1] and beg to extend my deepest sympathy to you and members of his family.   [Woodrow Wilson]

Printed in the *New York Times*, Feb. 23, 1921.
[1] William F. McCombs died on February 22, 1921.

A News Report

[*Feb. 22, 1921*]

WILSON TO DEVOTE HIS LIFE TO PEACE
He Tells Delegation of Harvard Students
He Will Give Remaining Days to Cause.

Washington, Feb. 22.—President Wilson expressed the determination today to devote himself upon retirement to private life to a continuation of his efforts toward world peace. In his first public utterance since the November election, the President, in receiving a delegation from the Woodrow Wilson Club of Harvard University at the White House, declared he had no intention of writing a history of the Paris Peace Conference. He added that was a task he preferred to leave to the professional historian, as the public might be prone to take into consideration the personal equation in any account of the peace proceedings he might write.

After their visit members of the delegation stated that they "were deeply impressed with the great heart of the President as he seemed in reflection to think over the question of peace. We were deeply touched by the President's faith in the ultimate accomplishment of his efforts toward peace and by the almost buoyant good humor with which he is leaving the White House."

They declared him as in good spirits and said they gained the impression that he was quite capable of conducting for a long time a vigorous campaign in behalf of world peace.

Robert C. Stuart, Jr. of Houston, Texas,[1] who headed the delegation, told the President that the club was organized on the second anniversary of the signing of the armistice, and that besides endeavoring to perpetuate Wilsonian ideas, it planned to collect historical manuscripts concerning his Administration and his activities at the Peace Conference to be placed in the Harvard University library.

The President received the delegation in his study, seated behind his desk. He shook hands with each of the six, apologizing for not rising, and in turn presented the visitors to Mrs. Wilson.

During his remarks the President removed his glasses several times and finally laid them down upon the desk. The college men said he spoke in a clear, well-modulated voice and with a fluency and wit which was afterward particularly remarked upon by the visitors.

Mrs. Wilson, who was standing beside the President, apparently much moved by the tribute expressed by the college men, expressed a wish that she might make a speech, but said she would not because she never had. She afterward escorted the delegation to the door. After thanking them for their visit she said:

"The President was deeply touched by your mission and your message." . . .

Printed in the *New York Times*, Feb. 23, 1921.
   [1] Robert Cummins Stuart, Jr., a senior at Harvard, who had organized a Woodrow Wilson Club at that university in November 1920. See, e.g., WW to R. C. Stuart, Jr., Nov. 20, 1920, Vol. 66.

From Oscar Wilder Underwood

My dear Mr. President: [Washington] February 22, 1921.

Since I received your letter[1] in reference to my making some suggestions concerning the veto of the so-called Emergency Tariff Bill, the bill has passed the Senate and has been sent to conference. I understand there are a great many differences among the Republican members of the conference committee, and I think it is entirely possible that they will not reach an agreement before the close of this session of Congress, and in the end the bill may not reach you at all. But on the other hand, it may be acted on hurriedly at any time. I am, therefore, enclosing herein a memorandum you requested and hope that it may be of service to you.[2]

I have not gone into the details of the bill but have only touched on the general principles involved. First, the abuse of the taxing power in exercising it for the benefit of special interests. Second, the effort to increase the cost of living when the natural tendency of the market should be downward instead of upward, and, third, the inevitable result that this class of legislation must have on the development of our foreign trade and the collection of the debts that European countries owe us. This bill is not only a bad piece of legislation from every angle but is admitted to be unwise by many of those who voted for it.

With best wishes, I am

Sincerely yours,   O W Underwood

TLS (WP, DLC).
   [1] See WW to O. W. Underwood, Feb. 5, 1921.
   [2] A T MS (WP, DLC). Wilson must not have liked Underwood's draft. In any event, Houston wrote the veto message printed at March 3, 1921. Houston, in his *Eight Years with Wilson's Cabinet, 1913-1920* (2 vols., Garden City, N. Y., 1926), II, 141-47, reprints the veto message.

From Bainbridge Colby

My dear Mr. President: Washington February 22, 1921.

I have been giving pretty constant reflection to the subject we have discussed, of "our" future. (I hope the word may be realized.)

I have done a little consulting with circumspect friends who are tried and true, and am ready to state my conclusions. I am for the plan thoroughly and unreservedly, and am confident that it will work out well.

It is an important decision and I have kept a tight rein upon my imagination, not to succumb to the lure of many possibilities in connection with the idea which instantly presented themselves to me. I have constantly reminded myself that it is largely a business question and must be approached in a pragmatic temper.

The proposal meets every test that I have applied to it, and it bristles with possibilities of the pleasantest and most substantial kind,—contingencies, to be sure, but right good and wholesome and friendly contingencies.

I have no hesitation about you or your part in it. Any sense of inadequacy in the technical branches of the law, because of the long interruption in your active practice of the profession, should not weigh in your decision. Proficiency in this field is largely mechanical. It could readily be supplied and you could command it at will. Furthermore, in practicing the profession as a man of your eminence would be called upon and expected to do, you would not be much, if at all, concerned with this aspect of the law. It would be wasteful of your energy and talent, and not judicious from the standpoint of your clients or yourself.

You would be a great lawyer,—indeed you are one now, because of your mind, your knowledge of life, of men, of great transactions, of the principles upon which human affairs are controlled, directed and decided, and the wide range and depth of your learning. Throughout the war and again during this precious year of association with you as a member of your Cabinet, I have continually been struck with your remarkable skill in handling facts. Your mind goes to the center of the most intricate and unfamiliar case with a true aim. I have never seen this faculty of yours equalled. And you do it without apparent effort, without retracing steps or requiring re-statements, and what is more, without any suggestion of lagging judgment or indecision. This is a rare power even among the foremost men at the bar.

You need have no apprehension that you would be subjected to undue demands upon your energy, which might arrest or retard the recovery of your strength. It would be unnecessary for you to keep hours at your office except as you felt inclined to. The fact that you could be consulted at your home by appointment, that you are in touch with your firm, that your attention and thought were enlisted in your client's service, and your name on the brief and in the case would be in themselves a very valuable service, leaving you to determine what measure of further service you would render and what role you cared to play in any matter of business that was in hand.

Your name would be the most valuable name, in my opinion, that a law firm could have. The firm would be a national one by reason of it, drawing its patronage from the widest possible field and enabling you to exercise a discriminating selection of the business you cared to undertake.

I am sure we would get remunerative business. Indeed I know it.

I hope you do not think I am going too fast,—getting "off side," as we used to say when I played football. When the resolving process is finished, and I feel from my point of view that it is, I am for getting ahead rather promptly. I think that an announcement should be made before you leave office, whatever the actual date may be on which you would think it well to inaugurate the arrangement. I think the firm should have an office in New York as well as here. There are many other details which greatly interest me, and which would be pleasant to discuss, at your convenience—I hope soon.

Sincerely always,   Bainbridge Colby

TLS (WP, DLC).

From William Edward Dodd

My dear Mr. President: Chicago Feby. 22, 1921.

Before you leave the high office which you have so greatly honored and elevated, I wish to [sic] you would let me, as one who has studied your career and work with as much care as I was capable of, say what I at any rate think of your services to this country and to all the world. Although what I say can have no more significance than the words of a plain citizen, I do, nevertheless, wish to let you know, just as you turn over the baton of office to another, how very highly I, and I believe nearly all other members of my profession, regard your legacy to all of us and all who must come after us. Only to-day I received letters from Professors Turner and Jameson[1] indicating their great admiration.

It has been rare that History has been just to many of those who have served mankind best. But in your case I am convinced that justice is going to be done you, and right speedily. There are ardent friends who think errors of tactics have been made. Of these History will not judge severely. It is the purpose, the intentions and the ideals that really form the basis on which the fame of a great man must rest—as well, of course, as upon his general equipment and ability.

There are three presidents who must be counted as unique, Washington, Lincoln and Wilson. There was one founder of a party, preacher of democracy, who stands alone in our hall of fame, Jefferson. To compare him with the other three is natural in some respects, but in others the comparison does not hold. I can not help thinking that your place is soon going to be alongside that of Washington. And it may be doubted whose fame will prove the more appealing as the decades pass. Turner says sometimes he fears it was a mistake to go to Paris. I tell him that to have pressed your ideals in Paris at the great and awful moment, regardless of the immediate consequences, is going to prove to be the great thing. You went into the very heart of cynicism and the old European order and begged men to look toward a better order. That they endeavored to destroy your influence; that the great and the powerful at home denounced you, will merely serve to prove to future generations your high purpose and your greater wisdom.

No; I can not consider that an error, except perhaps as to your own political fortunes. And what you did during those four years, after summoning all forward-looking men to your side, and what you urged men to do even in the midst of a world war, stands out a very marvel of accomplishment, more important far than the performance of any other president whatsoever. There is no comparison any where in our history. And to have done it against the violent opposition of the owners of four-fifths of our national wealth and with the aid of one of the least efficient and least co-operative of parties! That is the wonder. I sometimes think you and your work have saved us from a revolution.

There is not space in a letter, even if you had the time and patience to read, for me to say half what I think ought to be said to you from every home in this land. You have done a great work and done it nobly. You laid before the world a great and a wise programme, which the world has not accepted—because of our awful conduct—and these two things constitute your title to the high place that you enjoy now and shall surely enjoy hereafter. You have moreover inspired young men as young men have not been inspired since Jefferson. If they prove true, we shall all receive great benefit, or our successors shall do so.

May I close with one remark in reply to a question you raised when I saw you that day in bed. Do not fail to write as much of your story as you can write, and write it soon. You see how others are writing. You must not ever remain silent. Professor Turner wrote to ask if you were not going to prepare your story of Paris. I suspect he has written you.[2] George Creel was here to-day. We talked over the subject. When I saw you, you were disposed to leave it all to others, not write "another Jefferson's Anas."[3] You must not yield to that feeling, much as you might like to keep silent while so many small men shout.

After much thought, I have come to the conclusion that you ought to dictate something every day. Creel says you dislike dictating. I know that is a poor way to write good books. I have never been able to dictate a paragraph of anything but a letter. Only now you simply can not write and polish and mature all you say. There is too much to be said and you have undergone too much of a strain. After all, I believe your writing, even by this method, will be fine. You have written and spoken so much that is superb. At any rate write. Your work is going to be the source from which thousands of men will in the future draw information. Do not fail them.

As to your papers, I wrote your daughter, Miss Margaret,[4] when I tried to satisfy her about my stiff story of the early religious environment and so forth, that I hoped you would put your papers, every scrap, in the control of a commission of historians, say two in the field of American history and one in the field of European history. For the European I would, unless there is reason to the contrary, think that Haskins would be a good representative. These men should be such as have your utmost confidence; and they should be authorized to proceed at once to classify and calendar every bit of material you have. This material should be open, as they determine, to historians—at any rate it should be open to the committee.

If possible there should be a trained historian to do the work of classification and assist you in writing as many volumes as you feel able to write. Mr. Baker may be able to assist you in the work immediately in hand, that bearing on the Paris conference. But all the whole story of your two administrations needs to be told soon. Mr. Baker is not the man for that, good a man as I know him to be. Your work is going to be attacked with a bitterness almost unparalelled for some time to come. You need the very best of help in the preparation of your volumes—not defenses; I can not think of you in the role of defending yourself.

Mr. Creel says that he thinks financial assistance for all this work can be found. If so, that would enable you to do so much

more than you could possibly do otherwise. I hope he has found this aid; and I hope you will not refuse it. Pardon so long a story.
                    Yours sincerely,   William E. Dodd

TLS (WP, DLC).
    [1] F. J. Turner to W. E. Dodd, Feb. 19, 1921, ALS, and J. F. Jameson to W. E. Dodd, Feb. 19, 1921, TLS, both in the W. E. Dodd Papers, DLC.
    [2] Insofar as we know, he did not do so.
    [3] Jefferson, while Secretary of State, made informal notes on Cabinet meetings, his contemporaries, including Hamilton, etc. He later had them bound but never published them himself. The notes were subsequently published in part in editions of Jefferson's works. See the editorial note, "The Anas," in Charles C. Cullen *et al.*, eds., *The Papers of Thomas Jefferson*, Vol. 22 (Princeton, N. J., 1986), pp. 33-38.
    [4] W. E. Dodd to Margaret W. Wilson, Jan. 20, 1921.

To Jesse Holman Jones

My dear Jones: [The White House] 23 February, 1921

Your note from the Shoreham gave me very great pleasure. You may be sure that it was very delightful to us to be able to see Mrs. Jones and you, and we shall always remember the occasion with the greatest pleasure. Please give our warm regards to Mrs. Jones and, believe me, always
                    Your sincere and obliged friend,   [Woodrow Wilson]

CCL (WP, DLC).

From Breckinridge Long

My dear Mr. President: [Washington] February 23, 1921.

You will pardon, I hope, an intrusion upon your privacy at this time but it would not square with my conscience if I should permit these few remaining days to lapse without trying to express something of the admiration which your administration has aroused and some of the affection which a proximity to you has inspired in an humble but most sincere friend.

No glittering possibilities of reward now render it impolitic to record, nor can suspicion that the head speaks rather than the heart now cause a misconstruction to be placed upon a simple confession of an admiration, always publicly proclaimed, and of an affection which has grown deeper with the passage of years and events.

When I was an undergraduate at Princeton[1] you, in the lecture room, had an influence upon a character, then in its impressionable stage, which moulded it for life. You taught me a philosophy of life; you raised my eyes from the ordinary to the extra-ordinary;

you aroused my thought, my ambition—awakened a drowsing intellect;—you did that service for a man for which the beneficiary
can only be indebted for life and yet during all his life find his efforts inadequate to repay.

When you entered the world of politics and rose through succeeding successes to the position of preeminence in power and
prestige in the world, it was my pleasure to follow and in my little
way to help. I believed in your political theories, I believed in your
policies, I believed in you—and I still do.

You will go down to posterity as the great figure in American
history and as the one great outstanding statesman in the history
of the world. Your federal administration reached, in peace as well
as in war, the highest point of efficiency. When it came to the
Great Test, America rose under your influence and by virtue of
your leadership clove through a maze of war and made it possible
for the people of the world to realize peace once more.

The advantages of the peace you made possible have not been
realized because political opposition in its own dastardly and un-
wholesome form was able to mislead a public suffering from the
natural reaction of the war. It is said that your opponents have
won—but they have not. You have won, and their temporary accession to governmental control will afford them an opportunity to
prove beyond doubt, but by negative process, the correctness of
your position.

Your policies will survive and your administration will serve as a
beacon light for those which will follow. In a few years there will
be installed a government whose creed will be that of Woodrow
Wilson and whose leaders will follow the trail you have blazed.

My official service under you was the great honor of my life. It
was my constant regret that my ability was not commensurate with
my desire to handle the constant stream of questions which
coursed through the office, if for no other reason that you might be
relieved of some of the work which would ultimately find its way
to you; and I only fear that in my eagerness, as it occasionally developed and according to Departmental custom, I erred by proceeding too far.

I have looked forward to the time when I might speak without
fear of causing misapprehension. So, as your administration draws
to a close and as is being recorded the last line in the great epoch
of American history, I send you the free statement of an humble
servant and of a true friend, who wishes for you a full return to
health and the best that life holds.

Believe me, my dear Mr. President, while I live,

                Most sincerely,   Breckinridge Long

TLS (WP, DLC).
    [1] He was a member of the Class of 1904. We have only recently discovered that his full name was Samuel Miller Breckinridge Long.

From Joseph Taylor Robinson

My dear Mr. President: Washington, D. C. February 23, 1921.

I approach you in this matter with a great deal of diffidence, and with some embarrassment. You will know that Senator Kirby[1] and I have not been politically intimate in Arkansas, and I can easily understand why you personally, for reasons you have stated to me, would wish to turn with reluctance from any suggestion that had in mind the appointment of my colleague, Senator Kirby, to any position under the Federal government. Notwithstanding the foregoing, my colleague realizes his irretrievable mistakes in the early period of his service here, which mistakes were quite as repugnant to me as they could possibly have been to you, and for many months he has in every possible way cooperated with your friends in the Senate, until he is now regarded as one of the strongest among us.

In no sense extenuating, or in the least condoning, his conduct toward you in the early period of his service in the Senate, I feel that in view of all the circumstances it would be a gracious and generous act on your part and something which all of your intimate friends in the Senate, especially men like Honorable John Sharpe Williams, Senator Culberson, and myself would cordially appreciate.

The suggestion I have in mind is the appointment of Senator Kirby to the Tariff Commission. You probably know that under the situation now existing in the Senate no one but a member of that body will be confirmed if appointed to a membership on this Commission.

This is, probably, my dear Mr. President, the last official matter that I will address you on, and, before closing, let me say to you with what real pleasure I have served under your leadership and how sincerely and devotedly I know you have served the best interests of our country throughout both terms of your Administration as Chief Executive. No doubt it will gratify you, as it has me, to observe the reaction in sentiment which is occurring throughout the country, indicative of the fact that our people generally are approaching a time when their realization of your great public sacrifices and achievements will become thorough and complete. I have not only grown to have great admiration for your high ability, but I have learned to have a deep affection for you.

Believe me, my dear Mr. President,
Sincerely your friend,   Jos. T. Robinson.

TLS (WP, DLC).
¹ William Fosgate Kirby, Democratic senator from Arkansas, 1916-1921, who had failed of renomination in 1920. Among other things, on February 7, 1917, he had voted against the resolution approving Wilson's action in breaking diplomatic relations with the German Empire and was one of the "little group of wilful men," that is, the eleven senators who by filibuster defeated the bill authorizing Wilson to arm merchantmen in the closing days of the Sixty-fourth Congress.

Cary Travers Grayson to Cleveland Hoadley Dodge

My dear Mr. Dodge: The White House February 23, 1921.

I wish to thank you most heartily for your generous note. Since you insist on taking care of the automobile matter, I suggest that you send the check either to Mrs. Wilson or to me—I leave this to your good judgment.

I want you to know that I deeply appreciate your kind personal expressions.

With warmest regards,
Sincerely yours,   Cary T. Grayson

TLS (received from Phyllis Boushall Dodge).

To George Creel

[The White House] 24 February, 1921

Cannot be sure about Sunday but come and let us know of your arrival and I will if I can.   Woodrow Wilson.

T telegram (Letterpress Books, WP, DLC).

Cleveland Hoadley Dodge to Cary Travers Grayson

My dear Admiral Grayson: New York February 24, 1921.

I am delighted to get your note of yesterday, and to know that you can close the matter of the automobile. Seeing that I have had all the correspondence with you in the matter, I think it would be better to send the check directly to you, and am therefore enclosing check for $3500, which I understand will pay for the car, and that you will tell the President it is a gift from his five old stalwart

Princeton supporters, namely, Cyrus H. McCormick, Edward W. Sheldon, Thomas D. Jones, David B. Jones and Cleveland H. Dodge, all of whom have expressed a desire to participate in giving the retiring President his old accustomed car, to make him comfortable and happy. I think a little thing of this kind will please him almost as much as the larger matter which Mr. McCormick and Mr. Baruch are attending to. I unfortunately have not been able to see Mr. Baruch, but I have no doubt that he is communicating directly with you.

It must make you and the White House family very happy to feel the President is so near the end of his arduous work there, and I sincerely hope and trust he will not overdo matters, and use himself up in the last few days of his wonderful administration.

Thanking you for giving us this opportunity of expressing our love and affection for the great "old" man,

Very sincerely yours,   Cleveland H Dodge

TLS (received from James Gordon Grayson and Cary T. Grayson, Jr.).

To Joseph Patrick Tumulty

My dear Tumulty: [The White House] 25 February, 1921

As an expression of my great confidence in you and of my desire to see you placed where you will be most serviceable, I have taken the liberty of appointing you a Commissioner on the part of the United States on the International Joint Commission of the United States and Canada for the adjustment and settlement of all questions which are now pending or may hereafter arise regarding the use of boundary waters between the United States and the Dominion of Canada, as provided for in Article VII of the Treaty between the United States and Great Britain, signed at Washington, January 11, 1909. I hope that it will be agreeable and convenient for you to accept this appointment which I make with the greatest pleasure.[1]   Affectionately yours,   [Woodrow Wilson]

CCL (WP, DLC).
[1] Although Tumulty did not do so in a letter to Wilson, he declined this appointment.

To Joseph Taylor Robinson

My dear Senator: [The White House] 25 February, 1921

I hope that you already know how sincere my admiration for you is, indeed how genuine my affection.[1] You have been a wonderful friend and have excited my constant admiration as well as my loyal friendship. It, therefore, grieves me more than I can say to feel obliged to turn away from any suggestion you make, but I must frankly say (for I think friends ought above all things else to be absolutely frank with one another) that my observation of Senator Kirby convinces me that it would not be a service to the public to appoint him to any public office. I do not know any man who has more grievously disappointed me with respect to anything that might reasonably have been expected of him.

I know that you will understand, even if I disappoint you.

With the warmest regard,

Cordially and sincerely yours,   [Woodrow Wilson]

CCL (WP, DLC).
    [1] Wilson was replying to J. T. Robinson to WW, Feb. 23, 1921.

To Thomas William Lamont

My dear Lamont: [The White House] 25 February, 1921

Thank you for your letter of the twenty-first of February. I am very glad to have an authentic copy of your statement to the Press after you saw Mr. Harding. I did not read it at the time, because I was sure that whatever it contained was true, since it emanated from you. I have been very much puzzled how to give the whole matter publicity in detail without ruffling the sensibilities of some people on the other side of the water and making the situation perhaps a little more difficult than it is.

Do you think it would be wise to publish the memorandum of Keyne's [Keynes'] which was presented to me at Paris and my reply to it?[1] Or do you think that that would be bad manners in diplomacy?

In haste, with warmest regard to both Mrs. Lamont and yourself,

Faithfully yours,   [Woodrow Wilson]

CCL (WP, DLC).
    [1] Keynes' memorandum is printed as an Enclosure with D. Lloyd George to WW, April 23, 1919, Vol. 58. Wilson's reply was WW to D. Lloyd George, May 5, 1919, *ibid.* Lamont and Norman H. Davis had prepared the draft of this letter.

To Breckinridge Long

My dear Long: The White House 25 February, 1921

Your letter of the twenty-third has not only gratified me. It has deeply touched me. I am indeed proud to have excited such sentiments in you with regard to myself. You may be sure that in return I have given you my entire confidence and that I have admired the admirable way in which you have performed the duties of your difficult office. I shall always follow you not only with interest but with genuine and lasting friendship. It is hard to say good-bye.

With warmest regard,

Cordially and sincerely yours,   Woodrow Wilson

TLS (B. Long Papers, DLC).

From Roland Sletor Morris

My dear Mr. President: Washington February 25, 1921.

As I am closing out my work here at the Department my mind turns with profound gratitude to you for the permanent service you have rendered to our country and the world. I am so proud to have had a very small part in your administration, and for your kindness, your generosity and your leadership I thank you with all my heart.

May you be granted continued improvement in your health which means so much today in the cause of the world to which you have given your time and strength so unselfishly.

Mrs. Morris[1] joins me in every good wish to you and Mrs. Wilson.

Ever faithfully your devoted friend,   Roland S. Morris

TLS (WP, DLC).
[1] Augusta Shippen West Morris.

From the Shorthand Diary of Charles Lee Swem

26 February, 1921

The President received a letter from one of his relatives (Woodrow)[1] saying that the statement of the President's ancestry in the *Congressional Directory* was incorrect, that no one of the Woodrows ever emigrated to Ireland. They are wholly Scotch. The President replied that he had not known of the facts and that he was glad to have them called to his attention.

Therefore the President on his father's side is Scotch-Irish and on his mother's Scotch.

About the President's speech at the Jackson Democratic Club[2] before he was nominated, he said he would not prepare for it because he was not wanted there and wouldn't receive any attention anyway.

The President refused to grant Dudley Field Malone an interview for the purpose of discussing New York politics; referred him to Vance McCormick.[3] Malone was hurt and the President had to write him a long letter explaining.[4] He said after he had written it, "I wish people wouldn't have feelings in politics."

JRT transcript (WC, NjP) of CLSsh (C. L. Swem Coll., NjP).
[1] This letter is missing, but see WW to Marion Woodrow, Feb. 26, 1921. Marion was the daughter of James Woodrow and therefore Wilson's first cousin.
[2] He referred to Wilson's speech at the Jackson Day Dinner in Washington on January 8, 1912. His speech is printed at that date in Vol. 24.
[3] See D. F. Malone to WW, Aug. 2, 1916; WW to D. F. Malone, Aug. 3, 1916; and D. F. Malone to WW, Aug. 5, 1916, all in Vol. 37.
[4] WW to D. F. Malone, Aug. 8, 1916, Vol. 38.

To Roland Sletor Morris

My dear Morris: [The White House] 26 February, 1921

Thank you with all my heart for your letter of the twenty-fifth of February. I hope you know how I have valued your friendship and how delightful it has been to me to have an opportunity to show my confidence in you. I hope you know also how much I have admired the spirit and the success of your service in Japan.

Cordially and sincerely yours,   [Woodrow Wilson]

CCL (WP, DLC).

To Marion Woodrow

My dear Marion: The White House 26 February, 1921

Thank you for your letter of February twenty-third.[1] I must admit that I did not know that the statement in the Congressional Directory about my ancestry was incorrect and I am very glad to have the error called to my attention.

I am sincerely sorry to learn of Aunt Felie's illness and hope with all my heart that she is rapidly regaining her wonted strength.

Affectionately yours,   Woodrow Wilson

TLS (received from James Woodrow).
[1] It is missing.

From Newton Diehl Baker

Personal and Confidential.

My dear Mr. President: Washington. February 26, 1921.

I hope you will pardon my writing to you upon a matter about which you know more than I, and which is wholly outside the limits of my proper interest, but I think I can contribute some additional information. Senator Robinson, of Arkansas, has been to see me a number of times about the possibility of a favorable consideration by you of his colleague, Senator Kirby, for appointment on the Tariff Commission. In the early days, Kirby acted badly and joined forces with our adversaries, but from the day we declared war until now he has been as stalwart and constant a defender of the War Department and avocate of its policies in the Military Affairs Committee and in the Senate as we have had. Indeed, there has been no Senator to whom I could take the facts of any situation with as much confidence in his readiness to hear and his fairness to judge and to advocate our side of any controverted question. Senator Kirby, of course, is not a great man, but he has shown some of the elements of bigness in a very frank admission of his mistakes at the outset and in a very splendid and constant loyalty after he had seen the error of his early course. I know that Senator Robinson would deeply appreciate favorable consideration of Senator Kirby, if you found yourself able to give it, and as he could be confirmed, being now a member of the Senate, it is not too late for such an appointment to be made.

Respectfully yours,   Newton D. Baker

TLS (WP, DLC).

From Francis H. Robinson[1]

Dear Mr. President: The White House February 26, 1921.

Before you go out of office would it be asking too much to give me a letter of recommendation if you think me worthy of it? I would greatly appreciate it.

Thanking you for all the faovrs you have shown me and with best wishes for you and Mrs. Wilson, I am,

Sincerely yours,   Francis H. Robinson.

TLS (WP, DLC).
  [1] The White House chauffeur.

Stockton Axson to Edith Bolling Galt Wilson

Dearest Edith: Houston, Texas Feby 26, 1921

This is just a little "goodbye" note to you and the President as you leave the White House. I think the uppermost feelings in your mind will be relief, but there must be a touch of sadness too—I think it was Dr. Johnson (no sentimentalist) who said there is always sadness in doing anything the last time. So much has happened in these White House years that it will not be possible to leave the place indifferently. But, quoting Browning, "the best is yet to be"—happy, happy years in S Street—by the way, I fancy that it doesn't make any difference that I don't know the number—even Republican postmaster-generals will find the Woodrow Wilsons in Washington, I guess—without attachment of street-and-number address.

I had a little visit with Jesse Jones last night—just back—I haven't seen the "Mrs." yet. How good it was of you and the President to have them for lunch—you made them both very happy, and *he* will never forget that the President greeted him with "Hello, Jess!" He gave me my first news of Dr. Grayson's illness—hadn't heard a word of it—am sending the Doctor a note by this post.

Just because there happens to be lying on the table by me, as I write, a newspaper clipping, I am sending it.[1] Mrs. Hall, an elderly lady here who has always been one of my good friends (by the way, it is the Mrs. Hall who figures a good deal in the life of O. Henry[2]—it was on her ranch that he spent much time—indeed he came to Texas when Dr. & Mrs. Hall came down from their home in Greensboro, N. C., *his* home—and she "mothered" him). Mrs Hall handed me this after a lecture yesterday saying, "I don't suppose it is much as poetry, but read it." It is abominable poetry—no poetry at all—and even the *sentiment* the President won't like—he shrinks from that comparison, but I know it is just one of many thoughts in the same vein—you hear it everywhere. He leaves the White House with the hearts of the people in his keeping—by the way, did you know it was a Houston boy who led the delegation of Harvard students who called on the President and you the other day?[3]

If the Republican contingency think that the things Woodrow Wilson has stood for, and *stands* for, are dead they've another guess coming. We are just at the *beginning*! No President ever had the right to leave the White House with a conscience clearer than his—few with consciences so clear. He has suffered much, but not in vain—how does the scripture passage run?—though *he* wouldn't like that application either—"I shall see of the travail of my soul, and I shall be satisfied." He *will*, and he will have his great part in *making* it satisfactory too—may God spare him.

And you, dear, you have been, and are, most wonderful. Thank you for all you've done for me—and all of us.

With a heart full of love, for both of you   Stockton

P.S. I was with the Smiths[4] in New Orleans last week—they talk of "you all" all the time.

ALS (EBW Papers, DLC).

¹ The clipping is missing.
² About the relationship between Dr. and Mrs. James K. Hall and William Sidney Porter, see E. Hudson Long, *O. Henry: The Man and His Work* (Philadelphia, 1949), *passim*; and Richard O'Connor, *O. Henry: The Legendary Life of William S. Porter* (Garden City, N. Y., 1970), *passim*.
³ The "Houston boy" was of course Robert Cummins Stuart, Jr. For his and the Harvard students' meeting with Wilson, see the news report printed at Feb. 22, 1921.
⁴ Lucy Marshall Smith and Mary Randolph Smith of New Orleans, dear friends of Wilson and Ellen Axson Wilson.

From the Diary of Ray Stannard Baker

[The White House] Feby 28th [1921].

Still very busy at the White House. I had a talk with Mrs. Wilson & made arrangements for carrying on the work after they move into the new house in S. street. Certain rather disagreeable things have arisen which I learn about in a left handed way. Of course this work I am doing has been much coveted. The President was offered $150,000 for doing it himself¹—as he ought to do. George Creel, when he heard I was to do it, came down here & told Miss Wilson & Mr. Bolling, Mrs. Wilson's brother, that he could "make the President rich" out of these materials: that they were "worth half a million" &c&c. Of course they went straight to the President & Mrs. Wilson & urged the matter on them. But the President stood by his guns. He has made up his mind that I shall do it—and he will see it through. It would indeed be a terrible mistake for him to capitalize it in the way that George Creel would inevitably do it.—I cannot do it that way, nor make a fortune out of it.

¹ It is impossible to know precisely to what offer Baker was referring.

To Richard Jervis¹

My dear Jervis: [The White House] 28 February, 1921

Before leaving office, I want to express to you my warm personal appreciation of the attentive kindness with which you have taken part in watching over my safety and personal convenience. I hope that the best fortune will attend you in the future.

Sincerely yours,   [Woodrow Wilson]

CCL (WP, DLC).
¹ Of the Secret Service detail at the White House.

A News Report

[*March 1, 1921*]

President Bids Good-bye to His Cabinet;
Reviews Crowded Years at Last Meeting

Washington, March 1.—President Wilson said farewell to his Cabinet today at their last meeting. There was little formality about the proceedings, the session being devoted mainly to reminiscences of the eight years of President Wilson's Administration. All the members of the Cabinet were present, and the session lasted three and a half hours.

A good part of the time was taken up with a review by the President of the accomplishments of the Administration. What he said was described as impressive. He contended that it was necessary for the United States to enter the World War.

Members of the Cabinet joined in discussing phases of the President's policies, with the conclusion reached that the Administration had made a record to be proud of.

As a mark of affection the members of the Cabinet gave to the President the chair he had occupied at the Cabinet table during his two terms. This they bought from the Government.

In return the President gave to each member of his official family an autographed photograph of the Cabinet taken last week with the President at the head of the table.

After the meeting the President shook hands with the Cabinet officers and said to each a personal word of appreciation and farewell. At times the President's voice trembled as he extended his thanks for past services and good wishes for the future.

When the Cabinet members were gone the President remained behind for a few minutes to receive a delegation of the Valley Forge Historical Society, who presented to him a certificate as "Honorary Perpetual Benefactor" and the insignia of the organization, as a "teacher, writer and maker of history."

Raymond T. Baker, Director of the Mint, stepped into the room to wish the President farewell. "Take good care of the Mints," the President enjoined him as he shook his hand.

Rear Admiral Grayson, the President's physician, stopped long enough to wave a greeting, which the President acknowledged with a cheerful nod.

A few minutes later the President, leaning on his cane and limping slightly, passed slowly out of the executive offices where for more than six years before he was taken ill he thrashed out with his Cabinet momentous questions which faced the nation. It was probably his last visit to the offices and the leave-taking plainly af-

fected him. He descended the steps, and as he started down the
walk made a movement as if to return, but apparently reconsider-
ing the impulse, went straight forward and passed out of sight
around the corner of the building.[1]

Printed in the *New York Times*, March 2, 1921.
  [1] The following account by Houston, *Eight Years with Wilson's Cabinet*, II, 147-49,
is the only one by a member of the Cabinet:
  "Tuesday, March 1, 1921, we held our last Cabinet meeting. It had been decided to
hold it in the regular Cabinet room in the executive offices. I arrived a few minutes
early and saw the President coming through the White House grounds toward the
room. He was walking with great difficulty. It was a brave but tragic spectacle. I turned
away and walked into an adjoining room so that he might get seated, and then I entered
and took my place at his left. We discussed a few measures which were still before the
Congress, and something was said about the part the President would take in the exercises during the inauguration. He had not then had presented to him the full plans.
He made it clear that he expected and intended to carry out his full part in the exercises.
  "A brief pause ensued. Then one of the members of the Cabinet asked the President
how he was going to pass his time and if it was likely that he would write a history of
the Administration. The President replied that he would not write a history of his Administration, saying that he was too near the events and too closely personally associated with them to make it desirable or possible for him to do so. He said, in substance:
'I cannot write a history of these eight years. It is unnecessary for me to attempt to write
anything new. The people know everything that I have thought. There has been nothing which it was necessary or desirable for me to keep secret.' The same member of the
Cabinet said: 'But you must do something! What will you do?' The President reflected
a moment and said: 'I am going to try to teach ex-presidents how to behave.' Then he
added: 'There will be one very difficult thing for me, however, to stand, and that is Mr.
Harding's English.'
  "After the business was disposed of, our minds naturally turned to the experiences of
our eight strenuous years together and particularly to the President's personal struggles
and heroic endeavours. A short pause ensued. Then the Secretary of State, properly
speaking first, said in effect:
  " 'Mr. President, if I may presume to voice the sentiments of my colleagues, I have
the honour of saying that it has been a great distinction to serve you and with you in
the most interesting and fateful times of modern history. It has been a most satisfactory
and inspiring service. We shall keep watch of your progress toward better health with
affectionate interest and shall pray that your recovery may be rapid.'
  "It was then my part to say something. I turned toward the President and started to
speak but noticed that he was struggling under a powerful emotion and was trying to
control himself. His lips were trembling. He began to speak but hesitated a moment as
tears rolled down his cheeks. Then he said, brokenly: 'Gentlemen, it is one of the handicaps of my physical condition that I cannot control myself as I have been accustomed
to do. God bless you all.' This was a very touching statement. No greater trial could
come to a Scotch Presbyterian whose whole philosophy of life was self-control, to be
unable to master himself.
  "We got up quietly, shook hands with him, bade him farewell, and left the room. That
afternoon I returned to my office and dictated this letter which I sent him on Thursday."
  The letter just mentioned is DFH to WW, March 3, 1921.

To Finis James Garrett[1]

My dear Mr. Garrett: [The White House] March 1, 1921.

  My attention has recently been called to certain attacks made in
the House of Representatives, charging that certain men who rendered distinguished service in the war had profited out of the Government as a result of the fixing of the price of copper. These
charges and intimations have been satisfactorily answered, but a

statement of the facts in the matter of the fixing of the price of copper during the war, on my part, may further clarify the situation.

As a matter of fact, Mr. Bernard M. Baruch and Mr. John D. Ryan, whose names have been linked with irresponsible gossip in connection with the fixing of the price of copper, had nothing whatever to do with the price fixing negotiations, which finally resulted in the statement I made, fixing the price either at the time the price was fixed, or subsequent thereto. Judge Lovett[2] acted as Chairman of the Committee which considered the first price fixing of copper, and, after due consideration, recommended to the President, in September, 1917, that he had fixed the price at 23½ cents per pound, on condition that the wages of the employees of the copper producing companies should not be reduced below the then prevailing price, which was based on 27 cent copper.

A year later, a readjustment of the price was made necessary by an increase in the railroad rates and costs of supplies, and after negotiations which extended over many months, a further increase was recommended by Mr. Robert Brookings, Chairman of the Price-fixing Committee of the War Industries Board. Neither Mr. Baruch nor Mr. Ryan had any part in these two negotiations, which resulted in the fixing of the price announced by me and the prices were fixed only after an independent investigation and most thorough report by the Federal Trade Commission as to the costs of production.

For six months after the United States entered the war, the producers furnished all the copper necessary for our own war needs and all that was required by our Allies, without any price being asked or fixed, the producers taking the admirable position that they would furnish all the copper necessary for war purposes and adjust their business to whatever prices the Government would consider fair and just in the circumstances. The full production of the copper mines was placed at the disposal of the Government and the Allies, and, without unnecessary urging upon the part of the Government or the President, the production of copper was notably increased, this being an additional proof on the part of the men at the head of the copper industry of the country of their unselfish patriotism. It was their example of meeting the needs of the country that gave impetus to the movement to increase production in all the industrial plants of the country in the early stages of the war. To state that either Mr. Baruch or Mr. Ryan had influenced the action of the Federal Trade Commission in ascertaining the cost of production or attempting to dictate the recommendations either of the War Industries Board or any of the price fixing committees, is utterly foolish and without foundation of any kind. The price of copper was fixed solely by me upon the recommendations of the War Industries Board and the Federal Trade Commission, after full examination into the costs of production and without any attempt upon the part of copper producers or Mr. Baruch or Mr. Ryan to exert any pressure upon this Government or upon anybody connected with either of the Boards having to do with these vital matters.

I cannot allow this occasion to pass, my dear Garrett, without again expressing my great confidence in the gentlemen, Mr. Bernard M. Baruch and Mr. John D. Ryan, whose names have been unfortunately connected with this matter. There was not a suggestion of scandal connected with either of these gentlemen in any of the war activities in which they played so notable a part, and I wish, before the closing days of this Administration, again to say how admirably they served the needs of the Nation, and how unselfishly they devoted their fine talents to the Government in every crisis which faced us during the critical days of the war. In every transaction which they handled for the Government in the varied activities in which they played so distinguished a part, they were actuated by the highest patriotism. I know you share my opinion in this matter, for you have admirably covered it in your addresses in the House of Representatives.

With sincere regards,

Cordially yours,   Woodrow Wilson

TLS (Letterpress Books, WP, DLC).
   [1] We know nothing about the provenance of this letter. There is no correspondence in the Wilson Papers about its subject matter and no draft of the letter to Garrett. Someone obviously prepared a draft for Wilson, and it seems likely that Wilson added the last paragraph or emended it.
   On February 21, 1921, William Ernest Mason, Republican of Illinois, charged that Baruch and Ryan had profiteered in copper during the war and stirred up quite a furious debate in the House of Representatives. Garrett, on March 1, commented briefly on these accusations and then read Wilson's letter to the House. *Cong. Record*, 66th Cong., 3d sess., pp. 3564-67, 4200.
   [2] Robert Scott Lovett, about whom see the index references to him in Vol. 52.

From William Bauchop Wilson

My dear Mr. President: [Washington] March 1, 1921.

Referring to H.R. 14461, entitled, "An Act to Limit the immigration of aliens into the United States," I can not recommend its approval.[1]

No immigration emergency exists that would justify temporary legislation of this character. The total number of aliens admitted during the first eight months of the current fiscal year is estimated to be 547,000, quite evenly distributed into each of the months. If the same ratio continued for the balance of the fiscal year, it would make 821,000. The immigration in 1914 was 1,218,000, and the average annual immigration for the ten years from 1905 to 1914, inclusive, was 1,012,000. The present law was enacted February 5, 1917, to take effect, except as otherwise provided in Section 3, on and after May 1st of that year. Since that time we have either been actively engaged in hostilities or in demobilization and reconstruction to a peacetime basis, and there has been no opportunity to demonstrate the effectiveness of the Act.

Section 23 of that Act provides that the Commissioner-General of Immigration "may, with the approval of the Secretary of Labor, whenever in his judgment such action may be necessary to accomplish the purposes of this Act, detail immigration officers for service in foreign countries." No attempt has ever been made to apply that portion of the law. Because of the disturbed conditions due to the war, no appropriation has been asked for or given to carry it into effect. Yet it seems to me that it would be much more useful in restricting immigration on a selective basis than the plan proposed in this bill on a percentage basis.

The emergency alleged to exist growing out of the fear of the introduction of communicable diseases into the United States because of the underfed and unsanitary conditions of the people of Europe, particularly with reference to typhus, ought to be met by ample appropriation to the Public Health Service for quarantine and disinfecting purposes, rather than by a restriction of immigration. Restriction of immigration may reduce the danger, but can not eliminate it. The only way that that can be done is to stop immigration altogether, which the President has authority to do under the Act of February 15, 1893. (27 Stat. L. 449.)

The plan of admitting upon a percentage basis as proposed in the bill will be extremely difficult, if not impossible, of administration. Section 2 proposes, with certain exceptions, "(a) That the number of aliens of any nationality who may be admitted under the immigration laws of the United States in any fiscal year shall be limited to three per centum of the number of foreign born persons of such nationality resident in the United States as determined by the United States Census of 1910"; and "(d) * * * That the number of aliens of any nationality who may be admitted in any month shall not exceed twenty per centum of the total number of aliens of such nationality who are admissible in that fiscal year."

The number of aliens arriving from European ports has for many years, except during the period of the European War, been largely in excess of the percentage allotted. When the allotment has been nearly reached and vessels are arriving at several of our ports on the same day, the difficulty of determining which aliens should be permitted to land and which should be detained on their vessels or at immigration stations becomes immediately apparent. The great tragedy in connection with the immigration problem itself grows out of the necessity of detaining aliens when they have arrived in port or sending them back to the countries from which they came. That tragedy would be increased beyond the present conditions, unless the percentage is made so large that it is of no value for restriction purposes.

Section 2 of the bill excepts from the application of the percentage, "aliens who have resided continuously for at least one year in the Dominion of Canada, Newfoundland, the Republic of Cuba, the Republic of Mexico, countries of Central or South America, or adjacent islands." The effect of that provision would be to transfer a considerable amount of the passenger traffic from vessels trading in American ports to vessels trading in Canadian and Mexican ports. The Immigration Service is very seldom informed of the antecedents of aliens seeking admission into the United States. It has no machinery to make pre-investigations. To perform such a task successfully would require an organization far in excess of anything that Congress is likely to provide. Consequently, the immigration inspector would have to take the declaration of the alien himself concerning his length of residence in Canada, Mexico, or the other countries excepted. This would make our Canadian and Mexican Borders an easy means of access to the United States without running the chance of being debarred on account of the allotment having been exhausted.

Section 2 also exempts "aliens visiting the United States as tourists or temporarily for business or pleasure." It is not only conceivable but seems inevitable that thousands of persons will demand and must receive permission to enter after the quota fixed in respect to them as nationals has been reached. No burden of proof can be effectively imposed as to intention. Intention even when conceived in good faith and so declared is subsequently subject to change. Once in the country such aliens can remain permanently. No provision is made for their expulsion.

For these reasons I can not recommend the approval of the bill.

Faithfully yours,   [W B Wilson]

CCL (LDR, RG 174, 164/14, DNA).
¹ Tumulty had sent a copy of this bill to W. B. Wilson on February 28, saying that President Wilson would like to know if there were any objections to its approval. JPT to WBW, TLS (LDR, RG 174, 164/14, DNA). Wilson gave the bill a "pocket veto."

From Albert Sidney Burleson

Personal

My dear Mr. President: Washington March 1, 1921

I have this moment reached my office from the Cabinet meeting, and feel that I must send you a last line.

I was deeply touched by your parting words to your Cabinet, of which I have been a member for eight years.

It has been a great honor and privilege, My dear Mr. President, to have been associated with you during this epoch-making period while so much was being done by you for America and the World.

It can be truly said that no President in history has been confronted by such stupendous problems, and it can with equal truth be said that no one could have met those problems in a more masterly way than you have. Indeed, you have led America to higher standards. You surrender your great office, having at all times kept the honor of your Country unstained.

Now, the storm is over and it only remains for history to write its verdict. As one of your friends, permit me to say there can be no doubt as to what it will be.

Please do not tax your strength to reply to this letter.

With deepest affection for you, Mr. President, which I will carry in my heart to the end,   Faithfully,   A. S. Burleson

TLS (WP, DLC).

From George Madison Priest,[1] with Enclosure

Dear Mr. Wilson: Princeton, New Jersey March 1, 1921

Allow me to add to the enclosed that some of your friends in the Faculty are not in town this term, most notably Capps and Conklin and Hulett,[2] and hence their signatures are not included. I need not assure you that these three men are among the stanchest supporters and friends you have in Princeton or elsewhere.

I can also not refrain from telling you that the enthusiastic response which greeted the proposal of the enclosed letter has been a source of profound gratification and joy to the originators of the proposal. A majority of the signers have made a special trip to my room in order to secure the privilege of adding their names.

Believe me, Mr. Wilson,
                    Yours as always   George M. Priest

[1] Professor of Germanic Languages, Princeton University.
[2] Edwin Grant Conklin, Professor of Zoology, and George Augustus Hulett, Professor of Physical Chemistry.

182   MARCH 1, 1921

E N C L O S U R E

From Members of the Princeton University Faculty

Dear Mr. Wilson: Princeton, New Jersey February 26, 1921.

Some of your friends in the Faculty of Princeton University send you their greetings and congratulations as the term of your office as President comes to an end.

We have had the honor and the lasting inspiration of teaching in the University under your leadership, and we feel that we have understood the true meaning of your leadership of the nation the better for this experience. We have watched with admiration your great labors. We have seen what you have done to give meaning to our national life by bringing practice into conformity with ideals. In pursuit of this end we have seen you make every possible sacrifice and personal renunciation; and it is not only with admiration and reverence, but also with a deep feeling of personal sympathy and affection, that we have followed all the stages of your great career.

We hope, Sir, that you will find in private life all the refreshment and pleasure that your public services give you so good a right to enjoy.   Yours truly and sincerely

W. U. Vreeland	J. H. Westcott.	Henry B. Fine
Donald Clive Stuart.	Frank F. Abbott	William Libbey.
Douglas L. Buffum	Theodore W. Hunt	W. B. Scott.
Herbert S. S. Smith	Harvey W. Thayer	David Magie
Geo Mc Harper	G. T. Whitney	Morris W. Croll
David A. McCabe	Herbert S. Murch	C H Smyth Jr
W. B. Harris	William Foster	Charles G Osgood
F. C. MacDonald	Max F. Blair	John W. Basore
Henry van Dyke	Gordon Hall Gerould	Robert K. Root.
Harry F Covington	Walter M. Rankin.	E. H. Loomis
Luther P. Eisenhart	Duane Reed Stuart	Marcus S. Farr.
E. G. Spaulding	Henry R. Shipman	Wm Koren
E. P. Adams.	Edmund Y Robbins	Henry B. Van Hoesen
Allan Marquand	Raymond S. Dugan	Henry B. Dewing
	Oswald Veblen	R. B. C. Johnson per G.M.P.
		George M. Priest

TLS (WP, DLC).

From William Fosgate Kirby

Dear Mr. President: Washington, D. C. March 1st, 1921

Have just learned with amazement that you took offense at some remark I made to you or in your presence at a White House reception.

I have no slightest recollection of anything of the kind nor am I able to recall any word of mine that could have been so unhappily construed.

Certainly nothing could have been further from my intention than to do any such thing and of this fact you may be well assured.

Very sincerely   W. F. Kirby

ALS (WP, DLC).

From George Foster Peabody

Saratoga Springs, N. Y., March 1, 1921.

Have only to-day been able to read editorial Sunday's TIMES.[1] While I cannot agree as you will know, some portions of it, I am glad and proud to have its fine tribute published. It reflects honor upon American journalism to so evaluate your great administration and the manner of your impress of moral force upon the world. I send my cordial and affectionate greetings with earnest prayer for your welfare and early success to your work for world peace.

George Foster Peabody.

T telegram (WP, DLC).

[1] This editorial in the *New York Times*, entitled "WOODROW WILSON," occupied five columns of the editorial page of the issue of February 27, 1921. The writer was obviously well acquainted with many of Wilson's prepresidential writings, because he or she made the point strongly at first that Wilson was prepared for the presidency "by beliefs and convictions matured through a lifetime of labor, study and thought," and went on to quote from Wilson's writings at some length. Wilson's greatest task grew out of the challenges posed to him by the war and peace settlement. He was absolutely right, the writer said, not to plunge into the war until the great majority of Americans were prepared to follow him. However, all through the period of neutrality, Wilson's mind was occupied with the prevention of future wars, and the first evidence of his thoughts on this subject came out in his address to the League to Enforce Peace on May 27, 1916. Then, in the fullness of time, "with wonderful foresight and precision," he formulated the basic principles of the peace in his Fourteen Points Address of January 8, 1918. It was "incontestably" true that the body of Wilson's political principles "became the soul of the Treaty." Lloyd George, Clemenceau, and Orlando were won over to the American position, and the adoption of the Covenant of the League "was the crown and triumph of the cause of which he had made himself the champion."

The editorial then flashed back to three great domestic achievements of the Wilson administration: the Federal Reserve Act, the Underwood-Simmons Tariff Act, and the repeal of the measure which exempted American coastwise shipping from Panama Canal tolls.

In such an overview, the editorial went on, it was necessary to take account of Wilson's defects as well as of his qualities. Actually, Wilson's great loss of popular favor in the last two years was in large measure a result of party passion, which had not spared Washington, Jefferson, Lincoln, Cleveland, and Theodore Roosevelt. But Wilson had made mistakes by saying that there was such a thing as a nation being too proud to fight, by speaking in evenhanded terms of the war objectives of the Allies and the Central Powers, and by saying that the peace to be made had to be a peace without victory. However, Wilson had atoned for these mistakes during the war. Wilson also should not have shown his contempt for "pigmy minds" in the Senate so openly; it was unwise and inexpedient of a President ever to let a senator know just what he thought of him. Wilson's worst mistake, the editorial said, was not to take one or two eminent Republicans with him to Paris.

As the years rolled by and party and personal prejudices disappeared, and men forgot the small things and remembered only the ones that really mattered, the country would judge Wilson correctly. Wilson was never false to his ideals and noble aspirations. He fell grievously stricken on the field of battle. We cannot help thinking, the writer said, that, had Wilson been spared to continue the struggle, his powers of appeal and resources of leadership would have compelled a different result in the fight over the treaty.

"But Mr. Wilson's ideas survive, the Covenant lives, the cause for which he strove is deathless," the editorial concluded. Much noble work remained to be done, but, when it was completed, Wilson would stand through all time as its chief architect.

From the Diary of Ray Stannard Baker

[The White House] March 1 [1921].

Mrs. Wilson appeared this morning with a large bundle of documents & letters which had been discovered in some White House safe. They dealt with the years 1915, 16, 17 & early '18. So my labors are added to! But I am glad to have them. They let in new light on the roots of the war. A beautiful spring day, sunny & warm. To-morrow is my last day in the White House—I presume for a long time! I was there often during the Roosevelt regime, occasionally during Taft's administration, & much recently: but I imagine my contact with the Hardings will be slight indeed!

Wilson's Shorthand Draft of His Letter to Dr. Grayson

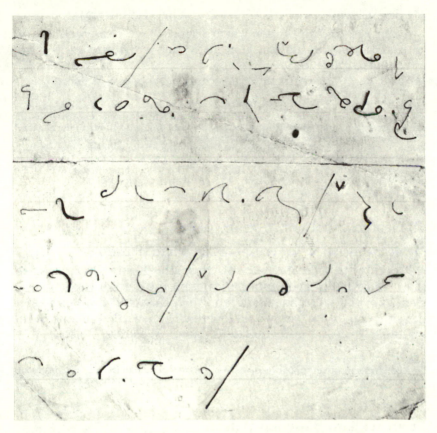

WWshL (received from James Gordon Grayson and Cary T. Grayson, Jr.).

To Cary Travers Grayson

My dear Grayson: The White House 2 March 1921.

I am not willing to cut the official threads of my service at the White House without first expressing to you my deep and grateful appreciation of the generous, watchful care you have shown for my health and welfare. I hope that the future holds every sort of happiness for you. I shall always wish you to regard me as your grateful friend.[1]   Affectionately yours,   Woodrow Wilson

TLS (received from James Gordon Grayson and Cary T. Grayson, Jr.).
[1] As the news report printed at Aug. 3, 1923, reveals, President Harding personally ordered the Navy Department to assign to Admiral Grayson the duty of serving as Wilson's personal physician. Thus the close tie between the two men continued until Wilson's death.

To Cleveland Hoadley Dodge

My dear Cleve: The White House 2 March 1921.

Again you and my other warm friends have overwhelmed me with an act of the highest generosity, and I write to express my affectionate gratitude.

Affectionately yours,   Woodrow Wilson[1]

TLS (WC, NjP).
   [1] Wilson was thanking his Princeton friends for the gift of the Pierce-Arrow touring car. He wrote the same letter, *mutatis mutandis*, to all the contributors to the car fund. The other letters are WW to C. H. McCormick, Jr., March 2, 1921 (with a Hw post-script: "I need hardly tell you how often my thoughts have been with you of late W.W."), TLS (WP, DLC); WW to T. D. Jones, March 2, 1921, TLS (Mineral Point, Wisc., Public Library); WW to E. W. Sheldon, March 2, 1921, TLS (Letterpress Books, WP, DLC); and WW to D. B. Jones, March 2, 1921, TLS (Letterpress Books, WP, DLC).

To George Creel

My dear Creel: The White House 2 March 1921.

I found with a great deal of distress, after looking into the case, that I could not in good conscience grant the pardon you suggest.[1] I am sure you will understand and that, if I could have explained the situation to you, you would feel that I was without blame in the matter.   Affectionately yours,   Woodrow Wilson

TLS (G. Creel Papers, DLC).
   [1] Creel had almost certainly urged Wilson to grant a pardon to Debs during his recent visit to S Street; G. Creel to WW, March 11, 1921, intimates that this occurred.

From William Bauchop Wilson

Dear Mr. President: Washington March 2, 1921.

Your administration is drawing to a close. It has been laid in the gravest crisis the world has ever known. It has been good to have the opportunity of service to our country and the world during such a period under your leadership, though the burden has been heavy.

The masterful manner in which you have handled the great domestic and foreign problems that have confronted you has developed the feeling of confidence and respect which your previous services had inspired within me to one of admiration and affection, which has grown with our service together, and will end only with our lives. May you live to see the day when a grateful country will recognize and appreciate the wonderful work you have done.

Faithfully yours,   W B Wilson

TLS (WP, DLC).

From Hamilton Holt

To the President: New York March 2 1921

As you are about to leave office I cannot let the event pass without writing to you to express in some degree my profound admiration for your service to the country and the world. I know no man in public life or in history who has appealed to my conception of a genuine statesman as you have, and I can sincerely say that I am proud to be a citizen of the same country that has produced you and that I am living in the same age with you.

I venture to enclose an editorial that will appear in this week's Independent,[1] dated Saturday, which will express in some measure my feelings as you leave the White House. I hope this may not be uninteresting to you.

Tho many of your countrymen have treated you shamefully, I can see the tide is already turning in your favor. The future is yours.

May God grant that you may be saved many years for the service of your country.   Respectfully yours,   Hamilton Holt

TLS (WP, DLC).
[1] Hamilton Holt, "Woodrow Wilson and the Service He has Rendered His Country and Humanity," *The Independent*, CV (March 5, 1921), 231-33. Holt recalled his first meeting with Wilson some fifteen years earlier, after Wilson had just finished writing his *History of the American People*. At the time, Wilson told Holt that his great ambition was to write the history of democracy. Democracy, Holt said, had always been the keynote of Wilson's life, the great cause that he had fought for at Princeton, in Trenton, and in the White House. Holt then briefly commented upon Wilson's accomplishments as President of Princeton University and as Governor of New Jersey and reviewed his notable domestic achievements during his tenure in the White House, which had made him the "champion and standard bearer of progressivism."
Once Wilson had taken the United States into the war, he soon gave moral leadership to the fight against Germany and became the spokesman of the entire Allied cause. His Fourteen Points Address rallied French and British working people and prevented a German victory in the spring of 1918. At great cost to himself, he won incorporation of the League Covenant in the Versailles Treaty. Even though he accepted changes in the Covenant proposed by former President Taft, Republican senators succeeded in "poison gassing" the Treaty. Then followed the Republican presidential campaign, in which misrepresentations and distortions of the truth about the League of Nations were the chief weapons. All told, the behavior of Republican senators under Lodge during the treaty fight, Holt said, "constitutes, in my judgment, the worst action of public men holding high public office in the history of the United States."
Wilson had his faults and had made mistakes, Holt said, and one of his chief mistakes was in assuming that the League issue would be decided solely on its merits. The time would certainly come when the American people would realize the real service Wilson had rendered his country and humanity. And when that day dawned, the United States would have taken her rightful place at the council table of the nations.

From Clarence Self Ridley[1]

My dear Mr. President: Washington, D. C. March 2, 1921.

With reference to the removal of articles from the White House I do not find any law bearing on the subject. Mr. Roosevelt took the chair he used at the Cabinet table, and Mr. Taft took three chairs. It has been the practice for Cabinet members to take the chairs used by them at the Cabinet table. In all of these cases, however, an exactly similar chair has been furnished by the person taking a chair to replace the one taken before the old one is removed. I do not see any objection to this practice. In fact it is a benefit to the United States inasmuch as it practically avoids the expense of maintenance of these chairs.

With regard to articles other than Cabinet and desk chairs I find no precedents. If such articles are of no historic value, are common articles of commerce and can be exactly duplicated before removal from the White House, I can see no possible objection.

Very truly yours,   C. S. Ridley.

TLS (WP, DLC).
    [1] Major, Corps of Engineers, U.S.A., Chief of the Office of Public Buildings and Grounds.

From Jessie Woodrow Wilson Sayre

Darling, darling Father,   [Cambridge, Mass.] March 2nd [1921].

Our love goes out to you as you come into your new home with the deepest hope that newness of health, and happiness, await you there. We wish to send our "Welcome Home" to you as you go in, and to tell you that the record of your eight years' great service have inspired and will always inspire not only the heart of the world but also your own little children and grandchildren. Dear Father, we are so proud of you, and our hearts beat higher and we are stronger and braver whenever we think of you which is constantly.

In spite of the hideous mess the world is in, the clue is in our hands and you have placed it there!

A kiss to dear Edith and to yourself from each and every one of us   Your adoring daughter   Jessie.

ALS (WC, NjP).

Ray Stannard Baker to Edith Bolling Galt Wilson

My dear Mrs. Wilson: The White House, March 2 1921

I find among the President's papers no copy of the report made by Mr. Swem of the Conference with the Senators on August 20:[1] nor any report of the Conference in March[2]—if any was made.

I presume the President has these elsewhere, as well as copies of his addresses made in the West.³ If he has not, it occurs to me that copies could be supplied before he leaves the White House.

I am going home for about ten days. I will communicate with you just before I return.

I want to thank you most heartily for your indulgence during these busy days.   Sincerely yours,   Ray Stannard Baker

ALS (WP, DLC).
¹ He meant Wilson's meeting with the members of the Foreign Relations Committee on August 19, 1919. Swem's transcript of that meeting is printed at that date in Vol. 62.
² No stenographic report of Wilson's meeting with the members of the foreign affairs committees of the House and Senate on February 26, 1919, was made. A long news report about this meeting is printed at that date in Vol. 55.
³ He did indeed: Swem's transcripts of Wilson's speeches on his western tour are printed as *Addresses of President Wilson: Addresses Delivered by President Wilson on his Western Tour, September 4 to September 25, 1919* . . . (Washington, 1919).

Nancy Saunders Toy¹ to Edith Bolling Galt Wilson

Dear Mrs. Wilson   Cambridge 2 March. 1921

Will you tell the President that on March 4th, a little group of his friends will meet in my little apartment to bid him *Vale atque Salve*. Mr. & Mrs. Sayre, Prest. Eliot, Mr. & Mrs. Moors,² and a few others, whose hearts have been always "true to Pole" will be thinking about him, will be talking about him, will be thanking God for him.   Yours sincerely,   Nancy Toy

ALS (WP, DLC).
¹ Wilson's old friend, the widow of Crawford Howell Toy, Hancock Professor of Hebrew and other Oriental Languages, Harvard University, 1880-1909.
² John Farwell Moors and Ethel Lyman Paine Moors. He was a broker of Boston.

Two News Reports

[*March 3, 1921*]

Mr. and Mrs. Harding at White House
Have Tea with President and Mrs. Wilson

Washington, Feb. [March] 3.—Mr. and Mrs. Harding paid a brief visit of courtesy early this evening at the White House and had tea with President and Mrs. Wilson.

The call lasted twenty minutes. Mr. and Mrs. Wilson received their guests in the Red Room at 6:30 o'clock. At 6:50 the President-elect and Mrs. Harding left the White House and returned to the Hotel Willard.

It was the first meeting between Mr. Harding and President Wilson since the Foreign Relations Committee of the Senate paid its famous visit to the White House in August, 1919, and questioned

President Wilson at length on the League of Nations covenant. Mr. Harding and the President then had a spirited discussion on the question of [the] obligation imposed on the United States by the covenant to go to war in possible future contingencies.

Since his election as President Mr. Harding has paid a call at the White House and left his card, but had not seen the President. Mrs. Harding, however, called a number of weeks ago and was shown over the White House by Mrs. Wilson.

In announcing in the afternoon that he and Mrs. Harding intended to make the call, Mr. Harding said that he was gladly conforming to a custom. The precedent for a brief visit of courtesy was set by President Wilson, who in 1912 declined an invitation to spend a week-end at the White House, but paid a brief call on President Taft on the eve of the inauguration. Before that time the outgoing President had sometimes dined the incoming one at the White House on the day before the inauguration ceremony.

[*March 3, 1921*]

WILSON AND COLBY TO START LAW FIRM
Announcement a Big Surprise to Washington—
Offices to Be There and in New York.

Washington, March 3.—President Wilson and Secretary of State Bainbridge Colby will form a partnership and begin the practice of law soon after they retire from office tomorrow.

Formal announcement to this effect was made at the White House today. It came as a great surprise to even the closest friends of the President and Mr. Colby.

The White House statement read:

"The President made the announcement today that at the conclusion of his term of office he would resume the practice of law, forming a partnership with the Secretary of State, Bainbridge Colby. The firm will have offices in New York and Washington."

No further details were forthcoming from the White House. Secretary Joseph P. Tumulty, who will also begin the practice of law shortly, said that the announcement spoke for itself. It is the intention of President Wilson and Mr. Colby to open offices in New York and this city as soon as the necessary arrangements can be made. Mr. Colby, it is understood, will be in active charge of the New York offices, making frequent trips to Washington to consult with President Wilson, who will spend most of his time here.

Printed in the *New York Times*, March 4, 1921.

A Veto Message

THE WHITE HOUSE,
The House of Representatives:　　　　*3 March, 1921.*

I return herewith without my approval H.R. 15275, an act imposing temporary duties upon certain agricultural products to meet present emergencies, to provide revenue, and for other purposes.

The title of this measure indicates that it has several purposes. The report of the Committee on Ways and Means reveals that its principal object is to furnish relief to certain producers in the Nation who have been unable to discover satisfactory markets in foreign countries for their products and whose prices have fallen. Very little reflection would lead anyone to conclude that the measure would not furnish in any substantial degree the relief sought by the producers of most of the staple commodities which it covers. This Nation has been for very many years a large exporter of agricultural products. For nearly a generation before it entered the European war its exports exceeded its imports of agricultural commodities by from approximately $200,000,000 to more than $500,000,000. In recent years this excess has greatly increased, and in 1919 reached the huge total of $1,904,292,000. The excess of exports of staple products is especially marked. In 1913 the Nation imported 783,481 bushels of wheat valued at $670,931, and in 1920, 35,848,648 bushels worth $75,398,834; while it exported in 1913, 99,508,968 bushels worth $95,098,838, and in 1920, 218,280,231 bushels valued at $596,957,796. In the year 1913 it imported 85,183 barrels of wheat flour valued at $347,877, and in 1920, 800,788 barrels valued at $8,669,300; while it exported in the first year 12,278,206 barrels valued at $56,865,444, and in 1920, 19,853,952 barrels valued at $224,472,448. In 1913 it imported $3,888,604 worth of corn, and in 1920, $9,257,377 worth, while its exports in the first year were valued at $26,515,146, and in 1920, at $26,453,681. Of unmanufactured cotton in 1920 it imported approximately 300,000,000 pounds valued at $138,743,000, while it exported more than 3,179,000,000 pounds, worth over $1,136,000,000.

Of preserved milk in the same year it imported $3,331,812 worth and exported $65,239,020 worth. Its imports in the same year of sugar and wool of course greatly exceeded its exports. It is obvious that for the commodities, except sugar and wool, mentioned in the measure, which make up the greater part of our agricultural international trade, the imports can have little or no effect on the prices of the domestic products. This is strikingly true of such commodities as wheat and corn. The imports of wheat have come mainly from Canada and Argentina and have not competed with the domestic crop. Rather they have supplemented it. The domestic demand has been for specific classes and qualities of foreign wheat to meet particular milling and planting needs. They are a small fraction of our total production and of our wheat exports. The price of wheat is a world price; and it is a matter of little moment whether the Canadian wheat goes directly into the markets of the other countries of the world or indirectly through this country. The relatively small quantity of corn imported into this country has a specialized use and does not come into competition with the domestic commodity.

The situation in which many of the farmers of the country find themselves can not be remedied by a measure of this sort. This is doubtless generally understood. There is no short way out of existing conditions, and measures of this sort can only have the effect of deceiving the farmers and of raising false hopes among them. Actual relief can come only from the adoption of constructive measures of a broader scope, from the restoration of peace everywhere in the world, the resumption of normal industrial pursuits, the recovery particularly of Europe, and the discovery there of additional credit foundations on the basis of which her people may arrange to take from farmers and other producers of this Nation a greater part of their surplus production.

One does not pay a compliment to the American farmer who attempts to alarm him by dangers from foreign competition. The American farmers are the most effective agricultural producers in the world. Their production is several times as great for each worker as that of their principal foreign rivals. This grows out of the intelligence of the American farmer, the nature of his agricultural practices and economy, and the fact that he has the assistance of scientific and practical agencies which in respect to variety of activity, of personnel, and of financial support exceed those of any other two or three nations in the world combined. There is little doubt that the farmers of this Nation will not only continue mainly to supply the home demand but will be increasingly called upon to supply a large part of the needs of the rest of the world.

What the farmer now needs is not only a better system of domestic marketing and credit, but especially larger foreign markets for his surplus products. Clearly measures of this sort will not conduce to an expansion of the foreign market. It is not a little singular that a measure which strikes a blow at our foreign trade should follow so closely upon the action of Congress directing the resumption of certain activities of the War Finance Corporation, especially at the urgent insistence of representatives of the farming interests, who believed that its resumption would improve foreign marketing. Indeed, when one surveys recent activities in the foreign field and measures enacted affecting the foreign trade one can not fail to be impressed with the fact that there is consistency only in their contradictions and inconsistencies. We have been vigorously building up a great merchant marine and providing for improvement of marketing in foreign countries by the passage of an export-trade law and of measures for the promotion of banking agencies in foreign countries. Now it appears that we propose to render these measures abortive in whole or in part.

I imagine there is little doubt that while this measure is temporary it is intended as a foundation for action of a similar nature of a very general and permanent character. It would seem to be designed to pave the way for such action. If there ever was a time when America had anything to fear from foreign competition, that time has passed. I can not believe that American producers, who in most respects are the most effective in the world, can have any dread of competition when they view the fact that their country has come through the great struggle of the last few years, relatively speaking, untouched, while their principal competitors are in varying degrees sadly stricken and laboring under adverse conditions from which they will not recover for many years. Changes of a very radical character have taken place. The United States has become a great creditor Nation. She has lent certain Governments of Europe more than $9,000,000,000, and as a result of the enormous excess of our exports there is an additional commercial indebtedness of foreign nations to our own of perhaps not less than $4,000,000,000. There are only three ways in which Europe can meet her part of her indebtedness, namely, by the establishment of private credits, by the shipment of gold, or of commodities. It is difficult for Europe to discover the requisite securities as a basis for the necessary credits. Europe is not in a position at the present time to send us the amount of gold which would be needed, and we could not view further large imports of gold into this country without concern. The result, to say the least, would be a larger disarrangement of international exchange and disturbance of international trade. If we wish to have Europe settle her debts, governmental or commercial, we must be prepared to buy from her, and if we wish to assist Europe and ourselves by the export either of food, of raw materials, or finished products, we must be prepared to welcome commodities which we need and which Europe will be prepared, with no little pain, to send us.

Clearly, this is no time for the erection here of high-trade barriers. It would strike a blow at the large and successful efforts which have been made by many of our great industries to place themselves on an export basis. It would stand in the way of the normal readjustment of business conditions throughout the world, which is as vital to the welfare of this country as to that of all the other nations. The United States has a duty to itself as well as to the world, and it can discharge this duty by widening, not by contracting, its world markets.

This measure has only slight interest so far as its prospective revenue yields are concerned. It is estimated that the aggregate addition to the Nation's income from its operation for 10 months would be less than $72,000,000, and of this more than half would arise from the proposed duty on sugar. Obviously, this and much more can be secured in ways known to the Congress, which would be vastly less burdensome to the American consumer and American industry.

The rates, however, have a peculiar interest. In practically every case they either equal or exceed those established under the Payne-Aldrich Act, in which the principle of protection reached its high-water mark, and the enactment of which was followed by an effective exhibition of protests on the part of the majority of the American people. I do not believe that the sober judgment of the masses of the people of the Nation, or even of the special class whose interests are immediately affected by this measure, will sanction a return, especially in view of conditions which lend even less justification for such action, to a policy of legislation for selfish interests which will foster monopoly and increase the disposition to look upon the Government as an instrument for private gain instead of an instrument for the promotion of the general well being. Such a policy is antagonistic to the fundamental principle of equal and exact justice to all, and can only serve to revive the feeling of irritation on the part of the great masses of the people and of lack of confidence in the motives of rulers and the results of government.   Woodrow Wilson.[1]

Printed in *Cong. Record*, 66th Cong., 3d sess., pp. 4498-9.
   [1] As has been noted (O. W. Underwood to WW, Feb. 22, 1921, n. 2), Houston wrote this message. Wilson's veto was sustained.

To Bainbridge Colby

My dear Mr. Secretary: The White House March 3, 1921.

   I beg to return the note received yesterday from the Japanese Government,[1] which I have read, in relation to the proposed mandate covering the Island of Yap.

My first information of a contention that the so-called decision of May 7, 1919, by the Council of Four assigned to Japan a mandate for the Island of Yap, was conveyed to me by Mr. Norman Davis in October last.[2] I then informed him that I had never consented to the assignment of the Island of Yap to Japan.[3]

I had not previously given particular attention to the wording of the Council's minutes of May 7, 1919, which were only recently called to my attention. I had on several occasions prior to the date mentioned, made specific reservations regarding the Island of Yap and had taken the position that it should not be assigned under mandate to any one power but should be internationalized for cable purposes. I assumed that this position would be duly considered in connection with the settlement of the cable question and that it therefore was no longer a matter for consideration in connection with the peace negotiations. I never abandoned or modified this position in respect to the Island of Yap, and I did not agree on May 7, 1919, or at any other time, that the Island of Yap should be included in the assignment of mandates to Japan.[4]

As a matter of fact, all agreements arrived at regarding the assignment of mandates were conditional upon a subsequent agreement being reached as to the specific terms of the mandates, and further, upon their acceptance by each of the Principal Allied and Associated Powers. The consent of the United States is essential both as to the assignments of mandates and the terms and provisions of the mandates, after agreement as to their assignment or allocation.

The consent of the United States, as you know, has never been given on either point, as to the Island of Yap.

Faithfully yours,   Woodrow Wilson[5]

TLS (SDR, RG 59, 862i.01/172, DNA).
[1] This note was a reply to NHD to Amembassy, London, Dec. 3 [4], 1920, printed as Enclosure III with NHD to WW, Dec. 3, 1920, Vol. 66. Davis' telegram to London was a vigorous reiteration of the position heretofore taken by the American government to the effect that Lansing and Wilson had not agreed to include Yap in the Pacific islands north of the equator to be assigned to Japan as mandates. A copy of this telegram was transmitted to Tokyo for delivery to the Japanese Foreign Office on December 6, 1920.
The Japanese note of February 26, 1921, pointed out that no Japanese representative was present at the meetings of the Council of Ten and of the Council of Four at which Lansing and Wilson entered reservations to the award of Yap to Japan, and said that the Japanese government had had no means of ascertaining the views of Wilson and Lansing expressed at those meetings. However that might have been, the note went on, the important question was whether the Supreme Council did or did not award Yap to Japan. Moreover, if the Supreme Council had not awarded Yap to Japan in its meeting on May 7, 1919, at which no Japanese representative was present, it could only be regarded as an act of "entirely bad faith." The most important fact of all, the note said, was that the Supreme Council had indeed awarded all the former German islands in the Pacific north of the equator to Japan, and the British and French governments had supported the Japanese government in this view in the current controversy over Yap. The note made several additional points to buttress Japanese claims to exclusive control of the island and concluded by saying that it could not agree to international control

over cables crossing Yap. E. Bell to SecState, Feb. 27, 1921, T telegram (SDR, RG 59,
862i.01/46, DNA), printed in *FR 1921*, II, 272-76.
    ² NHD to WW, Oct. 5, 1920, Vol. 66.
    ³ In a meeting with Davis on October 6, 1920.
    ⁴ Wilson did in fact approve the decision taken by the Supreme War Council at a
meeting on May 7, 1919, at 4:15 p.m. to award all former German islands north of the
equator under mandate to Japan, along with all other decisions concerning mandates.
He later recalled the meeting in a conversation with Sir Maurice Hankey. See M.P.A.
Hankey to WW, Nov. 23, 1921, n. 2. This was a very brief meeting held at the Trianon
Palace at Versailles following the ceremony of the presentation of the preliminary peace
treaty to the German delegation. The notes of this meeting are printed in *PPC*, V, 506-
509. It is entirely possible that Wilson's failure to note the decision concerning the islands mandated to Japan was another lapse due to his small stroke of about April 28,
1919.
    ⁵ This letter was drafted by Norman Davis; there is a CC of it in his papers.

To William Bauchop Wilson

My dear Mr. Secretary: [The White House] 3 March 1921.

It has given me real pleasure today to sign the commission¹
which accompanies this and I hope that you will accept the office
as an evidence of my unlimited confidence in your ability and public spirit. It has been very delightful to be associated with you and
I have learned to admire you more and more as the years have gone
by.

It was thoughtful of you to send me the photograph of yourself.
I value it highly, particularly because of the generous inscription
upon it.

    With warmest regards,
            Cordially and faithfully yours,   Woodrow Wilson

TLS (Letterpress Books, WP, DLC).
    ¹ As a member of the International Joint Commission of the United States and Can-
ada. After protests by Republicans in the Senate, William B. Wilson resigned this commission on March 19, 1921.

To Albert Sidney Burleson

My dear Burleson: [The White House] 3 March 1921.

I am giving myself the pleasure of sending you an affectionate
and grateful acknowledgement of your letter of the first of March
which has given me the greatest cheer.
            Cordially and faithfully yours,   [Woodrow Wilson]

CCL (WP, DLC).

To Hamilton Holt

My dear Mr. Holt: [The White House] 3 March 1921.

Your generous letter of yesterday gives me a welcome opportunity to say to you how proud and delighted I am to have won your confidence and how grateful I am to you for the several ways in which you have both publicly and privately expressed that confidence. I am, indeed, grateful and greatly cheered by it.

With warmest regards and good wishes,

Sincerely yours,   [Woodrow Wilson]

CCL (WP, DLC).

To Charles Lee Swem

My dear Swem: [The White House] 3 March 1921.

This is just a note of informal goodbye and to fulfill my desire to express to you the very deep and sincere appreciation I have of the long and excellent service you rendered me in which your skill and promptness and fidelity were of the greatest service to me.

I hope that in your new sphere and activities[1] you will have the most gratifying success.

Cordially and faithfully yours,   [Woodrow Wilson]

CCL (WP, DLC).
    [1] Swem had just joined the Gregg Publishing Company in Chicago to become editor of *The Gregg Writer. New York Times*, Jan. 29, 1921.

To Rudolph Forster

My dear Forster: [The White House] 3 March 1921.

As I am about to turn away from my executive duties at the White House, may I not send you a line to express the admiration for and confidence in you which I have learned to feel as I have watched and appreciated the faithfulness and loyalty and intelligence of the service you have rendered in the important post which you fill in the Executive Offices.

I am very happy, indeed, to subscribe myself,

Your sincere friend,   [Woodrow Wilson]

CCL (WP, DLC).

To Nancy Saunders Toy

My dear Mrs. Toy: [The White House] 3 March 1921.

It is always a real pleasure to receive a letter from you and I particularly appreciate your greetings under date of the second of March. This is the time when friendship seems to count most in my feeling and in my prospect of the future. Thank you with all my heart, and please give my most cordial and grateful greetings to the group of friends of whom you speak. I value their friendship and approval most highly and am greatly heartened by them.

With the warmest regards from all of us.

Cordially and sincerely yours,   [Woodrow Wilson]

CCL (WP, DLC).

To William Fosgate Kirby

My dear Senator Kirby: [The White House] 3 March 1921.

I have your letter of the first of March and beg to assure you that I do not remember any remark that you ever made anywhere, and therefore cannot have taken offence on such an occasion as you refer to.   Sincerely yours,   [Woodrow Wilson]

CCL (WP, DLC).

To George Madison Priest

My dear Priest: [The White House] 3 March 1921.

Your letter of the first of March has given me genuine and deep pleasure and you may be sure that the message from a group of my former colleagues on the faculty has been a source of unusual gratification and cheer to me. I wish I had the opportunity to express to them all the feeling of encouragement and happiness which their generous message has given me.

With warmest personal regards,

Sincerely yours,   [Woodrow Wilson]

CCL (WP, DLC).

From the Members of the Cabinet

Mr. President: [Washington] March 3, 1921.

The final moments of the Cabinet on Tuesday found us quite unable to express the poignant feelings with which we realized that the hour of leave-taking and official dispersal had arrived.

Will you permit us to say to you now, and as simply as we can, how great a place you occupy in our honor, love and esteem?

We have seen you in times of momentous crisis. We have seen your uncomplaining toil under the heavy and unremitting burdens of the Presidency. We have had the inestimable privilege of sharing some of your labors. At all times you have been to us our ideal of a courageous, high-minded, modest gentleman, a patriotic public servant, an intense and passionate lover of your country.

You have displayed toward us a trust and confidence that has touched us all, supporting and defending us, when under partisan attack, with staunch and untiring loyalty, and placing at our command, always in the most considerate way, the wisdom of your counsel. History will acclaim your great qualities. We who have known you so intimately bear witness to them now.

We fervently wish you, dear Mr. President, long life and the happiness that you so richly deserve and have so abundantly earned.

Bainbridge Colby	Josephus Daniels
D. F. Houston.	John Barton Payne
Newton D. Baker	Joshua W Alexander.
A Mitchell Palmer	W B Wilson
A. S. Burleson	
E. T. Meredith	

TLS (WP, DLC).

From David Franklin Houston

Dear Mr. President: Washington March 3, 1921.

I feel impelled to say just a word to you before I vacate my office and our official relations are severed. I need not tell you that I have felt greatly honored by my association with you in one of the greatest periods of American history. You conferred on me great distinction in making me first the head of the Department of Agriculture and later the head of the Treasury Department. These happen to be the departments of government dealing with activities in which my interests for many years have mainly centered. I have therefore derived immense interest, pleasure and satisfaction from supervising their activities, including not only the problems of rural life and of finance but also those of commercial and farm loan banking, not to speak of many others. At all times my problems have been numerous and difficult, but my tasks have been rendered tolerable by your unfailing support. I have had no doubt at any time of the principle by which I should be guided. I knew that the principle was the one by which you yourself are guided. I have known too long and been associated with you too intimately not to know that there is only one question in which you are interested, and that is whether a given course is right or wrong. May I say I have had knowledge of the fact that no other man has occupied your position who was so well prepared by training and experience to pass judgment on problems in this spirit or who had in higher degree the willingness and courage to follow the course deemed to be in the public interest? I am serenely confident that the sober judgment of the people of this nation now is that you have given the nation as effective and as clean an administration as it has ever had and that no man in the world has labored more valiantly and successfully than you to promote the higher interests of humanity. I know that the verdict of history will be to this effect.

I have deeply appreciated your many personal courtesies. I have been distressed that your numerous tasks weighed on you and almost overwhelmed you physically and I have followed with immense satisfaction your course of recovery. I hope that you will be rapidly restored to normal physical strength.

May I say just another personal word? I feel that I cannot close this note without an expression of indebtedness to Mrs. Wilson, and of admiration for the part she played and the judgment she has shown in dealing with important matters.

With great affection and gratitude, I am,

Faithfully yours,   D. F. Houston

TLS (WP,DLC).

From Edwin Thomas Meredith

My dear Mr. President: Washington 3/3/1921.

I have been trying to phrase some note to you, Mr. President, that would in some measure express what is in my heart, but I find myself unable to write anything that seems adequate.

You gave me the opportunity and privilege of sitting in your councils, and of coming in contact with you—an honor and personal satisfaction which I shall always cherish and which is the greatest heritage I give to my son. I am eternally grateful to you.

I cannot hope to put into words a proper estimate of the great service you have rendered to the nation and to humanity in the most trying and difficult period in the history of the world. All I can say is that I stand in awe. I feel very small, very worthless in the face of your wonderful vision and exalted example.

I am returning to Des Moines with a heart full of gratitude for your many kindnesses to me. You will ever be in my mind. If I can be of service to you in the future, I assure you that it will be a genuine privilege and pleasure to serve you in any way at any time.

Mrs Meredith[1] wishes to be remembered to you and Mrs Wilson and joins me in all good wishes to both of you.

With renewed expressions of appreciation, I am

Affectionately yours,   E. T. Meredith

ALS (WP, DLC).
  [1] Edna C. Elliott Meredith.

From Joshua Willis Alexander

My dear Mr. President: [Washington] March 3, 1921.

The hour is near when you will lay down the labors and responsibilities of the great office which you have filled with such distinguished ability for the last eight years.

To be a member of the cabinet of a President of the United States is an honor that any American citizen may well covet; but to have the honor of being a member of the official family of Woodrow Wilson, President of the United States, adds immeasurably to that distinction. I wish you to know I so regard the very great honor you have conferred on me by making me a member of your cabinet.

In time, when the exigencies of partisan politics have been severed, and your administration is viewed in the perspective, you should have no concern that it will be viewed in any other light than one of the greatest, if not the greatest, in the annals of this nation.

In my humble opinion for moral and intellectual greatness you are the premier of the statesmen of our time, and I firmly believe that when the history of your administration and of the peace conference is written the value of your service to your country and to humanity will assure you that merited distinction.

I beg you to permit me on behalf of myself and family to express for you and Mrs. Wilson our highest esteem and very best wishes for your future happiness and prosperity, and to express the hope that when relieved of your present duties and responsibilities you will rapidly regain your health and strength.

   With all good wishes I am
                           Sincerely yours,   J. W. Alexander.

TLS (WP, DLC).

Joseph Patrick Tumulty to Edith Bolling Galt Wilson, with Enclosure

My dear Mrs. Wilson: The White House, 3 March 1921.

   I tried in my letter to an old friend, a copy of which I enclose herewith, to express the feelings for the President that really lie in my heart, and I thought, perhaps, in a free moment, you might have a chance to peruse it.

   I cannot allow the curtain to roll down without telling you how deep my admiration and affection for you really goes. Your devotion to the President has touched me more than I can say, but the cold-ness of officialdom has prevented me from telling you, face to face, how much I really admire you. It has been a source of gratification to me to know that you have been always at hand—so generous and thoughtful of the President's interests, and always so ready and willing to listen to any matter in which I had a particular in-terest. I do not feel a bit lonesome today, before the events of to-morrow. I feel, like you, that we are close to the greatest figure in the world. There will be many comforting things about the close of my life here, and among them is the knowledge that I will have a chance to meet you and the President in a different way, and I want you to know that out of office I will give abundant proof of my loyalty and fidelity to you and the President.
                           Sincerely,   Tumulty

TLS (WP, DLC).

ENCLOSURE

Joseph Patrick Tumulty to James Kerney

My dear Jim: The White House March 2, 1921.

   Before the closing hours here and in the midst of the greatest whirl I have yet experienced I just want to reach my hand out and thank you, old fellow, for the fine way you have stood by me. I feel toward you as a soldier feels toward his comrade who has worked and suffered with him in the trenches.

You have the small credit, at least, of having discovered me and whether or not you are proud of the discovery, at least, I am very proud of the discoverer.

I never thought that I would live through these melancholy days that have followed so closely upon the election, but as we approach the journey's end there comes to me a serenity of mind and attitude I never thought I possessed. Perhaps it is my Irish temperament and a sense of humor which help me to bear up to the end.

How God must laugh at those who think the journey's end is the great consummation! I have faith to believe it is not. As I saw the President yesterday pass my window upon the conclusion of the Cabinet meeting, trudging wearily along, groping his way back to the White House, I felt that in this man, our great leader, fighting to the end, there was the real hope of the world. So, my dear Jim, I am not lonely. I, at least with those who have been with me, have walked in the presence of the great and only future events will pay him the tribute which is his due. Not until the tears are wiped from the eyes of the world can we grasp the vision of his greatness.

The City of Washington, so cold and indifferent at times, will, after the long siege here, be a beautiful place to live in. Here has been enacted the scene of one of the greatest tragedies in all human history. Here, in my opinion, have trod the feet of a man who tried to save the world, but beyond that cluster memories of men like Tom Pence, Billy Hughes, Ollie James and dear Old Doc Coughlin,[1] who walked with me in company with that great leader. We must with patience await the unfolding of the great plot. At least we can be proud in the years to come that at a dark hour in the life of the world we helped to lift the burden of him who sought to serve all humanity. At least you and I, who have kept the faith, have no cause for regret. Some times when I look at myself, after thoughtful friends pay tribute to my work, I marvel at what has been accomplished with such poor ability to utilize, but I am consoled in the belief that what I sought to do I did out of devotion to my chief and sympathy for the great things he sought to accomplish.

Please do not feel that on the Fourth of March I shall be lonely or sad or disspirited. My Irish temperament will hold me steady and after the parade is over and the curtain goes down on the last great scene, I hope that you in New Jersey can visualize me as one who is happy and content that he was privileged to serve.

Faithfully yours,   Joe

TCL (WP, DLC).
    [1] That is, Thomas Jones Pence, William Hughes, Ollie Murray James, and John William Coughlin.

From Bainbridge Colby, with Enclosure

My dear Mr. President: Washington March 3, 1921.
    At the request of the Polish Minister, I beg to enclose herewith the text of a cable addressed to you by the Chief of the Polish State.
    I am, my dear Mr. President,
                        Faithfully yours,   Bainbridge Colby

TLS (WP, DLC).

E N C L O S U R E

                                    March 3rd, 1921.
    I have the honor to most respectfully beg you to transmit to the President the cable just received from the Chief of the Polish State and which reads as follows:
    "The Honorable Woodrow Wilson, President of the United States.
Mr. President:
    On the eve of concluding the eight years of your presidency, which have marked a golden page in the history of Poland's resurrection, I, in my own name and in the name of the Polish people, have the honor to convey to you the expression of our deepest respect.
    Poland, bound to the great democracy of the United States of America by the deeds of their heroes that have fought for liberty, and by the labors of millions of Poles that have contributed to the prosperity of America, has indeed received, thanks to you and to your noble compatriots a never-to-be-forgotten help and support in bearing most difficult hardships and in surmounting every obstacle.
    The present moment is near to the day of peace on which our people will undertake that after-the-war creative effort which will strengthen and illuminate that independence which you, Mr. President, have assured to us in your historical declaration. As the head of the Polish Government, I am indeed very happy in the name of the whole Polish nation to be able today, Mr. President, to transmit to you the expressions of our profound thanks.
                        Pilsudski."[1]
Accept, Sir, the renewed assurance of my highest consideration.
                        Casimir Lubomirsky

TLS (SDR, RG 59, 811.001W69/967, DNA).
¹ The reply to this telegram, written by Colby, is BC to Amlegation, Warsaw, March 4, 1921 (SDR, RG 59, 811.001W69/967a, DNA).

A News Report

[*March 4, 1921*]

WILSON'S EXIT IS TRAGIC
Limping on Cane, But Smiling,
He Goes to Capitol with Harding.
Last Formal Statement Shows Coldness to Lodge—
Gets Big Ovation at His Home.

Washington, March 4.—Dramatic and touchingly pathetic were the circumstances and incidents connected with the departure of Woodrow Wilson from the Presidency into the rôle of private American citizen. During a large part of his incumbency of the White House he had been a towering figure in the affairs of the world. He had gone abroad to fight for the incorporation into the Treaty of Versailles of the project for a League of Nations; he had been received almost as a conquering hero, and, returning, faced a fight for the object dear to his heart, and so shattered his health that there was something tragic about the broken frame of the man who limped from the White House to accompany his successor to the Capitol.

While it had been the sincere desire of Mr. Wilson to participate to the fullest extent as a witness of the swearing in of the new Administration, the closing hours of his own term of office, both in the White House and at the Capitol, had fatigued the President to a point where, at the eleventh hour, he decided to forego the inaugural ceremonies, both within the Senate Chamber and on the eastern portico of the Capitol.

The first of these was scheduled to open on the stroke of noon. Five minutes before that hour the President left the President's Room, in the Senate wing of the Capitol, was escorted to a private elevator by Senator Knox, walked with a limp and a cane slowly to a waiting automobile, and was driven around the city to his new home.

He had accompanied Mr. Harding and the rest of the official inaugural party from the White House to the Capitol, under escort of a squadron of cavalry moving at a quick trot and with flying colors between the lines of people along Pennsylvania Avenue. But when he left the Capitol at noon he was accompanied only by Mrs. Wilson, Secretary Tumulty, Admiral Grayson, Secret Service men and a valet. There was no cavalry escort and the automobile of the out-

going President was accompanied only by two motorcycle policemen and a party of newspaper men. The route along Pennsylvania
Avenue toward the Capitol was retraced, there were flurries of applause, the party passed the White House, and before the ceremonies incidental to the inauguration of Vice President Coolidge had
been completed Mr. Wilson was at his residence at 2,340 S. Street,
Northwest.

There he enjoyed a brief rest and after luncheon he figured in a
series of ovations tendered by a throng of several thousand persons
who assembled in front of his home when the inauguration ceremonies for his successor had concluded. Delegations representing
the Democratic Central Committee of the District of Columbia and
the League of Nations Association of Washington marched to the
Wilson residence at 3 o'clock and for more than an hour participated in a demonstration in appreciation of his advocacy of the
League of Nations. The former President appeared more than a
dozen times at the front window and bowed or waved his hand in
acknowledgment.

There were demands for a speech, but he waved these aside. He
received a delegation of four from the two organizations who presented to him a large basket of flowers, and he told them how profoundly he was touched at these evidences of regard and esteem.

Woodrow Wilson was not by any means the tragic figure as he
bowed his salutations to the throngs before his private residence
that he was as he limped with the aid of a cane across the White
House front portico for the last time as President earlier in the day.
Whether it was because he had shaken the heavy burdens of the
Presidency from his shoulders or was inspired by the cheering of
the crowd, Mr. Wilson appeared to have gained in vigor. During
the hour that these demonstrations lasted it was difficult for the
President to remain away from the front windows of his new home.

Men who had served in his Cabinet and Congressional members
of the Democratic party were dropping in upon the ex-President in
a steady string as callers, but from time to time he appeared at one
and then another second-story window with Mrs. Wilson, who
raised the window sash while the President smiled, bowed or
waved his salutations. Twice the President drew a handkerchief
from his pocket and waved at the crowd. He appeared anxious to
deliver a speech, but was in control of his emotions. He was repeatedly urged by his physician, Admiral Grayson, not to tax his
strength.

Prior to the ceremonies at the Capitol Mr. Harding escorted President Wilson from the Blue Room of the White House to its front
door, but Mr. Wilson walked unaided across the portico to the wait-

ing automobile. He had to be assisted into the car. At the Capitol
Mr. Wilson did not accompany Mr. Harding's party up the main
flight of marble stairs outside the Senate wing, but entered
through a door on the ground floor, near that part of the Capitol
Building which houses the Supreme Court.

A wheelchair which had been doing service for Senator Boies
Penrose of Pennsylvania was used in taking the President from his
automobile up a small incline into a lower corridor of the Senate
wing. Senator Penrose had given his wheelchair man the slip by
entering the Capitol through another door, and the chair was used
principally because it happened to be there. Once within the building, Mr. Wilson walked the rest of the way to an elevator leading
to the President's Room, and when he left he retraced that route,
walking all the way, without again using the chair, although this
time it had been taken to the second floor and was ready for use if
he wanted it.

Aside from the demonstrations in front of his residence during
the afternoon and the pathetic picture of the former President
limping slowly out of the White House earlier in the day, one of the
outstanding incidents was the meeting between Mr. Wilson and
Senator Henry Cabot Lodge, leader of the anti-treaty fight, in the
President's Room at the Capitol, immediately before noon.

When Senator Lodge entered this chamber everybody gazed in
his direction. He had come offically to inform Mr. Wilson, who was
still President, that the Senate was ready to adjourn and to inquire
whether he cared to communicate any message to the adjourning
Congress. The appearance of Senator Lodge and all that his presence may have conjured up in the mind of Mr. Wilson brought
back a flash of his old fire.

"Mr. President," Senator Lodge declared, addressing Mr. Wilson,
"as Chairman of the Joint Committee I beg to inform you that the
two houses of Congress have no further business to transact and
are prepared to receive any further communications you may care
to make."

Mr. Wilson replied:

"Tell them I have no further communication to make. I thank
you for your courtesy. Good morning, Sir."

There was something in the voice of the President and the way
he uttered these words which left no doubt that he wished to make
only the most formal reply to Mr. Lodge. The President's response
was not uttered curtly or discourteously, but there was no mistak-
ing the rigidity of the response.

The human side of Mr. Wilson was revealed immediately afterward, when, after Mr. Harding and Mr. Coolidge had made their

farewell calls upon him, while voicing his regret that he did not feel able to witness the swearing in of Mr. Harding, he said to Senator Knox:

"Well, the Senate threw me down before, and I don't want to fall down myself now."

Mr. Wilson made an allusion in almost the same breath to the steepness of the grade of the marble stairs around the Capitol.

President Wilson was astir at 8 o'clock this morning, and after breakfasting with Mrs. Wilson, went to his study on the second floor of the White House, where he signed some bills. Those close to the President said that he was a little more tired than usual this morning, perhaps because he had worked until 10:30 o'clock last night considering or signing bills. A considerable number of these had been rushed to the White House during the closing hours of the legislative jam.

The Presidential party was delayed somewhat in leaving the White House for the Capitol. Under the escort of four troops of the Third Cavalry automobiles conveying the incoming presidential party drew up in front of the White House at 10:30 o'clock. The first automobile carried Mr. Harding, accompanied by Senator Knox and former Speaker Cannon,[1] representing the Congressional Joint Committee. There was a vacant seat in the car for use by Mr. Wilson. There were other automobiles in which rode Vice President-elect Coolidge, accompanied by other members of the Joint Committee, Mrs. Harding, Mrs. Coolidge[2] and George B. Christian, Jr.,[3] who is to succeed Mr. Tumulty as private secretary to the President. As each car swung under the porte-cochère of the White House its occupants entered the Mansion and were escorted to the Blue Room. They were greeted by Mr. Tumulty and remained in the Blue Room some time before President Wilson appeared. He was accompanied by Mrs. Wilson and Admiral Grayson.

There was an exchange of greetings and handshakings which delayed the departure of the party until 11 o'clock. Shortly before that hour Chief Usher Hoover appeared at the front door and signalled the Federal and municipal authorities that those within were ready. There were no high military officials present.

President Wilson walked out of the front door on the arm of Mr. Harding. On the porch Mr. Wilson used his cane and Mr. Harding dropped his arm. Mr. Wilson walked unaided a distance of about forty feet to the waiting automobiles. Senator Knox was on one side as his escort, while President-elect Harding followed, accompanied

[1] That is, Joseph Gurney Cannon, Republican of Illinois.
[2] Grace Anna Goodhue Coolidge.
[3] George Busby Christian, Jr.

by former Speaker Cannon. This little forty-foot trip for Mr. Wilson was a very trying ordeal.

The President smiled faintly at the onlookers surrounding the portico. It had been arranged that no moving pictures should be taken until after the Presidential party had entered the automobiles. Mr. Harding stood at the edge of the platform, while "Colonel" Arthur Brooks, the colored valet of the President, took tender hold of the President's right arm, at the same time handing the President's cane to a Secret Service man standing in the automobile. James Sloan, another Government Secret Service man, who had been serving with Mr. Harding since the election, aided Mr. Wilson to enter the car. Care had to be taken because it was quite a long stride for the President from the top of the steps to the running board of the automobile. Mr. Wilson was guided by the Secret Service man as the President stepped forward.

Mr. Wilson took the rear right-hand seat, and, as incoming President, Mr. Harding took the left-hand seat. Senator Knox and Representative Cannon rode in the same car. Mr. Cannon wore a brown slouch hat.

The whole attitude of Mr. Harding, as well as of Mr. Cannon and Mr. Knox, was one of great consideration for the outgoing President in his stricken condition. The expression on the face of Mr. Harding as he gazed upon the tragic figure of his predecessor slowly getting into the automobile was a very interesting study. There was something brotherly about Mr. Harding's look and an apparent realization of the real weight of the load that American Presidents cannot evade.

The battery of motion-picture men literally "went over the top" the moment Mr. Wilson and Mr. Harding were seated.

When the rest of the party came out of the White House it included Mrs. Wilson, Admiral Grayson, Secretary Tumulty and the military and naval aids to the President. From a second-story window Miss Margaret Wilson, and Ralph [Rolfe] Bolling, brother of Mrs. Wilson, looked down upon the scene.

As soon as he himself had entered the automobile President Wilson turned his head and looked up at Mr. Harding, who was still standing until certain that Mr. Wilson was comfortable. Mr. Wilson then lifted his hat to Mr. Harding, who responded with a bow.

The Presidential procession was wholly surrounded by cavalry on its way to the Capitol. Troop I rode ahead, Troop L to the left, Troop K to the right of the official vehicles, and Troop M brought up the rear. The cavalrymen rode with their new lance swords drawn. Inside this hollow square formation were eleven cars, six of them used by the official party, the other five occupied by Secret Service and newspaper men.

Not a strain of music was heard until after the party had swung past the Peace Monument at the base of Capitol Hill. One square north of this spot the Harding and Coolidge band of Washington was playing. The only other music was that furnished by the United States Band, seated red-coated in the Capitol Plaza, but none of its notes was heard by Mr. Wilson, as it did not begin to play until after Mr. Wilson had left the Capitol.

President Wilson's car did not halt at the main entrance to the Senate wing, but moved forward to the private and lower door, which it was arranged he should use to avoid the long climb up the stairs. The Harding and Coolidge party moved up the steps outside the Senate wing and took the second floor route, through the lobby, behind the Senate Chamber itself, to the President's Room, where Mr. Wilson was greeted on his arrival.

This was a few minutes later, perhaps five, because Mr. Wilson was not able to walk at an ordinary gait, and had to walk most of the distance through the first floor corridor under the main Senate floor to an elevator leading to the President's Room, which is on the main Senate floor, immediately northwest of the Senate Chamber, and entered through the latter's main lobby.

But from his automobile up an inclined plane to the ground floor door Mr. Wilson had the use of the Penrose wheelchair. While this was not down on the program, William M. Underwood, a negro messenger, had been waiting at that door for Senator Penrose, who, on account of his recent illness, has been making use of this chair when entering the Capitol Building. Penrose, however, had stolen a march on the messenger by walking to the Capitol through another door this morning. A negro laborer by the name of Barkley ran up to where Underwood stood with the chair and started off with it.

"Where are you going with that chair?" shouted Underwood.

"It is for the President," explained Barkley, and took it.

Mr. Wilson was not aware at the time that he had ridden in the Penrose wheelchair, and availed himself of its use only to the extent of saving a climb of several steps in entering the building. Once inside, Mr. Wilson left the wheelchair, and, using his cane, was escorted by Senator Knox to an elevator, accompanied by Admiral Grayson and Mrs. Wilson.

Mr. Wilson was in the President's Room at the Capitol from 11:18 o'clock to 11:55. He was greeted on his arrival by Mr. Harding and Mr. Coolidge, members of the Wilson Cabinet and others who had gone there ahead.

After being greeted by General Pershing, Admiral Coontz,[4] the

---

[4] That is, Robert Edward Coontz, Chief of Naval Operations.

ranking officer of the navy, and members of his Cabinet, Mr. Wilson divided his time in the President's Room between the signing of bills and receiving visitors, Mr. Harding and Mr. Coolidge having gone to another part of the Capitol. Later Mr. Harding returned with Mr. Coolidge to pay their respects again to Mr. Wilson, and Mr. Harding whispered something to Mr. Wilson.

What Mr. Harding said was not audible. Mr. Wilson's reply was, "I'm sorry, Mr. President, it cannot be done." Later it was learned that this was a reply to an inquiry whether Mr. Wilson thought he would be able to go into the Senate Chamber or to the Senate portico. It was also learned that during their automobile ride from the White House to the Capitol Mr. Harding told Mr. Wilson that he would quite understand if he should find it impossible to go through with all of the inaugural ceremonies. Mr. Wilson did not care to go to the portico, if he felt he could not remain until after Mr. Harding had been inaugurated, as he thought it would be ungracious to leave during the ceremonies. After he had become fatigued at the Capitol Mr. Wilson came to appreciate also that if he attempted to walk all the way to the portico the slowness of his stride might delay the movement of the rest of the program.

After the Lodge incident and Mr. Wilson's statement to Senator Knox that the Senate "threw me down before," Mr. Harding told Mr. Wilson how much he regretted the latter's inability to witness the ceremonies. Messrs. Harding and Coolidge both thanked Mr. Wilson for having come to the Capitol. Senator Knox then escorted Mr. Wilson to the elevator, and also thanked Mr. Wilson for his visit to the Capitol. On the way through the lower corridors, while walking slowly out of the building, Mr. Wilson halted once, as if to rest, and then moved ahead.

A floor above was the crowded Senate Chamber, where the oath was about to be administered to Mr. Coolidge. The galleries were filled with the fortunate card holders. There was a thrill of excitement in the chamber. The corridors below were absolutely deserted, except for policemen at the entrances, and half a dozen marines, standing in a side corridor, as an extra precautionary measure during Mr. Wilson's departure.

Mr. Wilson, on the arm of Mrs. Wilson, walked ahead of the little procession. Immediately behind them were Secretary Tumulty and Admiral Grayson. Then came two Secret Service men, and twelve newspaper men assigned to accompany Mr. Wilson to his home. The policemen bowed, the marines stood motionless. The President smiled and bowed to the Capitol policemen.

Outside waited one of the White House automobiles. This was not the hired inaugural committee's car in which Mr. Wilson had ridden to the Capitol, and which was standing at the same door to

convey Mr. Harding, once inaugurated, back to the White House.
The While House car which was available to Mr. Wilson for the
last time was one in which he has made many of his suburban
journeys around Washington. Mrs. Wilson, Secretary Tumulty,
Admiral Grayson, Brooks, the valet and Secret Service men accompanied Mr. Wilson on his ride as a private citizen.

Some officious marine officer had ordered the cars of the newspaper correspondents away from the space where they had been
parked. Secretary Tumulty turned his own car over to the correspondents in this emergency, otherwise no newspaper men would
have been in position to record the story of Mr. Wilson's ride from
the Capitol to his new home.

Instead of taking the direct short cut across the city two motorcycle policemen led the way for Mr. Wilson along Pennsylvania Avenue to the White House around Madison Place to Seventeenth
Street, to Massachusetts Avenue, to Sheridan Circle and to the
broad-fronted three-story residence for which Mr. Wilson recently
paid $150,000. At that time there were only a few persons in front
of the house. Nearly everybody else in Washington was along
Pennsylvania Avenue, or in the crowd of the inaugural stand at the
Capitol. No policemen were on hand in front of the Wilson residence, and when the crowds began to assemble there later they
were unable to learn whether Mr. Wilson had actually entered his
new home or was still at the Capitol.

This was the situation in front of the Wilson house from 12:15
o'clock, when he had entered the residence, until a few minutes
after 3 o'clock. By that time probably 500 persons were standing
on the sidewalk opposite the Wilson house, and at that moment
the crowd began to cheer, for Mr. and Mrs. Wilson had come to
one of the third-story windows. Mr. Wilson had rested a little and
taken nourishment. He looked a little refreshed and seemed to appreciate the demonstration. Admiral Grayson, his physician, and
Secretary Tumulty, who had lunched elsewhere, soon appeared,
accompanied by Raymond T. Baker, who has been serving as Director of the Mint. Mr. and Mrs. Wilson came to the window again
at 3:30 o'clock, when an organized but informal procession of
League advocates and personal admirers marched into S Street,
halting in front of the Wilson mansion.

This procession was headed by John F. Costello, Democratic National Committeeman for the District of Columbia. Behind him
walked J. Wilson Allen and C. D. Williams, members of the League
of Nations Club of the District of Columbia. They were carrying a
floral tribute, about three feet high, made up of red roses, red and
yellow tulips, lilacs and half a dozen other varieties of flowers, in a

white wicker basket. Behind them walked about a thousand members of the two organizations. There were many women in the procession. Some of them were well along in years, and some of the women carried banners or pennants bearing the legend "League of Nations" on a blue background—something quite different from the slogans on banners of suffragists and Sinn Feiners who some months ago had picketed the White House.

The tall figure of Colonel Robert E. Lee of Ravensworth, Va., a grandson of General Robert E. Lee, who is a Washington attorney, stood above the shoulders of the crowd as it halted in front of the Wilson house, awaiting developments. These came soon. Mr. Wilson, who had twice before come to the third-story window and bowed to the crowd that had assembled ahead of the arrival of this procession, now had descended to the second floor of the residence. He and Mrs. Wilson went to one of the windows. Three cheers were given for the ex-President. Mrs. Wilson responded by raising the window sash. Mr. Wilson smiled, bowed several times, and waved his right hand. The cheering stopped. A speech was expected. The President waved another acknowledgement, but did not speak. Then Mrs. Wilson lowered the window and the President withdrew from view.

The President sent out word that he would receive representatives of the delegation. Those who were sent in were Mr. Costello, the two men who had the flower basket, and two women from each of the two associations. These were Mrs. Kate Trenholm Abrahams and Mrs. Everard Todd of the League association, and Mrs. Mary Wright Johnson and Mrs. Rose Gouverneur Hoose of the Democratic committee. With their basket of flowers they ascended to the second story reception hall of the Wilson house, where they presented the flowers to Mr. Wilson without any attempt at a speech.

Mr. Wilson was seated when the delegation entered. The basket of flowers was placed at his feet. He smiled, reached out his right hand, and shook his visitors by the hand. "It makes me very happy to see you on this occasion," Mr. Wilson told them. "I am proud of you all."

He attempted no speech. When the delegation came out of the house a man in the crowd called for three cheers for the ex-President. Soon Mr. Wilson and his wife appeared at another one of the windows, which was opened, while he smiled, bowed and waved a white handkerchief.

Some one called for a speech. A hush fell over the crowd. For a second it seemed as if Mr. Wilson would respond. In the next instant he waved his hand negatively, raised his right hand to his throat with a gesture indicating that he did not consider himself able to respond, smiled and bowed several times again and then left the window.

Meanwhile former Attorney General Palmer, former Secretary Daniels and other members of the Wilson Cabinet and various Democratic Senators and Representatives began to arrive. They called as individuals, and were received by Mr. and Mrs. Wilson on the second floor of their residence. Several times Mr. Wilson came back to the front windows, but the crowd did not disappear until the policemen told them that there would be no speech. From 2 o'clock until late in the afternoon there was a steady stream of automobiles past the Wilson home, and scattered among them were occasional "rubberneck" cars, loaded with visitors.

A News Item

[*March 4, 1921*]

WILSON'S STOCK OF LIQUOR IS MOVED

Washington, March 4.—President Wilson's private stock of liquor is safely stored to-day in his new home. The stock is reported to be large.

Government guarantees of safety were stamped upon the big cellar stocks of President Wilson, Cabinet officers and Representatives in Congress when legal permits were given by Prohibition Commissioner [John F.] Kramer to remove the liquid joy to the new homes of the owners, now about to depart from official life.

How much liquor will be moved out of Washington by the change in Administration is subject to conjecture. Commissioner Kramer remarked rather dryly:

"Higher officials have fine stocks and in abundance. You should not expect me to divulge all the details of these permits, however. That is something in the nature of a private matter."

Commissioner Kramer's office during the last two days has been over-run with officials of every class who will join the exodus from Washington after to-day. One Representative listed several barrels, while the liquor shown to have been possessed by the average applicant rarely went below dozen case lots.

Prohibition officials treated these incidents with the greatest secrecy. Considerable interest attached to the details concerning the stock of White House liquors. These were removed from the Executive Mansion to the new residence of Mr. Wilson on S street. In the shipment was a whole barrel of fine Scotch whiskey, besides a variety of rare wines and liquors.

Printed in the *New York Times*, March 5, 1921.

From Newton Diehl Baker

My dear Mr President: Washington March 4, 1921

At the end of five wonderful years I lay down the responsibilities which you entrusted to me and which, without your constant confidence and as constant guidance would have been quite beyond my strength. I search my heart for assurance that I have, even measurably, done my part, only to feel sure that there must have been a thousand ways in which I could have made your burden lighter, if I [had] but been resourceful enough to discover them.

This note of personal and grateful leave-taking is no part of the history which you have been making, but you will understand, I am sure, the happiness with which I record the exaltation with which I have seen you remake the moral relations of nations and lead America, like a little child, to the altar of right there to return to the God of Nations, as a thankoffering, her contribution of unselfishness, enlightenment and a just spirit, to the saving of all that is worth while in the progress mankind has so far made. In all this, of course, I only shared the general benefit, but in your unfailing patience and your unbroken confidence I had an intimate and personal gift which I carry away as the priceless memory of the gran[d]est and the happiest years of my life.

It is my earnest prayer, my dear Mr President, that you may be spared for many years both to see how the tide of the time will bring your treasures home and to continue as our guide and captain in the years ahead, full as they must be of perplexity and struggle and needing, as they will need, all your comprehending knowledge and sympathy.

With grateful and respectful affection believe me, Mr President
Heartily yours,   Newton D. Baker

ALS (WP, DLC).

From John Barton Payne

Washington March fourth
My dear Mr President: Nineteen Twenty One, Ten oclock a.m.

May I say from my heart how thoroughly I have enjoyed working with you, and how deeply I appreciate the confidence you have imposed in me.

It has indeed been a joy and an inspiration and will be cherished always.

In the future I hope I may see something of Mrs Wilson and your good self. And if I can in any way be useful you will confer on me a lasting favor if you will command me.

Cordially and affectionately yours.   John Barton Payne

ALS (WP, DLC).

From Frank Irving Cobb, with Enclosure

Dear Mr. President: New York March 4th, 1921.

You probably will not see The World today, but I am sending you an Editorial in which I have undertaken to interpret you and your administration as I have understood them. I may have done it badly, but I have done it honestly.

With my best wishes for long years of life, happiness and public service,   Most sincerely yours,   Frank I. Cobb.

TLS (WP, DLC).

E N C L O S U R E

WOODROW WILSON—AN INTERPRETATION.
Hundreds of years hence Wilson's name will be one of the greatest in history.—Jan Christian Smuts, Premier of the Union of South Africa.

No other American has made so much world history as Woodrow Wilson, who retires at noon to-day from the office of President of the United States. No other American has ever bulked so large in the affairs of civilization or wielded so commanding an influence in shaping their ends.

The great outstanding figure of the war, Mr. Wilson remains the great outstanding figure of the peace. Broken in health and shattered in body, Mr. Wilson is leaving the White House, but his spirit still dominates the scene. It pervades every chancellery in Europe. It hovers over every capital. Because Woodrow Wilson was President of the United States during the most critical period of modern history international relations have undergone their first far-reaching moral revolution.

Mr. Harding is assuming the duties of the Presidency, but the main interest in Mr. Harding is still a reflected interest, which is concerned chiefly with the efforts that his Administration may make to adjust itself to the forces that Mr. Wilson has set in motion. Stripped of all the paraphernalia of his office, Mr. Wilson, by virtue of his achievements, remains the most potent single influence in the modern world; yet after his eight years in the White House it may be doubted if even the American people themselves know him better or understand him better than they did the day he was first inaugurated.

Neither Mr. Wilson's friends nor his enemies have ever succeeded in interpreting him or in explaining him, nor can any interpretation or explanation be satisfactory which fails at the outset to recognize in him the simplest and at the same time the most complex character in the greatest drama ever played on the stage of human history. Even his closest associates have never found it easy to reconcile a fervent political democracy with an unbending intellectual aristocracy, or to determine which of those characteristics was dominant in his day-to-day decisions.

No man ever sat in the President's chair who was more genuinely a democrat or held more tenaciously to his faith in democracy than Woodrow Wilson, but no other man ever sat in the President's chair who was so contemptuous of all intellect that was inferior to his own or so impatient with its laggard processes.

Mr. Wilson was a President who dealt almost exclusively in ideas. He cared little or nothing about political organization and rarely consulted the managing politicians of his party. When they conferred with him it was usually at their request and not at his request. Patronage hardly entered into his calculations as an agency of government. He disliked to be troubled about appointments, and when he had filled an office he was likely to be indifferent as to the manner in which that office was subsequently administered, unless his own measures were antagonized or his policies obstructed.

No man was ever more impersonal in his attitude toward government, and that very impersonality was the characteristic which most baffled the American people. Mr. Wilson had a genius for the advocacy of great principles, but he had no talent whatever for advocating himself, and to a country that is accustomed to think in headlines about political questions his subtlety of mind and his careful, precise style of expression were quite as likely to be an obstacle to the communication of thought as a medium for the communication of thought. That is how such phrases as "too proud to fight" and "peace without victory" were successfully wrested from their context by his critics and twisted into a fantastic distortion of their true meaning.

Mr. Wilson was likewise totally deficient in the art of advertising, and advertising is the very breath of American politics. He held himself aloof from all these points of public contact. The World's relations with him have certainly been as close and intimate as those of any other newspaper; yet during the eight years in which Mr. Wilson has been in the White House he never sought a favor from The World, he never asked for support either for himself or any of his policies, he never complained when he was criticised, he never offered to explain himself or his attitude on any issue of government. In the troublesome days of his Administration he often expressed his gratitude for services that The World had rendered in the interpretation of his policies, but he never solicited such interpretation or took measures to facilitate it. He was an eloquent pleader for the principles in which he believed, but he had no faculty whatever for projecting himself into the picture.

Mr. Wilson's enemies are fond of calling him a theorist, but there is little of the theorist about him, otherwise he could never have made more constructive history than any other man of his generation. What are commonly called theories in his case were the practical application of the experience of history to the immediate problems of government, and in the experience of history Mr. Wilson is an expert. With the exception of James Madison, who was called "the Father of the Constitution," Mr. Wilson is the most profound student of government among all the Presidents, and he had what Madison conspicuously lacked, which was the faculty to translate his knowledge of government into the administration of government.

When Mr. Wilson was elected President he had reached the conclusion which most unprejudiced students of American government eventually arrive at—that the system of checks and balances is unworkable in practice and that the legislative and executive branches cannot be in fact co-ordinate, independent departments. Other Presidents have acted on that hypothesis without daring to admit it, and endeavored to control Congress by patronage and by threats. Mr. Wilson without any formality established himself as the leader of his party in Congress, Premier as well as President, and the originator of the party's programme of legislation.

Senators and Representatives denounced him as an autocrat and a dictator. Congress was described as the President's rubber stamp, but Mr. Wilson established something that more nearly resembled responsible government than anything that had gone before, and Congress under his direct leadership made a record for constructive legislation for which there is no parallel. It was due to this kind of leadership that such measures as the Federal Reserve Banking Law were enacted, which later proved to be the one bulwark between the American people and a financial panic of tragic proportions.

But Mr. Wilson's domestic policies in spite of their magnitude have been obscured by his foreign policies. Had there been no war, these policies in themselves would have given to the Wilson Administration a place in American history higher than that of any other since the Civil War. What some of his predecessors talked about doing he did, and he accomplished it by the process of making himself the responsible leader of his party in Congress—a process that is simple enough in itself but capable of fulfilment only in the hands of a man with an extraordinary capacity for imposing his will on his associates. Mr. Wilson's control over Congress for six years was once described as the most impressive triumph of mind over matter known to American politics.

When we begin the consideration of Mr. Wilson's foreign policies we are entering one of the most remarkable chapters in all history, and one which will require the perspective of history for a true judgment.

The first step in the development of these foreign policies came in Mr. Wilson's refusal to recognize Huerta, who had participated in the plot to murder President Madero and made himself the dictator of Mexico by reason of this assassination. The crime was committed during Mr. Taft's Administration. When Mr. Wilson came into office he served notice that there would be no recognition of Huerta and no recognition of any Mexican Government which was not established by due process of law.

What was plainly in Mr. Wilson's mind was a determination to end political assassination in Latin America as a profitable industry, and compel recognition, to some extent at least, of democratic principles and constitutional forms. On this issue he had to face the intense opposition of all the financial interests in the United States which had Mexican holdings, and a consolidated European opposition as well. Every dollar of foreign money invested in Mexico was confident that what Mexico needed most was such a dictatorship as that of Huerta or American intervention. Mr. Wilson's problem was to get rid of Huerta without involving the United States in war, and then by steady pressure bring about the establishment of a responsible government that rested on something at least resembling the consent of the governed. Only a statesman of high ideals would ever have attempted it, and only a statesman of almost infinite patience would have been able to adhere to the task that Mr. Wilson set for himself.

Mexico is not yet a closed incident, but Mr. Wilson's policy has been vindicated in principle. For the first time since Mr. Roosevelt shocked the moral sense and aroused the political resentment of all the Latin-American states by the rape of Panama faith in the integrity and friendship of the United States has been restored among the other nations of the Western Hemisphere.

Of equal or even greater ethical importance was Mr. Wilson's insistence on the repeal of the Panama Canal Tolls Act, which discriminated in favor of American ships in spite of the plain provisions of the Hay-Pauncefote treaty. This was the more creditable on Mr. Wilson's part because he himself had been tricked during the campaign into giving support to this measure. When he began to perceive the diplomatic consequences of this treaty violation Mr. Wilson reversed himself and demanded that Congress reverse itself. Had he done otherwise, the American people would have had scant opportunity to protest against the German perfidy which turned a treaty into "a scrap of paper."

When Germany, at the beginning of August, 1914, declared war successively on Russia, France and Belgium, thereby bringing Great Britain into the most stupendous conflict of all the centuries, Mr. Wilson did what every President has done when other nations have gone to war. He issued a proclamation of neutrality. He then went further, however, than any of his predecessors had done and urged the American people to be not only neutral in deed but "impartial in thought." Mr. Wilson has been severely criticised for this appeal. The more violent pro-Germans and the more violent pro-French and pro-British regarded it as a personal insult and an attempt on the part of the President to stifle what they were pleased to regard as their conscience.

Mr. Wilson asked the American people to be impartial in thought because he knew as a historian the danger that threatened if the country were to be divided into two hostile camps, the one blindly and unreasoningly applauding every act of the Germans and the other blindly and unreasoningly applauding every act of the Allies. In the early years of its life the Republic was all but wrecked by the emotional and political excesses of the pro-French Americans and the pro-British Americans in the war that followed the French Revolution. The warning against a passionate attachment to the interests of other nations which is embodied in Washington's Farewell Address was the first President's solemn admonition against the evils of a divided allegiance. Mr. Wilson had no desire to see the country drift into a similar situation in which American rights, American interests and American prestige would all be sacrificed to gratify the American adherents of the various European belligerents. Moreover, he understood far better than his critics that issues would soon arise between the belligerents and the United States which would require on the part of the American people that impartiality of thought that is demanded of the just and upright judge. He knew that the American people might ultimately become the final arbiters of the issues of the conflict.

The United States was the only great nation outside the sphere of conflict. It was the only great nation that had no secret diplomatic understandings with either set of belligerents. It was the only great nation that was in a position to uphold the processes of international law and to use its good offices as a mediator when the opportunity arose.

For two years Mr. Wilson genuinely believed that it would be possible for the United States to fulfil this mission, and he never fully lost hope until that day in January, 1917, when the German Government wantonly wrecked all the informal peace negotiations that were then in progress and decided to stake the fate of the empire on a single throw of the U-boat dice.

Mr. Wilson perceived quite as quickly and quite as early as anybody the possibility that the United States would be drawn into the war, but he perceived also what most of his critics failed to perceive, that the immediate danger of the country was not war but a divided people. While he was engaged in framing the first Lusitania note he discussed the situation with one of his callers at the White House in words that have since proved prophetic:

I do not know whether the German Government intends to keep faith with the United States or not. It is my personal opinion that Germany has no such intention, but I am less concerned about the ultimate intentions of Germany than about the attitude of the American people, who are already divided into three groups: those who are strongly pro-German, those who are strongly pro-Ally, and the vast majority who expect me to find a way to keep the United States out of war. I do not want war, yet I do not know that I can keep the country out of the war. That depends on Germany, and I have no control over Germany. But I intend to handle this situation in such a manner that every American citizen will know that the United States Government has done everything it could to prevent war. Then if war comes we shall have a united country, and with a united country there need be no fear about the result.

Mr. Wilson's policy from that day to April 2, 1917, must be read in the light of those words. He plunged forthwith into that extraordinary debate with the German Government over the submarine issue—the most momentous debate ever held—but he was only incidentally addressing himself to the rulers of Germany. He was talking to the conscience of the civilized world, but primarily to the conscience of the United States, explaining, clarifying, elucidating the issue. His reluctance to countenance any extensive measures of preparedness was the product of a definite resolution not to give Germany and her American supporters an opportunity to declare that the United States, while these issues were pending, was arming for war against the Imperial Government.

When Mr. Wilson began this debate he knew something which his critics did not know and which for reasons of state he did not choose to tell them. Weeks before the destruction of the Lusitania two-thirds of the German General Staff were in favor of war with the United States as a military measure in the interest of Germany. They were under the spell of Tirpitz. They believed that the submarine would do all that the Grand Admiral said it could do. They argued that inasmuch as the Allies were borrowing money in the United States, obtaining food from the United States and purchasing great quantities of munitions in the United States, Germany, by restricting submarine warfare in answer to American protests, was paying an excessive price for what was in effect a fictitious neutrality. In their opinion the United States as a neutral was already doing more for the Allies than it could do as an active belligerent if free scope were given to the U boats. The American Navy, they said, could be safely disregarded, because with Germany already blockaded by the British Navy, and the German Grand Fleet penned in, the addition of the American Navy, or a dozen navies for that matter, would make little difference in respect to the actual facts of sea power. On the other hand there was not enough shipping available to feed the Allies and enable the United States to send an army to Europe. If the United States tried to provide troops, the British would starve. If the United States could not send troops, Germany would be quite as well off with the United States in the war as out of the war, and would have the priceless additional advantage of being able to employ her submarines as she saw fit regardless of the technicalities of international law.

In the fall of 1916 Mr. Wilson decided definitely that the relations between the United States and Germany were approaching a climax. If the war continued much longer the United States would inevitably be drawn in. There was no prospect of a decision. The belligerent armies were deadlocked. Unwilling to wait longer for events, Mr. Wilson made up his mind that he would demand from each side a statement of its aims and objects and compel each side to plead its own cause before the court of the public opinion of the world. This was done on Dec. 18, 1916, in a joint note which was so cold and dispassionate in its terms that its import was hardly understood.

The President said that the aims and objects of the war on both sides "as stated in general terms to their own people and the world" seemed to be "virtually the same," and he asked for a bill of particulars. Instantly there was wild turmoil and recrimination on the part of the Allies and their friends in the United States. The President had declared, they said, that the Germans and the Allies were fighting for the same thing. Mr. Wilson had expressed no opinion of his own one way or the other and the obvious discovery was soon made in London and Paris that the President had given to the Allies the opportunity which they needed of officially differentiating their war aims from those of the Germans. The German Government missed its opportunity completely, and by their own answer to the President's note the Allies succeeded in consolidating their moral positions, which was something they had never previously been able to do in spite of all their propaganda.

Informal peace negotiations were still in progress, although conducted in secret and carefully screened from the knowledge of all peoples involved in the conflict. On Jan. 22, 1917, Mr. Wilson made his last attempt at mediation in the "peace without victory" address to the Senate in which he defined what he regarded as the fundamental conditions of a permanent peace. Most of the basic principles of this address were afterward incorporated into the Fourteen Points. Here again Mr. Wilson was the victim of his own precision of language and of the settled policy of his critics of reading into his public utterances almost everything except what he actually said. He himself had insisted on giving his own interpretation of "peace without victory," and this interpretation was instantly rejected by the super-patriots who regarded themselves as the sole custodians of all the issues of the war.

When the armistice was signed one of the most eminent of living British statesmen gave it as his opinion that the war had lasted two years too long, and that the task of salvaging an enduring peace from the wreck had become well-nigh insuperable. It will always be one of the fascinating riddles of history to guess what the result would have been if Mr. Wilson's final proposals for mediation had been accepted. The United States would not have entered the war, and a less violent readjustment of the internal affairs of Europe would probably have resulted. There would have been no Bolshevist revolution in Russia and no economic collapse of Europe. Nor is it certain that most of the really enduring benefits of the Treaty of Versailles could not have been as well obtained by negotiation as they were finally obtained through a military victory which cost a price that still staggers humanity.

Be that as it may, the German Government, now fighting to maintain the dynasty and the Junker domination, took the issue out of Mr. Wilson's hands. Ten days after his "peace without victory" address the German autocracy put into effect its cherished programme of ruthless submarine warfare. The only possible answer on the part of the United States was the dismissal of Count von Bernstorff, the German Ambassador, and from that time war between the United States and Germany was only a matter of days. But Mr. Wilson had achieved the great purpose that he had formulated two years before. He had been balked in his efforts at mediation, but he had united the American people on the issues of the conflict. He had demonstrated to them that their Government had exerted every honorable means to avoid war and that its hands were clean. There was no uncertainty in their minds that the responsibility for the war rested solely on Germany, and Mr. Wilson now purposed to write the terms of peace with the sword.

Mr. Wilson's War Address on the night of April 2, 1917, was the most dramatic event that the National Capitol had ever known. In the presence of both branches of Congress, of the Supreme Court, of the Cabinet and of the Diplomatic Corps, Mr. Wilson summoned the American people not to a war but to a crusade in words that instantaneously captivated the imagination of the Nation:

But the right is more precious than peace, and we shall fight for the things which we have always carried nearest our hearts— for democracy, for the right of those who submit to authority to have a voice in their own government, for the rights and liberties of small nations, for a universal dominion of right by such a concert of free peoples as shall bring peace and safety to all nations and make the world at last free. To such a task we can dedicate our lives and our fortunes, everything that we are and everything that we have, with the pride of those who know that the day has come when America is privileged to spend her blood and her might for the principles that gave her birth and happiness and the peace which she has treasured. God helping her, she can do no other.

This was not Woodrow Wilson, the intellectual aristocrat, who was speaking, but Woodrow Wilson the fervent democrat, proclaiming a new declaration of independence to the embattled peoples.

No sooner had Congress declared war than Mr. Wilson proceeded to mobilize all the resources of the Nation and throw them into the conflict. This war was different from any other war in which the United States had ever engaged, not only by reason of its magnitude but by reason of the necessity for co-ordinating American military plans with the military plans of the Allies. The Allies were not quite agreed as to what they desired of the United

States aside from unlimited financial assistance, and the solution of the general problem depended more or less on the trend of events.

The test of any war policy is its success, and it is a waste of time to enter into a vindication of the manner in which the Wilson Administration made war, or to trouble about the accusations of waste and extravagance, as if war were an economic process which could be carried on prudently and frugally. The historian is not likely to devote serious attention to the partisan accusations relating to Mr. Wilson's conduct of the war, but he will find it interesting to record the manner in which the President brought his historical knowledge to bear in shaping the war policies of the country.

The voluntary system and the draft system had both been discredited in the Civil War, so Mr. Wilson demanded a Selective-Service Act under which the country could raise 10,000,000 troops, if 10,000,000 troops were needed, without deranging its essential industries. It had taken Mr. Lincoln three years to find a General whom he could intrust with the command of the Union armies. Mr. Wilson picked his Commander in Chief before he went to war and then gave to Gen. Pershing the same kind of ungrudging support that Mr. Lincoln gave to Gen. Grant. The Civil War had been financed by greenbacks and bond issues peddled by bankers. Mr. Wilson called on the American people to finance their own war, and they unhesitatingly responded. In the war with Spain the commissary system had broken down completely owing to the antiquated methods that were employed. No other army in time of war was ever so well fed or so well cared for as that of the United States in the conflict with Germany.

Mistakes there were in plenty, both in methods and in the choice of men, and errors of judgment and the shortcomings that always result from a lack of experience, but the impartial verdict of history must be that when everything is set forth on the debit side of the balance sheet which can be set forth Mr. Wilson remains the most vigorous of all the war Presidents. Yet it is also true that history will concern itself far less with Mr. Wilson as a war President than with Mr. Wilson as a peace-making President. It is around him as a peace-making President that all the passions and prejudices and disappointments of the world still rage.

Mr. Wilson in his "peace without victory" address to the Senate previous to the entrance of the United States into the war had sketched a general plan of a co-operative peace. "I am proposing, as it were," he said, "that the nations with one accord should adopt the doctrine of President Monroe as the doctrine of the world." He returned to the subject again in his War Address, in which he de-

fined the principles for which the United States was to fight and
the principles on which an enduring peace could be made. The
time came when it was necessary to be still more specific.

In the winter of 1918 the morale of the Allies was at its lowest
ebb. Russia had passed into the hands of the Bolsheviki and was
preparing to make a separate peace with Germany. There was
widespread discontent in Italy, and everywhere in Europe soldiers
and civilians were asking one another what they were really fighting for. On Jan. 8 Mr. Wilson went before Congress and delivered
the address which contained the Fourteen Points of peace, a message which was greeted both in the United States and in Europe
as a veritable Magna Charta of the nations. Mr. Wilson had again
become the spokesman of the aspirations of mankind, and from the
moment that this address was delivered the thrones of the Ho-
henzollerns and the Hapsburgs ceased to be stable.

Ten months later they were to crumble and collapse. Before the
armistice was signed on Nov. 11, 1918, Mr. Wilson had overthrown
the doctrine of Divine right in Europe. The Hapsburgs ran away.
The Kaiser was compelled to abdicate and take refuge in exile, justifying his flight by the explanation that Wilson would not make
peace with Germany while a Hohenzollern was on the throne. This
was the climax of Mr. Wilson's power and influence and, strangely
enough, it was the dawn of his own day of disaster.

For nearly six years Mr. Wilson had manipulated the Government of the United States with a skill that was almost uncanny.
He had turned himself from a minority President into a majority
President. He had so deftly outmanoeuvred all his opponents in
Congress and out of Congress that they had nothing with which to
console themselves except their intensive hatred of the man and
all that pertained to him. Then at the very summit of his career he
made his first fatal blunder.

Every President in the off-year election urges the election of a
Congress of his own party. That is part of the routine of politics,
and during the campaign of 1918 Mr. Wilson's advisers urged him
to follow the precedent. What they forgot and he forgot was that it
was no time for partisan precedents, and he allowed his distrust of
the Republican leaders in Congress to sweep him into an inexcusable error that he, of all men, should have avoided. The Sixty-fifth
Congress was anything but popular. The Western farmers were ag-
grieved because the price of wheat had been regulated and the
price of cotton had not. The East was greatly dissatisfied with the
war taxes, which it regarded as an unfair discrimination, and it
remembered Mr. Kitchin's boast that the North wanted the war
and the North would have to pay for it. There was general com-

plaint from business interests against the Southern Democratic control of the legislative department, and all this sentiment instantly crystallized when the President asked for another Democratic Congress. Republicans who were loyally supporting the Administration in all its war activities were justly incensed that a party issue had been raised. A Republican Congress was elected and by inference the President sustained a personal defeat.

Misfortunes did not come singly in Mr. Wilson's case. Following the mistake of appealing for the election of a Democratic Congress he made an equally serious mistake in the selection of his Peace Commission.

To anybody who knows Mr. Wilson, who knows Mr. Lloyd George, who knows Mr. Clemenceau, nothing could be sillier than the chapter of Keynes and Dillon in which they undertake to picture the President's unfitness to cope with the European masters of diplomacy. Mr. Wilson for years had been playing with European masters of diplomacy as a cat plays with a mouse. To assume that Mr. Wilson was ever deceived by the transparent tactics of Mr. Lloyd George and Mr. Clemenceau is to assume the impossible. It would be as easy to conceive of his being tricked and bamboozled by the United States Senate.

Mr. Wilson needed strong Republican representation on the Peace Commission not to reinforce him in his struggles with his adversaries at Paris but to divide with him the responsibility for a treaty of peace that was doomed in advance to be a disappointment. Although the popular sentiment of Europe was almost passionate in its advocacy of President Wilson's peace programme, all the special interests that were seeking to capitalize the peace for their own advantage or profit were actively at work and were beginning to swing all the influence that they could command on their various Governments. It was inevitable from the outset that Mr. Wilson could never get the peace that he had expected. The treaty was bound to be a series of compromises that would satisfy nobody, and when Mr. Wilson assumed all the responsibility for it in advance he assumed a responsibility that no statesman who had ever lived could carry alone. Had he taken Mr. Root or Mr. Taft or both of them with him the terms of the Treaty of Versailles might have been no different, but the Senate would have been robbed of the partisan grievance on which it organized the defeat of ratification.

Day after day during the conference Mr. Wilson fought the fight for peace that represented the liberal thought of the world. Day after day the odds against him lengthened. The contest finally resolved itself into a question of whether he should take what he could get or whether he should withdraw from the conference and throw the doors open to chaos. The President made the only decision that he had a moral right to make. He took what he could get, nor are the statesmen with whom he was associated altogether to blame because he did not get more. They too had to contend against forces over which they had no control. They were not free agents either, and Mr. Smuts has summed up the case in two sentences:

It was not the statesmen that failed so much as the spirit of the peoples behind them. The hope, the aspiration, for a new world order of peace and right and justice, however deeply and universally felt, was still only feeble and ineffective in comparison with the dominant national passions which found their expression in the peace treaty.

All the passions and hatreds bred of four years of merciless warfare, all the insatiable fury for revenge, all the racial ambitions that had been twisted and perverted by centuries of devious diplomacy—these were all gathered around the council table, clamorous in their demand to dictate the terms.

Mr. Wilson surrendered more than he dreamed he was surrendering, but it is not difficult to follow his line of reasoning. The League of Nations was to be a continuing court of equity, sitting in judgment on the peace itself, revising its terms when revision became necessary and possible, slowly readjusting the provisions of the treaty to a calmer and saner state of public mind. Get peace first. Establish the League, and the League would rectify the inevitable mistakes of the treaty.

It is a curious commentary on human nature that when the treaty was completed and the storm of wrath broke, all the rage, all the resentment, all the odium should have fallen on the one man who had struggled week in and week out against the forces of reaction and revenge and had written into the treaty all that it contains which makes for the international advancement of the race.

Into that record must also go the impressive fact that the Treaty of Versailles was rejected by the United States Senate, under the leadership of Henry Cabot Lodge, not because of its acknowledged defects and shortcomings, not because it breathed the spirit of a Carthaginian peace in its punitive clauses, but because of its most enlightened provision, the covenant of the League of Nations, which is the one hope of a war-racked world.

When people speak of the tragedy of Mr. Wilson's career they have in mind only the temporary aspects of it—the universal dissatisfaction with the treaty of peace, his physical collapse, his defeat in the Senate and the verdict at the polls in November. They forget that the end of the chapter is not yet written. The League of

Nations is a fact, whatever the attitude of the United States may be toward it, and it will live unless the peoples of the earth prove their political incapacity to use it for the promotion of their own welfare. The principle of self-determination will remain as long as men believe in the right of self-government and are willing to die for it. It was Woodrow Wilson who wrote that principle into the law of nations, even though he failed to obtain a universal application of it. Tacitus said of the Catti tribesmen, "Others go to battle; these go to war," and Mr. Wilson went to war in behalf of the democratic theory of government extended to all the affairs of the nations. That war is not yet won, and the Commander in Chief is crippled by the wounds that he received on the field of action. But the responsibility for the future does not rest with him. It rests with the self-governing peoples for whom he has blazed the trail. All the complicated issues of this titanic struggle finally reduce themselves to these prophetic words of Maximilian Harden: "Only one conqueror's work will endure—Wilson's thought."

Woodrow Wilson on this morning of the fourth of March can say, in the words of Paul the Apostle to Timothy:

> *"For I am now ready to be offered, and*
> *the time of my departure is at hand.*
> *"I have fought a good fight. I have*
> *finished my course, I have kept the faith."*

Printed in the New York *World*, March 4, 1921.

From Josephus Daniels

My Dear Mr. President: Washington. March 5. 1921.

This is the last line I write as Secretary of the Navy, and I wish it to be to you. During these eventful years you have overlooked my mistakes and been my inspiration and stone wall of strength. For the privilege of serving in your administration I am grateful. For your friendship I can say nothing except that [it] is my most valued possession and will be heritage which my children will prize as a legacy. We are too near the event to have a correct perspective, but already we can see that the great policy of world justice you incarnated will be hailed as the hope of mankind. One day it will be realized and the world will remember you with gratitude.

My wife joins me in love to you and Mrs. Wilson. Health and happiness to you both and long life.

With our sincere affection,

Your friend,   Josephus Daniels

ALS (WP, DLC).

From Edward William Bok

My dear Mr. Wilson: Merion Pennsylvania March 6 1921

May I just say to you that my faith in you and your ideals follow you into your private life the same as it was yours while President. I believe from now on the wheels of Time will move more rapidly to vindicate your Presidency and yourself, and that you will, within a few years, receive the homage due you from the people as a whole. The tide has already turned, and events from now will bring to your work a clearer understanding and to you a personal respect and devotion.

All your friends ask of you is that you will get well and enjoy in perfect health the reward for your work which is so certainly in store for you.

With the best of good wishes, and the assurance of my willing service whenever you need it, believe me,

Very sincerely yours,   Edward W. Bok

ALS (WP, DLC).

To Frank Irving Cobb

Dear Mr. Cobb: Washington D C March 7th 1921

You have been wonderfully generous to me in the great editorial in The World, and I thank you with all my heart.

It is very delightful to have your approval.

Cordially yours,   Woodrow Wilson

TLS (IEN).

To Edward William Bok

My dear Mr. Bok: Washington D C March 9th, 1921.

Your letter of March 6th has given me great pleasure, and I am very much cheered by your friendship and statements, as I hope you know.

Cordially and sincerely yours,   Woodrow Wilson

TLS (WP, DLC).

To Jessie Woodrow Wilson Sayre

My dearest Little Girl: Washington D C March 9th, 1921.

It was real thoughtful of you to send me the telegraphic message,[1] and you may be sure how it cheered and delighted me.

I am ever so anxious to have you come and see our new home, and help us make it feel like home.

With best love to you both;   Your affectionate,   Father

TLS (received from Francis B. Sayre).
  [1] It is missing.

From George Creel

[New York] March Eleventh,
My dear Mr. President: Nineteen Twenty-One.

Perhaps you do not like this form of address, but to me you will always be *the* President.

I would have answered your letter of March second before this but I did not want to give you another letter to read at that time.

I took up the matter of the pardon at the request of friends and felt that I had discharged my obligations of friendship when I secured consideration of the case. The reason that I suggested taking it up with the Attorney General for reference to you, was because I wanted the whole matter decided on its merits, and I feel that it was.

I do not know when I will be in Washington again, but please feel at liberty to call upon me at any time, whenever I can be of the slightest service.

With every dear wish for your new undertaking,

Always devotedly,   [George Creel]

CCL (G. Creel Papers, DLC).

From Charles William Eliot

Dear President Wilson: Cambridge, Mass., 12 March 1921

Your message vetoing that absurd Emergency Tariff Bill[1] is one of the best messages you have ever sent to Congress, its logic being unanswerable, and its style concise and vivid. If it does not change the policy of Congress in respect to protective duties, it will be because the majority in both Senate and House can neither see nor reason. The message is also highly satisfactory, because it expresses again your leading policies at home and abroad, including your policies at the Paris Conferences.

I take the liberty of saying also that your last days in office and your retirement to private life have been characterized by dignity and patriotic purpose. I feel strong sympathy with your apparent intention to leave to other people the discussion and estimation of the part you have played in this country and in Europe during the past eight years. When the other actors in the great events of the past seven years have told their stories and made all their "revelations," the competent historian, American or European, will have no need of any autobiographical narrative by you. The facts will speak for themselves. I have acquired during the last twenty years great distrust of autobiographies, because of the catastrophes that have befallen some of my friends and acquaintances who have indulged in that sort of self-revelation. All your friends here hope that return to private life will quicken your restoration to health and working power. Your purpose of returning to law practice is highly interesting. I had completely forgotten that you had ever studied or practiced law. You have selected a first-rate partner; and I hope you mean to let him do all the heavy or anxious work. I meet sometime in Cambridge society Mr. and Mrs. Sayre—always with great pleasure. They are both very charming young married people, and he a promising teacher of law.

Sincerely yours   Charles W. Eliot

P.S. On re-reading this letter I notice the tone, as of an old man's letter to a much younger friend. Please excuse me. I believe I am twenty-two years older; but you have had in three-quarters of my years a much more varied experience than I.

TLS (WP, DLC).
    [1] It is printed at March 3, 1921.

From Robert Jacob Bender[1]

My dear Mr. Wilson: Washington, D. C. March 13, 1921

Only a great press of work coming with the events of the last two weeks has prevented my writing a little note of affection and appreciation as you retire again to private life.

I wished you to know, however, the very deep gratitude in my heart for the many kindnesses shown me by you and those immediately about you during the eventful years just behind us. It is not the rule that a young newspaperman is accorded the privileges and many thoughtful bits of aid that were extended me during your administration. They were the direct means of effecting what success I may have achieved in my profession.

It is for these reasons as well as my deep sympathy for the great cause for which you have given so much that I intrude for a moment with an expression of pride that I might have lived and worked near you during these years. My hope and prayer is that you continue to gain in strength the better to carry on for the world's betterment.

With both affection and admiration I shall always remain,

Faithfully yours,   Robert J Bender[2]

TLS (WP, DLC).
[1] U.P. reporter; one of Wilson's best friends among the Washington press corps.
[2] Attached to this letter is the following draft of a reply: "my dear bender I was very much plsd to gt yr ltr of 13th and to lrn of yr friendsp and confdn. I hop that in the yrs to cm u wl fnd mny opprtntys to advance the ideas and idels which alone can digny the nation and gv it the world wide influence which all its thoughtdul leaders have sought for o it." T MS (WP, DLC).

To Josephus Daniels

My dear Daniels: Washington D C March 14th, 1921.

I have often had occasion to express to you my affection and friendship; but it is always a pleasure to renew the assurance, and I respond to your letter of March 5th with a very live feeling of gratitude that I have so entirely won your confidence and support.

Our association has been very delightful to me, and I hope in the years to come we will ever be able to renew our personal friendship and remind each other of the days of service together and our genuine affection for one another.

With warmest regards and best wishes for you all;

Your sincere friend,   Woodrow Wilson

TLS (J. Daniels Papers, DLC).

To David Franklin Houston

My dear Houston: Washington D C March 14th, 1921.

Your letter of March 3rd went to my heart.

None of my colleagues has filled me with a more complete sense of trust and confidence than you have.

It has been a pleasure not only, but always an inspiration, to be associated with you in the service of the country.

The sincere friendship now consummated between us will, I am sure, grow as the years pass, into a more delightful personal relation.

With the warmest heartfelt good wishes for the future to you and yours;   Gratefully your friend,   Woodrow Wilson

TLS (D. F. Houston Papers, NjP).

To Joshua Willis Alexander

My dear Judge Alexander: Washington D C March 14th, 1921.

Your letter of March 3rd brings me a most welcome message and trust.

I want to assure you that I have thoroughly enjoyed my official association with you, because I have felt throughout your steadiness and willingness in what is right.

I shall always cherish your friendship, and hope that in the years to come we shall often be brought together to renew our very delightful personal association.

With most cordial good wishes, in which Mrs. Wilson joins me, for both you and Mrs. Alexander;[1]

Gratefully yours,   Woodrow Wilson

TLS (RSB Coll., DLC).
[1] Roe Ann Richardson Alexander.

To Charles William Eliot

My dear Dr. Eliot: Washington D C March 15th, 1921.

Your letter of generous friendship and approbation brought me real cheer and comfort.

I value your friendship above that of others and it is very delightful to see that you view my actions with approval.

I am looking forward to my new carreer as a lawyer with great interest, and feel very confident about it, because I have the utmost confidence in the admirable man—my choosen partner—who has before been tested in high office.

Again begging to express my very deep appreciation of your friendship, and with high respect;

Cordially and gratefully yours,   Woodrow Wilson

TLS (C. W. Eliot Papers, MH).

From Frank Irving Cobb

Dear Mr. President: New York March 17th, 1921.

I thought it might interest you to know that the requests for copies of the Editorial of March 4th have been so insistent that we have reprinted it in pamphlet form.[1] Letters are steadily coming in with reference to it. Nothing is more evident than the swing of the pendulum in your direction; I find it everywhere. Mr. Ochs,[2] of the New York Times, told me the other night that all their letters indicated the same tendency.

The American people are in for a good stiff dose of normalcy, and the more of it they have to swallow the less they are going to like it.

You have seen the advance copies of Lansing's book[3] of course. It reminds me of McClellan's Own Story,[4] in which he set out to vindicate himself, and proved Lincoln's case against him.

With sincerest regards,   As ever yours,   Frank I Cobb.

TLS (WP, DLC).
  [1] *Woodrow Wilson: An Interpretation* (New York, 1921).
  [2] That is, Adolph Simon Ochs, publisher and principal owner of the *New York Times*.
  [3] That is, Lansing's *The Peace Negotiations*.
  [4] George Brinton McClellan, *McClellan's Own Story: The War for the Union, the Soldiers Who Fought It, the Civilians Who Directed It and His Relations to It and to Them* (New York, 1887).

From Edgar Odell Lovett

My dear President Wilson   Houston, Texas. 20 March 1921

We have received from Professor Axson the wonderful olive wood box from Athens which you have most generously sent us for preservation among the academic treasures of this new institution. I am especially grateful to you for allowing us to have also the address of presentation which accompanies the diploma.[1] We should like to deter public acknowledgment of your compliance with our request until June in order to include the announcement in the exercises of our sixth annual commencement. In the meantime I have taken the liberty of having several copies made of the presentation address, one of which I am sending to Mrs Lovett[2] and another to our former Princeton neighbour Professor Thilly[3] an equally loyal friend of yours.

And if the granting of one request might be presumed to prepare the way for the renewal of another, I should like to say that I have authority from the trustees of Rice and the founder of the Godwin lectureship to extend for the academic year 1921-22 an invitation which we had the honour to address to you and Mrs Wilson for the current year.[4] For the acceptance of this invitation we should be willing to meet your convenience in every way within our power. For example, if for any reason you should find the journey to Houston in conflict with any plans you may be making, would it not be possible for you to prepare a discourse on any subject of your own choosing and permit us to publish it in a limited edition of the Rice Institute Pamphlet, reserving for yourself all copyright privileges and accepting as partial compensation for so distinguished a service the flat honorarium which the lectureship bears, namely one thousand dollars.

I have made so many unsuccessful efforts to link your great name, either through the spoken or written word, into the early history of this institution, that I wish I could find some way to make this latest appeal a cumulative one. On the other hand, the knowledge of your goodwill has sustained me so often in my work, that I haven't the face, though I might still have the heart, to urge our invitation unduly upon you.

With a warm renewal of our invitation, pray accept our very sincere thanks for your gift, assure Mrs Wilson how deeply we appreciate her kindness in gaining your consent thus to honour us, and believe me to remain, with great respect

Faithfully yours   Edgar Odell Lovett

ALS (WP, DLC).
    [1] See E. O. Lovett to EBW, Nov. 21, 1920, and WW to E. O. Lovett, Nov. 26, 1920, both in Vol. 66. Wilson had sent Lovett the diploma from the University of Athens awarding him the honorary degree of Doctor of Laws, together with the decree of the university saying that Wilson's name had been added to the brief list of its recipients of honorary degrees. In addition, Wilson sent Lovett G[eorge] Z. Gazepe to WW, Dec. 10, 1918, TLS, which accompanied the above-mentioned items, and a typed copy of an English translation of the presentation address made by Gazepe, Rector of the University. The diploma is contained in a silver box, on the top of which in gold is the bust of Athena and three lines of Greek lettering in capitals of gold which read in English "The University of Athens to Woodrow Wilson, President of the American Republic." This silver box and the other items are contained in an olive wooden box, beautifully carved and polished. The box and its contents are in the Archives of Rice University. This information courtesy of Nancy L. Boothe, Director, Woodson Research Center, The Fondren Library, Rice University.
    [2] Mary Ellen Hale Lovett.
    [3] Frank Thilly, Professor of Philosophy and Dean of the College of Arts and Sciences, at Cornell University. He had served as Professor of Psychology at Princeton, 1904-1906, at which time Lovett had been Professor of Mathematics and then Professor of Astronomy at Princeton.
    [4] See WW to E. O. Lovett, July 27, 1920, n. 2, Vol. 65.

From the Diary of Ray Stannard Baker

[Washington] March 20 [1921].

They have given me a little comfortable room in the new house in S street. Mrs. Wilson showed me over her home. It is really a delightful place: with a small breakfast alcove giving upon a terrace-garden now green with new grass & bright with tulips. Mr. Wilson's study opens also to the rear & upon this garden: but he wants room for half his books. In the large front room Mrs. Wilson has hung the magnificent Gobelin tapestry, presented to her in France.[1] It covers all one end of the room & is so long that nearly half of it must be rolled up at the bottom

    [1] Baker was in error. Ambassador Jean Jules Jusserand presented the tapestry to Mrs. Wilson on behalf of the people of France in the White House on July 30, 1918. See J. J. Jusserand to S. J. M. Pichon, Aug. 1, 1918, Vol. 49.

Never was there such a swift change of public regard for a man than for Mr. Wilson since he left the White House. Not only in the newspapers, but in a hundred small ways (they showed me the extraordinary number of letters daily received) there are evidences of a return of appreciation for Mr. Wilson. All day automobiles & sight-seeing wagons go by the house—the caller-out shouting: "Just below on the left—not the house on the corner—is the new home of ex-President Wilson." Sometimes the cars stop entirely & there is much craning of necks & much pointing. This man, who was so low two months ago that there was scarcely any to do him honor, is now, again, coming into his own. The new Harding administration, thus far, is following exactly in the paths of his policy & thus confirming it (after such bitter attacks in the campaign): & they will have to follow it into the League of Nations.

It has been wonderful spring weather: positively hot: & this morning, in a tall tree at the top of the hill as I came over S street, a Kentucky cardinal was making the world glad. I stopped to tell him "good-morning."

—Mrs. Wilson brought me down this afternoon on her way to her first informal entertainment by Mrs. Harding.

[Washington] March 22 [1921].

Another perfect spring day: but not so oppressively warm. Working all day on the documents. Reading advance pages of Lansing's book: in which he gives a vivid picture of exactly what kind of a man he is. I lunched with Mrs. Wilson & Mr. Bolling, Mr. Wilson not being able to come down. We talked of her visit yesterday to the White House. The Hardings have been most cordial: they came here to call the other day in person. Mrs. Wilson looks much less careworn than she did in the earlier days at the White House: seems, indeed, to be greatly enjoying the new house.

After luncheon I went up stairs for a talk with Mr. Wilson. He was in bed, propped against a huge pile of pillows & looking inconceivably old, gray, worn, tired. His hair seemed unusually thin: & his face a kind of parchment yellow, with the skin drawn down over the temple & cheek-bones, bringing into new prominence the fine aquiline modelling of his face. Only the eyes seemed undimmed: very bright, clear, piercing: burning like living coals in the ashes of a spent fire. He has not been as well since he left the White House. He overstrained himself in the last few days: & since he came here has scarcely known what to do. He has been lost. Grayson told me that he had suffered somewhat from a recurrence of the trouble with the prostate gland. Yesterday he was in bed all day: out this afternoon, late, he got up & went for a drive with Mrs. Wilson. I may be wrong, but he seems to me to have failed much in the last two weeks.

He had a couple of electric flash lights on the stand near him, a book (of detective stories) and some chocolate. A very much worn Bible lay on the desk near the head of the bed. He could look out from where he lay across a pleasant, quiet room, to the garden, where spring is now breaking with rare beauty. Mrs. Wilson says the cardinal birds come to sing there: & just at the foot of the garden is a wondrous red-blooming shrub, like fire against the wall.

But he is bitter at heart. I told him of the change which was coming in the country toward him, but he was inclined to be skeptical & want cases: which I was abundantly able to give him. When I mentioned the greatly superior applause with which his picture was greeted at the moving picture houses over that of Mr. Harding, he said:

"But that was discourteous to the President of the United States."

"It showed how people felt," I said.

"Yes, I remember, how, in the early days of my presidency of being at the theater & of having Roosevelt's picture much more cheered than mine—although I was present."

He seems lonlier, more cut-off, than ever before. His mind still works with power, but with nothing to work upon! Only memories & regrets. He feels himself bitterly misunderstood & unjustly attacked: and being broken in health, cannot rally under it. He has not read Lansing's articles or book & does not intend to, but he knows that they are being published. He said, "I think I can stand it if Lansing can!"

I have not before had up with him any of the business aspects of the present work. I have felt delicate about it. But last week I began to realize what the financial possibilities might be: and I told him of my arrangements to date in regard to book, magazine & newspaper publication. I said that I thought there was going to be a good deal of money in it & that, of course, I could not consider taking it all: that my prime interest was in the book itself—in trying to lay a sound foundation of knowledge of what happened at Paris, as a basis upon which our future foreign diplomacy might be built.

He said, this [?], that he had asked George Creel to take charge of his literary business affairs & suggested that I talk with him— which I shall do.

I wish I could get rid of all these business matters. They worry me. Of course I want & must have pay for my work, and I should like a stake in all the future of the enterprise on its business side: but these matters of adjustment of dollar values of things that have no dollar standards of value—the intangible loyalties, enthusiasms [?], artistic impulses, friendships—make a miserable business. One thing only I shall demand & that is, freedom in writing the book. And I believe I can depend, in this, upon the President's word.

The President told me to-day that it was Col. House who suggested the institution of the Council of Four, in order to push business along. I had up a number of other questions with him. He does not readily remember times, or places: evidently has no *visualization* of the Conference in his mind: does not see it objectively or personally. What he recalls are arguments, and situations in the debates that went on. There is one period of the Conference—and a very important one—when the struggle between Wilson on the one hand & L.G. & Clemenceau on the other was at its sharpest—which is poorly documented. It was in the early days of the Big Four—about March 25 to April 10th—before any minutes of the meetings were made. It was in this period that, Grayson says, the President made his greatest speech.[2] I tried to get him to tell me about this, but he seemed not to remember it specifically at all.

He has little constructive faculty: but if one can give him a scheme, an outline, he is wonderful in annotating it, criticising it, casting its ideas into fine words. In the development of the League of Nations, he knew clearly the principles which he wished to apply: but when he came to construct an actual covenant he worked upon Baron Phillimore's draft, upon House's draft: and later upon Cecil's & Smuts'.

[2] Grayson might have been referring to Wilson's remarks in the Council of Four printed in Vol. 56, pp. 364-65.

From Franklin Delano Roosevelt

New York Mar 23 1921

Expect to be in Washington tomorrow May I come to see you at your convenience anytime except three o'clock Am at Forty seven East sixty Fifth Street New York City

Franklin D. Roosevelt.

T telegram (WP, DLC).

To Franklin Delano Roosevelt

[Washington] Mch. 23 [1921]

Regret that other engagements will prevent my seeing you to-morrow.   Woodrow Wilson.

T telegram (WP, DLC).

From Ida Minerva Tarbell

My dear Mr. Wilson: [New York] March 23, 1921

Will you permit a friend to welcome you back to private life; and in doing it to say some of the things that she has long been wanting to say?

The first will sound a little like self-glorification, I fear; but I do want to say that it is a matter of genuine pride to me that in the hard eight years that you are just finishing, I have practically always been in agreement with your view of every public situation and with your method of handling it. I take deep personal satisfaction in this.

More and more as time goes on I realize how right you have been at every grave moment, how deeply based your conclusions have been, how invulnerable they are before attack. Smoke and noise may have obscured or distorted them at times for a mass of onlookers; but, with the clearing of the smoke and the silencing of the tumult, they stand, and will continue to stand.

The long months of your illness have been hard for those of us who believe in you and in your work as I do. It was hard to see the country grow more and more bewildered, to see it take up with lesser things, to see it forfeiting its place in the hearts and minds of the men of other nations—we did so need your leadership!

And yet, personally, through it all—I think you will understand this—there has never been an hour when I have not had complete serenity, both as to the inestimable value of your achievement and as to your future position in the world's history.

As I see it, you have been the first to open the eyes of the world as a whole to the practical nature of the greatest of all men's ideals, that is, world peace. You took it out of the realm of the visionary and built it into men's minds as a reasonable, practical thing. It is now a world concept, not the dream of a few scattered groups of men and women. It can never be dislodged from the place that you have given it. It has become a part of practical human thinking and planning. You did that. It was consummate statesmanship to realize that the moment had come when this could be done, that it had to be done at that moment or not at all.

The supreme effort that you made in Paris seemed to me at all times like a conscious, willing sacrifice of yourself. You have had to pay a terrible price, dear Mr. Wilson, but you must believe that what you have done is worth all it has cost you. The country is already beginning to acknowledge your achievement—it has known it in its heart all the time. I am looking forward to happy years for you when the honor and effection [affection] which you have so nobly earned will be manifest not only here at home but the world over.

With all good wishes for your happiness, believe me

Faithfully yours,   Ida M. Tarbell

TLS (WP, DLC).

George Creel to Edith Bolling Galt Wilson

New York City
March Twenty-Third,
Nineteen Twenty-One.

My dear Mrs. Wilson:

I think you will believe me when I say that at the time I made my publication suggestion to the President I did not have any thought of personal profit, nor have I ever given that phase of the matter any thought. My only interests were the spread of the truth and the victory of our cause.

Because the President is the one man that the people want to hear from I felt that he must do the writing. Because there was no way in which this writing could be given free to the people and since money had to be made out of it, I wanted him to make the money.

The decision to give Mr. Baker exclusive rights to the President's material was, quite naturally, a bitter blow to me. I thought then and still think that the President was the only one to get any real value out of the material. For another thing, I did not think that the privilege should have been given exclusively to anyone. Even more, the strength given to Mr. Baker is not a strength that we can pass on to our movement, for he is not connected with it in any fighting capacity and has never been connected with it. However, I accepted the decision as whole-heartedly as I could and hoped for the best.

Today, however, I find this to be the situation: Doubleday Page and Company are going to bring out Mr. Baker's book, but before its publication it is to be run serially in the "World's Work"—also to be sold for serial publication in the daily press. A conservative estimate of the financial returns is about $100,000.

Mr. Herbert Swope saw me today and is very bitter about the whole matter. Mr. Brainard,[1] President of Harper and Brother, is handling the newspaper syndication for Mr. Baker on a fifty-fifty basis. The price that he wanted from the New York World for the New York City rights was $7,500. When Mr. Swope learned that the newspaper publication was to follow the magazine publication he refused to purchase.

Mr. Brainard, in explaining the high figure asked, stated that Mr. Baker's expenses in collecting the material had been very heavy and Mr. Swope gathered that he had been paying these expenses for Mr. Baker during his employment with the President in Washington. He exhibited the President's letters to Mr. Baker as further proof that Mr. Baker had been given exclusive rights by him for the marketing of these articles and Mr. Swope gained a very definite impression from him that the President was somewhat concerned in the division of profits.

I do not know how far the President has knowledge of all these things. What Mr. Brainard is doing in New York he is doing all over the United States, in every city. Nor do I know that you or the President has understanding of just how the whole transaction strikes those who have given love and devotion to the President. Doubleday Page and Company, despite the fact that Mr. Page[2] was so singularly honored by the President, is not a house that has been conspicuous for its loyalty to the President's beliefs. The "World's Work," throughout the war, had as its chief writer the press agent of the Republican National Committee,[3] and this precious scoundrel filled the pages of the magazine with every variety of administration attack. It was this same man in this same magazine that handled all of the Sim's articles[4] and all the Rathom articles.[5] Mr. Brainard, who gets fifty per cent of all returns from the newspaper syndication, can hardly be termed a militant follower of the President.

With every sincere wish for the health and happiness of the President, I am   Very sincerely,   George Creel[6]

TLS (WP, DLC).
   [1] Clinton Tyler Brainard.
   [2] That is, Walter H. Page.
   [3] Burton Jesse Hendrick, chief writer for *World's Work*. He was a strong supporter of Charles Evans Hughes in 1916; we have not been able to determine whether he was a press agent of the Republican National Committee in 1916, but it seems likely that he was. Joseph Frazier Wall, in his sketch of Hendrick in *Dictionary of American Biography*, Supp. 4 (New York, 1974), p. 368, writes: "Although he strongly supported the antimonopoly philosophy inherent in Woodrow Wilson's New Freedom (including its application to organized labor), Charles Evans Hughes, whom he had first met as the chief government counsel in the life insurance investigations, was the only national political figure to win his unqualified support."
   [4] That is, William S. Sims' series of articles entitled "The Victory at Sea," printed in

World's Work, XXXVIII-XL (Sept. 1919-July 1920). They were published as *The Victory at Sea* (Garden City, N. Y., 1920), with Burton J. Hendrick as collaborator.

⁵ John Revelstoke Rathom, Australian-born journalist and editor and general manager of the Providence, Rhode Island, *Journal* and *Evening Bulletin*. One of the most virulent anti-German publicists in the United States, he had made it the chief mission of his papers to enlist American support for the Allied cause during the period of American neutrality and had exposed a series of real and alleged German plots and conspiracies in the United States. Although he had contributed widely to leading American and foreign periodicals, the only article he wrote for *World's Work* during this period was "Germany's Plots Exposed," *World's Work*, XXXV (Feb. 1918), 394-415.

⁶ Attached to this letter is the following draft of Bolling's reply to Creel's letter:
"hv not given Baker exclu rights over material but have simply asked him to collate it for him and base a sober narrative upon it. Willing to leave to Creel and me all the business arrangement. Baker has been perfectly fair in telling him what he was going to do, and will not use Worlds Work. Yesterday he had a long talk with Baker in which B. told him that he didnt realize it was going into so much money as that had not been his object; but he found that the interest in it was so great that that feature would be very considerable; and that W. W. said at once that that was a matter he would leave to Creel, and asked Baker to get in touch with him. Suppose Bakr is doing that today as he has just gotten address from me. If he wants to come here and have talk with Baker and me it will be all right."

Jesse Frederick Essary¹ to John Randolph Bolling

Dear Mr. Bolling: Washington March 24, 1921.

Cardinal Gibbons passed away about two hours ago and I am wondering if Mr. Wilson would not feel the inclination to say a few words through The Baltimore Sun regarding this fine old citizen and churchman.²

Before writing this note to you I talked with Mr. Tumulty who suggested that I bring the matter to Mr. Wilson's attention through you and who authorized me to say that he felt it would be an appropriate thing for the President to do. Mr. Colby who happened to be in Mr. Tumulty's office at the time also agreed.

If Mr. Wilson looks with favor upon these suggestions you may communicate with me by phone (Main 7400) and I will send up immediately for what Mr. Wilson may have dictated.

I hope you will take occasion to express my personal good wishes to Mr. Wilson.   Cordially yours,   J Fred Essary

TLS (WP, DLC).
¹ Washington correspondent of the Baltimore *Sun*.
² "No reply" is penciled in the upper left-hand corner of this letter.

From the Diary of Ray Stannard Baker

[Washington] March 24 [1921].

Mr. Creel came here to-day at the President's request by long-distance telephone. It was planned that he & I should see the President this morning and talk over the publication arrangements: but the President had a hard night of it: very nervous & sleepless: and was unable to see us. So Creel, Bolling, Mrs. Wilson & I talked the whole matter over. I had made up my mind that I would leave the matter wholly to them in so far as my financial relationships went, but that if the question arose I should demand absolute freedom in handling the material for the book. *It must be my book*—this I am set upon. I worried a good deal about this last night: and having made up my mind to it—and decided that I could live & be happy even if I had to give the whole thing over—I went comfortably to sleep. After a general & frank discussion in which Creel seemed far too sanguine in his estimates of returns, I left them to discuss the problem. We lunched together later, the President not being there, but Mrs. Wilson was at her best. She has a delightful genius for mimicry and related her experiences at the White House tea the other day—with Mrs. Harding. There was not the slightest touch of malice in it, but it was a perfect picture of this new, small-town, middle-western woman transported suddenly into great place: her high, sharp voice with its western twang: and the way in which she played her part. Mrs. Wilson thinks her a very determined and dominant-minded woman.

After luncheon we talked again: Creel & Bolling proposed that we divide up all the proceeds of the book half & half between us, sharing all my expenses half & half. I accepted without a word: but made the point that I should wish to count upon the help of all of them—to the limit—in making a good book. It is worth everything to me to have the complete good-will & co-operation of the President & Mrs. Wilson in this work. And I know well, of course, that if it were not for the public understanding that I am working with the President's approval & with full access to his documents the book would command no such authority as it will have and yield no such financial return. I am of course putting against it my own intimate knowledge of what happened at Paris—& in the year previous—a great accumulation of documents & notes not in the President's collection—all my time & experience for a year or a year & a half—and a certain reputation for honest work. Probably the arrangement is fair enough. If the book goes reasonably well— as I hope—there will be a comfortable salary in it for me: if it goes big, as Creel's optimism suggests, why, there may be something more than "comfortable" for both Mr. Wilson & myself.

I dined tonight with the delightful Hapgoods.

I am glad to have these matters settled: though there remain many details which must be attended to.

[Washington] March 25 [1921]

The President was quite ill to-day—one of his attacks of nervous indigestion. In the flurry of telephoning for a doctor—because Grayson could not immediately be reached—the news got out & exaggerated reports were published in the evening papers. He is very far from well: and I cannot see that he is getting better. Everyone in the world is trying to get to him.

Two News Reports

[March 25, 1921]

WILSON OVERCOME BY FAINTING SPELL
Attributed to Indigestion

Washington, March 25.—Ex-President Wilson had a fainting spell today at his residence in S Street. He recovered quickly and was able to eat a light luncheon shortly afterward. Mr. Wilson kept to his room on the advice of his physician, but was able to move about. The attack was attributed to acute indigestion.

The attack came about noon. Mr. Wilson had eaten breakfast at 9 o'clock and apparently was in no worse physical condition than ordinarily. When the fainting spell came an effort was made to locate his regular physician, Rear Admiral Grayson of the Medical Corps of the Navy, who had attended him during his eight years' residence in the White House, but Admiral Grayson could not be found, and a hurry call was sent out for Dr. Sterling Ruffin, who had been Mrs. Wilson's family physician before she married Mr. Wilson. Admiral Grayson reached the Wilson residence before Dr. Ruffin, however, and applied remedies which quickly restored Mr. Wilson.

The attack was similar to spells of faintness from which Mr. Wilson suffered in his first year in the White House. He then suffered from biliousness and nervous indigestion which at times confined him to his bed. The activities of Mr. Wilson in his first year of office in putting through Congress the Underwood tariff bill and the bill creating the Federal Reserve banking system had much to do with his state of health at the time and at Christmas of 1913 he went with his family to Pass Christian, Miss., to recuperate. Regular exercise helped to overcome Mr. Wilson's tendency to nervous indigestion and there were very few recurrences of the attacks during the latter part of his service as President.

Since he left the White House Mr. Wilson has been receiving many letters from admirers and these he has attempted to answer personally. They came in a flood for a week or so after the Harding inauguration and since then have averaged about 200 a day. Some of Mr. Wilson's friends have felt that he should not have fatigued himself by attempting to answer every letter he received—the majority of them from strangers—but he had felt that courtesy demanded an expression of his appreciation.

It is said to be the opinion of Mr. Wilson's friends that he would help his recovery to health by undertaking as a regular occupation some writing for publication, particularly of his experiences as President, or his views on the conduct of Government born of his eight years service as head of the nation, but he has not consented to do this.

Mr. Wilson is said to have suffered somewhat from the reaction of a return to private life after the responsibilities of his eight years as President, and it is believed that a resumption of his literary labors would help him to overcome the effects of this reaction. There have been no signs that his gradual recovery from his long illness has been retarded since he left the White House, and nothing that was learned today indicated that his fainting spell was anything more than a sporadic occurrence.

Printed in the *New York Times*, March 26, 1921.

[*March 26, 1921*]

WILSON IS A "LITTLE WEAK."

Washington, March 26.—Former President Wilson was described today by his physician, Rear Admiral Grayson, as a little weak as a result of an acute attack of indigestion yesterday, but otherwise apparently recovered from the attack.

Printed in the *New York Times*, March 27, 1921.

John Randolph Bolling to Edgar Odell Lovett

Dear Dr. Lovett: [Washington] 26th March, 1921.

Mr. Wilson requests me to acknowledge your very kind letter of March 20th, and to assure you of the pleasure it has given him to present the Athens appreciation to the Institute.

With regard to the invitation you were good enough to extend to him and Mrs. Wilson, he directs me to say that he is planning an extended rest here and does not feel he can accept it. I am sorry to say that he does not think well of your suggestion to prepare a discourse for publication in the Rice Institute Pamphlet, as he feels that he does not want to make any literary engagements at the present time.

You will be interested to know that the three weeks' rest from his heavy responsibilities have resulted in a noticeable improvement in his condition; and I am hopeful that a continuation of this vacation will soon restore him to normal health again.

Cordially yours,   [John Randolph Bolling]

CCL (WP, DLC).

From Ernst Freund[1]

Dear Mr Wilson,   Chicago March 26/21

Information comes from Heidelberg, Germany, that the family of the late Professor Jellinek[2] is in great destitution. A number of those in this country who have derived profit and inspiration from Jellinek's work are trying to collect a small fund that may be used for food drafts. It has been suggested that you might be glad to be counted among the number, your work on the State being associated in the minds of students with Jellinek's Staatslehre.[3] Your participation in the tribute would be prized above others. If you care to make a contribution, I shall be glad to receive it.

Yours very truly,   Ernst Freund
(in 1915 Pres't Am Pol. Sc. Assoc'n)

ALS (WP, DLC).
  [1] Professor of Law at the University of Chicago Law School.
  [2] Georg Jellinek (1851-1911), distinguished legal and political philosopher, who had been a professor at the Universities of Vienna, Basel, and Heidelberg.
  [3] *Allgemeine Staatslehre* (1900).

To Ida Minerva Tarbell

My dear Miss Tarbell: [Washington] 29th March, 1921.

Your letter of March twenty-third gave me the greatest pleasure.

I have always valued most highly your friendship and approval, and it cheers me mightily to be so delightfully reminded of your generous attitude toward me.

With warmest regards;

Cordially and sincerely yours,   [Woodrow Wilson]

CCL (WP, DLC).

To Ernst Freund

Dear Professor Freund: Washington D C 29th March, 1921.

I am greatly distressed to learn from your letter of March 26th the sad plight of Prof. Jellinek and his family, and take great pleasure in enclosing herewith check for One Hundred Dollars as a contribution to the fund which you are raising.

With every good wish for your success in this most commendable undertaking;

Cordially and sincerely yours,   Woodrow Wilson

TLS (E. Freund Papers, ICU).

From Bainbridge Colby

My dear Mr. President: New York March 29, 1921.

The published account of your indisposition the other day gave us all a little start, but it was promptly followed by reassuring news. I hope it was nothing but what the papers stated, a little temporary upset.

I am deferring my departure for a few days because I am told that the proposal to admit you to the bar of this state by legislative act will come up for consideration this week. It has the cordial cooperation of the Governor,[1] who has taken the lead in the matter. I feel that it should be carefully watched, so that it can be suppressed if anything controversial or distasteful should develop,— which by the way I do not apprehend.

I have the record of your admission to the bar in Atlanta. You were admitted to the Superior Court, not the highest court of record, but admission to the Supreme Court follows as a matter of course, but requires a motion to be made. My correspondent, who has come from Atlanta this week to see me, says that the motion will not require your presence, and it can be quietly made at any time. I think he will be a good man to take care of this detail.

With sincere regards always,

Faithfully yours,   Bainbridge Colby

TLS (WP, DLC).
[1] Nathan Lewis Miller, Republican Governor of New York, 1921-1923.

George Creel to John Randolph Bolling

New York City
March Twenty-Ninth,
Nineteen Twenty-One.

My dear Randolph:

Brainard has not yet returned, but Baker came in yesterday and we spent the entire evening going over our matter. There is an explicit agreement between us as to the fifty-fifty division. I have stated also that Doubleday Page and Company must agree to a flat royalty of *twenty per cent* beginning with the sale of the first book.

Brainard, of course, is to continue in charge of the serial sales. I have a list of the newspapers, however, and will see to it that my recommendations are followed in the matter of assuring publication by our friends and not our enemies. Conservat[iv]ely speaking, this newspaper serialization ought to bring in well above $100,000.

I have told Baker, and he agrees, that all foreign rights are to be reserved pending a thorough examination of the situation. It may be that Doubleday Page can make us the best offer in the matter of publishing the book abroad, and it may be that Brainard is in the best position to handle the serial sales abroad. This remains to be proved, however, and I am collecting all possible data in order to bargain intelligently.

The "World's Work" arrangement has been wiped out entirely. This should get us a better price from the newspapers and will certainly make for a better feeling.

Mr. Baker and I have come to a very definite understanding as to the nature of the book. It is to deal entirely with the Peace Conference, touching nothing else. At no point will it deal with personal controversy, nor will it contain one single note of defense, apology, or attack. Reliance will be placed entirely upon the simple presentation of facts, supported at every point by facsimile documents.

Please assure Mr. Wilson that I am only too happy to be of this service to him and that I am convinced the present arrangement will work out satisfactorily and effectively.

With warmest regards to the President and Mrs. Wilson, I am
Very faithfully yours,   George Creel

Jugo-Slav matter in hand.

TLS (WP, DLC).

John Randolph Bolling to Bainbridge Colby

My dear Mr. Colby: [Washington] 30th March, 1921.

The President asks me to acknowledge your kind letter of yesterday, and to express to you his thanks for the interesting information which it contains relative to his admission to the bar. He bids
me say that he is sure you will handle the matter in the best possible way.

I could not resist the temptation to read to him your letter to me
regarding Mrs. Kruse;[1] and it would have done your heart good to
have seen the amusement it gave him. He said that he would size
up the lady as a "krusey" fool! It is a pity that I have to bother you
with such matters, but I think we agree that it is better they should
remain in the one channel. I am returning the Kruse letters herewith,[2] as it may be just as well to hold them in your files should
she try to get in touch with you again.

If you have made no decision regarding the organization of the
Washington office, may I suggest that you defer it until your return
and an opportunity is afforded me to talk over a plan I have in
mind?

You will rejoice to know that The President's slight set back on
last Friday has been almost entirely overcome, and I believe a few
more days of rest and diet will see him continuing the steady gain
we have noticed since about the middle of March. The sudden cold
snap keep [kept] him indoors yesterday, but he plans for a long
automobile ride this afternoon if the temperature permits.

Before going away, will you say to whoever you leave in charge
of your office not to hesitate to get in touch with me upon any
matter that they wish The President to pass upon? I think he thoroughly enjoys knowing all that is going on, and that a certain
amount of consultation work is beneficial to him.

With kindest personal regards, in which The President and Mrs.
Wilson join me;

Sincerely yours,   [John Randolph Bolling]

CCL (WP, DLC).
    [1] Probably Mrs. Georgia Fleming W. Kruse who in 1923 resided at 114 West 79th
Street, New York. At that time, she wrote Wilson to ask him to autograph her certificate
as a "founder" of the Woodrow Wilson Foundation. Georgia F. W. Kruse to WW, Sept.
26 and Oct. 24, 1923, both ALS (WP, DLC), and JRB to Georgia F. W. Kruse, Sept. 29,
1923, CCL (WP, DLC).
    [2] They are missing in the Colby Papers, DLC, as, indeed, are all documents that went
into Colby's legal files.

John Randolph Bolling to George Creel

My dear George: [Washington] 30th March, 1921

I have your letter of yesterday, and am delighted to know that you had such a satisfactory interview with Mr. Baker.

The arrangements you have made seem most satisfactory, from all sides; and I hope the foreign rights end of it will work out as you wish.

In my talks with Mr. Baker on Friday and Saturday (following our joint interview on Thursday) he seemed better satisfied—and more enthusiastic—than he had been before the business arrange- ment was taken up.

In my regular morning talk with Mr. Wilson I will give him the substance of your letter, without entering into the details of the business end of it. Mrs. W. agrees with me that for the present it is better to simply tell him it is satisfactory.

I am glad you came to such a definite understanding as to what is to be embodied in Mr. Baker's book. It seems to me that this clears a way for the other (and I believe even larger) matter we touched on briefly when you were here. Let this rest a while, and at the proper time I am sure it can be arranged.

Mr. Wilson has about recovered from his slight [in]disposition, but omitted his ride yesterday on account of the extremely cold weather. Given a few more days rest, and I am sure he will be all right again.

With kindest regards, in which Mr. and Mrs. W. join;

Sincerely yours,   [John Randolph Bolling]

CCL (WP, DLC).

From Bainbridge Colby

My dear Mr. President: New York April 2, 1921.

The National Democratic Club of this city are holding their an- nual Jefferson Dinner on April 9th. The Committee of which Mr. Frederick H. Allen[1] is Chairman has expressed its earnest hope that they may have a message from you which can be read at the dinner. I have been asked to transmit the request to you.

I am down for a speech on this occasion, having provisionally accepted the Club's invitation five or six months ago. I am not par- ticularly keen about making any speech at the present time and have relied upon my absence in London to get me out of this. I feel that I ought not to be off the scene, however, while the matter I wrote you about the other day is on the legislative program at Albany. If I am still here on the 9th I shall have to exercise my ingenuity to get out of this fix. I imagine that you would be inclined to concur with my feeling that this is not just the moment for speech making, at least for any attempt at significant or out-spoken utterance.

May be you will be kind enough to let me know how your mind slants on this subject when you give me your answer to Mr. Allen's request.

With best wishes always,

Faithfully yours,   Bainbridge Colby

TLS (WP, DLC).
[1] Frederick Hobbes Allen, lawyer of New York, active in Democratic party politics.

To John W. Scott[1]

Dear Sir: [Washington] 4th April, 1921.

The celebration of the birthday of Jefferson affords the party a happy opportunity once again to reinterpret, restudy and vigorously revive the great purposes of the founders of the Republic. They intended the Government to serve not only its own people but those who love liberty and believe in justice throughout the world; and it can yet be made the instrument for the realization of those great objects.

Cordially and sincerely yours,   [Woodrow Wilson]

CCL (WP, DLC).
[1] Physician of Springfield, Ill., president of the Jeffersonian Club of that city. Wilson was replying to J. W. Scott to WW, March 29, 1921, TLS (WP, DLC).

John Randolph Bolling to Bainbridge Colby, with Enclosure

Dear Mr. Colby: [Washington] 6th April, 1921.

Enclosed is copy of message to be read at The Jefferson Dinner on Saturday night. Mr. Wilson is sending the original to Mr. Allen by this mail.[1]

It is at my suggestion that Mr. W. allows me to send you this copy, since it occurs to me that it may suggest a line of thought upon which you may care to speak at the Dinner. Please keep the copy in the strictest confidence, and show it to no one.

This message is a special joy, since it indicates that Mr. Wilson is again in his old time form. Don't you think so?

Cordially yours,   [John Randolph Bolling]

CCL (WP, DLC).
[1] In WW to F. H. Allen, April 6, 1921, CCL (WP, DLC).

E N C L O S U R E

MESSAGE FROM HONORABLE WOODROW WILSON TO BE
READ AT THE ANNUAL JEFFERSON DINNER TO BE GIVEN BY
THE NATIONAL DEMOCRATIC CLUB, OF NEW YORK CITY,
APRIL NINTH, NINETEEN HUNDRED AND TWENTY ONE.

It is interesting and stimulating to reflect that when we celebrate the memory of one of the great founders of the Republic
we undertake, if we are sincere, a solemn obligation to perpetuate and set forward the work which he did.

Jefferson conceived it to be the mission and destiny of the
United States to make it easier for men everywhere to attain liberty and the blessings of genuine self government, and to render
justice imperative in the dealings of nations and peoples with
one another as well as in the dealings of governments with their
own subjects.

Do we? If we do, what do we mean to do about it?[1]

T MS (WP, DLC).
  [1] There is a WWsh draft of this message in WP, DLC.

From Robert Cummins Stuart, Jr.

Cambridge Mass 1921 Apr 7

Upon the fourth anniversary of the entry of the United States
into the war under your inspired leadership to establish justice and
peace as the basis for a new international conception of freedom
meetings are being held in the leading universities of America to
form Woodrow Wilson clubs dedicated to your ideals and in grateful appreciation of your generous service to humanity[1] The non-
partisan advisory committee on historical research headed by Dean
Charles H Haskins and including Professors A C Coolidge Director
of the Harvard University Library Bliss Perry C H McIlwain F J
Turner and W E Hocking[2] has just submitted an outline for the
historical work[3] in the carrying out of which the assistance of affiliated clubs will be had For this work an endowment of at least one
hundred thousand dollars will be raised

Robert C Stuart Jr

T telegram (WP, DLC).
  [1] According to Stuart, fifty-two such clubs had been organized, or were in the process
of being organized, by this time. *New York Times*, April 12, 1921.
  [2] Haskins, Coolidge, Perry, McIlwain, and Turner have appeared from time to time in
this and previous volumes in this series. William Ernest Hocking was the Alford Professor of Natural Religion, Moral Philosophy, and Civil Polity at Harvard.
  [3] See R. C. Stuart, Jr., to WW, April 13, 1921, n. 1.

To Robert Cummins Stuart, Jr.

[Washington, April 8, 1921]

Let me thank you most warmly for your telegram of yesterday, and assure you how greatly I appreciate the many kind expressions which it contains.

It is most gratifying to me to note the systematic and business-like manner with which the universities have gone about their work of organization, and I heartily congratulate you on the prog-ress which has already been made.

[Sincerely yours,   Woodrow Wilson]

Printed in the *New York Times*, April 12, 1921.

From Martin Luther Davey[1]

My dear Mr. President: Washington, D. C. April 8, 1921.

The Democrats of Akron are going to hold a big get together ban-quet within the next two or three weeks. It promises to be the big-gest affair of its kind ever held by the Democrats of Akron and vicinity. It is intended to draw the Democrats together in a solid fighting front and to rekindle the militant spirit of the party.

I have been requested to write you to ask if you will kindly dic-tate a message to the Democrats of Akron and vicinity which can be printed on the program for the evening. Such a message from you of about two hundred words in length would be exceedingly helpful, and I hope you will kindly comply with the request. Will you not please sit down and dictate a message immediately and send it to me at Kent?

With kind personal regards, I remain.

Sincerely yours,   Martin L. Davey

TLS (WP, DLC).
[1] Democratic congressman from Ohio, 1918-1921, 1923-1929. "Will send telgm." written at top of letter.

George Creel to William Edward Dodd

New York City

My dear Mr. Dodd: April Eighth, Nineteen Twenty-One.

Mr. Wilson refused absolutely to adopt my plan that called for an advisory committee and the establishment of a working force in connection with his papers. What was even worse, he gave Ray Stannard Baker a sort of roving commission among these papers and specifically authorized him to do a book on the Peace Conference. When this matter took some embarrassing turns he sent for me and again put all of his literary affairs in my hands. I have straightened out the Baker matter and expect to have another talk soon with reference to his papers as a whole.

Quite frankly, and very confidentially, I do not think that Mr. Wilson will be able to write. I will keep you in touch with things as they come up and if you have any suggestions please be kind enough to make them at any and all times.

Sincerely,   George Creel

TLS (W. E. Dodd Papers, DLC).

To the Democrats of Akron, Ohio, and Vicinity[1]

[Washington, c. April 11, 1921]

In conveying my warm greetings to the Democrats of Akron, please say to them that it seems to me there never was a time when it was more stimulating to be a Democrat, because the party is now fully identified with a great cause in which all free peoples are vitally interested and in regard to which all nations look to the United States under the leadership of the Democratic party to direct it into the paths of liberty and of freedom from the debasing fear of war and aggressive selfishness.

The world is on tiptoe to see the dawn of a day of redemption, and the Democratic party of the United States can bring that dawn if it be but true to itself and to the great task which circumstances have so clearly defined and so clearly called upon it to perform.

We need not look back to regret anything: we need only look forward and, shoulder to shoulder, press towards the great undertakings of policy which shall lift the world out of its present chaos and despondency and set it in the way to establish justice and find political redemption.

The forces of true liberalism must everywhere draw immediately together; are ready to draw together; and look to us to take the initiative and make the new program possible.

T MS (WP, DLC).
[1] There is a WWsh draft of this message in WP, DLC.

From the Diary of Ray Stannard Baker

Washington April 12 [1921].

Arrived this morning. I had it out, painfully, yesterday with both Brainerd & Doubleday. Brainerd has agreed to let me alone! And I am sure Doubleday will. Creel sees my case & will help me. I am to have another lease of life.

I dined with Doubleday at his beautiful home at Oyster Bay.

The President is better: but rests constantly. It is what he needs.

I think they all felt quite superior: & excused me as being "temperamental." I can stand even that if they will let me alone.

[Washington] April 13 [1921]

Grayson read me to-day Wilson's description of the aloneness or aloofness of Lincoln—in the speech at Hodgkinsville Ky Sep 4 1916[1]—which so clearly describes Wilson's lonliness. He is a man without intimates: without familiar friends. In all these days I have been so closely in contact with his life at the White House and in S Street (as formerly in Paris) it has been astonishing to me how little human contact he craves. No one comes to him merely because he is himself and for simple love for him: and he goes to no one because he desires him. He opens his heart to no one—scarcely I think even to his wife[.] Grayson tells me that he has had only fugitive glimpses within. The first Mrs. Wilson, even after she was mortally ill, insisted upon these contacts: insisted on having friends to dinner & events in the evening: but rarely without a protest from the President although he usually enjoyed the guests when they came. The present Mrs. Wilson has seemed more pliable: & herself seems less to care for friends.

[1] Wilson's speech on Abraham Lincoln at Hodgenville, Ky., accepting on behalf of the nation the log cabin in which Lincoln was born and a memorial hall enclosing the cabin. The speech is printed at Sept. 4, 1916, Vol. 38.

From Bainbridge Colby

My dear Mr. President: New York April 13, 1921.

You may have seen in the newspapers that I sailed yesterday on the Aquitania,—but I didn't. I canceled my sailing in order to watch our little matter at Albany, and engaged passage on the Cedric leaving Saturday, the 16th. This was the day it was announced some two weeks ago as the day on which the New York Legislature would adjourn. I am told that our matter is in fine shape and will

go through. You know how those things sometimes turn out, however. It is not a matter of vital moment, one way or the other, although I should like to see you admitted to the Bar in this state;
that would enable me to have the firm name on the door.

I ought not really for all material reasons to defer my departure
to London any longer. I shall not be gone long, and I hope to do
some substantial things from a professional standpoint while over
there. When I get back it will be a case of full speed ahead.

The delay as a result of the Albany situation has not been fully
wasted. Mrs. Colby[1] is out of the hospital to-day and home again,
which sends me away with a lightened heart. And I have had some
photographs of my teeth taken by X-Ray, the result of which is
reassuring. I will not afflict you with any copies of them. From
what I hear on every side this seems to be the thing to do in order
to stand off all kinds of ailments and premature disintegration. I
wonder if you have had it done. I really believe there is something
in it.

I had a little talk with Mr. Seymour on the telephone to-day. I
think your letter in acknowledgment of his was better than the one
I suggested.[2]

Your message to the Jefferson Day Dinner was received with
deafening cheers. It was the central feature of a fine gathering of
loyal Democrats.

As a watchful sentinel of your fame I am content in the fullest
sense of the word with the way things are going.

I will send you a telegram if I finally go on the Cedric Saturday,
and I shall be back just as soon as the business on which I go is
concluded.

With sincerest regards always,

Yours faithfully,   Bainbridge Colby

TLS (WP, DLC).
[1] Nathalie Sedgwick Colby.
[2] John Sammis Seymour (born 1848), formerly of the New York law firm of Dill,
Chandler & Seymour, who was seeking employment with Wilson & Colby. BC to JRB,
April 9, 1921, TLS (WP, DLC), enclosing a draft of a reply for Wilson to send. Bolling's
reply, which said that Wilson had sent Seymour's letter to Colby and suggested that
Seymour get in touch with him, is JRB to J. S. Seymour, April 11, 1921, CCL (WP,
DLC).

From Robert Cummins Stuart, Jr.

Cambridge, Massachusetts

My dear Mr. Wilson: April 13, 1921.

You will find enclosed a copy of a recent letter from Dean
Haskins[1] with attached memoranda from Professors A. C. Coolidge

and F. J. Turner[2] suggesting an outline for the historical work to be done by the Woodrow Wilson Club of Harvard and affiliated clubs which I thought would be of interest to you.

While our programme has not crystalized in final form, we now plan, however, to raise at least one hundred thousand dollars and possibly as much as two hundred and fifty thousand dollars. The income from this fund is to finance the historical research until it has been adequately carried out. The annual revenue from the endowment is eventually to furnish fellowships, which will bear your name, for foreign students desiring to study in the universities of the United States.

The clipping accompanying this letter[3] I sincerely hope is not objectionable. The newspapers made slight mention of the nation-wide movement for the organization of affiliated clubs upon April sixth but instead featured the historical work. Believing that this movement was deserving of public notice and feeling that this recognition would be stimulating and heartening to the other clubs I consulted Professor Sayre about the good-taste in making your letter public. As he thought you would not object, I took the liberty of giving its contents to the press.

Speaking of Professor Sayre has just made me think of the unusual sequence of events to-night. Early in the evening I heard Professor Sayre give a most interesting introduction to Dr. Iyenaga[4] and Jane Adams[5] who spoke on "Disarmament" after which I returned to my room to read for the first time your book on "Congressional Government" for my tutor in the morning and finally a letter to you yourself!

Again hoping that the news article is not offensive and with apologies for the length of this communication, I am,

Yours very faithfully,   Robert C. Stuart, Jr.

TLS (WP, DLC).
[1] C. H. Haskins to R. C. Stuart, Jr., April 2, 1921, TCL (WP, DLC). Haskins was responding to Stuart's recent request, on behalf of the Wilson Club, "for suggestions respecting the possible employment of a fund for collecting material relating to President Wilson and his work." Haskins reported that he had conferred with Bliss Perry, Frederick Jackson Turner, and Archibald Cary Coolidge, and that all were in "entire agreement as to the great value which such a collection in the Harvard Library might have for the future of President Wilson and his administration." He enclosed memoranda by Professors Turner and Coolidge which are discussed in n. 2 below.
[2] T MSS (WP, DLC). Turner's memorandum was a lengthy and wide-ranging discussion of source material for the study of the domestic policies of the Wilson administration, which the club might be able to collect for the Harvard library. He recommended the acquisition of the papers of individuals who had worked with Wilson and of newspapers from the various regions of the nation to facilitate the study of public opinion on the Wilson administration. Coolidge's briefer memorandum was more general in nature and stressed the importance of collecting materials from Europe while they were still readily available and relatively cheap, as well as the need for a staff to organize and catalogue the acquisitions.
[3] It was a clipping from the New York Times, April 12, 1921, which printed R. C. Stuart, Jr., to WW, April 7, 1921, and WW to R. C. Stuart, Jr., April 8, 1921.

4 Toyokichi Iyenaga, director of the East and West News Bureau of New York and a long-time Japanese publicist in the United States. He had studied under Wilson as a graduate student at The Johns Hopkins University in 1889-1890. See the index references to him in Vol. 6.
5 That is, Jane Addams.

To Bainbridge Colby

My dear Colby: [Washington] 14th April, 1921.

It is a great pleasure to me to have your letter of yesterday containing so much news of interest.

First let me tell you how glad we are that Mrs. Colby is out of the hospital; give her our love and assure her of our best wishes for a most speedy recovery.

I note what you say regarding the matter at Albany; I hope it will go through satisfactorily. Under any circumstances, however, I think you are right in not longer delaying your trip to London.

With my best wishes for a most comfortable and successful journey;   Cordially and sincerely yours,   [Woodrow Wilson]

CCL (WP, DLC).

John Randolph Bolling to the Macmillan Company

Gentlemen: [Washington] 15th April, 1921.

Mr. Wilson requests me to reply to your letter of April 14th and say that under no circumstances could he consider writing the article suggested by you.[1]

Yours very truly,   [John Randolph Bolling]

CCL (WP, DLC).
[1] "Could we interest you in the writing of a Life of Jesus, running 150,000 to 200,000 words in length? The historical problems connected with this piece of work would make most interesting study, while the problems of personality involved, would employ the full reflective strength of your powerful mind." W. H. Murray, Religious Books Department, Macmillan Co., to WW, April 14, 1921, TLS (WP, DLC).

John Randolph Bolling to Robert Cummins Stuart, Jr.

My dear Mr. Stuart: [Washington] 16th April, 1921.

Mr. Wilson asks me to acknowledge your letter of April 13th, and say that he had not the slightest objection to your giving out his letter of April 7th [8th] to the newspapers.

Mr. Wilson has read with interest the outline which you enclosed and thinks it excellent. He wishes me to say that he is sending it to Dr. J. F. Jameson, head of the historical department of the

Carnegie Institution, for an expression of his views, and comments. Dr. Jameson and Mr. Wilson are old friends, and he thinks that he may have some suggestions to make which will be of value.

Enclosed is copy of an editorial from the Spartanburg (S. C.) Journal of April 14th, which I think may interest you. It occurs to me that, if you have not already elicited the cooperation of the colleges mentioned (Wofford, Converse, &c.) they might be brought into line.   Cordially yours,   [John Randolph Bolling]

CCL (WP, DLC).

John Randolph Bolling to John Franklin Jameson

My dear Dr. Jameson: Washington D C 16th April, 1921.

Mr. Wilson asks me to enclose you a letter from Dr. Haskins, with memoranda attached, and request that you go over it and give him (Mr. Wilson) the benefit of your comments and suggestions.

These papers were sent Mr. Wilson by Mr. R. C. Stuart, Jr., President of The Woodrow Wilson Club of Harvard, and explain themselves.

Mr. Wilson is much interested in this matter, and I am sure will greatly appreciate your help and cooperation.

          Yours very cordially,   John Randolph Bolling.

TLS (J. F. Jameson Papers, DLC).

To Bainbridge Colby

My dear Colby: [Washington] 17th April, 1921.

I see in the action of the New York Legislature more the results of your generous work than of anybody elses influence, and I want to express to you my gratitude. It is wonderful to have such a friend.

We hope that Mrs. Colby continues to make progress toward complete restoration.

I need not tell you that my thoughts and earnest good wishes will follow and attend you on your errand across the water.

          Cordially and sincerely yours,   [Woodrow Wilson]

CCL (WP, DLC).

From Bainbridge Colby

My dear Mr. President: New York April 18, 1921.

I thank you for your pleasant and heartening little note of yesterday.

The Albany matter came through in the nicest possible way. I enclose the brief little message sent to both Houses of the Legislature by Governor Miller.[1] The bill admitting you to practice passed both Houses by a unanimous vote. There was a little splutter in the Senate, led by the Senator who represents Albany County, or more correctly, Mr. William Barnes,[2] but his statements were received with such a display of disfavor by both his colleagues and by the galleries that he finally asked to be excused from voting, and the record, therefore, shows the bill's passage without any recorded dissent.

There was applause when the message of the Governor was read in the Senate and again when the announcement was made that the bill had passed. I enclose also a little editorial paragraph from this morning's "World,"[3] in which the friendly activity of Senator O'Gorman is mentioned. I think undoubtedly you will want to send some little expression of appreciation to Governor Miller and also to Senator O'Gorman and to Judge Alton B. Parker. I have taken the liberty of dictating a little line to each of them,[4] which you can use as a suggestion and phrase according to your own impeccable taste in those matters.

I am very happy that the matter came through so handsomely. It has a great deal of significance from our point of view. It enables me now to go forward with a sense of complete freedom and to plan upon very much broader lines. I will not discuss this matter by letter, but I shall be giving it a great deal of thought while I am away and will promptly confer with you on my return.

I am off on Wednesday on the "Olympic." My address in London will be Claridges Hotel, Brook Street. I will cable you from time to time and shall not be away a moment longer than is necessary to dispatch the business that takes me over there. I have two or three matters, all promising, and I think I can do some real business, as well as get a little bit of rest and recreation.

I shall think of you constantly while I am away, and hope your steady gains will be uninterrupted. I am full of confidence about the future.

Please give my sincerest regards to Mrs. Wilson, and believe me always,   Yours most cordially,   Bainbridge Colby

TLS (WP, DLC).
[1] Governor Miller sent the following message on April 16: "I wish to recommend to

the consideration of the Legislature the passage of an act to confer on ex-President Wilson the right to practice law in the State of New York. . . . A lawyer by regular admission and practice in an American State, an eminent educator and author, President for eight years of a leading university, President of the United States for two terms, this distinguished citizen has a just title to a privilege the conferring of which, I believe, would be an eminently graceful act and one universally approved." *New York Times*, April 17, 1921.
    [2] Frank Lawrence Wiswall was the Republican state senator representing Albany County. William Barnes was the owner and publisher of the *Albany Evening Journal* and the conservative Republican party boss of Albany County and former chairman of the New York Republican State Committee. Barnes was reputed to have all Republican politicians of the Albany area under tight control.
    [3] Clipping, WP, DLC.
    [4] They are T MSS (WP, DLC).

To Bainbridge Colby

[Washington] April 19th, 1921.

Mrs. Wilson joins me in sincere good wishes for a safe and pleasant trip.   Woodrow Wilson.

T telegram (WP, DLC).

John Randolph Bolling to Bainbridge Colby

My dear Mr. Colby: [Washington] 19th April, 1921.

Your letter of April 18th, with enclosures, came this morning, and was heard with much interest by Mr. Wilson.

He has today written Governor Miller as per copy enclosed,[1] and which he believes will fully meet your views and wishes.

It is nice to know you will keep in touch with us by cable, and I am sure that any news from you will be received with the greatest interest and gratification by your "partner."

Please accept my sincere good wishes for a most pleasant trip, and believe me, always;

Faithfully yours,   [John Randolph Bolling]

CCL (WP, DLC).
    [1] WW to N. L. Miller, April 19, 1921, CCL (WP, DLC).

From Edwin Anderson Alderman

My dear Mr. Wilson: Charlottesville April 19, 1921.

It is hard for me to address my President in this familiar style of the long ago, but I do so with the same sentiments of respect and affection that I have always held for Woodrow Wilson. I beg to express the hope, at the outset, that release from care and responsibility is making for your progress towards health and strength. A portrait, and a very good portrait, of you, done by Duncan Smith, son of old Professor Francis H. Smith,[1] is now in my office, just received as a gift to the University from the alumni of Norfolk and Portsmouth. You may imagine how we shall care for and cherish it.

You are aware, of course, of our extensive preparation for the Centennial occasion, which occurs here at the approaching Finals. Thursday, the second of June, is our culminating day. The two principal addresses on that day will be made by His Excellency, the British Ambassador,[2] and John Bassett Moore, of the class of '80. I cherish the desire of reading, as the initial thing on the program of that day, before the speeches begin, a letter from you, however brief and simple, expressing whatever may be in your mind apropos of the One Hundredth Anniversary of the founding of this University. I believe the reading of such a letter would be an event of great significance to the occasion. I know that it would give pride and happiness to every alumnus of the University to be thus reminded at such a time of your connection with the University. You have served the nation and mankind as no other son of the University has ever served it. You have borne burdens and given direction to the life of the nation and of the world in such a way as to earn the gratitude of all good men, and most especially those who are brothers to you in the fellowship of University life.

Expressing the very earnest and confident hope that I may have the honor and pleasure of receiving and of reading this letter on this occasion, I remain,

Faithfully, your friend,   Edwin A. Alderman.

TLS (WP, DLC).
[1] Duncan Smith was an artist of New York. Francis Henry Smith, Professor of Natural Philosophy at the University of Virginia, 1853-1907, was still living at this time at the age of ninety-one.
[2] That is, Sir Auckland Geddes.

John Franklin Jameson to John Randolph Bolling

My dear Sir: [Washington] April 19, 1921.

I gladly comply with your request of April 16, to comment on the enclosed letter and memoranda which Mr. Wilson has received from Professor Haskins, but I suppose it is difficult for anyone to comment very definitely at present without more knowledge of the means which the Woodrow Wilson Club of Harvard University will have at its disposal.

One concrete suggestion, however, comes immediately to my

mind, and that is, that if the broad view is taken concerning the functions of the club which Professors Turner and Coolidge take, so that the club would expect to provide materials for understanding not only the personal aspect of Mr. Wilson's presidency but also its historical setting or background, then the club might very well provide the Library of Harvard University with a copy of the great collection of daily summaries of the German press, which were made by Dr. Victor S[elden]. Clark throughout the year 1918 and the first six months of 1919. Mr. Wilson will perhaps remember that this work, of subscribing for some twenty German (and Austrian) newspapers, of varied characters, studying them for material useful to our Government in the conduct of the war, translating portions so found, and systematically sending carbons of these translations to the various government offices where they would be useful, was undertaken at the expense of the Carnegie Institution of Washington on the basis of a letter which at my request he addressed to the President of the Institution. I believe that the work was distinctly useful to the government during wartime, Dr. Clark being a good all-around economist, who had worked in connection with various government departments, and had a small but good staff. But at all events, the results, of which he constantly preserved one set, must surely be useful to history, containing the cream of the information to be obtained from the enemy's point of view.

After hostilities ceased, and Dr. Clark went to other work (editor of the revived "Living Age") his main set of sheets, some 26,000 in number, if I remember rightly, was turned over to the *Manuscript Division* of the Library of Congress. The chief of that Division offered photostat reproductions of the whole series for about $700. to any libraries which wanted one. Six or eight were taken, but rather curiously none at Cambridge or Boston, or anywhere in New England. Harvard Library ought to have this set; the newspapers on which it rests would now be difficult, and in some cases impossible to procure, and even if one had them all, this collection of sheets furnishes the subject index to them.

In respect to more personal materials relating to President Wilson or those most closely associated with him, I should not like, in respect to any manuscript materials, to suggest anything running counter to the general principle that Washington is the place of ultimate destination for the papers of presidents, and of other public men whose activities have mostly been national in their scope. At present such papers are gathered into the Division of Manuscripts in the Library of Congress. When we have our national archives building, which we certainly shall have, and I think within a few years, it may be that such papers will be transferred to it from the Library of Congress, but in any case the papers of national statesmen help each other by being concentrated in Washington, rather than being dispersed over the country.

I wonder if a useful contribution to the knowledge of the proceedings at Versailles could not be secured by suggestion to these young men, many of whom probably combined some knowledge of shorthand with some knowledge of the history of those negotiations, that, after reading more thoroughly upon the subject, they should systematically interview all the more or less expert or technical Americans who accompanied the President to Versailles and served in the organization there. Some of these men have written something of their recollections already, others think they will—or will not; skillful questioning and note-taking might bring together for the future historian a considerable number of side-lights on what happened, such as, in 1915 [1815?] and the next ensuing years we got concerning the Congress of Vienna; but these we might get while they are fresh.

Perhaps better suggestions may come to me later. I am certainly interested.

Believe me,   Very truly yours,   [J. F. Jameson][1]

CCL (J. F. Jameson Papers, DLC).
  [1] Jameson had written a somewhat similar letter: J. F. Jameson to WW, Dec. 3, 1920, Vol. 66.

John Randolph Bolling to Edwin Anderson Alderman

My dear Mr. Alderman: [Washington] 20th April, 1921.

Mr. Wilson asks me to acknowledge your kind letter of April nineteenth, and to say that it will give him the greatest pleasure to send you a letter to be read on the final day of the Centennial celebration this year.

He was greatly pleased to receive in the same mail his "command" to be present at the celebration, and it is a great disappointment to him that he will be unable to attend.

I believe that the rest Mr. Wilson is taking is doing him a great deal of good, and he is out every day for long motor rides through the country.   Cordially yours,   [John Randolph Bolling]

CCL (WP, DLC).

From Abram Isaac Elkus

Dear Mr. President: [New York] April 20, 1921.

The Aaland Commission,[1] of which you did me the honor to appoint me a member, has finished its work, and we are ready to report to the League of Nations at its next session in May. The report is one hundred (100) pages of typewritten matter. It is soon to be printed, and I shall send you a copy, or if you prefer I will send you a summary, which I am having prepared.

The decision is in favor of Finland retaining the Islands and is unanimous. Special guarantees are provided as to their retaining the Swedish schools and language, and as to the neutralization of the Islands, and the appointment of a native governor. The decision is based upon historical and actual physical facts.

The principle of self determination, which was invoked by the Swedes and the Aalanders, we found did not apply in pursuance of the tests, which you so wisely specified. In view of the fact that the people of Swedish descent, numbering three hundred and fifty thousand (350,000) on the main land unanimously opposed the separation, was of itself a reason why this small body of Aalanders numbering twenty-five thousand (25,000) should not be separated from them.

The decision has not been announced and this reference to it is in confidence and for yourself alone.

Long ere this, I should have written you, felicitating you upon the great and remarkable achievements which you accomplished as President, had I not been seriously ill with "sleeping sickness" for the last three months, which I contracted while I was in Europe. I do congratulate you, and the country more than you, on what you have done for it. Your political enemies may have triumphed, but it is only a temporary triumph. In the end they will be forced to admit your achievement. However, you have a record of things accomplished of which you may well be proud. History will write you down as the greatest American President.

With kindest personal regards, I beg to remain

Very sincerely yours,   Abram I. Elkus

TLS (WP, DLC).
[1] About this commission and its work, see the index references to "Åland Islands" in Vols. 65 and 66.

John Randolph Bolling to John Franklin Jameson

My dear sir: Washington D C 21st April, 1921.

I am in receipt this morning of your letter of April 19, which Mr. Wilson has heard with the greatest interest. He desires me to express to you his appreciation of the attention given the matter, and to say that he heartily agrees in all you say.

At Mr. Wilson's suggestion I am sending copy of your letter by this mail to Mr. R. C. Stuart, Jr., President of The Woodrow Wilson Club at Harvard, that he may have the benefit of all you say.

Yours very cordially,   John Randolph Bolling.

TLS (J. F. Jameson Papers, DLC).

To Jessie Woodrow Wilson Sayre[1]

My darling Little Girl,   [Washington] 22 April, '21

It grieves me as much as it can possibly distress you that I cannot be present at dear little Woodrow's christening (God bless him!) but I could not without folly undertake a journey yet a while. But by all means go ahead. It ought not to be further postponed.

Our dearest love to all. I make a *little* progress.   Father

ALS (received from Francis B. Sayre).
[1] The letter to which this is a reply is missing. Wilson used a pencil to write his letter.

From Hamilton Holt

My dear Mr. Wilson   New York April 22, 1921

I enclose herewith an advance proof of an editorial I have just written on the forthcoming visit to the United States of Field Marshal Foch.[1] It will appear in The Independent dated April 30.

I venture to ask if you would be willing to send me a brief comment—less than three hundred words—on the suggestion made in this editorial so I can print it in a later issue of the magazine.

I am asking twenty-five prominent officials, military men and civilians thruout the land, to join with you in considering the best way to honor this greatest hero of the war. I would be very grateful if I could have your reply in hand not later than May 10th.

Very truly yours,   Hamilton Holt

TLS (WP, DLC).
[1] Tearsheet (WP, DLC). Entitled "Our Field Marshal," the editorial suggested that Congress might appropriately vote Foch an honorarium, make him an American citizen, or confer on him an honorary generalship in the United States Army.

A News Item

[*April 23, 1921*]

Wilson Attends the Theatre.

Washington, April 23—Woodrow Wilson attended the theatre[1] tonight for the first time since he retired from the Presidency. It also was the former President's first visit to the vaudeville house where he once was a regular weekly attendant since his illness in September, 1919.

Printed in the *New York Times*, April 24, 1921.
    [1] Keith's.

A Memorandum by Homer Stillé Cummings

Monday, April 25, 1921.

By arrangement made through Mrs. Wilson, I called at noon to see President Wilson at his home, 2340 S Street NW. Mr. Wilson was in bed throughout the interview and I think on the whole seemed more depressed than I had ever known him to be. It was with difficulty that he seemed to shake off a spirit of sadness and there was no disposition upon his part to relate amusing or witty anecdotes as is so characteristic of him. However, the family told me that he was very much better and did a great deal of work and it may have been simply a mood rather than anything more serious. Indeed the day was very hot and almost everyone seemed to feel it, and this may have accounted for his attitude. We talked very freely concerning the more serious aspects of international problems. He still retained his old determined and I may say uncompromising attitude toward the question of a proper settlement of foreign affairs. Secretary Hughes was cussed several times during the interview. The President said that he had been approached with a view to ascertaining whether he would be willing to confer and advise with Democratic senators and he wanted to know what I thought about it. I told him I thought it would be a very desirable thing to do if there was any prospect of unity of action amongst Democratic senators. I suggested that there had been no such complete unity heretofore and that that fact had prevented the ratification of the treaty. To this he agreed, saying that if the Democrats had unanimously stood firm, he thought the treaty would have been ratified but there were just enough to desert and just enough others who exhibited a weak spirit to encourage the opponents of the Treaty to continue the fight. He said he would be willing to confer with the senators if they were going to "play ball" but if not, he would rather not have anything to do with them. The President spoke of the deplorable consequences which had followed the failure to ratify the Treaty, and spoke of the relatively helpless attitude of our own country at the present moment when other countries were practically settling the affairs of the world or endeavoring to settle them. He expressed great apprehension concerning the present situation especially in France where he said the militaristic leaders had secured control of the government and were endeavoring to make a scrap of paper out of the Versailles Treaty. He expressed the belief that if the French troops occupied the Ruhr District for any considerable period of time, that it might produce an economic collapse of all Europe and in any event would be Alsace Lorraine over again, containing all the germs and seeds of a future war. He said that the course of events was leading inevitably to another world war. He said that we had abandoned "a fruitful leadership for a barren isolation." He spoke of General Foch, whose strong militaristic ideas now seem in the ascendant, and said that this was characteristic as they had "more trouble with Foch at the Peace Conference than with any other one person." He seemed full of determination however with reference to carrying on the work which he had undertaken. I spoke to him about our greatest domestic political difficulty, namely, the inadequate method of securing publicity. I told him that the Republicans were continually buying up newspapers situated strategically. He said he was aware of that but that it was a handicap we must accept without being discouraged.

I told him I had been in many political battles and had never felt depressed or disconcerted by defeat but that the cause of the League of Nations was a sort of religion with me and in its defeat in this country, I felt a curious kind of humiliation as an American. I then added: "It takes all of the philosophy that I can summon to endure it." He then said, "If I had nothing but philosophy to comfort me, I should go mad." I said "How do you feel about it?" This was a rather unfortunate question because it apparently cut pretty close home and his voice choked up so in answering me that I could not really hear what he said. His eyes filled with tears and he seemed on the verge of a breakdown. As near as I could gather it, he expressed the view that the matter was one in the hands of Providence and that we were only the instruments and he said "the very humblest instrument of a greater power and all that we can do is to make use [us?] as efficient instruments as possible." Seeing how he felt about it, I thought to turn the subject by suggesting that perhaps we were considering the matter too seriously or perhaps just now we ought not consider it at all. The conversation then drifted off on to various other matters of relatively less consequence. Amongst these was the question of the President's practising law and he related a mildly amusing conversation he had with Senator Knox on the day of the Harding inaugural when Senator Knox accompanied Mr. Wilson to his automobile.

The interview lasted, I imagine, three quarters of an hour. He asked me to come again and expressed the hope that I would stay to luncheon as he felt sure Mrs. Wilson would intercept me for this purpose on the way out. Mrs. Wilson did in fact intercept me and I remained for luncheon. Mr. Baruch came to lunch, Miss Margaret Wilson was there and also Mr. Bolling who now appears to be acting as his confidential secretary. In sharp contradistinction to my interview with Mr. Wilson which was a rather solemn affair, the luncheon was very delightful. Mrs. Wilson is always pleasant and gracious and considerate and we talked of various things, chiefly politics and in that respect principally with regard to the future of the party and the chairmanship of the Democratic National Committee. It was a pleasant gossipy luncheon and all went along very merrily. After luncheon, Mrs. Wilson showed me some chinaware which had been presented to her by the Queen of the Belgians. It was remarkably beautiful. There were I think 24 plates, each carrying individual paintings representing various scenes in Belgium. She also showed me the Gobelin tapestry which was the gift of France to Mr. Wilson prior to the entry of America into the war. It is an exquisite piece and is said to have taken five years to make. Later I saw Mr. Baruch at the Shoreham. He had seen Mr. Wilson after I left. He said I was right, that the President was very much depressed so I judge that he found him in much the same frame of mind as I found him in.

T MS (H. S. Cummings Papers, ViU).

To Hamilton Holt

My dear Mr. Holt: [Washington] 25th April, 1921.

I do not think it would be wise for me to comment on your suggestion regarding Marshall Foch,[1] because I was entirely disillusioned about him while I was in France. He proved himself in the Peace negotiations the most difficult obstacle to a peaceful settlement.

Some day I hope I may in conversation give you full information to what I refer. Suffice it to say for the present that he is the leader of the militaristic and imperialistic elements in France which are bent upon reversing the Alsace-Lorraine business in the Ruhr District. For the moment they are the worst enemies of the peace of the world.

Personally I could not receive Marshall Foch.

With kindest regards and regret I cannot help out in this matter;
            Cordially and faithfully yours,   [Woodrow Wilson]

CCL (WP, DLC).
    [1] Wilson was replying to H. Holt to WW, April 22, 1921.

From Lionel Golub[1]

My dear Mr. Wilson: New York City April 27th., 1921

In grateful recognition of the incomparable service which you have rendered Humanity by immeasurably advancing the cause of international peace, the students of New York University have to-day organized the Woodrow Wilson Club.

On the eve of the second anniversary of the promulgation of the Covenant of the League of Nations we respectfully greet you and dedicate ourselves to the glorious task of striving to effectuate your lofty concept of international relationship.

May you be spared, with restored physical and continued mental vigor, for very many years, so that your penetrating intellect and noble idealism may further contribute to the progress of Civilization.   Most sincerely yours,   Lionel Golub,
                    President of the Woodrow Wilson Club

TLS (WP, DLC).
    [1] A student at the New York University Law School.

Robert Cummins Stuart, Jr., to John Randolph Bolling

My dear Mr. Bolling: Cambridge, Massachusetts 27 April 1921

Many thanks for your letter of April the sixteenth with an editorial from the Spartanburg, S. C. paper. An organization was already underway at Furman College but our secretary has since communicated with the other colleges mentioned although it has been our practice to turn this work over to the most active club in the given state.

I have been in New York the past week conferring with Cleveland Dodge, Franklin Roosevelt and others in regard to combining the appeal of the Wilson Clubs for funds to take care of the historical work with that of the memorial committee.[1] It appears that we shall be able to co-operate and thus have one large inclusive testimonial.

We received a letter from Illinois the other day suggesting that the typewriter upon which the President wrote the notes to Germany and his address to Congress asking for a declaration of war would have considerable historical interest and should, if possible, be placed in some collection to be preserved for all time. Although having no concrete proposals to make I thought I should convey the idea to you for your consideration and judgement.

I am writing Mr. Wilson to-day acknowledging the letter referring to a collection of maps, photographs, and clippings which will be taken up with our librarian and answered very shortly.

Again thanking you for your thoughtful assistance, believe me,

Sincerely yours,   Robert C. Stuart, Jr.

TLS (WP, DLC).
¹ This is the first mention of what was to become the Woodrow Wilson Foundation. In a brief speech before a meeting of this organization on December 2, 1921, May Ladd (Mrs. Charles E.) Simonson recalled that, on November 3, 1920, one day after the presidential election in which she had worked for Democratic candidates, she had met Katrina Brandes Ely (Mrs. Charles Lewis) Tiffany, and they had agreed that some means should be found to honor Wilson. In later meetings, the two women discussed giving Wilson some material gift but discarded this idea. They met once again on November 21, 1920, the day on which the award of the Nobel Peace Prize to Wilson was announced in the newspapers. During their conversation, Mrs. Simonson remembered, they had hit upon the idea of establishing a similar humanitarian award in Wilson's name. They then proceeded to call a meeting of prominent women for December 23, 1920, to discuss the project. These women in turn brought the idea to the attention of Cleveland H. Dodge and other prominent men who might be interested in the proposal. T MS of Mrs. Simonson's remarks enclosed in H. Holt to WW, Jan. 4, 1923, TLS (WP, DLC).
The first public announcement of "a nation-wide tribute to Woodrow Wilson in appreciation of his great services for world peace" appeared in the New York Times, March 9, 1921. The article revealed that the project was "said to have been under consideration for several weeks" and that a meeting to discuss it would be held at the Hotel Biltmore in New York on March 15. Members of the preliminary committee on organization, the article continued, included Hamilton Holt, Thomas W. Lamont, Charles P. Howland, Edwin R. A. Seligman, Franklin Warner M. Cutcheon, Mrs. J. Malcolm Forbes, John Farwell Moors, Virginia Potter, Caroline Ruutz-Rees, Martha Carey Thomas, and Mrs. Tiffany. John Drinkwater and Edwin F. Gay were to speak at the meeting at the Biltmore, and others expected to attend included Ralph Pulitzer, Frank I. Cobb, Bliss Perry, Raymond B. Fosdick, the Rev. Harry Emerson Fosdick, Cleveland H. Dodge, Frank L. Polk, Constance Parsons (Mrs. Montgomery) Hare, Natalie Knowlton (Mrs. John Insley) Blair, Mrs. Simonson, Caroline Bayard Stevens Alexander (Mrs. Henry Otto) Wittpenn, and Florence Jaffray Hurst (Mrs. Jefferson Borden) Harriman. "Miss Potter said yesterday," the article concluded, "that the exact form of the proposed tribute had not been determined and would not be until after the formation of a permanent organization. She said that several plans had been suggested, none of them in the nature of a personal gift to the former President. It is intended to make the organization nation-wide, with branches in all the important cities of the country."
A second article in the New York Times, March 10, 1921, reported that the tribute to Wilson would probably take the form of a $500,000 fund to be contributed in small amounts, the interest on which would be devoted to "rewarding the one who during the year has done the greatest service to humanity." "The nature of the service," it continued, "for which the award will be made is to be defined by Mr. Wilson, who has been told of the project and has expressed himself as deeply appreciative of the honor paid him and of the purpose for which the money is to be used." The news report said that the idea behind the project had originated with women admirers of Wilson, especially "those who had worked in the last campaign to gain support for the League of Nations." It mentioned many of the names which had appeared in the previous article and added George Foster Peabody as one of the "ardent supporters" of the plan. It pointed out that the proposed fund, invested at 5 percent, would yield an annual prize, to be awarded by a jury, of $25,000, which compared favorably with the usual amount

of $40,000 of the Nobel Peace Prize. The article quoted Mrs. Wittpenn at some length. Among other remarks, she reiterated that Wilson had been informed of the plan and had endorsed it heartily.

The meeting at the Biltmore Hotel on March 15 formalized the plan to raise a fund of $500,000. However, the purpose or purposes to which the fund was to be put were left for a committee to determine. A steering committee, which was to appoint the larger committee, was chosen during the meeting and consisted of Franklin D. Roosevelt, chairman; Henry Morgenthau, Sr., treasurer; Dodge; Mrs. Forbes; Gay; Bernard M. Baruch; Mrs. Harriman; Adolph Simon Ochs; Polk; Miss Potter; Mrs. Wittpenn; Cobb; Holt; and Edward M. House. Herbert Sherman Houston, of Doubleday, Page & Co., suggested some of the possible uses to which the fund might be put: "A plan may be adopted for giving several substantial prizes each year to the college students of this country, possibly of the world, for the best papers on international subjects related to the development of the League of Nations. Some plan may be devised for encouraging constructive study of labor problems. . . . Everything that concerns the well-being of world democracy can properly come within the consideration of the committee in working out its plans." John Drinkwater made the principal speech at the meeting; it was a moving tribute to Wilson and his achievements. *New York Times*, March 16, 1921. Drinkwater's remarks are printed in *ibid.*, March 27, 1921, Sect. VIII, p. 2.

A Letter of Recommendation

TO WHOM IT MAY CONCERN: [Washington] 28th April, 1921.

Arthur Brooks served as my personal valet for eight years and I therefore had the best possible opportunity to test his capacity and his character.

He was invariably faithful, attentive and thoughtful, an unusual servant who did not wait to be told what to do. He had had a great deal of experience before he served me and it all told in his service.

I can speak of him in terms of the highest commendation. My interests shall always follow him. I hope he will always obtain the sort of employment which he deserves and which will enable him to show his unusual ability.

Very sincerely,   [Woodrow Wilson][1]

CCL (WP, DLC).
[1] There is a WWsh draft of this letter in WP, DLC.

From Robert Cummins Stuart, Jr.

My dear Mr. Wilson: Cambridge, Massachusetts 28 April 1921

The letter from Dr. Jameson[1] with suggestions regarding the historical work of the Wilson Clubs which you so kindly forwarded to me together with a recent communication from abroad was interesting and helpful.

I was in New York last week conferring with Franklin D. Roosevelt about combining the appeal of the Woodrow Wilson Clubs for funds to finance their historical programme with the nation-wide tribute which is being organized by the committee of which he is chairman. We tentatively agreed that a fund of $250,000, which would furnish an income of approximately $15,000 a year, should be assigned for our purposes.

Of this, $10,000 a year will be spent in purchasing material and defraying the expenses of a director who will assemble all data and documents at one place. The remaining income, or $5,000 a year, will be used to supply the smaller college libraries throughout the country with either transcripts of the more important material of the central collection or books relating to the period suited for a room dedicated to you.

At the end of ten or twenty years when the income was no longer needed it was thought that the proceeds might be employed for international fellowships comparable to those established by Cecil Rhodes.

As Mr. Roosevelt said he expected to see you this week you have, no doubt, had this plan outlined at some length and I shall, therefore, not sketch it more in detail.

Although my information (on the subject) is limited, it is, nevertheless, my impression that this is the first serious attempt ever made to collect all the possible material relating to a great historical period in order to have the background necessary for the true appreciation of the outstanding figure of that period. This being the case, we feel that such papers you may possess and are inclined to give to the public could be most appropriately placed with this central collection.

When this work has progressed sufficiently, it is our plan to solicit contributions of original material not only from American personages, but from the European Statesmen as well as those from Japan, Australia, and South Africa.

May I not, therefore, with all due respect and deference to the delicacy of the subject ask you to be so kind as to wait a few months until our national committee is organized and our programme financed before definitely arranging for the care of your material?

This plan, we feel, is bigger than any one club or institution and we are, therefore, constituting a committee of competent authorities from the entire country which will supervise the undertaking and which will decide upon the place where the central collection is to be located.

I am writing to Dr. Jameson this week inviting him to serve on the committee and should be happy to extend an invitation to any one you may suggest.

Yours very faithfully,   Robert C. Stuart, Jr.

TLS (WP, DLC).
 [1] J. F. Jameson to JRB, April 19, 1921.

John Randolph Bolling to Robert Cummins Stuart, Jr.

My dear Mr. Stuart: [Washington] 29th April 1921

Your letter of 27th April reached me this morning, and Mr. Wilson was interested in hearing its contents.

With regard to combining the appeal, Mr. Wilson says he fears it will bury and hide your movement which has a distinct dignity of its own.

I give you this comment for what it may be worth.

A letter comes to Mr. Wilson today from the New York University Law School, 33 Waverly Place, New York, advising him of the organization by the students of a Woodrow Wilson Club dedicated "to the glorious task of striving to effectuate your lofty concept of international relationship." In my letter of acknowledgment[1] I am (at Mr. Wilson's suggestion) telling them of your organization, and suggesting that it might be well for them to get in touch with you.

Yours very truly,   [John Randolph Bolling]

CCL (WP, DLC).
[1] JRB to L. Golub, April 29, 1921, CCL (WP, DLC).

To Edwin Anderson Alderman

My dear Dr. Alderman: [Washington] 30th April, 1921.

It is with heartfelt regret that I find myself unable to attend the great festival of the University.

I regard the University with genuine affection recalling as I do with the keenest interest and with many happy memories the profitable days I spent on her lawns and in the stimulating classroom where we used to gather about the great John D. Minor.[1] He was a great teacher, and I hold myself his permanent debtor.

May I not express the confident hope that, surrounded by her sons, the University may take on new life?

With affectionate loyalty to the noble University;

Faithfully yours,   [Woodrow Wilson][2]

CCL (WP, DLC).
[1] John Barbee Minor, Professor of Common and Statute Law at the University of Virginia, 1845-1895.
[2] There is a WWsh draft of this letter in WP, DLC.

To Irwin Hood Hoover

My dear Mr. Hoover: Washington D C 30th April, 1921.

I understand that on the sixth of May you will have completed your thirtieth year of service at The White House. During eight of those years it has been my pleasure to observe your work; for it has been a pleasure to observe your unfailing loyalty, your constant attention to duty and your really extraordinary resourcefulness in doing each thing assigned you.

I hope for you many more successful and happy years; and the years must be happy which are filled with work well done.

Cordially and sincerely yours,   Woodrow Wilson[1]

TLS (I. H. Hoover Papers, DLC).
[1] There is a WWsh draft of this letter in WP, DLC.

John Randolph Bolling to Robert Cummins Stuart, Jr.

My dear Mr. Stuart: [Washington] 30th April, 1921.

Mr. Wilson asks me to acknowledge your letter of April 28th, received this morning.

In regard to your conference with Hon. Franklin D. Roosevelt, and the plan outlined by you; Mr. Wilson seemes inclined to hold the view expressed to you in my letter of yesterday.

Yours very cordially,   [John Randolph Bolling]

CCL (WP, DLC).

From Charles Zeller Klauder

Dear Mr. Wilson: Philadelphia May 3rd, 1921.

I have not communicated with you since February 14th as I realized that you were probably fully occupied in getting settled in your new home on S. Street.

As I intend to be in Washington for the Convention of the American Institute of Architects (May 11th, 12th and 13th) it occurs to me that you might wish to look over the plans of your new house prior to that time and to confer with me when I arrive. It is needless to say I shall be very glad to do so, but whether or not the plans are to be discussed, I shall avail myself of the opportunity to call and see you.[1]

With warm personal regards to Mrs. Wilson and yourself, believe me   Sincerely yours,   Chas Z Klauder

TLS (WP, DLC).

¹ Wilson's reply to this letter is missing. However, the following words are written at its top: "can't get loans." This ended the correspondence between Wilson and Klauder about the large house on Conduit Road. It also seems to have ended Wilson's fantasizing about the project. In any event, he never mentioned it again in writing, except to acknowledge the return of certain photographs to Klauder in JRB to C. Z. Klauder, Feb. 9, 1922, CCL (WP, DLC).

From Bainbridge Colby

London May 5 [1921]

One of the great solicitors firms wishing to be our first English client has retained us in three admiralty cases each involving sixty thousand which we can handle well   Colby

T telegram (WP, DLC).

To Bainbridge Colby

Washington D C 5th May 1921

Thanks for messages; heartiest congratulations on business secured. Best wishes from all.   Wilson.

T telegram (WP, DLC).

From Robert Randolph Henderson

Dear Woodrow,   Cumberland, Md. May 5, 1921

Last May Bob Bridges, Will Lee, Hiram Woods and I had a little re-union at Ned Webster's at Bel Air. You were then overwhelmed with cares of state.¹ We are thinking of repeating the re-union this year at my house and I am naming tentatively the 26th of May. My plan is to pick the other boys up at Baltimore and bring them on by automobile. Of course, the re-union will not be complete without you. Now that you are free of official cares, will it be possible for you to join us? Nothing would give us all greater pleasure.

We are delighted to know that your health is so much better, and I am sure you are enjoying the freedom from the care and turmoil of official life.

With kind remembrances to Mrs. Wilson, in which Mrs. Henderson² joins me, I am,

Affectionately yours,   Robert R. Henderson

TLS (WP, DLC).
¹ About this reunion, see J. E. Webster to WW, May 7, 1920, Vol. 65.
² Louisa Patterson Henderson.

Edith Bolling Galt Wilson to William Edward Dodd

My dear Mr. Dodd: [Washington, c. May 5, 1921]

I have just read your little note,[1] and the clipping to Mr. Wilson and we both appreciate your thought in sending them—you are always having unusual and interesting experiences, and it is awfully nice to let us share them.

You spoke of a letter to my husband concerning his papers,[2] and he asks me to tell you he is sure the letter from you failed to reach him. So, if it is not too much trouble would you get your Secretary to send him a copy of it? For he is interested in what you say concerning a suggestion you made.

I hope you and Mrs. Dodd are very well. Please remember me to her.

I feel all you say regarding our country and the leadership so intensely that I am can't [sic] write about it. The conditions now going forward are beyond comment!

Faithfully yours,   Edith Bolling Wilson

ALS (W. E. Dodd Papers, DLC).
[1] It is missing.
[2] W. E. Dodd to WW, Feb. 22, 1921.

From Sid Houston[1]

Sir: Washington, D. C. May 5th 1921

A message from you to the men who served in the army or navy during the World War on Memorial Day would be greatly appreciated. Those men shall ever remember you as their Commander-in-Chief during those trying days when the fate of the world hung in the balance. They can never forget that message calling on Congress to officially recognize that war was being waged against this country by the Imperial German Government. And so on this Memorial Day when America stops to pay homage to her heroic dead, the men who served will look to you for some greeting.

We respectfully request that you use the columns of this paper for such a message in the issue of May 21st.

Very respectfully yours,   Sid Houston

TLS (WP, DLC).
[1] Although Houston wrote on the letterhead of *The Stars and Stripes* and signed himself as editor, there were no editions of that newspaper in 1921. Wilson's Memorial Day message was actually published in the *National Tribune* of Washington, published between August 20, 1881, and December 26, 1925, and as *National Tribune—Stars and Stripes*, January 7, 1926-January 31, 1963. Wilson's message was printed inconspicuously in the *National Tribune*, June 2, 1921.

To Sid Houston

My dear Mr. Houston: [Washington] 7th May, 1921.

Memorial Day has always been one of our most solemn and thoughtful anniversaries when we recalled great memories and dedicated ourselves again to the maintenance and purification of the Nation; but this year it has an added and tremendous significance because the memories and sacrifices of the great world war are now among the most stimulating of the recollections of the day.

We celebrate the immortal achiev[e]ments of the men who died in France on the field and in the trenches far away from home, in order that both our own people and the peoples across the seas might be delivered from the ugliest peril of all history. It is our privilege not only to indulge a high and solemn pride and grief for the heroes of that great struggle but also to rededicate ourselves to the achiev[e]ment of the great objects for which that war was fought. We shall not be happy; we shall not be able to enjoy the full pride of the Day's recollections until we have made sure that the duties that grew out of the war have been fulfilled to the utmost.

Are we sure? If we are not shall we not soon take steps to do whatever has been omitted?

Cordially yours,   [Woodrow Wilson][1]

CCL (WP, DLC).
  [1] There is a WWsh draft of this letter in WP, DLC.

To Charles W. Weiser[1]

My dear Mr. Weiser: [Washington] 7th May, 1921.

I am glad to send a greeting to Democrats[2] who are making a united effort to promote the great principles and causes which our party represents.

Every Democrat may look forward both to the immediate future and to the distant future with the utmost confidence, because his party represents the things that are permanent and which no human force can defeat. It represents justice and the right both for the people at home and for the people of all the nations of the world. It therefore stands with those who think justly and plan righteously everywhere in the world, and the future belongs to these.

Our immediate duty is to think in the most practical terms of achiev[e]ment. Justice and the right constitute a great ideal. We must make it our object to develop a program that will realize them for ourselves and for others.

Who can fail to take inspiration from such a view of present tasks and future triumphs?

Cordially yours,   [Woodrow Wilson][3]

CCL (WP, DLC).
[1] Wilson was replying to C. W. Weiser to WW, May 3, 1921, TLS (WP, DLC).
[2] The Democratic organization of Lehigh County, Pa., which was about to hold its annual meeting.
[3] There is a WWsh draft of this letter in WP, DLC.

To Charles Millard Starbird[1]

My dear Mr. Starbird: [Washington] 7th May, 1921.

Unhappily the state of my health renders it impossible for me to be present at the Convention which you are planning for the first week in July; but I shall be with you in heart, and only wish that I could convey to the young Democrats of Maine the vision that is in my own mind of the future of the Democratic Party.

It is of necessity the young man's party because its work is the work which must claim the devotion and absorb the energies of liberal statesmen throughout the world for the next two or three generations. No citizens can more properly, or I should think more enthusiastically, organize to assure its success than the young citizens of every forward looking community of our country.

Hoping and believing that the convention will be an unqualified success and greatly serviceable, not only to the State but to the country at large;

Cordially and sincerely yours,   [Woodrow Wilson][2]

CCL (WP, DLC).
[1] Wilson was replying to C. M. Starbird to WW, May 5, 1921, TLS (WP, DLC). Starbird, a senior at Bates College, invited Wilson to speak to the state convention of the Young Americans' Democratic League of Maine, to be held in Augusta sometime during the first week of July 1921.
[2] There is a WWsh draft of this letter in WP, DLC.

To Stanley White[1]

My dear Dr. White: [Washington] 7th May, 1921

As his classmate at the university, and his friend and frequent companion in subsequent years, I had abundant opportunity to know the fine qualities which endeared Halsey to his friends and the well deserved confidence of the Church.

I am deeply grieved that he should have been taken away; he will be missed in every relationship which he formed and not least by those of us who have known him longest and who entertain a sincere personal affection for him.

He will be remembered always as a man worthy of trust and affection.   Sincerely yours,   [Woodrow Wilson][2]

CCL (WP, DLC).
  [1] Wilson was replying to S. White to WW, May 4, 1921, TLS (WP, DLC). The Rev. Dr. Stanley White, Secretary of the Board of Foreign Missions of the Presbyterian Church, U.S.A., asked Wilson for a letter to be read at a memorial service for the Rev. Dr. Abram Woodruff Halsey at the First Presbyterian Church of New York on May 10. Halsey, who had died on April 20, 1921, was Wilson's classmate at Princeton and had been Secretary of the Board of Foreign Missions since 1899.
  [2] There is a WWsh draft of this letter in WP, DLC.

To Robert Randolph Henderson

My dear Bob: Washington D C 7th May, 1921.

It grieves me that I cannot join you and the other boys on the occasion you are planning.[1] It would be wholly delightful; and I find myself very often longing for the old companionships.

But I am sorry to say, my dear fellow, that the newspapers have given a quite msileading [misleading] impression of my improvement in health, and I have not yet the physical strength to venture so far afield even as Cumberland.

Please give my love to the boys, our warmest regards to Mrs. Henderson and believe me always,
                        Your affectionate friend,   Woodrow Wilson

TLS (photostat in RSB Coll., DLC).
  [1] Wilson was replying to R. R. Henderson to WW, May 5, 1921.

From Armistead Mason Dobie

My Dear Mr. Wilson: Richmond, Virginia May 7, 1921

You have been most gracious both in serving as a member of the National Committee of the University of Virginia Centennial Endowment fund, and in sending to us a commendation of the Endowment fund which was very helpful.[1]

I know, too, you will wish to make some contribution to this Centennial Endowment fund however small that may be, and we shall keenly appreciate any gift you may make. So I am taking the liberty of sending you a subscription blank, without any personal solicitation, trusting you will wish to fill it out and return it to us.

With sentiments of great respect,
                            Yours sincerely,   A. M. Dobie[2]

TLS (WP, DLC).
  [1] WW to A. M. Dobie, Feb. 16, 1921.
  [2] Wilson's reply is missing; however, a notation in the upper left-hand corner of Dobie's letter reads: "cant afford."

To Bernard Mannes Baruch

My dear Baruch: Washington, D C 10th May, 1921

We have learned with the greatest distress of your father's[1] illness; please give him our love and sympathy and tell him that in
common with all those who have learned to admire and feel a real
affection for him we expect and require of him that he take perfect
care of himself and get well.

We learn that you yourself have not been as well as you should
be; please be careful and report here in good shape as soon as possible.

With all affectionate messages from us both;
                    Faithfully yours,   Woodrow Wilson

TLS (B. M. Baruch Papers, NjP).
  [1] Simon Baruch, M.D.

William Edward Dodd to Edith Bolling Galt Wilson

My dear Mrs. Wilson: Chicago May 10, 1921.

The gist of what I wrote was that the President would confer a
great benefit upon those who seek to have his ideas carried home
again and again to the American people by depositing all his papers
with the Library of Congress where the writings of so many of his
predecessors are to be found.

Realizing that free use could not be made of them immediately
I suggested that three friends and scholars, at the same time, be
given access to them under such limitations as he might see fit to
fix. One of these ought to be an authority in the field of American
history, another should know modern Europe well and the third
might be some other friend, perhaps not especially a historian.

Do not think that I think professional historians are are [sic] the
last word in right thinking. But it so happens that the historians do
with all but unanimous accord agree upon the value and greatness
of the ideals and work of President Wilson, including some [of]
those who have been considered reactionary in their interpretations of life. The reason for urging such a disposition is that the
real Wilsonism may be understood before it is too late to harvest
some of the fruits.

The Library of Congress is the one place where scholars and
others expect to find the materials of our history. Most of us go
there frequently to work. And there the best care would be taken
of them for all time. I hope he may find it possible to agree with
me on this point.

The other point was the feasibility of empl[o]ying competent hands to go over all his correspondence, from early life to the present, with a view to the publication of an autobiography. Although he made plain to me the reasons that prompt him not to do this, I still feel that he ought to write a work in two or three volumes. There is every argument in favor of this and only two against it that occur to me. One against it is the charge of defending himself. With that feeling of his I sympathize, but not to the extent of being willing to have his work left without his own interpretation.

The other reason is the state of his health. My idea was to suggest a way that might be met to some extent, namely to employ someone of unquestioned standing as a historian (The name of S. B. Harding, a very able man and hearty admirer of the President was in mind) to do all the research and leave Mr. Wilson to dictate the narrative. That was all. I then thought, and still think, that means could easily be found to meet the expense of such a helper.

This was about all I wrote in the former letter. It was mailed to him the latter part of February. There was, I venture to mention, a similar letter, that is a memorandum, sent to him in the autumn of 1918 which he said he never saw.[1] As that letter dealt with a rather critical matter at the time and gave names and facts, I would be sorry to have it find its way into other hands than those intended. There must be a body of such correspondence in Mr. Tumulty's possession. In case there is, I submit whether it would not be best to have it all placed with the Wilson papers.

May I say in conclusion that I know every effort is being made by men of ability to pre-empt the public mind with books, writings and ideas of the late Colonel Roosevelt. This has been done in such a way as to tend to the misinterpretation of many of the greater movements of recent times. I have set myself as much as my time and vigor would allow to counteract this propaganda, a word than [that] I *hate*, if one may hate inanimate things or ideas. Aware, as Mr. Wilson must be, with the perversions of history by the most *respectable* characters, he must agree with me that he ought to cooperate with his friends as best he may.

I know Mr. Baker is doing a good work on the Peace Conference. That is as it should be. But Mr. Wilson's work concerns the whole great drift of our history these last twenty five years.

Yours Sincerely   William E. Dodd

If I could only hear that Mr. Wilson has recovered entirely or substantially!

TLS (WP, DLC).
[1] He describes the letter in W. E. Dodd to EBW, May 29, 1921.

From Bernard Mannes Baruch

My dear Mr. Wilson: New York May 13, 1921.

It is very good of you to think of my troubles and distress.

Father, evidently because of your charge to take care of himself, seems to be quite recovered. Indeed, his improvement was quite unexpected.

So far as I myself am concerned, I am all right and shall report at an early date.

With many, many thanks for your note, and with affectionate regards to yourself and Mrs. Wilson, I am, as always,

Sincerely yours,   Bernard M. Baruch

TLS (WP, DLC).

To Anne Wintermute Lane

[Washington] May 18th 1921

Our hearts go out to you in deepest sympathy in your tragical loss.[1]   Woodrow Wilson.

T telegram (WP, DLC).
[1] Her husband, Franklin Knight Lane, died suddenly on May 18, 1921.

David Lawrence to Edith Bolling Galt Wilson

Personal

My dear Mrs. Wilson: Washington, D. C. May 18, 1921.

Would you kindly give me about fifteen minutes of your time any day in the near future, as I would like to get your advice on a purely personal matter? It does not relate in any way to newspaper stories or business matters. I will be glad to come at any hour you designate after 11:30 A.M.   Cordially yours,   David Lawrence

TLS (WP, DLC).

From the Diary of Ray Stannard Baker

[Washington May] 18 [1921]

Lunch Wilsons'. With stenographer almost all day. Not well. Mr. Wilson worries about the situation in the country: thinks we are going wrong. Grayson says it is keeping him down physically. He is not well. He's in bed a great deal of the day: and sees almost no one outside of the family.

Edith Bolling Galt Wilson to David Lawrence

My dear Mr. Lawrence: [Washington] 19th May 1921

As I am not seeing anyone at this time, I suggest that you advise me by letter of the matter regarding which you write, and I shall be very glad to give consideration to it.

Cordially yours,   [Edith B. Wilson]

CCL (WP, DLC).

From Robert Cummins Stuart, Jr.

Cambridge, Massachusetts

My dear Mr. Wilson: May 20, 1920 [1921]

In deference to your judgment expressed in Mr. Bolling's letter of 29th April and in your letter of 30th April the Woodrow Wilson Club of Harvard has decided not to join with the committee headed by Hon. Franklin D. Roosevelt in raising one common memorial fund.

This change will require greater co-öperation and closer association of the affiliated clubs. To accomplish this a National Council of Woodrow Wilson Clubs composed of one representative from each club has been formed. An executive committee, of which I am chairman, has been fully empowered to constitute such committees and organizations as may be necessary to finance and execute the programme for historical research, memorial collections, and international fellowships as outlined in my letter of April 28th.

Among those replying this week accepting invitations to serve on the National Committee of Historical Research are Professors Walter F. Fleming (Vanderbilt), John H. Latané (Johns Hopkins), Charles Seymour (Yale), and Dean A. M. Thompson (Pittsburg)[1] who as a former student and friend of yours writes a most heartening letter.

Professor W. E. Dodd is co-öperating with the Chicago club in making a list of professors available in the west and with Cyrus H. McCormick in considering men to assist us in raising money in that section.

This work is meeting with such gratifying support that the Harvard executive committee is recommending through me to the national committee that the amount to be raised shall be substantially increased and more emphasis be placed on the international fellowships. The historical work, however, will not be slighted; it will be adequately financed and properly executed. The additional money will mean that the scholarships will begin immediately instead of waiting for the historical programme to be completed.

Last week requests were sent to all the clubs to hold meetings for the discussion of "Disarmament" and where sentiment was favorable to urge all members to wire or write to Washington urging an International Conference on Disarmament. In this way we hope to assist the focusing of public attention upon "The League" and thus co-öperate with the Pro-League Independents who are holding similar meetings—in Boston Sunday and the first of the week in Chicago.

We are also recommending that each club not only encourage its members as they leave college to continue their membership but welcome and earnestly urge all alumni of the respective institutions to become non-resident members. This, we feel, will extend the influence of the clubs more widely and by providing a nominal fee of one dollar a year each club should have ample funds for all reasonable activities.

Remembering that at the White House on February the twenty-second you expressed your intention to devote your time and energy "to furthering those ideals which grew out of the war," we felt that you might be disposed to suggest or outline from time to time a course of effective action whereby the affiliated clubs could exert an influence in shaping the political policies of the country. You have, therefore, Mr. Wilson, been elected Honorary President of the "National Council" for life.

Yours very faithfully,   Robert C. Stuart, Jr.

TLS (WP, DLC).
    [1] Walter Lynwood Fleming, Professor of History at Vanderbilt University; John Holladay Latané, Professor of American History at The Johns Hopkins University; and Alexander Marshall Thompson, Dean of the Law School of the University of Pittsburgh, Princeton class of 1893.

David Lawrence to Edith Bolling Galt Wilson

My dear Mrs. Wilson: [Washington] May 20, 1921.

I would be glad to write out all that I have in mind, but I am afraid it would be too long an epistle. While I an [am] a writer, I have not as much faith sometimes in the effectiveness of the written word as I have in the spoken.

I have heard that Mr. Wilson entertains for me a deep hatred and prejudice. I have had an opportunity from the beginning of knowing Woodrow Wilson. I have idealized and idolized him, and I have felt confident that Woodrow Wilson would do no man an injustice. When he was President, I did not feel it proper to take up this matter, as it might seem that I was seeking something—trying to curry favor. He is out of office now, he can do nothing for me in a business way, and my motive for wanting to straighten the matter our [out] at this time cannot be questioned. I hoped you might give me a few minutes of time, so that I might outline some phases of this affair, which, I am sure, in justice to me, you ought to know, and which afterwards, if you felt it desirable, you might communicate to Mr. Wilson.   Cordially yours,   David Lawrence[1]

TLS (WP, DLC).
    [1] "no reply" written at the top of this letter.

From Sylvester Woodbridge Beach

Winona Lake Ind May 21 1921

General Assembly rose to feet today and cheered for five minutes mention of Woodrow Wilson and League of Nations.[1]

Sylvester W Beach

T telegram (WP, DLC).
    [1] That is, the General Assembly of the Presbyterian Church, U.S.A. The demonstration was set off by the remarks of the Rev. Joseph Krenek of Czechoslovakia, who praised Wilson for his "attitude" on self-determination. *New York Times*, May 22, 1921.

From Edwin Anderson Alderman

My dear Mr. Wilson: Charlottesville May 21, 1921.

I may have written to your Secretary, but I must write to you to tell you how much happiness and satisfaction your handsome letter gave me.[1] I shall take leave to read it at our Centennial Celebration, and I know that it will be received with great appreciation by your fellow alumni who respect you for your great service to the nation and to the world, and have affection for you as a man and as a citizen.   Faithfully, your friend,   Edwin A. Anderson.

TLS (WP, DLC).
    [1] WW to E. A. Alderman, April 30, 1921.

Edith Bolling Galt Wilson to William Edward Dodd

My dear Prof. Dodd: [Washington] May 22, 1921

It was exceedingly kind of you to rewrite your suggestions in regard to Mr. Wilson's papers and files,[1] and he joins me in appreciation. He asks me to tell you he thinks the plan you outline very helpful, and when he gets back to literary works he hopes to carry out something along the lines you suggest[.] Just yet, things are still a burden that have to be thought out, but I think it is natural reaction from years of increasing burden and need for every ounce of driving force.

We join in sending warmest regards to you and Mrs. Dodd.

Faithfully yours,   Edith Bolling Wilson

ALS (W. E. Dodd Papers, DLC).
    [1] That is, W. E. Dodd to EBW, May 10, 1921.

John Randolph Bolling to Robert Cummins Stuart, Jr.

My dear Mr. Stuart: [Washington] 23d May 1921

It was very delightful to have your letters of May 20th,[1] received this morning; and Mr. Wilson was most interested in hearing the contents of both.

He asks me to say that while you cannot count on him for specific suggestions, he will be glad to make those which come to him. In this connection let me say that I believe the best way to secure his advice and cooperation will be for you to propound specific questions on which you wish information. I know his method of working so well, that I am sure you will obtain suggestions in this way that otherwise you will not.

He is glad to accept the office of Honorary President of the National Council—if you feel it will be of service for him to do so. I am sure that it will, and so I told him I would formally accept for him in this letter.

It seems too bad that you are not to have your trip to Europe this summer, but I can readily understand the importance of carrying on the work here while it is so well under way.

Please do not hesitate to write me (or Mr. Wilson) regarding any matters upon which you wish Mr. Wilson's views; and I am sure he will be only too happy to aid in any way that he can.

Sincerely yours,   [John Randolph Bolling]

CCL (WP, DLC).
    [1] The one not printed is R. C. Stuart, Jr., to JRB, May 20, 1921, TLS (WP, DLC).

From the Diary of Ray Stannard Baker

[Washington] May 25 [1921]

I had a long & very interesting talk with Mrs. Wilson after luncheon. The President was not down to-day. He lies in bed a great deal—Grayson thinks too much, & urges him to get at some work that will engage, even to exhaustion, his self-consuming mind. He seems to have no spirit for it. He reads a great deal—with his one

eye—mostly stories of vivid plot & action, just now Oppenheim.[1]
He seems not to want to know or think about what is going on, &
yet broods upon it! Grayson spoke to him yesterday about Col.
Harvey's speech in London[2] & referred to Harvey as a "skunk."
"No, no, Grayson," he said without the slightest smile, "you are
wrong: a skunk has a white streak."

He goes for a ride every day—and always the same ride—out
along the Conduit road. Mrs. Wilson told me he never seemed to
want to change. The country people & the children there have
grown accustomed to watching for his car, which runs on the minute, & come out & wave to him. He seems to take a kind of melancholy interest in waving to them in return, or lifting his hat. (I
think of him two years ago coming down the Champs Elysees in
Paris with the President of France, and the cheering thousands
who greeted him there.) He has always had a curious, almost ma-
chine-like precision in the regulation of his life. Never a moment
late at any time: meals, exercise, all the common acts of life, exactly according to rule and by habit. Never was such discipline of
the body & all the capacities by the mind: and now even though
the spark has been dimmed, the trained mechanism continues to
run on. He sees almost nobody, nor seems to wish any human contacts. He is the lonliest creature in the world. Letters come in
plenty but they are mostly the letters of strangers. I have a great
pity for this old man. (Yet never was anyone served with greater
devotion or more untiring zeal than he by Mrs. Wilson.)

Mrs. Wilson told me at length about all the much-talked-about
"break" of the President with Colonel House.[3] She said it was the

[1] E(dward) Phillips Oppenheim (1866-1946), prolific English writer of spy and ro-
mantic novels. Wilson was probably reading *The Great Impersonation*, which had just
been published.

[2] In a speech given at a dinner in his honor in London by The Pilgrims (a society of
notables dedicated to promoting Anglo-American friendship) on May 19, 1921, George
B. M. Harvey, the new Ambassador to Great Britain, said, among other things:

"Even to this day at rare intervals an ebullient sophomore seeks applause and wins a
smile by shouting that 'We won the war!' Far more prevalent until recently was the
impression—and this was and still is in a measure sincere—that we went into the war
to rescue humanity from all kinds of menacing perils. Not a few remain convinced that
we sent our young soldiers across the sea to save this kingdom and France and Italy.
This is not the fact. We sent them solely to save the United States of America, and most
reluctantly and laggardly at that. We were not too proud to fight, whatever that may
mean. We were not afraid to fight. That is the real truth of the matter, and so we came
along toward the end and helped you and your allies to shorten the war. That is all we
did and claim to have done."

Harvey also said that the question of American membership in the League of Nations
had been definitively settled by the election of 1920 and that the United States would
have nothing whatsoever to do with the League or with any of its committees or commissions. *New York Times*, May 20, 1921.

[3] The following account is in part substantially the same as the one told in Cary T.
Grayson, "The Colonel's Folly and the President's Distress," *American Heritage*, XV
(Oct. 1964), 4-7, 94-101, and Edith B. Wilson, *My Memoir* (Indianapolis and New York,
1938), pp. 250-52; see also the extract from the Grayson Diary and the notes thereto
printed at April 21, 1919, Vol. 57.

first time she had ever told anyone. And like so many things of this sort, a mountain has been made of a mole-hill. So far as she knows there have never been any words between the two men. The President, as I also know, felt at Paris that the Colonel was not supporting him as he should: and although, as he said more than once, he had a "great affection" for the Colonel yet he "felt disappointed in him." One of the chief troubles was the way in which the Colonel tried to force upon the President the services of his son-in-law, Auchincloss, & his brother-in-law, Dr. Mezes. Auchincloss was a hopeless misfit at Paris, as everyone knew except the Colonel. The actual "break," so far as there was any break, was not however with the President but with Mrs. Wilson. In the trying days of early April (1919) when the President had been ill & under fierce attack by the newspapers for delaying the peace, Mrs. Wilson had received copies of an article by Wickham Steed of the London *Times* (also published in America) in which Steed suggested (as she told me) that Mr. Wilson's illness was "diplomatic"—in short, that he was feigning to escape the decisions being forced upon the conference: & in the same article suggesting that a negotiator with more knowledge of European affairs—namely, Colonel House—ought to be intrusted with the settlements. (This is probably not a very accurate statement of the article but it was the impression strongly made upon Mrs. Wilson) Well, this cut Mrs. Wilson to the quick. She knew how the President was struggling & suffering! She also knew that Steed was a great personal friend of Colonel House's: & that Colonel House had even been appealing to the President to present Steed with a D.S.M. The Colonel had all along been on most friendly & even familiar terms with both the President & Mrs. Wilson He had stopped often at the White House & came in quite familiarly at Paris, to chat with Mrs. Wilson. He came in on the day in question, tapping on her door & asking if he might sit a moment while he waited for the President. In some way in the course of the conversation the London *Times* was mentioned: & Mrs. Wilson said that brought to mind Steed's article & she at once turned to the Colonel & said—for she had always talked to him with the greatest frankness:—

"Colonel, what about these articles by Mr. Steed? You are a friend of the President & you know how ill he has been."

"What articles?" asked Colonel House quickly.

Mrs. Wilson said he started up, & his face changed & colored vividly.

She opened the drawer of her desk & handed him one of them.

"They are very complimentary to you," she said to him, smiling.

He took the article quickly, glanced at it, & then jumped up, seized his overcoat and hat, and (she says) went rushing out with scarcely a word: and never, while at Paris, came to see her again.

She said she had absolutely no intent of offending him or of accusing him of any disloyalty.

"I have never been able since then to think of it without feeling that his conscience must have troubled him & he felt that I was accusing him when I was only telling him about one of the things that worried me—just as I had done in the past," she told me.

Of course the President felt uncomfortable about this incident when it was told to him: this with other intimations he had that the Colonel was attempting to advocate things that he knew the President would not approve (as in the Italian matter) certainly caused a coolness to grow up. It was said at the Crillon that the President's conferences were moved from the Colonel's offices to Secretary Lansing's because of this coolness, but Mrs. Wilson told me that it was not due to this at all. Henry White (& others) had told the President of the friction existing between House & Lansing & of the comments outside that the President was disregarding his foreign minister.

"Why," he said, "it never has occurred to me. It makes no difference to me where the meetings are held. We'll meet next time in Lansing's office."

It *did* matter: & that was the trouble! He never got the human significance of such a change: did not even think to explain it to Colonel House!

Later there was much talk of disagreement between the President & Colonel House about his returning home in the summer of 1919. The President advised him to stay: but he came. Mrs. Wilson said there was no hard feeling about this on the President's side: & the Colonel told me some time ago that there was no hard feeling on *his* side. But the President was ill & could not answer letters: & the Colonel was doubtful about his status at the White House—& there you are.

But to let such a friendship slip away for such trivial reasons! It is unfortunately too like the President not to make any advances, not to go half way not to make any explanations! He seems to have no imaginative grasp of the human aspects of such matters, or of the human feelings stirred up! The basis, of course, of the whole relationship from the beginning between the two men was the tenacious advances of the Colonel. He was friendly in spite of everything! He sought him out! He drove through the President's barricades! And if he had driven a little harder this last winter—he could, I feel certain, have done it again. Mrs. Wilson says she has none but kind feelings: there have been quite a number of exchanges of letters &c &c. I believe the President to-day would be glad to see the Colonel & if the Colonel were not in Europe I'd get a meeting somehow!

This, of course, is small talk, & yet it throws light on the character of both men. I think the Colonel understood the President better than most men: & wanted to serve him well: but got too little *explanation*, too little human sympathy & encouragement. It is a strange man, this President! Men have been fascinated by him, attracted & enthralled by his extra-ordinary intellectual powers, or his moral fervor: & have, like Colonel House,—but without his sincerity of purpose—broken through the President's barriers. Such, for example, were Col. Harvey, McCombs & Wm Bayard Hale:[4] all of whom attempted to use this grim old Scotsman for their own purposes: & when they got neither the benefits they expected, nor any human response: turned upon him with gall & worm wood & all three have attacked him fiercely in books or articles. Lansing's is a different case entirely & represents another facet of the President's nature. The President always hated to bother with human arrangements. He disliked to make appointments: but having made them he disliked any change! He would much have preferred to do the whole job himself. When Bryan went out Lansing was there—& he just let him be. He used him when he needed him, & let him be when he did not need him: and there was little or no real human relationship.

The President had vast labor to do, great legislative plans to work out, many speeches to make: and he was always at the edge of his physical capacity, always having to conserve his energy—and he let the cultivation of these ordinary human relationships (which are expensive in time, emotion, energy) slip by. Undoubtedly he underestimated their importance compared with the great moral ideas he was seeking to propagate. He never seemed to realize what an intensely human world this is!

Curiously in all these cases—Harvey, Hale, McCombs, Lansing—the hatred aroused has seemed to bring out all that was worst (truest?) in them, bitterest. In trying to give the world a bad opinion of Wilson they give it a worse opinion of themselves.

Never-the-less he represented & typified one of the great & eternal human attitudes toward life: that idealist, looking & struggling for a better world for all men to live in: where there was more liberty, justice, a greater sense of duty & responsibility. It will not be soon that the Wilsonian point of view is forgotten in America or in

[4] Wilson's first biographer and editor and special agent in Mexico; a paid propagandist for the German government until the United States entered the war. His *The Story of a Style* (New York, 1920), is an unflattering psychobiography of Wilson and a critical study of his style.

A much touched-up photograph taken during the last days in the
White House

Another much touched-up photograph

Wilson and his Cabinet, February 15, 1921

On his way to the Capitol, March 4, 1921, with Harding, Cannon, and Penrose

The house on S Street

The library in the S Street house

In the Armistice Day parade, 1921

Leaving his home on the arm of Isaac Scott

Out for a drive in his Pierce-Arrow

the world. He was against corruption always & everywhere: he was against the huge power of monied interests & so they hated him! He thought of the welfare of the great masses of men everywhere: but his next door neighbor he could not touch!

And he had a strange power—a veritable genius—for presenting these ideas so that they stole away men's hearts. I remember well the profound impression he made upon me the first time I heard him speak. He seemed to be everything I desired in a leader! And so he charmed, elevated, persuaded the whole world in 1917 & 1918. His words were worth army corps! This I shall always think pure genius. (Goethe in one of the Eckermann conversations makes a distinction I often recall between a "genius" and a "nature"—placing the latter on a higher plane.)[5] I sometimes wonder if I am not too close just now to see the President as he should be seen: a distant high peak, cold, snow-capped, with a kind of glittering beauty & power, reaching toward the stars—distant, distant! Such chit-chat as I have written above is not fair to him. We do not quarrel with Katahdyn[6] or the Grand Teton: we accept them! Why should Katahdin explain itself! Why should the Grand Teton clap us on the shoulder? To-day, in Washington, & indeed everywhere, Wilson is more discussed than Harding—and always will be! Men may hate him bitterly, as many do, or admire him, or try to explain him—but they can't get around him. There he is! And he will always be discussed, fought over, hated, admired, speculated about—

(But what a lonely thing it is to be Katahdyn! How cold and still & unhuman to be the Grand Teton!)

Mrs. Wilson told me about de-coding cablegrams while the President was ill, one very long one from Col. House which when she worked in [it] out in those hard-pressed days, were instructions for the opening of the Colonel's flat in New York which he requested be transmitted to Auchincloss! To do such little human kindnesses & ask others to do them for him is one secret of the Colonel's warm human approach. It is what he means by friendship: & it is what endears people to him. He is generous, & kind, & human and he assumes that all other people are also: and indeed by that very assumption stimulates in them qualities of kindliness. But think of sending to a President of the United States, who is ill & deperately over-wrought, a long cablegram, double-coded, containing instructions to his son-in-law for the opening of his flat! And think of the

[5] Johann Peter Eckermann, *Gespräche mit Goethe in den Letzten Jahren seines Lebens* (3 vols., Leipzig, 1836-1848). This work was frequently republished and translated into various languages. The passage referred to by Baker appears in the conversation of December 3, 1824.

[6] Mount Katahdin, in north central Maine.

President's wife sitting down for two hours of her anxious time, while she was nursing the President, to de-code what she thought must be a world important message! (There was a special secret code used by the President & Col. House) Isn't it amazing how we all suffer by the excess of our qualities! Here is the poor President suffering with inability to reach his nearest friends: to do the spontaneous, kindly, affectionate things—and being hated for it! And here is the Colonel over-doing these very loyalties! One of the troubles at Paris was due to the fact that the Colonel brought with him too many sons-in-law, brothers-in-law & the like! He had his whole family there in the Crillon & all in the Commission! And no two men there were such utter failures as Dr. Mezes & Auchincloss. Yet, he loved these friends, wanted them near him, desired to advance their interests. He tried to force Auchincloss on the President as a kind of secretary, sent him without consulting the President to London to make arrangements for the English trip, and in both cases to the point of utter irritation. In the same way he made more than loyal friends of such men as Wickham Steed & Sir Wm Wiseman—& tried to get honors from the President for both.

It was perhaps because these two men were at opposite poles of temperament: one cold & negative, the other warm & positive, that they so flew together, each recognising in the other what he lacked. Both had a kind of sincerity & disinterestedness—a greatness!—in his quality. People love House (I have that feeling myself) and he loves his friends: and is to-day, as he was at Paris, cheery, optimistic—yes, happy! He lives always in a kind of warm haze of good-feeling. What a contrast with the grim, bitter, tragic, lonely old man there in S. street! And yet twenty years from now he will be utterly forgotten (most people even to-day could not offhand mention a single thing of importance he ever said or did) except as he was a friend, a helper, of the President: an incident in the President's career & one of the men who reflected for a moment the light from that great figure and then suffered his displeasure.

What a world it is! How beautiful & strange are human beings!

David Lawrence to Edith Bolling Galt Wilson

My dear Mrs. Wilson: Washington, D. C. May 26, 1921.

Apropos of the letter I wrote you the other day, I wish you would read the enclosed letter which has just come to hand.[1] It is typical of other letters which we have received from time to time, and it only emphasizes the point that I have wanted to make to you—that I am paying a penalty for my convictions which are altogether different, I imagine, from the impressions that have been conveyed to you by others.

After you have read it, will you return the enclosed letter to me for our files?   Cordially yours,   David Lawrence

TLS (WP, DLC).
¹ Wilson's secretary typed at the top of this letter: "Letter was from The Monmouth Daily Atlas, Monmouth, Ill.; dated May 23, 1921. Returned to Mr. Lawrence on May 27th 1921 without reply. JRB"

From the Diary of Ray Stannard Baker

[Washington] May 27 [1921].

To-day coming out of the Wilson house in S. street I saw one of the big observation cars come swaying down the hill (the "rubber-neck wagons" all come through S. street these days to point out where Mr. Wilson lives) and the guide with his megaphone to his mouth was bawling: "On the left just below you will see the new home of Ex-President Wilson. He paid $150,000 for it—*or she did.*"!!

Each afternoon, now, at three o'clock (to the minute) when the President drives out there is a little group of people waiting, either in their cars, or sitting on the neighbors' flower-beds, to see him and Mrs. Wilson go by. There is always a cordial waving of hands.

From Newton Diehl Baker

My dear Mr. President: Cleveland May 29, 1921.

I hope Washington is keeping fairly cool and comfortable and that you are growing stronger day by day. All of us get an occasional word of your progress from some chance newspaper reference, but the news is a meager allowance upon a subject so near our hearts. Hurley was here a week or so ago, with late and comforting news of you, and whenever chance brings any of your old family together we swap news and compare notes, thus we constitute a sort of "News of Wilson" society which would please you and which gives us all a chance to air our pride in being a part of your elect!

Hurley, by the way, made a capital speech here. Much more thoughtful and suggestive than any I have heard from him before, and it created a fine impression. Redfield has been here twice recently, talking in the interest of the International Trading Corporation, and each time simply astounding his hearers with his encyclopedic information. I confess I was delighted with both of his addresses and informed too; may I therefore confess to you, as a

father confessor, that I have some times been guilty of the sin of
non-appreciation toward him, and be given absolution? I do not
mean that I have not always liked and admired Redfield, for I do
think him as zealous and high minded as any man I know, but it
has seemed to me sometimes as though all facts were of the same
size and importance to him, while I am afraid I am impatient of the
existence of any fact I cannot immediately use, and am disposed to
resent its being brought into my practical world at all. But any way
Redfield did finely here, and I was proud of him. And all such talk
is needed. How we Americans are ever to become even a little internationally minded, I do not know. We learn all we know from
newspapers, and our newspapers remind me of a remark Coleridge
made of DeQuincey when he heard that DeQuincey was writing a
book on Political Economy: "He not only knows nothing about political economy but all his life has been obstinately bent on learning
nothing about it!" I do not overstate the case much when I say that
we out here who depend upon the Plaindealer,[1] are little more in
touch with the real happenings in the world than was Robinson
Crusoe. I say this, it is true with a deep sense of grievance, but it
is worth saying as an explanation of much that has happened. As
a forecast of what of necessity will happen in the future I venture
the opinion that unless something radical happens to the newspapers of the country the mind of the next generation will have neither contents nor capacity for thinking. With such means as have
been at the disposal of the American people for learning the truth
and seeing things in their true proportions, I have ceased to wonder at their failure to act wisely. There is, however, one way in
which even a misled people learns, and that is by the consequences, and there are multiplying signs here in Cleveland that
some educating is going on. During the last campaign and during
the discussion of the Treaty two fundamental errors were drilled
into the common mind. One was that the making of a treaty was,
after all, a simple matter, and the other was that you had only to
wave some sort of a wand in Paris and you could have your way on
every subject. The book "What really happened in Paris" is being
widely read around here and it actually seems to get over the picture of the infinite intricacy of the questions and the mad intensity
of the passions that swirled about the Conference. Men are frequently saying to me now: "I never comprehended or imagined
that the task was so supremely complicated" and they usually couple it with some suggestion of regret. It is as good to sit by and see
the imponderables get their work in at last!

I dislike Harvey so genuinely that I can hardly trust myself to
write of him, but we really ought to be everlastingly grateful for
him. He has done more for the cause of right by being crudely,

impudently and offensively wrong that any body recently has been able to do by being eloquently right. I am getting letters from soldiers protesting against his misrepresentation of their purpose and motive, and my republican friends who are hardened enough to undertake a defense of all the other undertakings and outgivings of the administration, even to declaring Dr. Brigadier Sawyer a wise man, balk at Harvey.[2] Can you not see the glacial politeness of Mr. Balfour to the roughneck? To Englishmen, whose ancestors have not made a social blunder since the battle of Hastings, Harvey's manners will import a moral delinquency which he can never overcome. He may stay in England but he cannot live there, he is dead already and by a most appropriate death, self inflicted out of a composite of motives in which vanity malice and reckless mendacity all form parts. Like the thane of Cawdor "nothing in his life became him like the leaving it". Now I feel fine, having expressed my sentiments fully!

The industrial situation here is unimproved. Our industries are working on about a forty per cent basis and there are no signs of a pick up. Fortunately the Summer weather modifies the distress which so much unemployment would otherwise cause, and we are all hoping that the late Summer may see better times, but unless the foreign situation is cleared up the chances are not good, and nothing in the Plaindealer has yet indicated a policy in Washington on the foreign situation which has any medicine in it.

Please, Mr. President, do not feel called upon to answer or acknowledge this note; it is just an ad interim report to the chief and I shall feel freer to send them if I know that they impose no burden beyond the reading.

Mrs. Baker joins me in respectful regards to Mrs. Wilson
Heartily yours,   Newton D. Baker

TLS (WP, DLC).
  [1] That is, the Cleveland *Plain Dealer*.
  [2] Charles Elmer Sawyer, homeopathic physician of Marion, Ohio, who was now physician to President Harding, with the rank of brigadier general. Harvey's speech set off a storm of protest in the United States. See Willis Fletcher Johnson, *George Harvey: 'A Passionate Patriot'* (Boston and New York, 1929), pp. 295-99.

William Edward Dodd to Edith Bolling Galt Wilson

Dear Mrs. Wilson: [Chicago] May 29, 1921.

I wrote the President in November 1918[1] an account of a certain conference in Massachusetts which I suppose never reached him. You need not tell him, if you think it ought not to be told. But I want you to know it. I would have used it in my revised edition of the *Wilson and his Work*, if I had been able to bring my informant to give his consent.

On November 12, 1918 I had a phone call from former Senator Beveridge asking me to dine with him at the Blackstone. He wished my opinion about certain chapters in his *Life of Marshall*, then in manuscript. I accepted. When the professional conversation was over, he told me that Roosevelt, (I think Taft) George Harvey and himself, in conference at B's house at Beverly Farms, Mass, agreed as to the publication of *Harvey's Weekly*. He said that he, Beveridge, and Roosevelt, guaranteed Harvey 20,000 takers for the sheet. He also informed me then that Roosevelt was to be the nominee for 1920 and that he, Beveridge, was to be vice presidential candidate.

He was quite frank in a number of revelations which, he said were all a part of the game. That was the way of politics and he would have me understand it was not dishonorable. He said that Wilson was the ablest man they had ever had to do with and that he simply *must be destroyed*, not because he was wrong but because he was a Democrat. It was a sorrowful conversation which took away from me the real respect I had had for the speaker. Perhaps I ought to have said so then and there but I did not.

How Roosevelt, who had hated Harvey to the limit, fell into Harvey's arms, how Roosevelt, who had denounced Taft as a thief, wept a little later on Taft's shoulder in a New York hotel, how all of them hated Mr. Wilson with a consuming hatred is a part of my experience or information during those years, when I also knew the President fairly well and regarded him as the hope of the world against its worse self. It was made a matter of record with me. I give it to you now, not to annoy you or to be repeated if his health require otherwise.

At one time I had a notion that I, knowing public life somewhat as a historian and being devoted to the ideals and policies of Mr. Wilson, might like to offer myself for public position. These facts and the gullibility which the masses of men betrayed last November, cured me of all such desire, if my notion could be called desire. Yet I do not despair of a return of public sanity.

The concluding three chapters of my book are getting off tomorrow to Doubleday, Page and Company. They have taken a great deal more time than I had thought. It was so difficult to keep to the main track, to make fairly sure of the important events and to weave the study together. History of one's own time is the most difficult of all to write. If the historian can with so much pains discern the right path, perhaps one ought not to condemn untrained minds for not voting wisely, voting being nothing less than deciding what recent history is.

Of course what I have written may not be truth to Mr. Wilson who knows so many things that have not come to me. But my story seems to me true, historical rather than biographical in the strict sense. If when the work comes out, you or he discerns serious error, I hope you will do me the favor to let me know. The story moves me in spite of my authorship. I have not anywhere brought in Mr. Wilson's name as authority for anything.

I have a suspicion that the publishers will not wish to publish these new chapters. You know publishers are quite human in their attitudes. Won't you indicate our hearty good wishes to Mr. Wilson, our admiration quite as strong now as when he was director of the world's affairs, director as much as one man could be. Nor must you omit yourself from these warm regards.

Yours Sincerely   William E. Dodd

TLS (EBW Papers, DLC).
    ¹ Wilson, or someone else, must have destroyed the received copy of this letter. There is no copy of it in the Dodd papers, undoubtedly because it was an ALS; it does not seem likely that Dodd would have dictated so confidential a letter to a stenographer. Dodd's letter may well have been one of the most important Wilson ever received, since it may have caused, or helped to cause, him to decide against appointing Taft or some other prominent Republican as a peace commissioner. See WW to R. Hooker, Nov. 29, 1918, Vol. 53, for example, in which Wilson expressed his opinion of Taft and other prominent Republicans as potential peace commissioners.
    Dodd did write another letter to Wilson in November: W. E. Dodd to WW, Nov. 19, 1918, CCL (W. E. Dodd Papers, DLC). It does not conform in content to the letter that Dodd describes in his letter to Wilson of May 29, 1921.
    We have found no mention of the meeting on November 12, 1918, in any historical or biographical works dealing with this period. John Milton Cooper, Jr., who has done extensive research in the papers of Roosevelt, Taft, Beveridge, and other Republican leaders of this period, tells us that he has never seen any evidence to corroborate Beveridge's account. Whatever the truth about it may be, the important point is that Wilson undoubtedly believed that the account in Dodd's letter was true.

To the Rector and Board of Visitors of the University of Virginia

[Washington] 30th May 1921

As an alumnus of the University I shall be filled with foreboding to see the medical school moved to another place.¹ It would look like the beginning of disintegration, and I should expect to see other schools taken away afterwards. I should much rather see the University grow by the addition of schools—for example a college for women—than to see it pulled apart, piece by piece. I hope that this expression of opinion will be attributed to my affectionate interest in the University.

Woodrow Wilson

T telegram (WP, DLC).
    ¹ There had long been talk of moving the Medical Department to Richmond, or of combining it with the Medical College of Virginia in Richmond, on the ground that Charlottesville and the surrounding area did not provide enough clinical material for teaching purposes, and that the clinical facilities of the Medical Department were inadequate. Alderman, in 1912, had proposed to merge the two medical schools. A Commission on Medical Education held hearings on the question in early 1921, and it

seemed certain that it would recommend consolidation, although the location of the single institution was still in doubt.

It seems likely that Wilson's telegram was prompted by a letter (which is missing) or a telephone call from Theodore Hough, M.D., Dean of the Department of Medicine at the University of Virginia. Dr. Hough later wrote to thank Wilson for his telegram and said: "Your thoughtful action has great weight and may prove decisive in this paramount emergency." T. Hough to WW, June 15, 1921, TLS (WP, DLC). A bill to relocate the Medical Department and the School of Pharmacy and Dentistry in Richmond and to merge them with the Medical College of Virginia failed by a wide margin in the Virginia Senate in 1922. Efforts to move the medical school from Charlottesville thereafter ceased. Virginius Dabney, *Mr. Jefferson's University: A History* (Charlottesville, Va., 1981), pp. 69-72.

From Robert Bridges and Others

Cumberland, Md. May 30th 1921

We have had two days of pleasant journeying and good comradeship. All the old jokes have been recalled and some new ones devised. Hiram has been consistently late, Dan'l[1] has "leaned back," Chang[2] has hinted that his grandchildren are as good as any of Henderson's (he has one), and Bob B. has been carefully restrained in his loquacity. The Hendersons have fed us abundantly, and the whole reunion has been a great success.

We have missed you a lot, and want you to know that we think of you always with affection and admiration. It was fine [great?] to have known you all these years.

With our love   Robert Bridges
Robert R. Henderson
William B Lee
J. Edwin Webster
Hiram Woods

ALS (WP, DLC).
[1] That is, James Edwin Webster.
[2] That is, William Brewster Lee.

From the Diary of Ray Stannard Baker

[Washington] May 31 [1921]

Mr. Wilson was quite ill to-day & weak. Mrs. Wilson told me he was sick in the night: vomiting frequently although he eats next to nothing at all. Hopeful reports are given out to the public, but he seems to me to be losing ground. I am much pleased at making arrangements to-day so that I can take these documents, or a considerable part of them, home with me & work at Amherst. I have not been well.

[Washington] June 1 [1921].

Mr. Wilson ill again all last night. Grayson was with him. He was very weak. Better again this afternoon.

From Bainbridge Colby

New York June 1 [1921]

Reached house at noon well and keen Have some important matters for your opinion I plan to come down within day or two Your radiogram gave me a great deal of pleasure[1] Am eager to see you With best regards to Mrs. Wilson   Colby

T telegram (WP, DLC).
  [1] WW to BC, May 5, 1921.

To Bernard Mannes Baruch

My dear Friend: Washington D C 2nd June, 1921.

I am deeply sorry to disappoint you in the matter of the letter about Ochs,[1] but the truth is that I am entirely unfamiliar with the part he has played in shaping the character and policy of the "Times," and therefore anything I could sincerely write would necessarily be vague and without force. I am sure you will understand.

Ever since I entered public life I have been a pretty constant reader of the leading editorials in THE TIMES, and I have been much disappointed and disturbed to find that their utterances on financial and economic subjects were never liberal or progressive. They never contained anything that ought not to be perfectly acceptable to Wall Street, and to all the interests that resort to Wall Street for money and direction. This has prevented my having any enthusiasm with regard to the influence of the journal. You will see therefore how little good it would do Mr. Ochs if I expressed my opinion of the policy he has pursued in the editorial management of the paper.

I have heard with the deepest distress of your Father's present illness, and I hope with all my heart he is mending. Please give him my love.   Affectionately yours,   Woodrow Wilson

TLS (B. M. Baruch Papers, NjP).
  [1] The members of the staff of the *New York Times* were planning a celebration in mid-August 1921 of the twenty-fifth anniversary of Adolph Simon Ochs' management of that newspaper. Baruch sent telegrams to Bolling on May 31 and June 1 asking Bolling to call him collect in New York. Bolling must have called Baruch on the latter date, and Baruch must have asked him to ask Wilson to write the letter of tribute to Ochs. Letters written to or about Ochs were bound in a silver binding and presented to him at a dinner on August 18.

John Randolph Bolling to George White

My dear Mr. White: [Washington] 2nd June 1921

Mr. Wilson asks me to thank you for your kind letter of May 28th,[1] enclosing copy of one sent by you to the newly organized Woodrow Wilson Club of Portland, Maine.[2] He has noted the copy of your letter with a great deal of interest.

The Club sent Mr. Wilson a very cordial and loyal letter, to which response was made expressing his interest and good wishes.[3]

Mr. Wilson desires me to say to you that when he is a little more rested, he will be glad to have you run in and see him for a little talk. I will keep in touch with your office, and let you know a few days in advance when it will be convenient to have you call.

Cordially yours,   [John Randolph Bolling]

CCL (WP, DLC).
    [1] G. White to WW, May 28, 1921, TLS (WP, DLC).
    [2] G. White to the officers and women of the Woodrow Wilson Club of Portland, Maine, n.d., TCL (WP, DLC). This club was organized by women Democrats in Maine; Deborah Morton was president.
    [3] Bolling was confusing this organization with the Young Americans' Democratic League of Maine, to whom Wilson sent a message in WW to C. M. Starbird, May 7, 1921.

From Franklin Delano Roosevelt

My dear Mr. President   Hyde Park, New York June 2nd 1921

I am coming to Washington on Sunday to attend Frank Lane's Memorial service at four that afternoon, and would greatly appreciate the opportunity of greeting you while I am there. My wife & I get to Washington Sunday morning & will be at the Millers[1] house next door to you. If it is convenient for you to see me any time that day would you be good enough to have someone leave word at the Millers, as I shall be travelling during the next two days.

Please give our warm regards to Mrs. Wilson and believe me
                Always faithfully yours   Franklin D Roosevelt

ALS (WP, DLC).
    [1] Adolph Caspar Miller and Mary Sprague Miller, who lived at 2320 S St., N.W. He had been a member of the Federal Reserve Board since 1914.

To Robert Bridges

My dear Bobby: Washington, D C 3rd June 1921

It was a delight to get the letter you wrote from Cumberland, and which you and the rest of the gang signed. It was a great disappointment to me not to get over to Cumberland while you were there; but from the point of view of my slowly improving health it would have been folly to attempt even the moderate motor trip.

I hope you found the boys all well and in good spirits. It seemed very strange not to be part of such a re-union. I shall certainly seek some opportunity to recover the lost ground.

Please send my love to the gang when you get a chance, and tell them how proud I am to have won their confidence and admiration.   Affectionately yours,   Woodrow Wilson

TLS (WC, NjP).

From Louis Seibold

My dear Mr. President: Washington June 3, 1921.

As an accessory before the fact, I think you are entitled to all of the glory and at least fifty percent of the loot that came with the award to me of the degree from Columbia University for our joint interview a year ago[1]—furthermore, I am perfectly willing to put it all up on the foot race you and I are to run when I can get into proper form. You must remember you have been training in secret while I have probably disregarded every rule that the experts recognize.

I want to thank you for your many favors to me, not the least of which has brought me recognition that I most highly prize. I should like to come and see you at your convenience and without intruding. In the meantime, if I can serve Mrs. Wilson or you, you have only to command me.

With my best hopes for you always,
                    Faithfully,   Louis Seibold

TLS (WP, DLC).
[1] Awarded a diploma and the Pulitzer Prize for the best example of newspaper reporting by Columbia University for the year 1920. Seibold won the prize for his news report about and interview with Wilson printed at June 17, 1920, Vol. 65.

Joseph Patrick Tumulty to Edith Bolling Galt Wilson

My dear Mrs. Wilson: Washington, D. C. 3 June 1921.

About the car:[1]

You cannot realize how much pleasure I derive from serving the President and you. With me the old ties strengthen with each passing day and my only hope is that some time I can be of real service to you. If that service would only require some real sacrifice, I would feel much better satisfied. Everything we have, although small indeed, is yours for the asking.

Cordially,   J. P. Tumulty.

TLS (WP, DLC).
  [1] A taxicab had just damaged Wilson's Pierce-Arrow, and Tumulty had volunteered to handle the damage suit, probably gratis.

From Maurice F. Lyons[1]

My dear Mr. Wilson: Covington, Ky. June 3, 1921.

My attention has been called to the fact that a book which Mr. McCombs had intended to publish in 1915 or 1916, and which I informed Mr. Tumulty of at the time, is soon to be placed on the market by his sister, Mrs. Corinne Hardy, of Little Rock, Ark.[2]

I was ready to protect you then and I am ready to protect you now if necessary, though I am aware of your ability to handle this matter.

Please remember that I am always at your command,

Faithfully,   Maurice F. Lyons

TLS (WP, DLC).
  [1] Former secretary to William Frank McCombs, at this time an attorney of Covington, Ky., and Cincinnati.
  [2] Published as William F. McCombs, *Making Woodrow Wilson President*, Louis Jay Lang, ed. (New York, 1921), it is a self-serving and bitter account of his relationship with Wilson. It concentrated on McCombs' role as one of the persons active in the movement to make Wilson the Democratic presidential nominee and as chairman of the Democratic National Committee from 1912 to 1916.

To Bernard Mannes Baruch

[Washington] June 4th 1921

Our hearts go out to you in deepest sympathy at the death of your noble and distinguished father.[1] Please regard us as being with you in closest affection.   Woodrow Wilson.

T telegram (WP, DLC).
  [1] Dr. Baruch died on June 3. He was indeed distinguished. He served as a surgeon in Gen. Lee's army; after practicing in Camden, S. C., he moved to New York in 1881 and became a leader in the movement to build municipal bathhouses, a professor at the College of Physicians and Surgeons of Columbia University, and an internationally known authority on hydrotherapy.

From Lindsay Rogers[1]

Dear Mr. Wilson: Cambridge, Massachusetts 4.VI.21

Will you permit a sincere, and, to you, a hitherto silent admirer, to say how good it is to have you speak to the American people once more?

Your Memorial Day letter to the *Stars and Stripes*[2] was a breath of pure air after three months in a very stuffy atmosphere. To me, also, your message had a very personal appeal; for my brother— now one of those whom we can only remember—was, after the armistice, on the staff of the overseas *Stars and Stripes*.

So I have ventured to write to thank you.

Yours faithfully,   Lindsay Rogers

ALS (WP, DLC).
[1] Distinguished American political scientist; at this time lecturer on government at Harvard University and lecturer on public law at Columbia University; long associated with Columbia as Burgess Professor of Public Law.
[2] It is printed as WW to S. Houston, May 7, 1921.

To Newton Diehl Baker

My dear Baker: [Washington] 5th June 1921

Your letter of May twenty-ninth gave me a great deal of pleasure.

I was glad to get an expression of your opinion about the matters of which you wrote and happy to find that, as in the old days of our official association, my judgments coincided with yours.

By the way, you spoke of certain English families "whose ancestors had not made a social blunder since the battle of Hastings." Am I to infer that you regard Hastings as having been a social mistake? If you do I am inclined to agree with you. I am sure that a straight out Saxon race would have been socially very much more acceptable than the Saxon-Norman mixture we have been forced to put up with.

I had forgotten that God had ever made so great a fool as Harvey, and doubt if even He could make a greater. You remember the story of the Scotsman who smacked his lips over some delicious strawberries and exclaimed: "I dare say God could have made a better berry; I dare say he never did." I dare say God may have made a greater fool than Harvey; I dare say he never did.

Mrs. Wilson joins me in kind regards to you and Mrs. Baker.

Cordially and faithfully yours,   [Woodrow Wilson]

CCL (WP, DLC).

John Randolph Bolling to Maurice F. Lyons

My dear Mr. Lyons: [Washington] 6th June 1921

Mr. Wilson asks me to thank you for your letter of June 3d, and express his gratification and appreciation of your generous loyalty to him. He wishes me to say, however, that he feels no attack by Mr. McCombs will need a reply.[1]

I am sure you will be glad to know that Mr. Wilson is thoroughly enjoying his rest, and that he is out each day for long motor rides through the country.

Cordially yours,   [John Randolph Bolling]

CCL (WP, DLC).

  [1] In fact, Lyons did write a little book in anwer to McCombs: *William F. McCombs: The President Maker* (Cincinnati, 1922).

From Lawrence Crane Woods

Dear Mr. Wilson: Pittsburg, Penna. June 6, 1921.

I enclosed a copy of the Daily Princetonian of May 21, calling your attention to the Editorial.[1] I regard this as significant of the beginning of the honor which Princeton will ultimately pay to her greatest Son. I have repeatedly told the people down there that I expected to live to see the day when there was a great building, and innumerable portraits, memorabilia, etc., of Woodrow Wilson.

I was interested and delighted to hear from my son[2] that 45 out of the 60 members of the Faculty who had served under you ten years ago, had joined in a beautiful letter to you at the time of your retirement from the Presidency.[3]

I also learned from my boy that the Woodrow Wilson Club of Princeton, of which I am very proud to say he is the President, has enrolled a membership of some 600 undergraduates. Your ideals live at Princeton and will grow stronger and stronger as the years go by.

You might be interested in knowing confidentially that this Editorial was written by Charles Denby, Jr., a Republican, a nephew of the present Secretary of War.[4]

Mrs. Woods[5] joins with me in affectionate messages and all good wishes to you and Mrs. Wilson.

Sincerely,   Lawrence C Woods

TLS (WP, DLC).

  [1] He enclosed a clipping from the editorial page of the *Daily Princetonian*, May 21, 1921. The lead editorial, entitled "Woodrow Wilson," said that everyone, of every persuasion, had to admire Wilson's courage, vision, and idealism. It expressed its pleasure that a Woodrow Wilson Club of Princeton University had been organized on May 20.

  [2] Lawrence Crane Woods, Jr., of the Class of 1922.

3 See the Enclosure printed with G. M. Priest to WW, March 1, 1921.
4 Edwin Denby, actually Secretary of the Navy.
5 Rebekah Campbell Woods.

To Neal Larkin Anderson[1]

My dear Mr. Anderson: [Washington] 7th June, 1921.

I wish with all my heart that I might have the privilege and honor of being present on the occasion referred to in your letter of June second;[2] but unhappily it is not possible, and I must content myself with the few inadequate lines of this letter.

I account it my great good fortune to have known Dr. Axson whom my Father before me delighted to number among his valued friends and for whom he felt a real affection. Dr. Axson was a man of singularly pure and exhalted [exalted] spirit, and it must surely operate as a continuing inspiration to your Church to have had him as its pastor at so important a formative period.

With the pleasantest recollections of our association with one another from time to time;

Cordially and sincerely yours,   [Woodrow Wilson]

CCL (WP, DLC).
    [1] Pastor of the Independent Presbyterian Church of Savannah, Ga.
    [2] N. L. Anderson to WW, June 2, 1921, TLS (WP, DLC). Anderson invited Wilson to attend the unveiling in the Independent Presbyterian Church, on Sunday morning, June 12, 1921, of a tablet in memory of the Rev. Dr. Isaac Stockton Keith Axson, pastor of the church from 1857 to 1891 and grandfather of Ellen Louise Axson Wilson. In the event Wilson could not attend, Anderson added, "we should be gratified to have a few lines from you to be read at the excercises on June the twelfth."

To Thomas Nelson Page

Washington June 7th 1921

Our hearts sympathy goes out to you in fullest measure in this hour of your tragical loss and sorrow.[1]   Woodrow Wilson.

T telegram (WP, DLC).
    [1] His wife, Florence Lathrop Field Page, had died on June 6, 1921.

John Randolph Bolling to Lawrence Crane Woods

Dear Mr. Woods: Washington D C 8th June, 1921.

Mr. Wilson asks me to thank you for your letter of June 6th, and for your thoughtfulness in sending him the editorial from the DAILY PRINCETONIAN which he has noted with the greatest interest. He bids me send you his affectionate regards, and often refers to you as being among his best friends.

Mr. Wilson is enjoying his rest, and is out every day for long motor rides through the country.

May I add that such letters as yours are a source of the greatest pleasure and gratification to him.

Cordially yours,   John Randolph Bolling

TLS (WC, NjP).

A News Report

[June 10, 1921]

Wilson Militant and in "a Happy Mood,"
Chairman White Finds in Chat on Politics

Washington, June 10.—George White of Ohio, Chairman of the Democratic National Committee, called on ex-President Wilson at his home today and discussed national affairs with him for the first time since he left office.

Mr. White indicated afterward that the ex-President was watching public affairs with as much interest as when he occupied the White House. He said:

"Mr. Wilson retains his keen interest in public affairs and is imbued with a militant spirit. We discussed public affairs in general, and political matters. The former President was much interested to learn of the renewal of Democratic alignment in aggressive fashion. I found him well and in a happy mood, but obviously I cannot discuss his physical condition."

Chairman White told Mr. Wilson that he found Democrats throughout the country were getting back into a "fighting humor." Broadcast inquiries sent out by the Chairman had brought responses of a most cheerful character, he said. The Chairman told Mr. Wilson that everywhere Democrats were expressing satisfaction over what they termed the vindication of Wilson policies, the failure of the Administration to revive business, the prospect of failure to reduce taxes, and the absence of constructive policies.

That the Democratic leadership not only does not intend to forsake Mr. Wilson, but purposes to confer with him, was indicated by the conference today.

While Mr. White would not discuss the ex-President's health, other friends who have seen Mr. Wilson report an appearance of material improvement.

Although Mr. Wilson continues in seclusion, seeing few visitors and handling most of his correspondence through a secretary,

Washington does not forget the man who recently occupied the Executive chair.

There was an instance of this a few nights ago. The ex-President dropped into a popular vaudeville house downtown and for readier access to the door sat in the last row. His presence was noted only by those sitting near while the show was going on, but with the final curtain and upturned lights the audience discovered him.

Then followed an ovation which almost swept him off his feet. Attendants and police had to form a guard to keep the crowd back. The noise inside attracted people outside, who added their cheers when the former President emerged and continued until Mr. and Mrs. Wilson had entered their automobile and been driven away.

Printed in the *New York Times*, June 11, 1921.

To Bernard Mannes Baruch

My dear Baruch: Washington D C 10th June, 1921.

Thank you for your letter of June eighth.[1] Your attitude towards me touches and pleases me mightily, and you may be sure I shall always be glad to play any part in your life that you may wish.

I am looking forward with great pleasure to seeing you.

Affectionately yours,   Woodrow Wilson

TLS (B. M. Baruch Papers, NjP).
[1] It is missing in both the Wilson and Baruch Papers.

Stockton Axson to John Grier Hibben[1]

My dear Jack: Nashville, Tennessee June 11, 1921

Because you and Mrs. Hibben[2] were so solicitous (and lovely) about your old friend I want to give you both a brief report of his condition as I found him in Washington after seeing you in Charlottesville.

"Brief" the report must be because, to my regret, the condition is not greatly changed since I wrote to you last autumn in response to your kind inquiry. I had hoped to find more visible progress than appeared. However, I take comfort in these facts: first, that he is in no worse condition than last autumn, and secondly, that I saw him after a bad upset which he had suffered a week before my arrival in Washington. After Mrs. Wilson had told me of that attack (digestive) on my arrival at the house, I was prepared to see him worse than I actually found him. His color and expression were good (his face is now entirely normal, not "drawn" at all—this result of the original attack has completely disappeared), he was intermittently jocose and rather keenly interested in my account of the University of Virginia celebration.

But he is no more active physically than he was last autumn—in fact, not as much so, for he has not the long indoor walking spaces which he had in the White House hall-ways, and he declines to walk in the street or in the little garden of his new residence. I could see no improvement in his lame arm and leg.

All agree, physicians and family, that what he most needs now is systematic mental occupation, and yet one can easily understand how hard it is for him to resume the literary occupations which he practically abandoned twenty years ago when his administrative career began—I know, and doubtless you know, how hard it is to begin writing again after even a few months of cessation. I think his great problem is to get interested in writing, but of course he can't get interested until he by an act of volition begins to interest himself in the pursuit.

Strictly in confidence (because it is a business matter of which I should not feel free to speak except to his old friends—like you and Mrs. Hibben) I am taking hope along an entirely new line of mental occupation: it so happened that Mr. Bainbridge Colby arrived from Europe the day after I reached Washington, and he was full of legal plans in a large way; as he set forth some of the problems and projects which he proposed to lay before his senior partner, I could see much scope for our old friend's sagacity and genius for analysing and simplifying problems. Maybe he will get interested in *that*—God grant it!

In my hurried and interrupted visit I had no opportunity to discuss with Mrs. Wilson and Admiral Grayson yours and Mrs. Hibben's suggestion about the Mayo Brothers³—but will take it up with them on my return to Washington about the middle of July. This delay is of no consequence, for I know that no amount of persuasion can induce him to budge from Washington at present. Whether Mrs. Wilson and the Admiral can induce him to make a move later is a question. They are *both* wonderful—no less. Indeed, Mrs. Wilson's strength of body, mind, and cheerful will is almost miraculous.

It was so good to see you both in Virginia—and I am not going to try to tell you how much I was (and am) touched by the things you both said.

For the sake of your health and happiness I hope you will never visit Nashville in the summer. It must be in punishment for my sins that I, in a moment of amiable weakness, consented to lecture here[4] for five weeks—I hope it is not a foretaste of my eternal destiny,—though it is certainly a reminder of what *may* be. Outside of Yuma, The Needles, and Death Valley, it is surely the hottest place in America.

 With very warm regards for Mrs. Hibben and yourself,

Yours always sincerely Stockton Axson

ALS (photostat in General MSS, Misc., CO140, AM12871, NjP).

 [1] Axson and Hibben had remained close friends after Wilson's break with his "Dear Jack," and it was one of the great sorrows of Axson's life that he was never able to effect a reconciliation between the two men.

 [2] That is, Jenny Davidson Hibben.

 [3] That is, Charles Horace Mayo, M.D., and William James Mayo, M.D., renowned surgeons and physicians of Rochester, Minn.

 [4] At the George Peabody College for Teachers.

A News Item

[June 12, 1921]

Will 'Keep His Ideals Before the Public,'

Woodrow Wilson Tells Princeton Students

 Washington, June 12.—Former President Wilson, in receiving today a delegation of Princeton University students, was quoted as saying that he planned to "keep his ideals actively before the public."

 Mr. Wilson, his callers said, told them he was keeping in touch with political developments, but he did not indicate in what manner he planned to participate in public affairs.

 The former President and Mrs. Wilson received a committee of four Princeton undergraduates representing the newly formed Woodrow Wilson Society of Princeton. L. C. Woods Jr. of Pennsylvania, President of the association, presented to Mr. Wilson a letter signed by 600 Princeton students promising efforts for "due recognition by members of all parties to Woodrow Wilson as Princeton's foremost graduate for his leadership of America during the trying times of peace and of war and for the courage and idealism he showed in endeavoring to promote the peace of the world."

 Mr. Wilson expressed his appreciation of the tribute.

 The delegation, in addition to Mr. Woods, included Morgan C. Day of Missouri, C. T. Le Viness of Maryland and Sidney Sherwood of New York.

Printed in the *New York Times*, June 13, 1921.

To Arthur Francis Mullen[1]

My dear Mr. Mullen: [Washington] 13th June 1921

I would esteem it a great favor if you would make it convenient to see me here at my home in Washington (address given above) at three o'clock on the afternoon of Monday, June twentieth.

I hope that this is not asking too much of a busy man, as there are some matters I think we should talk over together.

Cordially yours,   [Woodrow Wilson]

CCL (WP, DLC).
[1] Lawyer of Omaha, Neb., member of the Democratic National Committee, 1916-1920, and member of the executive committee of the D.N.C., 1918-1920. His autobiography is *Western Democrat* (New York, 1940).

To George E. Brennan[1]

My dear Mr. Brennan: [Washington] 13th June 1921

I would esteem it a great favor if you would make it convenient to see me here at my home in Washington (address given above) at three o'clock on the afternoon of Monday, June twentieth.

I hope that this is not asking too much of a busy man, as there are some matters I think we should talk over together.[2]

Cordially yours,   [Woodrow Wilson]

CCL (WP, DLC).
[1] Successor to Roger Charles Sullivan as leader of the Democratic organization in Chicago and Illinois. He was of course a prominent "wet."
[2] Brennan replied that he could not come on June 20 but would be glad to come at a later date. G. E. Brennan to WW, June 20, 1921, T telegram (WP, DLC). After a further telegraphic exchange, Brennan came to S Street at 3 p.m. on June 24, 1921.

To Louis Seibold

My dear Seibold: Washington D C 14th June 1921.

The goods arrived as per Grayson schedule[1] and I am very grateful. You certainly know what is wanted and when.

With warmest regards from us all;

Faithfully and gratefully,   Woodrow Wilson

P.S. We were all delighted that you won the prize.

TLS (WP, DLC).
[1] Seibold, in an undated memorandum for Katharine E. Brand (T MS, WP, DLC), said that the "goods" were six bottles of rare Scotch whiskey which he had entrusted to Dr. Grayson for delivery to his distinguished patient. "Sometime later," Seibold added, "I personally delivered to Mr. Wilson's house some very good Rhine wine—Berncastler Doctor—as a gift from my father."

To Vance Criswell McCormick

My dear McCormick: Washington D C 15th June, 1921.

So many interesting things are happening nowadays that I find myself missing more than ever the little talks we used to have.

When you next come to Washington please let me know in advance of your coming and where I may get in touch with you after you get here. We ought to have one of our old time conferences.

Hoping that you and yours are well, and that you will give our sincere regards to your mother and sister;[1]

Cordially and faithfully yours,   Woodrow Wilson

TLS (V. C. McCormick Papers, CtY).
[1] Annie Criswell (Mrs. Henry) McCormick and Annie McCormick, both of Harrisburg, Pa.

From Bainbridge Colby

My dear Mr. President: New York June 16th, 1921.

I clipped the enclosed from the editorial page of the New York Evening Globe. I rather like its reference to the gropings of the Republican Congress to end the war "by indirection, hints and innuendoes."[1]

I had a little talk with Seibold at the hotel night before last, after I left you. He tells me that the Republicans are in a state of apprehensive nervousness arising from your unbroken silence since March 4th. There is an increasing sense of powerlessness to arrest and cope with the rising centrifugal tendencies within their party. According to Seibold, the hope is expressed that you may break your silence, so they may beat the old pre-election tom-toms, and thus renew the comfortable campaign sensation of unity on the platform of "anything to beat Wilson."

I told Seibold to have no fear, as you would never be caught in this trap.   Faithfully always;   Colby

TLS (WP, DLC).
[1] "GENTLEMEN WHO CRY PEACE," New York *Globe and Commercial Advertiser*, June 14, 1921. This brief editorial suggested that the "convenient and decent" way to end the state of war between the United States and Germany was for the United States to ratify, "with as many reservations as are required by the conscience of the present congress and executive," the treaties of Versailles and St. Germain. "The alternative," it continued, "is the absurd muddle which has been produced by the rival efforts of an overwhelmingly Republican House and an overwhelmingly Republican Senate to end the war by indirection, hints, and innuendoes." The substance of the war-ending resolutions passed by the two houses was, according to the editorial, "that the war is somehow over, that we are not certain why we went into it or who won it, but that we want to get out of it all that is coming to us."
The Senate, on April 30, 1921, adopted, by a vote of forty-nine to twenty-three, S.J. Res. 16, repealing the American declarations of war against Germany and Austria-Hungary and reserving to the United States all rights under the Armistice, the Versailles

Treaty, and the status of the United States as one of the Principal Allied Powers. These reservations were repeated concerning Austria. The House of Representatives referred S.J. Res. 16 to the Committee on Foreign Affairs, which reported an amended version that did not differ significantly from the Senate resolution. The House approved its own version of the resolution on June 13 by a vote of 304 to 61. The Senate and House resolutions then went to a conference committee, which agreed upon a measure. The only significant difference between the Senate and House was whether the resolution should stipulate that all property of the German and Austro-Hungarian governments seized during the war should be retained by the United States. The Senate insisted upon retaining this provision and prevailed. The Senate approved the conference report on July 1 by a vote of thirty-eight to nineteen; the House, on June 30, by a vote of 263 to fifty-nine. Harding signed the bill on July 2, 1921. This legislation was, of course, a forerunner of the Treaty of Berlin of August 25, 1921, about which more will be said later.

From Joseph Patrick Tumulty

Dear Governor: Washington, D. C. 16 June 1921.

Our friends are having their own troubles these days and these troubles seem to accumulate with each passing day.

Your policy of silence and apparent indifference to what they are doing is irritating them very much. My only suggestion is that you continue this policy of silence—say nothing, write nothing—that might in the slightest way be construed as a criticism of what they are doing. This attitude will only strengthen your position when it shall become necessary for you to strike.

No acknowledgment of this letter is required.

Affectionately yours,   J. P. Tumulty

TLS (WP, DLC).

Robert Cummins Stuart, Jr., to John Randolph Bolling

My dear Mr. Bolling: Cambridge, Mass. June 16, 1921.

The enclosure in your letter received this morning,[1] for which I am indeed grateful, will be of substantial assistance to us.

Do you think it would be possible to secure from the Democratic Committee a list of the contributors to the campaign last fall? To know at least those who "Matched-the-President" or gave larger amounts would be very desirable.

If this information could not be had directly do you suppose they would consent to give it indirectly—that is, "permitting" the turning over of a list of names to you without reference to amounts given and no indication as to the source.

My thought was, in short, some arrangement to secure the material without exposing the party to any fear of injury. I would consider this information confidential and am willing personally to pay the expense involved.

Saturday I leave for New York, where my address will be the Hotel Pennsylvania, to see four or five people in connection with our work. My present plan is to sail Wednesday the twenty-second from there to New Orleans on the S.S. Comus and continue to Houston, Texas where I shall be at 1916 Main Street until July fifteenth or August first.

It now seems it will take fully a month to select a chairman in each state and the ten or fifteen trustees which are necessar[y] before raising the fund. This correspondence, I thought, could be handled just as well from home.

Upon finishing this I was thinking headquarters might be established in some place centrally located and then, so far as possible, I should see those able to contribute substantially and secure from them pledges in advance so that when the colleges began actively to canvass in the fall enough would have already been raised to guarantee the complete success of the tribute.

I should be very pleased, if, at this time, you thought it advisable, to come to Washington to receive suggestions and help in planning the most effective work for the summer. I can conveniently remain in the east a week longer and if desired, the entire vacation.

It was found impractical to print the entire executive committee on the stationery as membership upon it is by clubs and several of these, as in the case of Princeton, are certifying one representative for the summer and another for the fall. Does this stationery meet with Mr. Wilson's and your approval?

The President of the Princeton Club wrote me of their inspiring testamonial and we were very glad to hear of their call upon Mr. Wilson.[2]

Both Mr. Colby and Mr. Tumulty have been written. This week I am trying to interest some prominent men in other countries in raising money for the fellowships. What they raised would probably be matched in this country and the income from the combined fund would be spent on the scholars from the given country.

Due to the pressure of this and the final examinations I am not sending Mr. Wilson a formal report of what has been accomplished since the small beginning upon last Armistice Day. Though we have come a long way, in looking ahead it appears that the real undertaking is now beginning. I hope Mr. Wilson will pardon the omission.

Thanking you for your kind assistance;

Faithfuly yours,   Robert C. Stuart

TLS (WP, DLC).

[1] JRB to R. C. Stuart, Jr., June 13, 1921, CCL (WP, DLC). The enclosure was a list of Cox-Roosevelt college clubs.

[2] See the news report printed at June 12, 1921.

From Alfred Lucking[1]

My dear Mr. Wilson: Detroit, Michigan June Eighteenth 1921

Knowing as I do that you are burdened with the consideration of a great many important matters, I would not attempt to add to those burdens by writing you at this time, except for the over-shadowing importance of the subject matter. You have, no doubt, noticed in the newspapers that the Ford-Newberry contest[2] is now reaching a critical stage and that the final determination must come very soon; and it is about this I am writing.

After more than two and one-half years of persistent demands for an investigation, the testimony has lately been taken; and the Senate Committee is now about to pass upon the same; later the Senate itself.

The stand-pat Republican Senators are determined to seat Mr. Newberry, notwithstanding the overwhelming evidence of corruption, fraud, vast unlawful expenditures, burning of books, papers and records and personal perjury of Senator Newberry. All of these things were proved incontestably and overwhelmingly.

Nothing will prevent the consummation of the outrage except a persistent, determined fight by the Democratic members of the Senate, thereby giving that publicity to the crime which will frighten the Republican majority from their otherwise set purpose.

I am trying to arrange for certain measures of publicity in the States of those Republican Senators, who may be said to be more susceptible to argument than such Senators as Watson[3] and Lodge.

Nevertheless, the all important measure is a determined fight on the floor of the Senate by a united body of Democratic Senators. This letter is written in the hopes of enlisting your co-operation. I know that a strong word from you, indicating your deep interest, to the Democratic Senators, will impel them to persist and arouse the Country, and this last is all that is necessary.

More infamous debauchery of the electorate and of the sources of public opinion, was never known, probably, in this Country. If Mr. Newberry can be un-seated, this will be doing the greatest possible service to the cause of pure elections.

It would be almost impossible for you to believe the tremendous and powerful influences which have been back of the purpose to keep Mr. Newberry in his seat; influences which have succeeded in very largely suppressing publicity, and in keeping the public in ignorance of the true situation.

Mr. Ford has personally no interest whatever in the seat, as such. In fact, in a recent telegram to the members of the Committee on Privileges & Elections, when it looked as if they were determined to suppress further investigation, he said:

"I personally care little or nothing for the seat for myself but I press my rights and insist upon the investigation in order to have it forever established that a seat in the United States Senate may not be purchased and that seats are not for sale to the highest bidders."

Except for the expenditures, Newberry would neither have been nominated nor elected. He was practically unknown in the State before their great campaign of purchased publicity began. Mr. Ford did not expend a single dollar. Nobody expended any money for him in the primary. The State Central Committee, after the primary, made a very good campaign and expended some moneys. These were perfectly lawful and were made in behalf of the entire Democratic ticket. The Republican State Committee did the same in larger measure, and of this no complaint has ever been made, on either side. The case thus presents the plain and undiluted issue whether seats in the United States Senate may be purchased outright. There can hardly be a greater issue.

I know that it is unnecessary to remind you that the seating of Mr. Newberry changed the political status of the Senate, enabled Lodge and his friends to pack the Committee on Foreign Affairs against your measures, and, in fact, changed the whole history of the World and brought about that train of calamities now so evident.

Pardon this long letter. Perhaps all might have been said in these few words that I hope you will personally see to it that the Democratic Senators are aroused to the importance of this great contest and that they awaken the Country and fight to the finish against this pollution of the Senate and of free government.

Hoping that I may have the honor of hearing from you and with assurances of my highest personal regards, I am,

As ever,   Faithfully yours,   Alfred Lucking.

TLS (WP, DLC).
[1] General counsel of the Ford Motor Co. and personal counsel of Henry Ford; Democratic congressman from Michigan, 1903-1905.
[2] About which, see n. 2 to the Enclosure printed with ASB to EBW, March 23, 1920, Vol. 65.
[3] That is, James Eli Watson of Indiana.

John Randolph Bolling to Bainbridge Colby

My dear Mr. Colby: [Washington] 19th June, 1921.

At Mr. Wilson's request, on Thursday last I got in touch with Chief Justice McCoy,[1] and he asked me to come to his apartment at 8.45 yesterday morning for a conference. I spent a very pleasant three-quarters of an hour with him, and told him that Mr. Wilson would like to be admitted on next Saturday, June 25th, to the local bar—the hour being set for 11.45 in the morning. Justice McCoy told me he would see the other Justices in the course of the day, and late last night advised me that the time would be okeh. Mr. Wilson then dictated the following telegram to be sent you, but as I knew your office was closed, I am embodying it in this letter:

"Time selected for the ceremony, Saturday morning, June twenty-fifth, at eleven forty-five. Will be glad to have you join me at the house beforehand."

I shall be obliged if you will acknowledge this message to Mr. Wilson, that he may know you will be on hand next Saturday. As we should leave the house not later than 11.30, my suggestion is that you get here a few minutes before that time. Sometime this week I am going to have our chauffeur go carefully over the ground, so that we can get Mr. Wilson in the building with the greatest privacy and the least fatigue.

Cordially yours,   [John Randolph Bolling]

CCL (WP, DLC).
[1] Walter Irving McCoy, Chief Justice of the Supreme Court of the District of Columbia since 1914.

John Randolph Bolling to Robert Cummins Stuart, Jr.

My dear Mr. Stuart: [Washington] 19th June, 1921.

Your letter of 15th June to Mr. Wilson[1] has come promptly, and he asks me to thank you for sending him the abstract of address by Mr. Holt, and copies of the "Crimson." He has asked me to put the Address on his reading table, that he may read it at his leisure this evening. When the copies of the "Crimson" come I will see that they are brought to his attention.

Your letter to me of June 16th is a most interesting one and I had a long talk about its contents with Mr. Wilson this morning (the better the day, the better the deed!)

To begin with, we both think you have a very dignified letterhead, and one reflecting the character of your purpose.

Mr. Wilson sees no objection to my taking up with the proper officers of the Democratic National Committee the matter of securing the list of contributors to the campaign fund last year. He is under the impression that the list was published; but whether it was or not, I will do my utmost to secure it for you. On my "Quick Attention" file I am putting this mission at the head of the list, and will try and get down to it early this week.

We both think you would be going to a great deal of unnecessary expense in establishing a separate headquarters. With the formation of your organization, you will of course appoint a national treasurer—to whom all contributions will be sent. This party can handle the entire financial end for you, in his own office; and even if it is necessary to employ a person to acknowledge contributions, &c. the overhead will be as nothing compared with setting up a separate and distinct establishment. Many of the largest war funds raised were handled in this way, and it is not only practical, but thoroughly economical. This method will mean that you can spend your summer at home—or such part of it as you wish—until you start out after the big contributors.

While it would be a pleasure to meet you personally, neither Mr. Wilson nor I see any use in your coming here at this time.

I want to work with you just as far as I can; and my twenty or more years of intensive executive and organization experience are at your disposal.

Have I ever mentioned to you Mr. Bernard M. Baruch—a great friend of Mr. Wilson's? He has a son at Harvard,[2] and if he is not already lined up as a member of your Club, you should certainly see him. At present Mr. Baruch and his son are in Europe—having sailed last Tuesday; but the senior will be back here in August, and I am sure would be interested in the matter. Make a memorandum of this, and let's get after him just as soon as he lands. He is very well to do—and one of Mr. Wilson's greatest admirers.

Let me hear from you, as to the progress you make; and I will be glad to keep Mr. Wilson in close touch with all that is going on.

Sincerely yours,   [John Randolph Bolling]

CCL (WP, DLC).
[1] R. C. Stuart, Jr., to WW, June 15, 1921, ALS (WP, DLC). Stuart enclosed an abstract of an address made by Hamilton Holt to the Woodrow Wilson Club of Harvard University on April 4, 1921.
[2] Bernard Mannes Baruch, Jr., Harvard 1923.

To Louis Dembitz Brandeis

My dear Brandeis: Washington D C 20th June, 1921.

How would the following do for one broadside:[1]

We insist upon the early resumption of our international obligations and leadership,—obligations which were repudiated and a leadership which was lost by the rejection of the Treaty of Versailles. That rejection was brought about by the influence of men who preferred personal and party motives to the honor of their country and the peace of the world. We condemn the group of men who brought this sinister thing about as the most partisan, prejudiced and unpatriotic coterie that has ever misled the Senate of the United States, and declare that the country will never be restored to its merited prestige until their work is undone.

Cordially and faithfully yours,   Woodrow Wilson

P.S. I spoke to Colby about our interview of the other day.

TLS (L. D. Brandeis Papers, KyLoU).
    ¹ This is the first mention in this volume of the joint effort to produce what later became known as "The Document," a statement of progressive principles for the Democratic party, which Wilson intended to use as the Democratic platform when he ran for a third term in 1924. There will be numerous other references to "The Document" in this volume and the next.
    Wilson broached the idea of the preparation of "The Document" to Brandeis in a meeting on, or shortly before, June 14, and Wilson requested Brandeis to confer with Colby and Thomas Lincoln Chadbourne, Jr., about the matter. However, Wilson never told his collaborators about the intended use of the document and managed to keep its existence secret. See Melvin I. Urofsky, *A Mind of One Piece: Brandeis and American Reform* (New York, 1971), pp. 127-29.

From Bainbridge Colby

New York June 20 1921

Will be on hand at your home Saturday morning in ample season to accompany you Will probably come to Washington the night before   Bainbridge Colby

T telegram (WP, DLC).

John Randolph Bolling to Bainbridge Colby

Dear Mr. Colby: [Washington] 20th June 1921.

Your telegram to Mr. Wilson has just come, and I am glad you will be here next Saturday as he requested. I need not caution you to keep the plan as quiet as possible, so as to avoid as much publicity as we can—until after the "ceremony" is over!

Mrs. Wilson asks me to send you the enclosed letter from Mrs. Merrill,¹ and say that she has written her you would go over the contents of it, and—if you felt her claim was valid—would advise her of a time when it would be convenient for her to come down from Stamford and have a talk with you. Mrs. Wilson told Mr. Wilson of the contents of the letter, and he suggested that it be handled in this way—Mrs. W. explaining to Mrs. Merrill that he had not yet entered upon active practice.

Kriz[2] was in my office this morning, and we are keeping right on the heels of the Bank building people to complete the offices.[3] Tomorrow I shall have a talk with a representative of the telephone company, and try and get the phones in promptly. My plan is to have a central box on Kriz's desk—with branches for three phones; one on your desk, one on Mr. Wilson's and the third on a desk in the middle room. I am also planning a series of call bells for both you and Mr. Wilson—so you can summon Mr. Kriz or your assistant without moving from your desk. I shall also have a call bell on Mr. Wilson's series—connecting with the room where his attendant will wait while he is at the office. Don't think I am bothering you with details; I just want you to know that we are getting things in ship-shape.

With kindest regards;

Cordially yours,   [John Randolph Bolling]

CCL (WP, DLC).
    [1] Mrs. Maud M. Merrill. For some details of her case, see BC to WW, July 1, 1921 (first letter of that date).
    [2] Edward C. Kriz, Bolling's stenographer.
    [3] The Washington offices of Wilson & Colby in the American National Bank Building at 1315 F Street.

From Arthur Francis Mullen

My dear Mr. Wilson: Washington June 20, 1921.

As soon as your note of June 13th reached me I started to Washington, arriving here this morning.

I will call, as you suggested, at three this afternoon.[1]

Yours very truly,   Arthur F. Mullen

TLS (WP, DLC).
    [1] About their meeting, Mullen later wrote (*Western Democrat*, pp. 201-205):
"About three o'clock in the afternoon of the twenty-first of June, 1921, I went to the house to which he had gone from the White House. As I went into the room into which Mrs. Wilson directed her brother, Randolph Bolling, to take me, I saw Wilson seated in a big chair near the fireplace. He looked hardly ill at all. His color was good. Except for the fact that his left hand rested on his knee and never moved through the time I was with him, and that a slight twitching showed occasionally on the left side of his face, he seemed in no way incapacitated. He used his right hand freely in gesture, and sometimes, when he grew emphatic, he pounded the arm of the chair vigorously.
    "Mentally, he was keen as a razor. He remembered everything of which he was speaking without effort. He even recalled relatively unimportant incidents of long-gone events. He was clear and definite in plans for the future.
    "He had sent for me, he said, because he wanted to have me take up the matter of getting some sort of effective organization worked out in the Democratic National Committee. His plan was to get George White of Ohio, then chairman of the committee as a hang-over from the Cox campaign of 1920, to resign. Then we could get a proper executive committee and thereby direct the affairs of the Democratic Party.
    "He said that he did not expect to have any definite organization out of Congress,

either in the House of Representatives or in the Senate. 'I understand,' he said, 'that there is no plan or proposed plan of organization in the House or Senate to work out a definite policy for the party or do anything to take care of the elections next year. The trouble is that most of the men up there are not Democrats and are more interested in their own personal campaigns than they are in the party.'

"I told him that I was not very enthusiastic about the prospects of getting anything done through the Democratic National Committee. It would be difficult to get George White to resign, I said, and if he did resign there would be something of a contest about choosing his successor.

"Wilson said that he thought Tom Chadbourne would make a suitable chairman.

"I thought there would be objection to Chadbourne because of the fact that he had been associated as attorney for large business interests in Wall Street. He came back at me with this: 'Of course, this is an objection, but it is not one that would weigh much. Chadbourne's connection with business is such as to give the party the right kind of standing with business, and those in opposition would be glad to cooperate with Chadbourne in making a plan of organization. He is a big man, capable of doing things, and is anxious to help.' I was still dubious, and he finally said:

" 'I want you to promise me that you will do what you can to help in this matter. The reason why I have sent for you is because you have some aptitude for this kind of work. Your connection with my administration was such that I can say that you are not acting for me or any one in my behalf. I am deeply interested in having something done. I know the necessity of having a strong Democratic organization. At present there is no way it can be done except through the Democratic National Committee.'

"I spoke to him of the League of Nations. He looked at me sadly. 'The League of Nations is dead,' he said.

"I told him that I thought that the treaty would be ratified, with reservations, after a time.

"He said, 'No, Lodge has power to defeat the treaty. It will never be ratified. Too much water has gone over the dam. While I regret that this is the case, we must meet the situation as it is. There is no sense in permitting these old complications to involve us in the future. My idea is that we ought to take the position that the Democratic Party demands that the United States resume its normal natural relations with all foreign countries and that it again take its place as leader among the nations of the earth. Adopt some sort of definite plan, and then work toward that plan. It should be broad enough so that details may be worked out as it develops.'

"I thought this might be worked out through a program of reduction of taxes.

"He said, 'No, nothing can be done in a campaign of economy.' A campaign of retrenchment and reduction of taxes is necessarily, he went on, a negative campaign. What we needed was a campaign of affirmation. We could not sit and wait for the opposition to turn things over to us in the Democratic Party. We must have vocal organs to express what we wanted. We must take advantage of the mistakes of the opposition, and we must have some concrete and definite plan of action.

" 'My idea,' he said, 'is that if Chadbourne is chairman of the Committee he will gather around him some men who can outline a definite program, a working platform, along conditions as they now exist, as well as along new lines, and get these out in the country to the working democracy. Through that we would be able either to influence or to direct our members of Congress along definite lines.'

"As he continued to talk of the selection of a chairman he swung into anecdote. 'I remember,' he said, 'when General Joffre was here. We had a conference at the White House. As he was leaving I asked him, "General, can you give me any advice that will be helpful?" The General said, "Yes, select the right men for the places." I told him, "I have tried to do that." '

" 'You were the only man with the power to do it,' I told him, ' who selected a general in the army who stayed all the way through.'

"Wilson smiled, 'Yes,' he said, 'I appointed the right man, and I stayed with him to the end. I didn't make many changes.' His smile deepened to irony. 'I didn't even change that ass of a Sims.'

"I suggested that the party should take some position on the railroad question. He said, 'Yes, that is a complicated question. It requires study and attention. It is important that we have an organization so that when the proper time comes we may be able to take an advanced position on that question and one which will be advantageous to the party.'

" 'I know that,' I said, 'but how are you going to fight this thing unless you get down and meet these people on common ground? There are two kinds of wrestlers, those who stand up and those who lie down. If you're fighting with the latter, you have to roll around with them on the earth and bite off their ears so they won't bite yours.'

"He shook his head. 'The temptation is great, but even to put Lodge in a hole we can not afford to act the part of demagogues. We can not afford to act as demagogues even to obtain a temporary advantage. I am not in favor of meeting Lodge that way. Let us get a definite plan along proper lines and work toward that plan. Then we can fight, and I am willing to do my part in that fight.'

"Before I left him he went back to his original intention. Would I, he asked me, promise to do what I could to get White to resign? I assured him I'd try, but that I had little hope of getting anywhere with White. He held out his hand, and thanked me for coming to see him. 'It was good of you to come,' he said. 'Heretofore, when I sent for men, I had power to do something for them. Now I have no power. I am only asking you to render a gratuitous service for me.' As I reached the door I looked back. He was lifting his shoulders as if to brace himself. The look on his face was one of weariness, of disillusionment, of desolation."

To Clarence Osborne Sherrill[1]

My dear sir: [Washington] 21st June, 1921.

Is it possible that it is true that a golf course is to be laid out in Rock Creek Park? I am loath to believe that such an unforgivable piece of vandalism is even in contemplation, and therefore beg leave to enter my earnest and emphatic protest.

That park is the most beautiful in the United States, and to mar its natural beauty for the sake of a sport would be to do an irretrievable thing which subsequent criticism and regret could never repair.   Very truly yours,   [Woodrow Wilson]

CCL (WP, DLC).
[1] Lt. Col., U.S.A., Corps of Engineers; in charge of the Office of Public Buildings and Grounds in the District of Columbia.

John Randolph Bolling to Alfred Lucking

My dear Mr. Lucking: [Washington] 21st June, 1921.

Mr. Wilson asks me to acknowledge your letter of June eighteenth and say he agrees with your estimate of the matter regarding which you write, and that he is fully awake to the critical importance of the whole situation.
                    Very cordially yours,   [John Randolph Bolling]

CCL (WP, DLC).

To Oscar Wilder Underwood

My dear Senator: [Washington] 21st June 1921

I hope you will not regard it as an intrusion on my part if I express the hope that when the Newberry case comes up in the Senate such a blaze of light will be turned upon the whole transaction as to reveal the nature of what the Republicans are doing in the case to the gaze and comprehension of the whole world.

It is the capital instance of the character of Republican politics and immorality. It was a process of fraud and corruption by which the history of the whole world was changed.[1]

Cordially and sincerely yours,   [Woodrow Wilson]

CCL (WP, DLC).
    [1] A somewhat exaggerated statement. If Ford had defeated Newberry in 1918, there would have been an even division in the Senate in 1919 when the Versailles Treaty came before that body. Vice-President Marshall would have been able to appoint a Democratic majority to the Foreign Relations Committee, and the Democrats would have controlled the hearings, etc., on the Treaty and prepared the majority report on it. All of this does not mean, of course, that they could have formed a two-thirds coalition in the Senate to obtain consent to ratification of the Treaty.

John Randolph Bolling to Robert Cummins Stuart, Jr.

My dear Mr. Stuart: [Washington] 21st June, 1921.

I have just returned from an hour's conference with the Secretary of the Democratic National Committee in regard to the list of contributors to the campaign last fall.

The Secretary showed me the list—several thousand pages, closely typewritten (single space) averaging I should say 50 names to the sheet. On a rough approximation, it would probably take ten typewriter oprators, working eight hours a day, several weeks to copy the list. We discussed taking out the larger contributors; but this would be an enormous undertaking. Again the lists are in constant use, and of course could not be removed from the headquarters. On the whole, I believe we had better figure out some other method; as this doesn't seem practical. The Committee wants to work with us, and will give us any assistance in its power. They are a fine lot of men, desirous of cooperating in any way that they can.

If you still favor securing these names, I imagine there would be no objection to our employing one or more typewriter operators and letting them go to the Headquarters and copy such parts of the list as are wanted.

If you have not gone over the plan with anyone else, it might be worth while writing some of the members of your organization (say Mr. Franklin D. Roosevelt) and see what they think of it.

I will be glad to help in any way I can.

Cordially yours,   [John Randolph Bolling]

CCL (WP, DLC).

John Randolph Bolling to Bainbridge Colby

My dear Mr. Colby: [Washington] 22nd June, 1921.

Mr. Wilson asks me to thank you for your letter of yesterday,[1] with its enclosures. He says he will be interested in looking over the papers, and he asked me to put them on his reading table where he can examine them this evening.

Mrs. Wilson is grateful for your prompt action in the Merrill matter. This is, of course, a "business" case—if you think it wise to take it up.

I note you expect to come down on Friday afternoon; if you can get here in time, Mrs. Wilson will be delighted to have you dine with us at seven-thirty o'clock.

Kriz telephones me this morning that the carpenters at the building have gone on a strike (more Republican prosperity!); I will run in there this afternoon and see just how things are going.

Cordially yours,   [John Randolph Bolling]

CCL (WP, DLC).
    [1] BC to WW, June 21, 1921, TLS (WP, DLC), enclosing Henry A. Forster to BC, June 11, 1921, TLS (WP, DLC).

From Arthur Francis Mullen

Dear Mr. Wilson: Washington June 22, 1921.

Mr. White will be here at the headquarters on Thursday or Friday of this week. I intend to have a heart-to-heart talk with him along the lines you suggested. In particular, I will point out the necessity of getting the right kind of momentum behind the Committee.

Mr. Brennan can, if he is in the right frame of mind, help very much in the matter of getting the present chairman to open a way for reorganization. However, there are reasons why it would not be expedient for you to mention the name of Mr. Chadbourne to Mr. Brennan. I understand that there are personal reasons why this would not be satisfactory to Mr. Brennan. In the matter of getting the present chairman to quit, Mr. Brennan can be of service. Stress that feature of the matter with him and say but little regarding the proposed successor.   Very truly yours,   Arthur F. Mullen

TLS (WP, DLC).

Robert Cummins Stuart, Jr., to John Randolph Bolling

My dear Mr. Bolling: Aboard S.S. Comus, June [c. 23] 1921.

In my last letter[1] it was not intended to give the impression that formal offices were to be established but rather a definite place selected for the center of activity.

Your suggestion[2] as to having the work carried on in the office of the treasurer seems good. From this I judge you would not consider a professional money raiser necessary to direct the canvass. Some members of the club at Harvard considered this essential. It was my impression, however, that as we should not have the public meetings, except at the universities, and as it was largely a question of personal interviews and letter writing this would be a needless expense.

For treasurer I am considering Thomas D. Jones of Chicago. Mr. Wilson at the beginning of his administration nominated him for The Federal Reserve Board. In view of his difficulties with the Senate is it likely he would be a burden to us?

Henry Ford ought to be interested in our work. How can we use or compliment him without arousing substantial antagonism?

I have been thinking a large advisory committee might be constituted to which such men might be invited. The committee could include everyone likely to give a large amount. Before giving out the details of the tribute as prepared by the committee of professors a copy of the report and a personal letter asking their suggestions might be sent.

By having this committee a man could be invited to become a member and while awaiting a reply additional information might be secured; besides his letter itself would furnish slightly better evidence as to his availability for a trustee or a state chairman.

It is difficult to get complete information about people over the country. You hear this man is prominent, wealthy and possibly in this or that business but you are not told he would be good for this or that particular function.

Among the names given me in New York were the following: E. L. Doheny (Los Angeles and New York—oil), Edward N. Hurley (Chicago—formerly of the Shipping Board), Samuel W. Fordyce[3] (St. Louis lawyer), Vance McCormick (Harrisburgh, Pa., former Chairman of the Democratic Committee), Norman D. Davis[4] (Stockbridge, Mass. and New York), Gavin McNab (San Francisco—lawyer and active Democrat). I have several more names but at present I can not locate my other cards.

Which of these do you think should be trustees? McCormick, Hurley, and McNab raise the question of having too many men of strong political affiliations.

Mr. Colby is willing to be a trustee. Mr. Candler[5] of Atlanta, the Coca-Cola man, has also been recommended for one. Do you know if there is any feeling between the two. Mr. Colby, I recall, sued the Coca-Cola Company for $500,000 about two years ago.

Before leaving Cambridge I wrote to Democratic Senators from twenty-seven states asking them for recommendations for chairmen and trustees. Judging by the very courteous and surprisingly prompt replies which came the day I left, there should be some good material in Houston when I arrive. These letters were written on the paper of the Harvard club for I feared the "Council" stationary might set some of them off.

Mr. Cleveland Dodge, whom I saw in New York, looked badly. Since March or even the last of April there has been a great change. He said he was "right on the ragged edge" and could serve on no other committees of any kind. He is on "The Committee of Ten,"[6] you know, of which Franklin Roosevelt is Chairman. He said since I saw him last some one had seen Mr. Wilson and talked over their tribute with him. Would it be possible for you to keep me informed as to how their work develops and especially if our tributes conflict or overlap.

Mr. Hamilton Holt, who is chairman of the sub-committee doing the greater part of the planning, said that they expected to raise their fund in one week ending on Armistice Day. He asked if our clubs would help them raise their fund!

I saw Mr. McAdoo in regard to a moving picture visualization of the tribute and the possibility of getting friendly actors to donate their services. As he is not now actively connected with these interests, he could not offer much assistance. Do you know anyone we might interest in working up something along this line?

Mr. Cyrus H. McCormick was stopping at the Plaza but as he did not return from the commencement exercises at Princeton before I left I was unable to see him.

Sir Charles Sykes, an intimate of Lloyd-George and large British newspaper owner, left for Montreal before my arrival. I had planned to see him about raising some money in England.

The New York Times mentioned a week or two ago that Mr. Gerard, the former Ambassador to Germany, had purchased some ground for a country estate at $180,000. Believing he might give us substantial assistance I called his office about eleven-thirty Tuesday morning. His secretary said he had not gotten down yet but would probably be in by twelve. Upon calling at twelve-thirty, getting his office, and waiting eight minutes by the watch for him to answer, I asked Mr. Gerard if during the afternoon he could see me for a moment. He said in a slow, sleepy, lifeless voice he was aufully buisy, was greatly rushed to get off to Europe on Saturday, to come back some time next September and he might see me.

Mr. Colby saw me at his office for a few minutes. As usual he was pleasant and gracious. He offered to do all he could for us.

When in New York last April I tried to see Mr. Baruch but he was in the west. Upon returning to Cambridge I wrote to invite him to address the club. He replied very cordially declining the invitation due to a full programme up to sailing for Europe. As he is on the "Committee of Ten" I think your help may be needed in connecting him with our movement. I shall make a note of him and write you about him when he is expected back.

Mr. Baruch's son is not a member of the Harvard club—unless he joined the last week or ten days. Though I do not know him we have several friends in common at the university. I shall see that he is asked to become a member at the opening of the fall term.

I did appreciate the free expression of opinion in your last letter and shall greatly value your advice and conclusions drawn from your long experience.

Our voyage has so far been calm and uneventful but exceedingly warm, in fact so warm I shall be glad to get to Texas!

Faithfully yours,   Robert C. Stuart

TLS (WP, DLC).
   [1] R. C. Stuart, Jr., to JRB, June 16, 1921.
   [2] JRB to R. C. Stuart, Jr., June 19, 1921.
   [3] Samuel Wesley Fordyce, also active in banking and business affairs; general counsel of the War Finance Corporation, 1918-1919.
   [4] He meant Norman Hezekiah Davis.
   [5] William Candler, secretary and treasurer of the Coca-Cola Co. of Atlanta.
   [6] Stuart was slightly confused and misinformed. F. D. Roosevelt was national chairman of the campaign to raise an endowment for what would become the Woodrow Wilson Foundation, and Hamilton Holt had agreed to serve as executive director. What Stuart called the Committee of Ten was actually the temporary executive committee, of which Dodge was chairman. Other members were Frank I. Cobb, Mrs. J. Malcolm Forbes, Edwin F. Gay, Florence Jaffray Hurst (Mrs. Jefferson Borden) Harriman, Edward M. House, Adolph S. Ochs, Frank L. Polk, Virginia Potter, and Caroline Bayard Stevens Alexander (Mrs. Henry Otto) Wittpenn. Baruch was not a member of this committee, as Stuart says later in this letter. See the *New York Times*, June 27, 1921.

A News Report

[*June 25, 1921*]

Wilson Goes to Court to Be Admitted to Bar;
Aided by Attendants, but Health Seems Better

Washington, June 25.—Woodrow Wilson was admitted to practice today before the bar of the District of Columbia Supreme Court during a ceremony that lasted less than fifteen minutes from the time the automobile of the former President drove up until he was again seated in it and driving away.

Mr. Wilson arrived at the Court House just before noon accompanied by his law partner, Bainbridge Colby, former Secretary of State, and Joseph Tumulty, his former private secretary.

The ex-President was assisted from the machine by an attendant. Another attendant handed Mr. Wilson his cane, and with an attendant on either side he made his way to the elevator.

Attendants assisted Mr. Wilson to enter the chambers, where Chief Justice Walter I. McCoy and the Associate Justices were waiting. Chief Justice McCoy met Mr. Wilson at the door and shook hands with him. Then the Associate Justices were introduced.

Mr. Wilson stood while Clerk Morgan H. Beach administered the oath. Then the ex-President sat down while he signed his name in the register of the court.

When that was done Mr. Wilson again shook hands with the Chief Justice and the Associate Justices, and was assisted to the elevator and descended to the ground floor of the Court House. As he entered the automobile an attendant grasped him about the waist with one arm. United States Marshal Maurice Splain, a Wilson appointee, stepped forward and shook hands with the former President, as did several deputy marshals.

Marshal Splain became indignant when two photographers stepped forward to take snapshots and ordered one of his deputies to drive the men away.

Before the arrival of Mr. Wilson Chief Justice McCoy ordered the photographers out of the building. They then camped about the east entrance waiting for an opportunity to get pictures.

Many Court House employes were on hand to witness the ceremony. Some of them said afterward that Mr. Wilson appeared to be in better health than on his retirement from the Presidency, though he relied much on his cane while standing and walking.

Printed in the *New York Times*, June 26, 1921.

To James Aloysius O'Gorman

My dear Senator O'Gorman: [Washington] 25th June, 1921.

Mr. Colby has kept me informed of your interest and courtesy in the steps looking to my admission to the bar of New York.

I wish you to know how sensible I am of your courtesy in this matter, and how much I appreciate it.

Sincerely yours,   [Woodrow Wilson]

CCL (WP, DLC).

To Walter Irving McCoy

My dear Mr. Chief Justice: [Washington] 25th June, 1921.

May I not express more adequately than I could today my deep appreciation of the courtesy and consideration shown me by you and the other members of your Court in arranging and effecting my admission to the District bar?

Please convey to your colleagues an expression of my grateful appreciation.

Cordially and sincerely yours,   [Woodrow Wilson]

CCL (WP, DLC).

From Louis Dembitz Brandeis

My Dear Wilson: Woods Hole. Mass June 25/21

Yours of 20th reaches me here. I am to pass through New York next week on my way West and hope to confer then with Colby and Chadbourne as you suggested.[1]

Most cordially   Louis D. Brandeis

ALS (WP, DLC).
[1] About their conference, see BC to WW, July 2, 1921 (second letter of that date).

To Edwin Thomas Meredith

My dear Meredith: [Washington] 29th June 1921

I have been wondering whom to thank for the gift of the chair I occupied at the cabinet table during my terms of office, and one of our colleagues of the Cabinet informs me that you were the most active in the matter. I therefore hasten to express my very deep appreciation, and beg that if you should have the opportunity you will hand on these expressions to our colleagues who were generous enough to participate with you in the gift.

I shall always prize the chair most highly, and it will always have many charming associations of memory.

Hoping that all goes well with you and yours, and taking it for granted you are as cheerful as all other Democrats;

Cordially and sincerely yours,   [Woodrow Wilson]

CCL (WP, DLC).

John Randolph Bolling to Clarence Osborne Sherrill

My dear sir: [Washington] 29th June, 1921.

Mr. Wilson asks me to acknowledge your letter of June 28th,[1] and say to you that he is greatly relieved at what you tell him regarding the location of the golf course in Rock Creek Park.

As your letter does not indicate the point in the Park where it has been suggested the course be laid out, Mr. Wilson is of course unable to make any suggestions regarding what might be done with the tract in question. While he appreciates your inquiry, I am sure that the matter can be safely left in your hands, and those of your office who have made a study of the entire situation.

Cordially yours,   [John Randolph Bolling]

CCL (WP, DLC).
[1] C. O. Sherrill to WW, June 28, 1921, TLS (WP, DLC). Sherrill said that "some mention" had been made recently of establishing a golf course in Rock Creek Park "with a view to determining the wishes of the public in this matter." However, no definite steps toward construction had yet been taken. The tract of land proposed for the course had never been open to the public, was overgrown with brambles and poison ivy, and was not suitable for scenic roadways. A golf course, Sherrill believed, could be so constructed on this site as not to mar the beauty of the park as a whole. Sherrill asked Wilson what use he would recommend be made of the tract, if it were not to be a golf course.

From Bainbridge Colby

My dear Mr President: New York June 29, 1921

Senator O'Gorman moved your admission to the Bar of this state this morning, appearing for that purpose before the Appellate Division of the First Judicial Department in this city. He has written you a letter today[1] enclosing a certified copy of the order directing your admission and also enclosing a Constitutional oath of office for you to execute. This should be signed and sworn to before the Clerk of the Supreme Court of the District of Columbia, the official who administered the oath to you last Saturday morning in Judge McCoy's chambers. I am quite certain that if Mr Bolling were to call him up he would be very glad to come to your house. It will doubtless occur to you that it might be well to offer to send your car for him at any time that will meet your mutual convenience. He should affix his seal as Clerk of the Supreme Judicial Court of the District and it would be well for Mr Bolling to remind him to bring his seal with him.

This oath after its due execution should be returned to Hon. John Proctor Clarke, Presiding Justice of the Appellate Division, 25th street and Madison avenue, New York City. Senator O'Gorman has suggested in his letter that a brief acknowledgment of

Judge Clarke's courtesy would be very appropriate, and has indicated a form of a little letter which would cover the situation.[2] I think it would be well to follow the form suggested by Senator O'Gorman, particularly as to its reference to himself, as one of the Judges this morning when Senator O'Gorman made his motion asked the somewhat routine question as to whether the motion was made upon due authorization from you. Senator O'Gorman had your letter[3] (which, by-the-way, he greatly appreciates) in his pocket and was able promptly to assure the Court that every step was taken at your instance and with your full authorization.

I was not in court, but Senator O'Gorman reports that the attitude of the Judges was most friendly and cordial. It is quite without precedent that the person whose admission is moved should not be present in the court. The reference, in the proposed letter to Judge Clarke, to the great inconvenience that this would involve for you at the moment is to support the explanation that was made on this point.

It is also customary that the person admitted to the Bar, either in the usual course or upon motion, should subscribe his name to the roll. The oath which you are requested to execute as above explained is to supply the omission of this signature and will be pasted upon the roll at a place reserved for it.

If I have not made these points perfectly clear Mr Bolling might call me on the telephone tomorrow, or if you wish to wait two or three days I will be in Washington to discuss with you any point that may occur to you. It seems, however, very clear to me and I think it would be well, if convenient for you, to get the letter off to Judge Clarke, together with the duly executed oath, as promptly as possible.

Some very pleasant remarks were made about you by the Judges and I think that in extending my own congratulations, my dear Mr President, I should say that there is no case in the history of the profession in this State in which any man was admitted to the Bar under quite these circumstances of welcome and consideration.

Cordially yours,   Bainbridge Colby

TLS (WP, DLC).

[1] J. A. O'Gorman to WW, June 29, 1921, TLS (WP, DLC).

[2] "May I thank you and your colleagues for your courteous consideration of my application for admission to the Bar?

"It would have given me great pleasure to be present when Senator O'Gorman moved my admission, had it been possible for me to do so at this time.

"I have taken the oath of office and beg to enclose it herewith." CC MS (WP, DLC).

Wilson made a few changes in this draft and sent it as WW to Judge Clarke. The retained copy in WP, DLC, is the emended letter, without date.

[3] That is, WW to J. A. O'Gorman, June 25, 1921.

From Franklin Delano Roosevelt, with Enclosure

My dear Mr. President: New York June 29, 1921.

I was delighted to read that you have again become a full fledged lawyer, and to know that in just one particular I have you at a disadvantage, because, in my eight years of absence from the Bar, I have had less time than you to forget the intricacies of the rules of practice.

You will remember that I spoke to you of the tentative "Purpose" for the Woodrow Wilson Fund, as follows:

"The Woodrow Wilson Award is to be given annually by a nationally constituted Committee, from the income of the Woodrow Wilson Fund as award or awards to individuals or organizations in recognition of distinguished public service."

I agree that this is vague, but it was made so because we feared that times and conditions would so change in the years and generations to come that a reference to anything which is of concrete present importance might restrict the usefulness of the fund later on.

I am enclosing suggestions for making the language more concrete. These were somewhat hastily gathered by Hamilton Holt. Frankly, none of them quite satisfy me though number 5 I like the best.

We cannot too closely emulate the Nobel Prize, and I wish we could get some language which would more clearly set forth the basic principles which underly the future success of the democratic form of government throughout the world.

Perhaps you will be good enough to help me. Whatever you write, will, of course, be for me only, but it would be most helpful if you could do for me in this what you did for the new Postoffice building inscriptions.[1]

Please give my cordial regards to Mrs. Wilson and tell her that I hope soon to be able to send her the old volume of travels by the Frenchman who visited Lady Bolling in Virginia just after the Revolution.[2]   Faithfully yours,   Franklin D Roosevelt

TLS (WP, DLC).
    [1] Wilson had revised the inscriptions written by Charles W. Eliot. See WW to WGM, Oct. 6, 1913, n. 1, Vol. 28.
    [2] François-Jean, Marquis de Chastellux, *Voyages de M. le Marquis de Chastellux dans l'Amérique Septentrionale dans les années 1780, 1781, & 1782* (2 vols., Paris, 1786). Roosevelt probably proposed to send a copy of one of the numerous editions of an anonymous English translation which first appeared in 1788. The visit referred to by Roosevelt appears in Volume II, Chapter 4, under the heading "April 25, 1782: Petersburg—Visit to Mrs. Bolling's."

ENCLOSURE

The Woodrow Wilson Award is to be given annually by a nationally constituted Committee from the income of the Woodrow Wilson Fund as an award to citizens of the United States or an American organization in recognition of distinguished public service, in promotion of

1. justice between individuals, classes, races or nations.
2. human rights, justice and democracy.
3. peace and justice, whether within nations or between them.
4. these principles of justice which make for democracy and peace whether within nations or between them.
5. these principles of justice which make for more democratic forms of life and government whether within nations or between them.
6. peace, whether of nations or of individuals.
7. human rights upon which all national and international welfare depends.
8. these principles of justice and human rights on which our Republic was founded and which when universally applied will be the salvation of the world.

T MS (WP, DLC).

From Lawrence Crane Woods

Dear Mr. President: Pittsburg, Penna. June 29, 1921.

You know you always will be *my* President. You were President of Princeton, and you were President of the nation, and forever and aye you will be "my President."

I have just come back from my 30th at Princeton. We had wonderful weather and some most delightful days. Our Class Spirit seems to improve as the years go by.

The thing that perhaps pleased me most of all was the universal approval of possibly a hundred different people that spoke to me about my boy organizing the Woodrow Wilson Club and taking the message to you.[1] On all hands I was told that Lawrence had served Princeton in taking the action which he had; and frankly, I was proud as to what he has done and the fact that I had not been consulted or influenced him in the least in the matter. Of course, I knew nothing about his plans to go to Washington, or I would not have written to you as I previously did.

But the most significant thing was when Ambrose G. Todd, '84[2] Chairman of the Graduate Council, who presided at the Alumni

Luncheon, introduced Roland Morris, '96, who had just gotten his Degree,[3] he spoke of the fact that he had received his appointment to Japan by the hands of Woodrow Wilson, '79. Your name was greeted with pronounced, hearty applause thruout the entire room.

This is but the beginning. I thank God that Princeton is returning to its respect, admiration and reverence for your ideals and your born leadership.

With affectionate best wishes, in which Mrs. Woods joins with me, to you and Mrs. Wilson,

Cordially yours,   Lawrence C. Woods

P.S. Just had a bully letter from Stockton Axson recently. What a fine chap he is!

TLS (WP, DLC).
[1] See L. C. Woods to WW, June 6, 1921, and the news report printed at June 12, 1921.
[2] Ambrose Giddings Todd of New York.
[3] That is, the honorary degree of LL.D.

From John Kelso Ormond[1]

Dear Mr. Wilson: Detroit, Michigan. June 29, 1921.

I am one of the sons of Professor Alexander T. Ormond, of Princeton,[2] and it is in connection with a posthumous book of his that I am writing to you. When he died, in December, 1915, he had completed a series of eight lectures on the Philosophy of Religion for the Eliot Lectureship at the Western Theological Seminary. Death prevented his delivering his lectures, but four of them were read at the Western Theological Seminary by one of his Grove City colleagues.

It was our intention to publish these lectures the year following his death, but financial matters and then the war intervened, and we have only now completed arrangements for their publication by the Princeton University Press. It is our plan to make this book something of a memorial to Father. His picture will appear as a frontespiece. A brief introduction to the lectures themselves has been written by Dr. James Kelso, president of Western Theological Seminary, explaining the circumstances under which the lectures were prepared.

We desire another introduction to the book in the form of an appreciation of Father as a man, a teacher, and philosopher, and it is with reference to this introduction that I am, with some hesitation, writing you. If you can see your way clear to writing such an introduction you will be doing us, his children, a great favor, and will be honoring the memory of one who was a firm friend of yours and a steadfast adherent of the ideals which you have so consistently represented, and for which you have so earnestly fought.

The length and form of this introduction will be entirely in your hands, if, as we very much hope, you may be willing to undertake this, and the state of your health will permit.

Sincerely yours,   John K. Ormond.

TLS (WP, DLC).
¹ Princeton 1906; M.D., The Johns Hopkins University, 1914; surgeon of Detroit.
² Alexander Thomas Ormond, Professor of Mental Science and Logic, 1883-1898, and McCosh Professor of Philosophy, 1898-1913, at Princeton; President of Grove City College, 1913 until his death on December 18, 1915. The book for which Wilson wrote the foreword was published as *The Philosophy of Religion: Lectures Written for the Elliott Lectureship at the Western Theological Seminary, Pittsburgh, Penna., U.S.A., 1916* (Princeton, N. J., 1922).

John Randolph Bolling to James Aloysius O'Gorman

My dear sir: [Washington] 30th June, 1921.

Mr. Wilson asks me to thank you for your letter of June 29th, with its enclosures. He will execute the oath of office, before the Clerk of the Supreme Court of the District of Columbia, and return it promptly to Judge Clarke—at the same time writing him along the lines you suggest.

You may be interested to know that Mr. Wilson's health has shown greater improvement in the past two or three weeks than at any time since his illness.

Yours very truly,   [John Randolph Bolling]

CCL (WP, DLC).

John Randolph Bolling to Bainbridge Colby

My dear Mr. Colby: [Washington] 1st July, 1921.

Mr. Wilson asks me to acknowledge your letter of June 29th— received this morning—and say that the matter of executing the Constitutional oath of office for Justice Clarke is "in course." As I told you over the 'phone this afternoon, I anticipate that the matter will be closed tomorrow, and that I will be able to return the paper to Justice Clarke tomorrow night, along with a nice letter from Mr. Wilson—substantially in the form suggested by Senator O'Gorman.

Mr. Wilson asks me to send you the enclosed letter from Mr. Lewinson,¹ that you may advise him whether he should join the Association—and if Mr. L. is the proper party to introduce him. He will be glad of a prompt reply, and your suggestions.

The work goes rapidly forward on the offices. The partitions have been re-located, and the plastering is now being put on. I shall keep in touch with the situation every day, and report progress.

I shall hope to receive in the morning your suggestions regarding the Announcements, and feel confident that Mr. Wilson will be glad to assist in the matter. This kind of work always appeals to him—not only the construction of the text, but the style of lettering, arrangement, &c. I shall solicit his views on as much of the detail as I feel will interest him.

With kindest regards;

Cordially yours,   [John Randolph Bolling]

CCL (WP, DLC).
[1] Benno Lewinson to WW, June 30, 1921, TLS (WP, DLC). Lewinson, treasurer of the New York County Lawyers' Association, invited Wilson to join "this great Democratic Association, which now has a membership of upwards of 3,900."

Bainbridge Colby to John Randolph Bolling, with Enclosure

Dear Mr Bolling: New York July 1, 1921

I have yours of the 29th.[1] I hope that the partitions have been straightened out and I am obliged to you for attending to this. I return herewith the proposed announcements of the firm which you handed to me some days ago. They are very good and would answer, I think, well. The enclosed form is I think a little more usual and I would like you to get Mr Wilson's impressions on the subject.

Do you think we should put the initials N.W. after "F Street"?

I am sending you under separate cover a number of engraved and printed notices which I have received, just as a guide. It may help Mr Wilson. I am inclined to think that a script form similar to the one enclosed is rather better than the Roman-type notices, although I confess to having no very well-defined preference.

The question of the number to be sent out is one that requires consideration. The President has countless friends who would be pleased to receive this notice, and some who would be offended if they did not. I wish you would get his ideas on this question. They should be sent very generally to the members of the Bar both in New York and Washington. I should think at least two thousand notices could be used without too fully covering this section of the field.

It oughtn't to take anything like two weeks to get these notices from the engraver or printer. I can get them done within four or five days here. We will have ample time to get them mailed before we are in our Washington office.

With kind regards,   Yours faithfully,   Bainbridge Colby

P.S. You will notice that in the form I have prepared I have reversed the order, mentioning the Washington office first. I think this is proper. The President's home is in Washington. He is the head of the firm. The notices should be mailed from Washington, and if one pauses to consider the question at all I think one comes to the view that this is the right order of mention.   B.C.

TLS (WP, DLC).
  ¹ JRB to BC, June 29, 1921, CCL (WP, DLC).

E N C L O S U R E

The undersigned beg to announce that they have formed a partnership for the practice of law under the firm name of
Wilson and Colby
with offices at 1315 F Street (American National Bank Building), Washington, D. C., and 32 Nassau Street, New York City. July 1, 1921   Woodrow Wilson
                                             Bainbridge Colby

T MS (WP, DLC).

Three Letters from Bainbridge Colby

My dear Mr President: New York July 1, 1921

I enclose an office memorandum of the facts stated to me by Mrs Maud M. Merrill, whose letter to Mrs Wilson was referred to me by your direction.¹ The publishing business in which Mrs Merrill's late husband had a very large if not an equal interest seems to have been liquidated with considerable profit to the surviving partner and with disastrous results to Mrs Merrill. The difficulty in the case is that there seems to have been a judicial proceeding in Montreal for the liquidation of the corporation, under which Mr Merrill and his partner Mr Parker conducted their business, and incidentally to these proceedings there has doubtless been a judicial ascertainment of the respective interests. I am writing to some of the persons named by Mrs Merrill from whom I can doubtless get a more reliable statement of the legal situation. Mrs Merrill's version of the transactions is general and inexact, quite however as you would expect. I am therefore writing to Mr Perron the Montreal lawyer who represented her in the liquidation proceedings; also to Mr Herbert a lawyer of Boston who represented her at one stage of the negotiations; and also to Mr Sherman Whipple whose name comes into the story. I think we may be able to do something for Mrs Merrill, although the fact that the liquidation proceedings in Montreal went to judgment throws a legal shadow over the situation.

Referring to the demurrage cases,[2] I received a cable from London a few days ago advising me that two of the cases were in course of adjustment and asking me to suspend activities with reference to the third until further instructed. I conclude that the third case also is regarded as susceptible of adjustment. From the standpoint of our clients, I think they are well advised in seeking a settlement if it can be had at a proper figure. We were proceeding diligently to collect the names of witnesses and prepare for the taking of evidence, and our instructions from London were received after we had reported our progress by cable. There should be a fee here, although it will be of less amount than if the case had gone to trial.

A couple of matters, each interesting and of importance, have been offered to me which I shall not undertake without first consulting you. I expect to be in Washington the early part of next week.

I am in correspondence with Mr Bolling about a lot of fussy and tiresome details about the Washington office, etc. and I hope you are not being bothered overmuch with such details.

I enclose the first page of yesterday's "Law Journal" which contains a mention of your admission to practice. This is the official journal of the Bar in this city and is a very important but not a very thrilling paper.

With kind regards,   Cordially yours,   Bainbridge Colby

[1] See JRB to BC, June 20, 1921, n. 1.
[2] See BC to WW, May 5, 1921. "Demurrage" as used in this context related to ships. The case must have involved three vessels seized by the British during the war.

My dear Mr President: New York July 2, 1921

Justice Brandeis, Mr Chadbourne and I had a meeting this morning at the Bar Association to discuss the matter about which you asked us to confer. I think the discussion was fruitful and that you will be interested when I relate its course to you. This I think I can do better when I see you, which I hope to do within a few days, and I will not therefore write you at length on the subject today. Both Justice Brandeis and Mr Chadbourne sent loyal and affectionate greetings to you. I think you will be satisfied with the results of our discussion.

    With kindest regards always,

                    Cordially yours,   Bainbridge Colby

My dear Mr President: New York July 2, 1921

    With reference to the enclosed letter from Mr Benno Lewinson requesting permission to propose you for membership in the New York County Lawyers Association, I am of the opinion that it would be a very gracious thing for you to join it and that it would be appreciated by your fellow-lawyers.

    I am a member of the County Lawyers Association, although I have little occasion to use its facilities, as I am also a member of the older association called the "Bar Association of the City of New York." You will undoubtedly be elected to the latter association, which is the older and more firmly established. Its building on 44th street between Fifth and Sixth avenues, you are doubtless familiar with. It has one of the largest libraries in the country, if not quite the largest, and is quite complete in its arrangements for comfortable and effective work.

    The County Lawyers Association was formed for the purpose of providing similar facilities to a large number of lawyers who found admission to the other association fraught with delay and difficulty. The County Association is very vigorous and I think a little more democratic in tone—if that means anything in this connection.

    If you decide to join the County Lawyers Association I think you should state your business address in New York as 32 Nassau street, using the white card.

    With kindest regards always,

                    Faithfully yours,   Bainbridge Colby

TLS (WP, DLC).

John Randolph Bolling to Lawrence Crane Woods

Dear Mr. Woods: Washington D C 2nd July 1921

    Mr. Wilson was very much pleased to have your letter of June 29th, which he thoroughly enjoyed. He asks me to say to you that it was a great pleasure to know your son, and that he "acquitted himself with dignity and propriety" in his delivery of the message from the undergraduates at Princeton.

Mr. Wilson desires that I convey to you his most affectionate regards, and tell you what a pleasure it is to him always to have your
letters.   Cordially yours,   John Randolph Bolling

TLS (WC, NjP).

John Randolph Bolling to Thomas Selby Henrey

Dear Sir: [Washington] 2nd July, 1921.

Mr. Wilson asks me to acknowledge your letter of 20th June[1] and
give you the following witticism which he thinks you may care to
include in your book:

My predecessor in the presidency of Princeton University, Dr.
Francis L. Patton, once said something to an anxious mother
which seems to me witty enough to deserve being recorded.

A lady who was just placing her son at the University—forget-
ting the large number of undergraduates, and knowing nothing
of the duties and preoccupations of the president of a university—brought her boy directly to Dr. Patton and insisted upon
placing him under his personal care.

"Madam", said the Doctor very gravely; "we guarantee satisfaction or return the boy."

Mr. Wilson is sorry he does not think of any other instance of
college wit at the moment which might be included in your new
edition. He will be glad to know when your book is out, and the
name of the publisher.[2]

                    Yours very cordially,   [John Randolph Bolling]

CCL (WP, DLC).
    [1] T. S. Henrey to WW, June 20, 1921, ALS (WP, DLC). Henrey, the vicar of St.
George's Church in Brentford, a neighborhood of Greater London, asked that Wilson
give him "one or two instances of wit—university or otherwise"—for a forthcoming enlarged edition of his *Good Stories from Oxford and Cambridge: The Saving Grace of
Humour* (London, 1918).
    [2] It was published as *Good Stories from Oxford and Cambridge and the Dioceses*
(London, 1922). Henrey quoted the second, third, and fourth paragraphs of the above
letter verbatim on p. 281. The publisher was Simpkin, Marshall, Hamilton, Kent & Co.

To Franklin Delano Roosevelt

My dear Mr. Roosevelt: Washington D C 4th July 1921

I am going to take the liberty of doing more than answer the
question contained in your letter of June 29th.

I have noticed that the fund is frequently referred to as a "memorial," which suggests a dead one; and inasmuch as I hope in the
near future to give frequent evidences that I am not dead, I have

ventured to formulate a title—not as a gratuitous attempt at self-appreciation—but with a desire to put into words the purpose I have understood my generous friends entertain. I therefore suggest the following title and description:

WOODROW WILSON ENDOWMENT

Created in recognition of the public services of Woodrow Wilson, twice President of the United States, who was instrumental in pointing out an effective method for the cooperation of the liberal forces of mankind throughout the world who love liberty and who intend to promote peace by the means of justice.

Now to answer your question: I suggest that the statement with regard to the award be that it will be made to—

The person who has made the most practical contribution to the liberal thought of the world with regard to human rights or international relationships.

My own hope would be that it should not be confined to Americans, but open to citizens of all countries.

Mrs. Wilson asks me to say that she will be glad to have the old book of travels when you find it convenient to send it.

Cordially and sincerely yours,   Woodrow Wilson

TLS (F. D. Roosevelt Papers, NHpR).

To Thomas William Lamont

My dear Mr. Lamont: [Washington] 4th July 1921

I congratulate you with all my heart on the result of the China Famine Fund relief effort.[1]

As an American I am very proud of it, and feel that a great deal of the personal credit is due to you.

Cordially and sincerely yours,   [Woodrow Wilson]

CCL (WP, DLC).
[1] Wilson was replying to TWL to WW, June 30, 1921, TLS (WP, DLC), enclosing a report of the American Committee for China Famine Fund, a CC MS (WP, DLC) dated June 24, 1921. The report said that the committee had raised $4,542,996.53 of the total monies sent by various Americans, the Red Cross, churches, etc. About the Chinese famine of 1920-1921, see G. Patterson to WW, Nov. 5, 1920, n. 2, Vol. 66.

Two Letters from John Randolph Bolling to Bainbridge Colby

My dear Mr. Colby: [Washington] 4th July 1921

Mr. Wilson asks me to acknowledge your letter of July 1st, and tell you he has read with the greatest interest the Memorandum of

Facts stated by Mrs. Maud M. Merrill, and notes your comments on them. He will be most interested to learn what information you receive from the parties to whom you have written concerning the matter.

Mr. Wilson suggests that I return the Memorandum to you herewith, fearing you did not keep a copy.

The announcement in the Law Journal was of interest to Mr. Wilson, and he has asked me to put it in his scrap-book.

Mr. Morgan H. Beach, Clerk of the Supreme Court of the District, came to the house at 4 Saturday afternoon; took Mr. Wilson's acknowledgment, and then we hurried back to the Court House to have him affix the seal (the seal itself was too big to bring here). I returned with the paper at 4.30; the letter (per copy attached hereto) was signed by Mr. Wilson, and at 4.40 the entire matter was in the mails—on the way to Judge Clarke. You will note that the letter is in substantially the form which Senator O'Gorman suggested, with a change or two which I think strengthens it.

Cordially yours,   [John Randolph Bolling]

My dear Mr. Colby: [Washington] 4th July 1921

Your letter of July 1st came on Saturday, and I have found Mr. Wilson not only interested, but glad to give us his views about the announcements.

He decides unreservedly on the form I got up—a copy of which I enclose—liking it because it is out of the usual, and does not follow the old beaten track. It is not necessary to put "N.W." or "Northwest" after the Street here, and it is always understood northwest unless otherwise specified.

Mr. Wilson also favors a very handsome card—of the size and quality on attached proof. Get in touch with your engraver on to-morrow, and have him give estimate for an initial order of 5,000— and then for additional thousands. I will get prices here, and then we can compare them.

Mr. Wilson has very definite ideas as to sending out these Announcements, and here is a partial list—made up when we first talked the matter over Saturday. Every hour, it seems to me, he is adding names:

Members of Congress (both houses)
Members Mr. Wilson's Class at Princeton
Members of Bar in Washington and New York City.
Ex-members Mr. Wilson's cabinets.
Members Democratic National Committee.
Ambassadors and Ministers at all legations here.

Members of faculties in Princeton, Johns Hopkins,
Yale, Harvard, Univ. of Va., Amherst and Williams.
Members of the Supreme Court of the U. S., and
all Courts in the District of Columbia and
New York.
Federal Judges in the United States.
Presidents of Banks in Washington and New York City.
Business concerns in Washington and New York City, in a very
general way.

I believe it would be a splendid piece of business—and Mr. Wilson agrees with me—if we could send an Announcement to all business concerns in Dun or Bradstreet, above a certain rating. Even setting the rating limit high, this would probably mean several thousand; but I feel if it takes weeks to cover the list, it will be well worth the expense and effort. I want to look into this a little more before making a definite recommendation about it.

Of the headings mentioned, I have (or am taking steps to secure) all the names except those of:

Members of bar in New York City.
Members of Court in New York.

From the telephone directory I gather there are about one thousand lawyers in Washington. Mr. Wilson feels that each one should be sent an Announcement, without exception.

As soon as we decide upon the firm who is to engrave the Announcements, we will have the envelopes put in hand at once, and let Kriz put in some of his present idle hours in directing them.

There is another class (which I have discussed with Mr. Wilson) where we will have to have several thousand more Announcements—if we conclude to cover it; but I shall not have definite information for a day or two as to whether the list is available. Will write you again when I know about it.

Cordially yours,   [John Randolph Bolling]

CCL (WP, DLC).

Robert Cummins Stuart, Jr., to John Randolph Bolling

My dear Mr. Bolling: Houston, Texas. July 4, 1921.

Your letter of June 21st. was awaiting me when I arrived in Houston and since then I have been reflecting upon its contents.

This morning I had a long talk with the President of the Houston Chamber of Commerce, D. W. Michaux,[1] a man who is now serving as a national officer of several large organizations and who was the first "Potentate" of the Shriner's temple here. He is widely known and his judgment is generally accurate. It was his opinion that it would be worth a substantial sum to secure the names of those giving over $1,000 to the campaign last fall.

I am enclosing my check for $100 to pay for the expenses in doing this work, provided you think for this sum at least 250 and possibly as many as 600 such names with their post office addresses could be had. If our fund is to be completed by November 11th.,[2] we must have the proper information and have it speedily. To exchange one or two letters with each state in order to get these names costs as much for stationary and typing and takes as much time as it will probable [probably] take to secure it from the Committee.

Mr. Michaux gave a practical suggestion. He said the best way to organize each state was through men who had received political favors and therefore could not say "no" yet whom we should not be obligated to place in our organization unless it suited our pleasure.

This raises the question of how to reach these men—outside of the southwestern states about which I either have or can easily secure satisfactory information.

Mr. Tumulty, as Mr. Wilson indicated, could furnish much of this information. Some time before leaving Cambridge I wrote him but no reply has been received. Though the letter seemed to me to be courteous I hope no offense was given.

Hon. Homer Cummings over a month ago wrote he was planning to go to South America, so it would be too late before he could help. Hon. Vance McCormack will probably do something but I never feel certain until there are tangible developments.

Please don't think my courage or enthusiasm is waning. The movement is growing and spreading daily. All the colleges on the list you sent are being cared for. The Executive Committee is going to divide the country into distrists [districts] and have every college listed and written before the beginning of the fall term. I consider myself under a personal obligation to Mr. Wilson to see that our tribute is worthy of his great service. I shall do my utmost to have it a complete success.   Faithfully yours,   Robert C. Stuart

P.S. Harvey W. Schmidt, President of the club at "George Washington," will probably be in Washington through the summer and I think he might give an hour or two daily to the work at the Committee. His address is 917-18th. N.W., Washington. I shall try to write him to-morrow about it.

Running short of stationary and as the strike here is bad have had to send back to Cambridge for the printing.

TLS (WP, DLC).
¹ Daniel W. Michaux, businessman of Houston; a leader in the building of Shriners' hospitals for crippled children.
² The date set by the executive committee of the "Woodrow Wilson Fund" for dinners across the country to raise the endowment. The date was postponed to January 15, 1922.

To Benno Lewinson

My dear sir: [Washington] 5th July 1921

Your kind letter of June 30th has come promptly to me, and I take pleasure in enclosing herewith my application for membership in the New York County Lawyers' Association, and check for Ten Dollars for annual dues.

Appreciating your thoughtfulness in writing me;

Cordially yours,   [Woodrow Wilson]

CCL (WP, DLC).

From Franklin Delano Roosevelt

Dear Mr. President: New York July 7, 1921.

That is splendid! I like both the Description and the Statement, and I believe that they put the whole purpose on the kind of high plane which will inspire. At the same time it is sufficiently practical to leave no one in doubt as to the definite good which it will accomplish in the years to come.

I have only had a chance to speak of the title and statement to Hamilton Holt and Frank Polk. They are in every way satisfied with the exception of the use of the word "endowment." Hamilton Holt does not like it, as he fears that it might suggest to some people that we are endowing you! Also, it seems a little too much like that word "memorial," and as we believe very thoroughly in your continued vitality, and our own, we are inclined to the idea of the word "foundation,"—that is not only permanent but is something on which to build. I hope you will agree with us in this.

In the meantime we are going ahead with the spreading of the gospel, and we are flooded with letters from impatient people who want to give some tangible expression to their feelings for the man and for the ideals they have believed in.

Faithfully yours,   Franklin D Roosevelt

TLS (WP, DLC).

From Bainbridge Colby

My dear Mr President: New York July 8, 1921

I understand from Mr Bolling that our Washington office will be ready for occupancy about the 15th.

I am in the toils of the plasterers and carpenters up here also. I have taken an additional room, which admits of a rearrangement of space and partitions, making an attractive and dignified office.

This is one of the best buildings in the city. It is the home office of the Mutual Life Insurance Company, admirably kept up and an excellent roll of tenants. The Mutual Life has a law library of 25,000 volumes, which is at the service of the tenants of the building and is a valuable facility.

I am sending to Mr Bolling tonight a sketch of our announcement made by a New York stationer. We can get delivery of the notices in 48 hours after giving the order.

I am receiving quite a number of letters similar to the one enclosed from Jacob Newman,[1] head of one of the leading firms in Chicago. I have some men under consideration from whom we can select one to take charge of the Washington office as soon as it is ready for us to move in. I shall want to discuss this with you before a decision is made.

I like your idea of an extensive distribution of our announcements.

I shall be in Washington on Monday and will have a good deal to talk over with you.

I saw Mr McAdoo at luncheon at the Bankers Club today. He was looking very well.

With kindest regards,   Yours ever,   Colby

TLS (WP, DLC).
[1] It is missing. Newman was a partner in the law firm of Newman, Poppenhusen, Stern & Johnston.

John Randolph Bolling to Bainbridge Colby

My dear Mr. Colby: [Washington] 8th [9th] July 1921

Mr. Wilson enjoyed very much your letter of yesterday, telling him of the plans in relation to the New York Office. I am sure you will have most attractive and dignified quarters when the changes are completed.

Mr. Wilson asks me to return the letter from Mr. Newman to you. This letter raises the rather pertinent question whether we shouldn't mail announcements to other law firms besides those in New York and Washington.

Your letter to me, with sketches enclosed,[1] came this morning. I spent sometime with the engraver here, and I think he will be able to get me up a sketch which will embody your ideas as well as Mr. Wilson's. This sketch is promised tomorrow, but I will hold it and let us go over it when you come down Sunday or Monday.

Kriz has just telephoned me (4 P.M.) that the electrical wiring in the American National Bank building was condemned in toto on yesterday, and that new wiring will have to be installed from top to bottom. This will necessitate a little delay in getting in the offices, but they are promised to us—without fail—on Tuesday, July 19.

I think it most wise that you come down the first of next week, that you may get the matter of furniture, &c. straightened out.

Get in touch with me as soon as you arrive.

With kindest regards from us all;

Cordially and sincerely,   [John Randolph Bolling]

CCL (WP, DLC).
  [1] BC to JRB, July 8, 1921, TL (WP, DLC).

John Randolph Bolling to Franklin Delano Roosevelt

Dear Mr. Roosevelt: Washington D C 9th July 1921

Mr. Wilson asks me to reply to your letter of July seventh and say his objection to the word "foundation" is that it has been used by both Mr. Carnegie and Mr. Rock[e]feller, whose foundations were both created with their own money. Carrying this thought a step further; is it not possible that Mr. Wilson's enemies would be unkind enough to say that the word was used with the deliberate intent to create the impression that he furnished the funds?

I have suggested to Mr. Wilson that he give further thought to the matter, and if another word occurs to him, I will be glad to communicate it to you.

Cordially yours,   John Randolph Bolling

TLS (F. D. Roosevelt Papers, NHpR).

John Randolph Bolling to John Kelso Ormond, with Enclosure

Dear Mr. Ormond: [Washington] 9th July 1921

I am happy to be able to enclose you the Foreword which Mr. Wilson found opportunity to prepare on July fifth.

Cordially and sincerely yours,   [John Randolph Bolling]

CCL (WP, DLC).

ENCLOSURE

I am glad to contribute a brief foreword to this volume because it affords me an opportunity to pay a tribute of affectionate admiration to my friend and colleague, Alexander T. Ormond.

He was a man of the most transparent sincerity and simplicity of character who could absolutely be relied upon in every relation of life. There was, besides, no lecturer in the University whose lectures were more worth while. All his work was characterized by the most honest industry and solid judgment.

I consider it a privilege and honor to have been his colleague.

WOODROW WILSON.

5th July, 1921.

CC MS (WP, DLC).

From Arthur Francis Mullen

My dear Mr. Wilson: Omaha, Nebraska July 11, 1921.

After a long delay I finally had a conference with George White at New York. He made a long statement which had neither aim nor purpose in it. He finally said that he did not intend to be crowded out of the position of Chairman. He thinks that there is a movement on foot to push him out. He stated several times that he wanted and intended to resign, but always attached a string to his resignation.

One of the things that he wants to know before resigning is who is slated as his successor. I suggested that an easy way for him was to announce that he intended to resign on a definite date in the future and, at the same time, issue a call for a meeting of the National Committee for the purpose of electing a Chairman of that body. He made some objection to this and finally stated in substance: "I intend to call a meeting of the National Committee about the first of September. In the meantime I can and will give most of my time to the Committee work. I want to confer with the leaders of the party and, in a general way, I intend to be guided by their advice and suggestions."

While he talks about resigning and indicates in this way that he intends to resign, I don't believe there is any chance of making any changes in the Chairmanship. Among other things, he told me that Governor Cox was opposed to making any changes in the Chairmanship of the Committee. He also intends to run for Governor of Ohio. I gathered from what he said that he wants to use the position of Chairman so that it will help him in his candidacy for Governor. If he were convinced that it would help his candidacy to resign, I feel sure that there would be no trouble in getting him to resign; but, if he thinks to resign would injure him, there is no chance of making any change.

Daniel Roper made a suggestion that might be helpful. It is this: A United States Senator is to be elected in New Mexico in November of this year.[1] If the local democrats in that State, who are interested in making an aggressive campaign for a Senator, request Chairman White to take some definite action towards helping them in the way of organization, literature and financial backing and insist that he do something or get out of the way and let somebody else in that can do something, that might bear fruit. Senator Jones[2] is the Democratic National Committeeman from that State. He is in a position to take this up with White and get some sort of an answer. I suggest that you see Senator Jones and request him to take this up with White.

With kindest regards, I remain

Yours very truly,   Arthur F. Mullen

TLS (WP, DLC).
[1] To fill the seat currently held by Holm Olaf Bursum, Republican, who had been appointed to fill the vacancy created by the resignation of Albert B. Fall to become Secretary of the Interior. Bursum was elected to the seat in November 1921.
[2] That is, Andrieus Aristieus Jones.

From Caroline Bayard Stevens Alexander Wittpenn[1]

My dear "Governor,"   Jersey City, N. J. July 12th, 1921

I do not know whether Deaconess Young or myself would be most gratified at your remembering the little incident I told about. Her response was so quick, and I know meant so much to her, that I am happy to know that it impressed you as it has me. Her name and address is Deaconess Virginia Young, Rescue Home for Girls, 17 Beekman Street, New York City. She is a very remarkable woman a real Christian, devoting her life to guiding the feeble steps of girls just released from penal institutions along the difficult path of right living. She is full of both ideas and idealism and it was no surprise for me to find her immediate response to the appeal of your name.

I had another very touching result of my visit to you yesterday. There is a bed ridden young man at Bernardsville, a son of the Squibb family,[2] well known as chemists, who are now in very straightened circumstances. He has always most ardently admired you and begged me to come and tell him of my visit, but I will say nothing further about this as Archie[3] proposes writing you about it. I think somewhat to show his skill as a "rival typist"!

I cannot tell you what a refreshing delight my half hour with you was last week. It will make it all the easier to continue the struggle, often somewhat discouraging, for all that you stand for. Mrs. Wilson also was more than kind and Archie and I vastly appreciate her gracious reception as well as yours.

With kindest regards to her and hoping to see you both before so very long.   Very sincerely yours,   Caroline Wittpenn

TLS (WP, DLC).
[1] Mrs. Henry Otto Wittpenn, an old friend and political supporter of Wilson. See the index references under "Alexander, Caroline Bayard Stevens," in Vols. 26-27. She had married Wittpenn, another old acquaintance of Wilson's, on January 6, 1915.
[2] The "Squibb family" of Bernardsville, New Jersey, was that of Charles Fellows Squibb, Margaret Dodge Squibb, and their seven children. The sons were Edward Robinson, John, and Paul.
[3] Her grandson, Archibald Stevens Alexander (1906-1979), son of Wilson's student, friend, and gubernatorial aide, Archibald Stevens Alexander (1880-1912).

To Vance Criswell McCormick

My dear McCormick: Washington D C 14th July 1921

I was distressed that we missed connections yesterday, and am sure that you will understand that a slow convalescence, such as mine, necessarily falls into a routine which must, from day to day, follow a definite schedule of hours—and that to vary that schedule requires a little preparation beforehand.

The next time you come down give me a little longer notice, and it will be a pleasure for me to arrange an hour for our interview.

With warm regards to your Mother, sister and yourself, in which Mrs. Wilson joins;
          Cordially and faithfully your friend,   Woodrow Wilson

TLS (V. C. McCormick Papers, CtY).

To Charles Evans Hughes

My dear Mr. Secretary: [Washington] 15th July 1921

When the Treaty of Versailles failed of ratification by the Senate the copy of the Treaty accompanying this note was returned to me personally with the official notification from the Senate that votes sufficient for the ratification could not be obtained.

This was at the time I was very ill, and the copy was put in my private fireproof files for safekeeping, and when my effects were transferred from The White House to my present residence this copy of the Treaty was of course transferred with other papers under the conditions of safety with which it had at all times been surrounded.

I beg now that if it is convenient to you, you will permit me to deposit it with the Department of State. I am therefore sending the copy by my secretary along with this letter.

Cordially yours,   [Woodrow Wilson]

P.S. I know that your judgment will justify me in asking the favor of having a formal receipt sent me for this copy.

CCL (WP, DLC).

John Randolph Bolling to Robert Cummins Stuart, Jr.

My dear Mr. Stuart: [Washington] 15th July 1921

Perhaps you'll forgive me for my rather tardy reply to your letter of June, written aboard the "Comus"—when you see what a nice list I'm enclosing you—in response to your later letter of July 4th.

It is rather a strange coincidence that on the day you wrote I "celebrated" by having an hour's talk with Mr. Wilson about the contents of your letter first referred to.

About the list; I am returning the check for $100 which you sent me, as I was glad to contribute the time of my secretary—and he his services—in spending two days at Headquarters here and making up the list for you. There are something over fifteen hundred names. Had we confined the list to contributors of large sums, it wouldn't have amounted to many names. So I set the limit at $100 and over, and you have the result. Here is a tip: the Democratic National Committee is already sending out to the entire list solicitation for funds, and I understand that Mr. Franklin Roosevelt is preparing to do the same thing for the Foundation. So it is up to you to get ahead of him, by writing a strong letter, and putting it in the mails as soon as possible. I believe you'll find that a short, separately written typewritten letter will pull 1000% more than the multigraph. Get up a little printed slip telling all about your organization, its object, &c., and then a 7 or 8 line letter—beginning "My dear Mr. Howard"—and sign it yourself. Good typewriter operators ought to be able to hammer these out at 20 or 25 an hour; eight hours 200 to 250 letters; or something like a week's work for a good worker.

With reference to Mr. Michaux's suggestion about organizing States; it seems to me as long as yours is a college organization it would be better to have college men and keep away from politics.

Mr. Tumulty is a pretty busy man, and I heard that he remarked the other day—when asked to help with some other organization work—that he was "too busy earning a living." However, I will speak to him when I see him, and ask him to write you. I am sure he is not offended, for he is not at all that type. He is probably occupied with other matters, and hasn't gotten around to yours. I feel about the same way as regards both Mr. Homer Cummings and Mr. McCormick. The former is busy with political matters, and the latter with large private interests; so I am afraid there is not much chance for active help from either.

I had a very nice letter from Mr. Schmidt, offering to help with the list; but I had already arranged to let my secretary do the work. I have written and thanked Mr. Schmidt.

I will now answer, paragraphically, your letter from the "Comus"—the answers being formulated after talking to Mr. Wilson and reflecting his views as well as my own:

It would be a great mistake to employ a professional money raiser, and if this was done the object would lose much of its interest for Mr. Wilson.

Mr. Wilson regards Mr. Thomas D. Jones of Chicago as one of the finest men he ever knew, and he thinks would make you an ideal treasurer if he can give it the time. He says his "difficulties with the Senate" would not prove of the slightest burden to you.

Henry Ford is rather a difficult man, unless he can be "it." He has a blind side—flattery—and if you can approach him from that angle, you may get some help.

Mr. Wilson does not favor a large advisory committee. He would like better a small, active committee—of wide awake college men—and believes you can get them. Of the names you mention he thinks well of all except Mr. Doheny. His choice of trustees would be Mr. Hurley, Mr. Davis and Mr. McNab. He would not care for Mr. Candler to be one, though he doesn't believe the suit to which you refer would interfere.

From what Mr. Wilson and I know of the Foundation, it does not in any way correspond or overlap your plans. I shall certainly keep you posted as to their progress, and as fast as they communicate with Mr. Wilson will let you know their plans.

Mr. Wilson does not think there is anything in the motion picture visualization of the tribute, and believes you had better not attempt it.

Mr. Gerard can be of no service to you; what you write about his "lifeless" telephone reply is typical.

Mr. Baruch will be back from Europe the end of this month, and the first time he comes down I will tell him about you. I think a fine way to get him interested will be through his son—who I am sure he would like to see identified with the movement.

This, I think cleans up pretty well all the matters contained in your letters; from this time out I will try and answer promptly.

The law firm of Wilson & Colby are getting their new offices ready here, and it has taken quite a bit of my time to work out the details of arrangement, furniture, &c. with the two partners. From the looks of things now they will be ready for business August 1; already quite a number of cases have been listed with them.

You will be glad to know that Mr. Wilson's health has shown greater improvement in the past three weeks than at any time since his illness. He loves hot weather, and we have had two weeks or more of intense heat. As long as he improves, however, I feel I would be willing to stand most anything!

Cordially and sincerely yours,   [John Randolph Bolling]

CCL (WP, DLC).

From Bainbridge Colby

My dear Mr President: New York July 16, 1921

I am indebted to Mr Bolling for sending me the enclosed copy of the message sent by the "World" to their Washington representative relative to the original copy of the treaty. The references to me and what I am alleged to have said, are wholly untrue, as I stated to Mr Bolling on the telephone yesterday when he spoke to me about this subject.

I was called up at my house on the telephone late one night last week by the "World" office and told, by someone whose identity I did not recognize, that an evening paper carried a story to the effect that search was being made for the treaty in the State Department. I was asked whether I knew if the treaty was in the State Department. I said I did not, as the matter had never been brought to my personal attention. The "World" man then said that probably Mr Wilson would know. I replied that I didn't know what Mr Wilson would know, and could not speak for him. I made no suggestion of any kind as to what the "World" might do, and brought the discussion to a very sharp close with the statement above repeated.

The following day Norman Davis called me on the telephone and said that the Under-Secretary of State Mr Fletcher[1] had phoned him from Washington asking if he knew the whereabouts of the original treaty, to which he replied in the negative. Davis then said (to me) that he supposed the treaty had possibly been packed up with books and papers at the time that you moved from the White House, and thought it might be a good idea to make a search for the treaty and return it to the State Department, mentioning the inquiry that had been made of him and your prompt institution of a search for the treaty, when he (Davis) reported to you the inquiry received from the Under-Secretary of State.

I transmitted this suggestion to Mr Bolling on the telephone and he has doubtless already discussed it with you. Of course I don't know what thought may be in your mind on the subject, and transmitted the suggestion for what it was worth.

I noticed with considerable surprise the publication this week of the letter written to you by Mr Lloyd George[2] in which there was some reference to the subject of mutual cancellation of the indebtedness of the Allies. I recall your decision not to publish your reply[3] at the time when your attitude on this question was a subject of discussion, on the ground that the letter of the British Prime Minister was personal and should be treated as confidential. Its publication quite independently of you opens the way to the publication of your reply if you deem that course advisable.[4] But as to this I am not clear. Your position was very frankly stated by Mr Lamont in an interview he gave out at the time the question was under discussion last autumn,[5] and it may be that the decision we then reached that there was no necessity for you to speak as your position had been made so clear, is still the right attitude, notwithstanding the publication of the Lloyd George letter. I merely write this to bring the matter to your attention, and in this connection enclose an editorial which appeared in this morning's "World" on the subject.[6]

I also enclose a brief account of some remarks made by Professor Dodd, in Chicago yesterday, which I like.[7]

With kindest regards always,

Cordially yours,   Bainbridge Colby

TLS (WP, DLC).
[1] Henry Prather Fletcher.
[2] D. Lloyd George to WW, Aug. 5, 1920, printed as an Enclosure with BC to WW, Aug. 18, 1920 (first letter of that date), Vol. 66. At a hearing of the Senate Finance Committee on July 14, 1921, Secretary of the Treasury Andrew William Mellon had made public that portion of Lloyd George's letter which dealt with the problem of inter-Allied indebtedness. It was printed, e.g., in the *New York Times*, July 15, 1921.
[3] WW to D. Lloyd George, Nov. 3, 1920, Vol. 66.
[4] Senator Lodge, on July 18, 1921, read into the *Congressional Record* that portion of Wilson's reply to Lloyd George which dealt with inter-Allied indebtedness. *Cong. Record*, 67th Cong., 1st sess., pp. 3951-52.
[5] The Editors have found no report of Lamont's interview of "last autumn." However, his interpretation of Wilson's position was undoubtedly the same as that in his statement summarized in T. W. Lamont to WW, Feb. 21, 1921, n. 1.
[6] It is missing, but it was "A PAINFUL LOSS OF INTEREST," New York *World*, July 16, 1921. This brief editorial noted that a frequent charge of the Republicans during the presidential election campaign of 1920 had been that Wilson had been "intriguing with the Allied debtors, and particularly Great Britain, to let them off with a clean slate." The recent hearings before the Senate Finance Committee had turned up only Lloyd George's suggestion to Wilson of a general cancellation of inter-Allied debts. "There followed," the editorial concluded, "a noticeable subsidence of interest in the matter on the part of Mr. [James A.] Reed and the Republican members of the committee. It became almost painfully observable when yesterday they were informed on the authority of Secretary Mellon's Treasury Department that all the evidence in hand indicated that President Wilson had never been inclined to regard the Lloyd George suggestion favorably."
[7] Dodd had spoken on the topic, "Woodrow Wilson, the League, and America's Present Duty." Brief extracts of his speech appeared in the *New York Times*, July 16, 1921.

William Gibbs McAdoo to Edith Bolling Galt Wilson

Dear Edith,   Huntington, L. I. July 17. 1921

I had to rush off somewhat precipitately the other day in order to catch my train and had no chance for a further talk with you, as I very much desired.

I wanted especially to tell you of my anxiety about you in all that Washington heat and with all the problems and burdens you have to face and carry. I wish with all my heart, I could do something to help you and I hope with equal fervor that you will never let anything that concerns me or Nell add to your cares. You must have every possible chance to take care of your own health and no one who loves you, as we all do, would consciously increase your anxieties or burdens. Wont you always feel that if I can ever be of the least assistance or comfort, you will make me very happy by calling on me without hesitation or reserve?

About political matters: I understand the situation at Washington. It is ironically tragic that one cant get a cooperation which would put the enemies of our great chief and of all his ideals, under foot and rehabilitate the party for future usefulness. It is not possible, I fear, in the circumstances. Our enemies—his enemies—by a singular turn of fate, have constantly claimed and with effect and with some show of truth—that he sympathized with this view of things. For instance—the Brennan letter,[1] although merely, as I understand it, an invitation to Washington, will be used as evidence of their claim that he is cooperating with them. It is painful to all his loyal friends and supporters to have these claims made with even the slightest semblance of verity but it cant be helped and we must make the best of it. I am saying this because I want you to know the facts not only but also to tell you that I am not going to let them affect my personal attitude in the slightest degree. So you must not worry about that. We must all "stand together" and do the best we can in the circumstances.

Frank & Jessie and two of their babies are here and we are all having a fine time—wish you and the "Governor" could visit us. Nell is swell as also are the babies and the Smiths.[2] Margie[3] is down for the week end. Sallie[4] is here too, so we have a houseful and a jolly crowd this week.

With dearest love for you and wishing all over again that I could do something to lighten your cares and increase your happiness, I am, dear Edith,   Very affectionately yours,   W G McAdoo

ALS (EBW Papers, DLC).
    [1] WW to G. E. Brennan, June 13, 1921.
    [2] Lucy and Mary Smith.
    [3] Probably Marjorie Brown King.
    [4] His daughter, Sarah Fleming McAdoo.

John Randolph Bolling to Bainbridge Colby

My dear Mr. Colby: [Washington] 18th July 1921

Mr. Wilson asks me to thank you for your letter of July 16th, and its enclosures, which he was interested in having this morning.

Enclosed is copy of a letter addressed by Mr. Wilson to the Secretary of State, which I delivered to the latter on last Friday afternoon, at 4 o'clock, together with the Treaty. My reception by the Secretary was most cordial, and he told me that he could fully understand exactly how this matter came about as it did. On Saturday Mr. W. received an official receipt for the Treaty, signed by the Secretary. This is, of course, for your ears only—and I am giving you the information at Mr. W.'s suggestion.

Mr. Wilson enjoyed the clipping from the Times about Mr. Dodd['s] lecture; Mrs. W. had a letter from Mr. Dodd this morning giving a wonderful account of the meeting.[1]

Kriz journeyed to Baltimore on Saturday; saw Mr. Kent[2] about the list, but he could give him only the names without addresses. Mr. Kent has written for the list with addresses, and promised Kriz to forward it to Mr. Wilson the moment it was received—possibly today.

Kriz was in the offices this morning; he telephones me they are putting the white plaster on partitions, and he feels encouraged at the progress, believing now that the offices will be finished next week, and that we can formally open them two weeks from today— August 1st. If the list of addresses comes promptly, I am hopeful that we will have the majority of the announcements ready for the mails when we get under way.

Mr. Wilson continues to improve, and always wants to be remembered most kind[ly] to you.

Cordially and sincerely,   [John Randolph Bolling]

CCL (WP, DLC).
[1] W. E. Dodd to EBW, July 15, 1921, ALS (EBW Papers, DLC).
[2] Perhaps he was Frank Richardson Kent, vice-president of the Baltimore *Sun*, who was a historian of the Democratic party and other political works.

From Franklin Delano Roosevelt, with Enclosure

My dear Mr. President: New York July 28, 1921.

I am sending you by express, insured, the books which I think I spoke to you about when I last saw you, and I am inclosing herewith the letter to you from Mr. Stan V. Henkels.[1]

I am sorry that you have never happened to meet Mr. Henkels himself. He is a very rare old man who has taken most of his rare qualities from the priceless documents which have passed through his hands during the course of more than fifty years as an auctioneer. It speaks well for his judgment that after the opportunity of perusing Washington, Hamilton, Madison, the Adamses and Jefferson in the original, he is more firmly convinced of the truth of the principles of the Democracy than ever.

Incidentally, he is one of the greatest admirers of yours whom I have ever met, and for over two years he has been talking about getting out these copies of Washington's Farewell Address in your special honor. He will be in the seventh heaven if you will write a few lines in his copy.

Also, he has been good enough to give one of these copies to me, and I don't need to tell you that I will greatly appreciate it if you will write a few lines in my copy too.

I hope all goes well with you and I know that you are not objecting to these very hot days.

                    Always faithfully yours,   Franklin D Roosevelt

¹ Stanislaus Vincent Henkels, a rare book and autograph dealer of Philadelphia.

E N C L O S U R E

From Stanislaus Vincent Henkels

Dear Mr. Wilson: Philadelphia, July 5, 1921

I am handing you through our mutual friend, Honorable Franklin D. Roosevelt, a little gift which I hope you will accept from me as a token of the high esteem in which I hold you. Knowing how studiously you have adhered to the advice given by the great Washington, I thought that I could not better please you than by presenting you with these copies of his Farewell Address. The one printed on vellum in the morrocco case, is a facsimile taken from the original letter he wrote to James Madison under date of May 20th, 1792. You will recollect that he intended to resign his office after his first term and he wrote this letter to Madison, requesting him to draw up a farewell address, which he thought was proper for him to make to the people, and he inculcated in the letter important items which he wished Madison would include in the address. But as his friends induced him to accept a second term, Madison was not obliged to comply. A little coldness originated between Washington and Madison, for some reason after this, and when he drew up his second farewell address, he sent the manuscript to Alexander Hamilton for him to review and to correct. Hamilton returned it with many interdelineations and alterations, but Washington struck out many of Hamilton's changes and made corrections of his own, and sent it to the printer. The late James Lenox of New york discovered that this original autograph address was in the hands of Zachariah Poulson, a newspaper publisher of Philadelphia, and he wrote requesting the loan of it, which was granted. He then made a verbatum copy of it, noting where Hamilton made corrections and where Washington crossed them out and made others, etc. Of this, he published a few copies, for private distribution among his personal friends, and the copy I am sending you, is the one he presented to Mr. Willing of Philadelphia. It is, of course, excessively rare, and I feel that you would like to have it, together with the one that I have published, and also for the reason that it shows how very little Alexander Hamilton had to do with the writing of the last farewell address, which, of course, is pleasing to us Democrats who do not take any stock in Hamilton or his aristocratic form of government.

On the binding of your book, I have caused an original signature of General George Washington, to be inlaid. You will notice that [it] is taken from a letter in which he signs himself, "I am your affectionate." He very seldom signed his letters in this manner, and only to dear friends, and the reason I give it to you, is that I feel if he were here in person, and were writing to you, this is the way he would sign himself. The frame around it is gold, so it will not tarnish.

Mr. Roosevelt will also hand you my copy, upon the blank leaf of which, I would like you to write in a few lines, giving your appreciation of General Washington and sign it with your name and say, "For my friend, Stan. V. Henkels," and believe me, my dear sir, I am truly your friend. You will notice by referring to the obverse of the title page that only six copies have been published of this, which of course, will make the book a greater rarity.

You will please excuse me for writing you this long and tedious letter, but I had to do it to fully explain the gift I am presenting you. It is my wish and prayer that God Almighty in His infinite goodness will confer upon you good health and that He will allow you a long life so that you may see your ideals realized, which I am fully confident will be the case.

Believe me to be,

Very sincerely your friend,   Stan V Henkels

TLS (WP, DLC).

From the Diary of Ray Stannard Baker

[Washington] July 29 [1921].

Again at S. street working with Kriz,[1] my stenographer. Early in the morning went down to see Grayson & with him to see Admiral Benson: to help get the documents regarding the call of the President for the *George Washington* on April 7 1919. I wish to show that Tardieu is a liar![2] I went up to see Mr. Wilson about noon & had a long & very interesting talk. He was sitting in his bedroom & having his luncheon, attended by Mrs. Wilson. Once during the meal he looked up at her & then over at me & said, "You see how well I am cared for!" Mrs. Wilson smiled & patted him on the head. She seems most happy these days: & I never saw her looking more beautiful. She goes about the house whistling like a leaf. The President wore a purple velvet jacket & his left hand was curled down & hidden by his side. He cannot use it. He is able enough with his right hand. His color is much better, more wholesome, than when I last saw him, & his voice is stronger: & he is far more cheerful. Mr. Wilson says that he enjoys the worst of the hot weather here: and Grayson told me that he was in the best health since he fell ill 18 months ago. He apparently expects to get well: goes at it with boundless courage!

I felt somewhat embarrassed as to what to talk about. He feels most pessimistic regarding the political situation (which is not surprising) & has no faith in the proposed conference for disarmament.[3] Thinks it not genuine.

We fell presently to talking about the Peace Conference: & finally, though I was fearful of unduly tiring him, I went & got the Inquiry Report of 1918 with his stenographic notes on the margin[4] & he went over all of them with me & read them—which I much desired. He even seemed to enjoy it & readily promised to read any others I might find. I was delighted to clear up quite a number of difficult points, as to the origin of his position on the mandatory system, his view of the rights of small nations, and above all to have him assure me again that I was to use *all* of the documents I have frankly as historical material. We got to talking about a title for the book & he had the same idea I have had: to express the contact of American ideals with European realities.

"Why don't you call it, 'America Meets Europe at Paris?' " he said.

Presently Mrs. Wilson & I were called to luncheon but had hardly got well started when Mr. Wilson sent his negro man Scott[5] down to ask me to come up to see him. He was now in bed propped high with pillows. As soon as I came in he said, without preface:

"In my notes on the Balkans (which he had previously interpreted for me) I speak of the relationships of the several Balkan states to one another as being determined by friendly council along 'historically established lines of allegiance & nationality.' This is important. I was thinking there of the great importance of tradition & habit in the settling of these problems. Habit is the basis of order. I am not an impractical idealist, nor did I, at Paris, want everything torn up by the roots & made over according to some ideal plan. I recognised always the importance of habitual relationships in cementing all of these allegiances."

From this our conversation drifted to the position of the Italians: and the President quite warmed to the enthusiasm I expressed in plans for the development of the book & of the service we might do with it in developing a better consciousness in America regarding international problems.

"It is the biggest work I ever attempted," I said.

"It is the biggest any American writer ever attempted," he said.

It was as near enthusiasm: warmth: toward me as I ever saw him get: not so much in the words as in the intonation & the expression. But at last, the barrier never goes quite down! One never quite gets to him! One feels like standing up as I did through all this conversation—at the foot of his bed!

When I got back the luncheon was about finished. Grayson took me down in his car & I caught the four o'clock train for New York. Rode up with President Bowman[6] of the University of Pittsburg. And so home again: & to work.

The new offices of Wilson and Colby are to open in the bank building at F & 13th streets next Monday. They have been refitted with a fine suite of rooms for Mr. Wilson with a private entrance.

---

[1] That is Edward C. Kriz, actually Bolling's stenographer.

[2] That is, a liar in what he said about Wilson's call for the *George Washington* in *The Truth about the Treaty* (London, 1921), p. 185: "In spite of Mr. House, the mendacious news is published that the *George Washington* has been hurriedly summoned to Brest." On this subject, see the index references under "*George Washington, U.S.S.*: WW's summoning," in Vol. 57.

[3] That is, the proposed conference on the limitation of naval armaments, to be held in Washington on a date still to be determined. The State Department had announced on July 10 that informal notes proposing such a conference had been sent to Great Britain, France, Italy, Japan, and China. All these nations had signified their acceptance of the proposal by July 14. At this time, Secretary Hughes was at work on the formal invitations, which were sent on August 11. See the *New York Times*, July 11-15, Aug. 11-12, 1921.

[4] They are printed, camera copy, in Vol. 45, pp. 476-82.

[5] Isaac Scott, Wilson's personal servant.

[6] Actually, John Gabbert Bowman was Chancellor of the University of Pittsburgh.

John Randolph Bolling to Franklin Delano Roosevelt

My dear Mr. Roosevelt: [Washington] 2nd August 1921

Mr. Wilson asks me to acknowledge your letter of July 28th, with one enclosed from Mr. Henkels; also the package of books which came by express on last Saturday.

By today's prepaid express, I am returning the copy of the book belonging to you, and Mr. Wilson wishes me to say that—in view of the fact that he has had to refuse to [so] many requests for autographs, &c.—he is sure you will excuse him from writing in the book as you ask. Since leaving office, I am sure I don't exaggerate when I say that he has been asked for thousands of autographs; and that books, papers, &c. by the dozen have been sent him with the request that he write in them.

Mr. Wilson's health continues to improve; in fact, I think he has shown greater improvement in the last month than at any time since his illness.

With kindest regards from us all;

Cordially yours,   [John Randolph Bolling]

CCL (WP, DLC).

John Randolph Bolling to Stanislaus Vincent Henkels

My dear sir: [Washington] 2nd August 1921

At Mr. Wilson's direction, I am sending you a book by today's prepaid express—recently received by him through Mr. Roosevelt. Permit me to call your attention to a note from Mr. Wilson that you will find inside of the package.

Yours very truly,   [John Randolph Bolling]

CCL (WP, DLC).

To Stanislaus Vincent Henkels

My dear Mr. Henkels: Washington D C 2nd August 1921

I need hardly say that your gifts, sent through Mr. Roosevelt, are greatly appreciated; but I do want to say that to me the most gratifying thing about them is the generous friendship which prompted you to send them.

Believe me, with grateful appreciation;

Your friend,   Woodrow Wilson

TLS (F. D. Roosevelt Papers, NHpR).

George Creel to John Randolph Bolling

New York City
My dear Randolph: August Third, Nineteen Twenty-One.

Baker came to town last Wednesday and I went with him to Garden City for a talk with Doubleday. Baker showed a disposition to put off publication until next fall but I pointed out the danger of this delay and proved its utter needlessness. Doubleday backed me up and it was agreed to publish the book about April first and to start newspaper syndication November fifteenth or thereabouts.

Last Friday night Baker called me up over the telephone on his arrival from Washington. He told me that before leaving New York he had had an interview with Brainard and Bradford Merrill, publisher of the New York American. Merrill, speaking for Hearst, offered $27,500 for the syndication rights for New York, Washington, Atlanta, San Francisco and Los Angeles. He recited various arguments in favor of the offer and told me that he had mentioned it to you and Mrs. Wilson. I told him that I thought he should have mentioned the matter to Mr. Wilson also, as the decision was entirely up to him. He seemed rather vague as to the next step and went off to Amhearst [Amherst].

Yesterday—Tuesday—I had luncheon with Brainard, and today I had luncheon with the World people. As a result of both interviews I think I am able to put the proposition in such form that Mr. Wilson will be able to make an intelligent decision as to what he wants to do.

There is no question that Hearst's offer has all the advantage as far as money is concerned. In Washington the Hearst paper is the Times, and the other customer is the Star: In Atlanta the Hearst paper is the Georgian and the other customer is the Journal: In San Francisco it is Hearst's Examiner against the Bulletin and in Los Angeles it is Hearst's Examiner against the Express.

Even if the World paid $10,000 for the New York rights I do not think that you could expect more than an additional ten thousand from the Washington Star, the Atlanta Journal, the San Francisco Bulletin and the Los Angeles Express.

There is also no question as to the value of the Hearst contract in connection with selling other papers. The very fact that Hearst has paid a high price for the use of the series in five of his papers, will have a big effect on other purchasers. There is also the point made by Mr. Baker that publication in the Hearst papers will bring the material before an audience that has been persistently poisoned by the lies of the past, whereas publication in friendly papers, like the World, only carries the material to those who are already of our way of thinking.

Now for those considerations that stand opposed to the Hearst offer: In the first place, there is the fact that Hearst has always been a bitter enemy of every Wilson policy and that he will continue to be. Secondly, to give the series to Hearst would take it away from true and tried friends, like the New York World and the Atlanta Journal. I do not think that any obligation is due to the Washington Star or the Los Angeles Express, but the San Francisco Bulletin is entitled to be classed with the World and Journal. Rightly or wrongly, these papers will bitterly resent the sale of the articles to Hearst and will blame it directly on Mr. Wilson.

Another thing, Hearst commences next Sunday the serial publication of the McCombs book,[1] or more properly, a book written by a Hearst employee[2] under the name of McCombs. From what I have learned from people who have seen the manuscript, it is about as vicious an attack on Mr. Wilson as has ever appeared in print. These, then, are the opposed considerations. I have tried to present them fairly and without bias. Please put this letter before the President at once, if you can.

Brainard has wired Baker to be in New York next Monday for the purpose of going to Washington Tuesday. He has also insisted upon my accompanying them. If the President desires to see the three of us for further discussion, please wire me at Manchester, Vermont, where I will be until Sunday morning. If, however, he makes a decision on the basis of this letter, please wire me and also wire Baker at Amherst so that we will not need to meet in New York Monday.

With warmest regards to Mr. and Mrs. Wilson and yourself, I am
                                        Always sincerely,   George Creel

Please regard this letter as *confidential.*

TLS (WP, DLC).
    [1] That is, *Making Woodrow Wilson President.*
    [2] Louis Jay Lang, Princeton 1881, sometime political editor of the *New York American*, appears on the title page of McCombs' book as "Editor." However, his obituary notice in the *New York Times*, Jan. 10, 1933, states that he was the "author of biographies" of Thomas Collier Platt and of McCombs.

John Randolph Bolling to George Creel

My dear George: [Washington] 4th August 1921

Your letter of August 3rd reached me this morning, and I at once laid it before Mr. Wilson. He says he can in no circumstances (nor for any amount of money) consent to the Hearst papers having the story. I have, therefore, wired you that it would not be necessary to hold the conference on next Monday, and am sending Mr. Baker a message to the same effect; also a copy of this letter. Mr. Linthicum[1] (Publicity Manager of the Democratic National Committee) has just informed me that he has been over the list of papers (he has had it since May) and will mail it to me tonight. I will forward it to your New York address.

We are all well and hope that you can run down to see us before long. With kindest regards;

Faithfully yours,   [John Randolph Bolling]

CCL (WP, DLC).
[1] Richard Linthicum.

To the Skandinaviska Kreditaktiebolaget

Gentlemen: [Washington] 5th August 1921

Please be good enough to forward me your cashier's check for the amount of my deposit with you, including interest on same as agreed.[1]

Your early attention will oblige;

Yours very truly,   [Woodrow Wilson]

CCL (WP, DLC).
[1] The bank replied that it enclosed to Wilson's order a check for Kr. 137,176.02 on the National City Bank of New York. Skandinaviska Kreditaktiebolaget to WW, Aug. 19, 1921, TLS (WP, DLC).

From Edwin Thomas Meredith

My dear Mr. Wilson: Des Moines, Iowa August 6th, 1921.

I have your letter of June 29th, acknowledged by my Secretary under date of July 5th and handed me upon my return to the office.

You give me more credit than I deserve in stating that I was more active than any others in the matter of the chair. The facts are that each and every one of the Cabinet members were equally interested, and our embarrassment was that we did not know how to properly give expression to the very great friendship we have for you and the deep obligation we feel we owe to you. I am sure there is no member of your Cabinet who does not prize as the greatest privilege that has ever come to him, the opportunity to serve under you.

I am sending each member a copy of your letter.

Will you kindly remember me to Mrs. Wilson?

With all good wishes, and assurance of deepest affection for both of you, I beg to remain   Sincerely,   E. T. Meredith

TLS (WP, DLC).

To Edwin Thomas Meredith

My dear Mr. Meredith: [Washington] 9th August 1921

Your generous letter of August sixth has given me the deepest pleasure, and I feel it is sufficient reward for the labors of office to have won the friendship and confidence of men like yourself and the other trusted colleagues of my cabinet. The chair will mean much to me.

Mrs. Wilson joins me in kindest regards to you and Mrs. Meredith.   Cordially and sincerely yours,   [Woodrow Wilson]

CCL (WP, DLC).

From Bernard Mannes Baruch

My dear Mr. Wilson: New York August 10, 1921.

This morning I talked to Tom Chadbourne on the telephone and he did not seem to be averse to the suggestion you had made regarding the chairmanship. But he feels that Roper¹ would make a better man. I am inclined to believe that Chadbourne as chairman would lend a great deal of dignity to the office. It might be possible then to get Roper as the active chairman in the field constantly visiting the various states and counties. This might make a wonderful combination.

I dislike very much to refer to the matter of the letter to Mr. Ochs of the New York Times because I know how strongly you feel about it. However, though it may be at the risk of causing you to be annoyed at me, I am going to make a suggestion. I myself have written a letter congratulating Mr. Ochs upon his twenty-fifth anniversary as publisher of the Times and wishing him continuing success and the enjoyment of his friends and associates.

After all, the New York Times has always been one of our strongest supporters even though it may not always have lent its support in the way we liked. It was one of the staunchest advocates of the League of Nations and even now is advocating this cause more actively than any other newspaper. I am wondering if you could possibly write something personally to Mr. Ochs congratulating him and wishing him further success, referring to the great news feature of the Times, which is indeed an almost encyclopedic compendium of the news of the day. What I have in mind is that we be careful not to alienate the support of such a powerful influence as the Times. After all, it has been friendly to us and particularly to you according to the way the light has broken upon them.

It was such a real pleasure to see you and Mrs. Wilson. I was particularly pleased to see such a rapid improvement in yourself.

Always with affectionate regards I am,

Devotedly yours,   Bernard M. Baruch

TLS (WP, DLC).
[1] That is, Daniel Calhoun Roper.

From John Firman Coar[1]

My dear Mr. Wilson: [At sea] August 10, 1921.

I am just returning from an extended trip of investigation through Germany, and am writing you this brief note before landing at Montreal.

It was my privilege to sit in numerous confidential conferences with the political, industrial, commercial, financial, agricultural, and labor leaders of Germany, and to obtain an intimate insight into the conditions of that country. What I have seen, the confidential reports, and the as yet unpublished statistics, together with much other material that came to hand, have filled me with foreboding, not of the kind usually discussed in our papers, but of a kind that causes me to regard the situation as little short of catastrophic.

I have hastened home, leaving my secretary in Berlin to gather up loose threads, convinced that there is only one way out, namely the effective and complete establishment of the idea for which you sacrificed so much.

If your health permits I should be glad to give you my observations, if not I trust you can put me in communication with those who, like myself, are willing to make some sacrifices for the coming generations. I expect to confer with Mr. Hamilton Holt and others in the premises. So far as my limited means permit I shall devote myself to the cause that ought to be dear to any American. Unhappily, I can do so only part of each year. Six months must be given to obtain the means to carry on the other six months.

Please do not reply if your health is not greatly improved. I shall manage somehow.

With the very best wishes and in sincere appreciation

Faithfully yours,   John F. Coar
Kingston, Mass.

ALS (WP, DLC).
[1] Professor of Germanic Languages and Literatures at the University of Alberta.

To Tom Moore[1]

My dear Mr. Moore: [Washington] 12th August 1921

It is delightful to have such generous friends, and I shall value the motion picture equipment not only for the entertainment it will afford me but also and even more as an evidence of your generous kindness.

I thank you and your associates from the bottom of my heart, and I want you to know that I am grateful for your constant interest in my entertainment during my convalescence.

With warmest good wishes;
Cordially and gratefully yours,   [Woodrow Wilson]

CCL (WP, DLC).
[1] President of Moore's Theaters Corp. of Washington. He had written to say that he had just sent Wilson "specially constructed motion picture equipment" for his residence. T. Moore to WW, Aug. 11, 1921, TLS (WP, DLC).

John Randolph Bolling to John Firman Coar

My dear Professor Coar: [Washington] 12th August 1921

Mr. Wilson asks me to express to you his deep interest and appreciation of your letter of August tenth, received this morning.

In order to secure a much needed rest, Mr. Wilson is making practically no appointments at this time. He suggests that you get in touch with Mr. Bernard M. Baruch, 508 Madison Avenue, New York City, and talk over matters with him. At Mr. Wilson's suggestion I am sending your letter by this mail to Mr. Baruch, asking that he arrange to see you.

Mr. Wilson will be glad to look over a synopsis of your observations, if you decide to put them in that shape.
Cordially yours,   [John Randolph Bolling]

CCL (WP, DLC).

John Randolph Bolling to Bernard Mannes Baruch

My dear Mr. Baruch: [Washington] 12th August 1921

Mr. Wilson asks me to say that your letter of August tenth is full of interesting suggestions which he will be glad to talk over with you the next time you come down.

Mr. Wilson requests that I send you the enclosed letter from Professor John F. Coar, Kingston, Mass., and copy of my reply. He is greatly interested in this matter, and will be glad if you will arrange to have an interview with Professor Coar at a time convenient to you both. The whole-hearted earnestness of the Professor's letter has greatly impressed Mr. Wilson and—in view of your recent visit to Germany—he feels you are specially qualified to see him.

With kindest regards from us all;

Sincerely yours,   [John Randolph Bolling]

CCL (WP, DLC).

Katrina Brandes Ely Tiffany to Edith Bolling Galt Wilson

My dear Mrs. Wilson: Montreal Canada August 12th [1921]

You were kind to act on Mrs. McAdoo's request so promptly and so satisfactorily and the Committee of the Woodrow Wilson Award[1] is correspondingly grateful. The photograph of Mr. Wilson[2] followed me here and, after enjoying it a day, I sent it on to headquarters for the committee's further consideration. It's a fine photograph and a *fine* likeness—but—I'm sorry to hear it's the best you and your husband can do for us! What we wanted Mrs. McAdoo to ask you for was a *list* of the portrayals that have been [made] of Mr. Wilson by free-hand artists—if I may so distinguish them from artist-photographers! I mean by that, portrait painters or sculptors. They tell us, for instance, that the Wedgewood pottery people have a bas-relief of Mr. Wilson which along with one of Clemenceau and Lloyd-George were given wide circulation in 1919.[3] Does Mr. Wilson happen to have one of the casts or know where we could find the original? Further, is the Jo Davison bust[4] a good portrayal & if so, where is that? And the Sir William Orpen portrait[5] etc etc.

We think we have an interesting plan for the certificate to be given donors to the award fund—or *founders* as we shall call them all, irrespective of the size of the contributions. We hope to make it a really good thing from the artistic as well as sentimental viewpoint and are inviting five or six of the most distinguished *etchers* to compete for the winning design. We propose to say to them, by way of specifications, "we want a portrayal of Mr. Wilson incorporated—in classic design or in portraiture & you may etch from the following representations" (giving a list of the two or three best).

We purpose further to have a jury of artists pass on the portrayals best suited to the purpose, finally, on the design itself and—*I*, at least, expect these etchings to become *very* valuable family heirlooms in a mere century or so besides being highly-prized household treasures to-day.

It's a crime to have written you at such weary length—in long hand, too! But—can you, will you, send to

Mr. Edward S. Morse[6]
Care Woodrow Wilson Foundation
150 Nassau St
New York

the list of portrayals & their whereabouts we've been needing?

With very warm greetings to your husband (if I may be so bold!) believe me to be

Very Sincerely Yours,   Katrina Ely Tiffany

ALS (WP, DLC).

[1] Contributors to the fund drive of the Woodrow Wilson Foundation, as it was now being called, were to receive certificates with Wilson's picture on it. The executive committee of the foundation had announced a limited competition to create the design of the certificate. The winner, to be chosen by a committee headed by Charles Dana Gibson, would be awarded a prize of $500. *New York Times*, Nov. 14, 1921.

[2] The Harris & Ewing "official" presidential portrait, made in 1916. A reproduction of it appears on the title pages of the volumes in this series.

[3] The Editors have not seen this bas relief.

[4] Jo Davidson executed his bust of Wilson in 1916. A reproduction appears in the illustration section of Vol. 37. See also J. Davidson to WW, June 13, 1916, Vol. 37.

[5] It is reproduced in the illustration section of Vol. 60.

[6] Executive Secretary of the Woodrow Wilson Foundation.

A News Item

[*Aug. 16, 1921*]

Wilson at His Law Offices for First Time;
He Sees Clients and Walks Without Help

Washington, Aug. 16.—Woodrow Wilson went today for the first time to the law offices of Wilson & Colby. The rooms were not quite in condition for occupancy, as the book shelves were empty and the decorators had not yet begun work on the walls, but the ex-President was said to have enjoyed the several hours he spent in them engaged in legal work.

The firm has its quarters in a big building at 1,315 F Street, formerly occupied by the Shipping Board and adjacent to the Adams Building, on the site of the residence of another President of the United States, John Quincy Adams. Mr. Wilson went to the offices in his motor car, accompanied by his secretary. He entered the building by a rear doorway and walked to the elevator and from the elevator to his offices without assistance.

Bainbridge Colby, his law partner, met him in the offices and they were busy for most of the afternoon engaged in seeing visitors, two of whom were clients. He left the building by the rear door.

The offices of Wilson & Colby have been fitted with fine desks and richly upholstered chairs and occupy much space. Mr. Wilson's friends are gratified over the interest he is showing in his law practice and in things generally, and believe that his new activities will have a beneficial effect upon his health.

Printed in the *New York Times*, Aug. 17, 1921.

To Edith Bolling Galt Wilson

Beloved,   [Washington] 17 Aug., '21
    You have filled these two years with happy memories   W.

ALI (WP, DLC).

John Firman Coar to John Randolph Bolling

My dear Mr. Bolling: Kingston, Mass. August 17, 1921
    Will you be kind enough to convey to Mr. Wilson my very warm appreciation of the interest he has taken in my recent letter apropos the German problem and the international situation? Your letter was the first to reach me in reply to numerous communication[s] I mailed at Quebec.
    I have written to Mr. Bernard M. Baruch, and hope for a favorable reply so that I may have the privilege of discussing the whole problem with him. As soon as the report is completed on which I am now at work, I shall send a copy to Mr. Wilson. Unhappily it seemed advisable to leave my secretary in Germany to complete certain details, so that I am obliged to do the whole work myself, and this rather delays matters. But I hope to finish before the week end.
    Kindly convey to Mr. Wilson my very sincere appreciation together with my profound conviction that his efforts of the past years will yet bear fruit. I wish him a speedy and complete recovery, and meanwhile a well-earned rest. Some of us others will carry on to the best of our ability.
                            Cordially yours,   John F. Coar

TLS (WP, DLC).

John Randolph Bolling to Edward S. Morse

Dear sir: [Washington] 17th August 1921

Mrs. Tiffany has requested Mrs. Wilson to send you certain information regarding likenesses of Mr. Wilson, which it is proposed to use in connection with the work of the Foundation.

Mrs. Wilson sent Mrs. Tiffany a photograph which both she and Mr. Wilson consider the best likness of him that they have ever seen. There is no other "portrayal" of Mr. Wilson that they like as well.

Mrs. Tiffany makes reference to a bas-relief reproduced by the Wedgewood Pottery people, but neither Mr. nor Mrs. Wilson recall having ever seen it. The Jo Davison bust is distinctly not satisfactory to either of them.

Mrs. Wilson appreciates fully that the trouble the Committee is taking is a sincere effort to produce something that will be artistic; but so many hundreds of people have tried the same thing and failed, that they believe it would be best to use a reproduction of the photograph. Thousands of them have been sent out, and it has become known as the "official" photograph.

If Mrs. Wilson can be of any further service in the matter, please advise me.   Cordially yours,   [John Randolph Bolling]

CCL (WP, DLC).

An Announcement

[c. Aug. 18, 1921]

Mr. Woodrow Wilson and Mr. Bainbridge Colby
announce the formation of a partnership for
the practice of law under the firm name of
Wilson & Colby
with offices at No. 1315 F Street American
National Bank Building, Washington D. C.
and No. 32 Nassau Street, New York City

Printed copy (H. A. Garfield Papers, DLC).

John Randolph Bolling to Brentano's of Washington

Dear sirs: [Washington] 18th August 1921

Kindly procure and send to Mr. Woodrow Wilson, at the above address, six copies of THE NEW REPUBLIC, issue of February 16th, 1918,[1] and oblige;

Very truly yours,   [John Randolph Bolling]

CCL (WP, DLC).
[1] "Labor and the New Social Order: A Report on Reconstruction by the Sub-Committee of the British Labor Party," *The New Republic*, XIV, Part Two, Feb. 16, 1918. This was the well-known manifesto and program of the Labour party for British postwar reconstruction.

From Cleveland Hoadley Dodge

My dear Woodrow: New York August Eighteen 1921

This is the first time for eight years that I have called you anything but President and it seems rather funny, but whilst you are, of course, an extraordinary citizen, in the eyes of the law you are nothing but an ordinary Washington attorney.

I am simply dropping you a line to tell you how overjoyed I am that you are really feeling well enough to get to your office and I wish you all sorts of happiness and success in your work there. I should think that probably you are better by having something regular to do, as I know whenever I get out of my regular habits, I commit some indiscretion and have to pay the consequences.

We have just come back from a delightful cruise on "Corona." My two daughters[1] were with us for the first time in a long while and it was a splendid opportunity to see them without interruptions, or telephone calls. I seriously thought of asking you and Mrs. Wilson to join us on the cruise, but I happened to meet E. P. Davis a little while ago and he told me that he would strongly oppose your running any risk of going off on a sailing yacht, and perhaps it was just as well, as we had one unfortunate adventure, running the yacht aground on the reef at the mouth of the Connecticut when the tide was going out. We had to wait for ten hours until the tide came in and floated us off. At dead low water we were at an angle of 33 degrees and it would not have been very pleasant for you. Looking out, though, on the mouth of the Connecticut and thinking of the old days when we used to go up to Lyme and get you, was quite interesting.

I would give anything to have a good, long talk with you. The way things are going in Washington must interest you exceedingly and the news in this morning's paper that the last country has come in[2] and that the International Court will be founded seems to make it very evident that this country will have to use the League of Nations, or be left out in the cold world. I hope the Democratic party in Congress is not going to play too much politics and go back to Bryanism. It is most significant that the moment your grip is taken off they wallow around as they used to years ago.

We think of you and talk of you and Mrs. Wilson very often and sincerely hope that your new venture will be a good thing for your health and most successful in every way. I wonder if you are ever going to be able to come to New York again. How would it do for you and Mrs. Wilson to come up to Riverdale to the anniversary of that gastly* Sunday when you sat in an armchair in my library and discussed what you would say to Germany about an armistice. I was pointing out that chair the other day to someone and said that I thought it would be an interesting thing to have a plate put upon it commemorating the great event.[3]

Grace joins me in much love to you both.

Yours affectionately,   Cleveland H. Dodge

* Pretty good for "gasless," but far from true. The best of stenographers will make mistakes so I leave it

TLS (WP, DLC).
  [1] Elizabeth Wainwright Dodge (Mrs. George Herbert) Huntington and Julia Parish Dodge (Mrs. James Childs) Rea. Mrs. Huntington lived in Constantinople, where her husband was professor at and vice-president of Robert College. The Reas lived in Pittsburgh.
  [2] It had been announced by the League of Nations in Geneva on August 17 that Spain had become the twenty-fourth nation to ratify the proposal for an international court of justice, thus enabling the League to proceed with its organization. *New York Times*, Aug. 18, 1921.
  [3] Wilson had lunch on Sunday, October 13, 1918, with the Dodges at Riverdale. The reply of the German government to Wilson's Armistice note of October 8 had just come in. Dodge later donated the armchair to Princeton; it had a plate on it saying that Wilson had written his reply to the German government of October 14 while sitting in the chair. The last time we saw the chair it was in great disrepair, and we assume that it was discarded.

John Randolph Bolling to John Firman Coar

My dear Professor Coar: [Washington] 19th August 1921

Your interesting letter of August 17th reached me this morning, and Mr. Wilson wishes me to thank you for your messages to him. He bids me tell you that he is most interested in your progress, and will look forward with pleasure to receiving a copy of your report.

I understand that Mr. Baruch has returned to New York, and I have no doubt you will be able to arrange an interview at an early date.

Cordially and sincerely yours,   [John Randolph Bolling]

CCL (WP, DLC).

To Cleveland Hoadley Dodge

My dear Cleve.:   Washington D C 20th August 1921

Your letters are always better than a tonic for me, and the one just received is delightful.

I thank you with all my heart for your thoughtful kindness. It would indeed be delightful if we could have a cruise on the "Corona" with you, but unfortunately I must deny myself such pleasure for the present.

Mrs. Wilson joins me in affectionate messages to you all. If your daughters are still with you please give them a special greeting from me. I wish I could share with you the pleasure of seeing them.

Faithfully and affectionately yours,   Woodrow Wilson

P.S. The next time you turn your face this way let me know in good time that you are coming so that I may arrange for an uninterrupted talk.

TLS (WC, NjP).

A Memorandum by Norman Hezekiah Davis

Williamstown, Mass., August 23, 1921.

At the request of Lord Bryce I went to see him last night at 9:30 after the evening address at the Institute of Politics and we talked until 11:30. At the beginning of our conversation we got into a discussion of the Treaty of Versailles. I told Lord Bryce that I agreed with most of his criticisms of the treaty provisions especially those of the Austrian and Hungarian treaties giving Tyrol to Italy, Thrace to Greece, Bessarabia to Roumania and the division of the Banat without plebiscite. I called his attention however to the fact that with exception of Tyrol which was agreed to by mistake the other transfers were made after U. S. was forced to or did withdraw from the Supreme Council—because of the Senate's attitude on the Treaty—and that the U. S. had been opposed to such annexations and settlements. I said I did not however agree with his condemnation of the Treaty made in one of his public lectures on the ground that it was so bad it had already required revision—that to my mind the principal virtue of the Treaty—aside from the Covenant of the League of Nations—was its susceptibility to revision; that it was intended there should be revision with the machinery provided therein in accordance with developments and improvement in public opinion and conscience. I then recalled to him the sudden changes following the Armistice, when the idealism and

exalted motives which sustained the peoples and carried them to
victory was obscured and overcome by the surging tide of passions
for revenge and selfish ambitions—accentuated by misinformed
and misdirected public opinion; that the political leaders in Europe
not only made no effort to stem this tide but increased its volume
by going with it until it became so powerful that no government
could remain in power which did not go with it. The peoples &
their leaders forgot all that they had stood for, and then under
these unfortunate conditions the Peace Conference was held in
Paris where this surging tide was at its highest. The one leader
who never for one moment lost the vision or sight of the true objective for restoring and maintaining peace harmony and stability
was Woodrow Wilson. The latter has been accused of obstinacy
because he was not willing to sacrifice his ideals; of holding his
position too grimly to make necessary compromises to get the
treaty ratified. Lord Bryce said he quite fully realized that in the
United States the fight on Wilson and the treaty was purely political but that he was anxious to know just why Wilson gave in to
Lloyd George & Clemenceau as much as he did in the treaty provisions and what he had in mind when he sent for his ship the
George Washington to be in Brest on May 1st, 1919. I told him the
President talked to me about this in April, when he was evidently
reaching a definite decision which he realized was most momentous. He had come to the conclusion that the British and French
Premiers were not willing or able to make settlements in complete
harmony with their moral pledges because they were hampered by
the secret treaties made before our entrance into the war which
they could not well cancel in respect to other nations without surrendering certain selfish ambitions which they held (altho he contended that in accepting his terms for the Armistice which were to
serve as a basis for peace they automatically cancelled all secret
treaties which conflicted with those terms) and that even if they
were willing in the face of existing adverse public opinion to make
a proper treaty it would probably fail of ratification and they would
be supplanted by political leaders even more reactionary and responsive to then prevailing inflamed public opinion. The President
had lost much confidence in Lloyd George and Clemenceau over
the Fiume incident. He told me they had both approved the statement he gave out on this and were to give out a statement the
following day supporting his position but that they didn't keep their
word.[1] Orlando had given warning that he would not return to a

[1] The most direct evidence of Lloyd George's and Clemenceau's reaction to Wilson's
statement on the Adriatic question of April 23, 1919, is found in Dr. Grayson's diary
entry of that date in Vol. 58. The statement is also printed at that date in *ibid.* The diary
entry confirms that the two Premiers did approve Wilson's manifesto, but they did not
give out their letter to Orlando, printed as Appendix III to the minutes of the Council

meeting of the big four and that he was going to make a public announcement which Wilson forestalled. In the conversation referred to the President said in substance that as a natural reaction from the war the people were confused; idealism was giving way to selfishness, prejudices and uncontrolled animosities which unscrupulous politicians were taking advantage of for their own selfish purposes; that even in the U. S. this was happening, as instanced by the resolution of the N. Y. legislature—on the preceding day—condemning his position on Fiume[2]—and other political activities. He realized with sorrow that with the unfortunate but probably temporary change in public opinion he could not count upon sufficient support to force through just the kind of treaty he wanted. Under such circumstances there were only two courses open to him—either to go home because he couldn't get what he wanted or to remain in Paris and get the best treaty possible. The former would undoubtedly be the popular thing to do. A statement to the American people that as the Allied Governments were still the same as of old—heaped in intrigue, selfishness & etc and unwilling to discard their old sinister diplomacy—he was unable to reach an agreement to which America could attach her signature and consequently had left them to stew in their juice— would be acclaimed with enthusiasm. This however would be an unwise step and the shirking of responsibility which would not stand the test of time and for which it would be impossible to escape blame for the moral and material damage resulting therefrom. Such a course taken by him would throw Europe into still greater turmoil with unforseen consequences. He felt that while this would just then be the popular course it would be the cowardly one and that while the American public might applaud it—being actuated by a traditional fear of European entanglements, distrust of European diplomacy, and by the reaction from the war—their approval would only be temporary because it would not accord with the real heart and soul of America. The latter course—which was finally adopted—seemed to be the only one which offered any hope and which certainly was the more honorable—namely—to remain in Paris, get the world at peace as soon as possible, get the League of Nations for maintaining peace, get the best treaty possible under

of Four printed at May 3, 1919, 10 a.m., *ibid.* Wilson told Grayson that Lloyd George had declared that he would "back up" Wilson's statement, but he did not say how he would do so. And Wilson commented to Grayson that the British Prime Minister was "as slippery as an eel," and that he "never knew when to count on him."

[2] Actually the joint resolution, signed by Governor Alfred E. Smith on April 7, 1919, requested that Wilson and the other American representatives at Paris support Italy's territorial claims, including those to Fiume and Dalmatia. The resolution is printed in *Treaty of Peace With Germany: Hearings Before the Committee on Foreign Relations United States Senate*, 66th Cong., 1st sess., Senate Document No. 106 (Washington, 1919), p. 1128.

the circumstances, and make provisions therein for improving it and adjusting differences growing out of it just as fast as developments required and as public opinion and conscience should permit and demand. He saw the all important necessity of getting the world at peace and had too much vision and practical wisdom to prolong that or jeopardize it in the face of adverse selfish aims and opinion provided he could secure adherence to the permanent provisions and principles which were so much more important than the little ephemeral claims which time would cancel. Lord Bryce expressed great interest in this information which gave him a clearer understanding of what happened. He asked if I had kept a diary in Paris. I told him that much to my regret I had not done so because I was simply too busy to do it but that I now intended to make notes of certain important happenings while still fresh in my memory. He said I must by all means write out what I had told him because it would be a most important contribution to history. We then discussed the "Khaki" Campaign conducted by Lloyd George in England—December 1918—the bad results and how Lloyd George had thus increased his difficulties in negotiating a just and workable treaty. He said this was inexcusable and unnecessary— that Lloyd George could have appealed just as successfully to the higher instincts of the British people, and that he had done a lot of harm. While admitting his vastly superior knowledge of England I expressed certain doubts—and instanced France, Italy and even the United States where idealism had given way at once to prejudices, greed, revenge, and political animosities and ambitions. I also recalled how a delegation from Parliament—representing a vast majority—had come to Paris to protest against Lloyd George making a sane and equitable settlement of the Reparations and other questions.[3]

I called Lord Bryce's attention to the fact that in spite of many unjust and unwise provisions in the treaty—the political opponents had been able to kill it in the U. S. by attacking the best part of it— its very soul—the League of Nations and that the Liberals here and especially in England who believed in the League and Wilson's principles had contributed to its defeat by a failure to realize the controlling factors which made it impossible to get a better treaty and by opposition to the treaty because it was not perfect.

(Copy) Norman H. Davis.

T MS (RSB Coll., DLC).
   [3] Davis' memory was faulty here. The parliamentary protest had actually taken the form of a telegram signed by 233 MPs and sent to Lloyd George in Paris on April 8, 1919. Davis was probably thinking of Andrew Bonar Law's flying trip to Paris on April 8 to discuss the parliamentary crisis with the Prime Minister. See ns. 1 and 5 to the extract from the Diary of Dr. Grayson printed at April 9, 1919, Vol. 57.

Brentano's of Washington to John Randolph Bolling

Dear Sir: Washington, D. C. August 25th, 1921.

Replying to your letter of August 18th for six copies of the New Republic of February 16, 1918, we would say the publishers have notified us that this edition is entirely exhausted.

This copy contained a special article entitled "Labor & New Social Order." If this is desired, we can secure a pamphlet of this article.

Awaiting your further instructions, We remain
                          Yours very truly,   Brentano's by H.N.

TLS (WP, DLC).

From Bainbridge Colby

My dear Mr President: New York City August 26, 1921

The enclosed telegram[1] addressed to you was forwarded to our New York office and I replied promptly by wire to the sender of the telegram, Mr W. H. Burson of Marion, Indiana, saying in effect that it was impossible for us to advise him as to his remedies or as to whether he had any basis for action at all, until we knew on what representations he had relied in making his investment.

Mr Burson is a retired farmer and stock-raiser living in Marion, Indiana.

He invested $50,000 in the preferred stock of the Haitian-American Corporation, a sugar concern operating a plantation and owning some public utilities in the Island of Haiti. The Company has suffered from the sensational decline in the price of sugar. There are at least two factions among its shareholders quarreling for control of the Company. The management of the Company is charged with incompetence and waste. Some heavy obligations, to-wit $3,000,000 to note-holders and about $700,000 to banks in addition, for current advances, have been incurred and are today obligations which take precedence over any interest of shareholders.

Mr Burson in response to my request has sent me the accompanying bundle of papers. It appears that he has deposited his stock with a Stockholder's Protective Committee of which Mr R[eginald]. B[ishop]. Lanier of Winslow, Lanier & Company, New York City, is chairman. This is a complication in any legal action that he may now take, but it is not an insuperable barrier.

Mr Burson is not, apparently, a well-educated man and his writing contains many misspelled words. I have not been able to get from him yet a connected statement of his case, but it is apparent that he has made a disastrous investment.

The Stockholder's Protective Committee proposes to buy in the property for the protection of the shareholders, and in order to do this has levied an assessment of $31.25 per share, which Mr Burson has been asked to remit. The Committee appears to have the power to assess the stock under the terms of the protective agreement.

Mr Burson is disinclined to pay the assessment. He wishes to be advised as to his chance of recovery against the promoters of the Company for misrepresentation of facts in connection with the sale of stock to him, or against the directors of the Company for mismanagement and waste.

I have today through our New York office obtained a two-weeks extention which will afford time to investigate the situation and determine upon a recommendation to Mr Burson.

I think you would be interested to run over these papers, not too minutely, as I have already culled their substance. As you will observe, the case is sent to you. I have made certain notes which will enable me to direct the investigation in New York, and when I see you next week we can have such conference as the matter then seems to warrant.

As you know, it is very hard to establish actionable waste and management on the part of a board of directors, as distinguished from general incompetence which is not actionable, particularly where the basic conditions in the business are known to have been so unfavorable as in the sugar business during the last year.

As to mis-statement of fact accompanying the sale of the stock to Mr Burson, I am unable to put my finger on anything that strikes me as an intentional and material misrepresentation.

Mr Burson however is in a tough position and I will interview the parties chiefly concerned in the matter in New York next week and sift the facts conscientiously.

Cordially always,   Colby

TLS (WP, DLC).
¹ It is missing.

A News Report

[Aug. 27, 1921]

WILSON IS CHEERED BY THEATRE CROWD
Former President Shows Marked Improvement
in His Physical Condition.

Washington, Aug. 27.—That Woodrow Wilson is steadily improving physically, was demonstrated tonight when, after seeing a vaudeville show at B. F. Keith's theatre and walking into and out of the playhouse unassisted, he stood up in an open automobile and waved his hat in response to the plaudits of a large crowd on the G Street side of the playhouse.

The former President was accompanied by Mrs. Wilson and by her two brothers, John Randolph Bolling and R. G. Bolling,[1] and occupied a seat on the left hand side of the main auditorium. When President, he usually occupied the Presidential box, which last night was occupied by President Harding, who went to the same theatre, accompanied by Mrs. Harding and Senator and Mrs. New.[2] Now the former President, who likes to be known as "Mr. Wilson," prefers to go to the theatre like the average citizen and will not use a box, although one would gladly be placed at his disposal at any time by the management of the theatre.

The demonstration for Mr. Wilson when he left the theatre was more notable than usual. The street was jammed with more than a thousand persons, most of them theatregoers who rushed out into the street to cheer and shout and watch the former President enter a waiting automobile, parked beside the theatre.

He was cheered half a dozen times as he went to his car, and the applause was such that, as he entered it, unassisted, he stood up and waving his flat-brimmed straw hat, bowed a cordial acknowledgement.

Inquiry revealed that Mr. Wilson has been going regularly to Keith's Theatre every Saturday night throughout the Summer and since Spring. He has his tickets reserved in advance and always occupies the same seats.

Tonight Mr. Wilson wore a Tuxedo and looked very much improved in health. While he still carried a cane and used it going into and out of the theatre, he did not limp nearly as much as when he left the White House on March 4 last. It was the subject of general comment that Mr. Wilson looked much better tonight than he did several months ago. He also seemed to relish the demonstration by the throng.

Further evidence of the improvement in Mr. Wilson's health came on Aug. 17 when, as senior member of the law firm of Wilson & Colby, he spent several hours in the firm's offices on the sixth floor of the building at 1,315 F Street, N.W., which formerly housed the United States Shipping Board.

After his first visit to the new law offices some Democrats at the Capitol began to wonder whether the opening up of large offices in Washington by Mr. Wilson and Bainbridge Colby meant that they contemplated acting as a sort of directing agency for the Democratic Party with a view to a Democratic reaction in the next three years. In response to that intimation, the statement was authorized that Mr. Wilson and former Secretary Colby had effected a law partnership and not a political organization.

Mr. Wilson has made subsequent daytime visits to his new law offices. When entering the building he has made use of the rear entrance to avoid gatherings of passersby on F Street, the main business street of the Capital, and because of the fact that it is more or less difficult for him to enter his automobile.

Printed in the *New York Times*, Aug. 28, 1921.
  [1] Actually, Richard Wilmer Bolling.
  [2] That is, Harry Stewart New of Indiana and Kathleen Milligan New.

From Bainbridge Colby

My dear Mr President: New York City August 27, 1921

I send you some editorials upon the treaty with Germany, clipped from last night's "Globe" and "Evening Post," of New York; also editorials in this morning's "Times" and "World," of New York.[1]

The New York "Tribune"[2] comes across with its usual rancor and partisan obeisance, but the New York "Herald" has no editorial allusion to the subject.[3] Mr Munsey[4] may be trying to ascertain what his long-cherished convictions are, or it is possible that the policy of scuttle is a little too rank, even for him.

Let us be of good cheer and hope as long as we can. The "Times" editor is evidently frightened at what he is doing, but nevertheless is trying to make a noise like a man. That you may know I am entirely in accord with your estimate of this paper, I might say that it reminds me of the lawyer of whom it was said that "he feels that he has completely severed his moorings when he says 'Perhaps.' "

I wanted to ask you yesterday what you thought of the Panama-Costa Rican incident.[5] With my impressions of South America still

  [1] All the editorials commented on the separate peace effectuated by the Treaty of Berlin, signed in the German capital on August 25, 1921. The *Evening Post*, the *New York Times*, and the New York *World* excoriated the treaty as "sordid," "humiliating," "a cash-register peace," etc., although the *Evening Post* said that the treaty was perhaps unavoidable in the present condition of American politics, and the *New York Times* said that the Senate should approve it because it established peace between the United States and Germany.
  [2] "Disentangled," *New York Tribune*, Aug. 27, 1921.
  [3] Actually, it did print a lead editorial on the treaty in its issue of August 26, 1921. It strongly favored a separate peace with Germany.
  [4] That is, Frank Andrew Munsey, owner of the *New York Herald*.
  [5] This "incident" was the latest manifestation of a dispute over the boundary line between Panama and Costa Rica which dated back to the nineteenth century, when Panama was still a province of Colombia. The matter was submitted by Colombia and Costa Rica to the arbitration of President Émile Loubet of France, who rendered his decision on September 11, 1900. However, the boundary line remained a subject of continuing friction following the establishment of Panama as an independent republic in 1903.

fresh in mind as the result of my trip last winter, I regret any action that tends to weaken our tenuous hold upon South American confidence and favor. One of the great things you succeeded in doing, which is possibly obscured by the greater things you did, was to plant the seeds of a genuine confidence in our attitude toward Latin America. I can't but feel that a relapse into the hectoring tone of the past and the quick recourse to words of finality and to a policy that has a clear note of coercion in it will prove a great setback for us throughout South America.

There is of course much to be said in favor of the general prin-

---

After repeated unsuccessful attempts by Panama and Costa Rica to negotiate a settlement based upon the Loubet decision, the two countries agreed in 1911, under the auspices of the United States Department of State, to submit the dispute to a second arbitration, this time by the Chief Justice of the United States, Edward Douglass White. White gave his decision on September 12, 1914. Panama immediately objected to his ruling, on the ground that he had exceeded the agreed-upon limits of the arbitration, and announced that it would never accept his award of certain disputed territories to Costa Rica. Here the matter rested, largely due to the upheaval of the World War, until early 1921. See William David McCain, *The United States and the Republic of Panama* (Durham, N. C., 1937), pp. 119-43. A translation of Loubet's decision is printed in *FR 1910*, pp. 786-87; White's decision is printed in *FR 1914*, pp. 1000–1015.

On February 21, 1921, Costa Rican troops seized the town of Pueblo Nuevo de Coto in one of the disputed areas near the Pacific Ocean. A Panamanian force retook the town on February 27. Further armed clashes took place at Pueblo Nuevo de Coto on March 1 and at Bocas del Toro, near the Atlantic coast, on March 4-5. Colby, on behalf of the Wilson administration, sent separate notes to Panama and Costa Rica on March 3, in which he urged both countries to refrain from further hostilities and advances in the disputed areas. The incoming Secretary of State, on March 5, reiterated to both governments the request for a cessation of hostilities. He also indicated that he considered the White arbitration award a definitive settlement of the boundary dispute, a position he was to repeat with increasing forcefulness numerous times over the next several months. The armed conflicts did cease, but the Panamanian government again stated that it could not accept the White decision. In response, Hughes sent a lengthy note to Panama on March 15, in which he defended the Loubet and White arbitrations and declared that Panama had to comply with the terms of both. This led Belisario Porras, the President of Panama, to appeal directly to President Harding in a telegram of March 18, in which he called the demand that Panama accept the White award "painful and humiliating." Harding responded on March 19 that he would be distressed if the Panamanian government had cause to "feel wounded," but that the communications of Secretary Hughes in the matter had been sent with his knowledge and "hearty approval" and that the decision of Chief Justice White "must be the unalterable position of this government." In response to another very lengthy note of protest from the Panamanian government, Hughes on April 27 sent a long note in reply, in which, after rejecting all the Panamanian contentions point by point, he demanded that Panama comply with the terms of the White award within sixty days. When the Panamanian government continued to procrastinate after the sixty days had expired, Hughes on August 18 informed that government that the United States saw no reason to advise the government of Costa Rica to delay any longer in taking possession of the territories assigned to it in the Loubet and White decisions. When the Panamanian government then asked if the United States would stand aside should hostilities be resumed between Panama and Costa Rica, Hughes on August 22 telegraphed the statement that the American government could not permit a renewal of hostilities by Panama against Costa Rica, should the latter take peaceful possession of the lands assigned to it. William Jennings Price, the American Minister to Panama, telegraphed Hughes on August 23 that Narciso Garay, the Panamanian Foreign Minister, had stated that there would be no further resistance to Costa Rica's taking possession of the territories in dispute.

The correspondence of 1921 on this matter is printed in *FR 1921*, I, 175-228, and all quotations are from that source. Virtually all of the correspondence was printed in the *New York Times*, and the notes in McCain, pp. 206-24, provide citations to the documents printed in that newspaper.

ciple that parties to an arbitration should abide by the award. On the other hand, our elaborate machinery of appellate review shows how tempered is our own regard for judicial inerrancy, and after all Panama's contention was tantamount to a motion for reargument on the ground that the Court, in the person of the late Justice White, had exceeded its jurisdiction and misapprehended material questions of fact. I half suspect that the present Secretary of State was influenced, maybe unconsciously, by a partisan feeling of loyalty to the Court of which he was so recently a member.

You doubtless know the circumstances under which Judge White's decision was reached and rendered. The record in the case, which was voluminous, was examined by comparatively a young lawyer (I think he is a member of the Washington bar) and his work was then submitted to Justice White, who adopted and approved it. I confess it has seemed to me, in view of the extreme sensitiveness of the small Latin States to any disregard of their sovereignty, that actual hostilities between Panama and Costa Rica could as easily have been deferred as they have now been prevented, and in view of the years that have elapsed since the White award a few months for the formal consideration of Panama's motion to reargue or to reopen would by no means have been wasted.

South America, to a large extent sincerely and to a very considerable extent as the result of hostile propaganda, regards our attitude toward the Latin-American nations as imperialistic. We are unfeignedly disliked and distrusted in influential quarters throughout South America, and the latest Panama incident will certainly accomplish nothing toward the softening of this attitude.

I am getting away on an afternoon train and tomorrow I expect to motor up to Stockbridge. I will not forget to give your message to Norman Davis. I am looking forward with pleasure to spending a day with him, and I shall hope to see you some day toward the end of the coming week.

I enclose some lines addressed to you from Mr Ralph R. Rice of San Francisco[6] which came in the mail this morning.

With kindest regards,   Cordially always,   Colby

P.S. I have just learned from Mr Bolling of your wishes in regard to the current mail coming to the office. This is good. B.C.

TLS (WP, DLC).
[6] It is missing.

To Bainbridge Colby

My dear Colby: Washington D C 28th August 1921

I must admit that my first impression regarding the Panama-Costa Rica trouble was that Panama was committing an offence in refusing to carry out any award that it had agreed to accept, which could not be countenanced. But your letter of yesterday modifies my view considerably.

I wish that we might be given another opportunity to set the country right in the view of Latin America.

Faithfully yours,   Woodrow Wilson

TLS (B. Colby Papers, DLC).

To Jessie Woodrow Wilson Sayre

My darling Jessie,   Washington D C [c. August 28, 1921]

This scribble is intended as a birthday letter and is freighted with love for you all. It's very difficult for me to manage a pen nowadays.[1] I think about you all constantly and am cheered to think of all the many things I love in you and your wonderful children. May God bless you all and bring to you, my sweet daughter, many, many happy returns!   Your devoted   Father.

ALS (WC, NjP).
    [1] He wrote this letter with a pencil.

To Joseph Patrick Tumulty

My dear Tumulty: [Washington] 3d September 1921

I would be very much obliged and gratified if you would press the claim against the taxicab company, for damage to my touring car, which I placed in your hands several weeks ago.

I don't see how the company can decently resist the claim, and it ca[u]ses me considerable mortification and chagrin not to be able to pay the people who made the repairs to my car.

Affectionately yours,   [Woodrow Wilson]

CCL (WP, DLC).

John Randolph Bolling to Franklin Delano Roosevelt

My dear Mr. Roosevelt: [Washington] 3d September 1921

In a letter[1] I have just received from Mr. Robert C. Stuart, Chairman, The National Council of Woodrow Wilson Clubs, he says:

"I also note in the paper that 'The Foundation' is preparing to appoint some one to take charge of raising their fund at the various colleges. * * * It is my impression that the prestige of our clubs at the colleges would be seriously affected if a rival appeal was directed there by a professional and it is unlikely that we could raise any considerable amount of money for some months thereafter."

Mr. Wilson suggests that I send the above quotation along to you for such action as you deem best.

Cordially yours,   [John Randolph Bolling]

P.S. Mr. & Mrs. Wilson join me in the hope that you have entirely recovered from your illness.[2]

CCL (WP, DLC).
    [1] It is missing.
    [2] Roosevelt had been stricken on August 10-11, 1921, at his summer home on Campobello Island, New Brunswick, Canada, with an illness which involved first the paralysis of his legs and soon his entire body below the waist. It was not until Dr. Robert Williamson Lovett, a noted specialist of Boston, was able to visit and examine Roosevelt on August 25 that his disease was correctly diagnosed as poliomyelitis (infantile paralysis).
    The *New York Times* reported on August 27 that Roosevelt had been seriously ill but was improving and on August 29 that he had "caught a heavy cold and was threatened with pneumonia." It was only on September 16, the day after Roosevelt was brought back to New York, that it was publicly announced that he had polio. Even then, it was said that he had a mild case which would not leave him permanently crippled. *Ibid.*, Sept. 16, 1921. See Geoffrey C. Ward, *A First-Class Temperament: The Emergence of Franklin Roosevelt* (New York, 1989), pp. 582-602, and Frank Freidel, *Franklin D. Roosevelt: The Ordeal* (Boston, 1954), pp. 98-102.

From Bainbridge Colby

My dear Mr President: New York September 3, 1921

I have an interesting letter today from Mr Henry Morgenthau who says:

"Now is the time for some courageous, constructive criticism. Let us tell the Republicans in unmistakable language that they must make good their promises to the millions of people whom they induced to vote for them on definite representations, or forever stand convicted of either wilful mis-representation, or total incapacity to cope with this, and the still greater crisis, that confronts this country. This is no time to mince words."

To quote further from his letter, he says:

"My idea is to demand of them that they carry through the Disarmament program as one of the few means by which they can plead palliating circumstances against the impending universal condemnation which they will receive from mismanaging the Government. You and I know that they will be unable to carry through the Disarmament program. The most that can be accomplished is a slight diminution of the naval programs of the larger Powers, so that a skilfully-worded demand, even giving them proper encouragement, and holding out universal appreciation if they should succeed, will be most effective. The fact that Hays[1] promised the business men of America that the Republicans would be a government for business management should be alluded to, so that business men realize how they have been buncoed, inasmuch as there have been no tax reductions, and no government aid to solve the problems confronting business. We must picture Wilson's wonderful foresight, and his earnest efforts to avoid present conditions by establishing the rule of right between nations, thereby avoiding the calamities of continued war and economic bankruptcy which now prevail."

I think Mr Morgenthau reflects a widening desire that we should unlimber our batteries pretty soon. I still agree with you unreservedly that the hour has not yet struck for this, but there is unmistakably a chafing desire among many of the more thoughtful Democrats to go over the top and a longing for the first streaks of dawn when they hope to hear the signal.

Cordially always, Colby

TLS (WP, DLC).
[1] That is, Will H. Hays.

John Randolph Bolling to Louis Dembitz Brandeis, with Enclosure

My dear Mr. Justice: Washington D C 6th September 1921

At Mr. Wilson's suggestion, I enclose a letter which he received this morning from Dr. Herman, Syracuse, N. Y. The letter contains so many delightful references to you that Mr. Wilson feels sure you will be interested in reading it.

Cordially yours, John Randolph Bolling

TLS (L. D. Brandeis Papers, KyLoU).

E N C L O S U R E

From Israel Herman

Dear Sir: Syracuse, N. Y. September 4/21

Now that the Zionist Congress is in session Carlsbad, Czecho-Slovakian, the world is to know the historic part played by you in realization of the Zionist ideals. When darkness and uncertainty enshrouded the so called Balfour Declaration on account of pressure brought to bear by unfriendly but powerful forces and the fondest dreams of Zionists seemed to hang in the balance; the majestic figures of Woodrow Wilson and Louis D. Brandeis have appeared on the horizon to illumine the way of a dispersed & persecuted race on its homeward journey. You have proclaimed to the world that a just cause must be respected and that a new era must be ushered in—if the world is to exist on basis of democracy. You have nobly demonstrated the true traditional spirit of Americanism and all that it stands for—namely the inalienable right of every individual or nation to enjoy freedom. The future historian will depict Woodrow Wilson as second to Abraham Lincoln and the Jewish race will add another illustrious name in the pages of its glorious history already so rich in names of men and women endowed with hearts and brains—that of Woodrow Wilson. Only men of noble soul and prophetic vision can achieve such distinction. May your health improve and your days lengthened to continue your work in the cause of humanity.

I remain   Most Respectfully Yours,   I. Herman

ALS (WP, DLC).

From Joseph Patrick Tumulty

Dear Governor: Washington, D. C. 6 September 1921.

Now that I have returned from my vacation, I will push your claim against the taxicab company with all possible speed.

I will drop in to see you in a few days.

With affectionate regards, I am,

Cordially yours,   J P Tumulty

TLS (WP, DLC).

To William Edward Dodd

My dear Professor Dodd: Washington D C 8th September 1921

A letter from you[1] is always welcome and I particularly appreciate the pains that you take in your letter of September seventh to send me a message of friendship and cheer. You are certainly doing a most generous work that you may be sure I estimate at its true high value.

I shall look forward with real pleasure to seeing the new edition of your book, though I read about myself with little zest. What I appreciate in such a book is the author more than the subject.

With warm regards and best wishes from Mrs. Wilson and myself;

Cordially and sincerely your friend,   Woodrow Wilson

TLS (W. E. Dodd Papers, DLC).
[1] W. E. Dodd to WW, Sept. 7, 1921, ALS (WP, DLC).

To Newton Diehl Baker

[Washington] Sept. 9th 1921

We have just seen in papers notice of your mother's death and our hearts go out to you in deepest sympathy.[1]

Woodrow Wilson.

T telegram (WP, DLC).
[1] Mary Ann Dukehart (Mrs. Newton Diehl, Sr.) Baker had died in Cleveland on September 6.

Louis Dembitz Brandeis to John Randolph Bolling

My dear Mr Bolling: Washington D. C. Sept. 9/21

The gratitude to Mr Wilson which Dr Herman has expressed, millions of Jews throughout the world feel.

Please thank Mr Wilson for letting me see the letter (returned herewith) and give him my most cordial greetings.

Sincerely,   Louis D Brandeis

ALS (WP, DLC).

John Randolph Bolling to Carter Glass

My dear Senator: Washington D C 10th September 1921

Mr. Wilson asks that you let him know when you get back to town, as he wishes to communicate with you. He does not wish you to make a special trip here, or shorten your vacation, as the matter is not an urgent one.

Yours very truly,   John Randolph Bolling

TLS (C. Glass Papers, ViU).

To Tasker Howard Bliss

My dear friend: [Washington] 13th September 1921

I see it stated in the Baltimore Sun of this morning that the administration will consult you as its chief military adviser during the approaching conference.[1] I hope with all my heart that this is true. It would seem to be the dawning of intelligence in high quarters. If it is true, the country is to be congratulated. Let us hope that the full light will come soon.

Cordially and sincerely your friend,   [Woodrow Wilson]

CCL (WP, DLC).
[1] The so-called Washington Naval Conference, which was to convene on November 12, 1921.

To Carter Glass

My dear Glass: Washington D C 15th September 1921

That was a bully letter to White,[1] and I am sincerely obliged to you for letting me see it.

The time has come for drastic measures, and we must put our heads together to devise the wisest method. I shall try to get hold of you as soon as you return to Washington.

Mrs. Wilson joins me in warmest regards to you and Mrs. Glass.[2]

Affectionately yours,   Woodrow Wilson

TLS (C. Glass Papers, ViU).
[1] C. Glass to G. White, Aug. 23, 1921, TCL (WP, DLC), enclosed in C. Glass to JRB, Sept. 14, 1921, TLS (WP, DLC). Glass urged White to call an immediate meeting of the Democratic National Committee to take action to support the Democratic candidate in the election of a successor to Senator Albert B. Fall in October.
[2] Aurelia McDearmon Caldwell Glass.

From Tasker Howard Bliss

My dear Mr. Wilson: Washington, D. C. Sept. 15, 1921

I have been deeply touched by the receipt today of your note of the 13th instant. As I am leaving the city very early tomorrow morning for a few days I am writing at once, and hastily, to thank you for your very kind words.

No, I do not think that what you read in the Baltimore Sun has any foundation. Beyond an apparently cordial, and quite unsolicited, statement made to me in the casual conversation of a moment, at the residence of a common friend, by the present Secretary of State, to the effect that he was disposed to concur in my views on the armament question, I have had no communication on the subject with any member of the present government.

My own view is that the less military men have to do with the matter the better. It is too much to expect of human nature. My opinions are probably as liberal as those of any of my profession but I can easily conceive of the limitations that may hedge me due to the long training in one line of thought.

There is an interesting dispatch from Geneva in today's press. It purports to give the criticism of a Scandinavian delegate on the lack of progress by the League's military committee on disarmament. If what he says is true, it justifies my criticism, made at the time that military committee was formed, that the parturition of the idea of general disarmament would owe little to the kindly offices of military midwives.

It seems to me that you, of all men, must look to the approaching Conference with absorbing interest, in view of what I think will be its certain reaction on the question of the League.

What will happen when one nation after another says "We can do little or nothing towards disarmament, unless armaments are replaced by some sort of a reliable guarantee against aggression?" When the people of the United States realize that that one thing alone—the refusal to check public war in the only way that we have been able to check private war—by the granting of a mass-guarantee against individual wrongdoing, I think the people of the United States will be heard from again.

Thanking you again for your letter, I remain, as always,
                        Cordially Yours,   Tasker H. Bliss

ALS (WP, DLC).

To Franklin Delano Roosevelt

My dear Roosevelt: [Washington] 16th September 1921

I have learned with distress from this morning's paper that you are not well and have deemed it wise to go to the hospital.[1] I write to extend my heartfelt sympathy, and to express the hope you are mending rapidly.

Mrs. Wilson joins me in cordial messages to Mrs. Roosevelt and you, and I am, as always,

Your sincere friend,   [Woodrow Wilson]

CCL (WP, DLC).
[1] This letter was addressed to Roosevelt at the Presbyterian Hospital, New York.

From Kazimierz Lubomirski

My dear Mr. Wilson: Washington September 16th, 1921.

I have the high honor to transmit to you herewith the diploma of the honorary degree of Doctor of Philosophy conferred upon you by the University of Cracow, in recognition of your distinguished services to mankind and as a testimonial of the gratitude of the Polish people for the supreme aid rendered by you in the restoration of the Polish State to its legitimate place among the nations of the world.

I feel singularly privileged by the chance that makes it my duty to convey to you this memorial for it represents perhaps the highest honor in the power of the Polish people. The University of Cracow since its foundation in 1364 has been a center of Polish culture. During the hundred and fifty years of our cruel oppression, it nursed the fires of that culture and of that idealism that sent some of the sons of Poland to these shores to aid the struggle for American independence. It is thus natural that, upon the reconstitution of its State, the Polish people, desiring to recognize the priceless aid of the great friend who made that reconstitution possible, should feel that its greatest gift should emerge from that center which has been instrumental in the preservation of those vital sparks for the hour of liberation.

The gratitude of Poland to you is immortal. As its representative to this nation, I can do little more than testify to it. Yet I do feel that I am rendering it a little more concrete to you by delivering into your hands this diploma with all its significance.

Believe me, Sir, with best wishes for your good health and with assurance of my highest regard,

Sincerely yours,   Casimir Lubomirski

TLS (WP, DLC).

Helen Hamilton Gardener to Edith Bolling Galt Wilson

My dear Mrs. Wilson: Washington, D. C. September 20, 1921.

I have just returned from a visit in New York with Mrs. Carrie Chapman Catt and other prominent men and women and have something of a message to deliver to Mr. Wilson. If he can see me it will be a pleasure to me to call at his convenience.

I hope that Mr. Wilson has greatly improved in health during the summer months.

He would have been greatly heartened, I am sure, if he could have heard some of the things that were said at the conferences in New York.[1]   Very sincerely,   Helen H Gardener

TLS (WP, DLC).
[1] Mrs. Wilson invited her to tea on September 27.

Isaac Thomas Jones[1] to John Randolph Bolling

My dear Mr. Bolling: Minneapolis, Sept. 21, 1921

It is commonly understood around the offices of the Woodrow Wilson Foundation in New York that Mrs. Charles E. Simonson, 404 Henderson Avenue, West New Brighton, Staten Island, New York, was the first to suggest the plan which has taken form as the Woodrow Wilson Foundation. I do not think there is now or can ever be any controversy as to the fact that she originated the idea.[2]

She is a very estimable, attractive, modest and effective woman of middle age and is intensely devoted, not only to the great principles that Mr. Wilson has advocated, but as well to Mr. Wilson personally.

She would not permit the fact that she had originated the idea to be given publicity in such a way as to come to the knowledge of the general public, but I am sure she would appreciate it greatly if the fact were reported to Mr. Wilson and that she would prize highly a personal letter from him in acknowledgement of the loyalty which led to her activity in the matter.

Please permit me to suggest that if such a letter is written that it should not commit Mr. Wilson to the direct statement that Mrs. Simonson originated this particular idea; not that I think there will ever be any controversy over this point, but there is always that possibility and it will be well to protect him against such a contingency.

The Woodrow Wilson Foundation movement is progressing very satisfactorily and I have no doubt will develop into a spontaneous and wholesome expression of the good will of his fellow men.

I recall with the highest degree of pleasure your many courtesies to me on the occasion of my recent visit and thank you again.

With kindest personal regards,

Cordially yours,   I. T. Jones

TLS (WP, DLC).

[1] Lawyer of Des Moines, Iowa, active in Democratic politics in his state. He had been "Assistant National Campaign Manager" of the League to Enforce Peace, 1919-1920, and had worked with Tumulty in arranging the itinerary of Wilson's western speaking tour in 1919. Roosevelt and Hamilton Holt had employed him in early August 1921 as a field agent to organize local groups across the country to raise money for the endowment of the Woodrow Wilson Foundation, and he was on a cross-country tour when he wrote this letter. See I. T. Jones to WW, Aug. 13, 1921, TLS (WP, DLC).

[2] For additional information about her, see R. C. Stuart, Jr., to JRB, April 27, 1921, n. 1.

An Unpublished Statement[1]

[Sept. 25, 1921]

A few months ago the American Ambassador at London, in his first public utterance after reaching his post, aroused the indignation and disgust of every patriotic and right-minded American by misrepresenting with the most impudent falseness the aims of the United States in entering the War.[2]

But now there is laid before the Senate an amiable treaty of separate accommodation with Germany which seems to afford conclusive proof that the Ambassador spoke the real mind of the President and Secretary of State, if his speech was not actually inspired by them.

We entered the war with definite purposes clearly and officially avowed and enthusiastically accepted by the whole country, with the exception of a few bitter and blinded partisans. All the world acclaimed both our entrance and our purpose.

The war ended, with an armistice brought about by a distinct statement of what would be exacted of Germany as the conditions of peace. That statement, made by our own Executive with the express authorization of our allies, corresponded exactly with our own statement, at the outset, of our purposes in taking up arms.

Republican partisans would fain cover up or ignore these facts, because they can extract no party boast and no party advantage from them. But the facts stand, nevertheless. They are known to all the world, and it is by them that the nations will assess our honour and our good faith to our allies.

WHAT WERE THOSE TERMS?

DOES THIS TREATY SECURE THEM?

It is not to be wondered at that this treaty was so readily and so rapidly negotiated and agreed upon. It is of the sort most familiar and most easily understood in Berlin, inasmuch as it is based upon the old Prussian principle of sacrificing the interests of every other nation, whether friend or foe, in order to gain your own object. We now figure as the pupils of Prussia!

T MS (C. Glass Papers, ViU).
    [1] The typescript of the following statement bears a note by Carter Glass that Bolling sent it to him on September 25, 1921. There is a WWT draft of the statement in WP, DLC.
    [2] About Harvey's speech, see n. 2 to the extract from the Diary of Ray Stannard Baker printed at May 25, 1921.

A News Report[1]

[*Sept. 26, 1921*]

Wilson, Stricken 2 Years Ago,
Now Puts In Healthy Man's Day

Washington, Sept. 26 (By the Associated Press.)—Woodrow Wilson fell a sick man two years ago to-day. Since then he has passed under the shadow of death and out of the White House. To-day, besides following the ways of a retired gentleman, with a lively interest in the world's affairs, Mr. Wilson lives by the eight-hour day which he once told Congress was "adjudged by the thought and experience of recent years a thing upon which society is justified in insisting, as in the interest of health, efficiency and contentment."[2] He aims to have eight hours for sleep, eight hours for work and eight hours for relaxation, and keeps to the schedule pretty well.

Seven o'clock in the morning is his rising time. He shaves and bathes, and then takes calisthenic exercise prescribed by his physicians as beneficial in restoring the use of nerves and muscles which were impaired. He has breakfast with Mrs. Wilson. Two years of illness and slow convalescence have not affected his appetite.

The morning papers never are neglected, whatever else may demand attention. Half a dozen of them are delivered early and Mr. Wilson reads them thoroughly.

Then comes the morning's work. About that time the mail carrier, six days a week, delivers quite a packet of letters. They come from a variety of correspondents. Old friends of Administration days write informal, friendly notes or discourse on the politics of

    [1] The following story was undoubtedly written by Lionel Charles Probert, A.P. White House correspondent.
    [2] In his address to a joint session of Congress on August 29, 1916, printed at that date in Vol. 38, p. 97.

the day. Schools and colleges ask for donations; individuals who feel the pinch of the times ask for some personal financial assistance. Others discourse on the shortcomings, as they see them, of the Republican party. Autograph hunters are represented in large number. Various gentlemen who think their ailment is the same as Mr. Wilson's want to know the names of his physicians.

Mrs. Wilson invariably goes over the morning's mail with her husband. Some letters are turned over to a secretary for reply. Most of them the former President answers personally, dictating to a stenographer who comes from his law office every morning. All of them he signs himself.

The work is done in the library. The old desk and chair and table Mr. Wilson used in his study at Princeton are there. Thousands of volumes which were packed away while he was in the White House are there. Through the windows may be seen the indigo blue strip of Virginia hills where he used to go golfing, and not far away hangs a bag of golf sticks, a reminder of a better day.

The former President and his inseparable companion always have their luncheon served in the dining room. Then comes a nap of an hour, and then, unless the weather is most inclement, a motor drive. Mr. Wilson while in the White House became attached to a certain automobile. It went back, as is the custom each year, to the manufacturer, from whom Mr. Wilson bought it as a "used car." He had it painted black, with orange trimmings—Princeton colors, and in this car, which he regards as an old friend, he goes driving. He dislikes exploring new routes, but rather enjoys driving over the same ground at about the same time.

Many folk in the country look for him; one quaint old woman recently held up the car and presented a sweater which she had knitted. A little girl gave him a knitted lap robe. Frequently the car stops at a farm and takes on a load of fresh vegetables, eggs and fowl. The party always is home before dark.

Dinner is an informal affair. Sometimes there are guests, always old friends or associates. Mr. Wilson no longer dresses for the occasion as he always did while President. But no meal in the Wilson household ever proceeds until grace is said. Mr. Wilson has always said it himself, and months ago, when he was so weak he could hardly stand without aid, and his voice was almost inaudible, he steadied himself on his chair and whispered the plea for divine blessing.

Friends remember him ever at meals. Frequently a Potomac River fisherman sends him a rare specimen from his catch. Once another friend sent him ducks out of season and paid the game warden a handsome penalty.

After dinner he goes in for reading or amusement. Once a week Mr. Wilson has a motion picture show of his own and frequently sees a film at the same time it is being shown at the theaters downtown. Occasionally he goes to a vaudeville show, his party taking seats in the last row, and entering and leaving with every effort to avoid ostentation. It rarely happens, however, that somebody fails to discover the visitors and a demonstration always ensues.

Evenings at home are passed in the family circle. The former President and Mrs. Wilson read a book together, or perhaps Mrs. Wilson reads aloud. Sometimes it is one of the detective stories of which Mr. Wilson was said to be so fond. They do not now form as large a part of his reading as may have been the case years ago. He takes to bed early, not to sleep, however, but to relax, to read and write. Like Mark Twain, he does much reading and writing in bed. Propped up by pillows and with a little writing board across his knees, he reads and makes notes, some of them voluminous and in shorthand. Nobody knows what they are about. He puts them away carefully. They are not notes for a book which many expect.

Unless Mr. Wilson changes his mind he will write no reply to Robert Lansing or any one else who has criticised his policies. A writer[3] who has been given access to Mr. Wilson's papers, of which there are almost a ton, is writing a book, but it will be his own, not Mr. Wilson's.

"I'll give you any material I have for your book," Mr. Wilson told him; "I'll answer any question you ask—but it's your book; I don't even want to see what you write."

However the evening may be spent, however tired he may be, there is one thing the former President never neglects. It is the reading of a few verses of the Bible. When he says "Good night" he invariably reads aloud some short passage from the book, which always rests on the reading table at his bedside.

Friends and admirers ask what is Woodrow Wilson's real condition now.

He will be sixty-five years old next December and has passed through an ordeal which few men survive. The measure of his progress toward health must be measured with those facts in mind. His normal weight in health while he was President was 180 pounds. He shows little departure from that figure now. His eyesight is good, although he has discarded his favorite nose glasses for spectacles. His hair has turned snow white, but it has not thinned. His appetite is too robust to please his physicians. Last March when he left the White House with President-elect Harding

[3] Ray Stannard Baker.

an attendant had to place his feet on each succeeding step from the portico. The other day he sent his attendant away and climbed alone, not without some effort, into his automobile, just to see if he could do it, and seemed pleased to find that he could.

Motor nerves and muscles of his left side have given more response to treatment than was hoped for. Of course they are not fully active now. He still walks with a cane most of the time, but frequently hangs the crook over his arms and "goes it alone."

Mr. Wilson is far from a weak [well?] man to-day. He was far from a well man when he entered the White House more than eight years ago. But in the last two years there have been times when his voice was inaudible and when he could not support himself alone. His condition to-day shows more improvement than his family and friends dared hoped for.

There are many angles to Mr. Wilson's present day psychology. Living in Washington and easy of access to party friends at the Capitol, he might give consultation on party policies, but he does not. Whatever a visitor may say in criticism of the Republican Administration Mr. Wilson never makes a reply, he never permits any one in his presence to speak what he regards as "disrespect of the President of the United States."

Somebody once raised the question "How do our ex-Presidents live?" Colonel Roosevelt had a comfortable fortune of his own, augmented by income from writings. Mr. Taft, until he became Chief Justice, had from time to time profitable sources of income.

Mr. Wilson brought with him to the White House the small savings of a life time, which he preserved. During his terms in the Presidency his royalties from books previously written mounted into rather handsome sums. Singularly enough they have shown a marked slump since he left the White House. While he was President circumstances helped him save money.

The war and suspension of social functions and entertainment were quite an item. It has been estimated that the former President's pocketbook was at least $25,000 richer because he was not called upon to wine and dine numerous dignitaries and official persons.

Upon his modest fortune he now lives simply with an establishment of only three servants and a "used car."

Printed in the *New York Tribune*, Sept. 27, 1921.

From Carter Glass

Confidential.   Washington, D. C.
My dear Mr. President: September 29, 1921.

I have not arranged to bring Senators Hitchcock and Gerry[1] to see you because I have a very definite suspicion that each of them treated my preliminary suggestion in a rather treacherous fashion.[2] In short, I have reason to suspect that each of them went immediately to Pomerene,[3] who is irrevocably committed to support the Germany treaty, and told him of the invitation. I think it was from this source that the newspapers derived the impression that you were endeavoring to influence the Senate; and the incident was used to stiffen the Wilson-haters among the Republicans and to weaken the same ilk among the Democrats. It does not matter much except that, as I view it, the action of these two gentlemen, if my surmise is accurate, betokens hostility.

The situation is improving every day. There have been two conferences and those of us who are opposed to the treaty are hammering hard. At the conference today things were distinctly better and it may be that we shall succeed in averting the disgrace of ratification of the treaty by Democratic votes. One finds himself utterly nonplussed to be told by a colleague that he thinks the treaty is infamous, but will vote for it. There is no effective appeal to such a perverted conscience. Nevertheless, we are hammering away and I will very likely communicate with you again soon.

With cordial regards and best wishes for your continued improvement in health, believe me

Devotedly your friend,   Carter Glass.

TLS (WP, DLC).
   [1] That is, Gilbert Monell Hitchcock and Peter Goelet Gerry.
   [2] The *New York Times*, Sept. 27, 1921, reported that some senators suspected that the sudden stiffening of opposition among Democrats to Senate approval of the separate peace treaty with Germany was due to Wilson's influence. One alleged bit of evidence of this fact was the announcement by John Sharp Williams on September 26 that he would vote against Senate approval. Another sign of Wilson's work, according to this report, was that Carter Glass was known to be a "strong opponent" of ratification. The *Times* reported on September 30 that Glass was "taking the lead" in the Democratic opposition to the treaty and would offer three reservations to it.
   [3] That is, Senator Atlee Pomerene.

John Randolph Bolling to Isaac Thomas Jones

My dear Mr. Jones: [Washington] 30th September 1921

Your letter of September twenty-first came promptly to me, and it was a pleasure to hear from you again.

In order that there might be no possible mistake, at Mr. Wilson's suggestion I have made some further inquiries regarding who first suggested the plan which has taken form as the Woodrow Wilson Foundation. From what I can learn, there seems just a bit of doubt as to whether the credit should go to Mrs. Simonson or Mrs. Tiffany, and in view of this Mr. Wilson feels some hesitancy in writing the letter you suggest. I am sure you will understand his position in the matter.

Mr. Wilson was delighted to hear of the progress of the Foundation. That I was not unappreciative of your letter from New York, I am enclosing copy of my reply which was returned from your hotel.

With kindest regards;

Cordially yours,   [John Randolph Bolling]

CCL (WP, DLC).

To Kazimierz Lubomirski

My dear Mr. Minister: [Washington] 3d October 1921

Nothing of the kind could gratify me more than the honor conferred upon me by the University of Cracow whose diploma you are kind enough to send me.[1]

Nothing connected with the Great War interested or concerned me more profoundly than the question of Poland, and it is very delightful to me to receive any evidence of the confidence and friendship of the great Polish people.

With much appreciation of your courtesy, and my best personal wishes;

Cordially and sincerely yours,   [Woodrow Wilson]

CCL (WP, DLC).
[1] Wilson was replying to K. Lubomirski to WW, Sept. 16, 1921.

From Warren Gamaliel Harding

(PERSONAL)

My dear Mr. Wilson: The White House October 4, 1921.

As you are aware, there is to be a rather unusual assemblage at Arlington Memorial Amphitheater on Armistice Day, when there will be conducted ceremonies attending the burial of an unknown soldier who served in the late World War. Undoubtedly it will be the part of the President to have a presidential party of a considerable number on that day and I have thought it would be fine if you could find it agreeable for you and Mrs. Wilson to accept an invitation to become members thereof. It has occurred to me, however, that I preferred to suggest this to you personally in advance of sending a formal invitation, such as will go out to those who are invited to become members of the party. I would very much like to have you present, and on the other hand I have thought it might be embarrassing to either or both of us if you felt it necessary to decline the invitation. I am sure you will understand the spirit which prompts me to address you in this wholly informal and confidential way. If you will only indicate to me your likely preference in the matter I will be governed accordingly.

Permit me to express the hope that you are constantly improving in health. Very truly yours, Warren G Harding

TLS (WP, DLC).

From Bainbridge Colby

My dear Mr President: New York City October 4, 1921

The firm's resources will stand a little distribution and I beg to enclose herewith a check to your order for $5,000.

Things are a little slow but I am not surprised. General conditions are not good and everyone is feeling the difficult times.

I am planning to be in Washington on Saturday and hope to see you. I can then review fully with you the matters we have in hand. There are several matters that I want to go over carefully with you and as to which I need your considered opinion.

There is a tremendous speculation everywhere about your course with reference to the Germany treaty. I suspect that you are not intending to depart from your policy of silence and non-interference, but it is none the less amusing to see the hosts of normalcy balk, shy and rear when they fancy they discern the shadow of your tall figure athwart their muddle-headed program. The persistent report of your gain in health and vigor is giving the enemy a case of nerves. Keep it up, my dear Mr President. You are doing your full duty to the firm at the moment by getting well.

With my best and kindest always,
Cordially yours, Bainbridge Colby

TLS (B. Colby Papers, DLC).

To Bainbridge Colby

My dear Colby: Washington D C 5th October 1921

Thank you for your letter of October fourth and the enclosed check for $5,000 (the receipt of which is hereby acknowledged) which was timely and welcome.

It is a pleasure to look forward to seeing you on Saturday; let me know when you get to town.

I shall be glad to discuss with you the business matters to which you refer.

Cordially and sincerely yours,   Woodrow Wilson

TLS (B. Colby Papers, DLC).

To Warren Gamaliel Harding

My dear Mr. President: [Washington] 5th October 1921

It is thoughtful and courteous of you to suggest that I join the party you are planning to take to Arlington on the eleventh of November, and I beg to express my sincere appreciation.

Inasmuch as my physical condition still makes it necessary that I should have one or two attendants, I think that it would be necessary if I am to have the pleasure of attending the exercises at all that I should form a small party of my own. I am sure you will understand the necessities under which I labor, and will not feel I am unappreciative of your kindness in coming to this conclusion.

Believe me, Mr. President, with entire appreciation;

Very truly yours,   [Woodrow Wilson]

CCL (WP, DLC).

From Jesse Holman Jones

My dear Friend: Washington, D. C. October 5, 1921.

It was a privilege that I fully appreciate, seeing you on yesterday, and I was pleased to see the decided progress that you have made since we were here in February. I realize that your disappointment at the turn things have taken, must be more of a tragedy to you than anything that could happen to you personally. You lifted the ideals of the people of the world to a high level, but was stricken before you could get the props all set. The pigmies that have undertaken to destroy what you had accomplished, have been—for the time being—successful. It appears, however, that Secretary Hughes has finally gotten the "address" of the League of Nations.[1]

I hope you will be willing to take the fight up again when you think the time is propitious, but in such a manner as not to be overtaxing to yourself.

The people are getting impatient with the present administration, but they have got a lot of disappointment coming to them. I do not believe that there is another man in the world that could have accomplished the things that you accomplished, and if you had kept your health you could have rendered a further service to the world, greater, perhaps, than can be imagined. You gave every ounce of your energy, mental and physical, therefore, any regrets you may have cannot be because of a lack of effort on your part. You are as much the ideal of right-thinking people who are not materialists, as you ever were. Nothing can take that from you. Personally, I would greatly prefer to be of your school—as it were— and in the minority for the time being, than to sit at the right hand of the present chief executive. My esteem, affection and profound admiration grows, as I more fully realize your greatness, and the power and influence for good throughout the world that you and your administration were. Mrs. Jones shares my sentiments, and we wish for you every comfort, and a complete restoration of health. Sincerely yours, Jesse H Jones

TLS (WP, DLC).
¹ Jones' comment was inspired by Edwin L. James, "WASHINGTON SENDS REPLIES TO LEAGUE," *New York Times*, Sept. 30, 1921. James reported from Geneva that, after consistently ignoring all communications sent to it by the League of Nations since February 1921, the State Department had suddenly sent fourteen form-letter replies with dates ranging from August 15 to August 29, 1921, to largely routine communications from the League, with dates ranging from February 4 to August 29, 1921. For the State Department's explanation of the delay of the replies, which attributed it to a "misunderstanding," see a separate news report in *ibid*. See also *ibid.*, Oct. 1 and 3, 1921, for further comment on the affair.

William Cox Redfield to Joseph R. Wilson, Jr.

Dear Mr. Wilson: New York City, October 5th, 1921.

Your kind letter of the 3rd to my former office has been forwarded here.

One of my outstanding recollections of your brother is his quick sense of humor and his pungent humorous way of putting things. I remember his saying once in the Cabinet that he did not like secrets because if you told them you lost your principle and if you kept them you lost your interest.

One evening when the Cabinet met in the study upstairs in the White House, after the meeting was over McAdoo and I were talking together, sitting on a table. President Wilson came and asked if we were talking business and said the business meeting had adjourned and it was no longer in order to discuss business. He then told how when he was President of Princeton he had been invited to make an address in Youngstown, Ohio, where he was entertained by an alumnus and his wife. The latter seemed painfully conscious that the President of the University was her guest and at dinner tried to maintain the conversation on a painfully high level. Your brother did what he could to get the lady down to earth but failed. Finally he made a plunge and said—"Have you heard my latest limirick"? The hostess gasped and said "no" and then, of course, had to ask what it was. "Well," said your brother, "it's this":

"There was a young monk of Siberia
Whose life it got drearier and drearier,
Till he burst from the cell
With a hell of a yell
And eloped with the Mother Superior."

He often expressed a strong distaste for making what he called "brutum fulmen." By this he meant writing useless letters or making useless statements on public matters that got nowhere. He felt that if you wrote or said anything it should achieve a purpose. He did not want to merely beat the air.

If the above are of value I shall be glad. Of course, do not use my name in connection with them.

Cordially yours,   William C. Redfield

TLS (received from Stuart I. McElroy).

From Isaiah Bowman[1]

My dear Mr. Wilson: New York October 6, 1921.

I should take it as a very gracious thing if you could find a moment in which to look at my book, "The New World: Problems in Political Geography."[2] I am mailing a copy today under separate cover.

It is the outgrowth of work for your government for several years, and may give the public some notion of the extraordinary complexity of the problems that confronted the Peace Conference, and that, thanks to the obstinacy of Lodge, now lie in a heap on the White House doorstep.

I fear it is too much to ask you to tell me your opinion of the book, but if you could do so I should be most grateful.

Sincerely yours,   Isaiah Bowman

Of course, a *review* of it from yourself would be glorious but I haven't the courage to ask for it. But if you should *offer* it, I should bless you forever!

TLS (WP, DLC).
    [1] At this time Director of the American Geographical Society of New York.
    [2] Yonkers-on-Hudson, N. Y., 1921.

From George Weston Anderson

Dear Mr. Wilson: Boston. October 6, 1921.

Last Saturday returning from Europe, where my chief objective was a study of the Assembly of the League of Nations at Geneva, I talked with Mr. McAdoo, who said he thought you would be interested in hearing briefly the impressions made on me as to the League. I limit myself, naturally, to generalizations, always more or less inaccurate.

(1) The League is, on the whole, a far more vital and working institution than I expected to find it. The delegates impressed me as a serious, intelligent body of men, intent on doing their best to work out an exceedingly difficult problem, and showing, on the whole, far more comprehension of the differing points of view of representatives of other races and other nations than I should expect under the circumstances. It was rather interesting to look at these delegates—100 to 150 in number—representing 40 odd nations, and to note that in personal appearance as well as in dress they were no more divergent from type than a like number of men in our national House of Representatives or in one of our State Legislatures. It gave me an increased appreciation of the possibility of the Aryan races assimilating to one type, physically, as well as in superficial manner. Moreover, if you analysed the attitude of the entire body—including those of different color of skin—towards political, social and moral problems, it was manifest that intelligent humans of whatever race or clime are very much alike. One did not feel that Kipling's statement that "East is East, and West is West" was fundamentally true.

(2) The working of the assembly, as related to the Council, seems to me to approve the judgment of the founders of the covenant. I think the powers are well balanced. The Assembly proved to be less of a mere speech-making, "leave-to-print" meeting than I had expected. Of course there was, and there ought to be, some chance for these delegates to make speeches for home consumption. But most of the speeches had a real reference to some problem in which the Assembly had some function to perform. There

was, as I assumed there would be, competition between the Latins and the Anglo-Saxons. The six votes of Great Britain are, as the Assembly was [has] worked, an advantage—an increase of power, not a decrease of power—to the United States, if it should ever have sense enough to go into the League. In the Assembly in a period of years competition will not be between the United States and Great Britain, but will be between Latins and Anglo-Saxons, with or without some more or less temporary side coalitions.

(3) The secretarian commissions (we would call them committees) were functioning publicly and, as it seemed to me, more efficiently than an ordinary American legislative committee. The utterances of the members seemed better prepared than I am accustomed to in America. The attitude of the members toward each other was most courteous and considerate.

(4) As to "super-government," greater nonsense was never talked. Small nations are as jealous of their sovereignty as the Irreconcilables in the United States Senate, but show more sense in expressing it. As I see it now, the danger is that the League will have too little, not too much, power, at least until, after considerably [considerable] experimentation, it becomes increasingly evident that only by enlarging the functions of what I may now call, though inaccurately, "world government" can peace and security for any part of the world be attained. But it is enough now to say that, as Mr. David J. Hill[1] noted over there, the League is no super-government. His remark was, in substance, that it was *intended to be a super-government, but was not so working out.*[2]

I might add much, but forbear. I will add, as a sort of general conclusion: I spent about two months in Europe. Through letters of introduction I saw a great many highly intelligent people, many of them occupying places of great official responsibility. Through the American Relief Administration I got at many of the poverty conditions resulting from the war. In Geneva of course I talked confidentially with a great many men from many different countries. My general conclusions are that, notwithstanding the manifested attempt of the American government to destroy the League, it will probably live, whether America is in or out, and will greatly assist in the possible rehabilitation of Europe. At any rate, if it does not, I see no possibility of any rehabilitation. Financially, Europe is a chaos. Only by long-time credits can it get what it needs and what America has in super-abundance. But no sane financier will recommend credits until there is financial stability, and there can be no financial stability until there is political stability, and there can be no political stability until the League of Nations is a more effective and more powerful disciplinary force, particularly over the small new nations that are now in process of developing national life—some of them with sophomoric recklessness.

Business conditions in America are the natural results of our foreign policy. We are "back to normalcy." Eliminating Russia, there is more unemployment in America than in all Europe, even including England. Undoubtedly America can survive under a policy of Chinese isolation, but the process of adjustment is obviously as painful as it is shameful. The outstanding fact is, that since your health broke two years ago there has been no world leader,—morally, politically, economically. When we shall develop leadership, and where, God only knows. I am pretty pessimistic.

With warm personal regards and hopes for your complete restoration, believe me,   Sincerely yours,   G. W. Anderson

TLS (WP, DLC).
   [1] That is, David Jayne Hill.
   [2] Probably Wilson's italicization.

John Randolph Bolling to Jesse Holman Jones

My dear Mr. Jones: [Washington] 7th October 1921
   Mr. Wilson says he cannot let your letter to him of October fifth pass without assuring you what profound gratitude it gave him; that it was a great pleasure to see you the other evening, and that he is sorry he could not see Mrs. Jones also.

Mr. and Mrs. Wilson send you and Mrs. Jones their kindest regards.   Cordially yours,   [John Randolph Bolling]

CCL (WP, DLC).

From John R. Mott

Dear Mr. Wilson: New York October 7, 1921.
   I venture to write you regarding a matter of real importance. You will recall that last year the World's Student Christian Federation conducted a campaign in the universities, colleges, and schools of America to enlist the generous gifts of the students and professors on behalf of the impoverished and suffering student communities of the nations of Central and Eastern Europe. At my request on the Sunday morning I called upon yourself and Mrs. Wilson at the White House, you kindly wrote me a personal letter which you permitted me to use throughout the student field.[1] I enclose a copy of that letter.

In view of the investigations which I made while in Europe not long ago and which have been supplemented by more detailed studies conducted by our representatives in such areas as Poland, Germany, Czechoslovakia, Hungary, Austria, the Balkan States, Russia, the Baltic States, and the foreign student communities of France and Switzerland, it has become very clear that we must raise another large fund this year to help meet the continued tragic need. Last year we secured from the American student community approximately a half a million dollars. We ought to provide even more this year. I know of nothing in the realm of American benevolence which has accomplished more real good than what we have been doing in this direction. Its value in promoting better international relations is very great indeed, quite apart from the relieving of the great physical and intellectual needs.

I venture to make two requests. One is that you may kindly consent to let us use your name as a member of a small cooperating or advisory or counselling committee, composed of leading university presidents and a group of men prominent in our public life; the other is that you may consent to send me a brief letter or telegram renewing your expression of appreciation of the invaluable national and international significance of this timely and unselfish ministry on the part of American students and professors. I shall appreciate more deeply that I can express your influential cooperation.

I am hoping to have the privilege of seeing you one of these days to report on some of my more recent experiences and some of my plans for the coming days.

With undying gratitude for all that your life and words have meant to me and to others through me, and with kindest regards to Mrs. Wilson,   Very sincerely yours,   John R. Mott

TLS (WP, DLC).
    ¹ WW to J. R. Mott, Nov. 22, 1920, Vol. 66.

Isaac Thomas Jones to John Randolph Bolling

My dear Mr. Bolling: San Francisco, October 7th, 1921.

Your letter of September 30th which also carried previous letter of September 7th reached me yesterday, forwarded from Des Moines, Iowa; I think I have forgotten heretofore to suggest that you reach me at 1416 23rd Street, Des Moines, Iowa, when another address is not available.

You were quite right in the course you pursued with reference to determining the person to whom credit is due for originating the idea of the Wilson Foundation; your course has removed any possibility of future controversy in the matter and of course I had this in mind in my previous letter on this subject.

The Woodrow Wilson Foundation will be much easier in achievement than I had anticipated; I find everywhere an eager enthusiasm which forecasts success.

Several things have occurred to me but I have decided that the better course will be to wait until I see you again and review them; for instance, there is the case of Mr. C. Samuel Jackson in Portland, Oregon; Mr. Jackson is the owner and editor of the Oregon Journal which is published at Portland; he has built an institution starting from nothing, and now has property valued at perhaps two millions of dollars; he has been a big up-standing man and a consistent advocate of the great principles which find their highest representation in Mr. Wilson and has at all times upheld Mr. Wilson's hand in the newspaper field which he covers; indeed, if I am correctly informed, he introduced Mr. Wilson on the occasion of his last visit to Portland, and if so Mr Wilson will readily recall him.

Mr. Jackson is now an invalid and while all of his work is done in his name, it must be done by subordinates of whom he has a large number who are very able men and which list includes his son, Philipp Jackson; some two or three years ago one of Mr. Jackson's son was drown[ed] accidentally and this has contributed to his present condition.

My thought in relating this to you is that it is one of the incidents wherein the human touch can be conserved by a kindly letter from Mr. Wilson to Mr. Jackson, written at the proper time; I do not think it should be done just now however because it might be construed as an effort to stimulate interest in the Woodrow Wilson Foundation inasmuch as Mr. Jackson is the titular leader of the movement in the state of Oregon; later, however, when the Woodrow Wilson Foundation movement is over, it would seem to me very desirable and I know it would be very cheering to Mr. Jackson to receive a little note from Mr. Wilson.

I am outlining this incident to you in detail for the purpose of indicating to you personally what I conceive to be an excellent method for bringing Mr. Wilson into a close and harmonious touch with his fellow-country-men; do you agree with me that this is a consummation to be desired? If so, I will when I see you point out several cases in various parts of the country where this friendly touch may be best applied. And please understand, dear Mr. Bolling, that I have no purpose in making this suggestion that is not based solely on personal friendship and interest.

I shall begin my journey eastward as soon as my work is completed in California, which will perhaps take another week; then I shall visit Nevada, Arizona, Utah, Idaho, Wyoming, Colorado and New Mexico in the order named and shall then return to my home in Des Moines, and after a little visit with my family, shall be in New York and Washington, at which time I shall hope to see you.

Cordially and faithfully yours,   I. T. Jones

TLS (WP, DLC).

John Randolph Bolling to George Weston Anderson

Dear Judge Anderson: [Washington] 8th October 1921

Mr. Wilson sends you his warm thanks for your interesting letter of October sixth, the contents of which he has noted with the greatest pleasure. He wishes me to add that there is nobody whose opinion on such matters he would rather have than yours.

I am happy to be able to advise you that Mr. Wilson's health is showing steady improvement, though his progress is slow. After all, however, if it is *sure* it is worth waiting for.

Cordially yours,   [John Randolph Bolling]

CCL (WP, DLC).

From George McLean Harper

Dear Wilson: Princeton, N. J. Oct. 8, 1921

The recent favorable accounts of your health encourage me to write you these few lines. While you were ill I was unwilling to add to the number of letters you may have felt it a burden to read; but now perhaps you may find some pleasure in hearing from old friends, whose affection is unchanged. Belle[1] & I have followed your course in the past nine years with an interest composed partly of concern for the public good & partly of a very deep regard for your personal well-being. If you ever permit a sense of disappointment to trouble you as you compare what you were allowed to do with what you tried to do, remember that we, & no doubt many others, are impressed rather with the extent & value of your achievements & convinced that their fruits will be more & more evident as time ripens them. To have made the idea of a League of Nations a question of practical politics, is to have helped mankind more, possibly, than anyone realizes at present.

It has at times been hard to live in Princeton amid the memories of great hopes unfulfilled & thinking constantly of what might have been. I see a ghostly group of colleges here which were never built, & am haunted by a vision of that intellectual pre-eminence which Princeton was on the point of attaining. But I learned long ago to resign myself to a hearty & cheerful performance of the obvious duties of my life & not let dreams annoy me.

The Westcotts[2] are enjoying a year's leave of absence. They have been in England all summer & have now gone to the Channel Islands on their way to France. We are all proud of our dear boy Jack[3] & his voluntary sacrifice.

Isabel[4] is a senior at Smith College. She broke off her course of training as a nurse when the war emergency ended, & decided to go to college. McLean,[5] who intends to teach Italian & Greek, is a graduate student at Harvard. Belle and I, for the first time, have neither child with us.

We have heard, with the deepest satisfaction, that you are in much better health. Please give our love to Margaret if she is with you. I venture to send my respects to Mrs. Wilson, whom I had the pleasure of meeting, one election day, in Princeton, but who probably does not remember me.

Ever sincerely yours,   Geo. Mc Harper

ALS (WP, DLC).
  [1] That is, Belle Dunton Westcott Harper.
  [2] That is, John Howell Westcott and Marian Bate Westcott.
  [3] John Howell Westcott, Jr. About his death in combat in the war, see WW to J. H. Westcott, Nov. 19, 1918, n. 1, Vol. 53.
  [4] His daughter, Isabel Westcott Harper.
  [5] His son, George McLean Harper, Jr., Princeton 1920.

John Randolph Bolling to Homer Stillé Cummings

Dear Mr. Cummings: Washington D C 9th October '21

Your letter of October 7th came on yesterday.[1] Mr. Wilson says he will be glad to see you at three thirty o'clock Tuesday afternoon, October eleventh.

Mrs. Wilson says for you to come to lunch with us on Tuesday, at one-thirty, if you can spare the time; so we will look for you at that hour. If it is not convenient for you to come to lunch, please telephone the office (Main 3614) and leave word with my secretary, Mr. Kriz.

It was thoughtful of you to send me copy of your letter to Mr. Haffer.[2] I have enjoyed so reading it that I am putting it on Mr. Wilson's reading-table, so he can see it, too.

Cordially yours,   John Randolph Bolling

TLS (H. S. Cummings Papers, ViU).
  [1] H. S. Cummings to JRB, Oct. 7, 1921, TLS (WP, DLC).
  [2] It was a letter to be read at a banquet to be given in Los Angeles on October 10.

To George McLean Harper

My dear Harper: Washington D C 10th October 1921

Please don't apologize for writing to me; your letters are always more than welcome. The one just received I have especially enjoyed.

I am so glad to get news of McLean and Isabel and of the Westcotts. Evidently you have reason to be proud of the children.

With warmest regards;

Always your sincere friend,   Woodrow Wilson

P.S. Those ghostly colleges will haunt some trustees to their graves.   W.W.

TLS (G. M. Harper Papers, NjP).

To Claude Augustus Swanson[1]

Confidential.

My dear Senator,   [Washington, Oct. 10, 1921]

Our conversation of last evening was of such importance (at any rate to me) that I take the liberty of sending you this memorandum,—

If the Democratic Senators will organize a caucus which can bind its members, and then care to seek my counsel, I will be glad to put at their disposal the utmost resources of my thought and judgment.

Otherwise, I should not feel justified in adding such a responsibility to the present tasks of my brain.

Cordially and gratefully Yours,

(Signed) Woodrow Wilson.

TCL (WP, DLC).
    [1] A note at the top of this letter says that it was a TCL of a WWT.

To Isaiah Bowman

My dear Bowman: [Washington] 10th October 1921

It is a real pleasure to receive a copy of your book, and I shall look forward with real zest to reading it whenever I have the leisure and energy to read anything.

I shall always remember you with satisfaction and pride, and am glad to have this opportunity to tell you how much I admire the efficiency and spirit of your own work.

I have no doubt that your book will enlighten those who desire enlightenment. The trouble is that those who most need it least desire it.

Cordially and sincerely your friend,   [Woodrow Wilson]

John Randolph Bolling to John R. Mott, with Enclosure

My dear Dr. Mott: Washington D C 10th October 1921

Mr. Wilson has taken a great deal of pleasure in writing the letter requested in yours of October seventh, and which I enclose herewith.

He asks me to say that he is entirely willing for you to use his name as a member of the cooperating or counselling committee that you have in mind.

It is a pleasure to tell you that Mr. Wilson's health continues to slowly improve. If you are coming to Washington at any time, let me know in advance, as I am sure he would like to see you.

Cordially yours,   John Randolph Bolling

ENCLOSURE

To John R. Mott

My dear Dr. Mott: Washington D C 10th October 1921

It gives me pleasure to express my deep admiration for the loyal support and cooperation of the students and professors in universities and colleges for the work in the Far East[1] which is being done through the World's Student Christian Federation, and to say it seems to me, beyond the immediate and immense good that such efforts have done and will do, their moral is even greater than their material value.

Cordially and sincerely yours,   Woodrow Wilson

[1] Mott wrote "Europe" above "the Far East."

From Herbert Sherman Houston

Dear Mr. Wilson: New York, October 10, 1921.

You are so staunch a friend that I want you to have the earliest possible information, direct from me, as to my future plans.

On November 1st I am withdrawing from the firm of Doubleday, Page & Company and selling to the company my interest in the business. My plans are not decided upon, but I feel sure that I shall go forward in the publishing business for I have built up and directed a half dozen magazines, which have usually had the decency to earn a fair income—and the publishing business is the only one I know. Through my association with you and other friends in the League to Enforce Peace, in the International Chamber of Commerce, and the Council on Foreign Relations,[1] and in the Japan Society, I have become imbued with the deep conviction that this country needs to be enlightened in regard to the rest of the world more than it needs any other thing; therefore I am strongly persuaded to develop some publishing enterprise that shall carry forward in a continuous and broad way the things that I know you believe in so profoundly.

At the present time I am not making any announcement of my intention to resign as Vice-President of Doubleday, Page & Co. and sell my interest in the business, but I am writing a few confidential letters to personal friends thinking that they might be interested in the tentative plans to which I have referred; I am thinking also that they might be prompted to make some suggestions that would enable me to direct my publishing experience toward educating this country along international lines.

It is a great pleasure to tell you I am devoting all of this month to the Ray Stannard Baker and Tumulty[2] syndicates in an endeavor to get the widest possible distribution for these two dramatic and interpretive series of articles on your great career. The New York Times has taken the publication in its territory.

I have been so delighted to read, as have all your friends, I know, the reassuring article in regard to the state of your health which the Associated Press sent out from Washington.[3]

With every good wish for the complete restoration of your health, and with kindest regards to Mrs. Wilson and to you, I am, my dear Mr. President, as always

Your faithful friend,   Herbert S Houston

TLS (WP, DLC).
    [1] About which, see JRB to R. C. Stuart, Jr., Oct. 18, 1921, n. 1.
    [2] Tumulty was writing articles for syndication that were published as *Woodrow Wilson As I Know Him* (Garden City, N. Y., 1921).
    [3] The news report printed at Sept. 26, 1921.

Robert Cummins Stuart, Jr., to John Randolph Bolling

My dear Mr. Bolling: Houston, Texas, 11 October 1921.

The copy of my letter to Prof. Duggan[1] which was sent you the other day I hope met with your approval. In paragraph one I substituted "requesting" for the word "suggestion" which you used in your letter to me of September fourth.[2] Though slightly stronger, I considered it justified by the evasion of Mr. Morse,[3] or the committee, in turning your letter over to the very man who was under discussion. Prof. Duggan appariently [apparently] tries to create an inaccurate impression in his first paragraph.

In paragraph four of my letter the quotations are from your letter last spring written in answer to one I wrote Mr. Wilson.

Since writing you on August 16th[4] I have felt that I made a mistake in not stating our case regarding a rival appeal at the colleges as forcefully as possible; especially as you could help more approp[r]iately by quoting. As you have so much to attend to, moreover, it was possible that the exact situation might not be evident.

Stating the question bluntly it might be asked: Has Mr. Wilson confidence in the college men and women carrying out their tribute as it has been conceived? If we have his confidence it is only common decency for the Foundation to leave the colleges to us.

Why? Because our tribute has a significance to the college men and women which theirs has not; because our funds must come largely from a limited reservoir, a reservoir of definitely restricted resources which can not be tapped by anyone else without serious injury to our cause, while they may secure funds from so many sources that to give up one would not materially affect them; because the Woodrow Wilson Foundation has a professional money raiser[5]—the man who raised the Harvard Endowment—directing their work against whom we could not make a satisfactory showing, whereas we are all amateurs and Mr. Wilson does not wish us to get a paid specialist.

Since the Foundation has men with big names in the business world on its committees we are unable to obtain substantial support outside of our restricted group (have any number of letters from people who wish our movement well but who have waited to accept places with the Foundation and do not think can participate in both. Some have become affiliated with us and later have gone over to the Foundation, as for instance Senator Glass). For the young men and women of the country to attempt an undertaking of such magnitude, an undertaking without precedence in the history of American colleges, should command a respect and defference which would not only veto competition but which would invite benevolent interest.

I believe we should insist upon the Foundation giving up their idea of making an appeal at the colleges. I feel so strongly in the matter that I am inclined to write a vigorous letter to Franklin Roosevelt and Hamilton Holt. In the event this consideration was not granted it seems to me we should give up the idea of our tribute for at least a year and I should resign as chairman but of course doing all I could on the outside to see that the clubs continued active. As the tribute has been so intimately linked with the clubs, however, it would be well nigh fatal to the movement outside of a very limited number of colleges.

If the colleges were reserved for us we should probably organize differently than planned earlier in the summer. We should first select a treasurer—in this case we hope it to be Mr. Goltra[6]—then assess a definite sum on each club to pay expenses. Each club would be asked:

1. To forward an alumni directory of the particular college;

2. To mark in this directory, or make a separate list of, the graduates who are prominent in their respective communities and who may be available for our state and local committees;

3. To prepare a list of those whom are known to be able to make a substantial contribution;

4. To forward the names and addresses of the parents of the members of the club so that we should have a list of people over the country who could be relied upon to help.

From this material state and local committees could be organized. All contributions would be credited to some college so that there would be rivalry between them to raise the most. Each college club could be relied on to make an intensive campaign among the students.

This plan I feel will work and with the list you sent this summer we should obtain our objective.

I saw by the Houston papers Mr. and Mrs. Jessie [Jesse] Jones had dinner with Mr. Wilson the other day. Dr. Axson thought he would make a good chairman for the Texas committee (and I did to[o]). I called upon him soon after getting to Houston. He was reclining way back in his chair, said it was too hot for the work, he was not as young as he used to be, was planning to take a trip (though he would not set a date) etc. If you think of it, tell Dr. Axson to get in behind Mr. Jones. I am determined for him to help us even if we waite for Dr. Axson to return to assist in applying the pressure. By the way could Dr. Axson go by Harvard and the University of Chicago on his way to Texas and give a talk about Mr. Wilson's home life—a few personal touches? Will try to write him about this if you don't get to see him.

I hope you do not misunderstand this letter. It was not intended to take up the question first raised by my letter of August 16th in order to get you to quote me further but to give the situation as it appeared to me for you to do as you saw fit. The question addressed to Mr. Wilson was rhetorical, not personal. If we are going to fall down, however, it is of course best to have the Foundation raise money at the colleges too but I am not going to admit defeat at the start.

If you still have Prof. Duggan's letter I should like to have it back but do not need the carbon of my reply as have another one.

Most faithfully yours for success,   Robert C. Stuart

TLS (WP, DLC).
    ¹ Stephen Pierce Duggan, Director of the Institute of International Education, New York. His letter to Stuart is missing.
    ² This letter is missing.
    ³ That is, Edward S. Morse.
    ⁴ This letter is also missing.
    ⁵ Stuart was confusing I. T. Jones with John Price Jones, Harvard 1902, former newspaper reporter and a pioneer in professional fund-raising. Thomas W. Lamont had hired him as general manager of the Harvard endowment campaign in 1919. Late in that year, Jones founded the John Price Jones Corp., which soon became the leader in the new field of fund-raising.
    ⁶ Edward Field Goltra, Princeton 1887, industrialist and banker of St. Louis, an old friend of Wilson.

John Randolph Bolling to Isaac Thomas Jones

My dear Mr. Jones: [Washington] 12th October 1921

Your letter of October seventh from San Francisco reached me this morning.

It is good to have such encouraging news of the way the Woodrow Wilson Foundation is progressing.

With regard to Mr. Wilson writing letters to Mr. C. Samuel Jackson and others; I don't think the idea is one that would meet with his approval—that is if he was told of the object. He knows Mr. Jackson quite well, and of his loyalty and good work.

Mr. Wilson's position regarding the Foundation and other organizations bearing his name is that he should remain silent; and I think it the proper one. I might add that as he grows stronger he is more and more drawing around him again his old friends. To put the matter concretely, I should say he is dictating personal replies to four times as many letters as he was even as recently as July or August.

The newspaper article (put out by the Associated Press) which appeared about two weeks ago has brought literally thousands of letters of congratulations and good wishes to him; letters which show how greatly he is admired among the thinking element of the country, and how steadfast and loyal they are to the ideals which he so wonderfully set up while President.

When you are in Washington again I can explain better in person the letter matter. Be sure to let me know in advance of your coming, for these are very full days with me—starting around eight in the morning and frequently not ending until close to midnight.

Cordially yours,   [John Randolph Bolling]

CCL (WP, DLC).

From Claude Augustus Swanson

My dear Mr. Wilson: Washington, D. C. October 12th, 1921.

I read with much interest your letter of recent date, which was delivered to me by your secretary, Mr. Bowling.

I have delayed making reply to your letter in order to give the matter full consideration and ascertain the situation among the democrats in the Senate regarding having another caucus in connection with the Treaty with Germany.

As you know, we have had two caucusses and the conclusion was reached at each it would not be wise to make a party measure of the Treaty. I have endeavored carefully to ascertain the sentiment among the democratic senators, and find there is no change of sentiment as expressed in caucus. There is certainly not sufficient change of sentiment to justify the calling of another caucus to make it a party measure at this time. This is frankly the situation, and I do not think anything can be accomplished by calling a conference and endeavoring to get a party declaration on the matter. The situation has not changed since the last time I saw you and it looks as though the Treaty will be ratified. Senator Walsh made a splendid speech today[1] but I have had no opportunity to ascertain its effect.

I can fully appreciate the wisdom of your decision not to take any hand in the matter unless the party will act in accord.

I enjoyed seeing you very much and was very much gratified to note your improvement.

With kind regards and best wishes, I am,

Your friend,   Claude A. Swanson

TLS (WP, DLC).
[1] For Thomas J. Walsh's speech in opposition to the Senate's consenting to the ratification of the Treaty of Berlin, see *Cong. Record*, 67th Cong., 1st sess., pp. 6248-57.

A News Item

COL. HOUSE CALLS, WILSON NOT AT HOME
Ex-President Was Out Riding at the Time—
House Leaves Cards for Him and Mrs. Wilson.

Washington, Oct. 13.—Colonel Edward M. House, who was a member of the American delegation to the Versailles Peace Conference, called this afternoon at the residence of Woodrow Wilson, and left cards for Mr. and Mrs. Wilson. Colonel House and Mr. Wilson did not meet, as the former President was out for his daily automobile drive at the time.

Colonel House has been in Washington since yesterday as a guest of Mr. and Mrs. Cyrus H. K. Curtis,[1] publisher of The Philadelphia Ledger, on Mr. Curtis's yacht, the Lyndonia, which is anchored in the Potomac. President and Mrs. Harding headed a company of notables who were guests of Mr. and Mrs. Curtis on the yacht today, and Colonel House was among those present at the luncheon.

Printed in the *New York Times*, Oct. 14, 1921.
[1] Cyrus Hermann Kotzschmar Curtis and Kate Pillsbury Curtis.

John Randolph Bolling to Claude Augustus Swanson

My dear Senator:　　　　　　　　[Washington] 13th October 1921

Mr. Wilson asks me to thank you for your letter of yesterday and express his profound regret at the conclusions you feel obliged to state.

With kindest regards and the hope that you will run in and see us again very soon;

　　　　　　　　Cordially yours,　[John Randolph Bolling]

CCL (WP, DLC).

To Frank Irving Cobb

My dear Cobb:　　　　　　　　[Washington] 13th October '21

I understand that you had a rattling editorial in Tuesday's paper (or was it yesterday's?) on the Senate.[1]

Will you not send me a copy; I missed it.

With the warmest regard;

　　　　　　　　Your friend,　[Woodrow Wilson]

CCL (WP, DLC).

[1] Entitled "Peerless Leaders," this editorial pointed out that Senators Lodge and Underwood constituted half of the entire American delegation to the forthcoming so-called Washington Naval Conference and declared that neither man had any substantial following in his own party. "Mr. Lodge and Mr. Underwood," it continued, "are men of more than ordinary ability, who go through the motions of leadership with grace and dignity. All they lack is followers." New York *World*, Oct. 12, 1921.

From Bainbridge Colby, with Enclosure

My dear Mr President: New York City October 14, 1921

I forgot to say when I was with you Wednesday that I entirely approved your comment on the report from Mexico City that the firm had been retained on behalf of Mexico in connection with its negotiations with this country.[1]

The Press Association here called me up on the same day and I made substantially the same comment.

Frank Cobb of "The World" said to me a little while ago that he intended to go to Washington shortly to spend a few days. He expressed the hope that a way might open for him to see you, but he did not ask me to request an appointment or say that he would seek it himself. He is the last man in the world who would want to disturb or weary you. But he is such an unqualified admirer of yours and so doughty and valiant a defender of all you stand for, that I think it would do a lot of good if you felt disposed to send for him some time when you feel just in the mood.

Here is a new idea in lawyers' letterheads. The rather good-looking firm whose letterhead I enclose uses merely the word "Counsel" to define its business. I think when we have our next batch of stationery printed we ought to put our registered cable address on it.

I did a little shopping around on the treaty situation before leaving Washington. I have embodied what I learned in a memorandum, which I enclose.

Since reaching New York I learn through reliable channels that Underwood's position is not likely to change. It rather accurately reflects, the desires and opinions, entertained in certain quarters where the Senator has been supposed at times to find his inspiration.

Cobb will continue to hit hard. I talked with him today.

Yours ever,   Colby

TLS (WP, DLC).
[1] We have not found this report.

ENCLOSURE

The following is the situation in brief at the moment regarding the ratification of the treaty.

A majority of the Democratic Senators will vote against ratification. It is indicated however that a sufficient number of Democrats will vote for ratification under the combined leadership of Underwood and Hitchcock to make up with the Republican Senators the necessary two-thirds.

It seems also to be the fact that if Underwood and Hitchcock should oppose ratification a sufficient number of Democratic Senators who are now listed as favorable to ratification would switch and ratification could be defeated.

The position of Underwood and Hitchcock should be stated with some particularity in order to be understood.

At the time Underwood was elected Democratic leader of the Senate[1] he announced that in all matters relating to the Versailles treaty or growing out of the armistice or the Peace Conference he still regarded Hitchcock as the Democratic leader. Hitchcock on the other hand will come up for re-election shortly. He has always shown a certain tenderness for the numerous German element among the Nebraska voters, and his present wobbly course is supposed to be dictated by a desire to curry favor with the pro-German elements in his State.

As to Underwood, it should further be said that he has not explicitly taken a position for or against the treaty, although it is everywhere assumed that he proposes to vote for ratification. His theory of opposition-leadership is that he should not frustrate the effort of the majority to discharge the responsibilities which the voters have placed upon it. He further is understood to feel that the Democratic conference has not sought to bind the individual Senators and that the Democrats should not take the responsibility of defeating the treaty's ratification, inasmuch as the country sighs for peace and business is anxious to see the impediments to its resumption with Germany removed.

Therefore, despite his party's declaration in the San Francisco platform against a separate peace; despite his private expressions of disapproval of the proposed treaty; despite the fact that a majority of his associates are opposed to the treaty, and notwithstanding he is the titular leader of the party in the Senate, he apparently proposes to vote for ratification in a parliamentary situation where his vote and the Democratic votes that will travel with him are essential to the success of the Republican program.

This is a very curious kind of leadership for an opposition leader.

I can see how a placid or timid opponent might arrive at the conclusion that he didn't care to resort to a filibuster or to dilatory ex-
pedients like reservations or parliamentary motions, but I fail utterly to see how under any theory of the duty of opposition it is
possible to lend to the majority party the votes admittedly necessary to effectuate the program of the majority, which but for the
support of a certain number of opposition Senators must fail.

Hitchcock's position is supposed to be influenced also by Mr
Bryan's advocacy of ratification. This is true also of the Florida Senators.[2] In view of Mr Bryan's recent adoption of Florida as his place
of residence and the general expectation that he will enter the fight
for nomination as a Senator from that State, the Florida Senators
are supposed to deem it circumspect to take up a position on the
treaty that is in line with Mr Bryan's. Senator Dial[3] and the two
Florida Senators are supposed to be influenced by the impatience
of the commercial community to resume exports of cotton and
other raw materials to Germany.[4]

T MS (WP, DLC).
  [1] On April 27, 1920.
  [2] Duncan Upshaw Fletcher and Park Trammell.
  [3] Nathaniel Barksdale Dial, Democrat of South Carolina.
  [4] As it turned out, the Senate consented to the ratification of the Treaty of Berlin on
October 18, 1921, by a vote of sixty-six to twenty. Fifty-two Republicans and fourteen
Democrats voted in the affirmative; eighteen Democrats and two Republicans voted in
the negative. Democrats voting for the consent resolution included Underwood, Robert
L. Owen, and Atlee Pomerene. Hitchcock was paired with his colleague from Nebraska,
George W. Norris, who if present would have voted against the consent resolution.
Hence Hitchcock, in effect, voted for it. *Cong. Record*, 67th Cong., 1st sess., p. 6438.

From John R. Mott

My dear Mr. Wilson: New York October 14, 1921.

On my return from Chicago I find awaiting me your invaluable
letter which you have so kindly sent and which I plan to use
among the students and professors of North America in enlisting
their cooperation on behalf of the destitute student communities of
Europe. Let me thank you with a full heart for this communication
and also for your generous willingness to associate your influential
name with the undertaking as a member of the cooperating committee.

With highest regard,

                    Very sincerely yours,   John R Mott

TLS (WP, DLC).

From Cordell Hull

My dear Mr. President: Carthage, Tenn. Oct. 15, 1921.

Thinking you might be interested in some phase of it, I enclose copy of a manuscript[1] which is self-explanatory. I turned it over to our Democratic National Committee Headquarters.

It is a great satisfaction to know that a general reaction is going on everywhere in favor of the principles and policies for which you stood.

In common with all good citizens I devoutly trust that you are rapidly regaining your health.

Very sincerely,   Cordell Hull.

ALS (WP, DLC).
  [1] This was the article that Hull summarized in his *Memoirs* as follows:
  "I prepared an article on the injurious effects of the defeat of the Treaty of Versailles. Some of its ideas occurred again in phrases I used as Secretary of State. I inveighed most sharply against isolation, employing the word a number of times. The Administration, I said, was following the idea that 'America should live in prosperity unto and within herself and have no sort of relations with the balance of the world.' This, I maintained, was impossible. Furthermore, it was in contradiction to the Administration's claim that the panic of 1921 over here was due to 'world causes.'
  "America's failure to ratify the Treaty of Versailles, I pointed out, delayed reparations by two years and prevented our extending even sound credits to European nations. Now, I said, 'there is—three years after the Armistice—still no disarmament, no reduction of war taxes, no treaty of peace with Germany, and no conditions of real peace in Europe.' 'Yet,' I said further, 'the League of Nations, or a league, or an association of nations, or an association with nations, whichever the dodging, insincere politician prefers—like Banquo's ghost—will not down.' " Cordell Hull, *The Memoirs of Cordell Hull* (2 vols., New York, 1948), I, 112-13.

To Edith Gittings Reid

Dearest Friend,   2340 S Street NW 16 October, 1921

It was characteristically sweet and thoughtful of you to write to me from Cambridge.[1] I am slowly improving, but so slowly that the process is scarcely perceptible even when measured by comparatively long periods; and I get desperately discouraged and in need of ch cheer such as your letters bring.

Please overlook the errors of this typing. i have the use of only one hand, you know, and am picking this l laboriously out only to get a message of grateful affection to you.

From a full heart,

Your devoted friend,   Woodrow Wilson

WWTLS (WC, NjP).
  [1] Her letter is missing.

John Randolph Bolling to Frank Irving Cobb

My dear Mr. Cobb: [Washington] 16th October 1921

Mr. Wilson asks me to say that he has just learned you expect to be in Washington in the next few days, and that he hopes you will let him know in advance of your coming so he can arrange to see you while here.

Cordially yours,   [John Randolph Bolling]

CCL (WP, DLC).

From Frank Irving Cobb

Dear Mr. Wilson: New York October 17th, 1921.

I am not quite sure which editorial you desired, so I am sending you all three of them.[1]

It seems evident that the Treaty would be beaten if Underwood and Hitchcock stood by their party record, but, of course, Underwood never stands by his party record. He is a Democrat only because he lives south of Mason and Dixon line. In any other respect he is about as much of a Democrat as Penrose.

I am more delighted to hear from Bainbridge Colby of your continued improvement in health and spirit. There is still a great deal of work for you to do in this world.

With sincerest regards, as ever your friend,   Frank I Cobb

TLS (WP, DLC).
[1] One was the editorial cited in WW to F. I. Cobb, Oct. 13, 1921, n. 1. Another was probably "Stupid Falsification of the Record," New York *World*, Oct. 12, 1921. The third editorial was almost certainly "A Mystery of American Politics," *ibid.*, which commented on Senator Borah's bill to exempt American coastwise ships from the payment of tolls through the Panama Canal. Borah's bill also figures prominently in the editorial cited in WW to F. I. Cobb, Oct. 13, 1921, n. 1.

To Herbert Sherman Houston

My dear friend: [Washington] 17th October, 1921

I am very much complimented that you should have taken me into your confidence regarding your personal plans, and with all my heart I wish you Godspeed in carrying them out.[1]

I like very much indeed what you say about them, and wish I had some counsel in my head that would be helpful.

What we need most to realize as a nation is that we cannot have the full exercise and enjoyment of a right without at the same time fully and ungrudgingly performing the reciprocal duty. I can imagine (and you can create) a magazine that would, in every number, illustrate these moral interlacings and reactions, and that would be great propaganda for righteousness, even for those who confine their education to the school of experience. I believe Benjamin Franklin said: "Experience is a hard school but fools will learn in no other."

Wishing you Godspeed in the great enterprise you are contemplating;

Cordially and faithfully your friend,   [Woodrow Wilson]

CCL (WP, DLC).
¹ Wilson was replying to H. S. Houston to WW, Oct. 10, 1921.

John Randolph Bolling to Bainbridge Colby

My Dear Mr. Colby: [Washington] 17th October 1921

Your letter of October 14th to Mr. Wilson, with its interesting enclosures, came promptly. He had me put your memorandum regarding the Treaty on his reading-table, and went very carefully over it last night.

Dr. Axson was here the night after your dinner at Mr. Tumulty's, and told of the very interesting talk you gave them. He characterized it as "simply wonderful."

Mr. Wilson says he does not like the letterhead which you sent—believing rather in the old-fashioned "Attorneys and Counsellors at Law"—a form which, I believe, has been used for years without number. If you would like the cable address put on some of the present letterheads, it can be very easily done.

We are just back from a two-hour ride in this glorious Fall weather, and Mr. Wilson's cheeks were as ruddy as an athletes when we came in.

Cordially and sincerely,   [John Randolph Bolling]

CCL (WP, DLC).

John Randolph Bolling to Robert Cummins Stuart, Jr.

My dear Mr. Stuart: [Washington] 18th October 1921

Your letter of October 11th came duly to me, and I had an opportunity this morning of reading it to Mr. Wilson.

Answering in the same spirit in which it is asked, the question contained in the fourth paragraph of your letter; Mr. Wilson wishes me to say that he has entire confidence in the college men and women carrying out their tribute, but he considers it most unfortunate for your organization to get in collision with the Woodrow

Wilson Foundation. The matter is one too delicate for him to express any opinion about, and I hope very much that in the future you will not embarrass him by quoting anything from letters which I write you. I am sure that a moment's consideration of the matter will convince you of the very trying position in which Mr. Wilson would be placed were he, even by intimation, to show anything but a most profound appreciation of the work which is being done by the Council,[1] the Foundation, and the other sp[l]endid movements which have been started as a tribute to him. When I write to you, I want to feel I can write frankly and fully—with no idea of your treating the contents of my letters other than in the strictest confidence. Where there is a matter which you wish Mr. Wilson to pass upon—something affecting the organization on which you wish to quote his views—then I will be glad to put it before him and advise you whether he feels he can give any expression regarding it.

I do not wish this letter to be interpreted as intimating that any harm has been done by the quotation from letter to which you refer; it is simply to guard against such a contingency in the future.

A very nice letter came to me a day or two ago from Mr. Cummings, indicating that he would accept the invitation to speak at Cambridge on November 11th. I wrote him of my letter to you—the day he was here—and I am sure if the matter is followed up you can secure him.

      Cordially and faithfully yours,   [John Randolph Bolling]

CCL (WP, DLC).
  [1] The Council on Foreign Relations, whose charter was approved by a New York court on July 14, 1921. Its objectives were to "afford a continuous conference on international questions affecting the United States, by bringing together experts in statecraft, finance, industry, education and science"; to create and stimulate international thought; and to cooperate with the United States Government and international agencies.
  The petitioners for the charter included many prominent Wilsonians, for example, Frank L. Polk, Edwin F. Gay, Oscar S. Straus, Hamilton Holt, Abram I. Elkus, etc. The first director of the Council on Foreign Relations was Hamilton Fish Armstrong.

John Randolph Bolling to Cordell Hull

My dear Judge Hull: [Washington] 18th October 1921

Mr. Wilson asks me to thank you very much for your letter of October 15th, and for your thoughtfulness in sending him copy of the article which you enclosed. He says there is nobody whose views he would rather have than yours; that he hopes in the near future he shall again have the privilege which he had in the past of working alongside of you for the things you both believe in.

Mr. Wilson's health has shown a steady improvement with the complete rest which he has been able to take since last March.

Cordially yours,   [John Randolph Bolling]

CCL (WP, DLC).

Frank Irving Cobb to John Randolph Bolling

Dear Mr. Bolling: New York. October 18th, 1921.

I expect to be in Washington Tuesday and Wednesday of next week. I should be very glad indeed to see Mr. Wilson if it is possible.

If it could be arranged, I should be greatly obliged.

Sincerely yours,   Frank I Cobb

TLS (WP, DLC).

John Randolph Bolling to Frank Irving Cobb

Dear Mr. Cobb: [Washington] 19th October 1921

Your letter of October eighteenth came promptly to me this morning.

Mr. Wilson asks that when you reach Washington you telephone my secretary, Mr. Kriz, at Main 3614; he will then put you in touch with me, and Mr. Wilson will appoint an hour when it will be convenient for him to see you.

I shall be glad of the opportunity that your interview with Mr. Wilson will afford me to meet you.

Yours very cordially,   [John Randolph Bolling]

CCL (WP, DLC).

From Jessie Woodrow Wilson Sayre

Darling, darling Father,   [Cambridge, Mass.] October 19, 1921

It hardly seems as if I could exist much longer without seeing you and I am writing this note especially to ask you if there is any possibility of your being able to have me come to see you any time soon. I haven't asked all these months because I didn't want to break in on your routine in any way and, I kept *hoping* you would let me know when to come at some time most convenient for you. Way up here I couldn't know when was a good time for you and

Edith, and there is so much pressure on you from all sides that I didn't want to be responsible for the tiniest bit more. But darling Father, it is nearly a whole year since I have seen you and I just can't bear it any longer, if there is the weeniest, teeniest, chance of seeing you I want to seize it. But please, please, be perfectly square with me and if its best for me not to come please say so.

Margaret is coming up on the 28th to see me. Oh I hope she really comes so that I can feel that some one of my blessed family has been inside our little home. How I wish that I could have the blessing of your presence here, dearest Father. Williamstown and Siasconset and New York always seemed more completely home after you had stepped inside.

With a whole heartful of devoted love to you both,

Adoringly, Jessie.

ALS (WC, NjP).

Unpublished Statements

[c. Oct. 20, 1921]

I cannot give my endorsement or support or my personal confidence in any form to a man who, at the end of a triumphant war, voted as a member of the Senate to accept national disgrace in the form of a separate treaty with Germany which repudiated every obligation to our allies and sought a selfish advantage out of victories which had been won by the combined forces of civilized mankind

◇

Certain intensely partisan groups of the opposite party try to ignore tsese facts; but the facts stand fast. Foreign nations are familiar with them and are certain not to lose sight of them. It will be in the light of these facts that they will judge the honour of our country and its good faith towards its allies

WWT MSS (WP, DLC).

To Jessie Woodrow Wilson Sayre

My darling Jessie: [Washington] 21st October 1921

You may be sure that I am as eager to see you as you can be to see me, and because of lack of space in the house here I am going

to make a very unusual request of you. If you will let me know
when you and Frank and the children can come, I will engage
rooms at The Shoreham and let you know when they are ready. Be
sure to let me know, without skimping, what accommodations you
would need.

If you think it wisest not to bring the children away from home,
of course we would have room for you and Frank here at the house,
and I need not tell you how delighted we should be to have you.

Lovingly,   [Father]

CCL (WC, NjP).

From Eleanor Randolph Wilson McAdoo

Darling, darling Father,   [New York] Oct 21st, 1921

I have been wanting ever since your precious letter[1] arrived to
write and tell you how happy it made me and how perfectly wonderful I think you were to remember my birthday and to send me
the check. But almost two weeks ago I poisoned myself with
swamp sumach and I haven't been able to use my hands at all until
to-day. I went into the woods to get some bright autumn leaves and
it seems I brought this horribly poisonous stuff itself home with
me! Wasn't that clever of me? I was too affectionate with Mac. too,
and patted his face that same day and so he has it too all over his
face! It's not dangerous, of course, only very annoying and painful
and we have been perfectly disgusted with life for days, but I am
practically well now and Mac nearly well and so we can live again.

You don't know, darling Father, what happiness it gave me to
get a letter written in your own hand—and such a dear one. If I
only knew how to tell you how much I love you and how proud I
am because I am your daughter and you love me. But I never
can—I haven't any words for it. Thank you with all my heart for
the wonderful present—just to have you remember my birthday is
enough to make me happy for weeks! And to have such a present
besides is too much!

Will you tell dear Edith that, if we hadn't been so miserable, we
wouldn't have been a day late sending her our love for her birthday. Will you tell her, too, that for the same reason, I am very late
sending a little giftie, but it will go soon.

You can't read this awful scrawl, I'm afraid, so I won't try to write
any news until I can do it better. If I may, I want to go down to see
you soon—it has been so long since I was there.

Mac sends his best love to you all and Ellen sends hugs & kisses

and I send my heart full of dear, dear love—and thanks to the dar-
lingest Father in the world.

Always your devoted daughter   Nell.

ALS (WC, NjP).
¹ It is missing. Her birthday was October 16.

To Bainbridge Colby,¹ with Enclosure

My dear Colby: Washington D C 24th October 1921

Enclosed you will find some sentences which I am taking the
liberty of sending as contributions to the document upon which
you and Chadbourne are engaged. When you find errors and defects in typing, please remember that I have the use of only one
hand (fortunately the right hand) and of no normal nerves whatever.   Cordially and faithfully yours,   Woodrow Wilson

TLS (B. Colby Papers, DLC).
¹ There is a WWsh draft of this letter in WP, DLC.

E N C L O S U R E

(I)

We demand the immediate resumption of our international obligations and leadership,—obligations which were shamelessly repudiated and a leadership which was incontinently thrown away
by the failure of the Senate to ratify the Treaty of Versailles and the
negotiation of a separate treaty with Germany.

We denounce the group of men who brought about these. evil
results as the most partisan, prejudiced, ignorant, and unpatriotic
group that ever misled the Senate of the United States.

◊

We shall use every legitimate means to advance to the utmost
the industrial and commercial development of the United States.
That development has already made the people of the United
States the greatest economic force in the world. It is as convincing
proof of their practical genius, as their free institutions are proof
of their political genius. It is their manifest opportunity and destiny to lead the world in these great fields of endeavour and
[a]chievement. Our opponents have sought to promote the accumulation of wealth as an instrument of power in the hands of individuals and corporations. It is our object to promote it as a means

of diffused prosperity and happiness and of physical and spiritual well-being on the part of the great working masses of our people.

◇

Without the systematic coordination, cooperation, and inter-change of services by the rai,roads the expanding, varying, and changeable commerce and industry of the cosntry cannot be prop-erly served. All of these conditions are now lacking because. our present laws deal with the railroads without system and altogether by way of interference and restriction. The result is a confusion which is constantly made worse almost to the point of faralysis by the multiplicity and intermittent conflict of regulative authorihies, local and national.

We need a Secretary of Tr.ansportation who shall rank with the heads of other great federal cabinet departments and who shall be charged with the formulation and execution of plns for the coordi-nated use and full development of the transportation systems of the country. He should be associated with a federal Transportation Board which should be invested with all the powers now lodged with the Interstate Commerce Commission and, in addition, with the authority to determine the occasions and the conditions of all loans floated and of all securities issued by the several railway and steamship lines. This Board should have the same powers of su-pervision and regulation over the steamshop lines of the United States that are now exercised by the Interstate Commerce Com-mission over the railways

◇

The present menace to political liberty and peaceful economic prosperity lies, not in the power of kings or irresponsible govern-ments, but in hasty, passionate, and irrational programmes of rev-olution.

The world has been made safe for democracy; but democracy has not yet made the world safe against revolution. It is the privi-lege and duty of ours, the greatest of all democracies, to show the way. It is our purpose to defeat the irrational programmes of revo-lution beforehand by sober and practical legislative reforms which will remove the chief provocations to revolution.

Among these we hold the following to be indispensable&:

A practical plan for a partnership between capital and labour.

A plan by which the raw materials of manufacture and the elec-trical and other motive power now universally necessary to indus-try shall be made accessible to all upon equitable and equal terms.

Such legal requirements of the manufacturer and the merchant as will serve to bring cost of prduction and retail price into a clearly standardized relationship known to the purchaser.

WWT MSS (B. Colby Papers, DLC).

John Randolph Bolling to William Lassiter[1]

Sir: [Washington] 25th October 1921

Referring to our conversation of this morning; I am requested by Mr. Wilson to ask that you will, at the earliest possible hour, communicate to the Secretary of War[2] his wish to join the procession on Armistice Day in a horse drawn vehicle.

Mr. Wilson also requests that you communicate to him the reply of the Secretary of War in writing.

Very truly yours,   [John Randolph Bolling]

CCL (WP, DLC).
  [1] Brigadier General, U.S.A., Assistant Chief of Staff. A typed note at the top of this letter reads: "Dict by WW."
  [2] John Wingate Weeks of Massachusetts, former congressman and senator from Massachusetts.

William Lassiter to John Randolph Bolling

Dear Mr. Bolling: Washington, D. C. October 25, 1921.

I would acknowledge the receipt of your letter of this date, stating that Mr. Wilson requests that his wish to join the procession on Armistice Day in a horse-drawn vehicle be communicated to the Secretary of War at the earliest possible hour.

I find that the Secretary of War has accompanied the President on a journey to the South and will not return to Washington until Saturday. I will take the earliest possible opportunity to conform to Mr. Wilson's request and lay his wish before the Secretary of War.

Very truly yours,   Wm Lassiter

TLS (WP, DLC).

From Bainbridge Colby

My dear Mr President: New York City October 26, 1921

The outstanding event of today is the receipt of your letter with its very interesting enclosures. These are great thoughts, greatly stated and as only you could express them.

The fact that you wrote them yourself and that you felt well enough to do so and to undertake such work, quite threw me into a state of excitement.

I have already tried to get into communication with Chadbourne and hope to before the day is done.

Congratulations, my dear Mr President.

I hope to be in Washington within a few days and of course to see you. Cordially always Bainbridge Colby

TLS (WP, DLC).

To Ralph Pulitzer

My dear Mr. Pulitzer: [Washington] 27th October 1921

It was very kind of you to remember me in sending out your invitations to the dinner you are planning to give to Mr. H. G. Wells, and it is a severe disappointment to me that I cannot hope to be well enough by November second to be present.

I have long desired to have the pleasure of meeting Mr. Wells; he must be very interesting and stimulating.

May I not ask you to present my personal compliments to him and also my hope that the pleasure to me of meeting him is only postponed?

With much appreciation;

Cordially and sincerely yours, [Woodrow Wilson]

CCL (WP, DLC).

From Herbert Sherman Houston

New York,
My dear and always esteemed friend: October 28, 1921.

As I told Ray Stannard Baker at the Harvard Club the other day, your letter of sympathy with and interest in my future publishing plans stirred me more deeply than anything that has come to me for a long time. It was most kind and generous of you to tax yourself to write me as you did, but I do want you to know how I appreciate your friendly interest from my heart.

I have now brought my ideas into such focus that I have been able to prepare a tentative plan for a publication which I believe would make a great success. In response to your cordially expressed interest, I am taking the liberty of sending a copy of this tentative plan[1] to you, in the hope you might find an opportunity to look it over. I read it to Baker the other day and he was greatly impressed with it.

Next Tuesday, November 1st, I am leaving Doubleday, Page & Company and then I shall have some time to concentrate attention on my own future plans. I am still convinced that I can render greater service to my country and to the world along international lines, toward which I have been urged by your own great example, than in any other way. I have had letters from Judge Taft, Dr. Garfield, Dr. Henry Van Dyke, and many others, which greatly encourage me to put my plans to the test of actual practice.

In the past two weeks I have been swinging about over the country placing the Tumulty series in the big newspapers with really astonishing success. My own belief is that their publication will have a profound effect upon public opinion. Everywhere, among Republican newspapers as well as among Democratic newspapers, I was tremendously interested, as a staunch friend of yours, to find the tide of interest in your great career steadily and surely coming back; in my judgment it will again come to the flood.

With kindest personal regards to Mrs. Wilson and to you, believe me to be as always, my dear "Mr. President,"

Your devoted friend and follower,   Herbert S. Houston

P.S. In the current issue of "The Woman Citizen" I have a little article which bears the rather challenging title "On Our Way to the League of Nations."[2] I am sending a copy forward to you under another cover.

TLS (WP, DLC).
   [1] This enclosure is missing, but for its subject matter, see WW to H. S. Houston, Nov. 4, 1921.
   [2] The Woman Citizen, VI (Oct. 8, 1921), 10-11.

A News Report

[Oct. 29, 1921]

Wilson Abed With Recurrence of Indigestion; Attack Is No Cause for Alarm, It Is Said

Washington, Oct. 29.—Woodrow Wilson is suffering from a recurrence of indigestion and sick headaches. He was in bed when Marshal Foch called at his home, 2,340 S Street this morning, and his personal physician, Rear Admiral Cary T. Grayson, had given orders that he was not to receive any visitors, whoever they might be.

Mr. Wilson was up and about the house for a time this afternoon, but was forced by the condition of his health to give up his customary trip to Keith's Theatre tonight. He has been a regular attendant for many weeks, occupying a seat in the rear row of the orchestra every Saturday night.

Dr. Grayson said tonight that Mr. Wilson had not been feeling as well as usual for the last two or three days. In the past he frequently suffered from indigestion and headache, and a few days ago the old trouble returned.

Mr. Wilson, however, had been rising early until this morning, when he was advised to remain in bed. Dr. Grayson was at the Wilson home in the morning and afternoon. It was his desire that the former President remain as quiet as possible and he considered it inadvisable that Mr. Wilson should receive any visitors.

So far as could be learned, Mr. Wilson's indisposition was not a cause for alarm. The belief was expressed that he soon would recover from the attack.

As soon as the news got about that Marshal Foch had been at Mr. Wilson's home and had not been received by the former President, attempts were made to set afloat stories that Mr. Wilson had declined to see the Marshal for various reasons which had nothing to do with his illness.

Printed in the *New York Times*, Oct. 30, 1921.

To Bainbridge Colby, with Enclosure

My dear Colby: Washington D C 29th October 1921

The enclosed should have come first among the sheets I sent you the other day, but I did not have it ready then; in fact had not even thought of it. So it must go as a sort of postscript. I beg that you and Chadbourne will receive it in the spirit of cooperation in which it is conceived.

Thank you for your last letter; I am glad I am to see you here soon.   Cordially and sincerely yours,   Woodrow Wilson

TLS (B. Colby Papers, DLC).

E N C L O S U R E

Suggested introductory paragraph.

We recognize the fact that the complex, disturbing, and for the most part destructive results of the great war have made it necessary that the progressive countries of the world should supply for the reconstruction of its life a programme of law and refo form which shall bring it back to health and effective order; and that it lies with the political party which best understands existing conditions, is in most sympathetic touch with the mass of the people, and is best qualified to carry a constructive programme through to take the initiative in making and pressing affirmative proposals of remedy and reform.

In this spirit and with this great purpose, the Democratic party of the United States puts forth, in deep earnestness, the following platform of principle and purpose and seeks to serve America and, through America, liberal men throughout the world who seek to serve their people.

WWT MS (B. Colby Papers, DLC).

Two News Reports

[*Oct. 30, 1921*]

Wilson Rallies After Attack,
But Remains in Bed All Day

Washington, Oct. 30.—Former President Wilson, who was unable to receive Marshal Foch yesterday because of illness, continues to improve, according to reports tonight. Mr. Wilson was confined to his bed all day, but is in no serious condition.

Mr. Wilson is suffering from a slight attack of indigestion, which occurs frequently by reason of the fact that he is unable to take any exercise. Reports that he had another attack of apoplexy were denied, and his physician, Rear Admiral Grayson, said that the ex-President would be able to take his customary drives shortly and attend the burying of the unknown American hero at Arlington on Nov. 11.

Printed in the *New York Times*, Oct. 31, 1921.

[*Oct. 31, 1921*]

Wilson Shows Improvement;
Will Attend No Functions

Washington, Oct. 31.—Ex-President Wilson was reported slightly improved tonight. Although no callers were allowed to see him, his physician, Rear Admiral Cary T. Grayson, said that his condition was rapidly submitting to treatment and constant improvement was noted throughout today.

While alarming stories were circulated last night and today as to

Mr. Wilson's ailment, his friends denied that there was any reason to be alarmed. They said that he was merely suffering from indigestion and a cold. The latter is very slight. The earlier report that he had suffered another attack of apoplexy was denied by his physician. In fact, his general health has been much better than at any time in recent months.

Although the friends of the ex-President are hopeful that he may be able to participate at least in the burying of the unknown American hero at Arlington on Nov. 11, it can be said authoritatively tonight that the ex-President does not desire to be present on this occasion. The reason given for this is that he intends to keep himself absolutely in the background and will remain a private citizen as far as possible.

In truth, his strength is not such as to justify his going into a crowd, and upon the advice of his medical director he will not make any extraordinary test of his physical strength.

Printed in the *New York Times*, Nov. 1, 1921.

From Bainbridge Colby

My dear Mr President: New York City October 31, 1921

I couldn't help phoning to Mr Bolling this morning, just to make sure that the published reports of your indisposition were exaggerated, although I thought I could read between the lines, and it was a relief to be definitely assured that all was well with you.

Frank Cobb telephoned me this morning in much distress of mind about the article which appeared in the New York "World" about your inability to receive Marshal Foch when he called.[1] Cobb said it was entirely the fault of the news-management of the paper; that he had expressed himself angrily about it and sincerely hoped that you would exonerate him from any responsibility for it. He said it was another case of "journalism of conjecture," which he said was one of your excellent phrases that he frequently employed. Cobb is your loyal friend and admirer.

I was very glad to receive your additional memorandum written Saturday. It is an admirable introductory paragraph for a declaration of the Party's program. It couldn't be better. I sent it at once to Chadbourne.

I told Mr Bolling on the phone that I would not get to Washington before Thursday unless called there earlier. I am invited to a dinner which is to be given to H. G. Wells on Wednesday and I rather think I would like to attend it. I believe there is to be an interesting company of men present and there will undoubtedly be much discussion of the forthcoming conference for the limitation of armament.

    With sincerest regards always,

Cordially yours   Bainbridge Colby

TLS (WP, DLC).

  ¹ A general article on Foch's reception in Washington on the front page of the New York *World*, Oct. 30, 1921, stated only that "Wilson's physician had given instructions that it would not be advisable for him to receive any visitors, as he was not feeling well." However, a second article, placed immediately below the first, speculated that Wilson's indisposition "was diplomatic rather than actually physical." The anonymous author noted that Wilson had been receiving visitors daily for some time and that often a later visit was scheduled if the first proved inconvenient. This had not been done in the case of Foch. The writer recalled that Wilson and Foch had clashed repeatedly during the peace conference and listed specific incidents. He asserted that, for Wilson, Foch represented the forces of militarism and imperialism. "It is generally known among those closest to Mr. Wilson," the author concluded, "that he resents and fears the exaltation of militarism that is involved in the ovations to Marshal Foch. It is for these reasons that deliberate, calculated purpose is read into yesterday's incident."

William Lassiter to John Randolph Bolling

Dear Mr. Bolling: Washington, D. C. October 31, 1921.

    I informed you under date of October 25th that the earliest possible opportunity would be taken to conform to Mr. Wilson's request that his wish to join the procession on Armistice Day, riding in a horse-drawn vehicle, be laid before the Secretary of War. You will recall that when you broached the matter in my office, I told you that I would at once take Mr. Wilson's message in to the Secretary of War, but you suggested deferring the matter until you had again seen Mr. Wilson. Unfortunately the Secretary of War had left Washington by the time your letter arrived the next day and the matter could not be presented to him until his return, when it was at once brought to his attention.

    The Secretary of War directs me to say that he welcomes the participation of Mr. Wilson in the processional march on November 11th and will make due arrangements in connection therewith.

    The assembly for the procession is to be at the east front of the Capitol; the march is to begin promptly at 8:30 a.m., so that everyone will be in place at Arlington at 11:15 a.m. The President will arrive in front of the east steps of the Capitol at 8:25 a.m., the Vice President, the Chief Justice of the Supreme Court, the Associate Justices, the Cabinet, the Members of the Senate and of the House will arrive at a slightly earlier hour so that they can form in the order just given and be in position when the President arrives. At 8:30 a.m. the President takes his place and the procession moves.

    It is proposed that Mr. Wilson, riding in a carriage, arrive opposite the main east entrance to the Capitol at 8:25 a.m., where an officer will meet and guide his carriage to the place appointed; and that in the procession his carriage shall immediately precede the Associate Justices of the Supreme Court.

Inasmuch as the streets northwest of the Capitol will be crowded with troops, it is suggested that Mr. Wilson's carriage should arrive by way of Massachusetts Avenue and First St. N.E.

When the procession reaches West Executive Avenue, the President, the Vice President, Members of the Cabinet, the Supreme Court, the Senate and the House will turn to the left down Executive Avenue and leave the procession, proceeding afterwards by motor via the Highway Bridge to Arlington. It is planned that Mr. Wilson shall conform to this movement, and leave the procession at the same point, moving either south through Executive Avenue or north through Jackson Place.

The War Department has reserved for the use of Mr. Wilson a box in the Amphitheatre at Arlington, which will be at his disposal, if he should desire to be present there during the ceremonies in the Amphitheatre and at the interment. As the entire plan for seating distinguished guests is involved, information is requested as to whether Mr. Wilson will occupy this box.

The Secretary of War would be glad to designate an officer to serve as Aide to Mr. Wilson for this occasion, who would make all preliminary arrangements for him. Mr. Wilson's wishes in this regard are requested.   Very sincerely,   Wm Lassiter

TLS (WP, DLC).

John Randolph Bolling to William Lassiter

Dear General Lassiter: [Washington] 31st October 1921

I have laid before Mr. Wilson the contents of your letter of this date, and he appreciates the very complete nature of your reply. He asks me to say:

That he will be in the place designated by you on Armistice Day as near 8:25 a.m. as he possibly can;

That it is his wish to accompany the body of the unknown soldier all the way to Arlington, and not to drop out of the procession at Executive Avenue as you suggest;

That he will be obliged if you will ask The President to excuse him from occupying a seat in the Amphitheatre during the ceremonies because of the extreme difficulty which he experiences in going up and down steps;

That he appreciates the offer of the Secretary of War to designate an officer as Aide, but does not feel that it is necessary for him to have one.

I believe that the above fully covers all the matters suggested in your letter under reply; should anything further occur to you, I shall be glad to bring it to Mr. Wilson's attention.

Cordially yours,   [John Randolph Bolling]

CCL (WP, DLC).

A News Item

[*Nov. 2, 1921*]

WILSON GOES TO MATINEE.
Former President Improved Enough
to Defy Inclement Weather.

Washington, Nov. 2.—Former President Wilson had so far recovered today from his recent slight indisposition that, despite inclement weather, he attended a matinee at a local theatre.

Printed in the *New York Times*, Nov. 3, 1921.

To Herbert Sherman Houston

My dear friend: [Washington] 2nd November 1921

At first your plan for THE NEW AGE and the Institute of Information¹ quite took my breath away, but the more I let its sober tone and high and serious aim sink into my consciousness the more confident I became that you could carry it out; and when you do you will have rendered a great service.

I wish I had known beforehand that you had Tittoni in mind as your "Interpreter" for Italy, because when I was in Paris I found no one had any confidence in him. But you have of course looked him up for this special purpose and have found [in?] him what you can use. The man in this country who knows him best is Henry White who, by the way, is one of the straightest and most loyal colleagues I ever had; I hold him in real affection.

I shall await with eager interest the launching of your enterprise, and hope that you will send me one of the first subscription blanks.

My heartiest good wishes will go with you throughout the whole development.

Thank you again for letting me know about it.

Cordially and faithfully yours,   [Woodrow Wilson]

P.S. I read with a great deal of interest your article, "On Our Way to the League of Nations," and thank you for sending it to me.

CCL (WP, DLC).

¹ Houston obviously soon discovered that *New Age* was the title of a long-established London review of politics, religion, and literature. He instead named the magazine which he published from 1922 to 1924 *Our World*. Apparently, the "Institute of Information" never materialized: it is not mentioned in his sketches in *Who's Who in America* or elsewhere.

From Charles Williston McAlpin

My dear Friend: New York City November 4, 1921

Much as I have longed to see you during the past three years, I have hesitated to intrude upon you, and I still hesitate to do so, but as I am planning to be in Washington for a dinner on Monday evening, November 21st, I am going to ask if it would be convenient for you to see me either on Monday afternoon, November 21st, or sometime on Tuesday, the 22nd.

You have been and are constantly in my thoughts and prayers, and I would love to see you if only for a brief interval, but if I am asking too much just say the word, for your word is still the law with me.

With kindest regards to Mrs. Wilson and affectionate greetings to you, believe me

Ever faithfully your friend, Charles W McAlpin

TLS (WP, DLC).

John Randolph Bolling to Charles Williston McAlpin

My dear Mr. McAlpin: [Washington] 5th November 1921

Mr. Wilson asks me to reply to your kind letter of yesterday and say he could never imagine you doing anything that would intrude upon him; that he was very glad to hear from you again.

As Mr. Wilson is making very few appointments, he finds it difficult to plan even two weeks ahead. If, however, you will communicate with him (by messenger) upon your arrival in Washington, he will try and arrange a time when you can run in and see him for a few minutes on one of the two days that you are here.

Cordially yours, [John Randolph Bolling]

CCL (WP, DLC).

To Ellen Duane Davis

My dear Friend: [Washington] 5th November 1921

The sheets completing the delightful calendar arrived safely and I congratulate you on the completion of what must I fear at times have been a very exacting task, and myself on possessing one of the most admirable calendars of its rare kind that I have ever seen. I certainly owe a vast deal to your thoughtful and affectionate friendship. Thank you with all my heart.

I am going along at the usual pace which is so slow that I am really not aware of any movement at all, but can only hope that nature is engaged upon some process that is not unfavorable.

Please give my love to E.P., and always think of me as
                    Your affectionate friend,   [Woodrow Wilson]

CCL (WP, DLC).

To James Henry Taylor[1]

My dear Friend: Washington D C 5th November 1921

You are extraordinarily thoughtful and kind; the birds hit my appetite at just the right stage. They will taste and agree with me all the better because of what their sweet flavor will remind me of.

With warmest regards;
                    Gratefully yours,   Woodrow Wilson

TLS (WP, DLC).
    [1] Pastor of Central Presbyterian Church of Washington, of which Wilson was a member.

John Randolph Bolling to John Wingate Weeks

Sir: [Washington] 5th November 1921

Mr. and Mrs. Woodrow Wilson desire me to thank you for the invitation[1] to be present at the ceremonies attending the burial of An Unknown American who died in the defense of his country in the Memorial Ampitheatre National Cemetery at Arlington on Friday morning November the eleventh at eleven o'clock, and the tickets enclosed for Box Number One.

Mr. and Mrs. Wilson regret that they will be unable to attend the ceremonies because of the difficulty which Mr. Wilson experiences in going up and down steps. I am, therefore, returning herewith the cards for admission to the box which you so courteously placed at their disposal.[2]

                    Sincerely yours,   [John Randolph Bolling]

CCL (WP, DLC).

¹ It is missing.
² A typed note at the top of this letter reads: "Read and approved by E.B.W. before sending."

To Louis Dembitz Brandeis, with Enclosure

My dear Mr. Justice: Washington D C 6th November 1921

Several times recently, as he has no doubt told you, I have sent to Mr. Colby sentences which I hoped might serve as contributions to the document upon which he and Mr. Chadbourne were collaborating.

Having learned to my great satisfaction that you and Mr. Colby have generously assumed the laboring oars in the all important enterprise, I take the liberty of sending to you a contribution to the same document which I hope may prove at least suggestive.

With grateful appreciation of the invaluable cooperation you have generously vouchsafed me;

Cordially and faithfully yours,   Woodrow Wilson

P.S. Please excuse the bad typewriting of the document enclosed; I have the use of only one hand, fortunately the right one.

TLS (L. D. Brandeis Papers, KyLoU).

E N C L O S U R E

"AMERICA FIRST" is a slogan which does not belong to any one political party, it is merely a concise expression of what is in the heart of every patriotic American. We enthusiastica cally incorporate it with this our declaration of principles and purposes. But it means different things in different mouths and requires definition. When uttered by the present leaders of the REPUBLICAN PARTY IT MEANS that AMERICA must render no service to any other nation or people which she can reserve for her own selfish aggrandizement.

When we use it we mean that in every international action or organization for the benefit of mankind America must be foremost: that Amarica must lead the world by imparting to other peoples her own ideals of Justice and of Peace and by rendering them material aid in the realization of those ideals.

WWT MS (L. D. Brandeis Papers, KyLoU).

William Lassiter to John Randolph Bolling

My dear Mr. Bolling: Washington, D. C. November 7, 1921.

Your letter dated October 31st has just been handed to me this morning. It arrived by messenger and I receipted to the messenger for it. Presumably there has been some delay on the part of the messenger in delivering this letter.

I have communicated to the Secretary of War the contents of your note and he directs me to say that he is glad to note that Mr. Wilson will be present in the procession on November 11th. The Secretary, however, directs me to say that the President and the other dignitaries of the Government will retire from the procession at West Executive Avenue, and, from thence on, the mourners immediately in rear of the remains will be purely military in character. He is, therefore, constrained to ask that Mr. Wilson conform to the plans arranged for the procession, which are that the President, the Vice President, the Chief Justice of the Supreme Court, Ex-President Wilson, the Associate Justices, the Cabinet, the Senate and the House will withdraw from the procession at West Executive Avenue.

I am   Yours very truly,   Wm Lassiter

TLS (WP, DLC).

John Randolph Bolling to Charles Evans Hughes

Sir: [Washington] 7th November 1921

Mr. and Mrs. Woodrow Wilson ask me to thank you for your kind invitation to attend the opening session of the Conference on the Limitation of Armament on Saturday morning the twelfth of November at half past ten o'clock, and express regret that the present state of Mr. Wilson's convalescence will not permit them to accept.

                    Cordially yours,   [John Randolph Bolling]

CCL (WP, DLC).

To Warren Gamaliel Harding

My dear Mr. President: [Washington] 8th November 1921

Under date of October fourth you were gracious enough to write me in regard to the ceremonies at Arlington on Armistice Day.

Presuming upon this, I got in touch with General Lassiter (who I understood was the official aide for that occasion) and found to my surprise that I must get special permission from the Secretary of War to join the procession in a horse-drawn vehicle—it being manifestly impossible for me to walk the distance. That permission was granted.

In view of the fact that I will not be able to attend the exercises in the ampitheatre (owing to the difficulty I experience in going up and down steps), it is my very sincere desire to accompany the body of the unknown soldier from the Capitol to Arlington. This wish was communicated to General Lassiter under date of October thirty-first, and I am now informed by him that The Secretary of War is "constrained to ask that" I retire from the procession at West Executive Avenue.

If this is the official decision I daresay it is best that I should not join the procession at all; but I am loath to accept it as the official decision until I am told that it is by you.

Yours very truly,   [Woodrow Wilson]

CCL (WP, DLC).

From Warren Gamaliel Harding

My dear Mr. Wilson: The White House November 8, 1921

I am just now in receipt of yours of even date. I think I have learned, as you doubtless have, the only way to solve an embarrassing situation confronting one is to meet it with entire frankness.

In the early stages of the preparations for the Armistice Day ceremonies and the burial of an unknown American soldier, it was thought by every one concerned that it would be most becoming to have you a participant. As your letter suggests, I wrote you an invitation to that effect and was desirous of making every possible provision to meet your wishes and convenience in the matter, and so directed those who have immediate charge. Subsequent developments are sufficiently outlined in your letter to me of this date. When it was understood that it was not convenient for you to attend the exercises at the Amphitheater, the officers in charge were quite unanimous in making an exception of your case and provided for your participation in the official parade as the one occupant of a horse-drawn vehicle. Because the official party from civil life can not be expected to make the full march from the Capitol to Arlington Cemetery, it was decided, quite in accordance with custom, to drop the official party out of the procession at Executive Avenue. I am sure you are so familiar with the practices in Washington processions to understand the desirability of this course. Since your participation is manifestly and distinctly that of one identified with the official civil life it was thought more seemly to have you adhere to the program adopted.

I fear a note of inharmony would be suggested, if one formerly in authority accompanied the procession to the Cemetery, when those who constitute the great body of the official division of the procession are dropping out according to the arranged program.

I should be sorry not to have you participate in any way, but I feel sure that this fuller recital will suggest to you that there is neither lack of courtesy or consideration in suggesting that we all adhere to the official plan.

Permit me to assure you, my dear Mr. President, that every one concerned is pleased at the thought of your participation and we really wish to do everything possible to accord with your preferences in that participation. You can understand, however, why those who are responsible for the program prefer to carry it out along the lines which have been carefully thought out.

Very truly yours,   Warren G Harding

TLS (WP, DLC).

From Louis Dembitz Brandeis

My dear Mr Wilson: Washington, D. C. Nov. 8/21

Let me thank you for the noble and penetrating note enclosed with yours of yesterday.

I am sending a copy to Mr Colby.

Most Cordially   Louis D Brandeis

ALS (WP, DLC).

From William Edward Dodd

My dear Mr. Wilson: Chicago, Nov 8, 1921

I am sending you by mail the revised and enlarged *Woodrow Wilson and His Work* which was to have been published on September 16. The delay came somehow in the office of the publishers, not because of anything I had done or neglected to do.

It is not by any means the full and satisfactory account I wish it were. There are doubtless many errors which you will detect if you find time to look it through; but they are not conscious omissions and certainly not perverted interpretations. What I have said of you at Paris and in the three chapters that treat the blunder of 1920, the crime, if one might say a people can commit a crime—and I disagree with Burke on this point—I can not help thinking substantially accurate. I wrote without access to the minutes of your discussions in Paris; but having now a copy of the digest of those discussions in my possession (in confidence), I am constrained to think my story an under rather than an over statement.

The revision had to be made without breaking the plates in most cases but I made some changes in the earlier chapters which I think your daughters will not dislike. All of us have drifted so far from the solemn religion of our fathers in the South after the great disaster of 61–65 that only a recurrence of the sermons, songs and printed conversations of the time can give us a sense of its seriousness.

If you ever get a moment's time from the calls of Fochs and Briands, won't you let me have a line from you as to my interpretation of the history, the events and the men of your great day?

The Iroquois Club[1] here asked me for a series of lectures on our recent history. Nos 4 & 5 are devoted to you and your leadership. George Brennan[2] keeps away, but his followers crowd the room and applaud with apparent enthusiasm. By the way Brennan tells what I take to be great lies about a visit to you last summer.[3] But he was completely undone at St Louis where he tried to direct the action of the National committee

Yours sincerely   William E. Dodd

P.S. I like Tumultys book very much so far, though I note some soft pedalling of Harvey and Wood

ALS (WP, DLC).
   [1] The club of the regular Democratic organization of Chicago.
   [2] About whom, see WW to G. E. Brennan, June 13, 1921, n. 1.
   [3] As n. 2 to the letter just cited reveals, Brennan did visit Wilson on June 24, 1921, at Wilson's request.

From Frank Irving Cobb

Dear Mr. Wilson: New York. November 8th, 1921.

Many, many thanks indeed for your kindness. I felt ashamed to bother you, and yet it was something that I wanted very much, and shall always appreciate.

It did me a great deal of good to see you again, and get your point of view.

I cannot say that I am increasingly pessimistic about the conference, because I have never been optimistic. The French delegation seems to have a characteristically naive programme of disarmament—which is to give the United States a coaling station in the

Pacific in exchange for a loan. It would all be joyous comedy, if it were not so tragic.

Again thanking you, I am, most sincerely your friend,

Frank I Cobb.

TLS (WP, DLC).

An Unpublished Statement[1]

[Nov. 9, 1921]

To the men who followed to France the flag for which I was at that time responsible:

It was of course my inclination and purpose to follow the body of our dead comrade to Arlington, but I find that it will not be possible for me to do so, and inasmuch as I feel that you will be interested to know the reason, I am taking the liberty of giving out the following letters, which, taken together, furnish the full explanation. I make this explanation because it is of necessity the only way in which I can pay my last tribute of respect to our dead hero.

⟨I am deeply distressed to find⟩ that ⟨I shall be excluded by⟩ the official arrangements ⟨from⟩ admit of no such modification as will permit my following the body of the unknown soldier to Arlington.

Both my feelings and my sense of duty as the one-time Commander in Chief of the forces to which my dead comrade belonged (for I regard every member of the great expeditionary force as my comrade), had impelled me to join the sad procession which is to go to Arlington on Friday.

⟨Unfortunately, I am unable to walk the distance from the Capitol to Arlington, or any great part of it; and it seems that the official arrangements render it impossible to give me a place in the procession after it reached the Department of War.

⟨I feel that my comrades of the expeditionary forces are entitled to this explanation of a circumstance which would in itself seem inexplicable.⟩

T MS (WP, DLC).
    [1] A typewritten note at the top of this document reads: "Dict. by W.W. Novr. 9th, 1921; not given out." Words in angle brackets struck out by WW. About Wilson's decision not to publish this statement, see WW to L. Seibold, Nov. 12, 1921, n. 1.

To Anna Eleanor Roosevelt Roosevelt

My dear Mrs. Roosevelt: [Washington] 9th November 1921

Thank you for your letter of November seventh.[1]

I am greatly relieved to hear of your husband's improvement and

wish you would convey to him my congratulations and the hope
that his recovery will be satisfactory and speedy.

Mrs. Wilson joins me in cordial regards to you both.

Sincerely yours,   [Woodrow Wilson]

CCL (WP, DLC).
¹ It is missing.

A News Item

[*Nov. 10, 1921*]

BRIAND FINDS WILSON OUT.
Calls on Ex-President and Also
Visits Washington Tomb.

Washington, Nov. 10 (Associated Press).—Premier Briand called
upon former President Wilson today but was informed that Mr. and
Mrs. Wilson were out. M. Briand left his card. . . .

Printed in the *New York Times*, Nov. 11, 1921.

A News Report

[*Nov. 11, 1921*]

WILSON IN TEARS AS 20,000 ACCLAIM
HIM WORLD'S HERO

Washington, Nov. 11.—Woodrow Wilson, War President, broke
his cold silence and aloofness to-day. Standing in the door of the
secluded home he chose when leaving the White House, he burst
into tears as more than 20,000 persons, standing bareheaded, paid
tribute to "the greatest soldier in the world." This was the unanimous appellation of those who had turned from paying a silent and
reverent tribute to America's Unknown Soldier to pay a reverent
but not silent tribute to the Unknown Soldier's Commander in
Chief.

This tribute at the home of Mr. Wilson came after another tribute that had been paid him as with Mrs. Wilson he rode down historic Pennsylvania Avenue behind the flag-draped caisson bearing
the body of the Unknown Soldier, and between the lines of veterans of the World War. Thousands lining the avenue were restrained in the presence of the soldier dead, but the pale face of the
man who gave his health and strength to uphold the same ideals
for which the Unknown Soldier died, seemingly unleashed the

pent-up emotions of the watchers. Growing from an excited whisper, as the carriage bearing Mr. and Mrs. Wilson entered the parade, gradually there spread a volume of applause that swept the length of the avenue and continued until the carriage turned out of line after passing the White House.

The homage paid the Unknown Soldier was that always accorded honored dead by Americans. The tribute to Woodrow Wilson, both in the funeral procession and at his home was a spontaneous and instinctive outburst to the high ideals for which he stood.

When former President and Mrs. Wilson left the funeral procession and went direct to their home, that residence became the mecca of thousands who were determined that he should be paid a fitting tribute on the anniversary of the armistice. No word of the impending demonstration had been given him, and he was not prepared for the huge throng that, soon after 1 o'clock, began forming in front of his home.

There was a tremendous outburst of enthusiasm when Mr. Wilson, a few minutes after 3 o'clock, suddenly appeared at the door. For nearly ten minutes the cheering, the shouting of greetings, interspersed with "Three cheers for the League of Nations!" "Three cheers for the greatest soldier of them all!" "Three Cheers for Woodrow Wilson!" swept over the quiet residential section.

Mr. Wilson leaned heavily upon a cane he carried in his right hand. His servant supported his left side, but the spontaneous outburst seemed to infuse the feeble frame with life and he disdained the help of his servant as he slowly came down the three steps to the side of an automobile drawn up in front of the door, where he greeted four disabled veterans of the World War.

At the urging of Mrs. Wilson, he finally consented to re-enter the house for a short rest before returning to the door to return the reception. The crowd was not to be denied, however, and a moment later the former President and Mrs. Wilson appeared at a window on the second floor.

Mr. Wilson was then informed that the committee of women who represented the Women's Committee of the District of Columbia for the Limitation of Armament, having the ceremony in charge, and the Women's Democratic Club of Baltimore, with their spokesman, Hamilton Holt of the League of Nations Association, had arrived. The former President returned to the front door.

Awaiting him at the door were a large number of children from Washington and Baltimore. These children, several hundred in number, had each contributed a flower, and these little Olive

Chace, daughter of an old friend, handed to the former President. She also handed him this letter: . . .[1]

After the ceremony, Mr. Holt delivered a short address on behalf of all those present. He told the former President of the burial of the Unknown Soldier in Arlington, which Mr. Wilson did not attend, and added: "Mr. Wilson, you were his Commander in Chief. You sent him into action with your blessing and imbued with the spirit of your ideals. We cannot let this day pass without coming here to tell you what is in our hearts. We haven't forgot the ideals for which we went to war and for which this soldier died.

"We wish to congratulate you—a wounded soldier of the war— on your regaining your health. We also wish to pledge to you our honor and our respect. Your work shall not die."

"I wish," Mr. Wilson replied in a voice clear but weakened by illness, "that I had the voice to reply and to thank you for the wonderful tribute that you have paid me. I can only say God bless you."

For a moment the silence continued and a booming voice shouted, "Long live the best man in the world!" Mr. Wilson could not restrain his emotion, and as the sentiment of the voice was echoed in a tremendous outburst of cheering, great tear drops rolled from his eyes. His right hand sought the hand of Mrs. Wilson, who has been his constant companion in adversity, and she too burst into tears. The grief of the trembling man seemed to reach out into the crowd and men and women also burst into cheers [tears?].

Mr. and Mrs. Wilson stood holding each other by the hand for a full minute, and then as the tune of "My Country, 'Tis of Thee" rang out upon the air they turned and slowly went into the house. As he entered, Mr. Wilson once more turned, and in a voice audible only within a few feet, murmured, "Goodby," and kissed his [her] hand.

Policeman in vain appealed to the throng to disperse with the statement that Mr. Wilson would not again appear, but for more than an hour there was hardly a movement except from those on the outskirts. Finally, however, those crowded densely at the door began slowly and with many backward glances to walk away.

In the parade Mr. and Mrs. Wilson rode in an open carriage drawn by two horses, one chestnut and one black. When they arrived at the Capitol the funeral procession already had started and the carriage was placed between two marching organizations of veterans of the World War. The former President seemed proud to

[1] Here follows the text of the next document.

have this place, rather than that directly behind Chief Justice Taft, to which he had originally been assigned, and a new firmness of step and squaring of shoulders came to the veterans as their former chief moved with them.

Mr. Wilson was dressed in a dark suit and overcoat and wore a high silk hat. In the lapel of his coat he wore a small red poppy. In his right hand he carried a light cane with which at times he tapped the floor of his carriage. His body inclined slightly toward Mrs. Wilson, who also was dressed in dark clothes and dark fur coat, topped by a three-pointed black trimmed hat. On her breast was pinned a large red poppy.

Mr. Wilson looked stronger than when he left the White House. His face has not the ruddiness it had a few months ago. His left arm was bent and held close to his side, but no artificial support was needed. He is lame in his left foot and leg, and, in walking, has to favor it. He was assisted in and out of the carriage.

Throughout the journey from the S Street home to the Capitol Mr. Wilson was constantly returning the bows of those who recognized him. As his carriage entered the procession, an excited whispering arose, then a faint ripple of applause which swelled into a continuous outburst as the procession marched down the avenue.

He acknowledged the salutes of his friends by constantly removing his hat. The spirited horses that drew his carriage gained on the marchers ahead and the ex-President went through a series of short halts, the last of which, immediately in front of the White House, was extended several minutes when President Harding and some of the other dignitaries withdrew from the parade. It was here that Mr. Wilson received one of the most pronounced demonstrations, which came in part from the policemen and employees of the White House, who were gathered in a reserved section along the avenue. Mr. Wilson lifted his hat while Mrs. Wilson nodded her greeting. Two or three admirers of the former President crowded out and spoke to him, while others waved their handkerchiefs in greeting. When the procession resumed its journey there was another ovation.

President Harding, Chief Justice Taft, the Cabinet and a number of Congressmen left the cortege at the White House, where Mr. Harding met the President and stood with him while he reviewed the remaining marchers. The greeting that passed between him and Mr. Wilson was formal, each lifting his hat and nodding. Mr. Wilson then left the procession, turning off Pennsylvania Avenue to the right at Jackson Place, the first street beyond the White House. He seemed to take little interest in his former home, glancing toward it only once or twice, and similarly, Mrs. Wilson appeared to be little interested, although she made a sweeping glance across the front grounds as the carriage approached.

When Mr. Wilson arrived back at home he was asked if he would comment on the ceremonies incident to the burial of the Unknown Soldier and his participation in it. At first he said, "no," but then added, "I was glad to have been there." At this point Mrs. Wilson joined in to say, "it was wonderful that the day turned out so perfectly for the ceremony."

Mr. Wilson was then reminded of the ovation he had received while coming down Pennsylvania Avenue and he said: "It was rather embarrassing because it was given in a funeral procession."

Immediately after he returned from participating in the parade Rear Admiral Cary T. Grayson, his physician, arrived at the house and examined the patient. He reported that Mr. Wilson had stood the trip well and did not seem unduly fatigued. When Mr. Wilson appeared a few hours later for the demonstration at his house he appeared even stronger than when he had left the house for the Capitol.

Printed in New York *World*, Nov. 12, 1921.

From the Children's Delegation

Dear Mr. Wilson,   Washington, D. C., November 11, 1921

We have come here today to let you know of the deep love the children of the nation have for you. Young as we are we have learned to admire you and the great principles for which you stand. In this basket of flowers we present to you, each flower is contributed by a child and with each flower goes the heart of the giver, for you represent the ideals so dear to America. We, as future citizens of the United States, will do our best to perpetuate these ideals you have fought for so bravely.

With best wishes for your future,
                                        The Children's Delegation.

ALS (WP, DLC).

To Louis Seibold

Dear Seibold: Washington D C 12th November 1921

Your counsel saved me from a very stupid blunder, and I thank you with all my heart.[1]
                                        Faithfully yours,   Woodrow Wilson

TLS (WP, DLC).
¹ Seibold, in an undated memorandum for Katharine E. Brand, attached to this letter, explains:

"The attached note written by Mr. Wilson on November 12, 1921 (eight months after he had ceased to be President), relates to a conversation I had with him on November 9 at his private residence on S Street in Washington, regarding the arrangements of the ceremonies attending the burial of the 'Unknown Soldier' in Arlington. General Rossiter [Lassiter], who had charge of the arrangements, stipulated that Mr. Wilson, who was in ailing health, should leave the funeral cortege at the city limits, to which Mrs. Wilson and he were to journey in an open horse-drawn Victoria. Mr. Wilson, who wished to be present at the final tribute to the American soldier who had served in the army of which Mr. Wilson was Commander-in-Chief, protested. His protest was ignored.

"During my conversation with him on November 9, Mr. Wilson turned over to me correspondence between himself and President Harding, as well as that with General Rossiter [Lassiter]. He also gave me an attached statement that voiced the indignation he felt over the treatment accorded him by President Harding and General Rossiter [Lassiter], and requested that I publish it in the newspapers; at the same time asking my advice as to the wisdom of such a course. I told him that I thought that it would create an unfavorable impression regarding the incident and provoke criticism that might reflect against himself. Therefore, I urged him to accept the conditions imposed by the War Department and participate in the tribute to the 'Unknown Soldier.' Mr. Wilson accepted this suggestion. Mrs. Wilson and her distinguished husband were the outstanding figures in the procession from the Capital to the city limits. Later in the day, a crowd of some ten thousand persons assembled before his residence and paid a great but silent tribute to him when he appeared on the balcony. Two days later I received the accompnaying [accompanying] note from him."

John Randolph Bolling to Maurice Drummond Peterson¹

My dear Mr. Peterson:			[Washington] 12th November 1921

With reference to your call of yesterday; Mr. Wilson will be glad to see Mr. Balfour at three-thirty o'clock on Monday afternoon, November fourteenth.

						Yours very cordially,	[John Randolph Bolling]

CCL (WP, DLC).
¹ Private Secretary to Arthur James Balfour, who at this time was Lord President of the Council and ranking member of the British delegation to the Washington Conference.

From John Sharp Williams

My dear Mr. President:			[Washington] November 12, 1921.

On yesterday my wife¹ and I went down and remained about three hours with the crowd which gathered about your house. I found a place where she could sit down and I roamed around in the crowd for the purpose of catching, as well as I could with my defective ears, the temper and tone of it. In addition to that, soon somebody who knew who I was started a conversation with my wife, introducing various people, so that she heard even more than I. It would please you very much to know with what cordiality and heartfeltness good things were being said about you; and if you are constituted like I am, it will do you almost as much good to know what bad things were being said about those who, actuated by political motives, had made a pretext out of American "sovereignty" and "independence," etc., to attempt to crucify you politically.

I noticed some people leaving their cards at the door, but unfortunately I had not brought any; but I want you to know that I was there, as I always am either in body or in spirit where your good name, your past record, or hopes for your future are concerned.

I have gotten so that I do not like to make political prophecies—I have made so many that didn't come true. I believe, however, that the recession of the tide, which followed its flood on the way to the land of world peace, has itself about stopped and the tide is beginning or soon will begin to flow landward again. I have been waiting for it, because I think no wise man struggles against a tide when by waiting awhile he can have the tide itself helping him on his way to his goal. However, I am not writing this for the purpose of horoscoping but merely that one good friend may know that another good friend on yesterday was interested in him.

I was struck with the patience of the crowd—its waiting three to three and one-half hours with nothing political or actual to be accomplished except to show good will to you for the present, faith in you for the future, and an endorsement of you in the past.

I am, with every expression of regard,

Very truly yours,   John Sharp Williams

TLS (WP, DLC).
    [1] Elizabeth Dial Webb Williams.

To John Sharp Williams

My dear Friend: Washington D C 14th November 1921

Your letter of November 12th gave me a great deal of pleasure.

I learned while the crowd was outside on Friday that you were in it, and sent out in the hope you might be found and brought in; but was told it was impossible without obliging you to struggle through the crowd in a way that would be most uncomfortable. I therefore felt it was most considerate of you for me to accept the disappointment of not speaking with you, and forced myself to be content with losing what would have been a great pleasure.

Mrs. Wilson joins me in warm regards to Mrs. Williams and you, and I am always, with affectionate esteem;

Your sincere friend,   Woodrow Wilson

TLS (J. S. Williams Papers, DLC).

To William Edward Dodd

My dear Friend:　　　　　Washington D C 14th November 1921

The revised copy of your generous biography of me is a most welcome gift.

I should not like to get out an enlarged, but I should very much like to get out a revised edition of the physical Woodrow Wilson. It is very much needed both for private and public circulation.

I find reading about myself very tedious, but I shall none the less look forward with real interest to reading your new edition.

With warm appreciation;

Cordially and sincerely yours,　Woodrow Wilson

TLS (W. E. Dodd Papers, DLC).

John Randolph Bolling to William Edward Dodd

My dear sir:　　　　　2340 S Street NW 14th November 1921

Mr. Wilson was interested in your reference to a "digest of the discussions at Paris" in your letter to him of November 8th. Will you be good enough to tell him what this digest covers, as he does not recall having ever heard of one?

Yours very truly,　John Randolph Bolling

TLS (W. E. Dodd Papers, DLC).

From Louis Seibold

My Dear Boss.　　　　　Washington, Nov 14, '21

The dear, dead Unknown private was no better soldier than his beloved Commander-In-Chief proved himself in a very trying situation.

I always knew you were a good sport

Affectionately,　Louis Seibold

TLS (WP, DLC).

From Martha McChesney Berry[1]

My dear Mr. Wilson:　Mount Berry, Georgia. November 14, 1921.

I know that you are interested in the Berry Schools and that you know that Mrs. Ellen Ax[s]on Wilson sold her pictures and endowed a day here, $1250., in memory of her brother.[2] The amounts that have come to me in this way has built up our endowment, and the interest on such amounts is used to help pay the expenses of boys and girls who are not able to pay.

I am enclosing a letter[3] from some attorneys here in Rome, Georgia, to the Governor of the State.[4] These men went to see the Governor and had him to sign a contract to give them 20% of all the money they could collect from the Berry Schools. I have had to beg all this money in the East and North and we are now having a hard struggle to keep things going and I feel that it is so unjust to make me pay these taxes after I have begged the money outside the State.

Feeling that you must know of the work we are doing and knowing what a hard struggle you have had and how many times you have been misunderstood, I believe a letter of encouragement from you would help me a great deal just at this time. For twenty years I have given my time and my strength to help the illiterates of Georgia and I am now facing a hard trial because these two men have found a way to make some moeny [money] for themselves by imposing a burden upon me. I have been to see the Governor and have done all that I possibly can without any success.

I hope that you are getting well and stronger. I know how to sympathize with you—I know what it is to give you[r] all and be misunderstood.   Sincerely,   Martha Berry

TLS (WP, DLC).
  [1] Founder (1902) and Director of the Martha Berry Schools at Mount Berry, Georgia.
  [2] Edward William Axson who, with his wife and young son, was drowned in the Etowah River near Creighton, Georgia, on April 26, 1905. See WW to R. Bridges, April 28, 1905, n. 1, Vol. 16.
  [3] It is missing.
  [4] Thomas William Hardwick, congressman from Georgia, 1903-1914; senator from Georgia, 1914-1919; and Governor of Georgia, 1921-1923.

To the Children's Delegation

My dear Friends: [Washington] 15th November 1921

Nothing could have given me more pleasure or pride than the lovely tribute of flowers which you brought me on last Friday.

It makes me very happy to think that the children of the country feel about me as they do, and I shall look forward with great pleasure to your cooperation in the future in realizing the ideals we all believe in.   Affectionately yours,   [Woodrow Wilson]

CCL (WP, DLC).

From Ellen Duane Davis

Philadelphia Monday 15th Nov. 1921

Thirty five years tomorrow E.P. & I began our life together, and strange to say, love each other more each day & grow more dependent upon each other. He is a "bad lot"—as you know & it takes a great deal of patience & and perseverence to keep him in order, but all things considered, he probably will say the same about me, so we are quits. I have been wanting to write to you ever since you wrote me that lovely letter about the Calendar,[1] but you are 27 days too soon! Dec. is yet to come, but you will [not] get the whole year until your birthday Dec. 28. E.P. and Kate Boyd our niece went up to Princeton and saw that wonderful game.[2] Wilder[3] had written begging him to go to a kind of reunion of "79" but alas there were so many *sons* of 79 in the 79 room that I fear E.P. did not enjoy it as much as if you & Cleve Dodge & a few others we might mention had been there. The game however was fine & I am only sorry last Saturday at New Haven was not as fine for Princeton.[4] Now I want you & Edith to let us come down to Washington when the Calendar is done and give it to you myself? E.P. is *horribly* busy & writing another book[5] (but not about you, he loves you too well for that) therefore he may not be able to come but may Kate Boyd come with me? I am better in health than for several years and made nine speeches for your kind of Democracy last week before Elections. I *may* run for U. S. Senator   I am nearly old enough & the campaign if I dont win out will give the Reps. a jolt! Please do not think my letter simply that of a fool, but we are so very proud of you and feel sure we shall be in *your* League of Nations before very long. With best love to Edith and with the knowledge that she grows prouder of you every day I am always

Most sincerely your friend,   Ellen Duane Davis

I wrote to Jessie last night. I really feel nearer & dearer to her and hers than anyone else except Kate. J. is a very wonderful woman.

ALS (WP, DLC).
[1] WW to Ellen D. Davis, Nov. 5, 1921.
[2] Princeton defeated Harvard, 10 to 3, in the football game played at Princeton on November 5.
[3] William Royal Wilder.
[4] Yale defeated Princeton, 13 to 7, in the football game played on November 12.
[5] Edward Parker Davis, *Complications of Pregnancy* (New York and London, 1923).

Arthur James Balfour to Edith Bolling Galt Wilson

My dear Mrs. Wilson   Washington. Nov. 16th, 1921.

Just a line of very sincere thanks for the kind letter with which you welcomed me to Washington.[1]

I need hardly say how anxious I am to have a chance of seeing you and Mr. Wilson at the earliest possible moment. Only the pressure of the Conference has so far made it difficult for a time to be arranged at which I can call on you; and I hope it will be practicable for me to see you both very soon. My Secretary is in touch with Mr. Bolling for this purpose.

Yrs ever   Arthur James Balfour

TLS (EBW Papers, DLC).
[1] It is missing in all collections and repositories.

To Martha McChesney Berry

My dear Miss Berry: [Washington] 17th November 1921

I am indeed sorry to hear you are encountering new difficulties. I do not know of any school that deserves more encouragement and support than yours does. Obstacles should be taken out of the way instead of being put in your way, and I hope the men who are now embarrassing you will come to see the folly and iniquity of what they are doing.

Cordially and sincerely yours,   [Woodrow Wilson]

CCL (WP, DLC).

William Edward Dodd to John Randolph Bolling

My dear Mr. Bolling: Chicago November 17, 1921.

Mr. H. C. Nixon[1] and Mr. Preston Slosson[2] had the task at Paris of making a copy of the proceedings of the Conference for each of the American Commission.

Nixon is a graduate student here. He has one of these copies which he loaned me in strictest confidence. When I was revising my book, which he had seen, he informed me on one or two points as to the position taken by Mr. Wilson. Some things I could not rewrite under the rule of the publishers; but there was no important misinterpretation, I am constrained to believe.

No other person, save Professor McLaughlin,[3] a close friend, has seen this document and Nixon would lose his mind if he thought Mr. Wilson were displeased—so loyal and patriotic is he.

Tell Mr. Wilson that I am sorry for Mr. Tumulty, a devoted friend in a most confidential position, because of certain traits of character. William B. McIlvain[4] of this city said to me yesterday that it seemed that everyone who wrote about Wilson ruined himself. I did not remind him of my performance! And George Foster Peabody, a noble soul I think, is greatly annoyed. But one may never be responsible for what one's friends may do.

After Lansing, McCombs and Tumulty, I begin to see what a President's job is. Well, somebody must be President and stand all this sort of thing, although there is some doubt in my mind whether the present head of the Nation will ever be disturbed by the authors of scores of volumes.

Pardon so much of a letter in response to your inquiry about the "digest."   Yours sincerely,   William E. Dodd

If Mr. Wilson were to have that physical revision of which he speaks in his letter, nothing would save him still other secretaries of state and supposed "makers." He would literally be drafted for the Presidency.   Wm E.D.

TLS (WP, DLC).
   [1] Herman Clarence Nixon, at this time a graduate student in history and political science at the University of Chicago. He does not appear in directories of the personnel of the American Commission to Negotiate Peace; he was probably one of the army officers or enlisted men assigned to assist in its work.
   [2] Preston William Slosson, at this time instructor in history at the University of Michigan. Slosson had been an assistant to James Thomson Shotwell in the history section of the A.C.N.P.
   [3] Andrew Cunningham McLaughlin, Professor and Chairman of the History Department at the University of Chicago.
   [4] William Brown McIlvaine, lawyer of Chicago.

John Randolph Bolling to William Edward Dodd

My dear Professor Dodd: Washington D C 19th November 1921

Thank you very much for your prompt and delightful reply to my letter asking about the digest. I read it to Mr. Wilson and he had a hearty laugh over what you said regarding the possibility of Mr. Nixon losing his mind if he thought he was displeased.

You have aroused Mr. Wilson's curiosity about the digest and he sends you this message:

"Tell Professor Dodd I never heard of such a digest. Ask him to let you know just what proceedings of the Conference are included in it—whether simply the plenary sessions or something besides."

Mr. Wilson's mail contains a mixture of comment on Mr. Tumulty's articles—some praising, some damning. As he is not reading the articles, I am withholding the comments until the book is out.

As a matter of fact, however, I doubt very seriously if he ever reads the book!

Your comment about Mr. Wilson being drafted for the presidency—should his health improve to the point where he felt he could again undertake such a task—bears out the prediction of literally thousands who have written him in the same vein since his appearance on Armistice Day. I realize, of course, that we may be seeing only the "Wilson" side of the picture; on the other hand, I sense this reaction in a most curious and positive way.

When you can spare a moment, kindly give me the details of the digest—as embodied in Mr. Wilson's question. I promise that nothing will happen to Mr. Nixon because you do so!

Very sincerely yours,   John Randolph Bolling

TLS (W. E. Dodd Papers, DLC).

From Edward Albert Filene

Dear Mr. Wilson: Boston November 22, 1921.

I am enclosing an article which may be of interest to you.[1] This year's study journey, as those of the past two years, has thoroughly convinced me that what the world needs most is to have the United States join the League of Nations.

I was very glad on my return this fall to get the impression that more and more people in this country are beginning to recognize this fact. I was most happy also when I heard the crowd acclaim you at the "Unknown Hero" Parade and when I saw how serious a tribute they gave you in front of your house that afternoon.

I shall be in Washington again next Saturday, possibly before, and I should like to come and tell you something of what I saw in Europe this summer, what the leaders say, and how it all confirms that your leadership as President was a very wise one. Of course, I don't want to come unless your health is such that you would rather see me than not. Will you please have your secretary drop me a line at the Cosmos Club and I shall understand if you are not free to see me.

With cordial regards, I am

Sincerely yours,   Edward A. Filene

TLS (WP, DLC).

[1] "TO PUT OUR UNEMPLOYED AT WORK ANEW, AND TO EXPORT OUR SURPLUS PRODUCTS, AMERICA MUST CO-OPERATE WITH EUROPE," New York *World*, Second News Section, Nov. 27, 1921. Filene reported on a long tour he had made of Hungary, Rumania, Yugoslavia, and Bulgaria; he also included his views on the future of Franco-German relations and of the League of Nations. The price of the peace and prosperity of the world, Filene said, was close cooperation between the United States and Europe.

From Sir Maurice Hankey

Dear Mr. Wilson,   Washington. 23rd November, 1921

I enclose, as promised this afternoon, a copy of the paper on Diplomacy by Conference to which I referred.[1] Of course, it was prepared for a British audience and as an official, I had to be very circumspect.

It was a very great treat and privilege to me to see you this afternoon.[2] Will you convey my kindest regards to Mrs. Wilson.

Perhaps you will excuse a dictated letter as I am in the throes of this Conference.   Yours very sincerely   M. P. A. Hankey

TLS (WP, DLC).

[1] A lecture which Hankey had delivered before the Institute of International Affairs (now the Royal Institute of International Affairs) in London on November 2, 1920. It was printed as "Diplomacy by Conference," *The Round Table: A Quarterly Review of the Politics of the British Empire*, XI (March, 1921), 287-311. See also Stephen W. Roskill, *Hankey: Man of Secrets* (3 vols., London, 1970-74), II, 194-95.

[2] Hankey reported on his meeting with Wilson in a personal letter to David Lloyd George written on November 24, 1921. The relevant portion of the letter reads as follows:

"I think you may be interested that I saw Mr. Woodrow Wilson yesterday for half an hour. I was rather shocked at his appearance, which somehow reminded me of a waxwork. Obviously he is paralysed on one side. . . . He apologised for not getting up, as he had 'a game leg.' I gave him kind remembrances from you, to which he very cordially responded.

"His mind was active and his memory fresh. He is extraordinarily bitter against his opponents, and said he was ashamed of his fellow-countrymen for throwing over the League. I reminded him of recent successes of the League, and begged him to take a long view and to believe that he had laid foundations on which some great scheme for world peace would be built; but he reverted almost at once to his bitter scorn for his opponents.

"The ex-President was also very bitter against the French, who, he said, were 'up to their old games.' Even for Foch he would not have a good word. He regards him as the ultimate author of all our difficulties. I said he was a first-rate General. To that he replied 'That may be, but at the time of the armistice the Germans had broken his spirit and he would not fight on.' This, no doubt, was harking back to Pershing's idea that we ought to have gone on with the war.

"He said that at present the British Empire and the United States were drifting towards leadership of the world, which he thought was rather dangerous. For yourself he seemed to preserve very kindly memories. He was so nice to me, and his private secretary had told me that he spoke so often of me, that I ventured to raise the question of Yap. . . . He at once violently repudiated the suggestion that any blame could attach to me, but said he feared he had been rather remiss in the matter. . . . He had quite forgotten the circumstances in which the decisions as to mandates were taken . . . though he recalled it when I reminded him.

"I left with the feeling that he was a terribly pathetic figure, but with the same liking for the man which I had in Paris. He is not unpopular here now. He has had a number of ovations—in the theatre, outside his house, and out driving. . . . If you ask me, I think all this is sentiment—devoid of much political significance, though undoubtedly the present Administration have lost popularity. . . .

"I have seen House—another pathetic figure. He has never been able to make it up with Wilson. Indeed, he has never seen him since Paris days." *Ibid.*, pp. 245-46.

John Firman Coar to John Randolph Bolling

Edmonton (South) Canada
My dear Mr. Bolling: November 23, 1921

You were kind enough, at the suggestion of Mr. Wilson, to put me in touch last September with Mr. B. M. Baruch of New York. In the several conferences I had with him it appeared that he and I were practically of one mind regarding the situation in Germany. We disagreed on the desirability of action at the present time, Mr. Baruch holding that the time for action was not yet ripe and I maintaining that we ought now to prepare so as to be ready when the proper time comes. The logic of the situation was, however, in both cases the same, viz

First, the present execution of the Treaty of Versailles is making Germany's recovery impossible, and is in addition storing up fuel for a future cataclysm;

Secondly, France's apprehensions are natural and excusable, but are nevertheless making the situation more difficult every day;

Thirdly, our own interests demand that the situation should be improved and this can be done only if France's apprehensions can be allayed by America's guarantee of protection against unprovoked aggression on the part of Germany;

Fourthly, this guarantee should be given on the condition that Germany be freed from the present restrictions and interference and that France's attitude toward Germany should be approved by the United States;

Fifthly, the guarantee should, however, be given only for a limited period to wit until such time as the League of Nations can be developed into a strong association of nations;

Sixthly, this presumes the entrance of both the United States and Germany into the League, and to this end it seems advisable to suggest our entrance into the League upon the condition that the Covenant be submitted at once for a thoroughgoing revision, in which both the United States and Germany shall take part, and that the revised Covenant be submitted for ratification to the legislative bodies of the several Powers;

Seventhly, the so reconstituted League shall then undertake to re-axamine [re-examine] the Treaty of Versailles and to bring about its revision in accordance with the best interests of all parties.

Having the foregoing in mind I undertook to write for the Weekly Review (now the Independent) a series of ten articles, which would set forth objectively and statistically the conditions prevailing in Germany and the probable consequences. This series is now running. Four of the articles have, I believe, been published.[1] The tenth article will draw what seems to me the logical conclusion as just set forth, and argue in favor of some such action as suggested.

But I also proposed to Mr. Baruch the desirability of bringing together strong men, independent of party lines, who would calmly consider the proposal and undertake to work together when the proper time comes. It was this part of my proposal that Mr. Baruch thought premature. I could not see it that way, and in the few days remaining before my duties called me back to this university, I conferred with other men in New York, business men of some prominence and all Republicans (for tactical reasons). It so happened that they were of the same mind with me—except as to the last point which I mentioned only to those whom I knew to favor the League. Unhappily I was called back earlier than I expected, so that a conference that was arranged with Mr. Kingsley[2] and some other influential men could not be held.

I ought to say that the proposed solution has been brought to the attention of Secretary Hughes and that copies of the MSS of the Independent articles have been put into his hands. I do not know his attitude, but the articles were backed by letters from some of his close friends, and may have given him some material worth while.

It is possible, though I doubt it, that something may result from the present Conference on the Limitation of Armaments that will tend to clear up the European situation, perhaps along the lines suggested. Meanwhile, I feel obliged to inform Mr. Wilson through you of the steps I have taken and am trying to take. It is very difficult at this distance to be as active as I should like to be, especially since my connection with a Canadian institution ties my hands somewhat. However, some of my Republican friends are interested in the program outlined and are working quietly. I hope to free myself early enough in the spring to bring together a number of strong men before I sail for Europe to look into some other conditions that I was unable to examine carefully last summer.

If there is anything in the foregoing plan or effort that seems to you or to Mr. Wilson undesirable, doubtful, or improvable, it would give me great pleasure to hear from you. Perhaps I ought to add that I have in mind reviving a plan which the gentlemen now interested undertook to forward just prior to the war, which was put into effect tentatively in 1916, but which was turned to war activities and necessarily became quiescent after peace. What that plan was is set forth in the little book "Democracy and the War,"[3] Chapter 4 or 5 (I forget which), all I need say here is that it contemplates the development of Americanism through a better general understanding and a more wholesome general practice of the principle of democracy. Even a League of Nations agreeable to the legislative bodies of all nations, and therefore more likely to have the backing of popular interest, is apt to become a mechanical thing, like too many governments, unless it can be made a vital idea in the minds of our people and kept vital.

Pardon the length of this communication. I should like to say to Mr. Wilson that the sanity and the generosity of his great purpose are bound to be approved by the American people, that they are approving it now in their support of the present Conference, and that, though he may not consider his own fortunes, there are many of us, officially or technically in the Republican ranks, who know that whatever good shall come of the Conference is Mr. Wilson's fine contribution to the cause of humanity and the glory of his country. I, for one, trust that he will be spared to rejoice in the gratitude of a great people. Will you kindly convey to him all the best wishes of one who can do little that is really worth while, but who purposes to do that little as much in the spirit of Mr. Wilson as possible.   Very sincerely yours,   John Firman Coar

TLS (WP, DLC).
[1] Of Coar's articles, the following had already been published: "German Actualities," New York *Review*, V (Sept. 10 and 24, 1921), 227-28 and 271-72; and "Upper Silesia: The Dilemma of the Powers," *Independent and Weekly Review*, CVII (Oct. 15, 1921), 60-62. *The Independent* published the balance as "Social Outlook in Germany," *The Independent*, CVII (Dec. 10, 1921), 253-55; "What May Happen in Germany," *ibid.*, CVIII (Feb. 11, 1922), 127-28; "Economic Outlook in Germany," *ibid.*, March 18, 1922, pp. 270-71; "Attitude of the German Industrialists to the International Loan," *ibid.*, July 8, 1922, pp. 578-79; "Is Germany Going to Pieces?," *ibid.*, CIX (July 22, 1922), 7-8; "Salvation for Germany," *ibid.*, Sept. 2, 1922, pp. 92-93; "Germany's Disastrous Prosperity," *ibid.*, Dec. 23, 1922, pp. 383-85.
[2] Darwin Pearl Kingsley, president of the New York Life Insurance Co., prominent in the civic affairs of New York and in the Republican party.
[3] J. F. Coar, *Democracy and the War* (New York and London, 1918).

A News Report

[*Nov. 24, 1921*]

Wilson Receives Visit From Balfour; Silent on Reported Feeling About France

Washington, Nov. 24.—The only foreigner Woodrow Wilson has received since the opening of the Washington conference is Arthur James Balfour, Lord President of the British Council, and ranking member of the British delegation to the conference in the absence of Premier Lloyd George, who has been detained in England by pressing affairs of state.

The visit of Mr. Balfour to the Wilson residence at 2,340 S Street Northwest took place about four days ago[1] and followed the delivery of Mr. Balfour's principal speech in the plenary session of the conference, in which he declared Great Britain's acceptance in principle of the Hughes proposal for limitation of naval armaments.

When Marshal Foch first came to Washington a few weeks ago he called, but was not received, the former President being reported ill at that time. When Marshal Foch returned to Washington a few days ago he did not again call on Mr. Wilson.

Mr. Wilson is alleged in a newspaper report published this morning to have said to a friend on Tuesday[2] that another war would soon be on us, and that it would "be caused by the policy of France." It was impossible tonight to learn whether Mr. Wilson had uttered such an expression or whether he would take notice of the attributed declaration.

Since his departure from the White House there has been no authorized statement of the views of Mr. Wilson with respect to so-called militaristic or imperialistic aspects of French national or foreign policy. It was recalled tonight that on March 8, 1920, however, approximately a year before he left the White House, Mr. Wilson, in a letter to Senator Hitchcock, charged that a "militaristic party" had regained control in France.[3] The Hitchcock letter was written in expression of his unqualified opposition to any attempt by the United States to evade obligations under Article X. of the League covenant.

Jules Jusserand, the French Ambassador at Washington, was at that time instructed to say to the State Department that the French Government was surprised at the references to the policies of France made by Mr. Wilson in his letter to Senator Hitchcock.[4] Mr. Wilson made no disclaimer.

Printed in the *New York Times*, Nov. 25, 1921.
[1] We have not found any report of this visit by Balfour in the repositories in Great Britain holding Balfour's papers, nor in the Foreign Office files in the Public Record Office. Dr. Grayson's memorandum (printed at Jan. 11, 1922), strongly suggests that Balfour's visit was purely social, and that he and Wilson did not discuss any matter of great importance.
[2] November 22, 1921.
[3] WW to GMH, March 8, 1920, Vol. 65.
[4] See, e.g., F. L. Polk to WW, March 13, 1920 (first letter of that date), *ibid.*

William Edward Dodd to John Randolph Bolling

My dear Mr. Bolling: University of Chicago November 24, 1921.

Having made a series of appointments to speak in Birmingham and at the State College of Mississippi this week-end, and my other duties accumulating a little at this time, I can not now give you full statement about the document now in my possession.

Mr. Nixon informs me this morning that it is what was known as the Annotation of the Treaty, that it was based upon the minutes of the Council of Four, the reports of some of the special commissions and, I think, of meetings of ministers and ambassadors. The work was done from stenographic reports by three or four people and for the benefit of the American commissioners, all of whom have copies.

What he meant by minutes of the Council of Four, I think, is what was submitted by someone to this group of workers for the American Commission. It may help a little if I say that page 10 of the part marked Shantung starts as follows: "President Wilson here made a statement that is given a summary of more than three hundred words in the minutes. He said he would like to repeat the point of view he had urged on the Japanese delegation a few days before" and so on. Baron Makino follows President Wilson in a statement about Shantung.

All through the document on Shantung the members of the Council of Four or the Council of Ten are reported in the third person. On the title page of the document I am referring to appear the following: Part IV. Shantung (section VIII), Articles 156 and 157. References: Council of Ten, BC-12, BC-13; Foreign Ministers, FM-4, FM-5; Council of Four: I.C. 175 C, and so on for several entries and then C.F. 62, C.F. 76 and C.F. 80. These are to indicate the sources for statements made.

Young Nixon I learn this morning did not bring this copy away from Paris, much as [he] coveted it. He found it here, in an office in the Ashland Block, in the hands of a friend of Mr. Wilson but apparently not held in the same esteem that Nixon held it. And Nixon borrowed it, kept it most carefully and loaned it to me when he came to study last October. He hesitates to give the name of the person from whom he borrowed it; but it is due to be returned. I asked Nixon to wait a while before returning it. He is willing for me to keep the document if the person who loaned it to him gives consent. I do not think that person has any great interest in it; nor do I think a copy has been made before it reached Nixon. I would give the name but Nixon feels that it would be a breach of honor and he thinks the person himself violated instructions when he brought it from Paris.

As I have said, only McLaughlin, whom the President knows, and myself have seen the document. We were greatly interested and feel that it would be a great benefit to all concerned if the facts were known, if Mr. Wilson's own words at the various critical discussions could get to the public. They would show how absolutely loyal he was to his great ideals, how watchful he was of his country's broader interests and how nearly he brought England and Japan to agree to retire bag and baggage from China.

But all know the reasons for keeping these documents from the public until the parties concerned give consent. So neither of us has shown the material to any one.

If only Mr. Wilson could recover his powers in full! How much might he not do? The French now playing their old game. The poor Japanese inviting China's millions to fall upon them some day.   Yours sincerely,   William E. Dodd

TLS (WP, DLC).

To Bernard Mannes Baruch

[Washington] Nov. 25 1921

We are deeply grieved to learn of your tragical loss,[1] and trust that the profound sympathy of loving friends may, in some degree, solace and support you.   Woodrow Wilson.

T telegram (WP, DLC).
    [1] Baruch's mother, Isabella Wolfe (Mrs. Simon) Baruch, had died on November 24 at the age of seventy-two.

To Ellen Duane Davis

My dear Friend: [Washington] 25th November 1921

We are delighted to know that we may before long have a glimpse of you and E.P.[1] and (answering your recent question) will of course be pleased to see your cousin if E.P. must send a substitute.

Mrs. Wilson joins me in warm regards to you both.
                    Faithfully yours,   [Woodrow Wilson]

CCL (WP, DLC).
    [1] Wilson was replying to Ellen D. Davis to WW, Nov. 15, 1921.

John Randolph Bolling to Sir Maurice Hankey

My dear Sir Maurice: [Washington] 25th November 1921

Mr. Wilson asks me to thank you for your thoughtfulness in remembering to send him a copy of your paper, "Diplomacy by Conference." He is looking forward to reading it with the greatest interest and pleasure.

Mr. Wilson wishes you to know how happy he was to see you again, and he has spoken several times of the pleasant twenty minute chat he had with you. He sends you his warm regards, in which Mrs. Wilson joins.

Cordially yours,   [John Randolph Bolling]

CCL (WP, DLC).

John Randolph Bolling to Edward Albert Filene

My dear sir: [Washington] 25th November 1921

Mr. Wilson asks me to thank you for your kind letter of November twenty-second, and the article which you enclosed.

If you will call at the house on Sunday afternoon next (November 27th) at three-thirty o'clock, Mr. Wilson will be glad to see you for a few minutes before starting on his daily automobile ride.

Cordially yours,   [John Randolph Bolling]

CCL (WP, DLC).

To Edward Albert Filene

My dear Filene: [Washington] 27th November 1921

I think the man you want is Brand Whitlock whom I made Minister to Belgium, who made such a stunning success there and who this unthinking Administration has misplaced. He is a man of the finest qualities, both in health [heart?] and mind, and I am sure you would find him a delight. I hope the suggestion will commend itself to you.

I enjoyed our little talk this afternoon and congratulate you on the work you are doing and the way you are doing it.

Cordially and faithfully,

your friend,   [Woodrow Wilson]

CCL (WP, DLC).

John Randolph Bolling to William Edward Dodd

My dear Professor Dodd: Washington D C 27th Novr., 1921.

I read Mr. Wilson this morning your very interesting letter of 24th November, and he says that it gives him an excellent idea of what the "Annotation of the Treaty" is. He sends his warm thanks for your trouble in giving him the details.

I quite agree with you that it would be a most wonderful thing if

Mr. Wilson was now fully restored to his normal health; but as long as we can see progress in that direction, from week to week, we can afford to wait.

Cordially yours,   John Randolph Bolling.

TLS (W. E. Dodd Papers, DLC).

To Cleveland Hoadley Dodge

My dear Cleve.:   Washington D C 28th November 1921

We were delighted to learn through Cyrus McCormick[1] that you expect before long to be in Washington, and doubly pleased when he told us you would let us know of your coming a few days in advance. That will enable us to make sure of a glimpse of you.

I am sure that you know there is nobody I would rather see.

I hope, my dear fellow, that you are constantly progressing toward assured health and strength again.

Mrs. Wilson joins me in cordial regards to you both, and I am— as always;   Your affectionate friend,   Woodrow Wilson

TLS (WC, NjP).
[1] In C. H. McCormick, Jr., to EBW, Nov. 23, 1921, TLS (WP, DLC).

From Cleveland Hoadley Dodge

My dear President: New York December 1, 1921.

I still address you as "President" because I get into the habit of doing so, and although you are not formally head of the Government, you are President of all our hearts and affections.

You are more than good to write to me and say that you will be glad to see Mrs. Dodge and myself when we come to Washington next week. I am getting so lazy that I think I would have cut the annual meeting of the Trustees of the Carnegie Institution if it were not for the fact that I want very much to see you, and Mrs. Wilson, too. Mrs. Dodge and I expect to go on to Washington next Thursday afternoon, but have meetings that evening and most of Friday, but as we both need a little change, we think we will stay over Saturday and Sunday, and if, sometime on either of those days, you and Mrs. Wilson would let us come and see you, either for afternoon tea, or perhaps, if you are good enough, for a meal, it would rejoice our hearts.

I had a little correspondence with Jessie lately about some friends of hers who want to get into Near East Relief work, and I had a lovely letter from her this morning, telling me of her visit to you, and speaking most encouragingly about your improvement in health, which rejoiced my heart, and I am doubly anxious to come down and see for myself, and Mrs. Dodge and I not only want to see you, but are particularly desirous of seeing Mrs. Wilson.

I am looking forward, especially, to hearing what you think about the Conference in Washington. I see that Senator Borah has got loose again,[1] and Mr. Harding will very likely have his troubles with some of the irreconcilables, just as you did.

Again thanking you for your delightful letter, with warm regards from Mrs. Dodge and myself to both you and Mrs. Wilson and looking forward to seeing you very soon

Yours affectionately,   Cleveland H Dodge

P.S. When I come to sign this, it strikes me that possibly this is too far ahead for Mrs. Wilson to make a definite appointment, so I hope she will not feel obliged to name any definite date immediately. We will be stopping at the New Willard Hotel, and of course she could let us know there when we arrive.

TLS (WP, DLC).
[1] The White House had announced on November 25 that Harding would soon formally propose that the conference be expanded to include more countries and should be simply the first of a series of annual meetings of an "association of nations" to deal with problems of common concern. *New York Times*, Nov. 26, 1921.
  Borah attacked Harding's plan in a statement and interview printed in *ibid.*, Nov. 28, 1921. He declared that the proposed association was really the equivalent of the League of Nations under another name. The only real question at issue, he asserted, was whether the United States should enter any organization of nations. If the answer to that question was "yes," the League of Nations would serve the purpose as well as any substitute. Indeed, he said, an organization with a written constitution or covenant was probably preferable to one without such a document. It was totally unclear, Borah stated, whether Harding's plan would leave the world with two leagues—one league and one association—or if the existing League would be merged into the new association. Moreover, Borah warned, the only way to bind the United States to any new association of nations would be through the means of a treaty, which would have to be approved by the United States Senate.

To Ellen Duane Davis

My dear Friend: [Washington] 3d December 1921

I am afraid that in my last letter to you, and in our recent conversation, I must have seemed to you to take rather lightly the idea of your running for the Senate. That was not my real feeling. I hope most sincerely that you will allow yourself to become a candidate, and I shall look forward with the keenest interest to the campaign.

It was a real pleasure to have you and Miss Boyd with us, and I hope you both enjoyed the visit as much as we did.

Please give my love to E.P. and believe me always,

Your partisan and affectionate friend,

[Woodrow Wilson]

CCL (WP, DLC).

To Louis Dembitz Brandeis, with Enclosure

My dear Mr. Justice: Washington D C 5th December 1921

I am taking the liberty to enclose another suggestion for the declaration of principles and purposes upon which we are endeavoring to concentrate common counsel.

With warmest regards and the hope that the approaching Christmas season will bring you and yours every sort of happiness;
          Cordially and faithfully yours,   Woodrow Wilson

TLS (L. D. Brandeis Papers, KyLoU).

E   N   C   L   O   S   U   R   E

Inasmuch as access by all upon equitable and equal terms to the fuel supply and to the raw materials of manufacture and also the availability to all upon fair and equal terms of the motive power supplied by electrical power companies and other similar privately owned and controlled agencies are indispensable to the unhampered development of the industries of the country, we believe that these are matters which should be regulated by federal legislation to the utmost limit of the constitutional powers of the federal government.

WWT MS (L. D. Brandeis Papers, KyLoU).

From Bainbridge Colby

My dear Mr President: New York City December 5, 1921

After much delay the business in London which I discussed with you briefly seems to have taken definite enough form to warrant me in proceeding, and I have booked passage on the Olympic sailing the tenth. My stay will be very short.

I shall be absent on your birthday anniversary—to my great regret, because when the hearts of all your friends turn to you with affection and gratitude and admiration,—I hate to be away.

In fact you can't imagine how I hate to be away—speaking generally. More often than you would suspect, the impulse seizes me to run down to Washington just to see you if only for the fewest moments. When things go better and I have heartening results to report, I will come over oftener. They will go better—I know it. Please believe it. But just at present I am a little mortified about myself,—that I haven't seemed able to force the pace. Times have something to do with it. But I am not disposed to stress conditions. A man ought to be able to make "conditions" behave.

Mr and Mrs Norman Davis took luncheon with us yesterday. Norman hoped to see you today, and said he was going to show you an article about you published in the New York Evening Post of Saturday.[1] I thought it quite charming. If he should forget, let me know. I have a copy of it.

This may turn out to be my last letter before sailing, so let me wish you all the happiness in the world, my dear Mr President, and a sweet and merry Christmas time.

Affectionately always Colby

TLS (WP, DLC).
[1] Christopher Morley, "CHRISTMAS CARDS I—To Woodrow Wilson," New York *Evening Post*, Dec. 3, 1921.

From Thornton Whaling,[1] with Enclosure

Dear Mr Wilson: Louisville, Ky. Dec 5th 1921—

I enclose letter which I received from one of the Davidson students, who serves as Editor-in-Chief of the College Magazine: I also enclose copy of my reply.[2] As a Davidson man myself, and a trustee of the old College, who was privileged to serve the school on the Executive Committee of its Board for many years, I can not refrain from writing a line to beg that you will send Mr. Richards, a few words expressing your interest in the College and your hope that generous friends will soon rebuild the Chambers Building[3]— by the way that is the building in which you roomed during your year at Davidson.

May I add my best wishes and prayers for your complete recovery. It must be increasingly evident to all observers that you are being vindicated in most remarkable ways, (and with what I beg to call a convincing divine irony), in your work for the League of Nations. Our country and the whole world will yet come to it. Your labors and sacrifices have not been in vain.

Cordially yours—Thornton Whaling

ALS (WP, DLC).
[1] Fellow student with Wilson at Davidson College, 1873-1874; at this time Professor of Apologetics and Systematic Theology and Dean of the Presbyterian Theological Seminary of Kentucky at Louisville.
[2] T. Whaling to J. M. Richards, Dec. 5, 1921, ALS (WP, DLC).
[3] As Richards said in his letter, Chambers Building, the main building of Davidson College, burned to the ground on November 28, 1921.

James McDowell Richards[1] to Thornton Whaling

Dear Sir: Davidson, N. C. Nov. 29, 1921.

It is the purpose of the staff of our college weekly, The Davidsonian, to publish in the near future an issue of the paper to be known as the Woodrow Wilson Issue. The first page of this paper would be devoted entirely to President Wilson. We had planned to run his picture and several articles about his life and achievements. The publication of such an issue would serve a double purpose: it would be an attempt on our part to render Mr. Wilson the honor which is due him, and it would serve as an advertisement for the college as well.[2]

In carrying out this plan we are relying very largely on you for assistance. In the first place we would like to have you write an article of about a thousand words for us on the subject of Mr. Wilson's life and record at Davidson, or anything connected with it that you might care to suggest.

We are also very anxious to have just a few words from Mr. Wilson himself if possible. We feel that he probably would not reply to a request from us to this effect but hoped that if you would make the request for us it might be granted. We do not ask for any article but merely for a word or two of greeting to the alumni or the college. The fact that Chambers building was burned to the ground yesterday morning would seem to make this an especially appropriate time for the message.

I know that this is a great deal of trouble to ask you to go to but am hoping that you can help us out. If you can write the article and the letter to Mr. Wilson for us we will appreciate it greatly, and we would also be very grateful for any suggestions you might make. On account of arrangements which have been made for special advertising the material for this paper will have to go to press on Dec. 17, so that it will be necessary for us to work quickly. Hoping to hear from you soon with regard to this matter and with all best wishes for yourself, I remain,

Respectfully yours,   J. M. Richards.

ALS (WP, DLC).
    [1] A senior at Davidson College, he was afterwards a Rhodes Scholar, Presbyterian minister, and President of Columbia Theological Seminary, Decatur, Ga., 1932-1971.
    [2] The Wilson issue was *The Davidsonian*, Vol. IX, Dec. 16, 1921. Dr. Whaling's article was entitled "Woodrow Wilson Was Well Prepared for Leadership." There were other articles by members of the Davidson faculty: Thomas Wilson Lingle, Joseph Moore McConnell, and Charles R. Harding. "It is a small token of our love and admiration," Richards wrote on the editorial page, "that the staff has decided to dedicate this issue of the Davidsonian to this most distinguished son of Davidson."

To Louis Dembitz Brandeis, with Enclosure

My dear Mr. Justice: Washington D C 6th December 1921

Here is another suggestion. I hope that it will not seem to you that I am firing these things at you with inconsiderate frequency and rapidity; they form themselves somewhere in the hidden recesses of my system and I am uneasy until I get them out.

With warm regards;

Cordially and faithfully yours,   Woodrow Wilson

TLS (L. D. Brandeis Papers, KyLoU).

E N C L O S U R E

We unqualifiedly condemn the action of the Republican administration in interrupting and in large part destroying the work of creating and developing an American merchant marine so intelligently begun and so efficiently carried forward by the Democratic administration and we demand the immediate rehabilitation of the Shipping Board and such appropriations for its use and such additions to its powers as may be necessary to put its work upon a permanent footing and assure its energetic and successful completion.

WWT MS (L. D. Brandeis Papers, KyLoU).

John Randolph Bolling to Bainbridge Colby

Dear Mr. Colby: [Washington] 6th December 1921

Mr. Wilson was greatly pleased and gratified to receive your delightful letter this morning, and sends his warm thanks for the many messages which it contains.

He says to tell you you need not think he is worrying over the progress of the law business as—with you—he feels sure it will come along in great fashion after the first of the year.

Our thoughts will be with you on your journey, and Mr. and Mrs. Wilson send you their affectionate greetings and good wishes for a safe and successful trip. I need hardly tell you how heartily I join them in these expressions.

Faithfully and sincerely,   [John Randolph Bolling]

CCL (WP, DLC).

To Christopher Darlington Morley[1]

My dear Mr. Morley: Washington D C 7th December 1921

I was deeply touched by your generous message to me of greeting and cheer which was printed in The Evening Post last week.[2]

I have read most (indeed I believe all) of your delightful published writings and therefore feel that I know you. It has given me the more pleasure and pride that you should think of me as you do. I feel now that I have ridden with you not only in Parnassus on Wheels but also on Pegasus on wings, and I thank you with all my heart for the ex[h]ileration it has given me.

Cordially and gratefully yours,   Woodrow Wilson

TLS (PHC).
  [1] Christopher (Darlington) Morley, at this time on the editorial staff of the New York *Evening Post*, already the author of numerous volumes of essays, verse, and fiction, including the novels *Parnassus on Wheels* (Garden City, N. Y., 1917) and *The Haunted Bookshop* (Garden City, N. Y., 1919), both of which are in the Wilson Library, DLC.
  [2] About which, see BC to WW, Dec. 5, 1921, n. 1.

To James McDowell Richards

My dear Mr. Richards: [Washington] 7th December 1921

I have of course not in the least lost my interest in Davidson.

I heard of the burning of the Chambers building with deepest distress, and I hope with all my heart that funds can be raised to rebuild it.

Please present my compliments to your fellow editors and believe me;   Sincerely yours,   [Woodrow Wilson]

CCL (WP, DLC).

To David Franklin Houston

My dear Houston: [Washington] 8th December 1921

A few Democratic friends and I have been more or less busy the last few weeks suggesting to each other items for a declaration of principles and purposes by the party when the next campaign comes, sharing the conviction which is very strong with me that it will be much more stimulating to the party, and serviceable to the country, to win on an explicit affirmative program than by merely taking advantage of the superabundant mistakes and misdeeds of the Republicans.

When I came to attempt something on the subject of taxation I was at once aware of my need of you.

Will you not be generous enough to send me something which will be a concise characterization of the taxation of the Republicans, and of the better way we should wish to follow? I will be very much your debtor for such a statement, and hope you will not think I am taking advantage of your kindness and good nature in putting such a burden upon you.

With warmest regards to Mrs. Houston[1] as well as to yourself, in which Mrs. Wilson joins;

   Faithfully and sincerely yours, [Woodrow Wilson]

CCL (WP, DLC).
 [1] Helen Beall Houston.

From Louis Dembitz Brandeis

My dear Mr Wilson: Washington, D. C. Dec 8/21

I am very glad to have your two letters with Enclosures. Copies of the latter I am sending today to Mr Colby.

The hope which you brought to an agonized world is bringing and making possible Christmas cheer and confidence that happier years will come.

With every good wish

    Most cordially Louis D Brandeis

ALS (WP, DLC).

From Edith Benham Helm

Dear Mr President   [Washington] December 8th [1921]

Mrs Wilson gave me a message yesterday. Thank you for it.

I can never think of you without her, or of her without you and something seemed very sadly missing with my lovely lady here alone. You and she have taught me so much of what real love is, I feel I am just so much better in my married life after living so close to you both.

Thank you for letting me have her yesterday and she was so beautiful please let me have her again

    Your loving little friend Edith Benham Helm

for I always feel just "little" beside you who see so much clearer & better than the rest of us

ALS (WP, DLC).

John Randolph Bolling to John Firman Coar

My dear Professor Coar: [Washington] 9th December 1921

I had an opportunity this morning of bringing to Mr. Wilson's attention the contents of your letter to me of November twenty-third, and I find that he does not concur with you in the statements which your letter contains; I refer particularly to those set out in numerical order on the first page.

I am sorry that I am unable to give you in detail the particularly [particular] points on which Mr. Wilson disagrees with you, but the program of complete rest which he is now following will not permit him to go into a detailed discussion of the matter.

With appreciation of your many good wishes.

Cordially yours,   [John Randolph Bolling]

CCL (WP, DLC).

To Bernard Mannes Baruch

My dear Baruch: Washington D C 10th December 1921

I am grateful for the ducks, and more grateful to have such a frieni [friend] as you who keeps me always in mind, and is always thinking of new kindnesses. It is very delightful to have such relations with you.

The Conference seems to be doing some good things at last, though it is amazing to see the Republicans lead us into a group alliance after the European fashion.

Always let me know, my dear fellow, when you may be expected in Washington so that I may be sure of successfully arranging an opportunity to see you.

Your sincere and grateful friend,   Woodrow Wilson

TLS (B. M. Baruch Papers, NjP).

To Anna Portner Flood

My dear Mrs. Flood: [Washington] 10th December 1921

May I not express to you my warm sympathy for you in the death of your distinguished husband,[1] as well as my own personal grief?

In my fortunate association with him I think I learned to appreciate his true quality, and I am saddened to think that I shall not again have the pleasure and benefit of association with him.

Hoping that every possible comfort may come to you;

Sincerely yours,   [Woodrow Wilson]

CCL (WP, DLC).
¹ Her husband, Henry De La Warr Flood, congressman from Virginia, 1901-1921, had died on December 8, 1921.

To William Byron Colver

My dear Colver: Washington D C 10th December 1921

Please don't feel too badly about that fake interview.¹ I am sure I understood from the first how you people had been imposed on, and never for a moment blamed you personally.

I feel as sure of your genuineness and loyalty as I ever did of any man's. Please forget the incident; I will.

What distresses me now is your illness, and I shall hope with all my heart for your rapid and complete recovery, for you can be of the greatest service to the country.

Of course I shall be most willing to help you outline an editorial policy at any time we may be able to get together.

With warmest regards;
                    Cordially and faithfully yours,   Woodrow Wilson

TLS (WC, NjP).
¹ Colver was at this time editor in chief of the *Washington Daily News*, which had begun publication on November 8, 1921. Wilson had written to him on November 22 to complain about an "alleged interview" with Mrs. Wilson which had appeared in the previous day's issue. "The whole thing," Wilson declared, "was fictitious from beginning to end—a shameless fake! Mrs. Wilson never has given, and never will give, an interview to anybody. I would appreciate it if you would caution your editor not to be imposed upon again. And the picture! It might just as well have been labeled 'Mrs. Harding' or 'Mrs. Champ Clark.' Pardon this outbreak from one who is simply trying to protect the person he loves most in a privacy which she values inestimably." WW to W. B. Colver, Nov. 22, 1921, CCL (WP, DLC).
Colver responded on December 8 with a letter of abject apology. He said that he knew nothing of the "cruel story" since he had been sent to a sanitarium in Battle Creek, Michigan (whence his letter was written) for "a rest." He promised to take measures to prevent any similar occurrence in the future. W. B. Colver to WW, Dec. 8, 1921, ALS (WP, DLC).

To Edith Benham Helm

My dear Mrs. Helm: [Washington] 10th December 1921

Thank you for your very sweet note of the eighth which pleased me mightily.

You may be sure that my dear lady will wish to come to you as often as possible, for both she and I are very grateful to you for the many quite invaluable services you have rendered us.

I shall always be happy to subscribe myself;
                    Your sincere and grateful friend,   [Woodrow Wilson]

CCL (WP, DLC).

From Edward Irving Edwards

My dear Governor: [Trenton] December 10th, 1921.

Yesterday at Newark, we had a very large meeting of people from all over the State, who came to meet the Chairman of the National Democratic Committee,[1] who, however, was not present owing to illness. It was a very representative gathering, having people from every part of the State and the large hall of the Washington Hotel was not able to accom[m]odate them all.

I thought you would be interested in knowing about this meeting, which was for the purpose of organizing the party for the fall election.

I venture to write to you because at every mention of your name there was spontaneous applause and the thought ran through my mind at the time that you were in the minds of the audience as proved by their applause, that the ideals for which you strove were now being justified by destiny as proved by the fact that these ideals were now being fulfilled at least in part by the action of the party in power at Washington.

I might also add that I have traveled all over the State and have made many speeches, in almost every one of which I have had occasion, owing to the nature of my talk to mention your name and in every place and in every gathering the response of the audience was instantaneous and sincere, showing that in the people's minds, at least in this State, your course in handling the destinies of our Country with an eye to the welfare of humanity, and with the approach of the coming election, your words and works seem to come more and more in the foreground and become very valuable possessions to the party in this State, and I hope that your thought is with us, as we are making in these troublous times a struggle to establish the principles for which the party stands, which we believe can alone bring industrial prosperity, social peace and human progress.

With kind personal regards, and fondest hope for your continued physical improvement, I am,

Yours very truly, E I Edwards

TLS (WP, DLC).
[1] Cordell Hull, who had been elected the new chairman on November 1, 1921.

From Ellen Duane Davis

My dear Friend,   Philadelphia. Pa. December 11th 1921

What must you think of my long silence, after receiving your letter last Monday regarding my running for Senator.

To make a long story short, I retired to bed on Sunday night with a cold coming on, which is continuing its weary way through bronchitis, and I have not been up since.

Your letter made me very happy, and is a source of great pride to me. Alas! When E.P. got home and read it, the roof of all my hopes and aspirations was blown off, as he seriously thinks I have neither the physical strength, nor the money to go into such a campaign.

He was truly in earnest, and, while not agreeing with him, as his wife, (although a voter, and strong suffragist), he is my husband, and his wishes must prevail.

Thank you for all your expressions of sympathy and interest, but you and Edith will both understand my attitude in the matter, and that my first duty is to E.P.

This does not mean I am to give up my State and County work, and you may rest assured that everything that I can do, I will do.

Have you anyone to suggest in Pennsylvania, as Democratic candidate for Governor, and also Senator? Probably you have a wider grasp of the whole State than I have.

I know we are pretty low down, and I feel terribly depressed, but I want you to realize that whatever I do, I will only do with Edward's consent and sanction.

I think he is rather pleased that I have this cold this week as a positive proof that I am physically unfit. (Don't tell him that!) But I shall never stop working until I die for the cause of True Democracy.

We did have such a good day in Washington, the memory of which will be with me always.

Best love to Edith, and tell her not to forget to send me that photograph, and she can send me one of yours at the same time, as I have no good one.

She will receive "A Woman's Hardy Garden"[1] this week, and I hope it will give her as much pleasure and profit as it did me.

Always your most grateful and sincere friend,

Ellen Duane Davis

I should be a very poor citizen if I am not a good wife.

TLS (WP, DLC).
[1] Helen Rutherford Ely, *A Woman's Hardy Garden* (New York, 1903). This book is in the Wilson Library, DLC.

From John Howell Westcott, with Enclosure

Dear Woodrow: Nice 11 Dec 1921

The other day I discovered this inscription on the frieze of a portico facing the Mediterranean. It pleased me so that I copied it to send to you. Mary[1] took a snapshot of it with her Kodak—if the print is successful, she will send it, but the camera is so small that it is not likely the inscription will be legible.

Having walked some miles in Paris in your avenue, we were glad to find others bearing your name in small towns—e.g., in Vienne on the Rhone, where history has left its traces in Roman remains, & where we found a *rue Wilson* to remind us of the great things you tried to do for the world. Marian[2] wants me to say she does not expect to find any Harding streets.

I say the Republicans will have to do most of the things you wanted done, & which they were too shabby to do when you advocated them.

We received some illustrations from Mrs Daniels,[3] of late doings in Washington, showing you apparently well & happy—& we hope you are feeling as well as you look.

We came to France primarily to visit Bony cemetery—in October. We spent five weeks in Grasse—a couple in Nice, & are now going on to Italy for the winter.

Ever yours faithfully   J H Westcott

There is a "Place Wilson" here, adjoining the main Post Office.

ALS (WP, DLC).
[1] His daughter, Mary Dunton Westcott.
[2] That is his wife, Marian Bate Westcott.
[3] Joan Robertson (Mrs. Winthrop More) Daniels.

E N C L O S U R E

VILLE DE NICE

POUR COMMÉMORER LA DÉCISION PRISE PAR LA RÉPUBLIQUE DES
ÉTATS-UNIS
SUR L'INITIATIVE DU PRÉSIDENT WOODROW WILSON
DE PARTICIPER AU CONFLIT MONDIAL DE LA CIVILISATION CONTRE
LA BARBARIE
LE CONSEIL MUNICIPAL DE NICE RÉUNI LE 30 AVRIL 1917
SOUS LA PRÉSIDENCE DE M. LE GÉNÉRAL COIRAN MARIE
A DÉCIDÉ D'APPELER Á L'AVENIR LE QUAI DU MIDI
QUAI DES ÉTATS-UNIS.

Hw MS (WP, DLC).

To Edward Irving Edwards

My dear Governor Edwards: [Washington] 12th December 1921

Thank you for your letter of December tenth. I am heartily glad to hear that hard work is being done to organize the party for victory in New Jersey.

I can't for the life of me understand how you and others see anything that the present Administration is doing which could be said to be fulfilling my ideals. I see nothing whatever; they are hurrying in the opposite direction.

May I not take the liberty of saying that it is going to be very hard for me to forgive you for supplanting the splendid man I put in for Superintendent of Education?[1]

Wishing the Democrats of the State every honorable success;

Sincerely yours,   [Woodrow Wilson]

CCL (WP, DLC).
[1] Calvin Noyes Kendall, whom Wilson had appointed New Jersey Commissioner of Education in 1911. Actually, Kendall, who had been ill for several years, had resigned from his post in the spring of 1921. He died of Bright's disease on September 2 of that year. Governor Edwards had appointed John Enright as *ad interim* Commissioner of Education on June 28, 1921, and later appointed him to a full five-year term.

To Margaret Woodrow Wilson

Dearest Margaret: [Washington] 12th December 1921

The enclosed came to us in a letter of a friend from the West, and I thought you ought to see it.

I must admit it has shocked me very much that the doctor you have been dealing with should have so abused your confidence. I am sure you will know better than I how to deal best with the matter as you are in communication with him. I need not suggest, after you see this, that you be very careful to select what you say to him in anything you write him in the future. The publication of a letter of this kind is, to say the least, highly unprofessional, and it means I am afraid that he will not hesitate to publish anything you may write to him.

Personally I feel very indignant, but my indignation I am sure you will understand is on your account and not on my own. The man can only do himself harm by the use of my name for advertising purposes, and is sure to make a most unfortunate impression on everyone who cares in the least for you or for me.

Lovingly,   [Father]

CCL (WC, NjP).

John Randolph Bolling to Claude Augustus Swanson

My dear Senator: [Washington] 13th December 1921

Mr. Wilson asks that you be good enough to see that he gets a copy of the test [text] of the new Four Power Treaty.[1] He will greatly appreciate your courtesy in having this sent to him.

I wonder if you have—or could get for me—a copy of the latest Congressional Directory? The one I have is dated last May, and I am under the impression that there have been many changes in it since then.   Cordially yours,   [John Randolph Bolling]

CCL (WP, DLC).
[1] The text of the so-called Four Power Treaty between the United States, the British Empire, France, and Japan, negotiated during the Washington Conference, had been made public on December 10. This agreement pledged the four powers to respect each other's rights in regard to their insular possessions and dominions in the Pacific Ocean, to have recourse to mediation in case of disputes among themselves over any Pacific question involving these rights, and to consult with one another to agree on a course of concerted action against any outside power which might threaten these rights. The treaty was to be in force for ten years after signing and to continue in force thereafter, with the proviso that any of the four powers could renounce it upon twelve months' notice. The full text of the treaty, which was signed on December 13, appeared in the *New York Times*, Dec. 11, 1921. See also John Chalmers Vinson, "The Drafting of the Four-Power Treaty of the Washington Conference," *Journal of Modern History*, XXV (March 1953), 40-47.

From David Franklin Houston,[1] with Enclosure

My dear Mr. Wilson: New York December 14, 1921.

What the Democratic Party should say about taxation is one thing. What it may be willing to say is another. The situation has its embarrassing aspects.

In May, 1919, in your message to Congress,[2] you pointed out the need of an early reconsideration of federal taxes. You suggested that they should be simplified and be made as little burdensome as possible. In December, 1919, in your annual message,[3] you repeated your recommendations and raised the question whether the higher rates of income and profits taxes could in peace times be effectively productive of revenue and whether, on the contrary, they might not be destructive of business activity and productive waste.[4]

Glass, in his annual report, dealt with taxation at length and made specific suggestions, strongly urging that the Excess Profits tax be repealed. In March, 1920, in a letter to the Chairman of the Ways and Means Committee, I pointed out the need of immediate action. I suggested the reduction of the Super-taxes, the repeal of the Excess Profits and the adoption of a flat tax on Corporations as a substitute. I urged also the adoption of four important administrative changes.

Secretary Mellon adopted our tax program and urged it before congressional committees. The recent act embodied its principal features, failing, however, to reduce the maximum surtax vote [rate] to as low a figure as I had suggested and to make the necessary modifications in the intermediate schedules.

Naturally I think the measure is in the right direction and is a decided improvement. The embarrassment arises from the fact that the noisy part of the Democrats, under Kitchen's[5] inspiration, instead of saying that they would accept a Democratic measure in principle, asserted that it was objectionable and would relieve the rich and burden the poor.

Their course, in my judgment, was a mistaken one. The representation is untrue. The supertaxes were losing their productivity. The rich had shifted and were continuing to shift their investments into tax-free securities. The Excess Profits tax also was losing its productivity. It was almost unworkable and was threatening an administrative breakdown. Also the new act raises the exemption for heads of families with incomes of $5,000 or less from $2,000 to $2,500, and that for each dependent from $200 to $400. Under the old law many individuals paid no income tax. The new exemptions affect over 2,000,000 old income taxpayers. Very many of them will pay much less under the new law than under the old.

The new law fixes the maximum supertax rate at 50% for incomes which accrue in 1922. The normal rate is left at 8%. I am convinced that it is unwise, in peace times, to try to take, through one federal tax, 58% of the income above $200,000 of individuals who also have to pay all other federal taxes and all state and local taxes.

I am interested in seeing the nation develop and retain a system of federal taxes which, as a whole, will in fair and reasonable measure be progressive. We must retain a progressive direct income tax; but it must be reasonable and workable. The difficulty of administrating in peace times will be insurmountable if the rates are very high. Certainly it will not yield the revenue expected or prevent individuals from enjoying large incomes, if its rates are high, and if, at the same time, the states are inviting people to invest in tax-free securities.

I enclose a summary statement which I hope you will find helpful. It sounds bromidic. I do not like it. I have not attempted to throw it into platform language. I hate platform language, and one reason why I dislike this statement is that it looks like a platform.

I am delighted to hear reports of your progress toward better health. Mrs. Houston and I think of you and Mrs. Wilson very often. We have the good fortune to see Mrs. McAdoo and Miss Wilson from time to time and they tell us about you. Our best wish for you this Christmas Season is that your health may improve even more rapidly, and that you may soon feel like your old self.

Mrs. Houston joins me in warmest regards to Mrs. Wilson and to you. Faithfully yours, D. F. Houston.

TLS (WP, DLC).
[1] He was at this time president of the Bell Telephone Securities Co., a subsidiary of A. T. & T.
[2] It is printed at May 20, 1919, Vol. 59.
[3] It is printed at Dec. 2, 1919, Vol. 64.
[4] All underlining in this letter by Wilson.
[5] Claude Kitchin of North Carolina, ranking Democratic member of the House Ways and Means Committee.

ENCLOSURE

Expenditure.

We pledge ourselves to enforce rigid economy in every branch of the Government's service, to reduce appropriations for existing services to the minimum needed for their efficient operation, and to subject to severe scrutiny all proposals for new enterprises. Only through decreased expenditure, can the necessary simplification and reduction of taxes be secured.

Taxation.

The burdens of federal taxation must be equitably distributed. They should be laid not only with due regard to the sacrifice which they will entail but also with a full recognition that extreme rates are abortive, and that they adversely affect the whole industrial life of the people and tend to break down the administrative machinery.

The tax arrangements which the Republicans built up before the war were unsafe and inequitable. Through the introduction of direct income taxes, the Democratic Party established a system which is sound in principle. It must be adjusted to peace conditions. We pledge ourselves to retain direct income taxation and a system which as a whole in reasonable and just measure will be progressive, and to resist all efforts to restore the former system of exclusive consumption taxes which unfairly burdened the masses of the people.

The Tariff.

We reaffirm our purpose to lay customs duties primarily for revenue. We will resist the reactionary movement to fix upon the people in the interest of special classes tariff rates in excess even of those under the Payne-Aldrich bill against which the people revolted in 1912. Such rates pernicious at any time would now be suicidal. We must adjust our economic life to changed conditions. The protection which our manufacturers and farmers mainly need is that which would be afforded by stable and extented [extended] foreign markets. If we wish to trade with foreign nations, particularly with those stricken by war and painfully struggling to recover, with meagre credit, and insufficient gold, indebted to us in huge sums, we must be prepared to import their commodities in large volume and to make extensive investments where conditions are satisfactory. In such manner we can serve ourselves and the world, and in no other way can we utilize the great merchant marine we have acquired.

We condemn as deceptive and destructive the American valuation plan.[1]

Hw MS (WP, DLC).
[1] That is, a widely held belief at this time that ad valorem tariff duties should be based on the American value of products rather than on foreign values, thus justifying higher rates.

From Edward Irving Edwards

My dear Governor: [Trenton] December 14th, 1921.

I beg to acknowledge receipt of your letter of December 14th, in reply to mine of December 12th.

I am very sorry to have to inform you that the splendid man you put up as Superintendent of Education passed away before his term expired. The present incumbent is an ad interim appointment, as you know no appointment could be made without the advice and consent of the Senate.

Yours very truly,   E I Edwards

TLS (WP, DLC).

From Stephen Samuel Wise

My dear Mr. President: New York Dec. 15, 1921

It is not possible to tell you how rejoiced all of us in the Executive of the Foundation[1] were to learn from Mr. Dodge of the gain in health that you have lately made and how hopefully we look forward to the day that shall find you restored to health and strength.

Your friends have probably followed the deliberations at Washington with an interest even greater than your own, for every day has brought to us some new testimony to that entire vindication which your purposes and plans are to have at the hands of history,—and history in the making.

I have tried to say something about your leadership in 1917-19 in the enclosure, especially pages 132-4,[2] which you may find a moment to glance over if you are not too utterly busy.

I shall have occasion in the near future to go to Washington, and the visit would be less mournful and far happier for me if I might see *my* President.

With heartfelt greetings to you and Mrs. Wilson,

Faithfully yours,   Stephen S. Wise

TLS (WP, DLC).
  [1] That is, the Woodrow Wilson Foundation.
  [2] The enclosure is missing, and we have not been able to identify it.

From Ray Stannard Baker

Dear Mr. Wilson: Amherst Massachusetts December 16, 1921.

I stopped in New York yesterday and made some inquiries regarding the progress of the syndication of our series. I thought you might be interested in hearing what is being done.

Mr. Brainerd [Brainard] is just beginning his intensive campaign so that we are not sure what the final results will be, but the arrangements thus far give us, it seems to me, a pretty good and well distributed selection of newspapers as follows:

New York *Times*,
Boston *Post*,
Springfield *Republican*,
Chicago *Daily News*,
Atlantic [Atlanta] *Constitution*,
Seattle *Times*,
New Orleans *Times Picayune*,
San Francisco *Chronicle*,
St. Louis *Star*,
Columbia *State*,
Pittsburg *Post*,
Omaha *World-Herald*,
Portland *Journal*,
Chattanooga *Times*,
Wilmington [N. C.] *Star*.

There are also several smaller papers.

The articles are to begin publication January first, and the contracts with these publications total $50.000. The Syndicate people seem to be sanguine that they will go much further, and the book, of course, upon which I rely more than the newspaper publication, is yet to come.

The Times editors have seen the earlier articles and tell me—I make allowances!—that they like them very much. At least they are going to do a first class job of advertising both in the newspapers and on bill-boards. Such advertising, I confess, always makes me flinch, but it seems to be necessary to get the results. The Times appears to be doing it with a full recognition of the importance and dignity of the material, and I hope if it comes to your eye you will not find it extreme or indecorous.

I regret that we could not have started publication sooner, though the articles may do fully as much good when the new treaties come up in Congress—at least the Times thinks so—as they would earlier, and we have a clearer stage and a more alert interest in foreign affairs. The fact is, I have found the task much greater than I had anticipated, and I am still a long way from being through with it. I felt that the importance of the material and of your record was far too great to be hastily treated, or to be treated for any purpose whatsoever, either financial or political, save to get down a true and complete account upon every part of which I could stand up and take my oath.

I know we shall be attacked for many things the record contains, but I hope not for misstatements of the facts. I comfort myself with a passage I ran across the other day in the life of Voltaire: "Whoso writes the history of his own times must expect to be blamed for everything he has said and everything he has not said."

I want to tell you in passing how an intensive study of the written records, upon which in any event future historians must base their conclusions, not only deepens my faith in the soundness and permanency of the principles and program you advocated at Paris, but confirms a conviction I had, during all those difficult months, of the sincerity with which you fought for them against impossible odds. You laid there the foundations of world unity upon which those who follow must inevitably build. You did at Paris what no one has dared to do at Washington—forced the discussion of ultimate standards, as to armament, and of a complete and logical program, dealing, not with fragmentary results of war, but with central causes. No matter what happens in the future, the world will be forced back always to a consideration of these fundamentals. What I am trying to do in this narrative is to keep those principles flying like a banner in every chapter. I shall, of course, show how the battle swayed hither and thither,—and that there were fearful losses,—and that it was after all not merely a battle but a war. If the story of how these principles had to meet the complicated traditions and necessities of the Old World is honestly set down, I believe it will be of very great help in shaping the still plastic judgment of this country in regard to our foreign affairs. And it is in itself a great record.

It was a pleasure to know at Washington that you were getting better and stronger. I can offer you no warmer Christmas greeting than the sincere hope that you will continue to improve during the coming year.

With much affection and loyal good wishes.

                    Sincerely yours,   Ray Stannard Baker

TLS (WP, DLC).

John Randolph Bolling to Edward Irving Edwards

My dear Governor Edwards: [Washington] 16th December 1921

Mr. Wilson desires me to thank you for your letter of December fourteenth, and say that he need hardly tell you that when he last wrote he had not heard of the death of Mr. Kendall. He is very grateful to you for your explanation.

                 Cordially yours,   [John Randloph Bolling]

CCL (WP, DLC).

To Stephen Samuel Wise

My dear Rabbi Wise: [Washington] 17th December 1921

Thank you for your letter with its enclosure. It gratifies me to know that your thoughts are following me still.

Let me say for your own ear alone that I can myself see no justification for the statement, I so frequently see made, that the present Conference is one of the fruits of my influence. Its works have no such flavor to my palate, but seem to me on the contrary the appropriate products of the minds of those who are presuming to represent us.

With warm greetings and best wishes for a very happy Christmas and profitable New Year;

          Faithfully and sincerely yours,   [Woodrow Wilson]

CCL (WP, DLC).

From James Edwin Webster

My dear Tommy: Bel Air, Md. December 20th, 1921

Doubtless you have seen in the papers of the passing of dear old Bob Henderson, and my mind naturally turns to the "Gang"[1] whose numbers are getting less as the years go by. Doc.,[2] Charlie[3] and Bob[4] leaves five out of the Eight.

You cannot imagine what a good time we had at Bob's last May[5] and how we wished for you, he was so genial and seemed so happy to have us with him. In late October he came down in his car and took Mrs. Webster[6] and me home with him, and after a most delightful week he brought us back home. Within a week or ten days after he left Bel Air he was taken sick, which illness terminated in his death this morning.

He had a most remarkable record on the bench, serving seventeen years, and only reversed twice by the Court of Appeals in all that time. For broadmindness and real intellect I ranked Bob second, only to yourself, out of the many great minds of the Class of '79. Every day I look at a little picture, hanging in my library, taken at one of our reunions, on the portico of "Prospect" and I have so often wished I had a larger picture of you to hang there, to hand down to my posterity, the only fear I have is it might cause some friction amongst them, as to whom it should go.

Some day possible [possibly] next Spring I want to take my twelve year old youngster[7] over to Washington and show him the sights and may call at your house to shake hands, only with the understanding that if busy or otherwise, you will not hesitate to be "out."

With kindest regards to Mrs. Wilson and love to yourself believe me   Affectionately yours,   J Edwin Webster

P.S. Best wishes for Christmas and the New Year.

TLS (WP, DLC).
[1] That is, the Witherspoon Gang at Princeton, about which, see WW to R. Bridges, June 13, 1894, n. 2, Vol. 8, and EBG to WW, Nov. 28, 1915, n. 3, Vol. 35.
[2] Charles Wellman Mitchell, M.D.
[3] Charles Andrew Talcott.
[4] Henderson.
[5] About this reunion, see WW to R. R. Henderson, May 7, 1921, n. 1.
[6] Dora Rouse Webster.
[7] John Rouse Webster.

From Francis Xavier Dercum

Dear Mr. Wilson,   [Philadelphia] December 20th, 1921.

Thank you very much indeed for your very kind and very thoughtful Christmas gift.[1] I prize it highly; for me it has a value and significance which is very personal. I cannot tell you, also, how much I appreciate the inscription which you have placed in the first volume above your signature. That I warmly reciprocate the sentiment which it conveys, you already know.

Pray believe me to be, with my kindest regards and my best wishes for the Holiday Season and the Coming Year, not only for yourself but also for Mrs. Wilson,

Very faithfully yours,   Francis X. Dercum

TLS (WP, DLC).
[1] Wilson had sent Dr. Dercum a set of his *History of the American People* as a Christmas present. See WW to F. X. Dercum, Dec. 12, 1921, CCL (WP, DLC).

John Randolph Bolling to the News Enterprise Association

Dear sirs: [Washington] 21st December 1921

In reply to your letter of December 19th;[1] Mr. Wilson requests me to say that he is at a loss to understand how you can say that a pure fake was the result of a "misunderstanding," and that his regret centers—not upon the fact that the newspapers gave currency to the fake—but that an association such as yours professes to be should have put it out. With regard to that he feels a deep resentment and begs you to understand that his feeling is that future "misunderstandings" of this sort might make it his duty to utter a public denunciation of their source.

Very truly yours,   [John Randolph Bolling]

CCL (WP, DLC).
[1] News Enterprise Association to JRB, Dec. 19, 1921, TLS (WP, DLC). The writer was replying to a copy of WW to W. B. Colver, Nov. 22, 1921 (summarized in WW to W. B. Colver, Dec. 10, 1921, n. 1). He apologized for the offending newspaper article and assured Wilson that Colver had been in no way responsible for it. The writer said that he would make amends if it were possible to do so. "But," he concluded, "I think you will agree that in a situation of this kind, so obviously the result of a misunderstanding, there is little if anything that can be done."

To Louisa Patterson Henderson

[Washington, Dec. 21, 1921]

The news of Bob's death has given me the keenest grief and my heart goes out to you in deepest sympathy

Woodrow Wilson

EBWhw MS (WP, DLC).

From Newton Diehl Baker

My dear Mr President: Cleveland December 21, 1921

If all the millions of people who love and follow you were to write you Christmas letters I fear even your patience would be exhausted, surely time would not suffice to read their messages. In any case you must just let us pour our hearts out and not make any attempt to answer or acknowledge our letters.

The return of reason among our people is daily more evident and I have no doubt you are enjoying the expressions of surprise which one hears on every hand that the Pacific Treaty[1] is after all our old friend Article X in much less frank and candid form and in much less effective association. Men here who appeared to regard Article X as the sum of all perils now look me straight in the face and say "But after all America cannot live alone! We must bear our share of the world's burdens if we are to enjoy the benefits of a common peace!" No matter in what form they put it I always say: "I am an optimist. The world is growing wiser and better—particularly now that I hear you quoting President Wilson!" It makes "the galled jade wince," but it is fair.

But this note is not about public things, its whole purpose is to carry to you and Mrs Wilson deep affection and the seasons greetings from Mrs Baker and me.

We heartily wish you health and happiness

Faithfully yours   Newton D. Baker

ALS (WP, DLC).
[1] That is, the so-called Four Power Treaty, about which see JRB to C. A. Swanson, Dec. 13, 1921, n. 1.

To James Edwin Webster

My dear Daniel: [Washington] 22d December 1921

It was delightful to get your letter. The "Gang" is indeed thinning out. It gave me keenest grief to hear of Bob Henderson's death. He was a most admirable and lovable character, and I had the warmest affection for him.

By all means bring the boy over to see me sometime. Let me know as far in advance as possible when you are coming so that I may be sure to be free for the enjoyment of seeing you again.

With all the best wishes of the season for you and yours;

Affectionately yours,   [Woodrow Wilson]

CCL (WP, DLC).

To Newton Diehl Baker

My dear Baker: [Washington] 24th December 1921

God bless you for your letter of December twenty-first. Your friendship and faith are very precious to me.

Mrs. Wilson and I join in wishing for Mrs. Baker and you every happiness in the Christmas season and every satisfying good fortune in the New Year and the years that follow.

Affectionately yours,   [Woodrow Wilson]

P.S. I myself do not see Article X anywhere in the War [Four?] Power Treaty. But then nobody knows what it means—not even those who wrote it by their own confession.[1]

CCL (WP, DLC).

[1] President Harding, when asked during an afternoon press conference on December 20 if the Japanese home islands were included in the phrase "insular possessions and insular dominions" in the Four Power Treaty, replied that they were not. That same evening, the White House issued a statement which said that Harding, following the press conference, had learned from the American delegation to the Washington Conference that they had "agreed to the construction which includes the homeland of Japan in the term 'insular possessions and insular dominions,' " and that he had "no objection to that construction." New York Times, Dec. 21, 1921.

To Ray Stannard Baker

My dear Baker: [Washington] 25th December 1921

Thank you for your letter; I regard it as a very satisfactory report of progress, upon which I congratulate you.

I hope that it is not necessary to tell you how deeply grateful I am by the sentences in regard to myself which your letter so generously discloses.

We join in heartfelt good wishes for the season, and the hope that your completed work will bring you lasting satisfaction and merited fame.

With warmest regards and sincere appreciation of the spirit in which all your work has been done;

Sincerely and faithfully yours,   [Woodrow Wilson]

CCL (WP, DLC).

To McLane Tilton[1]

My dear Mr. Tilton: Washington D C 25th December 1921

I am very much obliged to you for the handbook which you were kind enough to send me with your letter of December twenty-first.[2]

The question involved is of the deepest interest to me. I should deplore the removal of the Medical Department of the University of Virginia to Richmond as a very serious detriment to the University and also as a deplorable breach in the historical development of education in Virginia.

If the thing were done I should deplore it both as a wound to my pride as an alumnus of the University, and as distinctly contrary to my judgment as a student of education.

Cordially and sincerely yours,   Woodrow Wilson

TLS (ViU).
[1] Secretary-Treasurer of the General Alumni Association of the University of Virginia.
[2] M. Tilton to WW, Dec. 21, 1921, TLS (WP, DLC).

To John Howell Westcott

My dear John: Washington D C 27th December 1921

It was a real pleasure to get your letter from Nice, and to have news from you all.

I hope that when you get home again I shall have the good fortune to see you and yours again, and that the New year has in store for you all the most satisfying happiness.

I am not as well as some of the pictures make me look, but I believe I am slowly (and I hope surely) moving back in the direction of health again.

With warmest regards to you all;

Faithfully yours,   Woodrow Wilson

TLS (NjP).

From Ignace Jan Paderewski

Paso Robles Calif Dec 27 1921

On this solemn occasion my affectionate thoughts like those of many others go to you together with my most ardent wishes and prayers for your health and strength stop I beg to thank you once more and from the bottom of my heart for having been the joy of freedom to my people and to me the delight of gratitude stop With profound reverence admiration and heartfelt devotion

Paderewski[1]

T telegram (WP, DLC).
[1] Wilson's reply as sent is missing. However, his reply, as taken down in longhand (probably by Kriz) follows:
"Thank u warmly for yr mess u may be sure that my heart and best efforts will always be engaged on behalf of your much wronged country. may the new year bring her every bright fortune" Hw MS (WP, DLC).

From William Berryman Scott

Dear Mr. Wilson: Princeton, N. J. December 27th 1921

Let me send you a brief word of congratulation & good wishes on your birthday. I should very much like to write you a dissertation expressive of my unshaken faith in the solid greatness of your achievements as a stateman & of my gratitude to God that we had you at the helm throughout the great storm, but I will spare you, remembering that you will be fairly overwhelmed with letters tomorrow.

It is interesting to see how the whirligig of time is bringing around its revenges. Though the American people has failed to rise to the measure of their duty & their great opportunity, I feel assured that they will eventually shake off the apathy & sloth that have lain like a leaden pall upon them since the armistice, & take their true place in the world.

Wishing you all possible happiness & content, I am, as ever,

Very Sincerely Yours   W. B. Scott.

ALS (WP, DLC).

From Franklin Delano Roosevelt

New York City NY Dec 28th 1921

Woodrow Wilson Foundation extends to you heartiest congratulations on your birthday and sends best wishes for continued improvement of your health   Franklin D Roosevelt
                                        Chairman National Committee

T telegram (WP, DLC).

From Louis Dembitz Brandeis

My dear Mr Wilson: Washington, D. C. Dec 28/21

You were so deeply interested in the labor provisions embodied in the Clayton Act, that I am venturing to send you the recent opinions in the Truax Case.[1]

Possibly you may care to see also the opinions in the Duplex Case[2] enclosed.

With every good wish to you and Mrs Wilson for the New Year.
                    Most Cordially   Louis D. Brandeis

ALS (WP, DLC).

[1] Truax v. Corrigan, 257 U.S. 312. Chief Justice Taft, in an opinion rendered on December 19, had ruled unconstitutional an Arizona law restricting the use of injunctions in labor disputes on the ground that the denial of such injunctions was an infringement of property rights and denied property owners any real remedy as guaranteed by the due process and equal protection clauses of the Fourteenth Amendment.

Justices Oliver Wendell Holmes, Jr., Mahlon Pitney, and Brandeis filed separate dissenting opinions. In his dissent, Brandeis argued that property rights were not beyond legislative reach: such rights could be abridged or even destroyed for good cause. He said that the balance between property rights and other rights, such as those of labor, needed to be readjusted from time to time by legislative action. He also maintained that the Arizona statute did not in fact deprive the plaintiff of property without due process of law or deny him equal protection of the laws.

[2] Duplex Printing Press Co. v. Deering, 254 U.S. 443. In this case, decided on January 3, 1921, Justice Pitney delivered the opinion which held that the Clayton Act had not legalized secondary boycotts. Section 6 of the Clayton Act, he said, was not a full exemption of labor from the antitrust laws. It simply protected unions in "lawfully carrying out their legitimate objectives." Since secondary boycotts were unlawful, injunctions could be used to prevent them. Pitney further maintained that the restrictions upon the use of injunctions in Section 20 of the Clayton Act had to be construed to apply only to the immediate parties in a dispute. Thus, individual strikers might be exempt from an injunction, but a union was not.

Brandeis also wrote a dissenting opinion in this case, in which Justices Holmes and John H. Clarke concurred. Brandeis said that the narrow construction which Pitney had placed upon Section 20 of the Clayton Act would render that section nugatory. He asserted that it was the function of the legislature, not of judges, to determine the conditions of contests between employers and employees.

To Louis Dembitz Brandeis

My dear Friend: Washington D C 29th December 1921

I am very glad to get the decisions you so thoughtfully sent me, and thank you warmly for the courtesy.

I want to follow as closely as possible the application of the Clayton Act if for no other reason than to form an opinion of improvements that can be made in that Act—though I dare say you will form your own judgment on it, and later on I can get your own views on that matter.

Hoping that the New Year will bring you every lasting satisfaction.   Cordially and faithfully yours,   Woodrow Wilson

TLS (L. D. Brandeis Papers, KyLoU).

From Edwin Anderson Alderman

My dear Friend: Charlottesville December 29, 1921.

This University held you in mind with great affection and high remembrance on yesterday. You are honored and beloved here with a very deep and generous affection. We, at least, know how the years will treat you and we glory in it, for your sake and our own.

The boys are about to put a handsome bronze tablet on your old room in Dawson's Row.[1] They are doing it by private subscription and it is an independent impulse of theirs. They asked me for an inscription. I suggested, after the simple statement of facts, that splendid Horatian line 'Justum ac tenacem propositi virum,'[2] which seems to me to describe you in so far as one line could hope to do.

I am grateful to you for your ringing word about the removal of the Medical School. We shall win that fight, I think, for it is a fight of educational policy against superficial expediency.

Hoping for you increased strength and health, and rejoicing with you in the tide of appreciation and love which is flowing in to you from good men and women throughout the world.

                    Faithfully your friend,   Edwin A. Alderman.

TLS (WP, DLC).

[1] Wilson had occupied Room 158 in House F on Dawson's Row at the western end of the ranges during the academic year 1879-1880. He occupied 31 West Range during the autumn term of 1880. A tablet above the door of 31 West Range bears the following inscription:

IN THIS ROOM LIVED
WOODROW WILSON
1879-1881
PRESIDENT OF THE UNITED STATES
1913-1921

² A just man who sticks to his principles.—Horace.

From Donald C. Price

Dear Sir: Fort Wayne, Indiana, December 29, 1921.

I am a young man twenty-one years of age. I am setting the goal of "Success" far ahead. It will be my privilege to strive to attain that goal, sometime in the course of my life.

From one whom Experience and Success have dealt with great generosity, may I humbly seek the word that has been sounded as the keynote in a life that immeasurably has added to the gifts of mankind?   Your most humble friend,   Donald C. Price.

TLS (WP, DLC).

To Louis Dembitz Brandeis, with Enclosure

My dear Mr. Justice: Washington D C 2nd January 1922

The enclosed pages come from Mr. Houston, former Secretary of the Treasury, whom I asked to send them to me.

I have done little to them beyond touching up the phraseology here and there.

I hope they will seem to you worth while.

Cordially and sincerely yours,   Woodrow Wilson¹

TLS (L. D. Brandeis Papers, KyLoU).
¹ There is a WWsh draft of this letter in WP, DLC.

E N C L O S U R E¹

We share the disappointment and concern of the whole country at the failure and inability of the Republican party to effect a rational and business-like revision of the federal tax laws or develop any self-consistent or satisfactory method of economy. Economy, at all times imperative as a matter of plain duty, has become absolutely necessary as a matter of prudence. It should be carried to the utmost length compatible with the efficient conduct of the government and the development of the functions from time to time called forth by the diversified and constantly multiplying needs of the nation.

We pledge ourselves to enforce watchful economy in every

branch of the Government's service; to reduce appropriations for existing services to the minimum needed for their efficient operation, and to subject to severe scrutiny all proposals for new enterprises. Only through decreased expenditures can the necessary simplification and reduction of taxes be secured.

The federal tax laws needed simplication and the Republican Congress made them more complex. The excess profits tax had shown a cost of collection out of all proportion to its yield; had almost broken down in administration; and was likely, unless radically recast, to become a serious embarrassment to legitimate business. It ought to be repealed.

The burdens of federal taxation must be equitably distributed. They should be laid not only with due regard to the sacrifices which they will entail but also with a full recognition that extreme rates are abortive and that they adversely affect the whole industrial life of the people and tend to break down the administrative machinery.

The tax arrangements which the Republicans built up before the War were unsafe and unjustifiable. Through the introduction of direct income taxes, the Democratic Party re-established a system which is sound in principle. It must be adjusted to peace conditions. We pledge ourselves to retain direct income taxation and a system which as a whole in reasonable and just measure will be progressive and to resist all efforts to restore the former system of exclusive consumption taxes which unfairly burdened the masses of the people.

Since the close of the War large bodies of capital and the careful thought of enterprising merchants have been directed to the re-establishment and extension of our foreign trade. It is especially deplorable that just at this critical juncture the Republican Congress should have insisted on creating fresh tariff barriers and complexities.

We reaffirm our purpose to levy certain duties primarily for revenue. We will resist the reactionary movement to fix upon the people in the interest of special classes tariff rates in excess even of those under the Payne-Aldrich bill against which the people revolted in 1912. Such rates, pernicious at any time, would now be suicidal. We must adjust our economic life to changed conditions. The protection which our manufacturers and farmers mainly need is that which would be afforded by stable and extended foreign markets. If we wish to trade with foreign nations, particularly with those stricken by war and painfully struggling to recover, with meagre credit and insufficient gold, indebted to us in huge sums, we must be prepared to import their commodities in large volume and to make extensive investments where conditions are satisfactory. In such manner we can serve ourselves and the world. In no other way can we utilize the great merchant marine we have now acquired.

We condemn as deceptive and destructive the American valuation plan.

T MS (L. D. Brandeis Papers, KyLoU).
¹ The following document is Wilson's revision of the Enclosure printed with DFH to WW, Dec. 14, 1921.

John Randolph Bolling to Edwin Anderson Alderman

My dear Dr. Alderman: Washington D C 2d January 1922

Mr. Wilson asks me to express to you his warm appreciation of your delightful letter of December twenty-ninth last which he read with the greatest pleasure.

He is very touched by the action of the student body in marking his old room in Dawson's Row.

The possibility of the removal of the Medical School is giving him a great deal of concern, and if he can be of further service in helping to retain it at the University I am sure he will be glad if you will call on him.

Mr. Wilson's health is better now than at any time since his illness, and we note an almost daily improvement in his condition.

Cordially yours,   John Randolph Bolling

TLS (E. A. Alderman Papers, ViU).

From Douglas Wilson Johnson

My dear Mr. Wilson: New York January 3rd, 1922.

It has been my hope, ever since the Paris Conference, that at an appropriate time I could make known to the American people the whole story of the Adriatic controversy, in order that they might form a truer estimate of the tremendous difficulties encountered by their representatives in handling this question, and appreciate, as they do not now, that in this matter you were fighting for the cause of American idealism against a treacherous and discredited diplomacy. I thought the fact that I was a Republican, and as Chairman of the Executive Committee of the American Rights League had publicly opposed certain of your policies and acts before we entered the war, would free me of the charge of partisan bias, and together with a certain reputation for scientific accuracy which my friends credit to me, would gain for my statement of the issues a credence not always accorded the statements of one's political friends. I would like to have all the facts known as soon as they may with propriety be told, not merely in simple justice to you whose motives and reasons have been grossly misrepresented, but as an expression of my admiration for any man who fights magnificently for the ideals in which I believe, whether or not he be of my political faith; and most of all as an aid to my countrymen to see more clearly their mission to teach the world higher standards of international morality,—that between nations as between individuals, simple honesty and square dealing pay best in the long run.

On the other hand, I realize that my association with you as the principal adviser on territorial aspects of the Adriatic problem, might lay me open to the charge of bias from another angle. Furthermore, a heavy program of scientific work to which I am committed makes it problematical when, if ever, I could free my hands to write an adequate account of the Adriatic negotiations. It has therefore occurred to me that it might be best to place my records of this phase of the conference in the hands of my friend, Mr. Baker, for such use as he may wish to make of them. I assume that you have full confidence in his discretion, and his presentation of the facts will certainly have a far wider hearing than would anything I might write.

I therefore write to ask whether you see any objection to the suggested procedure. Of course I shall take the step, if I do take it, on my own responsibility; but I should appreciate your friendly advice in the matter (if I may venture to claim as friend the Chief under whom I am proud to have served), given confidentially. As Mr. Baker doubtless already has much of the material referred to in my records, and as I desire no publicity in the matter, I should ask him to treat any assistance I might be able to give him as merely an addition to your records, if this is agreeable to you.

With renewed assurances of my high regard, and with best wishes for continued improvement in health this New Year, I am
                    Very sincerely yours,   Douglas Johnson.

TLS (WP, DLC).

To Donald C. Price

My dear Mr. Price: [Washington] 4th January 1922

You may be sure if I knew any word that earned the secret of success I would be glad to send it to you; but I do not. Each man has to find that secret for himself; and it is my judgment it is best it should be so. It is a secret which cannot be communicated by precept or word of mouth.

I sincerely hope that you will find it out for yourself.

With best wishes for the New Year;

Sincerely yours,   [Woodrow Wilson]

CCL (WP, DLC).

From Edgar DeWitt Jones[1]

My dear Mr. Wilson: Detroit, Mich. Jan. 4, 1922.

It is certainly good news to the great host of your friends and admirers to know that your health is so much improved. I am one of that number who have believed in you all the way through the storm and the struggle. It is good now to see the beginning of the turn of the tide. Newspapers that had nothing but sarcasm and bitter criticism six months ago are considerably softened in tone, and a few of them are actually speaking kindly of you. This is significant in more than one way. However, whatever your critics may do or not do must be of little concern to one who has a sense of duty done and high purpose achieved.

If you were not already over-burdened with a heavy correspondence I should be moved to ask you to write me in a single paragraph your message to the young men in the Christian ministry of today. If it should be that you feel you could take the time to do this, it would gratify me deeply and serve a good purpose that I now have in mind.

With all good wishes for your restoration to health and deepest appreciation of your sacrificial services for a re-united world, I am,

Most sincerely yours,   Edgar DeWitt Jones.

TLS (WP, DLC).
[1] Pastor of the Central Church of the Disciples of Christ in Detroit; author of religious books.

From Martha McChesney Berry

Dear Mr. Wilson: Mount Berry, Georgia January 4, 1921[1922].

On the 13th day of this month will be celebrated the 20th anniversary of the Berry Schools. In twenty years the school has grown from a one room log cabin into an industrial school recently quoted in the "Review of Reviews" as having "no superior anywhere in the country." God has indeed blessed us!

Would it be asking too much of you if we ask you to help us

commemorate the day by sending us an autographed copy of one of your books for our library?[1] Also will you write a letter of cheer and good will, which will be published with other letters received on the 13th and made into a souvenir booklet?

Assuring you that I shall deeply appreciate the granting of this favor, and earnestly wishing for you a very happy New Year,

Sincerely, Martha Berry

TLS (WP, DLC).

[1] The following is typed at the top of this letter: "Wrote Jany. 7 had ordered book; would be autgrpd. by WW and sent soon as recvd. JRB."

To Franklin Delano Roosevelt

My dear Roosevelt: Washington D C 5th January 1922

Your telegraphic message[1] on behalf of the Foundation gave me a great deal of pleasure, and I thank you for it very warmly.

I am exceedingly proud of the proofs of friendship and confidence which the progress of the Foundation affords me, and your own friendship and unselfish devotion to its objects give me, as I hope you know, peculiar gratification.

I sincerely hope that your illness is being rapidly replaced by your accustomed health and strength, and that the New Year will add to the blessings of recovery every satisfactory happiness.

Mrs. Wilson joins me in kindest regards to Mrs. Roosevelt and you, and every good wish for you both.

Cordially and faithfully yours, Woodrow Wilson

TLS (F. D. Roosevelt Papers, NHpR).

[1] FDR to WW, Dec. 28, 1921.

To Douglas Wilson Johnson

My dear Johnson: [Washington] 5th January 1922

Of course I recall, and with real gratitude, the matter of the assistance you gave me in the matter of the vexed Adriatic question when we were in Paris; and the use you suggest making of your records seems to me just the right one.[1]

I have entire confidence in Stannard Baker, and I suggest you get in early communication with him and you and he together work out the best method of using your material. I sincerely appreciate your offer of assistance in this matter, and honor the motives which prompted it. No doubt you know Baker's address is Amherst, Massachusetts.

With pleasant recollections of our association in Paris, and most cordial good wishes for the New Year and the years to come;
    Cordially and faithfully yours, [Woodrow Wilson]

CCL (WP, DLC).
 ¹ Johnson wrote a 175-page history of the controversies over the determination of the Italian northern boundary and in the Adriatic area. For the main text of his memorandum, Johnson obviously quoted from a lengthy diary that he kept at Paris. This undated T MS is in the "personal letters" section of the R. S. Baker Papers, DLC.

To Ben Johnson¹

My dear Johnson: [Washington] 5th January 1922

I hope you will not think I am presuming on our friendship if I write to express my deep interest in the appropriation for a home for the feeble-minded in the District. The need for such a home is, I know, very pressing; and now that I am a resident of the District I am more deeply than ever concerned that its equipment in all matters of beneficence should be complete and unstinted.

Please consider this the liberty of an old friend, and let it have such weight with you as it may.

With best wishes for the New Year;
    Cordially and faithfully yours, [Woodrow Wilson]

CCL (WP, DLC).
 ¹ Democratic congressman from Kentucky and a member of the House Appropriations Committee. He had acquired a reputation of obstructionism in regard to anything connected with the District of Columbia. See Constance McLaughlin Green, *Washington: Capital City, 1879-1950* (Princeton, N. J., 1962), pp. 251-52.

William Edward Dodd to John Randolph Bolling

My dear Mr. Bolling: Chicago, Jan 5, 1922.

Would you mind saying to Mr. Wilson that he was unanimously chosen second vice president (president in due course) of the American Historical Association at the recent St Louis meeting. The committee on nomination of officers asked me a year ago to speak to him about the matter. This is the outcome. I hope he understands and that he will find it possible and agreeable to accept when the official notice is given.

Another matter of some moment to me: I was informed, when in St Louis, that my name was being canvassed by the proper authorities for the presidency of the University of Missouri.

Higher education being what it is in this country and the ordeals of university presidents, who do their duty, being what they are, I do not know whether I should be able to accept the appointment if made. It would seem like a sentence quite as much as an honor. But thinking it over I have concluded that I might render some better service to the country as a whole, if elected—perhaps gain a hearing for ideas and social purposes not now at my command.

Although I am not absolutely decided what would be best to do, I would be glad if Mr. Wilson could get word to some of his friends in Missouri what he thinks of the proposition. David R. Francis is president of the Board of Trustees. I do not know who are the other leading members of the body.

The enclosed clipping has probably come to your attention.[1] It was a dinner of extraordinary interest and enthusiasm. I never saw the like of it.   Yours Sincerely   William E. Dodd

ALS (WP, DLC).
[1] It is missing.

To Alexander Mitchell Palmer

My dear Palmer: [Washington] 6th January 1922

We have just learned of your tragical loss[1] and I hasten to send you this line of heartfelt sympathy.

I hope that every comfort that is possible in such circumstances may be vouchsafed to you. May God sustain you.

With deepest sympathy, in which Mrs. Wilson joins;

Sincerely yours,   [Woodrow Wilson]

CCL (WP, DLC).
[1] His wife, Roberta Bartlett Dixon Palmer, had died on January 4.

From Louis Dembitz Brandeis

My dear Mr Wilson: Washington, D. C. Jan 6/22

My thanks for your letter with its forceful and persuasive Enclosure.

Would it not be better to omit the third and fourth paragraphs?

Most Cordially   Louis D Brandeis

ALS (WP, DLC).

To Louis Dembitz Brandeis

My dear Mr. Justice: Washington D C 7th January 1922

Thank you for your letter of January sixth.

In reply to your question as to whether it would be best to omit paragraphs three and four from the memorandum of suggestions just sent you; let me say that I do not feel it safe to form any final conclusion about inclusions or omissions until we have conceived a complete document and can consider it in detail determining, among other things, the proper balance of its parts. The vital importance of such a document in the near future seems to me more and more evident as the days, empty of all political achievement, go by.

Among other uses to which it could be put, it has occurred to me to suggest to the Chairman of the Democratic National Committee that it be sent to Democratic candidates for Congress next year with the intimation that they select from it the declarations of policy and intention they were to include in their manifestos to the voters of their districts. In that way the thoughts of the party might, it seems to me, be drawn into common channels before the big tasks of nineteen hundred and twenty four demand immediate performance. I hope that the idea commends itself to your practical judgment.

Hoping, my dear Mr. Justice, that the New Year will contain for you every satisfying fortune and experience.

Cordially and sincerely yours,   Woodrow Wilson

TLS (L. D. Brandeis Papers, KyLoU).

To Edgar DeWitt Jones

My dear Mr. Jones: [Washington] 7th January 1922

I very much appreciate the kind personal sentiments of your letter of January fourth.

I do not know of anything I could say that would constitute such a message as I would be willing to send to young ministers. If you are a writer yourself you are no doubt aware that what you propose is the hardest thing in writing that there is to do. It was too hard for me when I was well; much more is it too hard for me now.

Sincerely yours,   [Woodrow Wilson]

CCL (WP, DLC).

To Martha McChesney Berry

My dear Miss Berry: [Washington] 7th January 1922

I heartily congratulate you on the twentieth anniversary of The Berry Schools. I know of no institution which has more excited my admiration, and I hope with all my heart that many more periods of usefulness, such as the last twenty years, will crown your unique and admirable enterprise.

Hoping that the New Year will be a particularly bright one for the Schools and for you;

                    Cordially and sincerely yours,   [Woodrow Wilson]

CCL (WP, DLC).

To Léon Dessez[1]

My dear Captain Dessez: [Washington] 7th January 1922

At last I am enabled to identify the young officer who so graciously spoke to me the other day on Sixteenth Street, and I want to give myself the pleasure of telling him how much I appreciated his greeting.

I like to consider myself a comrade of all the men in the service, and I am always very happy to have them entertain cordial thoughts of me.

May I not express the hope that the New Year will be filled for you with satisfying and fortunate circumstances.

                    Cordially and sincerely your friend,   [Woodrow Wilson]

CCL (WP, DLC).
    [1] Captain, U.S.A., a veteran of the battle in the Argonne, September-November 1918; at this time serving in the field artillery. He had written Newton D. Baker, telling him about meeting Wilson on January 1. He had been driving behind Wilson's car on Massachusetts Avenue, followed it up Sixteenth Street, where it stopped to deliver a card to some embassy, and impulsively jumped out of his car and introduced himself to Wilson. Wilson courteously acknowledged his greeting and then drove on. Dessez was visiting his family in Chevy Chase at this time. L. Dessez to NDB, Jan. 2, 1922, ALS (WP, DLC). Baker sent this letter to Wilson.

John Randolph Bolling to William Edward Dodd, with Enclosure

My dear Professor Dodd: [Washington] 8th January 1922

Your interesting and delightful letter of January fifth has just come to me, and I have this morning read it to Mr. Wilson.

He was so much interested in what you have to say about the presidency of the University of Missouri that he did not comment upon his election to the office of second vice president of the American Historical Association, though I am inclined to think he will accept it when the official notice reaches him.

Mr. Wilson feels with you that the presidency of the University of Missouri would open up new fields of service for you; and with his permission I am enclosing copy of letter which he is sending in this mail to Mr. Francis. Be sure to keep us posted as to developments.

Thanks for the clippings. I had had some sent me, but not as full accounts as those you enclose.

With warmest regards;

Cordially yours,   John Randolph Bolling.

TLS (W. E. Dodd Papers, DLC).

E N C L O S U R E

To David Rowland Francis

My dear Francis: [Washington] 8th January 1922

I understand that the trustees of the University of Missouri are considering, among other names, the name of Professor William E. Dodd of the University of Chicago for the presidency of the institution; and I cannot deny myself the pleasure of giving my testimony as to his character and fitness.

He is one of the most admirable men I know; sound in scholarship; sober in judgment and capable of the kind of steady and reserved enthusiasm which seems to me to have more dynamic force in it than any of the more demonstrative and effervescent sort.

I know from long experience in the field of university work that suitable presidential material is extremely scarce. Professor Dodd is one of the few men I know who seems to me to measure up to the requirements in character and fitness, and at the same time to have a suitable personality.

I hope that all goes well with Mrs. Francis[1] and you, and that the New Year will open up to you both only delightful and fortunate experiences.

Cordially and sincerely yours,   [Woodrow Wilson][2]

CCL (WP, DLC).

[1] Jane Perry Francis.

[2] Francis replied that he was no longer on the Board of Curators of the university; that the board had already elected John Carleton Jones, Professor of Latin, Dean of the College of Arts and Sciences, and Vice-President of the university, as Acting President; and that he, Francis, was sending Wilson's letter to Jones. D. R. Francis to WW, Feb. 4, 1922, TLS (WP, DLC).

From George Foster Peabody

Saratoga Springs N Y Jan 8, 1922

The beloved Ladye[1] has passed from our tender care to the true home which her life and words made so vivid to us and the multitude   Geo Foster Peabody

T telegram (WP, DLC).
   [1] His wife, Kate Nichols Trask Peabody, died on January 8.

To George Foster Peabody

My dear Friend: [Washington] 9th January 1922

Our telegram[1] was an attempt to express our sumpathy [sympathy], but did not afford us an adequate vehicle for expressing our sense of personal loss. Such a friend as she was—so fitted for counsel or delight, so thoughtful, so suited and so apt to inspire the best that was in one—can never be replaced.

Our hearts are very sad indeed that she is gone, and we feel impoverished by her loss.

May God vouchsafe you, my dear friend, every possible solace.

Mrs. Wilson is herself writing; I therefore need not add that she joins in this expression of bereavement and loss.

Please be assured always of our affectionate sympathy.

Sincerely and faithfully yours,   [Woodrow Wilson]

CCL (WP, DLC).
   [1] A draft of this telegram is attached to the telegram, just printed, from Peabody.

To Albert W. Kette[1]

My dear Mr. Kette: [Washington] 9th January 1922

I warmly appreciate the invitation of The Marion Democratic Club[2] to be present at their celebration of Jackson Day tomorrow evening, but unfortunately I am not well enough to accept. Pulling out from a breakdown of the nerves is proving to be a slow and tedious business; but it at least gives me time to reflect upon the prospects of duties of our party.

Those prospects were never brighter; those duties it seems to me never plainer.

I have no doubt that you and the other Democrats of Ohio share with me the confidence that we shall have early and repeated victories, and an opportunity to serve the country and the world with the best that is in us.

Confidently hoping for you and your associates a fortunate New Year;   Sincerely yours,   [Woodrow Wilson]

CCL (WP, DLC).
    [1] An insurance broker of Marion, Ohio, active in civic and Democratic party affairs.
    [2] A. W. Kette to WW, Jan. 6, 1922, T telegram (WP, DLC).

From Frank Irving Cobb

Dear Mr. Wilson: New York January 9th, 1922.

Here is something that I think will please you. Saturday the National Republican club had a meeting to discuss the Washington Conference, and asked me to come up and start the trouble, which I did, and told them the great value of this Conference is that it pushed the United States further toward the League of Nations.

Representative Fess,[1] of Ohio, who followed me, discussed the conference in detail, and at the close he said something like this (I cannot quite recall his exact words) "that Mr. Harding's place in history would be fixed by this Conference; that Mr. Hughes' place would also be determined by this Conference, but that all Republicans would have to admit that back of it all the man who had made it possible, the man who had focused the attention of the world upon this question of organized peace, and made it a vital question was Woodrow Wilson."

It will interest you most that nothing else said at the meeting received so much applause as this.

With sincerest regards,   As ever yours,   Frank I Cobb.

TLS (WP, DLC).
    [1] Simeon Davison Fess, Republican of Ohio.

From George Weston Anderson

Dear Mr. Wilson: Boston. 9th January, 1922.

Increasingly the four-party treaty seems to me not merely a negative, but a very *positive*, evil: a very dangerous retrogression. Why, if ratified, does it not commit us absolutely to a reversion to the old scheme of military and naval alliances and ententes,—alliances that have in all history been provocative of war and enlarged the scope of war? Reading the treaty, particularly in the light of Senator Lodge's speech,[1] it seems to me, in the main, an extension of imperialism in the Pacific: an appropriation of the finest lot of hitherto unappropriated islands for the benefit of the parties.

There is one aspect of this treaty that I have not seen discussed and want to bring to your attention: You will, of course, remember that the Versailles Treaty turned over the German islands to Mandataries,—Trustees, who must render an annual account of their trusteeships to the League of Nations. They were not turned over to Great Britain, France and Japan as dominions or possessions. They were to be regarded as a sacred trust for civilization,—held primarily for the benefit of their native inhabitants, secondarily for the world at large. Now, it is true, we are not in on the "sacred trust" theory; but what becomes of it when we make, with the Trustees,² an agreement "to respect their rights in relation of their insular possessions and insular dominions in the regions of the Pacific Ocean"? Plainly, we treat these islands as the "insular possessions or dominions" of the contracting parties. If we thus smash the "sacred trust" theory, may the trustees trade as to their trust estates as though they owned them? Offhand, it looks to me as though we were inducing the parties to the Versailles Treaty to make, at any rate by implication, an agreement utterly inconsistent with their obligations as trustees. This may be another of the numerous attempts made by this administration to destroy the League of Nations. But this important aspect of the situation has not as yet, so far as I have seen, been brought to the attention of the American people, or even of the American Congress.

You may be interested to know that on Saturday I had a considerable discussion of the situation with Gov. McCall,³ who was down there interpreting the Conference for the benefit of the Boston Post,—some 30 articles. *He* is under no delusions. In general, he regards the Conference as so far making more *for war* than for peace. It seems very plain that the attempts of the last few days to provide rules for making the Next War more gentlemanly,⁴ put us back to the foolish, futile fulminations of 20 years ago. Unless the situation is radically changed by the other treaties, I hope the Democrats will not help ratify this treaty. I think it will breed wars, and meantime tend to beguile and mislead the American people.

With cordial personal regards,

Sincerely yours   G. W. Anderson

TLS (WP, DLC).

¹ Henry Cabot Lodge, acting in his capacity as one of the American delegates to the Washington Conference, presented the Four Power Treaty to a plenary session on December 10. After reading aloud the full text of the brief treaty (about which, see J. R. Bolling to C. A. Swanson, Dec. 13, 1921, n. 1) Lodge went on to stress the explicitness and simplicity of the document. He pointed out that it contained "no provision for the use of force to carry out any of the terms of the agreement," and that no military or naval sanction lurked "anywhere in the background." He then spoke about the beauty and vast extent of the Pacific islands. However, he noted, many of the islands, especially the larger ones, contained great natural resources. "In a word," he said, "they have a very great material value, largely undeveloped, and where this condition exists the desires of men will enter; conflicting human desires have throughout recorded history

been breeders of war. . . . We make the experiment here in this Treaty of trying to assure peace in the immense region by trusting the preservation of its tranquillity to the good faith of the nations responsible for it." The full text of Lodge's speech is printed in *Conference on the Limitation of Armament, Washington, November 12, 1921-February 6, 1922* (Washington, 1922), pp. 158-66.

² Wilson's underlining.

³ That is, Samuel Walker McCall, Republican Governor of Massachusetts, 1916-1918.

⁴ He referred to discussions about requiring submarines, when acting as commerce destroyers, to obey the rules of cruiser warfare and to forbid the use of poisonous gases and chemicals in warfare. A treaty prohibiting the use of submarines as commerce destroyers was signed on February 6, 1922, but it was not ratified by France. The London Naval Treaty of 1930, which required submarines to observe the rules of cruiser warfare, was accepted by all naval powers before 1939.

From Ben Johnson

My dear Mr. Wilson: Washington, D. C. Jan. 9, 1922

I have the honor to acknowledge the receipt of your favor of 5th instant relative to a home for the feeble-minded of the District of Columbia.

The little I know about the subject already favorably inclines me toward it. Now that I have the benefit of your knowledge of its pressing need I shall feel safe in doing what I can toward its establishment.

Genuinely trusting that your health, sacrificed in a great cause, may be fully restored, I beg to remain,

Yours most respectfully,   Ben Johnson

TLS (WP, DLC).

To Frank Irving Cobb

My dear Cobb: [Washington] 10th January 1922

That was indeed a remarkable incident of which you tell me at the National Republican Club, and it was generous of you to write me about it. Thank you very warmly. You are the kind of friend it delights and strengthens me to have.

I hope that the New Year will open to you every door you care to enter.

With warm regard;

Cordially and faithfully yours,   [Woodrow Wilson]

CCL (WP, DLC).

From John Spencer Bassett[1]

My dear sir: Northampton, Massachusetts January 10, 1922.

It gives me great pleasure to inform you that at the last annual meeting of the American Historical Association, in St. Louis, December 30, 1921, you were unanimously elected second vice-president of the Association. You doubtless know that it is the custom of the Association to elect a man second vice-president with the expectation that in successive years he will advance to the presidency. It is by that means of choice that all our presidents, so far as I know, have been chosen. I mention this because it is understood that your election to the second vice-presidency is tantamount to your election to the presidency two years hence. I shall be very happy to have a line from you telling me that you accept service.

I cannot refrain from expressing my personal pleasure in being able to send you this notice; and I add my sincere desire that you will gratify your friends in the historians' craft by becoming our vice-president and president.

Yours sincerely,   John S. Bassett

TLS (WP, DLC).
    [1] Professor of History at Smith College and Secretary of the American Historical Association.

From Léon Dessez

                                        Chevy Chase D. C.
My dear Mr. President,   January 10, 1921 [1922].

You can never understand and I can never hope to be able to express to you my gratitude for your note which I received this morning. On New Year's day I meant a great deal more than I could say when I saw you and I wrote my friend Mr. Baker, who must have mentioned me in some way in one of his letters to you, I trust that, in spite of my very conventional words, my manner betrayed my real emotions and the message of my heart.

What I should have liked to express to you on New Year's day was that singularly complex emotion which every good soldier feels for his leader who has inspired and upheld him in time of danger and who is willing to risk personal sacrifice in order to be faithful to those whom he has led. This feeling I should have liked to express not only for myself but for the great mass of younger men in the Army with whom I share it. Unfortunately, like most of those men, I am as little able to express it as I am to analyze it— and I only hope that in some way I succeeded in making it felt.

Many of us were kept going in those terrible days in the Argonne by your utterances of courage and of hope—and our unquestioning loyalty to you then has only deepened with the increasing difficulties you have met with in fighting our battle for us. God knows, if there were a way, we would do anything to repay you for the sacrifices you have made for us.

I wish I might have the opportunity sometime to tell you about some of the interesting discussions we have in our regimental mess—of how the Third Field Artillery was a small but intensely militant Democratic island in Republican Illinois during the last Presidential campaign—of how our major, an "irreconcilable," was outvoted five to one by the junior officers in a discussion about the League of Nations.

My orderly in the battery—a rather quick-minded but uneducated youngster about nineteen years old met me in my quarters in Camp Knox one evening when I came back from supper with a book in his hand and won my heart as few men have ever done. "Captain," he said, "while you were out I started reading one of your books and it is so interesting I would like to sit down on your footstool over there and keep reading it until tatoo, if you don't mind." I told him I was not only willing but anxious to have him read all he wanted to. "By the way, Drummond, what are you reading?"—"A book by President Wilson, Captain, called the Triumph of Ideals[1]—it's a good book."

My own convictions are almost too strong to put down on paper. I went into the war for the League of Nations—I was willing to die for the League in 1918—and I am willing to die for the League now.

You have undoubtedly had many offers of service, Mr. President, but it won't hurt to have another one and, should you ever want to have anything done, I will do it.

Loyally and gratefully yours,   Léon Dessez

ALS (WP, DLC).
[1] The *Triumph of Ideals: Speeches, Messages, and Addresses Made by the President between February 24, 1919 and July 8, 1919 . . .* (New York, 1919).

To David Franklin Houston

My dear Houston: [Washington] 11th January 1922

I am ashamed to find there is no record of my having acknowledged your great kindness in contributing suggestions to the declaration of principles on which it is so important to concentrate common counsel. Notwithstanding my apparent indifference I appreciated your kindness and have already taken steps to put the suggestions in the declaration.

I hope that the New Year begins most happily for Mrs. Houston and you, and that all its auspicious signs will be fulfilled by a happy consummation.

With most cordial messages for you all from Mrs. Wilson and me;   Cordially and faithfully yours,   [Woodrow Wilson]

CCL (WP, DLC).

A Memorandum by Dr. Grayson

January 11, 1922.

I had luncheon with the Right Honorable Arthur James Balfour at 1:30 o'clock today (January 11, 1922) in his apartments at 1302 Eighteenth Street, N.W. Those present were: Mr. Balfour, Mrs. Grayson, Mr. Peterson (Mr. Balfour's Secretary), and myself. It was snowing and Washington was in the path of a heavy storm which was raging all along the Atlantic Coast.

Mr. Balfour came in about fifteen minutes late and expressed regret that he had been "button-holed" by several people as he was leaving the Conference on the Limitation of Armament, which was holding its final sessions. Sir Maurice Hankey was attending to some matters for Mr. Balfour so that he was unable, as Mr. Balfour said, to "unbutton" him, as he usually did on occasions of this kind.

Mr. Balfour, after apologizing for being late, remarked: "It is very fine to see you again, and it is particularly fine to see you looking so well." I told him that it gave me pleasure to be able to return the compliment—that he too was looking remarkably well. He responded by saying that he rather prided himself on the fact that he did not show that he was seventy-four years of age. He said: "I play tennis whenever I get an opportunity and also golf. My only trouble now is that I am a little deaf in my right ear."

Mr. Balfour suddenly turned the subject of our conversation. "Have you seen many of our old friends from Paris," he asked. After I had answered his question, he inquired as to Mr. Wilson's health. "I fancy," he said, "that Mr. Wilson's condition is much like that of Mr. Chamberlain's illness,[1] although I suppose Mr. Chamberlain was really worse than Mr. Wilson, for Mr. Chamberlain's speech was badly affected. I had considerable difficulty in understanding him, but he usually had one of his daughters present—they could understand him better than anyone else." He then dwelt upon the sadness of Mr. Wilson's illness, coming as it did at such an untimely period in the world's affairs. He said: "Mr. Wilson is unquestionably the greatest man of the age, and the things that he stood for—and I mean chiefly the League of Nations—are eternal. I am a firm believer in the ultimate success of the League. If it 'blew up to the skies' now, it would be well worth all that has been done. It has accomplished more—much more—than the people as a whole realize. It has stopped wars already—several wars—the most recent being between Serbia and Albania—by bringing economic pressure to bear. If anything could cause the defeat of the purposes of the League it would be the petty and sordid objections, magnified by political intrigue, against the paying of a very moderate tax for the maintenance of the League. Few have had vision enough to see that what this body is doing is for the good of all; in other words, that what is being done for any one part is naturally beneficial to the whole. I have been sent here on a different task, and, therefore, I must restrain myself, but I should like very much to have an opportunity to make a speech on the League of Nations. I have watched this country with the deepest interest and I firmly believe that the defeat of the League of Nations 'out here' was due to lack of understanding and to misrepresentation. I feel that I know as much about it (the League) as anybody, because I have made a thorough and exhaustive study of it—I have been a member of the Council and have attended nearly all of its meetings—and I must repeat that I feel that it is a decided success so far. Moreover, I am convinced that nothing can take the place of the League of Nations—nothing can be substituted for it."

Mr. Balfour was anxious to know how much of an interest Mr. Wilson was taking now in world affairs, and whether he kept in touch with the changing conditions not only in this country but in the world at large. He said: "I enjoyed my visit with Mr. Wilson very much. I hope that you are keeping notes about this important man. The things that may seem to you so very trivial now may be of very great importance later. You should write everything that you possibly can about him."

Mr. Balfour inquired whether Mr. Wilson read much. I told him that he had difficulty holding a book. He replied: "There are so many artificial means in the way of stands and book-rests that I hope he will not let his crippled hand interfere with his pleasure of reading." I said that Mr. Wilson was very fond of being read to, and that he had only recently told me how fortunate he was in having his brother-in-law, Dr. Stockton Axson, in Washington the past six months, Mr. Wilson remarking that it was a pleasure to have Dr. Axson read to him for he (Dr. Axson) was such an excellent reader and a man of letters. I also told Mr. Balfour that Mrs. Wilson frequently reads to Mr. Wilson, while in the evenings Mr. Wilson devotes a part of his time to reading the daily papers himself—more so than he ever did while in public life. . . .

T MS (received from James Gordon Grayson and Cary T. Grayson, Jr.).
   ¹ Joseph Chamberlain (1836-1914), former Principal Secretary of State for the Colonies, had suffered a stroke in 1906, which had left his body partially paralyzed and his speech permanently impaired.

To George Weston Anderson

My dear Judge: [Washington] 12th January 1922

Thank you for your letter about the four-party treaty; I find myself in agreement with it throughout, and have taken the liberty of putting it in the hands of one of our ablest and most trustworthy Senators.

Hoping that the New Year will treat you in every way kindly and generously;

             Cordially and sincerely yours,   [Woodrow Wilson]

CCL (WP, DLC).

To John Sharp Williams

My dear Senator: [Washington] 12th January 1922

I am taking the liberty of sending you the enclosed letter, because of its intrinsic interest and importance, and also because I know Judge Anderson to be genuine in every fibre. It was by my appointment he became Circuit Judge.

I am sending the letter on the theory (which I know is perfectly safe) that you are glad to see anything which throws light on public questions with which you have to deal as a Senator.

I hope, my dear friend, that the New Year has opened most auspiciously for you and yours, and that it will afford you every happy and fortunate experience.

With warm personal regard;

             Cordially and faithfully yours   [Woodrow Wilson]

CCL (WP, DLC).

To John Spencer Bassett

My dear Professor Bassett: [Washington] 12th January 1922

I need hardly say that I have always taken genuine interest in the work of The American Historical Association of whose birth I was a witness while I was studying at Johns Hopkins.¹

I feel it is a compliment that the Association should have chosen me one of its vice-presidents, and I accept the election.

With much appreciation;

Sincerely yours,   [Woodrow Wilson]

CCL (WP, DLC).
    ¹ In 1884. Arthur S. Link, "The American Historical Association, 1884-1984: Retrospect and Prospect," *American Historical Review*, XC (Feb. 1985), 1-2. Wilson was a charter member.

A Draft of a Telegram[1]

Telegram for Mrs. Sayre   [Washington, Jan. 12, 1922]

Favorite colour, orange
favorite flower, rose

WWhw MS (WC, NjP).
    ¹ "Sent to Jessie by EBW." EBWhw on document.

From Gilbert Fairchild Close

My dear President Wilson: Granite City, Ill., January 12th, 1922.

I have become quite interested in a campaign which is being conducted now throughout the State of Missouri for the purpose of raising a fund of about a million dollars for the benefit of the Presbyterian colleges of the State, and also to advance the Presbyterian student pastor work at the State University. Tom Evans,[1] Princeton '97, whom I am sure you will remember, is working on this campaign, and it is largely through him that I have become interested in it.

I am wondering whether you would find it possible to write a letter which we could use in the campaign, expressing your opinion of the importance of Christian colleges of this kind in developing character and Christian citizenship. Both of the Presbyterian colleges in Missouri, Westminster and Park, have had a very honorable record and are doing magnificent work in spite of lack of adequate equipment and adequate funds. It is really from colleges like these that a large proportion of the Christian leadership come, both ministers and laymen, and we are trying out here to put these colleges on a substantial basis. I am enclosing a letter head which is being used in the campaign which contains on it the essential facts about these colleges and what they are doing.

My only excuse for asking you to write such a letter is that I know it would be of tremendous help in bringing to a success this campaign, and because I know you are interested in things of this kind.

Whenever Mr. Howard[2] returns from his trips to Washington, I always ask him if he has seen you and Mrs. Wilson, and through him I have kept more or less in touch with you, and have been very glad to know that your health has been improving. I am sure that the American people are coming to realize more and more every day what a wonderful leadership you gave us as a Nation, and I am confident that your ideals for America will be realized.

I wish very much that I might have an opportunity to see you and Mrs. Wilson again, for I shall never forget the wonderful experiences which I had in Washington and Europe because of your kindness, and I shall always prize very highly the opportunity of association with you. It was wonderful for me, and I cannot tell you how deeply I appreciated and valued the time I spent in Washington with you.

Mrs. Close[3] and I unite in warmest regards and best wishes to Mrs. Wilson and yourself.

Always faithfully yours,   Gilbert F. Close

TLS (WP, DLC).
  [1] Thomas St. Clair Evans.
  [2] Clarence Henry Howard, president of the Commonwealth Steel Co. of St. Louis, with which Close was employed.
  [3] Helen Smith Farrer Close.

To Nancy Saunders Toy

My dear Mrs. Toy: Washington D C 13th January 1922

You may be sure that the birthday message sent by you on behalf of the Woodrow Wilson Foundation of Cambridge[1] was among the messages that gave me the greatest joy. What made it all the more delightful to me was that it seemed to speak in your own voice and to be in effect a personal message.

Thank you with all my heart and please—when you can—let those associated with you know how deeply I appreciated it.

I hope that the New Year will be for you one of unusually happy fortune.

Mrs. Wilson joins me in warmest regards and I am, as always;
Your sincere friend,   Woodrow Wilson

TLS (WP, DLC).
  [1] Nancy S. Toy to WW, Dec. 26, 1921, ALS (WP, DLC). She was secretary of the Woodrow Wilson Foundation, Cambridge Division.

To James Kerney

My dear Kerney: [Washington] 13th January 1922

I am sorry to be belated in replying to your generous birthday letter;[1] but I am sure you will understand and will believe me when I say that the letter gave me the greatest pleasure. After all, the thought and approval of old friends gives the deepest assurance to the heart.

You and I have been within sight of each other for so long that we can be sure of the genuineness of our comradeship.

I am sure that you are looking forward with confidence, as I am, to the early return of our people to their true ideals and of the policies which will restore the moral leadership of the United States in the world. We must spend all that is best in us when that time comes.

Hoping that the New Year will bring you everything that is worth having of satisfaction and success;

Cordially, your sincere friend,   [Woodrow Wilson]

CCL (WP, DLC).
[1] J. Kerney to WW, Dec. 26, 1921, ALS (WP, DLC).

A News Report

[Jan. 15, 1922]

WILSON REAFFIRMS HIS CONFIDENCE IN LEAGUE'S VITALITY

"It Will Take Care of Itself,"
and "Those That Don't Regard It" Must Beware.
SPEAKS TO CROWD AT DOOR.

Washington, Jan. 15.—Breaking the silence studiously maintained ever since he left the White House on March 4, Woodrow Wilson, former President of the United States, tonight renewed his profession of faith in the vitality of the League of Nations.

Responding to the greetings of several thousand men and women who marched to his S Street home this evening, after a mass meeting at the new National Theatre at which the local campaign for the Woodrow Wilson Foundation was launched, Mr. Wilson declared that "there can be no doubt as to the vitality of the League of Nations," that "it will take care of itself," and that "those that don't regard it will have to look out for themselves."

Samuel Gompers, President of the American Federation of Labor and a member of the official Advisory Committee to the American delegation in the Washington Conference on Limitation of Armament, as the spokesman for those who marched nearly two miles from the theatre to the Wilson residence, addressing Mr. Wilson on the latter's doorstep, declared that the demonstration furnished proof that the league was not dead, that those who had attended the mass meeting live in Mr. Wilson's spirit and that their activities in the future would mobilize public sentiment.

"Mr. Gompers, and fellow citizens," Mr. Wilson replied, "I need hardly tell you that such a demonstration and evidence of friendship makes me very happy. There can be no doubt as to the vitality of the League of Nations. It will take care of itself. Those that don't regard it will have to look out for themselves. I have no anxiety for it.

"My only anxiety is to see our great people turn their faces in the right direction and move with all their force. I thank you heartily for all this. I don't deserve it, but I enjoy it, nevertheless."

It was the first time Mr. Wilson had made any public oral pronouncement on the League of Nations since September, 1919, when he had a nervous breakdown while swinging through the West in his campaign for ratification without reservation of the Treaty of Versailles and the League of Nations covenant. It was the second time only that Mr. Wilson had said anything publicly since leaving the White House, the previous occasion having been a few weeks ago, when there was a demonstration in front of his Washington residence by admirers who called to pay their respects.[1]

The demonstration at the theatre in connection with the launching of the campaign in the nation's capital for the Woodrow Wilson Foundation was as real as that which occurred in front of Mr. Wilson's home. It was addressed by Dr. Samuel A. Eliot of Cambridge, Mass., a Unitarian minister and son of Charles W. Eliot, President emeritus of Harvard University; Hamilton Holt, editor and executive director of the Wilson Foundation; Samuel Gompers and John Temple Graves.

There was an outburst of cheering that fairly rocked the theatre when Samuel Gompers told the gathering that filled the playhouse to overflowing that "Woodrow Wilson is coming back."

The pilgrimage to the home of Mr. Wilson was the spontaneous result of a motion made by a man in the audience at the theatre mass meeting. The suggestion was put to a vote by Charles Edward Russell, the Chairman of the meeting, and was carried to enthusiastic applause.

A police escort was obtained quickly, and, led by a band, the people in the theatre filed into Pennsylvania Avenue, formed in lines four abreast, and started on the two-mile walk without further ado. Several United States Senators were in the vanguard of marchers, among them Senators Walsh of Montana, Fletcher of Florida and

Harris of Georgia. The band played, "Onward, Christian Soldiers," as it moved across the city to the Wilson home, at 2,340 S Street Northwest.

Charles Edward Russell, Chairman of the meeting, hurried ahead to the residence of the former President and apprised the family of the fact that those who had attended the mass meeting were marching across the city to pay a personal tribute to Mr. Wilson. The former President was assisted to the door by Mrs. Wilson, who shared with him the evident affection of the crowd which jammed the street, extending westward nearly to the home of Herbert Hoover, Secretary of Commerce, half a block away.

When Mr. Wilson appeared in silk hat and overcoat, Mr. Gompers stepped to the doorway and addressing Mr. Wilson, told him he had been asked to say a word.

Mr. Wilson stood in the doorway, leaning on his cane. Beside him stood Mrs. Wilson and his attendants. Mr. Wilson's voice, while lacking the volume of more vigorous days, was strong enough to carry to the centre of the throng and evoked cheer after cheer. His eyes were direct and clear. He moved with a little difficulty, but when part of the crowd that could not observe him because he was sheltered by part of the doorway called for him he moved down a step. He was urged to say more when he had finished his remarks, but contented himself with doffing his hat, all the while smiling happily.

So vociferous did his admirers become that Mr. Wilson sought to move toward them to shake hands, but was restrained by Mrs. Wilson, and, after more cheering, he retired inside the house. Not satisfied, the crowd continued the demonstration and dispersed only after Mrs. Wilson had twice opened a second floor window and waved her hand, and the former President had again appeared to bow acknowledgments from behind a closed window.

"We have not ceased to remember you, sir," said Mr. Gompers in beginning his address to Mr. Wilson, "not to feel in our minds that we should address you as 'Mr. President.'"

The applause that greeted these words forced Mr. Gompers to stop for a moment.

"Today," he continued, "we have held a great mass meeting in honor of you, sir, and the great achievements which have come to you and to your people. We live in your spirit, and our activities in the future will be to mobilize the public sentiment which we know exists among the citizenship of this Republic to your work and your watchword, 'Forward,' and to have them accentuated and become the daily rules of our everyday lives. . . ."

Printed in the *New York Times*, Jan. 16, 1922.
    ¹ See the news report printed at Nov. 11, 1921.

To Williamson Updike Vreeland

My dear Vreeland: Washington D C 15th January 1922

I hope you know how I have always valued your friendship. If you do you will know how welcome your letter of December twenty-third[1] was. I thank you for it most warmly, and hope that the New Year is opening in all respects most auspiciously and happily to you and yours.

Please present my kindest regards to Mrs. Vreeland[2] and give my love to May.[3]

It would indeed be delightful if I could visit Lime [Lyme] again, but if I did I am sure I would rather play on the old pasture course than the new course of which you speak. It was one of the most interesting courses I have ever known, and I often think of the pleasures of play and companionship which you and I had on it.

With warmest regards;

Faithfully yours,   Woodrow Wilson

TLS (received from Mrs. Henry A. Barton).
    [1] W. U. Vreeland to WW, Dec. 23, 1921, ALS (WP, DLC).
    [2] Alice May Brown Vreeland.
    [3] Their daughter, May ("Maidie") Vreeland.

John Randolph Bolling to Gilbert Fairchild Close

My dear Mr. Close: [Washington] 15th January 1922

Mr. Wilson asks me to reply to your letter of January 12th and express regret that he will be unable to send you the letter which you suggest.

I am sure that no one better than you realizes that Mr. Wilson is called upon constantly for letters and messages of all sorts. In the present state of his convalescence it is not possible for him to comply in every case, and he feels to comply in some and not in others would involve him in invidious distinctions which he does not feel at liberty to make.

He wishes me to assure you that he was glad to hear from you, and that he will always follow your career with the greatest interest.

With best wishes from us all;

Cordially yours,   [John Randolph Bolling]

CCL (WP, DLC).

To Edwin Grant Conklin

My dear Conklin: Washington D C 16th January 1922

Your letter of December 26th[1] is peculiarly gratifying—if you know, as I hope you do, how much I value your friendship and how much I have always admired and trusted you.

You needn't be told how much I value and am cheered by this message of faith from you.

I hope that the New Year has opened happily for you and yours, and that it will bring you all such happiness and fortune as are worth while and last.

With affectionate regard;

Faithfully yours,   Woodrow Wilson

TLS (E. G. Conklin Papers, NjP).
[1] E. G. Conklin to WW, Dec. 26, 1921, ALS (WP, DLC).

To William Berryman Scott

My dear Wick: [Washington] 16th January 1922

As I hope you know, I have always had the most affectionate admiration and regard for you; and therefore your generous letter written on the occasion of my birthday[1] has given me deep pleasure. Thank you for it most warmly.

My thoughts turn very often to you and your household, and I have nothing but happy memories of the old days when I was trying to do what I was not permitted to do for Princeton.

I hope that the New Year will bring all blessings to you and yours.   Affectionately yours,   [Woodrow Wilson]

P.S. If General Scott[2] is in Princeton, please given [give] him my affectionate regards

CCL (WP, DLC).
[1] W. B. Scott to WW, Dec. 27, 1921.
[2] Hugh Lenox Scott.

From John Sharp Williams

My dear Mr. President: [Washington] January 16, 1922.

I have your letter of the 12th and also the letter, written by Judge Anderson, which you enclosed for my perusal. I agree with him thoroughly about the "mandatory" part of what he says. His distinction between holding as a trustee and holding as an owner is indubitably well taken; and we ought to take care not to enlarge the rights either of Japan or of Australia by any outside act of our own, nor to give any pretext to others to regard them as enlarged. I say "outside" because *we* are outside.

I don't agree with Judge Anderson about the beginning of his letter, nor with Governor McCall, either. I don't think that the four-party treaty "leads rather to war than to peace." I have never imagined that you could have any binding covenant of any description between nations unless there was back of it potentially "the shadow of force." I have never imagined that even a justice of the peace could have his decrees regarded unless there was a constable, or a United States court, unless there was a marshal, and unless behind both stood the posse comitatus the constabulary *force* of the County in one case, or the Army of the United States in the other.

There must be an agreement to *guarantee* the possessions, at any rate, whether as owner or as trustee, of whatever a covenant *recognizes*. I was always more of a stickler for Article 10 of the Covenant of the League of Nations than I was for any other part of it. Indeed, I thought Article 10 a little too weak. Had I been wording it myself, I would have said that "any nation going to war with another nation without first submitting to arbitration or offering to do it, should be treated as an outlaw and each other nation in the Covenant should bring to bear against it all its forces, military and naval and aerial." There is only one way to treat an "outlaw" and that is to outlaw him. The very word means, put him outside of legal protection and proceed against him as a criminal—by force.

I return you Judge Anderson's letter, because I know you want to keep it. The man expresses himself with delightful clearness.

Your friend   John Sharp Williams

P.S. The reaction with the mob has set in. They are tired of the high priests & pharisees cry of "crucify him" & are pretty nearly ready to go back to their own old instinctive cry "Hosannah." Glad to see it—theatre & "movie["] mobs all are beginning to demonstrate it.   Again & always Yours   JSW

TLS (WP, DLC).

From Nancy Saunders Toy

[Cambridge, Mass.]

My dear Mr. Wilson   "The Zero Hour" [c. Jan. 16, 1922]

The clock has just struck twelve. All my fellow-workers are shouting and tumulting at a great W. W. F. mass meeting in Boston. Fate, with her accustomed "sweet Fanny's way" has slapped me on the one cheek by invaliding me home and caressed me on the other by sending me your letter—half mine, half the Committee's. It is stirring—isn't it?—to feel that so many people all over this big country are thinking about you at this minute and and [sic] are showing their faith by their works. Never have I enjoyed anything more than the scribbling of the past two weeks (I wonder if I haven't written your name almost as many times as you have!), the delightfulness of the fight (for isn't the pen *smitier* than the sword!), the sudden glimpses of what it all is about. x x x Three days ago I wrote, at the request of the Chairman,[1] solemn letters to each member of our Committee, a summons for tomorrow for a work conference—"it will be difficult to raise our quota" etc. etc Today comes the news that the quota *is* raised! and now we are going on to double it. x x x Jessie has looked and spoken like an angel at a recent W. W. F. lunch in Boston and a meeting in Cambridge. This comes to me from many people. Dr. Stevens,[2] my hardhearted doctor—and hers—kept me in my room, but consoled me with this extraordinary tale: a friend had just been in Washington where he dined in company with President Harding's doctor.[3] The talk turned on social science. "Social science," said the doctor, "is that the same thing as eugenics"? "Such a contrast to Dr. Grayson's all-round intelligence," commented my doctor, a dyed in the wool Republican, by the way.

Ah, this year 1922! I feel it in my bones that it is going to be a good year for all of us. If it is good for you, dear Mr. Wilson, that will mean that it is good for the world.

With affectionate regards to Mrs. Wilson

Your old friend   Nancy Toy[4]

ALS (WP, DLC).
[1] Jeannette Ennis Belo (Mrs. Charles) Peabody.
[2] Horace Paine Stevens, M.D., of Cambridge.
[3] That is, Dr. Charles Elmer Sawyer.
[4] She enclosed a handwritten manuscript entitled "Woodrow Wilson Day Jan. 16. 1922." In it she quoted from letters received from donors: Roland Thaxter, Professor Emeritus of Cryptogamic Biology at Harvard University; the Rev. Dr. Frederic Palmer, managing editor and secretary of the *Harvard Theological Review*; the Rev. Dr. William Henry Paine Hatch, Professor of the Literature and Interpretation of the New Testament at the Episcopal Theological School of Cambridge; George David Birkhoff, Professor of Mathematics at Harvard; Jeanne Cassard Bartholow (Mrs. Francis Peabody) Magoun; and Mrs. Charles Walter Gerould.

From Frank Irving Cobb

Dear Mr. Wilson: New York January 16th, 1922.

I am sending you this suggestion for what it is worth. It occurred to me that about March 4th, after a year of almost complete silence about public affairs, you might feel disposed to discuss not only the state of the nation, but the state of the nations, making a general survey of the political and economic conditions of the world.

The physical labor of preparing a statement, however, might be very irksome to you. What I had in mind was that if you felt like doing something of that kind, I should be very glad to go to Washington and help prepare it in the form of an interview, which could be carefully written there and as carefully revised by you personally. We could take as much time for it as seemed necessary. Then I could bring it back to New York, and could give it out to all the newspapers and the Associated Press for simultaneous publication throughout the country and in Europe.

This suggestion may not fall in at all with your plans and wishes, yet may be something you would like to consider. If you reject it, I shall understand.

That was a magnificent demonstration Sunday, and there will be others in the future still more impressive.

Most sincerely yours,   Frank I Cobb.

TLS (WP, DLC).

From John Spargo

New York NY 1922 Jan 16

Today[1] when your friends begin to express their devotion to you and your ideals through the Woodrow Wilson Foundation I am prompted to send this word of affectionate greeting All that has happened and the present international situation and outlook prove the wisdom of your leadership which will still prevail

John Spargo   Bennington Vermont.

T telegram (WP, DLC).
[1] This telegram was presumably written on January 15. It was dated 8:13 a.m., January 16.

To John Spargo

Washington D C Jan 16 1922

Thank you for your message Stop I am greatly cheered by your friendship and confidence which I hope may never be abated Stop Cordial best wishes   Woodrow Wilson

T telegram (J. Spargo Papers, VtU).

To Frank Irving Cobb

My dear Cobb: [Washington] 17th January 1922

I am heartily sorry to turn away from any suggestion of yours, but I must this time say I do not think it would be wise or opportune for me to break loose in any form next March.

After I had said to Congress on one occasion that we wouldn't stand for such and such an overt act from Germany (I have forgotten the exact definition) I was asked by one of the White House correspondents what I should regard as such an act. I replied that I could not define it hypothetically but I was sure I should know it when I saw it.

I feel the same way about the time for breaking my present silence; I cannot say now just what sort of occasion would justify it, but I feel confident I shall recognize such an occasion when it comes.

I know you will bear with me and wait for me.

The editorial page of THE WORLD continues to be an inspiration, and your confidence and friendship are among the influences that I value most.

With warmest regard;

Faithfully yours,   [Woodrow Wilson]

CCL (WP, DLC).

To Paul Bentley Kern[1]

My dear Dean Kern: [Washington] 17th January 1922

I esteem it a most gratifying compliment that the Committee in whose name you wrote your letter of January thirteenth should have desired that I deliver the 1923 lectures of the W. W. Fondren Lectureship on some aspects of the spread of the Christian faith both in our own country and abroad.[2]

To use your own phrase, I can easily "find it in my heart" to accept such an invitation but I cannot find it in my mind. Even if

I could predict with the least confidence the state of my health in 1923, I should still feel I was not able to undertake such lectures.

Frankly, I do not know enough about missions; and I should deem a lecture made up of sentiments in lieu of good-headed judgments unworthy of such a series as you have been fortunate enough to obtain the means for.

Please convey to the other members of your Committee my warm thanks, my sense of the honor they have done me and my sincere regret that I am bound in conscience to decline.

Cordially and sincerely yours,   [Woodrow Wilson]

CCL (WP, DLC).
   [1] Dean of the School of Theology at Southern Methodist University.
   [2] P. B. Kern to WW, Jan. 13, 1922, TLS (WP, DLC). Wilson would have had to deliver from four to six lectures on Christian missions for an honorarium of $1,000.

To Katherine MacDonald[1]

My dear Miss MacDonald: [Washington] 18th January 1922

I am sorry you worried about the advertisement, the copy of which you sent to Mr. Bolling with explanations.[2]

I think we have all formed a correct enough impression of your character to know that not only you yourself would have nothing to do with the origination of such an advertisement, and also that it would be most distasteful to you. It is not necessary therefore that we should consciously exonerate you; it never would have occurred to us to connect you with such a thing, and I beg you to believe that it distresses me less than it seems to have distressed you.

I hope that every good fortune will attend you during this New Year and in the years to follow, and that I shall often again have the pleasure of enjoying your pictures as I have always enjoyed them in the past. The last one we have had the pleasure of seeing was "Her Social Value." Are there later pictures than this?

Mrs. Wilson and I have often said to each other that we wished very much that your scenario writers would provide you happier parts. The parts in which we have generally seen you have been tragic and unhappy.

With most cordial good wishes;

Sincerely and respectfully yours,   [Woodrow Wilson]

CCL (WP, DLC).
   [1] A well-known motion-picture actress.
   [2] Her letter and enclosure are missing.

To Nancy Saunders Toy

My dear Mrs. Toy: Washington D C 19th January 1922

I need not tell you that your letter of the sixteenth gave me great pleasure. I like not only the cheering estimates you were kind enough to quote, but also and more especially the flavour of yourself which the letter bore throughout.

Your friendship and approbation are very dear to me indeed, and I feel highly honored you should have accepted a working part in the Woodrow Wilson Foundation organization. The objects of that Foundation are not quite as clearly and definitely stated as I could have wished, but will no doubt be more and more clarified in the administration of the trust.

Mrs. Wilson joins me in affectionate messages, and I am—as always;

Your affectionate and admiring friend,   Woodrow Wilson

TLS (WP, DLC).

From Frank Irving Cobb

Dear Mr. Wilson: New York January 19th, 1922.

My personal judgment coincides with yours. When I wrote to you, I had in mind various reports that you intended soon to take a definite stand in respect to certain matters. I thought that if those reports were true, an interview might prove the most convenient method. I think, however, that your judgment is wholly sound. Eventually, of course, you will have to break your silence, because the leadership of the Democratic party rests in you, but the longer you can avoid it, the more effective it will be when it comes. Nothing else worries those gentlemen at both ends of Pennsylvania avenue so much as your studied silence. It is something that they cannot deal with—something for which they have no answer. It is usually unwise to scrap anything that is working well, and your method is still working admirably.

There is no conflict of opinion between us on that point, and at heart I am glad that you have rejected the proposal that I made. My only desire in the matter was to be of service to you, in case you felt that the time was ripe for a public statement, but I am certain that you are very wise and farsighted in determining to say nothing.

Did you ever see anything so extraordinary as Hughes's abject surrender on his Chinese programme?[1] Why did he ever make it, if he intended to abandon it over night? Surely the best minds move in mysterious ways.

With warmest regards,

Most sincerely yours,   Frank I Cobb.

TLS (WP, DLC).
¹ Hughes, at a meeting on January 17, 1922, of the Committee on Pacific and Far Eastern Questions of the Washington Conference, had introduced a resolution intended to bind the nations represented at the conference to abide by the principles of the open door in China. The resolution restated those principles but also contained a provision for the establishment in China of an international "Board of Reference," to which any question involving the principles might, at the discretion of the parties involved, be submitted for investigation and report. The controversial portion of Hughes' resolution was its Article IV, which read as follows: "The powers, including China, represented at this conference agree that any provisions of an existing concession which appear inconsistent with those of another concession or with the principles of the above agreement or declaration may be submitted by the parties concerned to the Board of Reference when established for the purpose of endeavoring to arrive at a satisfactory adjustment on equitable terms." It was immediately pointed out that this retrospective provision would make possible the reexamination of such earlier concessions as those made by China to Japan under the terms of the so-called Twenty-One Demands (about which, see the index references under "China: and Japan's 21 demands on," in Vol. 32). Hughes vigorously defended his resolution and its Article IV during the ensuing discussion, saying among other things that he wished to make the open door "a fact and not a motto." For the text and discussion of the resolution, see the *New York Times*, Jan. 18, 1922.

On the following day, after an objection to Article IV by the Japanese delegation, Sir Robert Borden, of the delegation from the British Empire, moved that the article be deleted. Only the Chinese delegation spoke in favor of the article, and it was removed in short order. Far from defending Article IV, Hughes now agreed to the deletion on the ground that Article III, which established the Board of Reference, would allow any concession, past or future, to be referred to that body. The committee then voted to adopt the three remaining articles of Hughes' resolution. *Ibid.*, Jan. 19, 1922.

The authors of the news reports on the events of January 17 and 18 in the New York *World*, Jan. 19, 1922, interpreted the removal of Article IV as a serious defeat for both Chinese and American foreign policy and placed the responsibility for this dénouement squarely on Japan. Edwin L. James, the author of the *New York Times* reports cited above, was more discreet but came to essentially the same conclusion. So also did the anonymous author of the editorial "The Half-Opened Door," *ibid.*, Jan. 20, 1922. The New York *World* did not have an editorial on this subject.

To Gavin McNab

My dear McNab: [Washington] 20th January 1922

I am taking the liberty of sending you a letter just received by Mrs. Wilson which has excited our interest and sympathy.

Will you think it an imposition if I ask you through some instrumentality to have the case looked up? For the letter is lucid enough, and it may be a case of ignorance or injustice.

Knowing the bigness of your heart I venture upon this liberty.

With painful slowness I am, I think, coming back. At any rate I mean to take care of myself on that theory until it has proved untenable. I am greatly comforted in my illness by thinking of friends like yourself who have shown me entire loyalty and kindness.

I hope all goes well with you, and that the New Year—and all the years that follow—will reward you with happy experiences of fruitful and rewarding service.

I hope too that the future of the party seems as bright to you as it does to me. I would very much value a line from you to say what you think the immediate and most important duty of the party is. We must put and keep our heads together to bring the nation back to the exhalted [exalted] mood of service in which it went through the war.

With warmest regards;

Faithfully yours,   [Woodrow Wilson]

CCL (WP, DLC).

John Randolph Bolling to Frank Irving Cobb

My dear Mr. Cobb: [Washington] 20th January 1922

Mr. Wilson asks me to say that he has read your letter of yesterday with a great deal of interest, and is glad to find that you are in accord with his views.

With warm personal regards;

Sincerely yours,   [John Randolph Bolling]

CCL (WP, DLC).

To Stephen Samuel Wise

My dear Rabbi Wise: [Washington] 22d January 1922

I have not had the pleasure of seeing a copy of the speech on the Woodrow Wilson Foundation which you delivered in New York,[1] but many echoes of it have reached me and my daughter, Mrs. McAdoo, has spoken of it with especial enthusiasm.

I wish therefore to give myself the pleasure of telling you how deeply and sincerely I appreciate your confidence in me and your generous friendship. They contribute not a little to my courage and to my hope that I shall again have an opportunity to take up the work which was interrupted by so many at any rate superficial discouraging circumstances. I am happy to feel your comradeship in great affairs.

I hope that the New Year has opened most happily for you and your own exceedingly important work, and that the future will contain nothing but success and encouragement.

With warmest regard;

Your grateful friend,   [Woodrow Wilson]

CCL (WP, DLC).

¹ Actually, Wise had spoken at the opening of the local campaign for the Woodrow Wilson Foundation fund in Bridgeport, Connecticut, on January 16. He enclosed a printed copy of his remarks in S. S. Wise to WW, Jan. 25, 1922, TLS (WP, DLC). In his speech, Wise placed Wilson with Washington, Lincoln, and Theodore Roosevelt as one of America's great leaders. He hailed Wilson as a creator and spokesman of American ideals.

From the American Historical Association

Dear Sir: Washington D C January 23, 1922.

I have the honor to inform you that, at the annual business meeting of the American Historical Association held at St. Louis on December the thirtieth, you were elected to the office of Second Vice-President of the Association for the year 1922. I beg that you will notify me of your acceptance of the election at your early convenience.   Very truly yours,   Patty W. Washington
                                                      Assistant Secretary.

TLS (WP, DLC).

John Randolph Bolling to the American Historical Association

Gentlemen: [Washington] 25th January 1922

Mr. Wilson asks me to reply to your letter of January twenty-third and say he will be very happy to accept the office of Second Vice President of the Association for the year nineteen hundred and twenty-two.
                        Cordially yours,   [John Randolph Bolling]

CCL (WP, DLC).

From Joseph Patrick Tumulty

                                              Dayton O Jan 25 [1922]

The Jackson Banquet tonight will be one of the biggest political affairs in the history of the party All speeches center around your work It is the intention to pass resolutions complimentary to you I would suggest your sending immediately a telegram of greetings addressed to Governor Cox.   Tumulty.

T telegram (WP, DLC).

From Edward William Bok

My dear Mr. Wilson: Lake Wales, Florida January 25 1922
    I could not help thinking of you this morning when I read the following:

> He cut a path through tangled underwood
> Of old traditions out to broader ways;
> He lived to hear his work called brave and good;
> But, oh, the thorns before the crown of bays!
> The world gives lashes to its pioneers
> Until the goal is reached,—then deafening cheers!

    I like to think that the Woodrow Wilson Foundation is the first step toward the deafening cheers!
    With every good wish
                           Always sincerely yours   Edward W. Bok

ALS (WP, DLC).

Charles Horace Mayo to Cary Travers Grayson

                                        Rochester, Minn.
                                        January twenty-fifth
My dear Doctor Grayson: nineteen twenty two

    I note by the papers and the illustrated news that ex-president Wilson is getting about considerably more. I went away[1] feeling that I had left him somewhat depressed because of the lack of enthusiasm I showed regarding rapid improvement. When you next see him I wish you would give him my regards and tell him that it will be to his best interests to get about more, also to declare open house for some of his old friends and well wishers. With an active mind like his, so wonderfully stored with knowledge, and with his remarkable mental activities during the critical period of the world's history, he will not gain any advantage by dropping out of affairs; and the past two years have been much worse for him than imprisonment with hard labor. Urge upon him the need of mental occupation as well as physical exertions, as he will regain the use of his muscles in proportion to the exercise he gives them.
    With best wishes for an abundance of health and success in the New Year, I remain   Sincerely yours,   C. H. Mayo

TLS (received from James Gordon Grayson and Cary T. Grayson, Jr.).
    [1] From C. H. Mayo to C. T. Grayson, Nov. 28, 1921 (received from James Gordon Grayson and Cary T. Grayson, Jr.), it seems most probable that Dr. Mayo examined Wilson on December 16, 1921.

From Frank LeRond McVey[1]

Lexington KY Jan 26 1922

Bill has been introduced in Kentucky legislature with heavy penalty to prohibit teaching of evolution or use of books favoring evolution in all schools supported by public funds[2] Stop Wire collect
your opinion as to such a legislative act Stop To be used in opposing the bill   Frank L McVey

T telegram (WP, DLC).
[1] President of the University of Kentucky.
[2] This was one of the first fruits of William Jennings Bryan's campaign, begun in
1921, against the teaching of evolution in public schools, colleges, and universities. On
this subject, see Norman F. Furniss, *The Fundamentalist Controversy, 1918-1931*
(New Haven, Conn., 1954), pp. 76-83; Lawrence W. Levine, *Defender of the Faith,
William Jennings Bryan: The Last Decade, 1915-1925* (New York, 1965), pp. 258-92;
and Paolo E. Coletta, *William Jennings Bryan* (3 vols., Lincoln, Neb., 1964-69), III,
198-233.

To Jessie Bones Brower[1]

My dear Cousin: [Washington] 27th January 1922

I was mighty glad to get your letter.[2] We often think and talk
about you and Helen,[3] I am sorry to say, is no longer near enough
at hand to give us indirect news of you that we used to have
through her.

I am greatly interested in what you tell me about your present
engagement and am glad to infer that it is satisfactory.

There is little to report about myself. I believe I am slowly re-
covering, but the process is so slow its stages are hardly perceptible, and I sometimes wonder if any healing influences are at all at
work. I can only trust and wait. I try to curb my impatience but
find it increasingly difficult in view of the number of things which
are crying out to be done in the world, and some of which I think
I might do. Of course the wonderful lady who is constantly at my
side sees to it that everything possible is done for me, but even her
love and care cannot work miracles. The most that we can do is to
support each other's hope and await what Providence may have in
store for us. Edith joins me in all affectionate messages, and we
hope that sometime soon business if not inclination will bring you
to this part of the country so that we may have a sight of you again.

I need not tell you how often I think of the old days on the Sand
Hills.[4] I wish that we might be fortunate enough to go back there
some day together, if the old place is not so much changed that it
would sadden us to see it.

With all the love that you can desire;
                    Affectionately yours,   [Woodrow Wilson]

CCL (WP, DLC).
    [1] Wilson's first cousin, daughter of James W. Bones and Marion Woodrow Bones. Mrs. Brower was living in Peoria, Illinois, at this time and was manager of the Country Club of Peoria.
    [2] Jessie B. Brower to WW, Jan. 19, 1922, TLS (WP, DLC).
    [3] Her sister, Helen Woodrow Bones.
    [4] In Augusta, Georgia.

From Frank LeRond McVey

My dear Mr. Wilson: Lexington January 28, 1922.

I am just in receipt of your telegram saying that you are not at liberty to express an opinion about business pending the Kentucky Legislature.[1] To say that I am disappointed is to put the matter mildly. You can render a very great service to education and freedom of thought by saying something positive on this matter. This is not a question of business but a question of freedom of human thought.

William Jennings Bryan came to this State and spoke to the Legislature on the subject of "Enemies of the Bible."[2] His speech was full of misstatements and untruths. He made a profound impression upon the Legislature. He is engaged in a movement backed by reactionary forces to secure legal provisions limiting the right to teach and the right to think in the public schools in as many states as possible. The beginning is in Kentucky and Florida. As the foremost leader of America, I felt that I would secure from you an expression that would at least check Mr. Bryan's view. Mr. Bryan carries great weight with many people but your opinion would more than offset his views. To receive your telegram is, indeed, a disappointment and I trust that you will be willing to undertake to say something about this matter and to wire me again protesting against such legislation so that I may have your telegram to present to the committees before this coming Wednesday.

                    Very truly yours,   Frank L. McVey.[3]

TLS (WP, DLC).
    [1] A note on a sheet attached to McVey's telegram of January 26, 1922, says that the following was sent as a night letter to McVey on January 27: "I do not feel at liberty to express an opinion about business pending before Kentucky Legislature." There is no copy of Wilson's telegram in the McVey Papers in the University of Kentucky Archives.
    [2] On January 19, 1922.
    [3] "No reply WW" written at top of letter in an unknown hand.

From Norman Hezekiah Davis

My dear Mr. Wilson: [New York] January 28, 1922.

I have completed a revision of what I had written regarding the Disarmament Conference, the reading of which I inflicted on you. The suggested plan of getting these views adopted by some of our Senatorial friends is working rather slowly, and may not bring any early results.

Since talking with you, two of my friends have again urged that I give this out, say to the New York Times or other papers as an article by me. Their contention is that it is advisable for some such article to be published before the adjournment of the conference, and before the submission of the various agreements to the Senate. They believe that the presentation of certain facts at this time would have more influence in formulating public opinion than after the Conference adjourns, that as long as it is not a conference matter, the Democratic Senators would not take any exception, but would begin to think along the lines indicated, and that every opportunity should be used to show the necessity for the League.

There is, no doubt, much to be said in favor of their views. While our Delegates have already gotten themselves in a hopeless strategic position and have made serious blunders, from which, apparently, they will be unable to extricate themselves, I am exceedingly loath to jump into publicity and appear to criticize their actions while the Conference is still in session. I am not entirely convinced that it would do good and I certainly don't want to do it unless it will. I shall appreciate very much your confidential advice if you feel inclined to give it.

It was a pleasure to see you and Mrs. Wilson again. I had hoped to return to Washington this week, but was unable to do so.

With affectionate regards to Mrs. Wilson and yourself, I am, as ever,   Faithfully yours,   Norman H. Davis

TLS (WP, DLC).

To Elizabeth, Lady Bryce

My dear Lady Bryce: [Washington] 29th January 1922

May I not—as one who was a warm friend of your husband's and a sincere admirer of the large amount of useful and instructive work he had done and was doing—convey to you my heartfelt sympathy in your tragical loss[1] and say how serious a loss it seems to me to the best forces of politics that Lord Bryce should have been taken away.

I hope that it is possible for you to derive some solace from the universal admiration in which he was held, and the universal grief at his death.

With warm regard and most cordial good wishes;

Sincerely yours,   [Woodrow Wilson]

CCL (WP, DLC).
    [1] Viscount Bryce had died on January 22.

To Norman Hezekiah Davis

My dear Davis: [Washington] 30th January 1922

The matter referred to in your letter of January twenty-eighth has too many angles to it to be considered properly in an exchange of letters. I will think the matter over and be ready to express an opinion when I see you again, which I hope will be soon.

With affectionate regards from us both to you all;

Faithfully yours,   [Woodrow Wilson]

CCL (WP, DLC).

To Edward William Bok

My dear Bok: Washington D C 31st January 1922

I hope you know how much I am cheered and encouraged by your generous faith and friendship, and I thank you with all my heart for your letter of January twenty-fifth. It helps me to carry on.

With most cordial regard;

Faithfully yours,   Woodrow Wilson

TLS (WP, DLC).

To Harold F. Strong[1]

My dear Mr. Strong: Washington D C 1st February 1922

My interest in Berea College is of long standing and very deep, and only my physical weakness will prevent my attending the meeting about which you write.[2]

I am quite willing that you should, if you choose, quote me as a firm believer in the College and its work; and I hope that the present effort to raise a "Necessity Fund" may be completely successful.   Sincerely yours,   Woodrow Wilson

TLS (W. G. Frost Papers, KyBB).
¹ A fund-raiser for Berea College.
² H. F. Strong to WW, Jan. 31, 1922, TLS (WP, DLC). He wrote to invite Wilson to attend a fund-raising affair in Constitution Hall in Washington on February 13. Berea was trying to raise a million-dollar "Necessity Fund" to maintain its work.

From Norman Hezekiah Davis

My dear Mr. Wilson: New York—Feby 1st, 1922.

McAdoo, Baruch, Houston and Frank Polk, with whom I had discussed the matter referred to in my letter of Jan'y 28th to you, all recommended so strongly that I either publish an article or make a speech at once I was somewhat inclined to do so in spite of certain doubts. Your conclusion that the question has too many angles to be considered properly in an exchange of letters is so sound that I regret having attempted it.

I could have gone to Washington but my son Goode, 15 years old, who came home from school for last week end came down with pneumonia Saturday evening. While we are of course concerned about him the Doctor says he has developed no complications and that he expects him to reach the crisis by Saturday and then to begin to improve. I hope therefore to be able to go to Washington next week and to have the pleasure of seeing you all. It would be so much more satisfactory to discuss this matter a little more with you.

With affectionate regards to you all I am as ever
                        Faithfully yours   Norman H. Davis¹

ALS (WP, DLC).
¹ A typed note at the top of this letter says that the following telegram was sent to Davis on Feb. 3, 1922 (the following EBWhw): "We sympathize with you & Mrs Davis in the illness of your son & are greatly pleased to learn that there is prospect of his prompt recovery I shall look forward with great pleasure to seeing you soon & concluding our conference"

To Henry Jones Ford

My dear Ford: [Washington] 2nd February 1922

I did not know in which number of the Atlantic Monthly your article on the railroads¹ was to appear, and have therefore—I am sorry to say—missed it altogether. Will you not—so soon as you can get at it—formulate for me, as compactly as possible, legislative policy which you think ought to be pursued with regard to the railroads casting it, if possible, in a form that would be suitable for embodiment in a party platform. If you could do this sometime soon I would be greatly obliged to you.

With warm regards to Mrs. Ford[2] and yourself;

Cordially and faithfully yours,   [Woodrow Wilson]

CCL (WP, DLC).
    [1] Wilson was misinformed. Ford had not published an article in the *Atlantic Monthly* on any subject in the past several years. Wilson had named his former colleague at Princeton to the Interstate Commerce Commission on December 7, 1920. The Senate did not confirm his nomination, and Ford served only to March 4, 1921.
    [2] Bertha Batory Ford.

From Norman Hezekiah Davis

My dear Mr. Wilson: New York, Feby 3, 1922.

We very much appreciated your telegram today. The poor boy is having a hard time. His recovery has been delayed because the second lung became infected. The Doctor thinks however that he is doing as well as could be expected and that he will begin to turn the corner with another day or so.

I am particularly anxious to continue my last talk with you.

If you have not read Walter Lippma[n]n's article entitled "The End of a Great Illusion" in last Sunday's World[1] I recommend that you do so. This evidently is the opening gun showing the defense Hughes proposes to make. In substance he says that Hughes has turned his back on the Open Door policy because we could not enforce it, at least without the assistance of China and Russia and they cannot now give that. In exchange for the navy and the sovereign right to enforce that policy to the extent of securing respect for our own rights—we have chosen to cast our lot with England. After we pursuade [persuade] England to give up imperialism and accept our views that the rights of Russia and China should be respected we can ultimately with England's moral support bring about Japan's isolation and then with the growing pressure from China and Russia, Japan will have to pick up and go home.

While Lippman shows a woeful lack of information on some things he presents this case in a most subtle and plausible way. In the last analysis we are under this new policy—according to him— to rely entirely on public opinion and moral pressure.

No provision is made for ascertaining, crystallizing or applying public opinion but as this is to come only after we have pursuaded England to change her ways I presume there will be plenty of time to do that. He passes very lightly over the four power alliance and therefore fails to point out that such an alliance is unnecessary and utterly inconsistent with this new policy. He does not show why it was necessary for us to tie our hands without getting anything in exchange and thus put ourselves in a position where we might not be able even to assist China and Russia when they are ready to do their share. He overlooks the fact that our agreement to stop naval competition should have been more than sufficient compensation for a cancellation of the Anglo Japanese Alliance—and that England and Japan would have jumped at such an arrangement and would not have had the nerve to ask for more. As we gave them that at the outset—free of charge—then of course they could and did ask a big price for all they gave which was little. They are evidently becoming alarmed about the new alliance. The papers say now that letters will be written to Holland and Portugal offering to bring them under the umbrella. I hope to be in Washington Tuesday afternoon or Wednesday but cannot be certain yet. With warmest regards to Mrs. Wilson and yourself I am

Affectionately Yours   Norman H. Davis

ALS (WP, DLC).
[1] New York *World*, Jan. 29, 1922, Editorial Section, p. 1.

Cary Travers Grayson to Charles Horace Mayo

Dear Doctor Mayo: [Washington] February 10, 1922.

I owe you an apology for not answering before this your letter of January 25th, but I deferred doing so until I had some news for you.

I read your letter to Mr. Wilson and he was intensely interested in what you had to say. He gave me the following message to deliver to you: "Tell Doctor Mayo that I am doing my best to comply with his valued suggestions and thank him for the interest he is taking in me."

I again want to tell you how much I appreciate your kindness in visiting Mr. Wilson with me when you were here. The suggestions and advice which you gave him have helped decidedly. There was no sign of depression because of your plain talk. I, too, feared that he would be somewhat depressed, but, I am happy to say, his reaction was just the opposite. He is seeing more visitors and nearly all of them comment on his improvement in appearance, and particularly so in spirit. They all notice and are impressed by the fact that he is so much more animated while conversing than formerly.

I have taken occasion to tell his numerous Senatorial friends and others in public life here how much good your visit did him.

With warm personal regards to your brother[1] and to yourself, believe me,   Sincerely yours,   [Cary T. Grayson]

CCL (received from James Gordon Grayson and Cary T. Grayson, Jr.).
  [1] William James Mayo, M.D.

To Joshua Willis Alexander[1]

My dear Judge: Washington D C 11th February 1922

I know it will not be unwelcome to you if I occasionally express my interest in the party in Missouri. I like to keep in touch with my friends everywhere.

I have been pleased to learn of Breckinridge Long's candidacy for Reed's place in the Senate, and hope that you regard his chances as good. Reed is one of the worst influences in the party, and surely every effort should be made to consolidate and concentrate the opposition to him. I happen to know Long rather well and feel great confidence that he will truly and energetically represent and fight for the things that you and I believe in.

I would appreciate it very much if you would let me know from time to time whether there is anything you think I could wisely do to help in the fight.

With happy recollection of our association, and most cordial regard—in which Mrs. Wilson joins—to you and Mrs. Alexander;
                Cordially and sincerely yours,   Woodrow Wilson

TLS (RSB Coll., DLC).
  [1] This letter was prompted by one from Breckinridge Long, in which Long told Wilson of his interest in running against Reed for the Democratic senatorial nomination. Long said that he was sure he could defeat Reed in a two-way contest, but that Reed might win a plurality if other candidates entered the race. One potential candidate was J. W. Alexander, who would be a formidable candidate but could not defeat Reed. If Wilson was disposed to do so, it would be very helpful if he wrote to Alexander saying that he was eager to see Long defeat Reed. "It would have a very decisive effect," Long wrote. B. Long to WW, Feb. 9, 1922, TLS (WP, DLC).

To Nancy Saunders Toy[1]

My dear Mrs. Toy: Washington D C 13th February 1922

Perhaps the best way I can answer your question about the statements as to the object of the Foundation (on circular enclosed to Mrs. Wilson) is by repeating to you what I myself suggested to the national committee and which they seem either to have overlooked or rejected.

I suggested[2] that it be announced that the awards would be made to the person or group of persons who had, within a given time, made the most practical contribution to the liberal thought of mankind with regard to human rights or international relations. I hope that this will seem to you as it seems to me more definite and more serviceable than the formula which the committee has adopted.³ I of course have no desire to direct or to correct the actions of the national committee, but I must say that their formula leaves me exceedingly vague.

We are greatly disappointed that you cannot stop over on your way to Portsmouth, and unite in affectionate messages.

With warm regard;   Faithfully yours,   Woodrow Wilson

TLS (WP, DLC).
    ¹ The letter to which this was a reply is missing.
    ² In WW to FDR, July 4, 1921.
    ³ On August 5, 1921, the executive committee announced through Franklin Roosevelt that the foundation would make awards for "meritorious service to democracy, public welfare, liberal thought or peace through justice." *New York Times*, Aug. 6, 1921. A later announcement said that the Woodrow Wilson Award would be given to the individual or group "that has rendered, within a specified period, meritorious service to democracy, public welfare, liberal thought or peace through justice." *Ibid.*, Aug. 21, 1921. Frank Polk later explained that the object of the awards was not to exalt Wilson "but to keep alive his ideals and in such form that they will be both an inspiration and a reward to another man whose ambition it is to enable the world to live more amply, with greater vision, with a finer spirit of hope and achievement." *Ibid.*, Oct. 2, 1921.

From Norman Hezekiah Davis

My dear Mr. Wilson: New York, Feby 14th, 1922.

I am sending you an advance copy of the Comments and Reflections upon the Disarmament Conference which I am to give before the Council on Foreign Relations next Friday night.¹ This is a non-partisan organization and it will publish the address in pamphlet form and also furnish advance copies to all the papers. Some of [my] ideas have become more clarified in the last few days. The naval treaty really ought to have an amendment—namely that in order to maintain the relative ratio of strength the parties to the treaty shall be prohibited from forming an alliance which would upset it. After all the squirming to get the Anglo Japanese Treaty out of the way so that a naval ratio could be fixed one would think they would have prohibited the creation of another one. This of course then leads to a clearer view of the only way to get rid of such infections. France & England will have an Alliance. That will upset the naval ratio but how can we object to that? We either have to allow it or go along & give a guarantee to France or enter the League and make it such a factor that no further assurance could be asked.

In order to avoid your reading all of my document I have marked certain passages—especially those not heretofore raised.

With warm regards to Mrs Wilson & yourself I am

Affectionately Yours   Norman H. Davis

P.S. I am going to attempt at a Wilson Foundation Luncheon in Philadelphia tomorrow to say what I think of you.

ALS (WP, DLC).
[1] N. H. Davis, *Comments and Reflections upon the Conference on the Limitation of Armaments and Far Eastern Questions . . . Before the Council on Foreign Relations . . . February 17th, 1922* [New York, 1922].

After a few attempts to strike a nonpartisan and irenic pose, Davis then reviewed the various problems of the Far East, in their relationship to the United States, and assessed the degree to which the various Washington treaties had ameliorated them. Davis had high praise for the Nine Power Treaty, by which its signatories affirmed the principle of the open door in China and of respect for Chinese territorial and political integrity. He had only measured praise for the Five Power Treaty for the reduction of naval armaments. He said that he was of course in favor of disarmament in principle, but that the Five Power Treaty did in fact preserve the naval equilibrium in the Far East and effectually assigned naval supremacy to Japan, Great Britain, and the United States in their respective spheres. Davis was highly critical of the Four Power Treaty, by which Great Britain, France, United States, and Japan agreed to respect each others' insular possessions and dominions in the Pacific Ocean and to confer among each other if disputes among themselves arose or if they were threatened by outsiders. This treaty, Davis said, was either meaningless or effectual, and he was not at all sure as to whether any of the nations involved would use force to back it up.

Back of all of Davis' apprehensions about the Washington treaties was the, to him, most disturbing fact of all—Japan's occupation of Manchuria, eastern Siberia, and northern Sakhalin—and the additional fact that none of the treaties protected Russia and China against actual or future Japanese aggression. In addition, underlying everything that Davis said was his conviction that the United States could participate in an effective security system for the Far East only through close cooperation with or membership in the League of Nations. He was also fearful that the Four Power Treaty might be a reversion to a balance-of-power diplomacy.

To Edith Bolling Galt Wilson

My lovely Valentine   2340 S Street N W 14 Feb'y, 1922

I love you. You are my inspiration and my constant joy. Everything that is best in me does homage to you.

AL (WP, DLC).

From Anita McCormick Blaine

Dear Mr. Wilson: Chicago 15 February 1922.

I have been quite unhappy about part of the thought of the foundation that is being made in your honor.

I have thought of writing to you my feelings about it, but I have not been sure that I ought to do so until Mrs. Fairbank[1] and Mr. Jones[2] came to ask me to be on an advisory committee for the work in Illinois. Then I was confronted with my difficulties squarely and I knew that I must somehow express them to those in charge of the work and to you.

Mr. Holt is to be here tomorrow and I am to see him. I do not want to talk of it before I have written to you.

My thoughts are so much bigger than my power of words to express them. Will you please try to see what I mean better than I can say it?

There seems to me to be a clash between the wonderful thing they are doing, in creating a work to advance democracy in your honor, and the means that they are taking to advance it, in awarding prizes and especially prizes of money.

I think the prize idea for real human endeavor is one that will be eliminated and will some day seem to be a lowering element—consequently the higher the plane of the work the more I regret this feature.

Again, the plan of prizes cannot operate truly. The individuals who have done most for democracy can never be picked and in the very name of democracy I wish that that thought need not be incorporated.

Again, the tendency will be to pick persons without wealth in the effort to let the money do some real service and that will tend to create distinctions that are not real and lead away from the pure recognition of effort for democracy.

Again, the use of the money will be irrelevant to the cause the foundation is created to further.

There may be some danger of the prizes being worked for. That does not seem to me to be a strong reason for real work cannot be done in that way.

I feel the idea to belong to the old world and the former way, before democracy dawned on the human mind, and so I cannot help feeling sorry to have it joined to the crystallization of the thought of working for democracy which came out of your placing democracy on the mountain tops of the world.

I have tried to think what suggestion I could make as a substitute to the thing I regret.

It seems to me the whole thought could be changed over from the prize idea to the thought of helping constructive effort for democracy—with the fine recognition that would inhere in that.

It seems to me that it could be done with no jar to the work already begun, no setback to the beginning that is made, if, instead of the prize idea the scholarship idea could be incorporated in the plan so that the allotment of funds would be made on demonstrated plans.

In this way the funds would work for the cause. The best sort of recognition would be given to individuals because allotments would not be made except on the ground of confidence in demonstrated power and purpose, and the false elements would all be left out. It would not be rewarding people for results of high endeavor, but helping the high endeavor to achieve their results.

It is a great privilege to tell you my feelings about this and I know that you will understand that it is my intense interest in what is being started that leads me to want to do so.

I am faithfully yours   Anita Blaine

P.S. Since writing this I have seen Mr. Holt. I have had a fine talk with him and I am writing my ideas, at his request, to him, quite at length.

TLS (WP, DLC).
  [1] Janet Dyer (Mrs. Kellogg) Fairbank of Chicago.
  [2] That is, Isaac Thomas Jones, the fund-raiser.

To William Edgar Borah

My dear Senator Borah: [Washington] 16th February 1922

I had the pleasure of reading in this morning's paper the message you sent to the Woodrow Wilson Foundation in New York, in declining their invitation to dinner; and I take the liberty of writing to express my admiration of the qualities of heart and breadth of mind of which that message gives such interesting evidence.[1]

Allow me to subscribe myself, with sincere respect;

Your friend,   [Woodrow Wilson]

CCL (WP, DLC).
  [1] The Woodrow Wilson Foundation dinner was held on February 15 in the grand ballroom of the Hotel Commodore. Tumulty was the principal speaker. In his telegram, Borah wrote: "Difference of view on some questions of method has not, I trust, blinded me in the least to the great policies and principles urged and advocated by Ex-President Wilson in looking to a better and more peaceful world. I express the hope that the cause will succeed to the full satisfaction of its advocates." New York *World*, Feb. 16, 1922.
  In an interview with Charles H. Grasty a few days later, Borah reiterated his great admiration for many of the things for which Wilson had stood and fought: "disarmament, freedom of the seas, the right of all people to choose their own forms of government, and to live their own lives, anti-imperialism, the denial of one people to hand another about like chattels." "With searching power," Borah went on, "he went to the root of the criminal policies and practices which had brought the world to the brink of material moral bankruptcy. But as to the best method calculated to uproot and destroy these policies and practices—there was where the deep difference of views arose." *New York Times*, Feb. 19, 1922.

To Bainbridge Colby

My dear Colby: [Washington] 17th February 1922

I am sending you enclosed a copy of a letter I received a little while ago, and a copy of my reply;[1] because I feel that these papers should be in the office files in New York as well as in my files here.

I am sure that you will agree with me that we should accept no business which might involve us in dealings with the Government of Costa Rica.

I am greatly pleased to think of you as on this side of the water, and am relieved and delighted to hear that you are well. I hope you found Mrs. Colby and your daughters[2] well and happy.

I am looking forward with the greatest interest and pleasure to seeing you soon and hearing about your experiences on the other side.

Again with a heartfelt welcome and with affectionate regards;
Faithfully yours,   [Woodrow Wilson]

CCL (WP, DLC).
[1] Both the letter that Wilson received and the copy of the letter he sent to Colby are missing.
[2] Katharine, Nathalie, and Frances Colby.

From William Edgar Borah

My dear Mr. Wilson: Washington, D. C. February, 18, 1922.

I was greatly pleased to receive your generous message. The telegram expressed views I have always entertained.

I trust most sincerely your health is constantly improving.
With great respect,   Wm. E. Borah

TLS (WP, DLC).

To Anita McCormick Blaine

My dear Mrs. Blaine: Washington D C 18th February 1922

I not only fully appreciate the spirit of your criticism of the announced plans of the Woodrow Wilson Foundation, but am bound to say I think your criticism valid.

I have been afraid from the outset that the purposes were stated in too vague a form. You may be interested to know the formula which I suggested to the Executive Committee but which they did not deem it best to use.

Your interesting and suggestive criticism of the plan of conferring prizes not having occurred to me, I suggested that the statement be that prizes would be "upon that person or group of persons who had within a given period made the most practical contribution to the liberal thought of the world with regard to human rights or international relationships."

I feel of course that I am estopped from criticism or suggestion, but I am sincerely glad that you are going to supply Mr. Holt with a written statement of your ideas concerning the objects and methods of the Foundation. I feel sure that everyone who reads the statement will be impressed by it as I have been.

May I not say once more how much I value and how deeply I am gratified by your generous friendship and interest. With warmest regard;   Faithfully and sincerely yours,   Woodrow Wilson

TLS (C. H. McCormick, Jr., Papers, WHi).

To Edwin Anderson Alderman

My dear Dr. Alderman: Washington D C 18th February 1922

May I take the liberty of putting a thought into your mind with regard to the faculty of the University?

If at any time you should need a man in English literature who has had unusual success in interesting young men in *real* literature, and whose lectures have made an extraordinary impression both inside and outside academic halls, I suggest that you look up the record and characteristics of Stockton Axson, my brother-in-law, who is now at Rice Institute, Houston, Texas.

I will not write about him further now, but merely leave you to consider and pardon the suggestion. I make it in all fidelity to the University.

With the best wishes for yourself and the great University which we all love;

Cordially and sincerely yours,   Woodrow Wilson

TLS (E. A. Alderman Papers, ViU).

From Bainbridge Colby

My Dear Mr. President   [New York] Sunday [Feb. 19, 1922].

Your delightful letter gave me a real sensation of warmth and welcome. Thank you so much.

I am eager to see you and to feel in touch with you again. Would Tuesday be all right for me to come down? I could stay over Wednesday as it is a holiday, so if you find a place on your engagement list for Tuesday evening or any hour on Wednesday—we can have the talk I have so long looked forward to.

I can always however make my goings and comings conform to your preferences.

I have much to relate, and some substantial things to report.

I had rather a mean "go" with the "flu" in London. It laid me low for a couple of weeks, but I am all right again. There were as you will readily suspect many things requiring attention here, and my doctor thought I should defer even the short journey to Washington until the cold snap of the last few days moderated.

I hope Mrs. Wilson is well and that you will convey to her my particular and respectful regards.

> With a heart full of affection   Always—Colby[1]

ALS (WP, DLC).
[1] Typed at the top of the third page of this letter: "Telgm. Feb. 20: Mr. Wilson will be glad to see you at a quarter of one o'clock on Wednesday, Feby. 22d. Please confirm. J.R.B., Sec."

From Henry Jones Ford

My dear Governor: Princeton, N. J. February 20th, 1922.

I enclose herewith a draught of some suggestions and an accompanying memo.[1] on the matter presented by your letter.

There is a whole lot in this railroad situation. In proceedings before the Commission while I was a member the fact was brought out that Pittsburg had the same rate to San Francisco as Chicago, in disregard of the much longer haul. The trouble was that the railroads had to meet the rail and water rate from Pittsburg via the Panama canal. The West is dead sore over such rate anomalies and will rise with enthusiasm to greet corrective measures.

There is a big robbery going on in the matter of reparation claims. I did not think it wise to touch upon it in the draught I am sending, but I have it rather on my conscience that I ought to do what I can to start an agitation. I shall not make a move however until I get a chance to advise with you. I shall be in Washington on the 24th. inst. to remain for several days. If it will suit you to give me an appointment for some afternoon or evening I shall put the matter before you. I may be addressed at The Cosmos Club.

I trust that your health continues to improve. With warmest regards, I am, as ever,   Faithfully yours   Henry J. Ford

TLS (WP, DLC).
[1] "SOME SUGGESTIONS With Respect to Democratic Party Policy," T MS (WP, DLC). Ford, who was a Professor of Politics at Princeton and not an economist of any sort, began this memorandum with a prologue about the glories and achievements of

the Democratic party. His discussion of what he called "the transportation situation" is not altogether comprehensible. However, he did point out that the Interstate Commerce Commission had certain extensive powers, such as control over intrastate rates and the finances of interstate railroads, and that the commission's attempts to exercise these powers only produced "continual disturbance and immense litigation." He said, incorrectly, that the Transportation Act of 1920 gave the Railroad Labor Board authority to fix just and reasonable wages, etc.

From Cleveland Hoadley Dodge

My dear President: New York February 21, 1922.

When I crossed Broadway this morning, and looked up at the Woolworth Tower shining in the bright sunlight, I never saw it more beautiful and majestic, and it made me think of you and the wonderful come-back of the Wilson ideals all over the country.

I had an interesting experience the other evening. I had been reading so many new books about the war and the Peace Treaty and everything else that I realized I was neglecting my old friends, and I walked around amongst my books looking to see what I would read, and the first thing I struck was a volume of essays written by a young Princeton professor many years ago entitled "Mere Literature." I had not read the essays for years, and I had the keenest enjoyment, especially in the essay on the "Literary Politician." Then that suggested my Walter Bagehot, and I spent two or three delightful evenings with him. So you see even your old works are coming back!

A'Dios. Aff'ly C. H. Dodge

TLS (WP, DLC).

From Norman Hezekiah Davis

My dear Mr. Wilson: New York, Feb'y 22/22.

I will send you tomorrow or next day complete printed copies of my talk on the Conference. Cravath[1] tried unsuccessfully to combat my arguments about the four power pact and finally admitted that he would favor opening it up to include all powers interested in the regions of the Pacific—provided it would be acceptable. Roland Morris made a fine talk and said my analysis had convinced him. It is disheartening that we have no one in the Senate who seems inclined or able to take the lead. Some of them don't seem to know the fundamental difference between alliances and a League.

On account of the damage done by the Republicans, to say nothing of the moral aspects, in the fight on the work of the Paris Conference I had hoped the Democrats would not find anything sufficiently bad in the Washington treaties to justify them in offering any opposition, but the more I study the four power treaty and learn how it came about the more I am convinced that it was unnecessary and unwise. Since it has been signed however I think it ought to [be] accepted provided the fundamental defects can be eliminated. The Republicans have already set the precedent by offering reservations to this treaty and the Democrats could do a really constructive work and avoid a lot of harm by offering an intelligent and necessary reservation. They could show how much better it would be to invite all the powers interested in the Pacific or its regions to join this treaty and to attend all conferences relating to questions arising there and that the exclusion of any powers will inevitably arouse suspicions and cause the big powers to ignore their rights or interests. From what I can gather Hughes made up his mind that he couldn't get us in the League and deliberately decided as an alternative that the big powers would have to dominate the world by alliances. He thinks his alliances will be different because these big powers will work for the good of all—small, big & weak—although they will not give a voice to the small powers. That is typically Republican. The great influence of America has been due in such large measure to the principles we have stood for and particularly to the assertion that the rights of peoples and nations are not proportionate to their power, wealth or size; and also to our freedom from alliances or agreements with any nations which prevent us from being impartial or taking the side of the oppressed. Even if the four power pact is nothing more than an agreement to confer, the mere fact that we should agree to confer along with the three powers which have done most to exploit and violate the rights of China and Russia will lower our prestige and influence for good in those Countries. It will arouse suspicions and make those peoples feel we have abandoned them. Completely aside from the principle involved and the harm to the movement for worldwide cooperation, this is a bad thing from a purely selfish standpoint. We can do more for China and Russia and get more out of them in the long run by acting with them while they are trying to work out their salvation. The Democrats can offer something constructive which would appeal to the ideals and imagination of the peoples and I think they ought to do it. They should praise all the good that has been done and show that their proposal would preserve the good and avoid the bad.

I think a reservation should provide that all powers interested in the Regions of the Pacific Ocean will be invited to join the four power treaty; that it's [its] maintenance shall be contingent upon the compliance with the other treaties and pledges relative to the Far East; and that an alliance or Diplomatic agreement in the future by any party to this treaty with one or more other powers which might create a community of interest shall be cause for those omitted to reconsider or renounce this four power pact.

I have been told on good authority that Root has passed the word around that the treaties must be pushed through in a hurry because if much discussion ensues over the four power treaty it will be killed. An alliance really appeals to the Republican mind, not all of them, but they love the exercise of power. Some of them who profess to be advocates of the League have told me unguardedly that it would be a fine thing for England and America to dominate the world and that the Washington Conference will lead to that.

I hope I haven't wearied you with this but I wanted to let loose some of my thoughts and feelings where they would be understood.

I may go to Washington again in a few days.

With warmest regards to Mrs Wilson and yourself I am

Affectionately Yours   Norman H. Davis

ALS (WP, DLC).
¹ That is, Paul Drennan Cravath.

From Jessie Woodrow Wilson Sayre

Darling, darling, Father,   [Cambridge, Mass.] Feb. 22, 1922

Woodrow was quite thrilled by receiving a really truly telegram himself. How sweet of you to send him one and lure on his warmest, lovingest, Thankyous.

This is the first time, of course, that he has appreciated a birthday, and he entered into it all with a zest and a spirit that were perfectly delicious. We had three little tots in for supper and games. The Brooks twins very shy and clinging to each other and their grand mother, and Moses Ware, an adorable brown bud of four with whom Woodrow is very intimate. Woodrow was like a golden butterfly darting in and out among them, and Eleanor and Francis looked like grown ups beside them. Some fascinating George Washington hats with comical white pig tails hanging down behind broke the ice and every one was happy and even the twins when they went away seemed to have forgotten the teary beginning of the afternoon and promised gaily that they would come again.

It was good to hear of you from Bliss Perry who was most enthusiastic about you in every way and so wonderfully happy at being allowed to see you.

Dearest love from us all to you both, darling wonderful Father. I am so *glad* I have a little son named after the nicest, noblest, wisest, man in all the world!   Your devoted   Jessie.

ALS (WC, NjP).

To Cleveland Hoadley Dodge

My dear Cleve,   Washington D C 23d February 1922

I am heartily glad to find that you are turning to Bagehot for stimulation. I do not know where else you can get it in such delightful form. It pleases me to think that I should have had the good fortune to introduce you to him, and it also makes me happy to think of you as looking for and finding enjoyment.

With warmest regard from both Mrs. Wilson and myself to Mrs. Dodge[1] and you;

Your affectionate friend,   Woodrow Wilson

TLS (WC, NjP).
[1] That is, Grace Parish Dodge.

From Bainbridge Colby

My dear Mr President: New York City February 23, 1922

I enclose a copy of the powerful paragraph which you wrote on the subject of railroads and transportation.[1] I think this is what you referred to yesterday.

I came back on the midnight train last night all the better for my talk with you. I was surprised to find when I left your room that I had been there an hour. I think this is a little too long. By-the-way, did you notice that an English newspaper reproved Ambassador Harvey for the length of his speech the other night at the Pilgrim dinner to Mr Balfour? It appears that Mr Harvey spoke forty minutes, and according to the London "Standard" the attention of his auditors wandered, and much that he said was completely lost. The fact that Mr Balfour the guest of the evening spoke but fifteen minutes, was mentioned by way of contrast.

I thoroughly agree with you that the hour has not struck for breaking the silence which those of us who watch you closely have observed for the last few months, and yet there are one or two speeches that I find it difficult to turn down. They do not involve controversial discussion, or political allusions, and you may agree that I could make them without violence to the reasoning that underlies our silence.

I want very much to make one speech for the Wilson Foundation and am strongly pressed to go to Utica on Saturday evening to assist the managers of the Fund in Central New York, which might be called the enemy's country. I don't know of any section of the country where the spirit of Republican partisanship is more stiff-necked and hard-shelled than in this part of up-State New York. I have refrained from an active part in this great movement whose success is now so abundantly assured. In fact, I think I have never spoken of it to you. I have thought that possibly, in view of my close professional relation with you, I should refrain from an active part in the work on grounds of good taste. However, I would like very much to make this speech. It will be brief and I think unobjectionable on any of the grounds that I have mentioned.

There is another affair in Albany on the 16th of March. The legislative correspondents at Albany give a dinner on that date and have two speakers, one a Republican and the other a Democrat. The speeches are not reported. The Republican speaker is to be Governor Miller and he has expressed a hope that I would be the Democratic speaker. The Governor behaved so handsomely in the matter of that special statute which your admission required in this State that I'd like to do this as a little mark of appreciation.

The only other thing I have in mind is an invitation from the University of Minnesota, of which my old kinsman Dr William Watts Folwell is the president emeritus. The date they suggest is toward the end of April and of course I can speak without touching any matter of political or party moment.

I suppose things like this do not come within the scope of our brief talk on this subject yesterday, but if you think a rigid and unbroken silence is better I can readily extricate myself from any one or all of these engagements.

With kindest regards always,

Cordially yours   Bainbridge Colby

TLS (WP, DLC).
[1] It is printed as an Enclosure with WW to L. D. Brandeis, Feb. 27, 1922.

To Bainbridge Colby

My dear Colby: Washington D C 24th February 1922

I unaffectedly hesitate to advise you with regard to speechmaking, because I know the taste and good judgment which you always display in your public utterances. But, to use your own phrase, "a rigid and unbroken silence" seems to me for the present an imperative counsel of wisdom on the part of those of us who may be called the inner circle of the last Democratic administrations. I believe that upon reflection you will yourself think this the course of true expediency, using the word expediency as Burke would have used it, to mean the wisdom of the circumstances.

Thank you for the copy of the statement about the railroads. I had not kept even my original shorthand version, and wished to discuss the statement with one of the best equipped members of the I. C. C.

It was delightful to see you again and most reassuring to see you looking so vigorous.

With all regard and confidence;

Faithfully yours,   Woodrow Wilson

P.S. This morning the following telegram[1] turned up:

"Boston, Mass. Feb. 24, 1922.

Hon. Woodrow Wilson
Washington, D. C.

Please deny horrible report which fills newspapers that Woodrow Wilson firm will defend Pelletier.[2] Your friends who hold you in reverence above all other men are overcome by this news. It is unbelievable that your name can be associated in any way with this type of man. Faithfully your friend   Virginia MacMechan."

And the reply was:

"Washington, D. C. Feb. 24, 1922.

Miss Virginia MacMechan,
Boston, Mass.

Mr. Wilson directs me to say his firm has had no dealings of any kind with the person named.

John Randolph Bolling,   Secretary."

I do not even know who Pelletier may be.

TLS (B. Colby Papers, DLC).
    [1] Virginia MacMechan to WW, Feb. 24, 1922, T telegram (WP, DLC).
    [2] Joseph C. Pelletier, a Massachusetts district attorney, accused of and tried for bribery and malfeasance; removed from office by the Supreme Court of Massachusetts in February 1922.

From Elizabeth, Lady Bryce

Dear Mr Wilson   London. Feb. 24. 1922.

I have not been able sooner to acknowledge your letter of the 27th [29th] January & to thank you for your sympathy in my great loss. I am still stunned by the shock & am overwhelmed with letters. The blow fell with absolute suddennes; no illness & no warning. Lord Bryce had been well & active as usual, full of work & taking his walks each day, & that last night when he went to bed there was no sign that there was anything the matter, nor did he call me during the night. When I awoke the next morning I found that he was gone. He had passed away quite peacefully in his sleep, from failure of the heart. That death should have come to him so gently, with no pain & in the full strength of his mental & physical powers, I am deeply thankful. He was working to the last, & the end came as he would have wished, in peace & calm, after a long life of faithful service.

It is some comfort to me to know how much he was beloved & how widespread was the influence of his character & personality.

With my thanks, & my remembrances to Mrs Wilson, believe me
very sincerely yours   E. Marion Bryce.

ALS (WP, DLC).

To William Calhoun

My dear sir: [Washington] 25th February 1922

Having read your letter of February twenty-third,[1] and having seen several films attempting the sort of thing you suggest with regard to Washington, I am constrained to say that I think it would be unwise to make the attempt.

I for one should not wish the children of the country to get the impression of Washington which they would certainly get from such an attempt to depict him unless some histrionic genius has recently been born of whom I have not heard.

Very truly yours,   [Woodrow Wilson]

CCL (WP, DLC).
[1] W. Calhoun to WW, Feb. 23, 1922, TLS (WP, DLC), asking about the advisability of producing a movie based on George Washington's life.

To Ida Minerva Tarbell

My dear Miss Tarbell: Washington D C 26th February 1922

I have been told, and would fain believe, that you wrote the editorial in a recent number of Collier's Weekly entitled "The Man They Cannot Forget."[1]

I wish to express to you my pride and deep pleasure that you should entertain such thoughts of me. It is the favourable verdict of minds like your own which everyone dealing with high and difficult affairs should desire and strive for.

Hoping that I shall many times more have the pleasure I had at Shadow Lawn of exchanging thoughts with you personally,[2] and with best wishes;   Gratefully yours,   Woodrow Wilson

TLS (Ida M. Tarbell Papers, PMA).
    [1] "The Man They Cannot Forget," *Collier's*, LXIX (Feb. 18, 1922), 14. As will soon become evident, Miss Tarbell did indeed write this editorial. Why, she asked, did so many people, people of all sorts and kinds, still revere Woodrow Wilson? Among other reasons, she gave the following:
    "Woodrow Wilson means something to the people of the United States: something profound, something they cannot forget. People think of him now as the man who was behind the inspiration of their greatest moments; who stirred them to a fresh understanding of the meaning of words that had become mere patter on many tongues—'democracy,' 'union.' He made them realities, personal, deep—showed them as the reason of all that is good in our present, all that is hopeful in our future, the working basis on which men may strive to liberty of soul and peaceful achievement. He made them literally things to die for, lifting all of our plain, humble thousands who never knew applause or wealth or the honor of office into the ranks of those who are willing to die for an ideal—the highest plane that humans reach."
    [2] Miss Tarbell visited the Wilsons at their summer home on the New Jersey shore on September 28, 1916. The result of that visit—her article—is printed at Oct. 3, 1916, Vol. 38.

To Louis Dembitz Brandeis, with Enclosure

My dear Brandeis: Washington D C 27th February 1922

This time I am sending you a suggestion of a statement of policy about the railroads. It may have already reached you through Colby, but I do not know that it has and am acting on the principle of "safety first,"—a rule of practice not unknown to lawyers though of little practical interest to a member of a court of final resort.

I think it only fair to send you at the same time a memorandum prepared at my request by my able and thoughtful friend, Henry Jones Ford, at Princeton, who was a member of the Interstate Commerce Commission until the recent triumph of Obscura[n]tism. You may think it wiser to follow his lead than to follow mine. I can at least vouch for the fact that he knows what he is talking about.

Always with the warmest regard;
                        Faithfully yours,   Woodrow Wilson

TLS (L. D. Brandeis Papers, KyLoU).

E   N   C   L   O   S   U   R   E

Without the systematic coordination, cooperation, and interchange of services by the railroads the expanding, varying, and changeable commerce and industry of the country cannot be properly served. All of these conditions are now lacking because our present laws deal with the railroads without system and altogether by way of interference and restriction. The result is a confusion which is constantly made worse almost to the point of paralysis by the multiplicity and intermittent conflict of regulative authorities, local and national.

We need a Secretary of Transportation who shall rank with the heads of other great federal cabinet departments and who shall be charged with the formulation and execution of plans for the coordinated use and full development of the transportation systems of the country. He should be associated with a federal Transportation Board which should be invested with all the powers now lodged with the Interstate Commerce Commission and, in addition, with the authority to determine the occasions and the conditions of all loans floated and of all securities issued by the several railway and steamship lines. This Board should have the same powers of supervision and regulation over the steamship lines of the United States that are now exercised by the Interstate Commerce Commission over the railways.

T MS (L. D. Brandeis Papers, KyLoU).

To McLane Tilton

My dear Mr. Tilton: Washington D C 28th February 1922

The news brought me by your letter of February twenty-seventh of the defeat of the effort to remove the Medical School from the University to Richmond[1] is most gratifying. I rejoice that it should be true, and am indeed gratified that you should think that my letter on the subject contributed to the fortunate result.

Thanking you for your thoughtfulness in sending me the good news, and with all good wishes;
          Cordially and sincerely yours,   Woodrow Wilson

TLS (ViU).
[1] M. Tilton to WW, Feb. 27, 1922, TLS (WP, DLC).

Ray Stannard Baker to Edith Bolling Galt Wilson

                                        Amherst
Dear Mrs. Wilson: Massachusetts February 28. '22

I expected to go to Washington last week, but I find I can save time by getting two or three more chapters in hand before going. I was in New York, however, and had a number of interesting conferences with Norman H. Davis, Professor Shotwell and others covering certain aspects of the Conference where I needed more light. One of the pleasantest aspects of this work to me has been the generous interest and confidence of many of the men who were at Paris with us and who have not only been willing to give me information, but to place their documents at my disposal. All of these things help greatly.

I saw Justice Brandeis in New York & he told me he had seen Mr. Wilson and was astonished at the improvement shown. This is truly good news. I hope the betterment will continue.

I expect soon now to have the report, complete, from the Syndicate for the first two months of our series. I will then send on a statement to date with a remittance for the amount due.

There is an expectation of a still wider circulation of the Syndicate material: but I am placing my chief hope for getting really effective results, and substantial influence, from the book publication.

Please remember me cordially to Mr. Wilson.

Sincerely yours,   Ray Stannard Baker

ALS (EBW Papers, DLC).

From Bernard Mannes Baruch

My dear Mr. Wilson: New York March 2, 1922.

The things which I think the farmer should have are the things which will place him on an equality of footing with other pursuits.

All other business have a more or less ready access to credit for orderly marketing and for productive purposes. You have, through the Federal Farm Loan Bank, increased the radius of the personal credit of the farmer on farm mortgages so that a farmer in an out of the way farming district can place his mortgage in the Federal Farm Loan Bank, and have investors bidding for it in the central credit markets of the world. This is what I should like to see done for the orderly marketing of the farmer's products and for production. Therefore, I recommend that the Federal Farm Loan Bank system be enlarged to permit the farmer to borrow money on a short-time obligation with which to market his crop in a more orderly manner. This he would do as follows:

He places his grain in an elevator or his cotton in a warehouse where it is graded by a neutral grader. Heretofore, many of the greatest abuses came about through under-grading. Often the farmer saw his products re-sold as of a higher grade than he had been paid for. To proceed, the farmer takes this certificate of his warehoused product and places it as collateral in the Federal Farm Loan Bank, which places this note in its treasury and issues its own obligation against it. This note should be subject to rediscount if purchased by a member of the Federal Reserve system.

I suggest that a plan following the German system be adopted here whereby an association of farmers can mutually endorse one for the other for the purchase of cattle, machinery, seed or such things. This local association would pass its note on to a regional association, which, in turn passes it on to a national association, which, in its turn, sells its own notes or obligations, secured on the farmers' notes, in the credit markets of the world.

These two credit institutions, one for production and the other for the purpose of creating an orderly marketing system, can be perfected by an enlargement of the principle underlying the Federal Farm Loan Bank.

Very truly yours,   Bernard M. Baruch

TLS (WP, DLC).

From Bainbridge Colby

My dear Mr President: New York City March 2, 1922

I am so much obliged to you for your charming little note in which you gave me the benefit of your advice in language that was so modest and considerate on the subject of speech-making. I feel that you are absolutely right, and immediately upon receipt of your letter I cancelled my engagement for Utica and have taken steps to cancel the other two engagements that I mentioned. It would be a pleasure to me merely to accede to your wishes, but I unreservedly assent to your judgment also.

That was a delightful reference to Burke. The "wisdom of the circumstances" is a first-class definition of expediency. I was reading Morley's essay on "Compromise"[1] some time ago and I recall his distinction between the petty, immediate, individual expediency and that larger, ultimate and complete expediency which is "akin to principle."

I came across a good line last night in Gilbert Murray's new book. The words are translated from Aristophanes' "Knights" and are put in the mouth of Demosthenes.

"A blood-shot voice, low breeding, huckster's tricks—
What more could man require for politics?"[2]

There is a bit of truth in this, isn't there?

Thank you again for your kind letter. I hesitated to bother you about the matter at all, yet now I am very glad I did.

With sincerest regard always,

Cordially yours,   Bainbridge Colby

TLS (WP, DLC).
  [1] John Morley, *On Compromise* (London, 1874).
  [2] Gilbert Murray, *Tradition and Progress* (Boston and New York, 1922), p. 49.

From Eleanor Randolph Wilson McAdoo

Darling, darling Father,—   [New York] March 2nd 1922

I couldn't go down to Washington to tell you good-bye—not because there wasn't time, but because I couldn't bear to say good-bye to you.[1] This is the only way that I can stand it at all—going so far away from you. It isn't as if we won't be back before long on a little visit—we'll probably be here in the fall, but I feel as if I were chopping a great big piece off of my heart when I put four days, instead of five hours between you and us. I don't see how I'm going to stand it, Father darling. I love you more than I have ever been able to tell you and I owe you so much in every, every way that I shall never, never be able to repay it all. I wish I knew how to tell you what you and your love mean to me.

I can't write very much—for I am too sad—this is just a little note to tell you that I love you and that we'll be back soon.

Will you give dear, dear Edith a big hug and kiss for me and ask her to hug you for me?

Ellen sends her heart full and so does Mac—to you both—

With oh so much love darling darling Father from

Your adoring daughter   Nell.

We are leaving to-morrow—Friday—and our address will be

Hotel Huntington
Pasadena
California

ALS (WC, NjP).
  [1] McAdoo had decided to move permanently to California in order to continue his law practice there and to improve his chances for the Democratic presidential nomination in 1924.

To Bainbridge Colby[1]

My dear Colby: Washington D C 3rd March 1922

My judgment concerning Nortoni's[2] proposal to occupy a portion of our offices here corresponds with yours exactly.

Judge Nortoni took pains to have himself thrust upon my attention repeatedly while I was in office, and it would be a great nuisance to have him under my nose. I do not mean to suggest any odor except that of the busy politician. What he proposes is no doubt with a view to getting an inside track for a partnership which would of course be out of the question. He is a very pushing person, and in this case will have to be pushed out.

I hope you realize how deeply gratified I am by your confidence in my judgment in the matter of the "wisdom of the circumstances," and I appreciate your decision most deeply.

Always, with affectionate regard,

Faithfully yours,   Woodrow Wilson

TLS (B. Colby Papers, DLC).
[1] Wilson was replying to BC to WW, March 2, 1922, TLS (WP, DLC).
[2] Albert Dexter Nortoni, former judge, leader of the Progressive party, lawyer of St. Louis.

From Louis Dembitz Brandeis

My dear Mr Wilson: Washington, D. C. March 3/22

I am very glad that you are turning your thoughts to the railroad problem. The need of constructive action is becoming daily more manifest.

The wisdom of the principle of "safety first" finds confirmation: for Colby had not sent me a copy of your statement.

Let me thank you also for sending me Prof. Ford's suggestive memorandum returned herewith. I am particularly impressed with his proposals in regard to water transportation. A high development of coastwise and inland transportation is essential to an adequate system.

You had so large a part in giving us Woman Suffrage, that you may care to see these opinions which establish the Nineteenth Amendment as a part of our Constitution.[1]

And possibly you may be interested also in the Lemke case,[2] where a promising effort of a State to protect itself met its doom.

Most Cordially   Louis D Brandeis

ALS (WP, DLC).
[1] Lesser v. Garnett, 258 U.S. 130, and Fairchild v. Hughes, 258 U.S. 126. Brandeis delivered the opinions in both these cases on February 27, 1922. In the first, he held

that the Nineteenth Amendment was in fact a valid part of the Constitution. His major argument was that the Nineteenth Amendment was "in character and phraseology precisely similar to the Fifteenth," and had been adopted by the same method. The Fifteenth Amendment, he noted, had been recognized as valid for over half a century; hence, the Nineteenth Amendment was also valid. He also rejected several legal technicalities which had been raised in regard to the ratification of the amendment. In the second case, in which the plaintiff, Charles S. Fairchild, sought also to have the Nineteenth Amendment declared void on legal technicalities, Brandeis declared that Fairchild had no valid standing to bring such an action.

² Lemke v. Farmers Grain Co., 258 U.S. 50, also decided on February 27, 1922. This was a suit brought against William Lemke, Attorney General of North Dakota, on the ground that that state's Grain Trading and Inspection Act of 1919, one provision of which required all grain for sale to be inspected, was an undue restraint on interstate commerce, since virtually all grain produced in North Dakota was shipped to points beyond its boundaries. Justice William R. Day agreed in the majority decision. Brandeis dissented and was supported by Oliver Wendell Holmes, Jr., and John H. Clarke. Brandeis argued that the North Dakota law was a valid application of the state's police power, especially since Congress had not legislated on the subject.

From Ida Minerva Tarbell

My Dear Mr Wilson: [Peoria, Ill.] March 5 1922.

I have received today here in Peoria, Illinois, your letter of February 25. I cannot tell you how deeply it touched me or how much it cheered me.

Yes, I wrote the editorial in *Collier's Weekly*, "The man they cannot forget"—wrote it without dreaming it would ever come to your eyes. That it has and that it pleases you makes me both proud and happy.

I have never doubted for a moment, dear Mr Wilson, that your place in the minds and hearts of all right-thinking people—not only in this country but throughout the world—was secure. You have done what the world will never forget. That you have paid the price of your health has been a great grief to me though I know very well that you would have given your life cheerfully to have secured all you hoped in Paris. Feeling all this you see how glad I am if a word of mine has brought you a moment of satisfaction.

I would value it as a great privelege [privilege] to see you again and talk with you freely as in 1916 at Shadow Lawn; and since you are good enough to suggest that you are willing to see me, I am going to let you know in advance when I am next in Washington— it will probably be in April—hoping that if you are strong enough you will let me call.

May I ask you to give my best wishes to Mrs Wilson. I am very proud of her.

Sincerely and Faithfully yours   Ida M. Tarbell

ALS (WP, DLC).

To Eleanor Randolph Wilson McAdoo

[Washington] March 6th 1922

My heart has followed you to California. This is meant as a loving message both of goodby and welcome to your new home. We are as usual but shall miss you, Mac and the children more and more.   Father.

T telegram (WC, NjP).

John Randolph Bolling to Bessie P. Britt[1]

Dear Madam: [Washington] 6th March 1922

Mr. Wilson asks me to express to you his warm appreciation of your letter of March first[2] and say he thinks it only an act of justice to a very fine person to say that the idea of the Woodrow Wilson Foundation originated with Mrs. Charles L. Tiffany (according to his best advices), of New York, and not with Mr. Franklin Roosevelt. He wishes me to add, however, that Mr. Roosevelt has put his whole heart and energy into the movement in a most admirable spirit of unselfishness.

With every good wish;

Cordially yours,   [John Randolph Bolling]

CCL (WP, DLC).
  [1] Mrs. L. R. Britt of Norfolk, Va.
  [2] Bessie P. Britt to WW, March 1, 1922, ALS (WP, DLC).

To Ida Minerva Tarbell

My dear Miss Tarbell: Washington D C 7th March 1922

I have had the pleasure of reading your generous letter from Peoria. In it you promise just what I would have wished—that you will let me know in advance of the time of your next visit to Washington—and I shall look forward with pleasure to arranging to see you then.

With warmest regard, in which Mrs. Wilson joins;

Cordially and sincerely yours,   Woodrow Wilson

TLS (I. M. Tarbell Papers, PMA).

To Eleanor Axson Sayre

My dear Eleanor: Washington D C 9th March 1922

Your letter[1] gave me a great deal of pleasure. It was very nicely written, and I am glad that you are learning to write.

Yes indeed I do love you, and very often wish that I might see you again. I hope that I shall see you very often in the days to come; you will then have a chance to know how much I think of you. We shall be great friends.

I saw a photograph the other day in one of the Sunday papers of Woodrow's birthday party. It was a picture of you, Francis and Woodrow sitting at a round table. Woodrow had a big cracker in his hand and his mouth very full of something. I hope it was something very good, and that the party was a great success. Did you think only of Woodrow or also of George Washington whose birthday it was too?

Give lots of love to your mother and father, and to Francis and Woodrow. I hope you are all well.   Lovingly,   Grandfather

[1] It is missing.

To Francis Bowes Sayre, Jr.

My dear Francis: Washington D C 9th March 1922

I enjoyed your letter.[1] You may be sure that I love you very much and think of you very often.

Your letter was very nicely written, and I was very glad to see that you were learning to write.

Give my love to all.   Lovingly,   Grandfather

TLS (received from F. B. Sayre).
[1] It is also missing.

To Bernard Mannes Baruch

My dear Baruch: Washington D C 10th March 1922

I read with great interest your letter on what the farmer needs and find myself (so far as I can understand a subject which I have had no opportunity to study) in agreement with you on what I take to be the essential points. Unfortunately we are not in a position now to inaugurate such a policy as you sketch, but we shall be before long; and I shall expect then to turn to your letter again as a guide to my thought and purpose. In the meantime, will you not do this for me: Will you not sum up the suggestions of your letter in as brief a form as possible suitable to constitute the plank of a platform, something after this order:

The farmers of the country should be put on a footing of perfect equality with the other producers of the country in the matter of the command of credit. We therefore advocate, &c. &c.,—not going into particulars but using such phrases as could be easily translated into particulars by those who are on the inside and really understand the subject.

I am collecting such suggestions on the various matters which have to be dealt with presently if our economic society is to be placed upon a basis of perfect equity and advantage. At an opportune time I shall assemble these suggestions in a program which can be submitted for the consideration of those who are to determine the policy of the party. I have asked Chadbourne, for example, for a similar statement with regard to the policy which ought to be pursued for the correction and reasonable settlement of relations between capital and labor; Houston for suggestions about the tariff, &c.

I hope that you will not find it too onerous to contribute what I have just now suggested. If you find it too difficult to satisfy yourself with the wording of the brief summary statement, send it to me in as rough a form as you choose and I will try to help with the phrasing.

The partridges suit my palate and my digestion perfectly, and I am greatly your debtor for your kindness in sending them to me. If their flavour is drawn from the atmosphere of South Carolina, South Carolina would certainly be greatly to my taste.

Mrs. Wilson joins me in warm regard, and I am as always;

Affectionately yours,   Woodrow Wilson

TLS (B. M. Baruch Papers, NjP).

To Marion Edmund Melvin

My dear Mr. Melvin: [Washington] 15th March 1922

I have your letter[1] with accompanying document and am of course interested in the movement to which you refer, but I am by far from approving of it.

I believe it is a radical mistake to move an educational institution which has become generally known from the place where it first took root and became known and with which its graduates associate their days of study in it. I am confident that my father would have felt the same way. He expressed himself very fully about a similar attempt some years ago to remove the institution to Louis-ville.[2]

I appreciate your courtesy but feel bound in acknowledging it to speak my real opinion. I have had some experience in educational matters and express the opinion with real conviction.

Sincerely yours,   [Woodrow Wilson]

CCL (WP, DLC).
[1] M. E. Melvin to WW, March 13, 1922. The Rev. Dr. Melvin, director of the "One and One-Half Million Dollar Rebuilding Fund to Rebuild and Enlarge Southwestern Presbyterian University at Memphis—the Strategic Center of the Mid-South," and Sec-retary of Stewardship of the Presbyterian Church, U. S. (southern).
[2] Southwestern Presbyterian University at Clarksville, Tenn., was removed to Mem-phis in 1925 and renamed Southwestern, the College of the Mississippi Valley (the name was shortened to Southwestern at Memphis in 1945). One of the architects of the new campus and its Gothic-style buildings was Wilson's friend, Charles Z. Klauder. The college was renamed Rhodes College in 1984 in honor of Peyton Nalle Rhodes, Professor of Physics at and President of Southwestern, 1926-1965.

Henry Morgenthau to Cary Travers Grayson

My dear Doctor: New York March 15th, 1922.

I am extremely anxious to use in my book the information you gave me about President Wilson, and your having come to the con-clusion that he should resign, and how he was influenced by Mrs. Wilson to give up this plan, about which you and he had already arranged all the details.[1] I think the public would be keenly inter-ested.

Kindly let me know whether you have any objection to my doing so, and if you have none, ascertain how the President would feel about it.[2]

With kindest regards to Mrs. Grayson and yourself, I am

Sincerely yours,   H Morgenthau

TLS (received from James Gordon Grayson and Cary T. Grayson, Jr.).
[1] About Grayson's initiative, see the extracts from the diaries of John W. Davis and Ray S. Baker printed in n. 1 to the extract from the Diary of Ray Stannard Baker, printed at Feb. 4, 1920, Vol. 64.
[2] There is no copy of a reply from Grayson in the Grayson Papers, and no letter of reply in the Papers of Henry Morgenthau, DLC. Moreover, there is no mention of this subject in the Morgenthau pocket diaries and other materials in the Morgenthau Pa-pers.

From Bernard Mannes Baruch, with Enclosure

My dear Mr. Wilson: New York March 16, 1922.

I am enclosing you the memorandum, which I intended to send you sometime ago; but, unfortunately, I have had a recurrence of a little cold I had in the South, and I have again been confined to my bed. I am sitting up dictating this to you.

With kindest wishes to Mrs. Wilson, and affectionate regards to yourself, I am,   Sincerely yours,   B M Baruch

TLS (WP, DLC).

ENCLOSURE

MEMORANDUM

The farmers of the country should be put on a footing of perfect equality with the producers of the country in the matter of the command of credit. We therefore advocate that, for the purpose of orderly marketing of his crops, there should be an enlargement of the Federal Farm Loan act whereby the radius of the personal credit of the farmer can be enlarged by having access to the short-time credit markets of the world as he now has to the long-term markets through the Federal act covering mortgages.

We advocate the establishment of a system whereby the farmer can receive enlarged credit for the production of his crops and for the purpose of raising cattle.

T MS (WP, DLC).

To Joseph Taylor Robinson

My dear Senator: [Washington] 21st March 1922

Please do not be alarmed that I am sending you the enclosed letter.[1] It does not mean that I am going to unload my correspondence on this subject on you. It merely means that I regard you as the real moral and intellectual leader of the Democrats in the Senate and would feign submit to you occasionally such sincere expressions of opinion and suggestions of argument as Mr. Fuller's letter contains.

But explanations are not necessary. I know that you will understand; you always do.

With warmest regard;
           Faithfully yours,   [Woodrow Wilson]

CCL (WP, DLC).

[1] The enclosure is missing, but a note on JRB to H. H. Fuller, March 21, 1922, CCL (WP, DLC), says that the original of Fuller's letter was sent to Senator Robinson on March 21, 1922. Fuller cannot be identified except to say that his permanent address was Madison, Wisc. About the contents of his letter to Wilson, see J. T. Robinson to WW, March 27, 1922.

From James Weldon Johnson[1]

Dear Sir: New York March 21, 1922

It is unnecessary for me to call to your attention the danger of lynching and mob violence in the United States and the humiliation in the eyes of the civilized world which it causes all American citizens. You yourself have already expressed these facts in the most forceful manner possible in the statement on lynching and mob violence which you issued to the country on July 26, 1918. In that statement you truly said:[2]

"There have been lynchings and every one of them has been a blow at the heart of ordered law and humane justice. No man who loves America, no man who really cares for her fame and honor and character, or who is truly loyal to her institutions, can justify mob action while the courts of justice are open and the governments of the states and the nation are ready and able to do their duty."

In the last thirty years mobs have arrogated to themselves the sovereignty of the state and the functions of law and put to death 3,443 persons accused of crime (known cases), sixty-four of whom were women. In 1921 sixty-four persons were lynched, two of whom were women and four of whom were burned at the stake.

States have proved their inability to cope with this form of anarchy, and to remedy this condition there has been introduced in the Congress a bill which would make lynching a crime against the United States. The bill was passed by the House of Representatives on January 26, by a vote of 230 to 119, and is now in the Senate.

We are asking your signature to a Memorial to the United States Senate urging the prompt enactment of this measure which is designed to remove this stain and reproach from the name of America. We, therefore, earnestly request that you sign the enclosed form and return it to us.

We are sending you a copy of the bill in order that you may know what its provisions are.

              Yours very respectfully,   James Weldon Johnson

TLS (WP, DLC).
[1] American poet and writer; Secretary of the National Association for the Advancement of Colored People.
[2] It is printed at that date in Vol. 49.

John Randolph Bolling to the National Association for the Advancement of Colored People

Sirs: [Washington] 22d March 1922

In reply to your letter of March 21st, Mr. Wilson requests me to say that, as the whole country already knows, he is deeply interested in all measures calculated to rid our country of the disgrace of lynching; but that he does not put his name to the paper you send because—as is also well known—he does not feel at liberty at present to exert any influence in matters of national legislation.

Very truly yours,   [John Randolph Bolling]

CCL (WP, DLC).

From Bainbridge Colby

My Dear Mr. President.   New York Mch 22 [1922].

We have rather an interesting piece of business on the ways—the reorganization of Ecuador's finances involving a loan of some millions, which some bankers here are considering with a prospect of favorable action.

I don't like to say much about it until it is assured, and will have more to say in a few days. I have been very busy on it for the last fortnight. Norman Davis is helping.

This is a [sic] just a line at the end of the day as I am about to hurry uptown to take Mrs Colby to dinner at the Houstons.

Affectionately   Colby

ALS (WP, DLC).

John Randolph Bolling to Bainbridge Colby

Dear Mr. Colby: [Washington] 22d March 1922

Mr. Wilson asks me to thank you very warmly for your note of yesterday [sic], and say he is much interested in what you tell him about the matter upon which you are working. He will be obliged if you will keep him posted as to developments.

You will be glad to know that he felt well enough to go with Mrs. Wilson to matinee this afternoon—to see Milne's "Mr. Pim Passes By."

I was at the office this afternoon, and everything is all right there.

With warmest regards from us all;

Faithfully,   John R Bolling.

TLS (B. Colby Papers, DLC).

To James Watson Gerard

My dear Gerard: [Washington] 24th March 1922

You ask in your letter of March 23rd,[1] just received, how I prefer to be addressed; but you use the form I prefer in that very letter, namely, Mr. Wilson.

I must ask you to indulge me in the matter of the photograph. I have recently found it always so difficult, and sometimes so painful, to use a pen that I have felt obliged to decline to send autographs to a great many persons whom I know and whom I would have been glad to please; and now I feel bound in a sort of loyalty to them not to make exceptions. I am subjecting myself to a very exacting routine of convalescence, and do not think I am asking too much when I ask my friends to indulge me in matters of this kind.

I need hardly tell you that I have very much appreciated your activities in behalf of the Foundation.

Sincerely yours, [Woodrow Wilson]

CCL (WP, DLC).
[1] J. W. Gerard to WW, March 23, 1922, ALS (WP, DLC).

To John Nance Garner

My dear Garner: [Washington] 24th March 1922

You are certainly right in assuming that my heart goes out to Senator Culberson in the warmest friendship and sympathy.[1] But my conscientious judgment is that the Texas Democrats ought to [be] left to exercise a perfectly independent judgment as to returning him to the Senate.

The circumstances are so extraordinary that I myself find it very difficult to form a conclusion as to what is most in the public interest in a case like this.

I am sure you will understand, for I can always count on you to do that, and that you will know it is through no lack of loyal friendship and admiration for Senator Culberson, but only from conscientious public motives that I feel constrained to take this position.

I sincerely hope that everything goes well with you, and wish again to assure you how happy and proud your constant support and assistance have made me. You are the kind of a comrade in affairs that is worth having.

[Sincerely yours, Woodrow Wilson]

CCL (WP, DLC).
[1] Wilson was replying to J. N. Garner to WW, March 22, 1922, TLS (WP, DLC). Culberson, a veteran Texas progressive, had been in the United States Senate since 1899.

Garner asked Wilson to support Culberson in the primary fight. He was defeated for renomination in 1922 by Earle Bradford Mayfield.

From Christopher Darlington Morley

Dear Mr Wilson: New York, N. Y. March 24, 1922

I have just got back to my desk, and cannot resist the impulse to thank you for your great kindness in letting me call. My little talk with you in the great sunlit room, the charming graciousness of Mrs Wilson, and the happiness of knowing that you are gaining strength after your long and painful trouble—all this, and the privilege of seeing you face to face, was something that I shall never forget.

Perhaps you, in your youth, may have had that experience of going to visit someone whom you had long honored and loved from a distance. If so, you will remember the honest emotion of youth. Rudyard Kipling described, somewhere in his *From Sea to Sea*, how as a young man he went to call on Mark Twain, and his pride and happiness when Mark laid his hand on Kipling's shoulder. No matter what happens to me, said Kipling, no matter what a failure I may make in life, I shall always have something to boast about— Mark Twain put his hand on my shoulder.

There are many of us younger men who, whatever our blunders and pitiful errors, sincerely believe that we are better men because we have lived in a time when we saw and admired your courage.

I am sending you, as I promised, the detective story written by a friend of mine who has written a number of excellent books of that sort. You will pardon its being a battered copy: it has not been published in this country, and this is the only copy available at the moment. But do not bother to have it returned. And, if you and Mrs Wilson have not read a book called THE LUNATIC AT LARGE,[1] you might ask Mr Bolling to let me know: I should like to send it to you, for it is ideal for diverting reading aloud.

I hope Mr Bolling's neuralgia is better; I was much touched by his courtesy to me when I could see that he was suffering greatly.

I hope I have not trespassed upon your patience; I could not refrain from thanking you again for your kindness and generosity. I had a curious feeling yesterday as I wandered about Washington in the sunshine—it seemed to me that behind those beautiful buildings, so grave and yet so uplifting, I could feel at work and pervasive something of the spirit which you infused into the government of this country; it seemed more real and potent now than ever. It is no credit to a man to love his country: we do so by instinct and naturally; but to love her unselfishly and with the courage to try to deny her some of the things on which she seems at time[s] to have set her heart, that is the true patriotism!

With genuine gratitude and homage to Mrs Wilson and yourself,

Yours indeed,   Christopher Morley

TLS (WP, DLC).
[1] Joseph Storer Clouston, *The Lunatic at Large, A Novel* (Edinburgh, 1899).

To Robert Bridges

My dear Bobby: Washington D C 25th March 1922

You will presently receive a call from a young man named Vail Motter[1] who is a Princeton graduate and whom I promised to introduce to you.

Mr. Motter wants I believe to go into some work such as a newspaper editor or magazine publisher might give him. I have strongly advised him not to connect himself with a newspaper for I think (and I believe you agree with me) that the newspaper "profession" is no profession at all. But you will know better than I how to talk to the lad after you have heard his own views and hopes.

My own instinct is to rescue him.

Affectionately yours,   Woodrow Wilson

TLS (Meyer Coll., DLC).
[1] Thomas Hubbard Vail Motter, born March 7, 1901. A.B., Princeton, 1922; Ph.D., Yale, 1929. Teacher, author, and editor. Consulting Editor, *The Papers of Woodrow Wilson*, July 1, 1964-June 30, 1967. Died April 1, 1970.

To Herbert Sherman Houston

Dear Friend: [Washington] 26th March 1922

I congratulate you on the first number.[1] It is good in itself and gives confident promise of even better things to follow.

I have no doubt that you will work out the admirable purpose you have in mind in a way to command the universal attention and exercise very wide influence. I with all my heart bid you Godspeed in the enterprise and shall hope to see the magazine become one of the chief instruments for rousing our people to a realization of their true moral relations to the rest of the world. God grant the day may come soon, for we are now wallowing in the sloughs.

With warmest best wishes not only, but confident expectation of your complete success;

Gratefully and faithfully yours,   [Woodrow Wilson]

CCL (WP, DLC).
[1] Of *Our World*.

To Christopher Darlington Morley

My dear Friend: Washington D C 27th March 1922

The copy of The Fugitive Sleuth[1] has come safely to hand, and I shall look forward with pleasure to reading it. Thank you for your kindness in remembering to send it.

May I not say how much I was gratified by the generous way in which Mrs. Wilson tells me you spoke of me in your lecture last Thursday. It is very delightful to have such assurances of your approving judgment and warm feeling towards me.

I hope that our friendship will steadily ripen in the years to come. I am hoping that some day I shall be really free to cultivate and enjoy my friends again.

Do not forget your promise to let me know when you again turn your steps this way.

May all happy circumstances attend you, and your varied work develop just as you wish it to.

Mrs. Wilson joins me in messages of sincere regard, and I am happy to subscribe myself;

Your sincere friend,   Woodrow Wilson

TLS (PHC).
  [1] Hulbert Footner, *The Fugitive Sleuth* (London, 1918).

From Bainbridge Colby

My dear Mr President: New York City March 27, 1922

I am returning herewith your proposals for a Party platform, having arranged them in the order which seems to me to be a logical one, and inserting some suggestions of my own which I have indicated in red brackets.[1] I don't think I have added much of value to what you have already written. The test of a proper attitude, it strikes me, on the part of our candidates is contained in your fine sentence beginning, "We demand the immediate resumption of our international obligations and leadership."

I am also sending you a few pages of hurried and disconnected jottings from some little reading I have been doing, more particularly on the question of labor and the aspirations of the workers.[2] It might interest you to run your eye over these memoranda, and if any idea seems to you to merit development or fuller expression I will be very glad to try my hand at it.

I think the matter you prepared is quite sufficient as a test-oath. The real indictment against the Republican Party is that it is not facing any of the realities of the present world-situation. Our national policy is a writhing, wriggling effort to square our course with the stump-speaking commitments of some Republicans who find themselves in office. The attempt is being made to reach solutions without entering the field where the problems lie. I think your declarations are basic and therefore adequate and require no enlargement. However, if it was your idea to enlarge upon them I would be very glad to submit something to you by way of fuller statement, although, as I say, I do not believe it necessary.

I also think your general references to the labor problem, labor unrest and necessity of reaching some accommodation between capital and labor are sufficient and, considering the trend of men's thoughts at the moment, tactful. The great number of men, I think, fail to realize that the tactics of labor are really those of a belligerent seeking to nibble and undermine a social and industrial system which they think spells slavery or at least deprives them of that freedom of life and self-expression to which the workers aspire. While this idea may not be understood fully by the rank and file of labor, I think it is pretty definitely in the minds of the leaders and accounts for the frequency and recurrence of strikes. It seems very patent to me that labor is not so much seeking the redress of demonstrable grievances as waging war against a system which it believes to be doomed.

On the other hand, I think among many well-meaning men there is a feeling of impatience with labor's position at the moment. The need of larger production is keenly felt in business circles. The indifference of the workers to this need is resented and one hears frequently the remark that labor must be liquidated.

The Democratic Party however must keep the balance even and must seek to interpret the highest practical conception of justice to the manual worker.

I shrink very much from adding to what you have written on that subject.

If it is your idea that the platform should be built up to the conventional stature of platforms in general, paragraphs might be added on quite a variety of subjects, such as Republican traffic in offices, with resultant demoralization of the civil service; the bonus, the tariff, etc., but, as I understood you, your idea was a basic definition of principle to which intending candidates might be invited to give their adhesion.

I would be glad to receive a memorandum containing any fresh suggestions that occur to you and I will endeavor to respond with promptness. I have given a little more work and thought to this material than you would ever suspect,—somewhat distracted however by the work-a-day duties at the office.

I may go to Chicago on Wednesday to spend only a day, if the client desires to pay the sum I have asked him for.

Always with best wishes and regards,

Cordially yours   Bainbridge Colby

TLS (WP, DLC).
¹ See BC to WW, April 5, 1922.
² Again, see BC to WW, April 5, 1922.

From Joseph Taylor Robinson

My dear Mr. Wilson: [Washington] March 27, 1922.

I cannot tell you how sincerely your letter of the 21st is appreciated.

The fight in the Senate against the Four Power Treaty was lost in the beginning because of the attitude of Senator Underwood and his followers.¹ We never had a chance to prevent the Senate from advising and consenting, although the efforts of the treaty advocates in the debates were pitiably feeble. You have pursued a wise and dignified course in refraining from participation in the Senate controversy. This is the unanimous opinion of your friends in and about the Senate. If we could have prolonged the contest for another month, the reversal in public sentiment which probably would have resulted might have enabled us to prevent ratification. This, however, could not be done without filibustering, and I am sure for us to have engaged in that would have offset other advantages to be derived from a frank and legitimate fight.

I am leaving for Arkansas tomorrow, and upon my return to Washington will ask the pleasure of seeing you at sometime when it may be convenient to you.

With assurances of profound esteem, I am

Very truly yours,   Joe. T. Robinson.

TLS (WP, DLC).
¹ The Senate, on March 24, 1922, had voted to consent to the ratification of the Four-Power Treaty by a vote of sixty-seven to twenty-seven. Fifty-five Republicans and twelve Democrats voted in the affirmative; twenty-three Democrats and four Republicans voted in the negative. Democrats voting for the consent resolution included Underwood, Owen, Pomerene, and John Sharp Williams. *Cong. Record*, 67th Cong., 2d sess., p. 4497.

From Henry Waldo Coe

My Dear Sir: Washington Mch. 27 1922

Subject to your approval the T.R. Committee has placed your name as an ex-president upon the program for the unveiling ceremonies relative to the Roosevelt Statue,[1] as to which please find enclosed advance proof. I trust this liberty may not meet your disapproval.   Sincerely yours   Henry Waldo Coe

ALS (WP, DLC).
[1] To be held in Portland, Ore., on August 5, 1922. President Harding was scheduled to deliver the dedicatory address. Wilson and other dignitaries were listed as "vice chairmen."

From Robert Bridges

My dear Tommy: New York March 27, 1922.

I shall be glad to receive your young man, Vail Motter, and give him the benefit of any special knowledge that I may have accumulated.

It is a pleasure to hear from you, and also to have had a talk with Lee[1] on Saturday about his delightful conversation with you. You and he no doubt recalled many pleasant times. His chief Exhibit for me was the photographs of four grandchildren.

With best wishes always,
                    Faithfully yours   Robert Bridges

TLS (WP, DLC).
[1] That is, William Brewster Lee.

To Breckinridge Long

My dear Long: Washington D C 28th March 1922

The information contained in your letter of March 25th[1] just received is very cheering to me.

You may say to Mr. Roberts[2] (to whom I hope you will feel at liberty to show this letter) that I consider Reed my implacable opponent in everything that is honorable and enlightened. He has been false to his own character on the few occasions when he has affected to support me, and has generally opposed me. I regard him as a discredit to the party to which he pretends to belong but to which he has no true allegiance. He can indeed have no true allegiance to anything or anybody, for he is essentially false. I have never dealt with a man who more thoroughly and completely earned my distrust, and I should consider it a discredit to the party and an unhappy omen for the country if he should be returned to the Senate.

These are strong words, but this is a critical time when weak and bland words are faithless words. It is high time to put on our war paint and fight for the right things, and I for one mean to do so without compromise of any kind or degree.

I am sure that both you and Mr. Roberts, since you know me, will understand the spirit in which I have thus sought to reveal my whole mind.

Paranthetically, Mr. Fordyce[3] is not only not in my confidence but is in no way in a position to interpret my thought or any part of my purpose.

With hearty congratulations on the prospects as you tell me of them;   Cordially and faithfully yours,   Woodrow Wilson[4]

TLS (B. Long Papers, DLC).
[1] B. Long to WW, March 25, 1922, TLS (WP, DLC), saying that he would have a clear field with James A. Reed and would defeat him.
[2] John C. Roberts, connected with the International Shoe Co. of St. Louis and owner and publisher of the *St. Louis Star*.
[3] In his letter to Wilson of March 25, Long said that Fordyce was a friend of Tumulty.
[4] Wilson wrote an equally strong letter in WW to J. W. Alexander, March 30, 1922, TLS (photostat in RSB Coll., DLC), and invited Alexander to show the letter "to any responsible Democrat."

To Bainbridge Colby

My dear Colby: Washington D C 29th March 1922

I have your letter of March twenty-seventh, but may I not say that it would be much more like business if you would go over the whole matter with Brandeis and let me have some formulation which would be the result of the joint judgment of the two of you.

As you know, I regard this as a critical and even exigent matter, and I am sure you will be willing to effect common counsel upon it as early as possible.

In haste, with affectionate regard,
                    Faithfully yours,   Woodrow Wilson

TLS (B. Colby Papers, DLC).

John Randolph Bolling to Henry Waldo Coe

My dear sir: [Washington] 29th March 1922

Mr. Wilson asks me to reply to your letter of March 27th and say that he seriously objects to his name being used by any one without first obtaining his consent, and that he must insist upon its being removed from the program, proof of which you enclosed.
            Yours very truly   [John Randolph Bolling]

CCL (WP, DLC).

From William Howard Taft

My dear President Wilson: Washington D. C. March 29, 1922.

The Lincoln Memorial Commission directs me to invite you to be present on the occasion of the dedication of that Memorial, to take place on the afternoon of Decoration Day, May 30th. It is hoped that the Memorial will then be entirely completed, and that the mirror or reflecting pool on the side toward the Washington Monument will be ready. We have taken Decoration Day because it is an appropriate holiday, when the Houses of Congress will not be in session, and their members will be at liberty to attend. We have arranged with the members of the Grand Army of the Republic so to time their services at Arlington upon that day as to be with us in the afternoon.

The Commission has arranged a short program, which will consist of a commemoration service by the Grand Army of the Republic, not to last more than ten minutes, an address of fifteen minutes by a representative negro, an address by yourself, if you are willing, some remarks by myself as Chairman presenting the Memorial to the President, and an address by the President in receiving the Memorial on behalf of the people of the United States.

I hope that this program will approve itself to you and that you will advise me of your acceptance of this invitation.

With great respect, believe me,

Sincerely yours,   Wm H Taft

TLS (WP, DLC).

To William Howard Taft

My dear Mr. Chief Justice: [Washington] 30th March 1922

I warmly appreciate the invitation which you extend to me on behalf of the Lincoln Memorial Commission to be present and take part in the exercises which are to be held on the thirtieth of May in connection with the presentation of the Lincoln Memorial to the head of the Government, but I am sorry to say that it would be an act of great imprudence on my part to promise to be present and I must beg that the Commission will accept my sincere thanks and excuse me.

Will you not extend my congratulations to the Commission on the completion of the beautiful building and the expectation that the surrounding improvements will also be completed.

Sincerely yours,   [Woodrow Wilson]

CCL (WP, DLC).

From Bainbridge Colby

My dear Mr President: New York City March 30, 1922

I am in receipt of your letter of yesterday with enclosures and have written Justice Brandeis saying I will come over to Washington tomorrow if he can arrange to see me.

I have not received a word of concrete suggestion from either Brandeis or Chadbourne, and with much misgiving and too much delay, I concluded that I would have to see what I could do by myself, if you were to get any support whatever in the preparation of this material.

As I said in my former letter, I think what you have written is splendid and that nobody can improve it or add much of value to it, considering your specific aim with reference to its use.

I was asked the other day to go into the enclosed matter,[1] which is a proposal by two firms of high standing to build a railroad in the Republic of Colombia in conjunction with the Colombian government. You will notice, however, the marked passages on the fifth and seventh pages, from which it appears that the business is predicated upon the ratification of the treaty between this country and Colombia, and more explictly upon the sum received by Colombia as a solatium or indemnity.[2] I suppose without any question we must decline employment in this matter, in view of the fact that the policy of this treaty was a feature of your administration. I might say also that one of the last speeches I made during my term of office was at the meeting of a commercial congress in Washington at the New Willard Hotel, in which I predicted the ratification of the treaty and deplored our long delay.

                                        Cordially always,   Colby

TLS (WP, DLC).
    [1] This enclosure is missing.
    [2] The Wilson administration had long been pressing the Senate to give its consent to the ratification of the Treaty of Bogotá of 1914, by which the United States had expressed its "sincere regret" for anything that had occurred to mar the good relations between the United States and Colombia, had made an award of $25,000,000 to Colombia, and had granted certain other concessions to that country. The regret clause of the treaty was generally interpreted to be an apology for the participation of the United States in the secession of the Province of Panama from Colombia and its establishment as an independent republic in 1903. One of President Harding's first actions was to urge the Senate to approve the treaty, which in 1919 had been amended with Colombia's consent by the elimination of the regret clause and other changes. The Senate gave its consent to ratification of the amended treaty on April 20, 1921, by a vote of sixty-nine to nineteen. After a spirited debate in Bogotá, the Colombian Congress also approved the treaty, and ratifications were exchanged on March 1, 1922. For references to the Treaty of Bogotá, see the Index references to "Colombia and the United States" in Vols. 39, 52, and 69 of this series; see also E. Taylor Parks, *Colombia and the United States, 1765-1934* (Durham, N. C., 1935), *passim*.

To Bainbridge Colby

My dear Colby: Washington D C 31st March 1922

As usual your instinctive judgment is quite correct about having anything to do with business matters which have anything to do with the treaty with Colombia. I think it would lead to endless embarrassment to say nothing of good taste in the matter. But you need no suggestions or counsel on the matter.

I greatly appreciate the effort you are making to go ahead with Brandeis and Chadbourne in the preparation of our material, and I have no doubt that what you have done will be of great service when we finally bring about the conferences which should bring the matter to a conclusion. If I know the men, Brandeis and Chadbourne will be willing to make some sacrifice of convenience to bring about the conferences. I think therefore that you can confidently apply to them in even an insistent way.

With affectionate regard,

Faithfully yours,   Woodrow Wilson

TLS (B. Colby Papers, DLC).

To Bernard Mannes Baruch, with Enclosure

My dear Baruch: Washington D C 31st March 1922

I have had the temerity to sum up from your letter about the farmers a statement for the form of party policy and I enclose it for your comment and criticism. Please remember in noting the typographical blunders that I had the use of only one hand in using the typewriter.

I know you will always be frank in your comment and tell me if you think this is a clear and frank statement of what should be done for the farmers.

Affectionately yours,   Woodrow Wilson

TLS (B. M. Baruch Papers, NjP).

E N C L O S U R E[1]

By affording them such access to the use of capital as they never had before, the farm loan banks, instituted upon the initiative of the Democratic Administration, have rendered the farmers of the country an inestimable service; but they are still at a slight economic disadvantage as compared with producers and merchants in other branches of industry and in the matter of access to credit for productive purposes and for orderly marketing. We therefore favour legislation which will secure to the farmer a just and accurate grading of his grain or cotton at the elevator or warehouse and ready access to short term credits on the basis of his actual assets; and for these purposes we favour the assistance of legislation in the creation of the necessary machinery in the way of credit institutions in the form of mutual associations formed among responsible farmers themselves to facilitate production and assist orderly marketing.

Have I covered all?   W.W.

T MS (B. M. Baruch Papers, NjP).
    [1] The following reproduces a typed copy of the WWT MS, which is missing.

To Vance Criswell McCormick

Dear Friend: Washington D C 31st March 1922

We have been greatly shocked and deeply grieved to hear of your Mother's death.[1] By some singular fatality we had indeed no news of it until today. We know her unusual quality and have therefore some partial means of judging your loss and the loss of the communities in which she played so influential and useful a part. Our hearts go out to you and your sister in heartfelt sympathy.

I hope that the memory of her wonderful life will serve in some small part to console you and compensate you for the great loneliness you must be feeling, and I trust that the affectionate sympathy of friends like ourselves will also help. I feel that it was a privilege to know her and that her death deprives us of a friend whom we could value with deep and reverent affection.

Mrs. Wilson and I join in the most affectionate messages to you and I am as always
                    Your affectionate friend,   Woodrow Wilson

TLS (V. C. McCormick Papers, CtY).
    [1] That is, Annie Criswell (Mrs. Henry) McCormick.

From Bernard Mannes Baruch

My dear Mr. Wilson: New York April 3, 1922.

It was such a pleasure to hear from you. You have been continually in my mind and indeed I have been in hopes of coming down to see you. This I am going to do the coming Sunday if it is convenient to you.

As far as the memorandum you sent me is concerned, may I suggest the following:

"By affording them such access to the use of capital as they never had before, the farm loan banks, instituted upon the initiative of the Democratic Administration, have rendered the farmers of the country an inestimable service; but they are still at an economic disadvantage as compared with producers and merchants in other branches of industry in the matter of access to credit for productive purposes and for orderly marketing. We therefore favor legislation which will secure to the farmer a just and accurate grading of his products at the elevator or warehouse, and ready access to short-term credits on the basis of his actual assets; and for these purposes we favour the assistance of legislation in the creation of the necessary machinery in the way of credit institutions in the form of mutual associations formed among responsible farmers themselves to facilitate production and assist orderly marketing."

Sincerely yours,   Bernard M Baruch

TLS (WP, DLC).

Henry Waldo Coe to John Randolph Bolling

My dear Sir: Washington, D. C. April 3, 1922.

Replying to your favor of the 29th of March, permit me to hand you herewith another proof of the dedication exercises and unveiling of statue of Theodore Roosevelt in which you will note that as per your advice the name of Mr. Wilson has been removed.

These programs will not be published until July. This proof is full of errors, but in view of the acceptance of all of the others from whom I have heard, I hope that I may be authorized by Mr. Wilson to include him in this list as one of the vice-chairmen. I fear that if this is not done that it may be taken as an intentional slight upon Mr. Wilson, whom I had hoped to honor in this appointment.

No one in Washington knows when Congress will be through, but the printer in Portland apparently thinks he knows because he has fixed the date of the unveiling for August 5th. In an interview with President Harding yesterday, I told him that these exercises as to the date were not like St. Patrick's Day which must be held in the morning of the 17th of March, but that they would be fixed to accommodate the President's itinerary, if Congress shall adjourn in time to permit him a seasonable visit to Alaska.

With very high personal regards to Mr. Wilson and with my compliments to yourself, I am

Sincerely yours,   Henry Waldo Coe.

TL (WP, DLC).

From the Diary of Ray Stannard Baker

Washington April 4th [1922]

On Monday I worked at S Street, had a long talk with General Patrick[1] on the aeronautical conventions: & at dinner went up to see Mr. Wilson. Both in voice & in the appearance of his face he seems much better, but I can see no change in the condition of his stricken arm. His left hand is still useless. I found him much more cheerful in spirit, with his old liveliness of mind. We got on the subject of Edmund Burke of whom he is a great admirer: & he was positively brilliant in his comments on Burke's service. He spoke of him as knowing, profoundly, "the wisdom of concession." We talked of Mrs. Gaskell & Miss Mitford—for Mrs. Wilson is now reading aloud Jane Austen. I told him about the old farmer who came to see me sometime ago & having asked if I was chairman of the Woodrow Wilson foundation committee said he liked Mr. Wilson's "ideas." He "wa'n't no politician" but he thought "Mr Wilson had the right of it" & he wanted to help him. So he got out his old worn pocket-book & handed me a two-dollar bill. Mr. Wilson was much affected by this incident & said: "I am more pleased to hear of such a gift as that than I am of Henry Ford's $10,000." We talked of the Harding treaties which are just now being ratified by the Senate. He is strongly opposed to them: thinks them "alliances" & dangerous.

"They are accepting arrangements which the Democrats will have to carry out."

He spoke again of the time "when the Democrats come in."

He is fully convinced that the Democrats are coming back into power in 1925—refers to it as a certainty—and, more than that, seems actually to think of himself as the leader. I got this impression quite strongly & afterwards, when I talked about it to Grayson, he confirmed it: said Mr. Wilson was plainly thinking of another presidential campaign. The sheer spirit of the man! Here he is, paralyzed, blind in one eye, an invalid, 66 years old & sees himself leading a campaign in 1924!

I told him something—rather guardedly—about my work, but he gave no indication that he had read any of the articles so far, though I know Mrs. Wilson has. When I spoke jokingly of the attacks being made on me for certain things I have said, he remarked

"Pay no attention to them. Treat them as though they did not exist. That has always been my policy."

He said of one of the men who is writing these attacks:

"Why, Baker, he is a skunk."

He gave the same impression of masterly power that he has always given: indomitability of will! There is yet in him a tremendous fight or so—if he does not drop dead before he gets to it! The democrats pressed him hard to take part in the present treaty fights.

"The time has not come yet," he said to me. "I shall know when the time is ripe."

And he will! He will know when the big issues are ripe.

He reads the papers more than ever, dictates many letters, goes to ride every day & to theater once or twice a week. Mrs. Wilson worries about him because he has nothing to occupy his consuming mind. She even urged him hard to write a life of Hugo Grotius for a series which Bok is getting up.

Mrs. Wilson is certainly as convinced as he, that there are great things ahead of him.

There is no doubt that the country is changing toward him. Miss Tarbell, who has been lecturing in the middle west from Minnesota down to Oklahoma told me that she found everywhere evidences of this change, together with a more serious attention to our responsibilities for foreign affairs.

[1] Maj. Gen. Mason Mathews Patrick, U.S.A., chief of the Air Service.

To Breckinridge Long

My dear Long: Washington D C 4th April 1922

I have your letter of April first.[1] Much the best way to make my attitude towards Reed known would be for some real friend of ours to ask him at a public meeting if he was willing that he, the questioner, should write to me and request my endorsement of him, Reed. If the questioner did write to me afterwards I could send you a copy of my reply and that would be the letter to use rather than the one to you which would be in danger of being discounted as addressed to the rival candidate himself.

I am heartily glad to hear your estimate of the prospects and of course wish for you the most abundant and complete success.

I wrote a letter to Judge Alexander the other day in which I expressed my opinion of Reed as unreservedly as in the letter to you which I suggested you show to Mr. Roberts.

Cordially and faithfully yours,   Woodrow Wilson

TLS (B. Long Papers, DLC).
[1] B. Long to WW, April 1, 1922, TLS (WP, DLC).

John Randolph Bolling to Henry Waldo Coe

My dear Dr. Coe: [Washington] 4th April 1922

In reply to your kind letter of April third, Mr. Wilson asks me to say that he deeply appreciates the honor you are seeking to do him but that he feels in honor bound to say to you in confidence that he feels it would be an act of insincerity on his part to consent to the use of his name in the program because he was never one of Mr. Roosevelt's admirers and would therefore be put in a very false light. He nevertheless hopes that the most fortunate circumstances and the best success will attend the unveiling ceremonies which you are planning.

Mr. Wilson directs me to say that he is deeply gratified by every evidence of your generous friendship. Thank you for sending me copy of your letter to Mr. Smith, at Portland—which Mr. Wilson noted with interest.

With every good wish;

Cordially yours,   [John Randolph Bolling]

CCL (WP, DLC).

To Katrina Brandes Ely Tiffany

My dear Mrs. Tiffany: [Washington] 5th April 1922

Of course I will sign the engraving as you request and shall consider it a very slight token of the gratitude I owe you for the many generous evidences you have given me of your confidence and friendship.[1]

I cannot help feeling sorry that so great an engraver as Cole[2] should have used his gifts on this particular work of Sargent's which I have regretted ever since it was painted.[3] But that you value the engraving is sufficient for me and I am more than willing to put my signature upon it.

With warm regard,

Your grateful friend   [Woodrow Wilson]

CCL (WP, DLC).
 [1] Wilson was replying to Katrina B. E. Tiffany to WW, April 2, 1922, ALS (WP, DLC).
 [2] Timothy Cole of New York.
 [3] A reproduction of John Singer Sargent's portrait of Wilson is the frontispiece in Vol. 47.

From Bainbridge Colby, with Enclosures

1315 F STREET   32 NASSAU STREET
WASHINGTON D C   NEW YORK CITY

WILSON & COLBY

ATTORNEYS AND COUNSELLORS AT LAW

NEW YORK CITY

April 5, 1922

My dear Mr President:

In the matter of Platform proposals, I beg to return the
material upon which I have been engaged, in three sections:

1st.   Your material without change or addition.   I
have numbered each of its paragraphs for easier reference.

2nd.   The Brandeis suggestions, which I have endeavored
to reduce to expression.

3rd.   Some additional matter of my own, which I venture
to submit for what it may be worth.

I have indicated by brackets the Brandeis suggestions and
have rewritten in full the paragraphs where they belong, so that
you will have the amended paragraph in its entirety before you.

I have pursued the same plan with reference to my own suggestions.

Judge Brandeis suggested that there should be no "denunciation" in the paper and this would apply to your paragraph
"6".   I think, however, that this paragraph should not be
omitted.   It is clearly cognate to what precedes, and is strong
and valuable.

I have endeavored to arrange this material in a way that
will not harass your mind by any confusion, in which attempt
I hope I have measurably succeeded.

With sincerest regards always,

Cordially yours

Colby

Honorable Woodrow Wilson

TLS (B. Colby Papers, DLC).

E N C L O S U R E S[1]

Mr Wilson's material. (Intact)

1.   We recognize the fact that the complex, disturbing,
and for the most part destructive results of the great
war have made it necessary that the progressive countries
of the world should supply for the reconstruction of its
life a programme of law and reform which shall bring it
back to health and effective order; and that it lies with
the political party which best understands existing conditions, is in most sympathetic touch with the mass of
the people, and is best qualified to carry a constructive
programme through to take the initiative in making and
pressing affirmative proposals of remedy and reform.

2.   In this spirit and with this great purpose, the Democratic party of the United States puts forth, in deep earnestness, the following platform of principle and purpose
and seeks to serve America and, through America, liberal
men throughout the world who seek to serve their people.

3.   "AMERICA FIRST" is a slogan which does not belong to
any one political party; it is merely a concise expression of what is in the heart of every patriotic American.
We enthusiastically incorporate it into this our declaration of principles and purposes.   But it means different things in different mouths and requires definition.
When uttered by the present leaders of the Republican
Party it means that America must render no service to
any other nation or people which she can reserve for

---

[1] All handwriting on the following pages Wilson's.

2

her own selfish aggrandizement.

4.   When we use it we mean that in every international
action or organization for the benefit of mankind America
must be foremost; that America must lead the world by
imparting to other peoples her own ideals of Justice and
of Peace and by rendering them material aid in the realization
of those ideals.

5.   We demand the immediate resumption of our international obligations and leadership,--obligations which
were shamelessly repudiated and a leadership which was
incontinently thrown away by the failure of the Senate
to ratify the Treaty of Versailles and the negotiation
of a separate treaties with the Central powers.

6.   We condemn the group of men who brought about
these evil results as the most partisan, prejudiced,
ignorant, and unpatriotic group that ever misled the
Senate of the United States.

7.   We shall use every legitimate means to advance to
the utmost the industrial and commercial development
of the United States.   That development has already made
the people of the United States the greatest economic
force in the world.   It is as convincing proof of their
practical genius as their free institutions are proof
of their political genius.   It is their manifest opportunity and destiny to lead the world in these great fields

3

of endeavour and achievement.   Our opponents have sought
to promote the accumulation of wealth as an instrument
of power in the hands of individuals and corporations.
It is our object to promote it as a means of diffused
prosperity and happiness and of physical and spiritual
well-being on the part of the great working masses of
our people.

8.   Without the systematic coordination, cooperation,
and interchange of services by the railroads the expanding, varying, and changeable commerce and industry of
the country cannot be properly served.   All of these
conditions are now lacking because our present laws
deal with the railroads without system and altogether
by way of interference and restriction.   The result
is a confusion which is constantly made worse almost to
the point of paralysis by the multiplicity and intermittent conflict of regulative authorities, local and
national.

9.   We need a Secretary of Transportation who shall
rank with the heads of other great federal cabinet departments and who shall be charged with the formulation and
execution of plans for the coordinated use and full development of the transportation systems of the country.
He should be associated with a federal Transportation
Board which should be invested with all the powers now
lodged with the Interstate Commerce Commission and, in
addition, with the authority to determine the occasions

3

4

and the conditions of all loans floated and of all securities issued by the several railway and steamship lines.
This Board should have the same powers of supervision and
regulation over the steamship lines of the United States
that are now exercised by the Interstate Commerce Commission over the railways.

10. The present menace to political liberty and peaceful economic prosperity lies, not in the power of kings
or irresponsible governments, but in hasty, passionate,
and irrational programmes of revolution.

11. The world has been made safe for democracy; but
democracy has not yet made the world safe against revolution.   It is the privilege and duty of ours, the
greatest of all democracies, to show the way.   It is
our purpose to defeat the irrational programmes of revolution beforehand by sober and practical legislative reforms which will remove the chief provocations to revolution.

12. Among these we hold the following to be indispensable:
13. A practical plan for a partnership between capital and
labour.

14. A plan by which the raw materials of manufacture
and the electrical and other motive power now universally necessary to industry shall be made accessible to
all upon equitable and equal terms.

15. Such legal requirements of the manufacturer and the

5

merchant as will serve to bring cost of production and
retail price into a clearly standardized relationship
known to the purchaser.

Nelson

Brandeis
(9)

16. 7. We unqualifiedly condemn the action of the Republican administration in interrupting and in large part destroying the work of creating and developing an American
merchant marine so intelligently begun and so efficiently
carried forward by the Democratic administration, and we
demand the immediate rehabilitation of the Shipping Board
and such appropriations for its use and such additions to
its powers as may be necessary to put its work upon a
permanent footing and assure its energetic and successful
completion.

17. 18. Inasmuch as access by all upon equitable and equal
terms to the fuel supply and to the raw materials of manufacture and also the availability to all upon fair and
equal terms of the motive power supplied by electrical
power companies and other similar privately owned and
controlled agencies are indispensable to the unhampered
development of the industries of the country, we believe
that these are matters which should be regulated by
federal legislation to the utmost limit of the constitutional powers of the federal government.

5

Brandeis

4.   When we use it we mean that in every international action or organization for the benefit of mankind America must be foremost; that America, [by developing within her own citizenship a sensitive regard for justice in all the relations of men, must
lead the world in applying the broadest conceptions
of Justice and of Peace, of amity and respect, to
the mutual relations of other peoples, and in rendering them material aid in the realization of those
ideals.]

6

Brandeis

7.   We shall use every legitimate means to advance
to the utmost the industrial and commercial development
of the United States.   That development has already
made the people of the United States the greatest economic force in the world.   It is as convincing proof
of their practical genius, as their free institutions
are proof of their political genius.   It is their
manifest opportunity and destiny to lead the world in
these great fields of endeavour and achievement.   Our
opponents have sought to promote the accumulation of
wealth as an instrument of power in the hands of individuals and corporations.   It is our object to
promote it [not only] as a means of diffused prosperity
and happiness and of physical and spiritual well-being
on the part of the great working masses of our people,
[but as a means of that individual development which
will nourish and sustain our progressive democracy
with a constantly improved material for responsible
citizenship.]

Brandeis

13.   A practical plan for a partnership between
capital and labour, [in which the responsibilities of
each to the other, and of both to the nation, shall
be stressed quite as much as their respective rights.
Our industrial system must command the interest and
respect of the wage-earners as an avenue to those liberties and opportunities for self-development, which
it is the nature of free men to desire.   Justice must
reign over it, and its dignity as one of the foundations
of the national vigor and as a great training school for
democratic citizenship must be recognized and cultivated.]

Brandeis

16.   We unqualifiedly condemn the action of the
Republican administration in interrupting and in large
part destroying the work of creating and developing an
American merchant marine so intelligently begun and so
efficiently carried forward by the Democratic administration, and we demand the immediate rehabilitation of
the Shipping Board and such appropriations for its use
and such additions to its powers as may be necessary
to put its work upon a permanent footing and assure its
energetic and successful completion.

[An efficient and adequate merchant marine is vital
to the nation's safety, and indispensable to the life
and growth of its commerce.   In close relation to the
upbuilding of our overseas trade is the development of
our inland waterways.   We demand therefore the unprejudiced and scientific study of this vastly important
field of national expansion, and the prompt inauguration of adequate and effective measures to bring to the
service of our producers in the interior States, a sys-
tematized, cheap, and efficient transportation by inland
water routes, including the development of ship canal
communication with the Atlantic seaboard.]

9

Colby

OKeh N.N. (For insertion between Paragraphs 4 and 5 as an additional paragraph)

We are suffering in common with the nations of
the world from the industrial and commercial prostra-
tion which succeeded the great war.   Bound up with
world-conditions from which we cannot extricate ourselves, the Republican Administration still prates of
isolation.   Unwilling to use our accumulated strength,
our savings and our matchless resources in the rescue
of our sister nations, from which alone our own recovery can arise, we not only fail to display the generosity of a great nation to a world stricken with calamities which it could neither foresee nor avoid, but we
persist in the ignorant delusion that we are untouched
and unaffected by these all-encompassing conditions.
Unwarned by our dwindling foreign commerce, our tied-up
shipping, and the helplessness of our debtors among the
nations, we brandish our contracts and clamor for payment, indifferent to the fact that we hold the gold of
the world in our chests and will not receive the goods
of our debtors, with which alone their debts can be discharged.

10

Colby

5.   We demand the immediate resumption of our
international obligations and leadership,--obliga-
tions which were shamelessly repudiated and a leadership which was incontinently thrown away by the
failure of the Senate to ratify the Treaty of Versailles and the negotiation of a separate treaty
with Germany, [in which we exact every privilege and
benefit secured to us under the terms of the Treaty
of Versailles, while at the same time we refuse all
participation in its enforcement and repudiate every
responsibility which devolved upon us not only as one
of the victors in the war, but as a member of the
family of nations, charged with duties to mankind,
which are measured by our enlightenment and power,
and which we cannot without dishonor and vast material
hurt fail to perform.]

\\

Colby
(For insertion between Paragraphs 6 and 7 as an
additional paragraph)

We point to the lamentable record of incompetence, evasion
and political truckling of the present Congress, dominated in
both the Senate and House of Representatives by a commanding
Republican majority.   No step has been taken toward the redemption of the pledges made by the Republican party.   Despite
the crying needs of the hour and the hopes of the people, it
has not enacted a single piece of constructive or ameliorative
legislation, although for the last three years it has controlled
both Houses of Congress.

The demand for a revision of the tax laws, although made
three years ago by a Democratic President upon the conclusion
of the armistice, is still unheeded, and the burdensome and un-
equal war tax, born of and justified only by a great emergency,
still persists, thwarting the normal processes of post-war
recovery, and robbing the frugality and industry of the people
of their just rewards.

A budget still unbalanced, and distended beyond the requirements of efficient and economical administration in time
of peace, shows no sign of contraction, and every day brings
the report of some fresh conspiracy against the public treasury.
We promise studious and disinterested approach to the problems
of national relief and rehabilitation and denounce the cal-
lousness and levity with which the Republican party has sub-
ordinated the duty of resolute attack upon these vital problems to the petty contentions of partisan politics.

12

Insert ~~between~~ after 15.

16. By affording them such access to the use of capital as they never had before, the farm loan banks, instituted upon the initiative of the Democratic Administration, have rendered the farmers of the country an inestimable service; but they are still at an economic disadvantage as compared with producers and merchants in other branches of industry in the matter of access to credit for productive purposes and for orderly marketing. We therefore favor legislation which will secure to the farmer a just and accurate grading of his products at the elevator or warehouse, and ready access to short-term credits on the basis of his actual assets; and for these purposes we favour the assistance of legislation in the creation of the necessary machinery in the way of credit institutions in the form of mutual associations formed among responsible farmers themselves to facilitate production and assist orderly marketing.

T MSS (B. Colby Papers, DLC).

From Joseph Patrick Tumulty

Dear Governor: Washington, D. C. 5 April 1922.

On Saturday evening of this week, April eighth, the National Democratic Club of New York City will have its Jefferson banquet at the Hotel Commodore in New York. Thomas E. Rush, whom you appointed Surveyor of the Port of New York, is chairman of the dinner committee, Bainbridge Colby, Gerard, Elkus, Morgenthau and Frank Polk are expecting to attend, and I am intending to go to New York for the affair.

It would hearten and inspire everybody if a message from you could be read at the banquet. It could take the form of an acknowledgment of the invitation and an expression of regret at not being able to attend. Will you advise me of your feeling in the matter? Mr. Rush's address is 40 Wall Street.

Cordially and sincerely yours,   J P Tumulty

TLS (WP, DLC).

To Joseph Patrick Tumulty

My dear Tumulty: [Washington] 6th April 1922

I feel that a message to the New York dinner which you suggest would be quite meaningless unless I made it a serious expression of my views and feelings about the present national situation, and I do not feel that the occasion is a specially appropriate one for breaking my silence.

Thank you nevertheless for telling me about it.

Faithfully yours,   [Woodrow Wilson]

CCL (WP, DLC).

From Bainbridge Colby

My dear Mr President: New York City April 6, 1922

My mind is in the tangle-grass of speechmaking again today. A couple of invitations just received present the subject in a little different light from that in which we have discussed it. May I bother you with the subject a little further?

I sent regrets to the Jefferson Day banquet committee of the Democratic Club. The occasion was entirely political and every consideration that you and I have discussed, indicated that it was good judgment not to speak on this occasion.

The Broadway Association is giving a dinner on the 19th. It is an association of leading business men and the occasion is wholly municipal and civic. National politics would be altogether out of order. The thought occurs to me that such an occasion as this is not to be despised as an opportunity of bringing oneself agreeably into contact with men worth knowing and thus freshening and enlarging useful acquaintance. Life is a good deal of a show-window, and complete abstention from these contacts often results in being forgotten in quarters where it is useful to be remembered.

I am also invited to deliver an address at the U. S. Grant Centennial under the auspices of the Missouri Historical Society in St Louis on the 27th. This, as you know, is my old home town and I have some genuine and useful friendships there which it is well to touch up at intervals.

These commemorative addresses are rather stale and empty, and yet what I have said about the New York City speech applies in a certain degree to the Missouri speech.

Do not think that I am inconstant in my full accord with your attitude on the subject of political speaking just at this time. If you think it better not to discriminate too closely between invitations, then I think so also.

I do not exaggerate in saying that I have declined about a hundred invitations during the last year. Many of these invitations I am sure come to me because of my association with you, and I suspect strongly that the committees feel that if they can't get you they may at least get me as a sort of pallid and lunar reflection.

I will call up Mr Bolling tomorrow afternoon on the telephone hoping to get your judgment on these matters, as I should send replies without delay.   Always most cordially   Colby

TLS (WP, DLC).

From Franklin Delano Roosevelt, Cleveland Hoadley Dodge, and Hamilton Holt

New York Apl 6 1922.

America today celebrates the fifth anniversary of her entrance into a war for idealism Stop You as spokesman of the ideals for which we fought voiced the will of the entire nation Stop The principles you enunciated stand today unchanged Stop The members of the executive committee of the Woodrow Wilson Foundation dedicated to the perpetuation of these ideals of public service, liberal thought, the extension of democracy, and peace through jus-

604 APRIL 7, 1922

tice send their respectful greetings on this anniversary and pledge
their loyalty to the struggle for their attainment.

Franklin D. Roosevelt, National
Chairman
Cleveland H. Dodge, Chairman
Executive Committee,
Hamilton Holt, Executive Director
for the Executive Committee.

T telegram (WP, DLC).

John Randolph Bolling to Bainbridge Colby

My dear Mr. Colby: [Washington] 7th April 1922

I return herewith the two letters sent to Mr. Wilson in yours of
April 6th to him, and confirm his reply—given you over the 'phone
this afternoon:

"Tell Colby I don't think it is wise to discriminate too nicely
among invitations. It would be quite contrary to everybodys expectation for him to speak without reference to national problems. The
safest thing is to reserve our forces for the one great offensive."

With warmest regards from us all;

Faithfully,   [John Randolph Bolling]

TLS (B. Colby Papers, DLC).

To Hamilton Holt and Others

[Washington] April 7th 1922

The message from you and other members of the executive com-
mitt. of the Foundation has given me the deepest pleasure and
gratification. I have the assured faith that the ideals with which we
entered the war are still consciously held and earnestly believed in
by the whole body of our people and that we are upon the eve of a
notable reassertion of the principles for which we sacrificed so
much. In this revival a very great part will undoubtedly be due to
the splendid men who have organized and developed the Foundation. Warmest greetings to all.   Woodrow Wilson.

T telegram (WP, DLC).

ADDENDA

A Memorandum by Stockton Axson

["one Sunday night in August, 1919."]

There was a long conversation on the rear portico of the White House Sunday evening (no record of date) after dinner, there being present besides the President only Mrs. Wilson, Miss Wilson and myself, Doctor Grayson being still absent with his family in Connecticut. There was a good deal of talk about the third term, to which both Mr. and Mrs. Wilson are instinctively very much opposed, though Mr. Wilson's opposition to it does not rest on the two-term tradition. He said that if he were a younger man he would be inclined to break that tradition just for the sake of breaking it; that he thinks that the American people should always have the right to choose for President whomever they wished to choose. And he said that he finds that a good many of his close and sincere friends really hold an idea about the office of the Presidency which he is sure is wrong, namely, that the office itself is so powerful that it would be dangerous to let any man occupy it for more than eight years. Said he: "I insist that the office in and of itself is not one of the most powerful of offices; it is nothing like so powerful as the Premiership of England for the simple reason that the Prine [Prime] Minister of England can at any time dissolve Parliament and appeal directly back to the British people, and it is this knowledge on the part of Parliament that the Prime Minister can at any time make this appeal back to the people that undoubtedly whips Parliament into supporting the Prime Minister in many things in which they would not otherwise support him. And thus he has a hold on Parliament utterly unlike and superior to the hold which the President has on Congress." "Suppose," said he, "I could dissolve Congress now and appeal to the people to support the Treaty, is there any question that the Treaty would be immediately ratified? I would not have to dissolve Congress. The mere fact that I had the right to do it would bring Congress around at once." Surely this seems to be the soundest kind of analysis. Now, the President added to all this: "The Presidency is what the incumbent makes it. If he is a small and compliant man it is a small office; if he is a real leader, it is an office of leadership. There is nothing dangerous about the office. The only danger is the man you put into office."

This conversation led to a consideration of Presidential possibilities. The President asked me this question: "Suppose you yourself could name the next President of the United States, (not considering his chances of being elected—not considering him as a candidate, but actually as President in the chair), whom would you name?" I replied: "You mean excluding yourself." He bowed assent. "Well," I said, "I know whom you would name, or I think I know that you would name one of two men—either Mr. Baker or Mr. Houston—neither of whom could probably be elected President." Again the President nodded assent, it being his opinion that neither man has the qualities to make a winning candidate. I continued: "I do not know either of these gentlemen in the way in which you know them, and, therefore, cannot have your conviction about the inherent qualities of each for the office, and I cannot help taking a very personal view of the matter and cannot rid myself of the thought and hope that if you are not available, Mac (meaning Mr. McAdoo) would be the nominee of the party for the next President." To this the President replied: "In anything that I have ever said about Baker or Houston I do not mean for a moment to rate them above Mac. I do not consider them abler men than Mac. But there is this one thought in my mind which troubles me: They are both *reflective* men—and I am not sure that Mac is a reflective man. There is no man who can devise plans with more inspiration, or put them into operation with more vigor, than can Mac, but I never caught Mac reflecting. Now, I may be wrong. It may be that when I have been with him, he has simply been so busy with the things in hand or immediately to come that I could not perceive the reflective elements in his nature. I am only saying then that dear Mac may not have the quality which I believe is going to be essential to a successful and wise administration in the near future. And I think Baker and Houston both have that quality—the quality, in short, of seeing the picture as a whole, the whole country in all its diverse elements, and understanding all these elements before they decide on any action at all. The action of the future may be very dangerous if it is precipitous and not based on long reflection on the condition of the country as a whole."

He then went on to make an analysis that was one of the most searching things I have ever heard even from him. He said: "The labor people are the only internationally-minded people in our country. The rest of us (and he used the pronoun 'us') are provincials. The labor people see what the provincials do not see—that the fundamental questions of the future are questions which do not belong particularly to one country or another, but questions in which all countries are concerned. Now, this leads to a socialistic view, and I need hardly say that as between socialism and individualism, I favor individualism. But that does not mean that I do not see the inevitability of a part of the socialistic program in order to give just the opportunity to the individual that he ought to have. For instance, I am perfectly sure that the state has got to control everything that everybody needs and uses. This means that the state must control the means of distribution—the transportation facilities, the railroads; that the state must control the coal mines and the iron mines; that the state must control the water sources, the lighting facilities, (he named several others but I will not undertake to recall them)." Said he: "These things must be controlled by the state in order to secure equality of opportunity among individuals. For instance, the railroads under private management favor large shippers as against small shippers, give rebates, say that a man who takes a whole car should have more favorable rates than the man who sends only a single parcel. But on the principle of equality of privilege that is not true. The little man must have just the same rights as the big man, and state control provides for this." "Now," said he, "I go up to this point with the labor people, and, you may say, with the socialists, but there is a point beyond which I cannot go with the socialists, because in my opinion their further programmes are not for the individual benefit of the individual. The man who is going to direct the future of America as an able President should always direct it, has got to be a man who reflects long and deeply on these complicated relationships of our time and the time immediately pending. He must not jump at conclusions; he must not be too speedy."

T MS (received from James Gordon Grayson and Cary T. Grayson, Jr.).

A Memorandum by Oscar Solomon Straus

CONFERENCE WITH PRESIDENT WILSON
AT THE WHITE HOUSE
-RE-
LEAGUE OF NATIONS AND THE PEACE TREATY
AUGUST 6TH, 1919.

The League to Enforce Peace called a meeting of the Executive Council on July 22nd to determine what action had best be taken to further its efforts and propaganda for the ratification of the Peace Treaty which was being debated in the U. S. Senate. There were present former Secretary of the Treasury Wm. G. McAdoo, former Attorney General Wickershaw [Wickersham], Talcot[t] Williams and some 25 others. It was decided that it would be best to confer with the President. Mr. Vance McCormick Chairman of the War Trade Board was also present.

It was finally decided that Mr. McCormick and I should be a Committee to confer with the President. Mr. McCormick and I decided it would be well if President Lawrence Lowell should also be invited if it were agreeable to the President; which Mr. McCormick, who was to see him in advance to make the appointment, was to ascertain.

The appointment was arranged for August 6th at 2.15 at the White House. At the appointed day we met in Washington, Lowell, Dr. [William Harrison] Short, Secretary of the League and I, met at the Luncheon at the Metropolitan Club as the guests of McCormick and from there went to the White House. At a few minutes after the appointed time the President joined us and after a pleasant greeting, told us while he was somewhat tired, he felt fit. He told us of the Conferences he had held with individual Senators of the opposition and the explanations he had given regarding to the disputed points, The Monroe Doctrine provision Art. XXI, Art. X guaranteeing against external aggression, the right to withdraw from the League, etc., being the four points of reservation formulated by the moderate group headed by Senator Kellog[g] of Minnesota, etc.[1] The explanations the President made were quite in accord with these reservations. It was suggested if the President could make in some public and formal way the explanations regarding these points, it would facilitate matters. The question was how this could be best done. One suggested if made by the President to the press, another by a communication to some Senator. It was suggested that it would be more advisable, and such communication would have more effect, if made to a Senator of the opposition party—and which would be preferable if made in reply to requests to the President from such Senator asking his views. The President seemed to prefer this plan provided the letter of inquiry was so framed as to enable the President to give his views as expressed without having to dodge any of the inquiries for reasons that might cause irritation or embarrassment to the Allies.

It was agreed that McCormick, Lowell and I should call on Senator Hitchcock the Democratic leader of the minority of the Committee for Foreign Relations who could best steer us regarding what member of the Republican majority on the Committee it would be best to see. We went to the Senate and found the Committee for Foreign Relations in session exam[in]ing Secretary of State Lansing. Hitchcock suggested Senator McCumber, but it was found he was not in Washington. Mr. Hitchcock after mentioning one or two other Senators, whom neither I or Lowell personally knew, then he mentioned Senator Kellog. As I knew Kellog very well and had conferred with him on the subject of the League when last in Washington in June shortly after my return from Paris—(when former Senator Burton and I went there as a Committee of the League to confer with some of the opposition Senators)—it was decided Senator Kellog would be the best man to see. Mr. McCormick thought because of his close connection with the Administration—because he was the former Chairman of the National Democratic Party—it might be better that Lowell and I being Republicans, should see Kellog. This we did, Short went with us. We found Kellog in favor of the League and told us on the following day he was scheduled to make his speech in the Senate advocating the ratification of the Covenant and the Treaty with the reservations his group had formulated; which reservations he felt confident were not in the nature of amendments, but interpretive only and therefore would not require resubmission to the Plenary Conference and to Germany.

Lowell and I outlined our plan to have a letter written to the President as stated above. Kellog personally favored this plan, but said he would have to confer with the members of his group—and he believed they would be favorable. We then suggested whether the President's answer of clarification would not serve the purpose of making reservations unnecessary. Kellog said no, but the reservations could recite they were based upon the President's interpretations. It appeared to us that reservations under such conditions would be in the nature of clarification—as distinguished from reservations which might have the effect of amendments, or form a precedent for other nations to make reservations—as distinguished from clarifications; which would disintegrate the Covenant. In order to meet the President's views as well as our own as to the form of the letter, we arranged that Kellog in conjunction with Hitchcock should prepare such a tentative letter of inquiry, which Hitchcock should show the President, and if he approved Kellog would address the President to which the President would reply giving his interpretations upon the clauses of articles in question. Kellog stated his relations with Hitchcock were entirely confidential. After leaving Kellog we again called on Senator Hitchcock and as "honest brokers" for the League, to use Lowell's phrase in speaking with Kellog, we gave an account of our interview and left it with him and Kellog to work out. Hitchcock thought very favorably of our plan and believed it would work out advantageously.[2] Lowell and I felt satisfied and gratified with our days work.

Our Conference with the President lasted a full hour—he was very frank, confidential and outspoken. He said he was preparing

a message to Congress on how to regulate the high cost of living,
in which he would point out how the delay in ratifying the Peace
Treaty tended to unrest and to the disturbed conditions we are suffering, as well as other countries.[3]

T MS (O. S. Straus Papers, DLC).
    [1] About these reservations, see the news report printed at Aug. 2, 1919, Vol. 62.
    [2] These negotiations apparently came to an end as the result of the statement by Sen-
ator Hitchcock on August 15, following a conference at the White House, that Wilson
thought that talk of reservations was premature until all amendments to the Versailles
Treaty had been defeated. See the news report printed at Aug. 15, 1919, ibid. Wilson, on
August 13 and 14, 1919, prepared a draft of a letter about controverted provisions of the treaty
to be sent to Senator Lodge (it is printed at the latter date in ibid.), but later decided not to
send this letter and instead incorporated it in a statement that he read to the members of the
Foreign Relations Committee when he met with them at the White House on August 19,
1919. A transcript of Wilson's statement and the conversation that followed at this meeting
are printed at that date in ibid.
    [3] Wilson's address to a joint session of Congress on the high cost of living is printed at Aug.
8, 1919, ibid.

Abbott Lawrence Lowell to William Howard Taft

Dear Mr Taft: [Cambridge, Mass.] August 7, 1919

Having been prevented from being at the meeting of the Executive Committee of the League to Enforce Peace by a wreck on the
track which delayed our train six hours, I did not receive your letter until my return from Washington this morning.

I should assuredly not think for a moment of presenting to the
Committee your resignation as President of the League; and for
the League to accept it would be as absurd as a man's accepting
the resignation of his own eyes or tongue.

Moreover, I agree with your attitude more nearly than most
members of the Executive Committee do. At the meeting before
last I was thoroughly persuaded that it was better not to advocate
any compromise in the way of reservations or interpretations; but
I thought the vote at the last meeting went too far, because I believe that the only way to bring about an ultimate ratification is to
draw together the more moderate Republicans who insist on interpretations, and the Administration Democrats. Something of this
sort we tried to do when we saw the President yesterday. He was
willing to answer a letter that might be addressed to him by some
one of the most conciliatory Republicans, in which he (the President) should state his opinion in regard to the meaning of the
treaty on the four points where they wish interpretations, which
would show that his view of the treaty at the present time coincides
with what they would like it to be. The President, however, said
that he wanted to see the letter to be written to him before it was
sent, in order that he might be sure that it involved no questions

that it would be indiscreet for him to answer. We then saw Senator Kellogg, who was well disposed towards the writing of such a letter, but wanted to consult the other members of the group of seven to which he belongs. If they agree to his doing so, he will present a draft of the letter to Senator Hitchcock, whom we also saw, and who will act as the channel of communication with the President.

There is one difference in the points of view of the President and Senator Kellogg. The President hopes that by this means it may be unnecessary to make the reservations that they want. They do not think so; but in any case, such a public correspondence would very much simplify the solution; because even if interpretations to that effect are ultimately put into the treaty, they would not carry at all the same criticism of the President that they would if he had not said that they expressed his own views upon the treaty. And what is much more important, they would not tend to encourage other nations to put in their reservations or interpretations; because if only a formulation of what one of the Big Four states was always intended, they stand on a very different footing from any attempt to pervert the meaning of the treaty.

If Mr Houston is with you, will you not show this letter to him, as it is really an answer to his letter enclosing yours, as well as to your letters which he enclosed.

Very truly yours,   [A. Lawrence Lowell]

CCL (A. L. Lowell Papers, MH-Ar).

Two Letters from R. A. Rogers[1] to Francis Xavier Dercum

Dear Sir   The White House December 13th/19.

I was so glad to get a chance to speak to you to day, even at that was not able to report anything as they exist to you, this is my second letter The first I tore up as was afraid it would be seized by some malicious person here going through the different hands ect, as one of my letters was held up for several days here in one of the departments.

I have nearly lived down the opposition to which I met when arrived here. I waited untill after 11 pm oclock that night to see Dr Grayson, when he arrived he eyed me over & detailed a man to show me to my room by saying would see me at 10 am following am, at that time he said there was absolutely nothing to do for the President but hand him the urinal occasionally. The next day he told me to have a good time as he did not know if [he] would be able to use me or not. Then Wednesday am, he told me he did not think he would be able to work me in. I said very well Dr that will be all right, only let met know as Dr Dercum has other patients waiting for me, & it is useless to me to waste my time here, well I will see he said, up to this, I had not seen the President Mrs Wilson nor nurses. On Thursday am he sent for me, to introduce me to patient & Mrs Wilson. They were both very nice to me. I gave first treatment that Pm, patient was so pleased to think there could be something more to be done for him. The opposition party were so surprised that the President took to me. I quoted you to Dr Grayson as saying to me that the time had arrived when patient ought to have, bed baths passive movements, massage, resistive movements ect, is he having them I said No the reply, but that his skin was fairly clean, he would admit that he might have more baths. Well I said if you dont get busy soon, you might as well close the book as they will do no good later. Well then Dr G said we might as well get busy then. I quote few of findings.

Patients body about 3 coats dead epidermis Very uncomfortable, & no attempt made to try to get back use of limbs ect. I give your prescribed treatment, and patient asks me what you would do & I tell him then we will do it he says, he has periods of forgetfullness allso seeing two objects in room at times. Very weak & soon tires, spells of dizziness even when in bed. Patient likes Dr G. to give Electricity & there is no objection as that has been mere pretense

They are some party here alltogether they are to be pitied because they do not know any better, you sir were right in your first statement to me

Mrs Wilson runs the case Dr G is afraid to speak to patient or Mrs W. The head usher runs Dr G & the usher, likes the skirts especially women nurse as is seen, he is the one who helps to lift patient in & out of chair. Now your treatments have brought about such decided improvements that they are all taking a back seat even Mr Wilson is astonished at the gain. it make the president feel so happy about himself. I have gained patient confidence he is nice to me talk & chats & remembers things that happened when I first met them ect. Mrs Wilson thinks or did that it was all in the entertaining the patient untill she said to me laughingly now he goes to sleep till four am, & that is enough for any one. I said not for the patient as he might sleep for a few days & night & it would not do any harm, & that there was a great deal of hard work to be done to get the President on his feet again, & now she sees & steps aside, for his treatments, but they have no system in anything. It takes me two hours 4 to 6 with aid of Nurse to give the patient treatment he ought to have, he is very heavy & takes three to lift him in &

out of bed, but is improving right along, now he likes you very much & is looking forward to your visit, he says you cheer him up so. They seem to be opposed to another man just yet. I have sounded them all. I think that they are going to try to work in his valet as soon as can, especially if present improvement continues. I will do my best for your plans as occasion arrises Mr Axson told me patient is very fond of me Now everybody is treating me fine, excuse long letter but I knew you never knew how things were running here I wish you were nearer thanking you very kindly

I am Sir very Sincerely   R A. Rogers

Dr I will drop short report to you Sir occasionly to keep you posted. <u>I do not expect answer</u>

---

[1] A physical therapist employed by Dr. Dercum to work with his stroke patients.

Dear Sir   The White House Dec 17/19

The President is making steady progress, he is more cheerful & hopeful about himself now, he can stand his weight on right leg & with my support throw the left leg out & put some weight on it for few steps, can help himself more not quite so heavy to lift, expect to have him strong enough to use commode soon, allso at your suggestion sit up for one meal in chair to start with, ect.

There is one trouble patient is liable to rush too much, as there is little arterial tension at intervals, which makes him very restless & nervous for periods, cannot relax nor sleep when wants.

he goes to bed when wants usually about 9 Pm or rather goes to sleep, then at 4 am wakes up very restless & nervous then worries in the time At breakfast, such is doing him harm. The left arm is still very sensative especially below the shoulder blade. I have used electric prod to warm it well before massage good effect, think the electric battery is doing it harm now, as he complains burning sensation & severe irritation whole arm. I notice when bowels disturbed there is Cortical irritation allso. I can massage left leg for toes up to groin no complaints allso rotate & resist ect. he confides in me about things & told me they dont give him any rest at all I rely on you sir when you visit as these people dont know and some dont care a dam. They are all falling to the fact now that they ought to have let you done what wanted before.

They are all delighted at the improvement in ten days already. I am doing as you said, doing my work professionally & gentlemanly nice to everyone high & low & I get the return, everybody nice to me even the servants cant do enough to make me comfortable, it will not be long before we will be able to control whole situation

I offer these reports for your visit, need attention for patients benefit

Dr Axson came in to day asking kindly for you & family, he expects to see you some of visits soon he looks well, too stout

I give best can under circumstances

Bed Bath, Massage, Passive exercises Resistive movements, ect. & help them all can I can hold patient back some when needs it, he says all right hell do it

I am Sir Sincerely   R A Rogers.

ALS (received from Steven Lomazow).

Franklin Knight Lane to Cary Travers Grayson

Personal

My dear Admiral: Washington January 5, 1920.

As you know, I am contemplating resigning. It has been my purpose to wait until such time as the President was well enough to see me and talk the matter over with him. I understand from Mr. Tumulty that the President is prepared to name my successor and that it would not in any way add to his embarrassment to fill my place in the immediate future. I would like to know if this is the fact, for my course will be shaped accordingly. Two years ago I had an offer of $50,000 a year which I put aside because I thought it my duty to stay while the war was on. When Mr. McAdoo resigned this offer was renewed but I then thought that I should await the conclusion of formal peace, which all expected would come soon. While the President was West I promised that I would take the matter up with him on his return, and since then I have been waiting for his return to strength. I need not tell you that I am delighted to know that he is in such condition now as to turn to matters that in the best of health are vexatious, if this is the fact.

My sole reason for resigning is that I feel that I am entitled to have assurance as to the future of my family and myself. I have been in public life twenty-one years and have less than nothing in the way of private means, not enough in fact to pay my way back to California. And having given the better part of my life to the public I feel that I must now regard the interest of those dependent upon me.

I wish you would be absolutely frank with me, for I would do nothing that with your knowledge you would think would make against the welfare of our Chief.

Cordially,   Franklin K. Lane

TLS (received from James Gordon Grayson and Cary T. Grayson, Jr.).

From Jessie Woodrow Wilson Sayre

Dearest, dearest Father,   [Cambridge, Mass.] Jan 20, 1920

I find I have only note-paper in the house but I must drop you at *least* a note to tell you I have not vanished utterly into the great unknown. It seems when I come home after a brief vacation that there are so many threads to pick up the days are not half long enough and much is left undone.

I collected innumerable stories of the children for you and even they have fluttered away as the days flew by—only one or two "sticking by."

We happened to mention that a friend of Frank's who had visited us had just died and that night at prayers Eleanor informed God, "Oh God, Mr. Safely has just gone up to you. Please mend him." The next night as Francis prayed for Miss Larkin Eleanor said "Please bless Dizzybelle. You know, God, Miss Larkin and Dizzybelle are the same one."

I have been sick in bed with a cold for three or four days and Eleanor was much concerned. "There are two of 'em sick now, so I think I'll go down to Washington and make grandfather well." "How will you make him well?" Eleanor is never at a loss for an answer and makes one up as she goes along "I'll take my snow shovel and shovel all the badness out of him into the garbage can, that's what I'll do."

Francis has coined a new word "Now, Elliebai, don't 'intercorrect' me" He meant interrupt of course but I think his version isn't bad!

Francis had a beautiful party on his birthday. Two little boys came in and all played with perfect amiability. Frankie's velocipede enraptured him. "That makes two wonderfully special presents this year, my vicaterola and my velocipede." Even the snow has lost some of its charm and he is eager to have it go so that his velocipede can have full play.

Thank you dear dear Father for it. He associates it entirely with grandfather's name and it has quite surpassed everything else (except the vicaterola) in his love.

He dresses and undresses on it and rides it to his bath and to his meals and adores it.

We are all well again now but quite snowed in. Four snow storms in succession have piled layer on layer and it is great fun for the children. Between times it is clear and cold and quite what winter should be.

The papers give good news of you, and I hope its all true.

The five of us send dearest heart's love to you darling darling Father.   Devotedly your daughter   Jessie

ALS (WC, NjP).

Richard Martin Boeckel[1] to Hamilton Holt

Dear Mr. Holt: Washington, March 4, 1920

I had to fall back on Roper[2] again in this week's message. What with cabinet changes, politics, treaty and the general uncertainty, everything in Washington is in confusion. I was disappointed on three other articles before I got Roper. I am hoping, however, that things will straighten out in a few weeks.

Will you let me tell you a few things about the treaty situation I think you ought to know if you do not know already? You may want to do something about it. The only hope for the treaty now seems to be that Wilson will let a sufficient number of Democrats in the Senate know that he will not kill them outright if they vote for the Lodge reservations to muster a two thirds majority.

If the Democratic tactics can be changed quickly there is still some chance that the Lodge reservations can be modified in some particulars. But there can be no change without some assurance from the President.

After a conference with the mild reservationist Republicans ten days ago Bernard M. Baruch went to the White House and urged the President to give the necessary Democratic votes. He was coolly received and the conference came to a close when he hinted that the President should feel some gratitude toward the middle ground Republicans, because they had worked harder than almost any other group for ratification. The President felt differently.

Mr. Baruch thereupon advised Democratic senators to "make the best bargain possible" and supply the votes to send the treaty to the White House. He believed he and the President's other advisors could do something with the President after the Senate had acted but not before. But he found the Democrats afraid.

It was about this time that the mild reservationists announced that they would adhere to the Lodge program, feeling that the treaty was gone and the next thing of importance was to preserve party solidarity for the campaign.

Mr. Baruch met the mild reservationists again a few days ago and said they were making a mistake. They urged him again to go to the President in one last effort, but he refused. However, Mr. McAdoo, who had just come to town, would go.

Mr. McAdoo has a deep interest in the matter. He wants to be a candidate, and Mr. Baruch is supporting him, but he cannot be a candidate on an issue calling for unreserved ratification. He wants the treaty out of the way. The only man who can put it out of the way is Wilson.

Mr. McAdoo is supposed to have seen the President last night.

How far he got I do not know. I judge, however, that he made little progress for he never had had any assurance in going to the President on other matters and always has been prepared to fall in with the President's view. His attitude may have changed since he left the cabinet, but if Mr. Baruch made no progress I very much doubt whether Mr. McAdoo had any greater success.

Ten days ago (and this is confidential) Mrs. Wilson called up the New York Evening Post and asked that Ray Stannard Baker be sent to the White House for a conference. Mr. Baker came. He talked with Mrs. Wilson and received the distinct impression that she was running the White House. I don't know how hard he tried, but he was unable to convince her that the people were not solidly behind the President in his opposition to any but interpretive reservations. In this he judged she reflected the view of the President, this also accounted, he thought for the President's desire that the treaty be made a campaign issue unless the Lodge reservations were modified.

A few days ago Mr. Baker was again called to the White House and this time he conferred with Tumulty and Greyson [Grayson]. They urged that he get Mr. Ogden,[3] who was in the city to write a letter to the President outlining the exact situation and stressing the necessity of his letting Democratic senators know he would accept something like the Lodge reservations as the conditions of ratification.[4]

The letter was written and Dr. Greyson guaranteed that he would put it in the President's hands. It was delivered at the White House yesterday. Whether Greyson and Tumulty had not the courage to tell the President the situation themselves, or had told him, without result, or thought the advice would be more effective coming from some outside source I do not know. Nor do I know whether they have asked for other letters along this line.

One thing seems to me to be clear from all this. That is that the President has no present intention of surrendering, or of sending the ratification to Paris if it is by any chance adopted with the Lodge reservations, which seems altogether unlikely. He has made up his mind that the treaty shall go into the campaign if he cannot get it ratified approximately the way he wants it.

If the treaty is not ratified this time, I am convinced, it is dead. If it goes into the campaign the President will have to dominate the San Francisco convention and probably be the candidate. The only other possible candidate on this issue is Hitchcock. Palmer will run on this or any other issue, but be cannot hold the campaign to the treaty issue. If he is the candidate the issues will be free speech, espionage, his relations with the interests and labor issues.

And besides the treaty cannot win in the campaign. Already it is being rewritten just as fast as it can be. It should have been written with the object of opening up Europe's sources of raw materials and rehabilitating Europe's industry—all Europe's industry—as quickly as possible. It was written on a very different theory—and so written that to carry out its settlements needed American support.

But American support has been withheld and may never be available, so that Europe is changing the entire theory of peace. This will be evident to all the American people long before the campaign comes to an end. There will be no Treaty of Versailles—except for the League of Nations covenant—left to ratify.

If ratification of this treaty is to come at all it must come now. The time is short. The only thing that will save the treaty is a surrender by Wilson within the next ten days. In the opinions I have given you may not be interested, but in the facts I thought you would be.

It may be that letters to Wilson will do no good. I am far from convinced that he would not regard their writers as his enemies for life. However, with these facts before you, and others you already have, I thought you might want to consider writing him some advice.

There are several other matters I want to talk to you about, but I'll not burden you with them in this letter. I am glad you are coming to Washington soon.

Faithfully yours, (Signed)   R. M. Boeckel

TCL (A. L. Lowell Papers, MH-Ar).
[1] Author and journalist, at this time Washington correspondent of the *New York Times* and of *The Independent*.
[2] That is, Daniel Calhoun Roper.
[3] Rollo Ogden, editor of the New York *Evening Post*.
[4] This letter has apparently not survived.

David C. Williams[1] to Mrs. Baer

Dear Mrs Baer: The White House. June 1st-1920

I had no difficulty in finding the car and getting to the White House on the 24th.

Have gradually been broken in on the case. So far have not heard any comments on the way I am getting on. It is not exactly the work one has to do here that is hard, it is the way we have to do it.

At present it is impossible to work Dr Dercum's method exactly. However we think later on we will be able to do it.

We have a scheme which if we are allowed to follow will do very well and give both of us a chance to rest.

I do not know how Rogers has stood it all these months. He had not been able to talk to anyone that even a chat with me relieved his mind, and since he has had a chance to take some rest says he feels like a new person.

You realize how guarded one has to be in what they write and talk.

There are lots of things I would like to say but am afraid that in some way mail might be held up.

Best regards to all

Yours very Sincerely   David C. Williams

ALS (received from Steven Lomazow).

[1] Another physical therapist who worked for Dr. Dercum. Mrs. Baer unidentified.

INDEX

NOTE ON THE INDEX

THE alphabetically arranged analytical table of contents at the front of the volume eliminates duplication, in both contents and index, of references to certain documents, such as letters. Letters are listed in the contents alphabetically by name, and chronologically within each name by page. The subject matter of all letters is, of course, indexed. The Editorial Notes and Wilson's writings are listed in the contents chronologically by page. In addition, the subject matter of both categories is indexed. The index covers all references to books and articles mentioned in text or notes. Footnotes are indexed. Page references to footnotes which place a comma between the page number and "n" cite both text and footnote, thus: "418,n1." On the other hand, absence of the comma indicates reference to the footnote only, thus: "59n1"—the page number denoting where the footnote appears.

The index supplies the fullest known form of names and, for the Wilson and Axson families, relationships as far down as cousins. Persons referred to by nicknames or shortened forms of names can be identified by reference to entries for these forms of the names.

All entries consisting of page numbers only and which refer to concepts, issues, and opinions (such as democracy, the tariff, money trust, leadership, and labor problems), are references to Wilson's speeches and writings.

Four cumulative contents-index volumes are now in print: Volume 13, which covers Volumes 1-12, Volume 26, which covers Volumes 14-25, Volume 39, which covers Volumes 27-38, and Volume 52, which covers Volumes 40-49 and 51.

INDEX

644 INDEX

United States Congress (cont.)
Treaty, 577,n1; and Treaty of Bogotá, 581,n2; see also under the names of the individual committees, such as Finance Committee
United States Constitution: and woman suffrage amendment, 563,n1
United States Grain Corporation: see Grain Corporation (U.S.)
United States Mail Steamship Co., Inc., 124n1, 125
United States Railroad Labor Board: see Railroad Labor Board
United States and the Republic of Panama (McCain), 382n5
United States Shipping Board: and statement for The Document, 593, 595
United States Supreme Court: and Debs case, 98
United States Tariff Commission: see Tariff Commission (U.S.)
United War Work Campaign Fund, 74-75, 87-88, 96-97, 97
Upper Silesia: The Dilemma of the Powers (Coar), 463-64,n1
Urofsky, Melvin I., 319n1
Uruguay, 23,n1
Utica, N.Y.: and WW Foundation, 555; Colby cancels speech in, 561

Valley Forge Historical Society, 175
Vanderbilt University, 285,n1
Van Dyke, Henry, 182, 434
Van Hoesen, Henry Bartlett, 182
Vargas, Manuel, 132
Veblen, Oswald, 182
Vénisélos, Eleutherios Kyrios, 10, 11, 105n3
Versailles Treaty, 15n1, 324n1, 599; R. S. Baker organizes WW's documents on, 89; Hines on river shipping decision under, 93; on German obligations to Belgium, 145; various comments on failure to ratify, 227-29, 268-69, 324n1, 423,n1, 430; editorial supports ratification of, 313n1; question of location of original copy, 351-52, 354-55, 357; N. H. Davis on discussion with Lord Bryce on, 375-78; Straus on meeting with WW on plans to insure ratification, 607-10; Boeckel on strategy for ratification, 616-18; A. L. Lowell on ratification plan, 610-11
Victory at Sea (Sims), 242n4
Villard, Oswald Garrison, 37n1
Vinson, John Chalmers, 484n1
Virginia, University of: WW on endowment fund effort, 138-39,n1; and centennial of, 263,n1, 265, 275, 310; WW solicited for donation to, 281,n2; proposed move of medical school, 299,n1, 495,n1, 498,n1,2, 501, 559; and Wilson & Colby announcement, 344; plaque on WW's room at, 498,n1,2, 501; WW recommends S. Axson as future faculty member at, 549
Voyages de M. le Marquis de Chastellux dans l'Amérique Septentrionale dans les années 1780, 1781 & 1782, 333,n2

Vreeland, Alice May Brown (Mrs. Williamson Updike), 524,n2
Vreeland, May (Maidie), 524,n3
Vreeland, Williamson Updike, 182, 524
Vrooman, Carl Schurz, 139-40,n1, 139n1, 140

Wagenknecht, Alfred, 99,n2
Wallace, Hugh Campbell: on U.S. representation on European commissions, 33, 34-36; and French unknown soldier ceremony, 131, 133; and fund-raising efforts for WW's S Street home, 137n3; and Yap controversy, 147, 153-56
Wall, Joseph Frazier, 242n3
Wall Street: WW on New York Times and, 301
Walsh, David Ignatius, 37n1
Walsh, Thomas James, 70,n1, 522; and Treaty of Berlin, 418,n1
Wanamaker, Rodman, 128
war chests, 87-88, 96, 97, 110
War Department: and army recruiting issue, 97n1
Ward, Alan J., 52n1
Ward, Geoffrey C., 386n2
Ware, Moses, 553
War Finance Corporation, 25n2,3, 70; issue of revival of, 16-17, 25n3, 192, 193; WW's veto of revival of, 18-22; Lamont on veto override, 27-28
War Industries Board: and copper price fixing, 177-78
War-Time Journal of a Georgia Girl (Andrews), 75-76,n1
Washington, George, 76, 128, 135, 162, 183n1, 533n1, 566; Farewell Address, 220, 358, 358-59; WW on not making movie on, 557,n1
Washington, Patty W., 534
Washington, D.C., 505,n1, 513
Washington: Capital City, 1879-1950 (Green), 505n1
Washington Daily News: alleged interview with EBW, 479n1, 492n1
Washington Naval Conference: see Conference on the Limitation of Armament
Washington Sends Replies to League (James), 402n1
Washington Times, 363, 364
Watson, James Eli, 316,n3
Watson, William, 105n3
Ways and Means, Committee on (House on Reps.), 121n2, 191, 484, 485n5
Webster, Dora Rouse (Mrs. James Edwin), 491,n6
Webster, James Edwin (Ned), 277, 300, 493-94; on death of Bob Henderson and memories of "Witherspoon Gang," 491
Webster, John Rouse, 491,n7, 494
Weeks, John Wingate, 432,n2, 442
Weiser, Charles W., 279-80
Wells, H. G. (Herbert George), 433, 437
Wertz, Edwin Slusser, 100-101,n5
Westcott, John Howell, 182, 411, 412, 494; on inscription found in Nice, 482

WOODROW WILSON

Woodrow Wilson, cont.

Kirby, 166-67, 168-69, 171-72; and Canadian Commission, 168,n1, 196,n1; at last Cabinet meeting, 175-76,n1; Lane on resigning, 614

CABINET

Daniels records meetings, 9, 25-26, 70-71, 90-91, 109; on reparations and tax on German exports, 109,n1; unwilling to accept resignations, 109; time for resignation letters, 124; photograph taken, 126,n1, 138; WW's first meeting with in Cabinet room since illness, 138; letter of farewell from, 150, 199; bids farewell at last meeting of, 175-76,n1; practice of retiring members to replace table and chairs, 187-88; receives gift of chair, 330, 365, 366; and Wilson & Colby announcement, 343; proposes a Secretary of Transportation, 431, 559, 591; Lane's wish to resign, 614; photograph of, *illustration section*

FAMILY AND PERSONAL LIFE

EBW's love for WW, 5; Nell's Christmas and birthday greetings, 5-6; plans for mansion, 7-8, 30-31, 47-48, 84-85, 86-87, 105, 136; news from Aunt Felie, 11; thanks McAdoo for birthday greetings, 14; answers Aunt Felie, 16; granddaughter thanks for Christmas gift, 18; responds to granddaughter's note, 22-23; responds to McAdoo on family, 22; R. S. Baker on relationship between EBW and, 82; contributes to S. W. Beach's gift fund, 91, 123-24; on lucky number *13*, 105, 115, 125; guest list for housewarming, 105n3; on name of his mansion, 105; EBW reveals love for in letter to K. Trask, 106-107; news from Jessie, 107-109; suggests law partnership to B. Colby, 107,n1; and granddaughter's poem, 108-109, 125; friends buy Pierce-Arrow for, 116-17,n1, 148, 156-57, 167, 167-68, 186,n1; visits new home and prepares for move, 127; arrangements for Nobel Prize money, 131-32; Valentines to EBW, 133, 545; friends' fund-raising effort for S Street house, 137,n3, 148-49, 157; and law practice with Colby, 160-61, 161; ancestry of, 170, 171; S. Axson's news and thoughts on WW and EBW, 172-73; Jessie's praise and good wishes in new home, 188; arrives at new home, 206; private liquor stock moved to new home, 214; eager to have Jessie see new home, 231; unable to attend christening of grandson, 267; plans for mansion end, 276,n1; unable to attend reunion of "Witherspoon Gang," 277, 281, 300, 302-303; University of Virginia solicits for donation, 281,n2; and Pierce-Arrow accident claim, 303,n1, 385, 388; on EAW's grandfather, 307,n2; receives liquor from Seibold, 312,n1; McAdoo's concern for

Woodrow Wilson, cont.

EBW's health and burdens, 356; receives rare copy of Washington's Farewell Address, 357-59; love for EBW, 371; Dodge's invitation and reminiscences, 373-74; birthday greetings to Jessie, 385; a normal day's routine, 395-98; life style and finances, 398; news of Harpers and Westcotts, 410-1, 412; Jessie's desire to see WW, 427-28; on arrangements if entire Sayre family visits, 428-29; Nell's news and thanks for birthday greeting, 429-30; cheering crowd brings tears to WW's eyes, 449-53; and Berry Schools, 456-57, 459, 503-504, 507-508; news from Ellen D. Davis, 458; Edith Helm on WW and EBW, 477; concern over publication of letter from doctor, 483; J. E. Webster on death of Bob Henderson and memories of "Witherspoon Gang," 491; favorite color and flower, 519; and Cousin Jessie Brower, 536; recommends S. Axson as future faculty member at University of Virginia, 549; Jessie on son Woodrow's birthday, 553; Jessie happy son named for, 554; Nell on love for WW and on her move to California, 562; sends Nell love and welcome to her home, 565; letters to grandchildren, 566; Jessie's news of grandchildren, 615; S Street house, *illustration section*

HEALTH

W. E. Dodd on, 68; R. S. Baker on, 71, 237-38, 245, 300-301, 360, 585; various comments on improvement of, 71, 148, 308, 360, 397-98, 401, 585; loss of initiative, 103-104; Swem on WW dwelling on past triumphs, 103-104; ventures out in cold, 111-12; Harding on participation in inauguration and, 149; and last Cabinet meeting, 175-76,n1; uses cane, 175, 205, 206, 208, 329, 381, 450; memory lapse on Yap possibly due to small stroke, 195n4; uses wheelchair at Capitol, 207, 210; prostate problem, 237; attack of nervous indigestion, 245, 246; importance of exercise, 245, 395; Bolling on improvement, 247, 336, 354, 357, 362, 410, 413, 427, 470, 501; rests constantly, 256; depression, 268, 270; on his slow improvement, 281, 423, 442, 495, 507, 510, 532, 536; R. S. Baker on WW's isolation and, 284; S. Axson on, 309-10; gets little exercise, 310; advanced planning to avoid fatigue during Washington bar admission ceremony, 318; mentally keen, 321n1; uses only one hand, 360, 423, 430, 443, 582, 585; improvement evident at law offices, 370-71, 381-82; walks unassisted, 370, 380-81, 397-98; improvement evident at theater, 381,n1, 440; attack of indigestion and headaches, 434-35; rallies after attack but remains in bed, 436, 436-37; difficulty with stairs, 439, 442; unable to attend